LEVELS OF PROCESSING IN HUMAN MEMORY

Edited by

LAIRD S. CERMAK

BOSTON V.A. HOSPITAL

BOSTON UNIVERSITY

FERGUS I. M. CRAIK

UNIVERSITY OF TORONTO

 LAWRENCE ERLBAUM ASSOCIATES, PUBLISHERS
1979   Hillsdale, New Jersey

DISTRIBUTED BY THE HALSTED PRESS DIVISION OF

JOHN WILEY & SONS

New York   Toronto   London   Sydney

Lawrence Erlbaum Associates, Inc., Publishers
62 Maria Drive
Hillsdale, New Jersey 07642

Distributed solely by Halsted Press Division
John Wiley & Sons, Inc., New York

Library of Congress Cataloging in Publication Data

Main entry under title:

Levels of processing in human memory.

  Papers presented at a conference held in 1977 in
Rockport, Mass.
  Includes bibliographies and indexes.
  1. Memory—Congresses.   2. Human information
processing—Congresses.   I. Cermak, Laird S.
II. Craik, Fergus I. M.
BF371.L39   153.1'2   78-27848
ISBN 0-470-26651-1

Printed in the United States of America

Contents

v

PART III: LANGUAGE PROCESSES

PART IV: DEVELOPMENTAL ISSUES

Preface

Levels of processing as a conceptual framework for the investigation of human memory has enjoyed a great deal of popularity since its introduction in 1972. It has served as an impetus for literally hundreds of experiments and has been used as an "explanation" for a wide range of retention phenomena. As a consequence, a wealth of data and theorizing has emerged within a very short period of time, and few have had the time to assimilate and—more importantly—to evaluate this information. In order to achieve such an evaluation, a group of individuals— some proponents and some outright opponents—of the levels notion were brought together to discuss this topic.

The incentive for this conference was originally generated as a result of several meetings between the editors of this volume. These meetings generally revolved about issues related to similarities and differences in the editors' viewpoints and gradually extended to an investigation of others' theories and research as well. It was then decided to gather together as many of these individuals as possible to formally discuss these topics. Eventually the concept was extended to include discussions of the levels notion within the areas of developmental memory, language processing, and amnesia. The results of this conference, i.e., the papers that were presented for discussion, constitute the chapters of this book.

Support for the conference was provided by the National Institute of Child Health and Human Development through the awarding of a grant #NDMH 10807-01. The site chosen for the conference was the Seaward Inn in Rockport, Massachusetts—a secluded spot on the waterfront that provided an ideal atmosphere for the contemplation of depths, levels, elaboration, distinctiveness, and such other cerebral imaginings. We are grateful to NICHD for their participation in this conference both financially and through the participation of Dr. Grace Yeni–Komshian, a representative of that organization. We also appreciate the New England hospitality extended to us by Mr. and Mrs. Cameron, proprietors of the Seaward Inn, and by Mrs. Olson and the staff at the Inn.

The conference consisted of six sessions spread across the course of three days. Within each session, either two or three related papers were presented. This was followed by an open discussion stimulated by the predesignated discussant and revolving primarily around points that were chosen as critical by that discussant. All participants had received preconference drafts of each presentation, so discussion was not totally off the cuff but instead sprang from earlier consideration. This same organization has also been used as the basis for the structure of the book, which includes each participant's revision of his/her original presentation. Discussants were shown these final revisions before writing their formal discussion sections; thus their comments are based upon the revised chapters. The final chapter was written following the conference, and it represents a reflection upon the proceedings in general.

We wish to record our gratitude for the contribution made to the conference by Dr. Robert Shaw and Dr. Michael Turvey. They presented a paper at the meeting, but the paper is not included in the present book as the authors wished to develop their theoretical views more completely before publishing them. We are grateful to Bob Shaw and Mike Turvey for their major intellectual (and social!) contribution to the Rockport meeting.

In addition to our appreciation to NICHD and to the Rockport Inn, we would also like to acknowledge the help of David DeLuca, who provided the audiovisual technology as well as postsession refreshment, and to Lynn Reale, who organized travel arrangements for all participants. Finally, the authors extend continuing appreciation to their wives, Sharon and Anne, for their support and encouragement in this undertaking.

L. S. CERMAK
F. I. M. CRAIK

LEVELS OF PROCESSING
IN HUMAN MEMORY

THEORETICAL AND
EMPIRICAL DEVELOPMENTS

1

Effects of Elaboration of Processing at Encoding and Retrieval: Trace Distinctiveness and Recovery of Initial Context

Larry L. Jacoby
McMaster University

Fergus I. M. Craik
University of Toronto

One central point made by Craik and Lockhart (1972) in describing a levels-of-processing framework for the study of memory was the intimate association between memory and perception. In their view, the memory trace was characterized as the record of operations carried out initially for the purposes of perceiving and interpreting the stimulus array. It was also proposed that deeper, more meaningful analyses of perceived events would be associated with more durable memory traces than would relatively superficial analyses of the sound or appearance of incoming stimuli; and in support of their proposal, Craik and Tulving (1975) showed that words for which meaningful decisions are made show higher levels of retention in an incidental memory task than do the same words after decisions about their sound or appearance. However, although the levels-of-processing view has had some success in describing general features of remembering in many situations, some difficulty has been encountered in specifying precisely what is meant by "deep" and "meaningful." Further, the view does not readily allow for distinctions to be made within the domain of meaningful analyses; it simply postulates that all events processed in terms of their meaning should be well remembered. In some instances, however, types of meaningful processing have been associated with quite poor retention (e.g., Mandler & Worden, 1973). Given a set of tasks, each requiring subjects to deal meaningfully with presented items, the original levels framework provides no basis for predicting differences, although such differences are found.

In later papers (Craik & Jacoby, 1975; Craik & Tulving, 1975; Lockhart, Craik, & Jacoby, 1976), the original levels formulation has been altered in a

1

number of ways. Differences in retention are no longer explained purely in terms of depth of processing; additional mechanisms have been introduced. First, it has been suggested that processing differs in breadth or degree of elaboration as well as in level, thereby allowing an account of differences in retention that arise within a level of processing. Lockhart et al. also implicated discriminability as an important determinant of retention. By this was meant that the memory of a particular event must be discriminable from those of other events. Discriminability in turn was related to differences in the "depth" and "elaboration" induced by initial processing.

The present paper expands on these and related notions. First, the role of distinctiveness of encoding is examined more fully; the idea that distinctiveness is not an absolute characteristic but is always relative to some particular background or set of items is emphasized. Following from this idea is the second point—that the original context must be recreated at output if the encoded distinctiveness is to be effective in allowing discriminability of the wanted trace from others. Third, the notion is developed that retrieval, like encoding, is a matter of degree; just as an encoded item can be elaborated to a greater or lesser extent, so can retrieval information be processed more or less extensively. For example, the degree to which the initial encoding context is retrieved is largely under task control. Fourth, the point is made that some forms of recognition do not depend on retrieval of the encoding context; the parallels between context-dependent and context-free recognition on one hand and Tulving's (1972) notions of episodic and semantic memory on the other are explored. These ideas are illustrated by the results from some recent experiments.

Encoding Distinctiveness

One of the major difficulties with the original levels framework comes from the way that meaning was treated. Although not explicitly defined, there was a tendency in that paper to treat meaning as if it were a fixed entity; *the* meaning of a word was said to be either encoded or not encoded, depending on task demands. By this commonsense approach, each word has a single meaning or at most a few meanings. Such an approach quickly runs into difficulty, as can be seen in the simple situation of naming a given object. As pointed out by several writers (e.g., Brown, 1958; Garner, 1974; Olson, 1970), a concrete object does not have a single name or description. Rather, what an object is called or how it is described depends on the other objects from which it is to be discriminated. For example, a chair is a chair; but it is equally a piece of furniture, a thing, a wooden artifact, and any number of other descriptions, depending on what the chair is to be distinguished from. Similarly, the meaning of a word in a given context depends on distinctions that are to be conveyed by that word in that context.

The dependence of meaning on the distinctions to be conveyed is easily illustrated in considering synonymy. Anyone who has ever tried to construct a list of synonyms soon becomes convinced that there are no true synonyms in English. Paradoxically, however, almost any pair of words can carry equivalent meaning in some context. To the driver of a car, the consequences of a statement such as "Look out for the ___" are equivalent if the blank is filled by *tree, house, truck,* or generally any other concrete object name. Clearly, however, the words would not be synonymous in all other contexts. In contrast, words such as *woman* and *lady* seem more truly synonymous, because it is more difficult to imagine a context in which the choice of one word over the other would be meaningful. However, contexts that would distinguish the two words can clearly be found.

In perceptual research, several theorists have come to view perception as the process of describing a stimulus (e.g., Rock, 1975). In many cases, contextual factors such as the alternatives from which a stimulus is to be discriminated influence the description and, consequently, the perception of that stimulus. If we return to the original levels notion that memory for a stimulus is the record of perceptual analysis, we can then claim that the memory trace is functionally a description, or set of contrasts. The resultant view is similar to that advanced by multicomponent (Bower, 1967) or attribute (Underwood, 1969) memory theorists. The major difference between the present view and the previous ones is the claim that description is necessarily relative to a given context. That is, meaning is not simply an attribute that is or is not encoded. Rather, meaning is a set of contrasts resulting from distinctions required when interpreting the item in the context of some task.

It is useful to contrast the notion of distinctiveness with that of elaboration. By elaboration, it is often meant that a change in encoding is largely quantitative; that is, more information is added to the trace. By distinctiveness, however, we mean to emphasize the contrastive value of information. For example, learning that a particular person has a high school diploma adds information but has no contrastive value unless other people in the appropriate set failed to complete high school. Our notion is that perception and, consequently, memory move forward by a set of contrasts. If several events are described with highly overlapping or redundant dimensions, the events are not well-distinguished from each other. Additionally, if the same events are described with dimensions that do not overlap at all, they are also not distinguished because they have never been contrasted.

Distinctiveness requires change against some background of commonality. The phenomenon of proactive inhibition in short-term memory (e.g., Wickens, 1970) can be used to clarify this point. The buildup and release from proactive inhibition is likely to depend on characteristics of the whole series of lists rather than simply on the characteristics of words that appear in adjacent lists. If a set of lists is made up of unrelated words, one would expect no release from proactive inhibition to result when, for example, *dog* is followed by *coat*. This is true despite the change in category that is produced by this sequence of words. A change in category will be noted and serve as a basis for distinctiveness only if the commonality among prior words has been sufficient to establish a category that can serve as a background for change. Tversky (1977) has recently made a related point by demonstrating the importance of contrast for scaled similarity. In his experiment, the judged similarity of pairs of European countries (e.g., Italy – Switzerland) was increased when the list also included pairs of American countries (e.g., Brazil – Uruguay) that were to be judged rather than when it included only additional pairs of European countries. In the absence of variation with regard to continents, two countries being parts of the same continent added relatively little to their judged similarity. Tversky used the term *diagnosticity* to describe the above effect of contrast among other effects found in judged similarity. The work reported by Tversky makes it clear that judged similarity depends on diagnosticity and on the intensity or salience of attributes as well as on the number of attributes that two events potentially share. In considering memory performance, the notion of elaboration is insufficient to the extent that it denotes only a difference in the number of attributes encoded and ignores factors such as the diagnosticity of those attributes. By using the term *distinctiveness,* we mean to emphasize the importance of relationships among events—particularly the importance of contrast.

It is attractive to consider a memorable encoding as one that is easily discriminable or highly distinctive in the memory system. It seems quite possible that deeper, more elaborate encodings are more distinctive in this sense; a similar view has recently been put forward by Klein and Saltz (1976) and by Wickelgren (1977). The idea is that deeper encodings will be more discriminable from other encoded events and will be more easily retrieved, provided also that an appropriate retrieval cue is given (Tulving, 1974) and that the information is encoded in an organized, "recoverable" form (Norman & Bobrow, 1977). To make this point clearer, again consider the case of describing an object. The details of an object are more fully described when the object must be discriminated from a set of very similar objects; the description of a circle will be more complete if it is to be discriminated from other circles that differ in size and location than if it is to be discriminated from a set of squares. A more complete description results in the utility of the description being less reliant on reinstating the original set of alternatives. That is, the fuller description would also serve to specify the object among any less similar set of alternatives (within the same encoding dimensions, at least). Thus, more complete descriptions confer both greater distinctiveness and greater generality as a basis for discriminating one object from others. Similarly, in the case of memory for words, a more complete encoding or description of a word allows that word to be discriminated from a larger set of alternatives. The memory confusability of words that are similar, such as *lady* and *woman,* depends on the distinctions that are compelled by the study task and context. If *lady* were encountered in a list and *lady* and *woman* later appeared as alternatives on a recognition test, we would expect a high number of false recognitions of *woman* (Underwood, 1965). However, if the initial task required encoding of *lady* in terms of deportment as well as sex, fewer false recognitions of *woman* should result.

Let us stress again that distinctiveness is a context-relative term. A description that is highly distinctive for a particular set of alternatives is not necessarily distinctive for another set. Consequently, the distinctiveness of the description of an event cannot be specified without considering the alternatives from which it has been contrasted. If the set of alternatives is changed drastically, a previously distinctive description may be of very little use. A similar point has been addressed by Tulving and Thomson (1973) as encoding specificity. In agreement with Tulving and Thomson, we feel that it is necessary to focus on interactions between the manner in which initial encoding was carried out and the demands of the particular situation in which memory is assessed. However, it seems too extreme to argue that *all* aspects of the encoded trace are drastically modified by the context in which an event occurs (that is, that all aspects of the encoded description are relative to the specific context); presumably, some aspects are relatively invariant across contexts. It has been suggested, for example, that physical and structural aspects of words are relatively insensitive to changes in context, whereas semantic aspects are modified by context to a greater degree (Jacoby, 1974; Nelson & Brooks, 1974). The assumption that some aspects of an encoding or description are relatively invariant across contexts proves useful in a later discussion of retrieval processes.

Retrieval Processes

These ideas of distinctiveness and discriminability must be tied to some notions of how retrieval processes operate. We will assume a simple "feature overlap" model of recognition; that is, the probability of recognition increases with an increase in the number of common features activated at encoding and retrieval (or as a function of repetition of the same mental operations; Kolers, 1973). It follows that reinstatement at retrieval of the original encoding context enhances recognition by leading to an increase in the number of activated features in common between the study and test situations. Even out of context, re-presentation of an item may lead to some degree of recognition, and in this situation recognition can be enhanced by active reconstruction of the initial context. In this case the partial recognition may lead to constructions of plausible contexts ("Where might I have seen that person before?"); to the extent that one general line of reconstruction is associated with increased feelings of familiarity ("probably somewhere around the university"), that line is pursued until recognition reaches some acceptable level ("a student in my Introductory Psychology class"). In this sense, episodic and semantic information are thought to interact to enhance recognition (Lockhart, Craik, & Jacoby, 1976). One main point to be made here, and developed later, is that retrieval is not to be thought of as an all−or−none, automatic process. Rather, retrieval operations can be elaborated on or curtailed depending on task demands. The second point is that a distinctive encoding enhances recognition, because in this case when the encoding context is fully reinstated as retrieval information, such retrieval cues specify the prior event more precisely.

A number of memory effects can be described in terms of the interactions between distinctive encodings and adequate retrieval information. First, if the original encoding is difficult to accomplish, later memory of the event will usually be good. It is argued that the initial difficulty is associated with the formation of a more complete "description" of the stimulus and thus with a more distinctive trace of the event. As initial encoding becomes easier (with practice, say), there is a concomitant decrease in the level of recognition (Kolers, 1975). The effects of difficulty of *retrieval* on subsequent retention of the event can also be described in this way (Gardiner, Craik, & Bleasdale, 1973; Götz & Jacoby, 1974). The role of distinctiveness in explaining effects of depth of encoding, of difficulty of retrieval, and of interference is described more completely later in the paper.

Our ideas on retrieval start from the assumption that successful recognition involves the activation of some critical number of features or operations that are then matched with the record left by the event on its previous occurrence. If there is a sufficient degree of overlap between the features encoded in the trace and the features presently active, then recognition occurs. We also assume that the trace of the event's initial occurrence incorporates information about both the event itself and its context. If the event is re-presented in the same context on the second occasion, there will be a greater degree of overlap between trace information and test stimulus information; and the probability of recognition will be increased. Further, due to the more precise description of the original event, fewer new events will be falsely recognized. However, rather than treat recognition as all or none, with the probability of the "all" state increased with increasing degrees of overlap, we prefer to think of degrees of recognition; that is, the present stimulus is judged to be more or less familiar depending on the degree of overlap.

So far, this description of recognition makes it appear a rather automatic, passive process. However, we would like to stress the *active* nature of the processes involved and also the likelihood that retrieval processes, like encoding processes, can be modified both by the subject's strategies and by task demands.

We assume that the encoding processes that occur on presentation of a stimulus for recognition are partly driven by the stimulus itself but also occur in part through more creative, reconstructive efforts on the subject's part. That is, the stimulus evokes its habitual, "normal" encoding, but this more or less automatic encoding response may be elaborated by further processing. The purpose of the more elaborate encoding in an intentional recognition situation is presumably to reconstruct the initial context in which the event occurred, thereby enhancing the overall likelihood of successful recognition. The question immediately arises as to how the system goes about reconstructing the initial context if the stimulus itself is uninformative in this respect. We assume that such further processing is a "bootstrapping" operation with creation of very general, plausible contexts occurring first; if one such general context is associated with an increase in recognition familiarity, then the reconstructive operations will be refined in this direction until either full recognition occurs or the reconstructive efforts lead to no further increase in familiarity. In this sense, the record of the initial occurrence can be thought of as guiding and shaping reconstructive retrieval processes (Lockhart et al., 1976). This account should be distinguished from "generate—recognize" models of remembering (described by Tulving, 1976) in that such models argue for complete generation of possible encodings that are then matched with the trace; in contrast, the present account stresses the interactions between reconstruction and trace information while the reconstruction is being carried out.

The two points we wish to stress at present are—first, the notion that retrieval processes, like encoding processes, can be elaborated to a greater or lesser degree and that greater degrees of elaboration (of the correct qualitaive type) increase the likelihood of overlap with the trace information and thus of successful recognition. The second point is that retrieval processes can be split into two components—those processes induced rather automatically by the stimulus itself and those directed by task demands. We refer to these two aspects of retrieval as "spontaneous" and "directed" retrieval, but it should be stressed that these labels refer to portions of an underlying continuum: The stimulus itself spontaneously induces a certain amount of encoding, and this by itself may be sufficient to recognize the event; if it is not, and if the situation demands it, the system is directed to make further reconstructive efforts in an attempt to achieve recognition.

A third point concerns the type of information about prior occurrences of the event evoked by the present stimulus. Either rather general information or more specific detailed information of the initial context can be retrieved. This distinction corresponds repsectively to Tulving's (1972) notions of semantic and episodic memory, although we would wish to give greater emphasis to the continuity between the two types of information. That is, the total record of a common event's many past occurrences will contain some information common to all occurrences (e.g., a word's spelling), some common to groups of occurrences (usual settings in which the event occurs), and some specific to each particular context in which the event has occurred. At the time of test, more or less of this stored information will be retrieved: If only the general information is retrieved, the subject will feel that he or she "knows" the event, it feels familiar; if specific details of the initial context are retrieved, then the event will be recognized as having occurred at a particular time and place. Task requirements, as well as the subject's set and motives, are seen as directing the system to retrieve greater or lesser amounts of such past information. It is interesting to speculate on the relative ease and difficulty with which different types of stored information can be evoked; plausibly it is the general "semantic memory" information that is more easily and spontaneously evoked by the stimulus, whereas "episodic" information may be more difficult to retrieve and is thus evoked only when directed by task demands or when facilitated by re-presentation of the same context.

It should be noted that whereas we have described retrieval as a somewhat one-way process in which the records of past experience are elicited by present stimulation and by reconstructive activities, it is considered more likely that stored information and the present stimuli affect each other in a more interactive fashion. That is, it seems probable that the cumulative record of past experience serves also as an interpretative framework within which the present stimulus is understood. When a stimulus elicits (or interacts with) general "semantic memory" information, we talk about the process as *comprehension*; when, in addition, specific details of the initial context are evoked, we talk about episodic *memory* of the event. In common with others (e.g., Bransford, McCarrell, Franks, & Nitsch, 1977; Kolers, 1973; Restle, 1974), we are thus stressing the essential similarity between processes of perception, comprehension, learning, and memory.

In summary, retrieval is seen as a process in which the encoded trace is matched with the presently active encoding. The present encoding, in turn, is partly driven by the stimulus and partly reflects the results of more elaborate reconstructive operations. Thus retrieval operations vary in their extensiveness; habitual encodings are evoked spontaneously and automatically by the stimulus, whereas further elaborate processing is evoked if directed by task demands or by feelings of partial recognition. It is assumed that retrieval processes mirror initial encoding processes and may thus also be described as varying in depth, elaboration, and distinctiveness. This point of view suggests studies of "incidental retrieval" in which retrieval processes are controlled by orienting tasks in the same way that encoding processes have been controlled in many recent studies. Also, for the distinctiveness of an encoded trace to be effectively utilized at retrieval, it is considered necessary to reinstate the original encoding dimensions.

A stimulus may be recognized on the basis of its general familiarity; in this case, recognition is "context free." If a more specific retrieval question is asked, however, retrieval operations must be expanded by more active reconstructive activities in an attempt to reconstruct the original episodic context; in this case, recognition is "context dependent." The final point was made that past experience may interact with present processing in two major ways. In the first, attention is focused on the current pattern of stimulation, and past learning serves as a context for interpretation of presented stimuli (that is, past learning aids present comprehension). In the second case, attention is focused on specific episodic details of the past experience, and the present stimulus is used to specify the type of information required (that is, present stimuli act as cues to evoke memories of past events). Whether the interactions between past learning and present stimulation result in "comprehension" or "remembering" will depend in turn on the subject's set, goals, and motives.

Bransford et al. (1977) have stressed the "stage-setting" role of past learning in allowing degrees of differentiation of present stimuli; this role corresponds to the "comprehension" mode described above. We agree that this is one way in which the system can operate but suggest the system can *also* operate in the more traditionally accepted manner of the stimulus functioning as a retrieval cue to evoke contextual details of an event's past occurrences.

EMPIRICAL ISSUES

Some important empirical effects can be described in terms of the foregoing analysis. Brief descriptions of such effects are now given before proceeding to outline some further recent studies.

Selective Encoding vs. Emphasis

The levels of processing framework, as originally formulated by Craik and Lockhart (1972), claimed that the orienting task acts to select particular attributes of an event for encoding. An attribute (e.g., the sound of a word) will be encoded only if the orienting task requires the subject to deal with that attribute. It now appears that this original selective encoding position is too extreme; attributes in addition to those involved by the orienting task are encoded. In retrospect, the original levels experiments provide evidence that this is the case. Those experiments demonstrated that retention is higher after decisions about the meaning of a word (e.g., Does the word refer to an animal?) than after decisions about the physical characteristics of a word (Is the word in upper or lower case?). As claimed earlier, these results illustrate that retention performance is tied to the nature of input processing. However, the important thing to note for present purposes is that retention performance in the conditions where subjects judged the "case" of presented words was substantially above zero. If in making case decisions, subjects had described the words only as having appeared in upper or lower case, retention performance should have been essentially zero; this is true because remembered information regarding case alone would be of no help in the later test of memory for the particular words that were presented. The nonzero level of retention performance provides evidence that information beyond the minimal amount necessary to accomplish the orienting task must have been encoded. Nelson (Chapter 3, this volume) provides more direct evidence that information that does not appear to be involved by the orienting task is, nonetheless, encoded.

If orienting tasks do not act solely to select particular attributes for encoding, what do they do? Nelson's answer to this question is that orienting tasks have their effect by emphasizing the attributes that are involved by them. Recent work by Spyropoulos and Ceraso (1977) can be used to expand on this suggestion. Spyropoulos and Ceraso demonstrated that a manipulation of orienting tasks can influence the accessibility of an encoded trace. In their first experiment, for example, a colored shape was classified by either its color or its shape. After this task, one property of the colored shape was presented as a cue for recall of the other property. Recall was found to be substantially higher when the property that had been used as a basis for classification, rather than the unclassified property, was presented as a cue for recall. Results of additional experiments, reported in the same paper, lend convincing support to the conclusion that this greater cue effectiveness of the classified dimension was due to a difference in accessibility; the classified property was more effective at providing access to the trace, although—as a colored shape is an integral stimulus—both the classified and the unclassified properties were available in memory. Spyropoulos and Ceraso suggested that when a unit is stored, it is also classified; direct access to the unit is then only possible via cues that are specified in the classification system. That is, attributes of an event that are emphasized by an orienting task comprise a classification system within memory, and this classification system must be used to gain access to unemphasized attributes. The effect of contrast in determining distinctiveness can also be considered in this light. Contrast acts to emphasize an attribute and to increase the probability that that attribute is involved in the classification system; the classification system is based on attributes with the greatest diagnosticity. By this view, our earlier discussion of description and distinctiveness characterizes the classification system rather than the memory trace of an event.

A combination of the selective encoding and emphasis positions is desirable. It may well be that what is originally a difference in emphasis develops into selective encoding as a result of further experience with a given task. The idea is that processing is inefficient when a subject first engages in a task. As a consequence, attributes are dealt with in addition to those that are strictly required by the task; complete ignoring of these "irrelevant" attributes is accomplished only through extensive experience with the task. Returning to the original levels experiments, retention performance after subjects had made decisions about the case of presented words would be expected to reach zero only after subjects became highly experienced at making case decisions. In line with these notions, recent research and theorizing by Mackintosh (1975) make the point that learning to ignore aspects of an event plays an important role in selective attention. The effects of practice on a task are considered more fully in the following section.

Practice effects.   As a result of practice, performance of a task usually becomes more efficient; the task is accomplished smoothly, rapidly, and with less effort. It may be suggested that the subjects has learned to become more selective in terms of the aspects of the incoming stimulus being dealt with; also, individual parts of the task are integrated into the task as a whole and so lose their individual identity. Whereas these changes are to the subject's advantage for performance of the task at hand, they lead to a decrement in later memory for individual occasions on which the task was performed. Through practice, the subject need perform fewer and less extensive analyses—particularly of peripheral (contextual) information. Also, he or she has learned to operate in terms of classes of events rather than with individual events. Overall, it is suggested that greater efficiency is gained at the expense of memory for the individual occurrences of the task. Perception of words and other events can be considered as skilled tasks and thus amenable to the same theoretical analysis. Kolers (1975) has described his experiments on reading transformed texts in these terms.

Spacing effects. It is possible to interpret the spacing effect (or "lag effect"; Melton, 1967) in the above terms. The idea, basically, is that whereas repetition of an event confers a benefit for later recall, this benefit is attenuated progressively with proximity of the two events in time. That is, if an event is repeated closely after its first presentation, the system need perform less extensive analyses on the second occasion. For example, if you are given an arithmetic problem, $47 + 15 + 36 = ?$, and after working out the answer, you are immediately given the same problem again, the answer can be given with less effort and with the involvement of many fewer operations. Similarly, the less extensive analysis of the repeated event attenuates the positive effects of repetition. The attenuation itself decreases as the events are spaced further apart, and the subject must indulge once more in a full analysis. Other plausible analyses of the spacing effect have been advanced by Hintzman (1974) and by Lockhart (1973).

Isolation effects. It has been known since the experiments of Von Restorff were reported that dissimilar or incongruous items in a set are better remembered than are the background items. What processes underlie this effect? Cooper and Pantle (1967) have claimed that the retention advantage of an isolated item is due to its greater rehearsal; the subject spends more time rehearsing the isolated item. By the present analysis, in contrast, isolating an event has its effect by necessitating fuller processing of the isolated event than of its background events (or that of a control event presented against a different background). The background events "set" the subject to deal with events of a particular class; because the isolated event is not a member of this prepared class, the isolated event must be dealt with more extensively. This fuller processing may occur in part as the result of an attempt to resolve the incongruity associated with the different event. Again, task demands or the general cognitive context will determine the effort put into the resolution of ambiguity. For example, readers will either struggle to find meaning in vague and obscure statements or dismiss them as nonsense, depending on the credibility of the source (cf. Mistler-Lachman,

1975). It would be expected that occasional nonsense coming from a usually credible source would benefit from extensive processing and be well remembered. Given that the anomalous item has been processed extensively and a distinctive trace formed as a consequence, good retention will also depend on the presence of an effective retrieval cue.

Decision difficulty.   A difficult initial decision will usually be associated with high levels of retention for the reasons given above; namely, the difficulty necessitates more extensive processing, which then results in the formation of a more distinctive trace. Again, the level of retention will depend on other factors also; for example, the congruence of the retrieval cue with the encoded trace (Craik & Tulving, 1975) and the specificity of the relation between cue and trace (the "cue-overload effect"; e.g., Watkins & Watkins, 1976). Illustrations of the relation between initial decision difficulty and later retention levels have been provided by Gardiner, Craik, and Bleasdale, 1973; Kolers, 1975; and Epstein, Phillips, and Johnson, 1975, among others. A parallel series of demonstrations has related the difficulty of initial *retrieval* to subsequent retention level (e.g., Bjork, 1975; Götz & Jacoby, 1974; Lockhart, 1973).

Distinctiveness in study and retrieval processes.   Several investigators have attempted to eliminate differences in retention by controlling study processing. The usual procedure is to do what is essentially a levels experiment employing subjects from two different populations. If the performance of subjects from the two populations does not differ on the incidental test, it is argued that effects found with more traditional intentional learning procedures are due to differences in level of processing that are eliminated by means of employing orienting tasks and incidental learning instructions. If differences between the two populations remain with the incidental test, it is argued that some factor other than differences in processing is responsible for effects in retention. This strategy has been used to investigate developmental differences in memory among children (e.g., Brown, 1975), to assess the effects of aging (Craik, 1977), and to compare the memory of hospitalized individuals of different types with that of normals (e.g., Cermak, Chapter 6, this volume).

A weakness in the strategy just outlined is that it ignores potential differences in the processing of retrieval information. An experiment conducted by Karen Reay, under the guidance of the first author, can be used to illustrate this point. That experiment investigated age-related differences in memory among elementary-school students; level of processing was factorially combined with the form of the subsequent retention test. Effects of age were found to be larger when retention was tested by means of cued recall rather than by free recall. This was true although encoding processes are thought to have been equated across ages by means of orienting tasks and incidental learning instructions. A conclusion that can be drawn is that children of different ages differed with regard to the extent that they processed retrieval information. Just as younger children are less likely to extensively process items during study when they are instructed to learn, they are also less likely to fully process retrieval cues when they are instructed to recall. Variations in the distinctiveness of encoding during study will have relatively little or no effect if retrieval information is superficially processed. Further, due to an apparent similarity of the processes, deficits in retrieval processes might be expected usually to accompany deficits in encoding processes. To rule out processing or strategy deficits, it is necessary to attempt to equalize processing at retrieval as well as at encoding. Incidental testing procedures may be necessary to accomplish this end; there is no reason to believe that instructions to recall or recognize necessarily equalize processing among populations to any greater extent than do instructions to learn.

EMPIRICAL STUDIES

Three recent studies are described to illustrate some of the theoretical points already made.

Experiment 1

The point of this study was to examine the effects of initial decision difficulty on subsequent cued recall and recognition, while also varying the degree of association between the "decision" word and the word used later as the retrieval cue.

On each trial, the subject was given a card that had one word (the "focus word") printed on one side and two words printed on the reverse side. The subject's task was to study the focus word, then turn over the card and pick the word from the two that was more highly related to the focus word. Words on the reverse side were either high or low associates of the focus word or were unrelated to the focus word; the two words were either both highly related to the focus word (High−High), one high associate and one low associate (High−Low), or one high associate and one unrelated word (High−Unrelated). Similarly, other conditions were Low−Low, Low−Unrelated, and Unrelated−Unrelated. Decision difficulty was assumed to depend on the relative degrees of association of the two words to the focus word; thus difficult decisions would be involved in the High−High, Low−Low, and Unrelated−Unrelated cases; the easiest decisions should occur in the High−Unrelated case. Thus, for example, if the focus word was *water* and the two words on the reverse were *lake* and *ocean* (High−High), the decision was assumed to be difficult; if the focus word was *chair* and the two words were *table* and *grass* (High−Unrelated), the decision was assumed to be easy. The word picked out is referred to as the *target* word. The initial (incidental learning) task was followed by either cued recall—in

which focus words were presented as cues for recall of the chosen target word—
or by recognition of *focus* words, followed by recognition of *target* words.

The results (Fig. 1.1) show that both initial decision difficulty and the strength
of prior association between focus and target words have strong effects on cued
recall. Recognition of focus words is consistently higher than recognition of
target words (possibly reflecting either the greater attention paid to focus words
or the fact that target words were recognized later in the test sequence), and
both sets of recognition values are less affected than are cued-recall scores by the
strength of association between focus and target words. Decision difficulty does
have some effect on recognition of focus words but essentially none on recognition of target words. Finally, it should be noted that cued-recall scores are
higher than recognition scores for the highly associated focus—target materials
but that this superiority of cued recall drops for low associates and reverses for
unrelated words.

The main points we wish to make from this study are that retention level is a
function both of the nature of encoding and of the effectiveness of the retrieval
information to enable formation of mental operations that will match the trace.
Decision difficulty is assumed to affect the distinctiveness of the encoded trace,
but clearly the ease with which the focus word can facilitate reconstruction of the
focus—target complex is important too. In line with the preceding theoretical
analysis, it is argued that more difficult decisions required the target words to be
described more precisely—to be differentiated to a greater degree. Thus not all
aspects of meaning are encoded "automatically"; encoding depends on task
demands.

Since the focus words are given as a cue for the target words, those aspects of

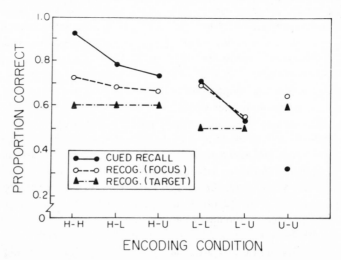

FIG. 1.1. Proportions of words recalled and recognized as a function of
experimental condition (Exp. 1).

the encoded trace concerned with focus−target interactions are particularly relevant for cued recall. However, recognition of target and focus words is less dependent on these aspects of the trace; other features of the general experimental context plus context-free aspects of the encoding may also help to facilitate recognition. The finding that recognition of focus words *is* affected by decision difficulty to some extent suggests that in this case retrieval processes are "expanded" to make some use of the focus−target interactions that took place at encoding. The crossover between recall and recognition levels emphasizes that retention level depends both on the distinctiveness of the trace and on the effectiveness of the retrieval cue to reconstitute the encoded information at the time of retention. This last point is taken up again in Experiment 2.

Experiment 2

The point of this study was again to vary both initial decision difficulty and the effectiveness of retrieval information to reconstitute the trace in recognition and recall. Decision difficulty was manipulated by asking a category question (e.g., "Is the word a type of tree?" "Is the word a type of cloth?") and then presenting a target word in a tachistoscope, ostensibly in a decision-latency experiment. Of the 72 question/word trials, 24 led to "no" responses; these were filler items and are not considered further. In the remaining 48 trials, 16 questions were each used 3 times throughout the total 72 trials. These 16 questions were category labels for the Battig and Montague norms, and the 3 different target words for each question were drawn respectively from the top, middle, and bottom thirds of the normative lists. It was assumed that category decisions would be easiest for high-ranking exemplars, more difficult for middle exemplars, and most difficult for low-ranking exemplars. In order to avoid a confounding with word frequency in the language, words were chosen that were matched for frequency across the three levels of decision difficulty. After the initial task was completed, half the subjects were reprovided with the 16 relevant category names and asked to recall the target words; the remaining subjects were given a recognition sheet with the 48 target words mixed randomly with 144 lures (the lures were 9 nonpresented words from each of the 16 tested categories). The subject was asked to check exactly 48 items—those that he or she had seen earlier. Recall and recognition thus both followed incidental learning.

It was predicted that since low-ranking exemplars involved greater decision difficulty, and thus the formation of more distinctive traces, these words would be best recognized. On the other hand, the greater ease of reconstructing high-ranking exemplars from the category label (as indexed by the norms) might reverse the effect for recall.

The lefthand panel of Fig. 1.2 shows that decision latencies increased systematically from high to low exemplars. Arguably, then, decision difficulty increased from high to low. The righthand panel of Fig. 1.2 shows that recognition also

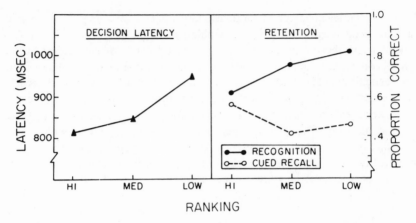

FIG. 1.2.   Decision latency and proportions recalled and recognized as a function
of ranking (Exp. 2).

rose from high to low but that cued recall was highest for the high-ranking exemplars. The interaction between rank and recall/recognition was significant
$(F, 2.60 = 15.1, p < 0.01)$.

The conclusions are the same as for Exp. 1. Greater decision difficulty is
associated with higher levels of retention, but this effect must be qualified by the
congruence or coherence of retrieval information with the encoded trace. In the
present case it is argued that the beneficial effects of a difficult decision are
swamped in cued recall by variations in the effectiveness with which the retrieval
cue can reconstitute the trace. The same effect is seen in the recall data of Exp. 1
when a difficult decision with an ineffective cue (U−U) is compared to an easy
decision with an effective cue (H−U).

Experiment 3

This final experiment was designed to illustrate the ditinction between spontaneous and directed retrieval. The notion is that recognition of an event does not
necessarily involve retrieval of that event's prior local context; as with study processes, retrieval processes are under the control of task demands.

The effects of repetition on cued recall were studied in situations that did or
did not require retrieval of the first encoding context at the time an item was
repeated. A long list of words included pairs of synonyms (e.g., *baby−infant*)
with the members of a synonym pair appearing successively in the list. In some
cases (Single Item) the second member of the pair was not repeated, but in other
cases (0-spacing) the second member of the pair was repeated immediately (e.g.,
. . . *baby infant infant* . . .). In still other cases, a varying number of unrelated
items (3, 6, or 12) intervened between repetitions of the second member of a
synonym pair (e.g., . . . *baby infant . . . . infant*). The subject's ostensible task

was to detect whether or not a synonym of each word had been presented. In a "1-back" condition, subjects were instructed to detect this similarity with respect to the immediately preceding word only; that is, each word was compared only with the word that immediately preceded it. In an "*n*-back" condition, similarity was to be detected with respect to all previous words in the list. Thus, the spaced repetitions of the second member of a synonym pair were accompanied by the requirement to retrieve the first member of the pair (the prior local context) only in the *n*-back condition.

Subjects were later given an unexpected cued-recall test, with the second member of each synonym pair serving as the cue for recall of the first member. It is argued that the beneficial effects of repetition will require that the prior local context be retrieved at the time an item is repeated; repetition should facilitate later cued-recall only in the *n*-back condition. In contrast, relatively context-free recognition, of the type expected to result from repetition in the 1-back condition, might interfere with later cued recall. This is true, because repetitions of an item in that condition are embedded in totally separate contexts on their two presentations; for recall of the first member of a synonym pair (context of the first presentation of repeated items), this is roughly equivalent to an A−B, A−D retroactive inhibition paradigm. Another question of interest was: Does massed repetition enhance later cue effectiveness? The results are shown in Fig. 1.3.

It is clear that cue effectiveness is not enhanced by repetition in the

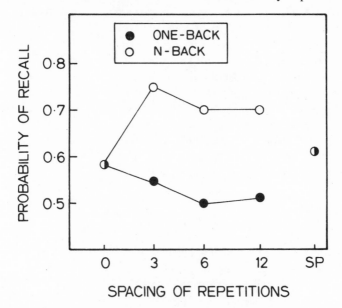

FIG. 1.3. Probability of recall as a function of spacing and experimental condition (Exp. 3).

"0-spacing" case; immediate repetition results in no further useful encoding. With spaced repetition, cue effectiveness is enhanced relative to the single item case only under n-back conditions. The point again is that retrieval of the previous synonym during presentation of a repetition does not occur "automatically" but is under task control. In contrast, under 1-back conditions, spaced repetitions interfere with later cued recall. This interfering effect of repetitions provides evidence that there is recognition of repetitions in the 1-back condition. However, recognition in this case must be relatively context-free, since otherwise facilitation rather than interference would be expected. Further, there is also a "spacing effect" for repetitions in the 1-back condition. In the 1-back condition, however, that spacing effect reveals increasing interference rather than increasing facilitation. It is clear that in this situation, at least, the direction of the spacing effect is under strategic control. When prior local context must be retrieved, increasing the spacing of repetitions enhances cued recall; this is possibly due to greater difficulty of retrieval under spaced conditions. When the retrieval of prior local context is not required but comparison with an irrelevant word is, increasing the spacing of repetitions interferes with cued recall.

Overall, this experiment provides a demonstration that retrieval of a past event is a matter of degree—prior local context is retrieved to the extent that the task demands it. Recognition of one member of a previously presented synonym pair does not necessarily involve the other member of the pair. This is true even though in free recall a synonym pair fulfills the requirements for being considered a unit; members of a synonym pair are grouped in recall, and either both, or neither, of the members of a pair are typically recalled (e.g., Jacoby & Goolkasian, 1973). Thus, the incidental procedures employed in the present experiment demonstrate a degree of independence in retrieval that is not revealed by intentional-recall tests. Retrieval is regarded as being quite analogous to a second encoding; just as study processing is under the control of task demands, so is retrieval processing. A difficult initial encoding requires more work to differentiate the specified item from other alternatives; a difficult retrieval requires more operations to specify the desired trace from others in the memory system. In both instances, the further operations result in more distinctive traces, which help to enhance future retention performance.

CONCLUSIONS

What relation do these ideas bear to levels of processing? In our view, the present paper, as well as suggesting new directions, develops some of the ideas suggested by Craik and Lockhart (1972) and by Lockhart, Craik, and Jacoby (1976). The notion of "depth" is still retained to describe qualitative differences in encoding processes and to suggest that semantic processes are generally more abstract, less tied to specific input channels, and more interrelated. Such processes are "deeper" in the system in the sense that they typically require more attention and effort to achieve. However, further thought was needed on such issues as the reasons underlying different levels of retention within semantic processing.

The ideas emphasized in the present paper are—first, the notion that greater depth and greater degrees of elaboration of the stimulus allow formation of a more distinctive, discriminable trace. As others have also suggested (Eysenck, Chapter 5, this volume; Klein & Saltz, 1976; Norman & Bobrow, 1977; Wickelgren, 1977), the different levels of retention associated with structural, phonemic, and semantic processing may reflect differences in the underlying descriptive dimension of distinctiveness. (But beware!—we are not back to unidimensional, crypto-strength models. Distinctiveness requires specification of the qualitative dimensions in which distinctiveness is achieved; a green object may be more easily distinguished from a background of white objects than is a circle from a background of ellipses, but it would not be satisfactory to describe the green object as "stronger" than the circle. "Strength" is a shorthand notation for performance level, whereas "depth" and "distinctiveness" attempt to describe the processes underlying performance; they reflect different explanatory levels from "strength".)

Other ideas stressed in the present paper are that encoding and retrieval processes are very similar in many ways. In particular, whereas practice and familiarity with a stimulus lead to some aspects being encoded spontaneously and "automatically," the degree to which the resulting encoding is elaborated (both during input and retrieval) is optional and under task control. Greater degrees of elaboration at input lead to formation of a more distinctive trace; since this distinctiveness is relative to a particular context or encoding dimension, this dimension must be reinstated at retrieval. Also at retrieval, information provided by the retrieval cue is elaborated by "reconstructive processes" to a greater or lesser degree depending on task demands. Finally, it was suggested that the extent to which episodic information is retrieved may also be under strategic control; the focus of attention is either on the present stimulus—with the general aspects of past experience serving as an interpretive background—or the focus is on specific details of past experiences—with present stimulation serving as a retrieval cue.

ACKNOWLEDGMENTS

The work reported in this chapter was supported by grants from the National Research Council of Canada to the authors.

REFERENCES

Bjork, R. A. Retrieval as a memory modifier: An interpretation of negative recency and related phenomena. In R. L. Solso (Ed.), *Information processing and cognition*. Hillsdale, N.J.: Lawrence Erlbaum Associates, 1975.

Bower, G. H. A multicomponent view of the memory trace. In K. W. Spence & J. T. Spence (Eds.), *The psychology of learning and motivation: Advances in research and theory* (Vol. 1). New York: Academic Press, 1967.

Bransford, J. D., McCarrell, N. S., Franks, J. J., & Nitsch, K. E. Toward unexplaining memory. In R. Shaw & J. Bransford (Eds.), *Perceiving, acting, and knowing*. Hillsdale, N.J.: Lawrence Erlbaum Associates, 1977.

Brown, A. L. The development of memory: Knowing, knowing about knowing, and knowing how to know. In H. W. Reese (Ed.), *Advances in child development and behavior* (Vol. 10). New York: Academic Press, 1975.

Brown, R. W. How shall a thing be called? *Psychological Review*, 1958, *65*, 14–21.

Cooper, E. H., & Pantle, A. J. The total-time hypothesis in verbal learning. *Psychological Bulletin*, 1967, *68*, 221–234.

Craik, F. I. M. Age differences in human memory. In J. E. Birren & K. W. Schaie (Eds.), *The handbook of the psychology of aging*. New York: Van Nostrand Reinhold, 1977.

Craik, F. I. M., & Jacoby, L. L. A process view of short-term retention. In F. Restle, R. M. Shiffrin, J. J. Castellan, M. R. Lindman, & D. B. Pisoni (Eds.), *Cognitive theory* (Volume 1). Hillsdale, N.J.: Lawrence Erlbaum Associates, 1975.

Craik, F. I. M., & Lockhart, R. S. Levels of processing: A framework for memory research. *Journal of Verbal Learning and Verbal Behavior*, 1972, *11*, 671–684.

Craik, F. I. M., & Tulving, E. Depth of processing and the retention of words in episodic memory. *Journal of Experimental Psychology: General*, 1975, *104*, 268–294.

Epstein, M. L., Phillips, W. D., & Johnson, S. J. Recall of related and unrelated word pairs as a function of processing level. *Journal of Experimental Psychology: Human Learning and Memory*, 1975, *104*, 149–152.

Gardiner, J. M., Craik, F. I. M., & Bleasdale, F. A. Retrieval difficulty and subsequent recall. *Memory & Cognition*, 1973, *1*, 213–216.

Garner, W. R. *The processing of information and structure*. Hillsdale, N.J.: Lawrence Erlbaum Associates, 1974.

Götz, A., & Jacoby, L. L. Encoding and retrieval processes in long-term retention. *Journal of Experimental Psychology*, 1974, *102*, 291–297.

Hintzman, D. L. Theoretical implications of the spacing effect. In R. L. Solso (Ed.), *Theories in cognitive psychology: The Loyola Symposium*. Hillsdale, N.J.: Lawrence Erlbaum Associates, 1974.

Jacoby, L. L. The role of mental contiguity in memory: Registration and retrieval effects. *Journal of Verbal Learning and Verbal Behavior*, 1974, *13*, 483–496.

Jacoby, L. L., & Goolkasian, P. Semantic versus acoustic coding: Retention and conditions of organization. *Journal of Verbal Learning and Verbal Behavior*, 1973, *12*, 324–333.

Klein, K., & Saltz, E. Specifying the mechanisms in a levels-of-processing approach to memory. *Journal of Experimental Psychology: Human Learning and Memory*, 1976, *2*, 671–679.

Kolers, P. A. Remembering operations. *Memory & Cognition*, 1973, *1*, 347–355.

Kolers, P. A. Memorial consequences of automatized encoding. *Journal of Experimental Psychology: Human Learning and Memory*, 1975, *1*, 689–701.

Lockhart, R. S. *The spacing effect in free recall*. Paper presented at the annual meeting of the Psychonomic Society, St. Louis, Missouri, November 1973.

Lockhart, R. S., Craik, F. I. M., & Jacoby, L. L. Depth of processing, recognition and recall:

Some aspects of a general memory system. In J. Brown (Ed.), *Recall and recognition*. London: Wiley, 1976.

Mackintosh, N. J. A theory of attention: Variations in the associability of stimuli with reinforcement. *Psychological Review*, 1975, *82*, 276–298.

Mandler, G., & Worden, P. E. Semantic processing without permanent storage. *Journal of Experimental Psychology*, 1973, *100*, 277–283.

Melton, A. W. Repetition and retrieval from memory. *Science*, 1967, *158*, 532.

Mistler–Lachman, J. L. *Some psycholinguistic studies of vagueness*. Paper presented at the Psychonomic Society meeting, Denver, Colorado, November 1975.

Nelson, D. L., & Brooks, D. H. Relative effectiveness of rhymes and synonyms as retrieval cues. *Journal of Experimental Psychology*, 1974, *102*, 503–507.

Norman, D. A., & Bobrow, D. G. Descriptions. A basis for memory acquisition and retrieval. Technical Report 74, Center For Human Information Processing, 1977.

Olson, D. R. Language and thought: Aspects of a cognitive theory of semantics. *Psychological Review*, 1970, *77*, 257–273.

Restle, F. Critique of pure memory. In R. L. Solso (Ed.), *Theories of cognitive psychology: The Loyola Symposium*. Hillsdale, N.J.: Lawrence Erlbaum Associates, 1974.

Rock, I. *An introduction to perception*. New York: Macmillan, 1975.

Spyropoulos, T., & Ceraso, J. Categorized and uncategorized attributes as recall cues: The phenomenon of limited access. *Cognitive Psychology*, 1977, *9*, 384–402.

Tulving, E. Episodic and semantic memory. In E. Tulving & W. Donaldson (Eds.), *Organization of memory*. New York: Academic Press, 1972.

Tulving, E. Cue-dependent forgetting. *American Scientist*, 1974, *62*, 74–82.

Tulving, E. Ecphoric processes in recall and recognition. In J. Brown (Ed.), *Recall and recognition*. London: Wiley, 1976.

Tulving, E., & Thomson, D. M. Encoding specificity and retrieval processes in episodic memory. *Psychological Review*, 1973, *80*, 352–372.

Tversky, A. Features of similarity. *Psychological Review*, 1977, *84*, 327–352.

Underwood, B. J. Face recognition produced by implicit verbal responses. *Journal of Experimental Psychology*, 1965, *70*, 122–129.

Underwood, B. J. Attributes of memory. *Psychological Review*, 1969, *76*, 559–573.

Watkins, M. J., & Watkins, O. C. Cue-overload theory and the method of interpolated attributes. *Bulletin of the Psychonomic Society*, 1976, *7*, 289–291.

Wickelgren, W. A. *Learning and memory*. Englewood Cliffs, N.J.: Prentice–Hall, 1977.

Wickens, D. D. Encoding categories of words: An empirical approach to meaning. *Psychological Review*, 1970, *77*, 1–15.

2 The Flexibility of Human Memory

William F. Battig
University of Colorado

Recent research on human memory has shown marked increases with respect to virtually every conceivable dimension or characteristic, although the obvious growth both in quantity and range of memory research may well represent its only feature on which all of us would be in complete agreement. We are continually being flooded with a torrent of new phenomena, paradigms or methodologies, types of measures, theoretical interpretations, and empirical data that are often inconsistent if not conflicting. Thus anyone who is interested in studying the effects of continuous memory overloads could hardly find a richer source thereof than those memory researchers who try to keep abreast of all the relevant literature.

This plethora of recent research on memory has at least one unfortunate consequence—namely, that most of us have become either generalists—with little specific knowledge or concern with detailed analyses of any single aspect of memory—or else specialists—with expertise limited to some specific subarea(s) of memory. To make matters worse, we must continually cope with radical shifts in research emphases, such that today's hot research topic may well be of little if any concern tomorrow. Rarely if ever do these changes in research emphases reflect any satisfactory resolution or understanding of an important problem or topic. Instead, they more typically represent an acknowledgment of the high complexity or limited generality of what originally had been conceived as a relatively straightforward research problem, causing researchers to move on to some new problem in their continual search for something that will be maximally productive and viewed as important particularly by their peers. Such "new" problems or approaches, of course, may represent little more than alternative ways of conceptualizing or relabeling old problems or phenomena, such that the

23

underlying commonality is obscured. More is said about this latter point later in this chapter.

Some of the foregoing introductory comments surely will elicit substantial disagreement but very little if anything in the way of disconfirming evidence. For present purposes, their primary relevance may be viewed as trying to justify or rationalize my own fixation of several years upon two widely demonstrated characteristics of human memory that I have found to be especially interesting and important. Both of these, however, appear quite counterintuitive, unnecessarily complex, and/or suggestive of inadequacies in current theorizing about memory. Consequently, they have also been widely ignored if not actively suppressed by most memory researchers.

The first of these two old but poorly understood aspects of human memory is that materials that are particularly difficult or presented under conditions of high interference, which nonetheless must be learned adequately, will typically show delayed retention that is at least as good and often better than for easier materials learned under noninterfering conditions. Secondly, individuals are remarkably inconsistent within themselves, typically using two or more quite different types of processes or strategies across different individual items of the same type and even across successive presentations or trials for exactly the same item. Moreover, such "within-individual differences" are most apparent for those more difficult items that must be learned under interfering conditions leading to improved long-term memory (as just described).

This is not the place to go into detail on the substantial body of evidence supporting these two phenomena, especially since general descriptions thereof are available elsewhere (Battig, 1972, 1975). In the 15 years since we first noted the phenomenon, there have been well over 40 different kinds of experimental demonstrations, especially of superior long-term memory and occasionally of greater intertask transfer following original learning under conditions of high interference and/or task difficulty as produced by such factors as interitem similarity or various types of task or contextual incompatibilities or inconsistencies. The majority of these experiments actually have come from other laboratories that typically attach little if any significance to such results, a notable exception being Nitsch's experiment as described in Chapter 15 by Bransford, Franks, Morris, and Stein.

With regard to within-individual processing differences, we have never failed to find these in abundance; nor have the few other researchers who have considered the matter directly. At best a small minority of individuals show complete consistency in their processing across even a maximally homogeneous set or list of items or other units, even at the level of such general types of strategies as verbal, imaginal, etc.

Our research on both phenomena (Battig, 1972, 1975) has been distinguished especially by its lack of impact on most memory researchers and theorists, although a closely related very recent concern with the importance of varied (and mutually interfering) types of learning contexts or conditions for producing effective memory can be seen in Chapter 15 by Bransford et al. Moreover, several other contributors to this book do acknowledge the typicality of multiple and variable types of processing of which any individual subject is capable to a much greater extent than has typified most recent writings on memory or other topics. Some (e.g., Jacoby & Craik, Chapter 1; Nelson, Chapter 3; Bransford et al., Chapter 15; and Anderson & Reder, Chapter 18) even begin to take into account within-individual variations whereby multiple processes can be used differentially across individual items under essentially the same conditions. Yet none of these, nor any other memory researchers known to me except Neimark (1976), explicitly tries to cope with the far-reaching theoretical implications of such within-individual processing differences. As is elaborated more fully later in this chapter (as well as in Battig, 1975), however, most if not all current cognitive information-processing theories can be viewed as completely correct— but only for some individuals on some occasions. Unfortunately, these within-individual inconsistencies also make all such theories incorrect, even for these same individuals on other occasions. Such inconsistencies clearly call for more complex and flexible theories incorporating multiple processing mechanisms that can be and typically are employed variably within as well as across individual tasks. This may be the most important single point of this chapter, and we return to it later.

Thanks to the initial encouragement provided by the Craik−Tulving (1975) and Lockhart−Craik−Jacoby (1976) modifications of the original Craik−Lockhart (1972) depth-of-processing view, and by the "contextualism" approach developed by the Minnesota group (e.g., Jenkins, 1974), I have recently begun to try to develop a general conceptualization of memory that may lead ultimately to a satisfactory explanatory framework—not only for within-individual processing differences but also for improved long-term memory for materials that are learned under interfering conditions or are difficult to learn for other reasons. In this context, I should further note that my preference for levels-of-processing and contextualism over other simpler or more explicit theoretical approaches is precisely due to the flexibility and other theoretical insufficiencies that have been so strongly criticized by others (e.g., T. O. Nelson, 1977).

The key features of this conceptualization of memory as it has developed to date are summarized briefly in the following section. Since some of these features are common also to other memory conceptualizations presented in this book and elsewhere, the sections that follow elaborate only upon those features that I judge to be especially unique or significant or for which we can present some relevant supporting data or other potentially useful elaboration. This chapter is concluded with a discussion also of some potentially important methodological points intended to increase the informativeness or relevance of future memory experiments.

A GENERAL CONCEPTUAL FRAMEWORK FOR
MEMORY RESEARCH

For present purposes, the key features of my current conceptualization of human memory are presented as eight closely interrelated encoding, processing, and/or retrieval characteristics associated with effective long-term memory in general and in particular with within-individual processing differences or with memory facilitation produced by contextual interference during learning. Because many of these eight features are consistent with (and, in some instances, directly influenced by) the views of other contributors to this volume, each point is followed in parentheses by a listing of other chapters known to emphasize the same or similar features of effective memory.

1. *Multiple Processing.*   In common with most memory theories presented in this book and elsewhere, any item is assumed typically to be encoded in terms of two or more distinguishable mechanisms or processes, which can operate simultaneously as well as sequentially.

2. *Variable Processing.*   In addition to multiple types of processing, the typical individual subject is quite capable of and typically uses quite different processing strategies even for different individual items of the same general type and even across repeated instances of exactly the same item.

3. *Elaboration and Organization.*   Especially under conditions of high contextual interference and variety, adequately processed items typically receive increased amounts and greater elaboration of processing, often consisting of organization of two or more items into larger units that may incorporate also other items or knowledge extraneous to the list or task (see also Anderson & Reder, Chapter 18).

4. *Distinctiveness.*   Particularly for recognition memory, an item must be encoded and processed in a distinctive fashion relative to other items in order to be remembered. Although greater elaboration can and often does produce a more distinctive and thus more memorable encoding, elaboration especially in the form of organization is likely to produce no greater (or even less) distinctiveness of any single item (see also Jacoby & Craik, Nelson, and Eysenck, Chapters 1, 3, and 5).

5. *Contextual Factors.*   The specific context(s) within which an item is presented, as well as the more general context of other items and task components (and in multitrial experiments also the previous encoding attempts for that item), are all assumed to be major determinants of the use of multiple and variable processing and of any consequent elaboration or distinctiveness of encodings.

6. *Contextual Interference.*   Especially across repeated trials in the typical list-learning experiment, any given item is subjected to varying but often very

substantial amounts of interference produced by the context of other items and the ways in which they are processed. Items subjected to minimal contextual interference may require little processing to meet the task requirements, but this processing may be insufficient for them to be remembered after a long retention interval. Items subjected to larger amounts of contextual interference require more processing, are learned more slowly, and within most experimental paradigms may receive insufficient processing to be learned and remembered as well as those easier items with less contextual interference. Items learned well enough to overcome this contextual interference, however, typically are remembered as well as or better than under low-interference conditions (see also Jacoby & Craik, Chapter 1).

7. *Contextual Variety.* Contextual changes within or across repeated encounters with any given item represent a principal source of contextual interference that has the further effect of increasing the contextual independence of the encoding(s) of that item and of facilitating its memory under changed contextual conditions (see also Bransford et al., Chapter 15).

8. *Encoding—Retrieval Congruence.* Memory for an item is importantly determined by the extent to which the original study and processing conditions produce an encoding that is consistent with (and can be retrieved under) the often-changed conditions or context that prevails at the time of retrieval, so that congruence of encoding with retrieval conditions is an especially important determinant of effective memory (see Tulving and Bransford et al., Chapters 19 and 15).

VARIABLE PROCESSING AND WITHIN-INDIVIDUAL DIFFERENCES

Although information-processing theorists typically postulate several different processing mechanisms even in very simple types of tasks, they have been curiously silent with respect to the availability of multiple ways of using these mechanisms to perform any given task. This probably reflects the tremendous complexity and indeterminacy such multiple and variable processing would add to the whole information-processing enterprise—for researchers as well as the individual subject. In my view, however, we can make no real progress until we acknowledge within-individual variations as well as multiplicity of processes and consider the important questions relating to how and why these multiple and variable processes exist and operate.

As mentioned earlier in this chapter, the existence of substantial processing variations within as well as between individuals (Battig, 1975) indicates the futility of searching for a single way in which information-processing mechanisms typically operate. Such simplistic research strategies can lead only to inconclusive results or interpretations and often to artefactual confrontations between two or more allegedly incompatible theories under conditions where all of these may represent a small part of a complete and satisfactory multiprocess theory. Thus rather than asking whether a particular theory is right or wrong, the kinds of questions we should be raising concern how often and under what conditions do individuals behave in accordance with the theory. With respect to the individual subject, the most fundamental questions should be at the following levels:

1. What are the several kinds of processing mechanisms or strategies in the subject's repertoire, and to what extent do these differ qualitatively rather than quantitatively along one or more dimensions?

2. What is the relative strength and/or range of usage for each of these processing mechanisms or strategies?

3. What are the principal determinants of which ones will be used in any particular task or situation?

We have nothing remotely resembling satisfactory answers to any of these questions, although it is only very recently that we have given them serious consideration in designing our experiments, and some preliminary evidence is presented in this and the following section. Perhaps most basic is the question of *why* individuals do show such variability in processing techniques even under conditions where a single fixed optimal strategy may appear quite sufficient for succesful performance. It may be helpful to approach this question from the perspective of the typical individual subject, for whom any memory experiment most likely represents a kind of problem-solving task, with the problem being to complete the task as quickly and effectively as possible or to impress the experimenter. Problem solving is of course demonstrably most effective for subjects capable of using a wide range of alternative strategies and of selecting the one(s) most appropriate to the requirements of the particular problem, being typically defined in these terms. Consequently, multiple processing might be expected to have similar adaptive qualities in improving subjects' performance in memory experiments.

The potential facilitation of memory resulting from changes in type of processing over a series of items is especially well demonstrated in a recent series of experiments by Bird (1976, 1977), using the PI-release paradigm developed so extensively by Wickens (1972) as an index of relative strength of component dimensions or attributes represented in the encoding of an item to be remembered. Bird modified this technique to show that shifts in type of processing (e.g., between pleasantness and number-of-letters judgments) led to memory improvements at least as large as did changes in actual item attributes (e.g., Wickens, 1972). These results clearly demonstrate how individuals can produce more distinctive and memorable encodings by shifting between different types of processing across successive items.

Further evidence of superior memory for subjects and items incorporating two or more different processing strategies comes from secondary findings in three unpublished doctoral dissertations from our laboratory, all concerned primarily with other problems. Particularly demonstrative of such effects is Shu-in Huang's (1976) finding that word pairs for which subjects switch strategies across repeated study (and strategy description) trials show superior uncued pair recall (but not cued response recall) after a week, even though such pairs were more difficult and probably not learned as well initially. Furthermore, Kay Barrow (1976) found number of reported strategies to be correlated 0.71 with paired-associate cued recall for individual subjects, increasing to 0.99 for different word pairs varying systematically in both concreteness and pleasantness. Also noteworthy in this context is Patricia Lauer's (1975) finding that in a free-recall task, number of different processing strategies is correlated 0.69 with subsequent recognition for elderly subjects, but only 0.06 for college students.

Correlational comparisons based on subjective strategy reports, like those of Barrow (1976) and Lauer (1975), admittedly provide far less than a direct assessment of the extent to which individuals actually making optimal use of multiple processing techniques show better memory as a result. In addition to the well-known limitations of such correlational analyses, reports of multiple strategies probably are made not only by subjects using these to improve their memory performance but also by poor or unmotivated memorizers who respond unsystematically or inaccurately in reporting their strategies. Similar confoundings may also occur for subjects reporting more consistent strategies across items. Better indices clearly are required to identify those individuals who make effective use of multiple strategies to generate more distinctive and memorable encodings as shown experimentally by Bird (1976, 1977), and some preliminary research along these lines is described in the following section.

Before concluding this section, however, we should consider within-individual processing variations as related to between-individual differences in memory deriving from more classical research on individual differences. A recent master's thesis at Colorado by Michael Masson (1977) can be used as a point of departure for this discussion. Masson's research constitutes a major correlational and factor-analytic investigation of individual differences in memory, including 30 memory performance measures on tasks covering the entire range of those typically used in any type of memory performance or test and 243 male undergraduate students providing data for each of these 30 measures. Despite the close comparability within certain subsets of these 30 tasks, their pairwise correlations were surprisingly small, with a median r of less than 0.17 and only 3% as large as 0.5. These low correlations obviously offer little evidence for consistent between-individual differences across tasks in memory abilities or processes. Such low correlations across tasks, however, are exactly what would be expected if individuals typically employ a wide range of multiple encoding and processing strategies, although such an interpretation is very indirect and subject at least to the same limitations on correlational evidence for within-individual differences as discussed in the preceding paragraph.

Consistent with Masson's evidence, however, are the unimpressively small differences at the level of basic information-processing mechanisms between college students selected from high and low extremes in verbal intelligence in the extensive research program by Hunt and his associates (e.g., Hunt, Lunneborg, & Lewis, 1975), which can at best account for only a small proportion of the individual-differences variance in the typical memory experiment. Moreover, most if not all of the differences demonstrated by Hunt et al. could be accounted for in terms of individual differences in the range of available processing mechanisms or strategies and the ability of the individual to select and use those strategies that are most effective for the task at hand. Thus within-individual processing variations may also provide a more fruitful source of important between-individual differences than the typical search for specific mechanisms or processes characterized by consistent differences between individuals, although major conceptual and methodological changes from current approaches to individual differences in memory and related topics would clearly be necessary prerequisites. First, however, researchers concerned with individual differences must be convinced of the necessity of taking into account differences within individuals, which is the intended message of the present (and to some extent, also the following) section of this chapter.

ELABORATION AND DISTINCTIVENESS

The importance of elaboration and distinctiveness for effective memory represent major emphases elsewhere in this book. Some relevant information about elaboration and distinctiveness has emerged also from some of our recent experiments, which were originally intended to get at the effects of multiple and variable processing upon recall and recognition memory. These experiments all employed the incidental word-processing paradigm characteristic of much levels-of-processing research, requiring subjects to process a given word on one or more semantic dimensions varying systematically in their relatedness to one another. The resulting variations in dimensional relatedness or distinctiveness were combined with different levels of elaboration produced by requiring multiple processing of the words on separate presentations in two or more ways or contexts.

In our first exploratory experiment (Battig & Einstein, 1977), each subject rated three otherwise equivalent subsets of 12 words on either one, two, or three different semantic dimensions. For the *related* group, these three dimensions were highly correlated (concreteness, imagery, and categorizability). The weakly correlated dimensions used by the *unrelated* group were concreteness, pleasantness, and number of attributes. After 48 hours, all subjects were tested for free recall followed by recognition of the 36 rated words. In addition to marked increases from one to three different word ratings, Table 2.1 shows significantly superior recognition by the unrelated group irrespective of how often the word was rated. Recall, however, showed no significant group differences, with the related groups slightly superior for words rated on all three dimensions for which memory should be most facilitated by the increased elaboration and distinctiveness presumably provided by multiple processing of words on less related semantic dimensions (Klein & Saltz, 1976). Instead, Table 2.1 shows the unrelated superiority to be maximal for twice-rated words on both recall and recognition, as well as being larger for once-rated than thrice-rated words.

This last result led directly to our second experiment (Battig & Weiss, in preparation), which required subjects to make single ratings of 72 words, 24 on each of the three related or unrelated semantic dimensions used by Battig and Einstein (1977). Due to the low recall levels for once-rated words shown in Table 2.1, only a 3-to-5-minute retention interval was used prior to successive recall and recognition tests for all rated words. During this interval, subjects read (and answered four true—false questions about) one of two stories containing non-overlapping halves of the 72 rated words. The relevance of this experiment derives from the word's encoded distinctiveness being greater for the unrelated than for the related groups, whereas subsequent reading of rated words in a meaningful story represents a type of nondistinctive elaboration of these words.

As shown in the last row of table 2.2, both recall and recognition differences favoring unrelated over related groups correspond closely to the Battig—Einstein (1977) results in Table 2.1, except that the present recall differences are somewhat larger and marginally significant. Of particular interest, however,

TABLE 2.1
Mean Proportion Correct in 48-Hour Recall and Recognition
(Battig & Einstein, 1977).

| | Number of Ratings | | | |
	One	Two	Three	Total
Recall				
Related group	.030	.121	.292	.148
Unrelated group	.050	.167	.263	.160
Total	.041	.145	.277	.154
Recognition				
Related group	.431	.638	.837	.635
Unrelated group	.510	.750	.887	.716
Total	.472	.696	.863	.677

TABLE 2.2
Mean Proportion Correct Recall and Recognition of Words Present and
Absent from Interpolated Story by Related and Unrelated Groups
(Battig & Weiss, in preparation).

	Recall			Recognition		
Words	Related	Unrelated	Total	Related	Unrelated	Total
Story	.391	.438	.424	.795	.873	.834
Nonstory	.341	.344	.342	.790	.894	.842
Total	.367	.401		.793	.883	

are the differences between recall and recognition for words contained within
the interpolated story. This latter type of elaboration significantly facilitates
subsequent word recall, and it is only those words elaborated by the interpolated
story that show any recall superiority for the more distinctive unrelated over the
related processing tasks. Recognition, however, is totally unaffected by the
interpolated story elaboration, showing a large unrelated-group superiority that is
closely comparable for nonstory and story words.

In interpreting these results, unrelated and related processing dimensions can
be viewed respectively as higher and lower levels of processing distinctiveness,
with subsequent inclusion of these words in a meaningful story representing a
kind of elaboration that should, if anything, reduce the distinctiveness of
individual words. Thus the results in Table 2.2 indicate that increased distinctiveness of processing facilitates recall only for those words receiving subsequent
nondistinctive elaboration. Alternatively, added elaboration appears to aid recall
primarily for words with more distinctive encodings. Such elaboration, however,
has no apparent effect on recognition performance, which is markedly facilitated
by the more distinctive unrelated processing conditions. These results offer
support especially for Eysenck's (Chapter 5, this volume) emphasis on distinctiveness as particularly important for recognition and on elaboration as more
important for recall, as well as demonstrating that elaboration does not necessarily
produce more distinctive encodings and that greater distinctiveness is not produced
only by more elaborate processing. Further research is in progress to follow up
on these apparent differences in elaboration and distinctiveness across recall and
recognition following related and unrelated multiple processing, as indicated by
the Klein—Saltz (1976) and Battig—Einstein (1977) studies.

The Battig—Weiss data also revealed that words rated for pleasantness were
recalled and recognized significantly better than words rated for any of the other
four related and/or unrelated dimensions, in line with previous results (e.g.,
Postman & Kruesi, 1977). Moreover, exclusion of the 24 words rated for
pleasantness eliminated any unrelated-group superiority for recall, although the
unrelated recognition superiority shown in Table 2.2 remained significant for

words rated on the other two unrelated dimensions of concreteness and number of attributes. Because of this apparent nonequivalence between individual semantic dimensions, a subsequent experiment (Packman & Battig, in press) compared recall and recognition following ratings on only one of the seven semantic dimensions used for 2,854 words by Toglia and Battig (1978), including the five used by Battig and Einstein (1977) plus meaningfulness and familiarity. Table 2.3 shows that pleasantness ratings once again produced significantly better recall and recognition than for any other dimension. That this superiority may be attributable to the greater distinctiveness of pleasantness from other semantic dimensions is indicated by the large negative correlations (all r's $\geqslant 0.83$) between each of the memory measures in Table 2.3, and the average of the six pairwise correlations of word ratings on each individual dimension with ratings on the other six dimensions as reported by Toglia and Battig (1978) and presented in the last column of Table 2.3. This suggests that the importance of distinctiveness for effective memory extends beyond the individual encoding and applies also at the level of distinctiveness of the dimensions or attributes on which the encoding is based.

CONTEXTUAL INTERFERENCE AND VARIETY

The preceding two sections have dealt primarily with concepts and research relevant to variable processing and within-individual differences with little direct relevance to our other major concern with greater interference or difficulty during original learning or processing as a possible source of facilitated delayed retention or transfer. The present section attempts to redress this imbalance by

TABLE 2.3
Mean Proportion Correct Recall, Recognition, and d' Measures for
Each of Seven Semantic Dimensions
(Packman & Battig, in press).

Dimension	Recall	Recognition	d'	Mean r[a]
Meaningfulness	.148	.835	2.42	.595
Categorizability	.153	.785	2.01	.612
Imagery	.177	.816	2.38	.638
Number of Attributes	.187	.865	2.48	.524
Concreteness	.189	.832	2.38	.519
Familiarity	.200	.799	2.34	.501
Pleasantness	.264	.928	3.17	.288

[a]These r values are the averages of the six correlations of word ratings on the row-designated dimension with the six other dimensions based on 2,854 words (Toglia & Battig, 1978).

discussing the important roles of contextual interference and variety for effective memory.

Until very recently, we had conceived of "intratask interference" as localized directly in the task itself and particularly in the interitem similarities or inconsistencies that lead to learning difficulty. Recent research in our laboratory, however, has indicated similar kinds of memory facilitation after very long delays for materials learned under interference produced by an additional concurrent processing task (Einstein, 1976), as well as showing that subjects' processing activities may modify or even eliminate the nominal interference inherent in the task itself (Lauer, Streby, & Battig, 1976).

Such results have led us to a broader and less direct conceptualization of functional interference including not only the interfering aspects of the task and materials but also factors extraneous to the task and inferred interference-related processing activities. Consequently, the original intratask-interference label becomes somewhat misleading and recently has been replaced by *contextual interference*. This latter designation seems especially appropriate in view of the important role of context in my general conceptualization of memory and the important roles of contextual factors, both within and extraneous to the subject's memory task and processing activities, in determining what does and does not constitute functional interference.

One major consequence of such an expanded view of contextual interference is to tie it closely to changes across trials in the experimental and processing contexts as potential covariates if not determinants of contextual interference. For present purposes, we will label such changes as *contextual variety* and suggest that increased contextual variety can produce more elaborate and distinctive processing that leads to better delayed retention, especially under changed contextual conditions at the time of retrieval. This emphasis on contextual variety as a source of improved long-term memory relates very closely to the Bransford et al. discussion of transfer-appropriate processing (Chapter 15). It also can be viewed as a way of overcoming encoding specificity and dependence of memory on reinstatement of the original encoding context (see Tulving, Chapter 19), by making the encoding less context-dependent and more likely to be retrieved under new or different contextual conditions.

The importance of contextual variety as a determinant of memory is demonstrated especially well by Hans Brunner's (1978) master's thesis research in our laboratory. Brunner used an experimental task requiring subjects first to study a polysemous target word in the context of a sentence biasing one of the word's meanings. Immediately thereafter, this target word was rated repeatedly as to how closely each of six different feature words related to the target word in its sentence context, with varying proportions of these six feature words appropriate and inappropriate to the original sentence context. The expected result was that subsequent memory for these target words would increase systematically with increased numbers of context-appropriate feature words.

Brunner's results, however, show higher proportions of subsequently recalled targets with two (0.683) and four context-appropriate feature words (0.675), whereas appropriateness of all six feature words (0.613) leads to recall comparable to all six feature words associated with a different meaning of the target (0.607). Stated another way, subjects exposed to a context that requires processing relevant to both meanings of the polysemous target word showed significantly higher recall than was found for feature-word processing involving only one target meaning, even when all targets had been studied and processed under substantial levels of contextual variety. Clearly, systematic variations in contextual variety offer a promising experimental technique for inducing and evaluating the effects on memory produced by multiple and elaborated processing, as well as contextual interference.

This section concludes with some discussion about why and under what conditions contextual interference and variety may lead to processing or learning that is more effective for subsequent memory or transfer tasks. As noted previously, such effects are most evident with lists or items that are difficult to learn but nonetheless get processed and learned to a high level. Further discussion of the importance of difficult items, however, is deferred to the following section.

The context and task requirements of the memory or transfer tests obviously represent critical determinants of whether or not memory will be improved due to the types of additional processing produced as a result of contextual interference or variety. Although the matter is obviously far more complex, we can illustrate this by contrasting two quite different ways in which contextual interference may develop. One is through such variables as increased interitem similarity, which induces additional processing consisting primarily of the formation of organizational and discriminative transformations that are of little value if the retention context is markedly changed. Such conditions, which predominated in our early research on intratask interference (Battig, 1972), are likely to aid memory primarily when the retrieval task maintains the key features of the learning context or reinstitutes enough of the original interference so that the additional processing used to overcome this interference is effective also for the memory test(s). Under such conditions, it is doubtful that markedly changed memory testing conditions would show much facilitation of retention, although this remains to be investigated directly.

A second quite different source of contextual interference involves increases in contextual variety like those of Nitsch as described in Chapter 15. If the subject is forced to process items in a variety of different contexts, changed contextual conditions should show greater facilitative effects on subsequent memory than conditions identical to original learning, as indicated by Nitsch's research.

Finally, we should revive within the present context our earlier interpretation, whereby interference which normally would produce forgetting is overcome as a result of the intratask interference present during learning, and thus becomes less effective during the retention interval so that subsequent memory is facilitated. This appears quite consistent with a distinctiveness interpretation of effective encoding, supplemented by an encoding—retrieval correspondence not only of the contextual features included in the encoding but also of those potentially interfering contextual factors that have been effectively discriminated from the encoding per se.

The basic point, however, is that increased contextual interference and variety can and often do lead not only to more effective original processing and learning but more importantly, to better subsequent retention and transferability of this information. Any satisfactory explanation of effective memory clearly must account for this phenomenon, and after 15 years of seeing it treated with skepticism or disbelief by most researchers, I welcome all of those who recently seem to be finding it of enough interest and importance to merit serious consideration.

THE NEGLECT OF DIFFICULT MATERIALS

The importance and generality of the effects of elaborated multiple processing and of contextual factors in human memory become especially convincing when we consider the strong evidence for them despite general usage of experimental designs and procedures ideally designed to obscure and prevent direct observation of such effects. The avoidance of ceiling effects is a key requirement of any serious memory experiment, which necessarily means that everything we know about how things are remembered is based entirely upon the subset of items that are remembered correctly. Consequently, we know little or nothing about any processing (or lack of same) for the often substantial subset of items that are not remembered correctly, especially when a recall measure is employed. It would not be inaccurate to characterize memory research as the psychology of memory for relatively easy items, especially within the typical single-trial procedures that characterize virtually all research based upon levels-of-processing or contextualist formulations, as well as most other recent memory experiments.

This limitation to a subset of easily processed and remembered items becomes problematical, of course, only to the extent that processing or memory levels change substantially with increased item difficulty. My suggested conceptualization of memory, however, is predicated upon the existence and importance of such differences, since it contends that effective memory depends heavily on multiple and variable processing and on contextual interference and variety. Such effects cannot help but be more evident within those more difficult items that are insufficiently processed after a single restricted study period and that require more time or trials to produce sufficient processing for subsequent memory.

Since item difficulty may be inseparable from differences in processing, as well as being a consequence rather than a source of other experimental variables, I have no intention of arguing for its theoretical significance. Rather, it represents a gross and sometimes post hoc basis for distinguishing between items that probably differ in other important ways as well, which for present purposes serves to help identify a badly neglected subset of materials of special importance for the observation and analysis of some critical aspects of memory. In addition, a greater focus on more difficult materials could contribute importantly to specification of the major determinants of such difficulty. Besides being a useful source of general information about memory, more difficult materials surely must correspond more closely to the kinds of everyday memory tasks and problems to which basic laboratory research should be applicable.

In the present context, however, probably the most important point is that greater levels of item or task difficulty can produce greater amounts and/or elaboration of processing even under conditions where study time or original learning level is comparable to that for less difficult items. Two recent unpublished experiments at Colorado can be cited to illustrate this point. One represents an effort Einstein and I made to manipulate interference within a multitrial free-recall task by presenting the target words in alternation with other words given directed-forgetting instructions, with interference varied in terms of the semantic similarity between words in these alternating sets. Much to our surprise, similarity had little if any effect either on learning or 1-week delayed memory for the target words. Further analyses, however, revealed significantly greater incidental delayed recall of the high-similarity than low-similarity to-be-forgotten words, which was localized entirely in those words presented in adjacent serial positions to the targets to which they were related. In other words, high-similarity conditions clearly produced greater recall of nontarget words without affecting target recall, which indicates more extensive and possibly different kinds of total processing under these conditions.

The second experiment, a 1978 master's thesis by Mark McDaniel, represents a more direct difficulty variation within each individual item. McDaniel's principal variable involved otherwise comparable sentences being presented either in normal or self-embedded forms, with identical semantic processing requirements for each type of sentence and subsequent memory tests for both semantic and surface properties of these sentences. Despite single presentations of each sentence for equivalent time intervals and identical semantic processing tasks, self-embedded sentences not only showed better memory for surface features but also were no different from the normal sentences in semantic memory. Clearly there was more extensive total processing for these more difficult self-embedded sentences.

In concluding this section, it should be noted that research directly concerned with memory for the most difficult items will probably require substantial methodological changes. In addition to the obvious increases in number of trials or learning criteria, potentially more effective means of accomplishing this may involve selectively presenting difficult items more often than easier items or making subsequent presentations contingent upon number of previous errors made on earlier trials. Having pioneered in the development of such drop-out procedures for paired-associate tasks even before the development of computer-controlled techniques for automatizing such contingencies (Battig, 1965), we hope to incorporate them where appropriate in our future research.

THE IMPORTANCE OF LONG DELAYED AND MULTIPLE TYPES OF MEMORY TESTING

In this section, it is argued that future memory research should examine much longer retention intervals than are typically employed in most research allegedly concerned with long-term memory, as well as making greater use of several different kinds of memory tests explicitly designed to assess various types of information contained within or reconstructable from whatever is remembered.

I have always been uncomfortable with the qualitative distinctions drawn by many memory theorists between short-term and long-term memory stores or stages, which appear to have outlived their usefulness and currently represent a serious impediment to the research evaluation of what I consider to be the important questions about memory. A major attraction for me of the levels-of-processing approach has been its provision of a much more appropriate and flexible means of conceptualizing the memory changes that take place over time. Thus I would prefer to see the levels-of-processing approach and terminology replace rather than try to coexist with the postulation of separate short-term and long-term memory stages. My principal objection derives from the tendency to emphasize the hypothesized sharp qualitative distinction between short- and long-term memory to the point where changes within long-term memory are neglected. Thus the typical "long-term memory" experiment is based on retention intervals of an hour or less and often no more than a few minutes. Such limited long-term memory experiments undeniably have shown interesting and important differences when contrasted with immediate memory. Nonetheless, memory after a few minutes often differs at least as much from memory after intervals of 1 or more days, weeks, or months (e.g., Einstein, 1976).

In any event, my entire conceptualization of memory as presented in this chapter is predicated upon major differences between performance on allegedly immediate memory tests (which in many experiments probably come closer to long-term than short-term memory) as compared with memory tests after longer delays. Since such differences and relevant evidence have recently been discussed elsewhere (Battig, 1975), only a single recent instance of some typical levels-of-processing research showing substantive changes over delay intervals longer than a few minutes is presented here (McDaniel & Masson, 1977). This research showed that the widely demonstrated equivalence of incidental semantic processing to intentional learning conditions in immediate memory can change markedly after 24 hours. More specifically, the McDaniel−Masson results show greater memory losses and inferior delayed recall for their incidental than intentional subjects, but only when categorized rather than unrelated word lists are used and subjects perform a different processing task on each word within a single conceptual category. Clearly incidental−intentional comparisons were substantially and differentially affected as a function of length of retention interval.

The other important methodological question I would like to discuss briefly concerns the insufficiency of any single type of memory measure and the desirability of including within any given memory experiment as many different kinds of measures as possible. Such multiple measures obtained in succession often encounter objections on the grounds that the first measure necessarily contaminates any subsequent measures and thereby reduces or eliminates any usefulness of the latter. Our usage of multiple measures, however, has indicated any such contamination to be relatively minor, especially when the sequence of multiple measures is carefully arranged so that any information provided to the subject as part of the previous measurement procedure is available also for any subsequent measure (e.g., cued recall following free recall or recognition following recall). Although such previous measures may well influence overall performance level, they rarely affect the comparisons between groups or conditions that are usually of primary concern.

There already exists an abundance of cases where more than one type of memory measure obtained for a single individual has proved to be particularly valuable and has even become standard practice. Measures of recall followed by recognition have characterized much of our research discussed in this chapter, as well as being important to the research of several other contributors to this volume. Our experiments also frequently include other types of measures, particularly (but not exclusively) when these appear useful for purposes of the particular experiment. Especially when such additional measures are not introduced until after the principal memory measure(s) have been completed, they can only add some potentially useful information that would not otherwise be available, as demonstrated by the following example.

In addition to illustrating the value of both recall and recognition measures, the previously discussed Battig−Einstein (1977) experiment also included as a post hoc measure subjects' judgments of the number of processings for each of the words they recognized as having been processed previously. Despite the superior recognition for words processed more broadly on unrelated dimensions, such words also elicited significantly smaller and less accurate frequency judgments than did words processed on highly correlated dimensions. Had we not obtained these frequency judgments, which on a priori grounds appeared irrelevant to our purposes in doing the experiment, we would have missed some potentially valuable information indicating a noncorrespondence between elaboration or distinctiveness and perceived frequency of multiple processings. Clearly there is much to be gained, and little if anything to lose, if we obtain as many different memory measures as feasible. Moreover, there may be added dividends from trying out new and different types of measures even when these may bear little relevance to the primary goals of the experiment, although these may introduce additional problems discussed in the following section.

"TRANSFER" AS RELATED TO MEMORY RESEARCH

Since a major theme of this book concerns major decrements in memory performance resulting from even relatively minor changes of retrieval from original learning or encoding conditions, and since Bransford et al. (Chapter 15) have reintroduced to modern memory research the old but infrequently used concept of "transfer" to refer to such changes, a few relevant historical and methodological points about transfer research appear appropriate here.

Probably the oldest and least controversial fact deriving from transfer research is that *any* type of change from the original learning to the transfer task typically produces marked decrements in performance relative to maintenance of the original learning task and conditions. This is clearly shown by Osgood's (1949) "transfer surface" depicting the decremental effects of changes in stimulus and/or response similarity, along with numerous verbal statements in the transfer literature such as "Improvement in any single mental function rarely brings about improvement in any other function, no matter how similar."

This latter quotation, from Thorndike and Woodworth's (1901, p. 250) pioneering report on experimental research on intertask transfer, suggests that especially Tulving's encoding-specificity principle represents merely a restatement if not a special case of a very old and general principle. Moreover, this principle comes from two of the most prominent early American representatives of the functionalist and associationist traditions that modern cognitive psychology allegedly has rejected and replaced. Another Thorndike—Woodworth (1901) quotation could even be viewed as stating the basic tenets of the levels-of-processing approach. "Attention to the meaning of words does not imply equal attention to their spelling, nor attention to their spelling equal attention to their length, nor attention to certain letters in them equal attention to other letters [p. 249]."

The essential point, however, is that current memory research on relationships between encoding and retrieval conditions obviously has much in common with classical transfer research, so we should take full advantage of what is known from previous transfer research that can be helpful in current research on memory. Thus three such points will be presented and discussed briefly.

The first is merely an extension of the previous Thorndike—Woodworth (and

Tulving) message. To the extent that even minor changes from encoding to retrieval conditions produce marked decrements in memory performance, it follows that such changes must yield performance measures that produce gross underestimates if not distortions with respect to what and how much is remembered. The intent here is not to discourage the use of such changes in memory testing conditions but merely to suggest that their negative effects need to be taken into account and, if possible, corrected. Perhaps the best way of doing this is to include multiple measures in the same experiment (as advocated in the preceding section) that systematically vary with respect to their congruence with the original learning or processing tasks or conditions, especially when the latter are also systematically varied.

A second relevant point made in several discussions of transfer research (e.g., Battig, 1966; Postman, 1968; Voss, 1968) is that performance, especially under drastically changed transfer or retrieval conditions, may provide information mainly about whether and how the original processing can be transferred or adapted to the different requirements of the transfer task, rather than providing any direct information about the original learning processes themselves. Consequently, it must be recognized that, for example, a forced-choice recognition test may elicit a correct response due to factors at best indirectly operative during the previous study and encoding processes.

Finally, transfer has classically been defined not only in terms of changes from the original learning to the transfer task but also in terms of learning on subsequent practice trials on the transfer task. Although Bransford et al. (Chapter 15) use transfer tasks that at best incorporate only the first of these two criteria, multiple-trial transfer tasks can also yield valuable information for memory researchers. Numerous instances could be cited where multitrial transfer effects have represented phenomena of direct research interest, such as the continuing research activity generated by Tulving's (1966) surprising finding of negative transfer on later trials of a free-recall list produced by previous learning of a part of this list.

That multiple-trial transfer tasks can also yield new insights on important problems not obtainable by other methods is especially well illustrated by Conover and Brown's (1977) recent transfer-based evaluation of serial-position differences in free recall. As an alternative to the final free recall for all of the several individually presented and immediately recalled lists typically used to demonstrate a "negative recency effect" for items in terminal serial input positions (e.g., Craik, 1970), they constructed for different groups separate transfer lists consisting either of items from the beginning, middle, or end serial positions in the original lists. In sharp contrast to their finding of negative recency for those transfer items that had been correct in immediate free recall, originally nonrecalled items actually showed significantly higher transfer performance if taken from the end than the beginning or middle positions. The Conover–Brown transfer results thus implicate selective processing and recall of easier items as important determinants of free recall except for terminal serial positions, where recency of presentation and/or priority of free recall of the end items are the primary determinants of immediate free recall. These differences between serial-position effects for immediately recalled and nonrecalled items could be evaluated only through a relearning transfer task, which also provides evidence supporting our previous arguments for the special importance of evaluating memory for difficult as well as easy items.

SUMMARY AND CONCLUSIONS

In an effort to increase our understanding of the widely demonstrated phenomena of interference during original learning as a source of facilitation of subsequent memory or transfer, and of within-individual processing variations especially for more difficult items, effective memory is conceptualized as incorporating multiple and variable processing, elaboration and organization, distinctiveness, contextual interference and variety, and encoding–retrieval congruence. Selective evidence and discussion is presented concerning the operation primarily of those factors that are especially important or unique to the present conceptual and research approaches to memory, many of which overlap extensively with other chapters in this book. More specific methodological discussions subsequently concern the importance of: (1) difficult items for the assessment of important memory processes; (2) greater attention to long-delayed and multiple memory measures; and (3) the role of transfer in memory research. Though making no pretense of providing a complete framework for future memory research, the points emphasized in this chapter are judged to be necessary components of any minimally adequate interpretation of memory. This latter goal clearly will be approached most effectively by trying to combine together most of what is presented in this book (as well as other present and future ideas about memory), rather than the more typical tactic of deciding either to accept or reject apparently conflicting and overly simplistic theoretical alternatives.

ACKNOWLEDGMENTS

This is Publication No. 70 of the Institute for the Study of Intellectual Behavior, University of Colorado, and is based primarily upon research supported by Research Grant BNS 72-02084 from the National Science Foundation. A number of present and former ISIB graduate students also made important contributions to the research and thinking that underlie this chapter. Most of these are identified directly in the test, but Gilles O. Einstein deserves special appreciation for his helpful comments on an earlier version of the chapter.

REFERENCES

Barrow, N. K. H. Word affect and imagery effects in recognition and recall memory. Unpublished doctoral dissertation, University of Colorado, 1976.

Battig, W. F. Procedural problems in paired-associate learning research. *Psychonomic Monograph Supplements*, 1965, 1, No. 1.

Battig, W. F. Facilitation and interference. In E. A. Bilodeau (Ed.), *Acquisition of skill*. New York: Academic Press, 1966.

Battig, W. F. Intratask interference as a source of facilitation in transfer and retention. In R. F. Thompson & J. F. Voss (Eds.), *Topics in learning and performance*. New York: Academic Press, 1972.

Battig, W. F. Within-individual differences in "cognitive" processes. In R. L. Solso (Ed.), *Information processing and cognition: The Loyola Symposium*. Hillsdale, N.J.: Lawrence Erlbaum Associates, 1975.

Battig, W. F., & Einstein, G. O. Evidence that broader processing facilitates delayed retention. *Bulletin of the Psychonomic Society*, 1977, 10, 28–30.

Bird, C. P. On the role of processing requirements in short-term memory. *Journal of Experimental Psychology: Human Learning and Memory*, 1976, 2, 234–243.

Bird, C. P. Proactive inhibition as a function of orienting task characteristics. *Memory & Cognition*, 1977, 5, 27–31.

Brunner, H. Context and breadth of processing. Unpublished master's thesis, University of Colorado, 1978.

Conover, J. N., & Brown, S. C. Item strength and input location in free-recall learning. *Journal of Experimental Psychology: Human Learning and Memory*, 1977, 3, 109–118.

Craik, F. I. M. The fate of primary memory items in free recall. *Journal of Verbal Learning and Verbal Behavior*, 1970, 9, 143–148.

Craik, F. I. M., & Lockhart, R. S. Levels of processing: A framework for memory research. *Journal of Verbal Learning and Verbal Behavior*, 1972, 11, 671–684.

Craik, F. I. M., & Tulving, E. Depth of processing and the retention of words in episodic memory. *Journal of Experimental Psychology: General*, 1975, 104, 268–294.

Einstein, G. O. Effects of simultaneous interference upon free recall learning and retention. *Memory & Cognition*, 1976, 4, 701–708.

Huang, S. I. Effects of concreteness on long-term retention: Differences in concreteness or in types of idiosyncratic processing. Unpublished doctoral dissertation, University of Colorado, 1976.

Hunt, E. B., Lunneborg, C., & Lewis, J. What does it mean to be high verbal? *Cognitive Psychology*, 1975, 7, 194–227.

Jenkins, J. J. Remember that old theory of memory? Well, forget it! *American Psychologist*, 1974, 29, 785–795.

Klein, K., & Saltz, E. Specifying the mechanisms in a levels-of-processing approach to memory. *Journal of Experimental Psychology: Human Learning and Memory*, 1976, 2, 671–679.

Lauer, P. A. The effects of different types of word processing on memory performance in young and elderly adults. Unpublished doctoral dissertation, Uniersity of Colorado, 1975.

Lauer, P. A., Streby, W. J., & Battig, W. F. The effects of alphabetic organization on the acquisition and delayed retention of semantically similar words. *Journal of Experimental Psychology: Human Learning and Memory*, 1976, 2, 182–189.

Lockhart, R. S., Craik, F. I. M., & Jacoby, L. Depth of processing, recognition, and recall. In J. Brown (Ed.), *Recall and recognition*. London: Wiley Interscience, 1976.

Masson, M. E. J. A multivariate approach to the study of memory and problem solving. Unpublished master's thesis, University of Colorado, 1977.

McDaniel, M. A. Memory for the meaning and surface of sentences as a function of processing difficulty. Unpublished master's thesis, University of Colorado, 1978.

McDaniel, M. A., & Masson, M. E. Long-term retention: When incidental semantic processing fails. *Journal of Experimental Psychology: Human Learning and Memory*, 1977, *3*, 270–281.

Neimark, E. D. The natural history of mnemonic activities under conditions of minimal constraint. In A. Pick (Ed.), *Minnesota Symposium* (Vol. 10). Minneapolis: University of Minnesota Press, 1976.

Nelson, T. O. Repetition and depth of processing. *Journal of Verbal Learning and Verbal Behavior*, 1977, *16*, 151–172.

Osgood, C. E. The similarity paradox in human learning. *Psychological Review*, 1949, *56*, 132–143.

Packman, J. L., & Battig, W. F. Effects of different kinds of semantic processing on memory for words *Memory and Cognition*, in press.

Postman, L. Association and performance in the analysis of verbal learning. In T. R. Dixon & D. L. Horton (Eds.), *Verbal behavior and general behavior theory*. Englewood Cliffs, N.J.: Prentice–Hall, 1968.

Postman, L., & Kruesi, E. The influence of orienting tasks on the encoding and recall of words. *Journal of Verbal Learning and Verbal Behavior*, 1977, *16*, 353–369.

Thorndike, E. L., & Woodworth, R. S. The influence of improvement in one mental function upon the efficiency of other functions: I. *Psychological Review*, 1901, *8*, 247–267.

Toglia, M. P., & Battig, W. F. *Handbook of semantic word norms*. Hillsdale, N.J.: Lawrence Erlbaum Associates, 1978.

Tulving, E. Subjective organization and effects of repetition in multitrial free-recall learning. *Journal of Verbal Learning and Verbal Behavior*, 1966, *5*, 193–197.

Voss, J. F. Serial acquisition as a function of number of successively occurring list items. *Journal of Experimental Psychology*, 1968, *78*, 456–462.

Wickens, D. D. Characteristics of word encoding. In A. W. Melton & E. Martin (Eds.), *Coding processes in human memory*. Washington, D.C.: Winston, 1972.

3 Remembering Pictures and Words: Appearance, Significance, and Name

Douglas L. Nelson
University of South Florida

Many researchers accept the assumption that words are represented in memory in terms of their distinctive features, attributes, or dimensions, a conjecture that has been extended to incorporate pictures within its domain (Bower, 1967; Nelson, Reed, & Walling, 1976). These features are usually conceptualized as being qualitatively different and independent, and accordingly, they can be classified into three general types: visual, phonemic, and semantic. Visual features characterize the stimulus as it exists in the physical world, its appearance. These features refer to the visual configuration produced by the lines, curves, angles, brightness, etc., making up both words and their corresponding pictorial referents (Gibson, 1971; Nelson, Reed, & Walling, 1976). Phonemic features refer to the phonemes associated with the name code for the stimulus and include both acoustic and articulatory attributes (Hintzman, 1967; Wickelgren, 1969). Finally, semantic features characterize the significance of the stimulus, referring to its denotative, connotative, associative, and conceptual meanings (Anderson & Bower, 1973; Johnson, 1970; Osgood, 1968; Rumelhart, Lindsay, & Norman, 1972).

THE SENSORY–SEMANTIC MODEL

The theoretical viewpoint described in this chapter embraces a process–feature orientation to memory and expresses this orientation within a relatively broad framework, the sensory–semantic model. The model is an evolving conceptualization developed by my students and myself over the past 10 years and represents our attempt to understand how the features of words and pictures might be

45

processed in different tasks, particularly sensory features. It is similar in some respects to our earlier coding−access−recognition conceptualization (Nelson, Wheeler, Borden, & Brooks, 1974), and therefore, it is compatible in many ways with levels-of-processing approaches (Craik & Tulving, 1975; Paivio, 1971; Posner & Warren, 1972) and with current explanations for retrieval (Jacoby, 1974; Tulving, 1976). The model achieves its unique qualities more in its characterization of the details of assumptions and in the facts that it purports to explain than in the invention of new ideas. Nevertheless, the conceptualization is different enough to warrant its presentation.

The sensory−semantic model is described by four major assumptions. These assumptions concern the types of features processed, their relative orders of activation, the role of selectivity, and finally, the effects of the distinctive and interactive qualities of activated encodings.

Types of features.   The types of stimulus features and their relative orders of activation are depicted in Fig. 3.1. As this figure illustrates, all three general types of attributes can be processed for both pictorial and verbal stimuli: visual, phonemic, and meaning. As indicated, meaning codes for simple pictures and

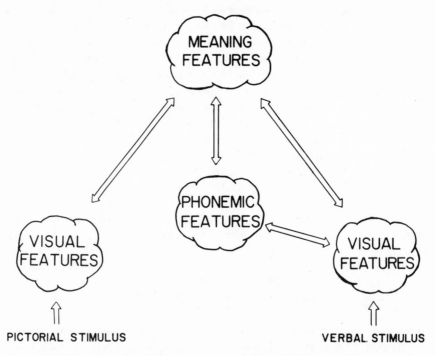

FIG. 3.1.   The sensory−semantic model of picture and word encoding. (From Nelson, Reed, & McEvoy, 1977a, © (1977) by the American Psychological Society. Reprinted by permission.)

their corresponding verbal labels are assumed to be functionally identical (Nelson, Reed, & Walling, 1976). The meaning of the concept *buffalo* is functionally the same whether it is activated by a line drawing or by its verbal referent. Of course, this assumption requires that the line drawing possess an unambiguous label or verbal description, and therefore, emphasis is placed upon having abstract and simple pictures.

Relative order of access.   Figure 3.1 also indicates that there are constraints on the relative order of access from the nominal stimulus to the various types of features. In a visual encoding task, the processing of both pictures and words usually begins with visual features, with appearance. However, access to phonemic features is different for the two kinds of stimuli. For pictures, access to these attributes is indirect, occurring only after access to meaning. Before a picture can be named, it must be meaningfully identified or understood. In contrast, phonemic access for words is direct and does not require prior processing of meaning features (Nelson & Brooks, 1973b; Nelson & Reed, 1976; Potter & Faulconer, 1975; Seymour, 1973).

However, regardless of the order of processing the types of features, encoding does *not* proceed in a series of dichotomous steps with the requirement that each successive step be completed before the next begins. Antecedent features do not have to be fully redintegrated into complete functional codes prior to processing succeeding features (e.g., Craik & Tulving, 1975; Posner & Warren, 1972). Encoding is assumed to be continuous, occurring through time, with several independent types of features being processed at any given moment in time (Kendler & Kendler, 1962). For example, referring to Fig. 3.1, picture processing begins with visual features; but before the total set of visual features are redintegrated into complete and detailed visual codes, the processing of meaning and phonemic features can proceed. A subset of features is sufficient for activating information for succeeding codes. Words are encoded in a like manner. Before a visual code is fully developed, the processing of phonemic features can be initiated, processing that is based upon the activation of a subset of the visual attributes. Similarly, the processing of meaning features can proceed from the activation of only subsets of activated visual or phonemic features. Note that with verbal stimuli, meaning access is achieved either directly from visual features or after some amount of phonemic processing. This issue is unresolved (cf. Kleiman, 1975; Meyer, Schvaneveldt, & Ruddy, 1974; Rubenstein, Richter, & Kay, 1975). However, at least for tasks involving the presentation of individual words without the benefit of meaningful context— tasks that are most germane to this review—it seems reasonable to assume that at least minimal phonemic processing is usually carried out prior to meaning access (Nelson, Brooks, & Borden, 1974). This view does not require that phonemic features be redintegrated into name codes prior to meaning access, only that some subset of critical phonemic features be activated.

Focal codes. The third assumption concerns the role of selectivity, with the model assuming that encoding efforts can be selectively directed. Additional and possibly conscious effort devoted to particular types of features increases the likelihood that those features will be redintegrated into focal mnemonic codes. These focal codes presumably can be controlled by externally directed environmental contingencies, by biases induced in the learning situation. Thus, encoding operations can be directed to specific types of codes by instructions to use interaction imagery or repetitious rehearsal (Paivio, 1971), by requiring subjects to answer different questions or to make different judgments about items (Craik & Tulving, 1975; Hyde & Jenkins, 1973), or by using different types of cues that bias encoding operations toward certain features (Nelson, Wheeler, Borden, & Brooks, 1974; Tulving & Thomson, 1973). Encoding operations also can be influenced by the requirements of the task itself—by whether it primarily involves recognition, paired-associate or ordering processes, etc.; by expectations for testing, and by whether it requires the acquisition of new skills (e.g., Frost, 1972; Kolers, 1975; Nelson, Reed, & McEvoy, 1977a; Nelson, Reed, & Walling, 1976; Tversky, 1973).

Encoding operations ostensibly determine the qualitative nature of the focal code. However, the encoded representation for any given nominal item is not exclusively controlled by these operations. Even though encoding efforts may be directed toward a particular type of feature, other attributes of the stimulus events may be activated with consequent effects upon performance. The model assumes that the processing of any feature activates corresponding representation. The activation of these other features is affected by order of access constraints and by habitual modes of processing. For example, if the task requires naming pictures, the relative order of access assumption suggests that both visual and meaning features of the pictures will be activated. Even though the focal codes may be the names for the pictures, attributes activated prior to these name codes will affect performance (Nelson, Reed, & McEvoy, 1977a). Similarly, even though processing efforts are directed toward activating meaning representations for word pairs, their visual and phonemic features may be activated also (Nelson, Reed, & McEvoy, 1977b; Nelson, Wheeler, & Brooks, 1976). And, finally, even though processing may be selectively directed toward encoding the sensory attributes of word pairs, the individual meanings of the words also may be activated because of habitual modes of semantic processing that subjects bring to the laboratory. Thus, although the sensory−semantic approach recognizes that encoding processes can be selectively directed, some degree of independence is assumed between the specific encoding operations or strategies used to process stimulus events and the functional representations of those events in memory. Put simply, encoding operations directed toward meaning features do not result in only meaning codes, and operations directed toward sensory features do not result in only sensory codes.

Distinctiveness−interactiveness. The fourth and final assumption of the model concerns the relative distinctive and interactive qualities of activated features or codes (e.g., Eysenck, Chapter 5, this volume; Lesgold & Goldman, 1973; Moscovitch & Craik, 1976; Paivio, 1971; Saltz, 1963). Retention level is assumed to be a direct function of the relatively unique and unified nature of the study trial encoding *and* the degree to which the retrieval environment recapitulates this encoding. Distinctive or interactive encodings are presumably easier to remember, because they are less susceptible to interference from competing encodings established prior to or during the task (Battig, 1968). The two notions—distinctiveness and interactiveness—are conceptually separable on logical grounds, but they are not altogether independent. It seems reasonable to assume that the encoding of a stimulus event can result in a distinctive representation that is not interactive; however, interactive encodings by their very nature are more distinctive. Both concepts seem to be necessary to provide a full account for recognition and recall findings.

This distinctiveness – interactiveness principle can be used to explain apparent differences in mnemonic effectiveness between various types of features (Craik & Tulving, 1975; Nelson, Wheeler, Borden, & Brooks, 1974). For example, given a list of unrelated word pairs and activation of specific visual, phonemic, and meaning codes for a particular target word, its meaning representation would typically be more effective for its retention. Relative to all other targets being encoded in the task, its meaning code would simply be more uniquely descriptive, differentiating, and more interactive with its context or cue. For example, suppose the item to be remembered was the word *leg*. This item might be encoded in the context of a visual – phonemic modifier (*KEG LEG*) or in the context of a semantic modifier (*ARM LEG*). The visual – phonemic modifier presumably would effect little change in the mnemonic representation of the sensory features for the word *LEG*. Whatever inherent distinctive features this item possesses would go relatively unchanged in the presence of a sensory cue that simply recapitulates the identical sensory attributes shared by the two items, the "*-eg*" ending. Such is not the case for semantic modifiers. The mnemonic representation of the semantic features for the word *LEG* would be specifically modified by the cue word *ARM*. The representation of the word *leg* is now distinctively related to a specific body part usually associated with primates. The potential meanings of *table leg* or *chicken leg* are not functionally activated.

The feature orientation of this model suggests that the process of cued recall is reconstructive in nature (e.g., Horowitz & Prytulak, 1969; Jacoby, 1974; Nelson, 1972). Words are not simply recalled as phonemic entities directly elicited as responses to nominal cues. Rather, they are redintegrated or reconstructed out of information contained in the retrieval cue itself, including associated extrastimulus temporal – contextual information. Accordingly, when a cue is presented, *its* sensory and semantic features are processed, and the activated information provides the basis for redintegrating information related to it prior to or during encoding. The effectiveness of this cue can be partially under the control of instructions indicating what features are relevant, or "focal." However, the effectiveness of this cue is primarily determined by the extent to which it reactivates specific sensory and meaning features processed during encoding. The more likely a given cue uniquely specifies its target by recapitulating features or codes activated during study, the greater are the chances that the target will be redintegrated (Fisher & Craik, 1977; Tulving & Thomson, 1973).

This conceptualization suggests that retrieval is a very specific process, easily disrupted. Since the features of the cues are processed during test, any reduction in the individual distinctiveness of the cues themselves should produce concomitant reductions in recall. If they share visual, phonemic, or semantic features, the processing of these common attributes at test will disrupt contact between the nominal version of the cue and its functional code as activated during study. On the positive side, this view suggests that cues that are strongly related or highly integrated with their target representation will be more effective than those that are weakly related or poorly integrated with their targets. Strong cues will be superior to weak cues, and semantic cues will *usually* be superior to sensory cues. The emphasis upon the word *usually* is intentional. One implication of the reconstructive access assumption is that semantic information will not invariably provide superior redintegrative information. Depending on encoding operations, the retrieval environment, and other constraints allied to processing time and task, visual–phonemic cues may specify potential targets more precisely than semantic cues. This differential effectiveness should be directly reflected in measures of recall under certain conditions (Bransford, Franks, Morris, & Stein, Chapter 15, this volume; Eysenck, Chapter 5, this volume; and Nelson, Wheeler, Borden, & Brooks, 1974).

SENSORY (VISUAL–PHONEMIC) FEATURES

According to the sensory–semantic model, encoding in a visual task typically begins with the processing of the visual features of both words and pictures, with the perceptual analysis and encoding of the appearance of the physical stimuli. When combined with the idea that all amounts of processing activate corresponding mnemonic representation, this conception suggests that sensory information may have a high degree of functional effectiveness. In fact, a substantial literature indicates that these features should not be characterized as transient or shallow. The processing of sensory features can result in the activation of tenaciously effective functional representations for both words and their pictorial referents.

Words

Evidence attesting to the significance of sensory attributes in word processing tasks comes from a variety of sources. The results of experiments using probe recall, short-term recognition, and release from proactive inhibition all support the generalization that these attributes represent effective components of the memory code under conditions ostensibly involving short-term storage (e.g., Bruce & Murdock, 1968; Kintsch & Buschke, 1969; Shulman, 1970). Other research findings suggest that sensory information is effective even under experimental conditions that primarily involve long-term storage. In free-recall tasks, phonetic relationships among words embedded in the middle of a list of other words facilitates their recall (Craik & Levy, 1970; Glanzer, Koppenaal, & R. Nelson, 1972). In paired-associate and serial-recall tasks, both positive and negative transfer effects have been obtained when items in successively learned lists were homophones (Laurence, 1970; Nelson & Davis, 1972; Wickens, Ory, & Graf, 1970). In recognition memory tasks involving delays that could exceed 5 to 6 mins, reliably more false recognitions are obtained on homophones of items appearing during study as compared to control items (Nelson & Davis, 1972; Raser, 1972). Other studies show that sensory features inherent in both intralist and extralist rhyme cues are highly effective as retrieval aids (Arbuckle & Katz, 1976; Nelson, Wheeler, Borden, & Brooks, 1974; Tulving & Watkins, 1975). Finally, and most impressively, there appear to be reliable savings for sensory information over intervals of up to a week (T. Nelson & Rothbart, 1972). The combined results of all of these studies encourage the inference that sensory attributes are effective components of the memory codes for words processed within the defined constraints of both short- and long-term storage.

Another source of evidence implicating the functional importance of sensory attributes can be found in research involving manipulations of the number of letters shared by a set of items, defined as *formal similarity*. The greater the sharing, the higher the degree of similarity. High amounts of such similarity can either facilitate or impair performance, depending on the situation. For example, facilitation occurs when learning to associate words that share letters with their stimuli, as in the pairs *cactus—carrot, instep—influx* (Nelson, Fosselman, & Peebles, 1971). Interference occurs when stimuli that share letters must be discriminated from each other. As part of a larger experiment, Nelson (1968) varied the amount of similarity among sets of words serving as stimuli for a word—number paired-associate task. The high-similarity stimuli were generated by using all combinations of two different first and last letters with three vowels (e.g., *ban, bat, ben, bet, bin, bit, pan, pat*, etc.). This list was four times as difficult to learn relative to a low-similarity control list. Thus, formal similarity among words substantially increased difficulty, despite the fact that each word was associatively and semantically distinct.

The magnitude of this interference effect was unexpected and, at the time, annoying. It did not seem to fit with the prevailing theoretical belief that sensory information was quickly lost through normal processes of decay and interference (e.g., Baddeley, 1966, 1972). Thus, this finding provided the impetus for a long series of paired-associate experiments dedicated to understanding the phenomenon and the limits of its existence. These studies were directed toward three particular problems: isolating the nature of the sensory representation, identifying the source of the sensory interference effect, and finally, determining the effects of processing strategies upon its potential elimination.

Nature of the sensory representation.   Our work on the nature of the sensory representation supports the inference that as a sensory entity, a word is structured and possesses a characteristic organization. Difficulty of learning a paired-associate list is not only affected by the amount of sharing among the stimuli but also by the location of the sharing (Nelson & Rowe, 1969). Difficulty is greater when first letters of the stimulus cues are identical than when last letters are identical (e.g., *tag, tea, tin*, etc. as compared to *mat, pet, bit*, etc.). Least difficulty is encountered when the similarity is located within middle positions (e.g., *bag, ham, mad*, etc.). This pattern can be completely reversed by confining the location manipulation to paired-associate pairs instead of to stimuli (Nelson, Fosselman, & Peebles, 1971). Thus, performance is best when word pairs share first letters (*tag−tea*), intermediate when they share last letters, and poorest if they share middle letters.

This first−last−middle pattern seems to be relatively invariant. It occurs with both three- and six-letter words and with concrete and abstract words, and it occurs regardless of whether the words are presented visually or aurally (Nelson & Brooks, 1973a; Nelson, Brooks, & Fosselman, 1972). The effect also appears to be independent of encoding time and type of response (Nelson, Brooks, & Fosselman, 1972). Finally, the pattern appears in a number of different tasks. It is found with both free- and serial-recall procedures (Nelson, 1969). It appears in tachistoscopic word identification (Bruner & O'Dowd, 1958), in word recall from a tip-of-the-tongue state (Brown & McNeill, 1966), and in word regeneration from one of its parts (Horowitz, White, & Atwood, 1968). Thus, the first−last−middle pattern emerges under a variety of conditions and methodologies.

However, this phenomenon appears to be dependent on processing the sensory code as an integrated entity. It is eliminated when processing efforts are focused upon individual letters or parts of an item. If the task is given a concept-formation aspect such as "words with the same first letter have the same response, etc.," the typical pattern is not found (Nelson, Bercov, & Leslie, 1970). Nor is the pattern obtained if nonsense syllables are used and presented visually so as to encourage cue selection based upon individual letters (Nelson, Brooks, & Fosselman, 1972; Runquist, 1968). Finally, when first graders are learning aurally presented pairs of words, the typical pattern emerges when the words are monosyllabic but not when they are bisyllabic (Wheeler, 1978). In this case, learning is fastest with middle-letter overlap. Going grade by grade, the usual and adult pattern for bisyllabic words does not clearly emerge until the fifth grade. Apparently, such words are initially treated as though they consisted of two distinct phonemic units, and with practice, they become integrated into single holistic representations.

All of these findings suggest that adults typically process English words as if they possessed a characteristic organizational structure, a structure that apparently involves sensory features and that conforms to a first–last–middle pattern. A number of explanations for this effect have been considered, empirically evaluated, and judged inadequate (Nelson, 1972). At the time it seemed reasonable to conclude that words are represented, at least in part, as phonetic sequences, as serial codes analogous to miniature serial lists. However, in all of these studies, manipulation of formal similarity confounded visual with phonemic similarity, a confounding that was regarded as unimportant. Subjects rarely mislabeled the stimuli when naming them during test trials, and therefore, visual features were considered to be relatively inconsequential. But when this assumption was finally tested, it was found to be false.

In a series of paired-associate experiments, both visual and phonemic similarity was independently manipulated at both initial and terminal letter positions. In addition, these lists were presented visually or aurally (Nelson, Brooks, & Borden, 1974). The results were straightforward. Under conditions of visual presentation, both types of similarity disrupted performance. Under conditions of auditory presentation, only phonemic similarity disrupted performance. These findings were independent of where the similarity was located, at word beginnings or ends. Thus, the functional sensory representation of a word apparently contains both visual and phonetic components when items are presented visually. It apparently contains only phonemic components when items are presented auditorily. As far as words are concerned, hearing what is seen appears to be more likely than seeing what is heard. Thus, the assumption that the first–last–middle pattern reflects the processing of a word as a serially structured code or sequence remains tenable. What is no longer tenable is the simplifying assumption that this sensory representation is only phonetic in nature. Visual information, or appearance, also seems to be encoded.

Source of the sensory interference effect.   The second problem examined in attempting to understand the sensory interference effect concerned the identification of its source. High levels of stimulus similarity in a paired-associate list conceivably could disrupt performance during one or both of two phases. Other than by chance, the test cue will evoke its target only if it contacts its representation as established during study and then only if this representation leads to the correct target (Martin, 1967). Thus, the interference that occurs when words look and sound alike may arise during the retrieval test itself, or alternatively, it may reflect a disruption of what was encoded in the first place.

According to the retrieval assumptions of the model, the features of each cue are processed at test. If so, then the processing of attributes common to other cues will occasionally lead to the activation of stimuli that share those features. For example, given the cue *BANK* at test, the processing of the sensory features of this item may inappropriately activate the functional encoding of *BRICK*, another list item. These list cues are nominally similar and presumably have similar functional representations within the domain of sensory attributes. Alternatively, the interference that occurs when cues are similar may emanate from what was encoded during study itself. For example, the processing of *BANK–HOUND* when this pair is on the screen conceivably could activate relationships between other similar stimuli, and the currently present response, between *BRICK–HOUND* and *BEAK–HOUND*. In this way, each response could become associated to each similar stimulus, resulting in considerable interference at test.

The traditional method for separating the source of effects consists of adding a stimulus–recognition task to normal paired-associate procedures (Martin, 1967). If a correct recognition response is given to a list cue, contact with the functional encoding of that item is assumed. Hence, if similarity disrupts correct cue recognition, then sensory overlap among the stimuli presumably interferes with the contact process during the test for retrieval. Alternatively, if similarity disrupts recall of the target only *after* correct cue recognition is established—that is, if it disrupts contingent recall—then encoding processes taking place during study would be implicated.

Using this general approach but avoiding certain problems (e.g., Runquist, 1974), Nelson, Brooks, and Wheeler (1975) varied sensory similarity among the cues as well as associative relatedness between cues and their targets. Word pairs were associatively compatible as in *BANK–VAULT*; they were unrelated, or they were incompatible. In the latter case, compatible items were simply mispaired.

The results indicated that high similarity disrupted stimulus recognition and had no effect whatever upon contingent recall. Thus, when one word is presented as the cue for another, the processing of attributes common to other *cues* impairs contact with its appropriate internal representation. An error in the Höffding step occurs, and nominal recall of the target is reduced. However, once contact with the appropriate representation of the cue is achieved, similarity seems to have no effect. Sensory similarity among the cues does not appear to disrupt encoding processes taking place during study. Thus, the results of recognition and contingent recall measures indicate that the sensory interference effect is limited primarily if not only to the retrieval phase. In contrast to these findings, associative compatibility between cues and their targets facilitated both stimulus recognition and contingent recall. Both measures indicate that performance is highest when pairs are compatible, next highest when they are unrelated, and lowest when they are incompatible. The processing of unique and differentiating features of the cues during study facilitates both functional contact at retrieval and recall of the target once contact is achieved. In fact, both functional contact and associative recall processes seem to be facilitated when the cues and their targets share letters, meanings, or interactive imaginal links (Dempster & Rohwer, 1974; Ellis & Tatum, 1973; Runquist & Evans, 1972).

Processing strategies and sensory interference. The results of research discussed up to this point suggest that the sensory representation of a word is organized as a sequential code reflecting the activation of both visual and phonetic elements and that interference produced by the sharing of these elements occurs primarily during the test for retrieval, during the process of contacting the representation activated during encoding. Our third area of research concentration has centered about attempts to experimentally eliminate sensory interference effects (Nelson & Borden, 1973; Nelson, Wheeler, & Brooks, 1976).

Initial findings suggested that sensory interference is remarkably tenacious. It is not eliminated by using concrete words, relatively long encoding and retrieval times, or, most unexpectedly, by using associatively compatible word pairings such as *BANK.–VAULT*. Other studies (Nelson & Brooks, 1973a) indicated that the interference still occurred when subjects were given concrete word pairs and were trained in using interactive imagery. Thus, although the "focal" encoding was directed to meaning, the activation of antecedent visual and phonemic features continued to influence memory performance.

However, in the earlier studies, the slowest study rate used was 3.0 sec per pair. Although this rate seemed adequately long for meaning processing, Nelson, Wheeler, and Brooks (1976) felt that even longer encoding times might be required, especially with interactive imaginal encoding. In the first study, a single study–test trial was given on a long list of concrete word pairs. Stimulus similarity, rate of presentation, and encoding strategy were manipulated, and responses were either associatively unrelated or associatively compatible and related to their stimuli. Presentation rate was 2.0 or 5.0 sec and the test trial was self-paced. The instructions either encouraged imaginal encoding or they were neutral in that no specific strategy was mentioned. The results indicated that slowing the rate, associative compatibility, and imaginal encoding all facilitated performance. Finally, sensory interference was present—present regardless of the status of the other variables. Nevertheless, its effects did appear to be lessened when imagery instructions were provided *and* the amount of allowed study time was 5 sec. Several additional experiments confirmed this trend, including one involving the use of verbal mediation instructions. Thus, sensory interference was statistically nullified but only when a long encoding interval was *combined* with encoding strategies that encouraged the use of interactive meaning encoding, either imaginal or verbal mediation.

According to the assumptions of the sensory–semantic model, the activation of the sensory features of the stimuli during encoding and the processing of these features again during testing lead to the apparent tenacity of their effects. Experimental elimination of sensory interference is accomplished only when sufficient time is allotted during study for the development of highly effective meaning mnemonics. Interactive processing of the pairs during encoding seems to increase the likelihood that specific and distinctive meaning features of the cues will be processed at test. The chances are greater that the encoded meaning representation for *cannon* will be contacted at test, not the sensory referents for *carton, cavern*, etc. However, even under relatively optimal conditions of semantic encoding, there are usually slightly but not significantly more errors made on the similar lists.

These results suggest an interesting implication. Though processing strategies may influence the nature of the focal encoding, other types of features appear to be functionally activated. This possibility was recently tested (Nelson, Reed, & McEvoy, 1977b). Several paired-associate studies were designed to compare the effects of different encoding strategies upon two types of interference, sensory and associative. Sensory interference was created by mispairing rhymes (e.g., *PAIL—SKUNK, JUNK—WITCH, DITCH—MAIL*, etc.) Associative interference was created by mispairing associatively related words. In control lists, the pairs were unrelated. The instructions to the subjects either encouraged interaction imagery or repetitious rehearsal.

The results of these studies indicated, as usual, that imaginal encoding facilitated recall. However, at both short and long encoding intervals (2 or 5 sec), mispairing rhymes and mispairing associates produced equivalent amounts of interference, regardless of whether pairs were encoded through interactive imagery or through repetitious rehearsal. Encoding strategy, therefore, did not influence the amounts of sensory and semantic interference. This finding seems inconsistent with the notion that encoding strategies or operations applied to verbal material can completely determine the nature of what is remembered (Craik & Tulving, 1975; Jenkins, 1974; Kolers, 1975). Overt rehearsal does not appear to activate only sensory encodings, and imaginal processing does not appear to activate only meaning representations.

Taken altogether, the results of all of these studies on processing strategy suggest that there is at least some degree of independence between processing strategies or operations and the types of codes that are activated as a result of applying those strategies. Sensory and semantic interference effects persist even though pairs are imaginatively encoded. Semantic interference is obtained even though instructions emphasize sensory attributes. Thus, although instructional set may determine what types of features are focal to the task, other types of features are apparently independently activated.

Pictures

Manipulation of visual—phonemic or sensory features indicates that processing these word attributes activates functionally effective codes. Manipulation of the visual features of pictures leads to a similar conclusion (Bencomo & Daniel, 1975; Frost, 1972; Nelson, Reed, & McEvoy, 1977a; Nelson, Reed, & Walling, 1976). In fact, the typical finding that pictures are easier to remember than their verbal labels, the pictorial superiority effect, may be accounted for in terms of the relative distinctiveness of their visual features (Nelson, Reed, & Walling, 1976). This result has traditionally been explained by the assumption that pictures are simply more likely to be dually encoded as both imaginal and verbal representations, as both visual codes and verbal label codes. This conceptualization presupposes that the pictorial superiority effect is directly produced by code redundancy (Paivio, 1971). One implication of the dual code hypothesis is that the superiority effect should be eliminated when it can be shown that the pictures are not labeled and therefore not dually encoded.

Nelson and Brooks (1973b) tested this possibility using pictures or their labels as paired-associate stimuli, with unrelated words serving as responses. Sensory similarity *among the labels* was varied. This manipulation was made possible by drawing pictures of objects that did not look alike themselves but whose labels were phonemically similar when pronounced—e.g., *parrot, puppet*, etc. Presumably, if the pictures were being named, then high relative to low *label* similarity should have disrupted performance. The results indicated that high label similarity impaired acquisition when instructions required naming the pictures aloud during test. However, when the instructions made no reference to such naming, high label similarity failed to generate any interference whatever. Furthermore, when shown each picture, the subjects reportedly did not name them, because they allegedly "already knew what they were." In conjunction with the verbal report findings, this experiment indicated that the pictures were not labeled and not dually encoded, and yet the pictures produced reliably higher levels of performance.

The generality of this finding was explored in a series of experiments. First, an attempt was made to determine if the naming process would be involved in learning to reconstruct the relative order of a sequence of pictures (Nelson, Brooks, & Borden, 1973). Paivio has suggested that the verbal system is most suited for processing sequential information (Paivio & Csapo, 1969). If this assumption is correct, then acquisition of the ordering of a set of pictures may require or at least encourage naming the pictures. A serial reconstruction task was used to test this possibility. In this task, stimuli are presented during study in some fixed order, and during test, copies of the stimuli are given to the subject, who attempts to reconstruct their relative order. For this experiment, mode of representation during study was factorially combined with mode of presentation at test, generating four conditions: picture—picture, picture—word, word—picture, and word—word. Label similarity was either low or high. The instructions made no reference to naming the pictures; and conceivably, when pictures were shown during study and then provided again at test, the task could be performed without such naming. However, label similarity disrupted performance in every condition, and the great majority of the subjects reported that they consistently named the pictures.

At this point, the findings suggested that the naming process is deployed in learning the order of a sequence of pictures but not in learning what unrelated word goes with what picture. Three additional paired-associate experiments were designed to explore other conditions in which the naming process might be utilized (Nelson & Reed, 1976). Picture-word, paired-associate lists were constructed, and relationships between the labels or names for the pictures and their responses were varied. The stimuli were pictures of common objects; and their corresponding responses were associatively unrelated (*BED − FLAG, BELL − COOKIE*) or associatively related (*BED − SLEEP, BELL − RING*), or they rhymed with the labels for the pictures (*BED − SLED, BELL − WELL*). Label similarity and naming instructions also were manipulated in order to assess the involvement of the labeling process.

As in the earlier study, when the instructions required naming at test, high label similarity disrupted performance. When the instructions made no references to naming, high label similarity had no effect. This pattern of results was obtained when the picture − word pairs were unrelated and when they were associatively related, suggesting the interpretation that the meaning of a picture is conveyed directly without apparent mediation through a verbal naming process (e.g., Potter & Faulconer, 1975; Seymour, 1973). The meaning allied with the picture of a *bed* is conveyed without having to name it. This direct access is illustrated in Fig. 3.1. In contrast to these findings, the results of the experiment in which rhymes were used as responses indicated that the pictures were named regardless of instructions. High label similarity produced equivalent disruptions of performance whether the instructions required naming or did not mention it.

The results of this whole series of experiments suggested that simple pictures of common objects are not automatically and consistently named, not spontaneously labeled. Pictorial naming appears to be an ancillary process, partially under the control of the information processor, to be used primarily in certain tasks and under certain conditions of encoding. This finding does not mean that labeling cannot play a facilitating or even a necessary role. However, this result is difficult to reconcile with the simplest version of the dual code hypothesis, one that attributes the pictorial superiority effect to dual picture − name redundancy (Paivio, 1971; but see Paivio & Csapo, 1973). Alternatively, the relative ease of remembering pictures might be explained in terms of inherent differences in the distinctiveness of either their visual or their meaning features. The visual representation for a simple picture may be more differentiating than the visual representation associated with its label. Similarly, the meaning representation allied with the picture of an object may be more distinctive than that associated with its label. Nelson, Reed, and Walling (1976) attempted to isolate the source of this superiority effect using pictures or their labels as paired-associate stimuli and unrelated words as responses. Visual similarity among the pictures was either high or low, and the stimuli were selected either from the same conceptual category or from different conceptual categories.

When visual similarity was high, all of the pictures looked alike, sharing a common configuration; and when it was low, the pictures were drawn to share a minimum of visual attributes. When conceptual similarity was high, all the stimuli of a given list belonged to the same taxonomic category, and items were selected so that they could be drawn to appear visually similar or dissimilar. Representative stimuli are presented in Fig. 3.2. Thus, kind of stimulus, visual similarity among the pictures, and conceptual similarity among all items were varied in a factorial design. In addition, since it seemed plausible that all variables might vary in effectiveness with amount of encoding time, rate of presentation was fast (1.1 sec) or slow (2.1 sec) during study.

The logic of the experiment was tied to the relative effects of visual and conceptual similarity for the two kinds of stimuli. If pictures are easier to remember than words because their visual codes are superior, then high visual similarity was expected to eliminate this superiority effect. Alternatively, if their visual configurations are not processed or if the resulting sensory codes are very transitory, then visual similarity among the pictures was expected to have little influence. Interest also was focused upon the relative amounts of conceptual interference produced as a function of kind of stimulus. Equal amounts of

Similarity Conditions

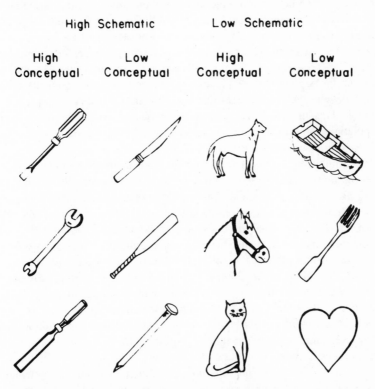

FIG. 3.2.   Representative pictures for similarity conditions (From Nelson, Reed, & Walling, Jr., 1976, © (1976) by the American Psychological Society. Reprinted by permission.)

conceptual interference could be taken to mean that similar meaning representations were processed for simple pictures and their verbal labels, and different amounts of interference would have suggested that the functional meaning codes were different.

The results of this experiment indicated that high visual similarity eliminated the pictorial superiority effect at the slow study rate and completely *reversed* it at the fast study rate. When the pictures looked alike and encoding time was limited, recall was reliably worse when pictures served as stimuli. In contrast, equal amounts of conceptual interference were produced for pictures and their labels at both rates of presentation. When embedded in a list of articles of clothing, a picture of a hat generates the same amount of conceptual interference as the word *hat*. Meaning interference seems to be independent of the kind of stimulus producing it, a picture or its label. This evidence is sketchy, but it suggests that functional meaning representations are identical for both pictures and words, a possibility that is reflected in the sensory−semantic model.

The results of manipulations of visual and conceptual similarity suggest that the primary difference between pictures and their corresponding verbal labels is inherent in their expression as physical stimuli. The visual code for a picture is apparently more differentiating than that associated with its label, and this distinctiveness may be reflected during retrieval processes operating at test (Wicker, 1970). Reducing this normally available distinctiveness by increasing visual similarities among the pictures generates substantial amounts of interference, despite the obvious fact that each picture possesses a unique meaning encoding. This finding is completely analogous to the effects of comparable manipulations of visual similarity among words (Nelson, Brooks, & Borden, 1974; Nelson, Wheeler, & Brooks, 1976).

The cumulative results of these picture studies suggested three inferences, inferences that ultimately led to the incorporation of pictorial stimuli into the sensory−semantic conceptualization. First, pictorial labeling does not appear to be a required, automatic, and consistently applied process. Secondly, the relative ease of remembering pictures does not appear to result because they evoke different and superior semantic encodings. Conceptual meaning codes seem to be very similar, if not identical. Finally, the relative ease of remembering pictures clearly has something to do with their visual features, with their appearance. The visual representations for a set of simple pictures appear to be more differentiating than the corresponding visual representations for their labels.

Each of these inferences has been integrated into the assumptions of the sensory−semantic conceptualization. Furthermore, in formulating this approach, access to phonemic features was assumed to be indirect for pictures, with label or name codes accessible only *after* meaning processing was initiated. For words, however, access to these features was assumed to be direct with no need for prior meaning activation. Nelson, Reed, and McEvoy (1977a) tested the relative order of access assumption using serial reconstruction and serial-recall tasks. In the first three experiments, some subjects learned to reconstruct the order of a series of pictures, and others learned to reconstruct the order of their labels. Since this task apparently requires the activation of label codes, the relative order of access assumption leads to the expectation that different types of features will be processed for pictures as compared to their labels. As shown in Fig. 3.1, visual, meaning, and phonemic features must be processed for the pictures. However, only visual and phonemic features need be processed for the words. Whereas similarity among visual and phonemic features should disrupt the sequential learning of both kinds of stimuli, high conceptual similarity should produce a relatively greater impairment of picture than of word reconstruction. The activation of meaning is more likely for pictures than for their labels in this task.

Stimuli were pictures or labels, and in different experiments, study rate, label similarity, visual similarity, and conceptual similarity were manipulated in various combinations. Thus, rate during study was three items or one item per sec, and all types of similarity were varied at extremes of low or high. The results indicated that high label similarity impaired serial ordering equally for pictures and words, independently of all other variables. This finding confirms the apparent usefulness or necessity of redintegrating verbal label codes in attempting to remember serial order. However, despite the fact that labels were more directly accessible for words than for pictures, reconstructing the order of the pictures was easier than reconstructing the order of their labels. The fast, three-item-per-sec rate did not eliminate this effect. According to the model, this superiority effect could be maintained, because the visual codes for the pictures were more discriminating or because processing meaning was more likely. If so, then high visual or high conceptual similarity should eliminate pictorial superiority. The results indicated that such was the case. When pictures were visually similar and shared a similar configuration or when pictures were all taken from a common taxonomic category, serial ordering performance was worse with pictures than with words. Finally, although conceptual similarity impaired the serial reconstruction of pictorial order, it had no apparent effect whatever on reconstructing word order. These effects of visual and conceptual similarity were completely replicated in a fourth experiment in which serial recall of the labels was directly required. Thus, in agreement with the relative order of access assumption, conceptual similarity had a greater disruptive effect upon pictures— suggesting that with these stimuli, the processing of meaning was more likely.

One final point about this series of experiments should be mentioned. The serial reconstruction and serial-recall tasks both emphasize the acquisition of order information and appear to require the activation of verbal labels, a process that seems to be most suitable for encoding discrete sequential events (Paivio, 1971). Thus, an argument might be made that the focal mnemonic code for these tasks is the verbal label. If this assumption is correct, then the results associated with pictures provide additional support for the selectivity assumption of the sensory—semantic model. Although the nature of the two tasks requires selective encoding of phonemic information, features activated prior to this code continue to affect mnemonic performance. As in the paired-associate experiments, even though the encoding operations may focus processing efforts toward one particular type of feature, the processing of antecedent features seems to activate functionally effective codes.

SENSORY VERSUS SEMANTIC FEATURES

Cuing with Rhymes and Synonyms

Research findings associated with words and pictures as stimuli converge upon the same conclusion. Their appearance as physical entities is analyzed, and this processing consistently leads to the activation of functionally effective visual encodings. This inference is supported in experiments designed to produce either interference or facilitation. Reduction in the visual distinctiveness of paired-associate stimuli disrupts the retrieval of associated information, regardless of whether this reduction is produced through letter sharing among words or through configuration sharing among pictures. Similarly, increases in the sensory distinctiveness of individual word pairs produced by letter sharing between them facilitates the retrieval of the related item. These effects are obtained under a wide variety of encoding strategies, tasks, encoding intervals, and semantic constraints. At the very least, this research indicates that there are a large number of conditions under which sensory features form an integral portion of the information processed about a stimulus.

Granting this mnemonic effectiveness and the qualitative division between sensory and semantic types of features, a question naturally arises, one that concerns the relative functional importance of each type of feature. Namely, what type of information produces the best memory performance, sensory or semantic? The work of Craik and his colleagues and the studies reported by Hyde, Jenkins, and their colleagues indicates that encoding operations directed toward meaning seem to invariably produce higher amounts of recall and recognition (e.g., Craik & Lockhart, 1972; Craik & Tulving, 1975; Hyde & Jenkins, 1973; Till & Jenkins, 1973). Craik and Lockhart (1972) suggest that the mnemonic effectiveness of a stimulus is a direct function of the "depth" to which that stimulus is analyzed during encoding, with superficial levels corresponding to the analysis of sensory features and with deeper levels concerned with the analysis of meaning features. According to this levels formulation, physical, phonemic, and semantic questions about the stimuli induce progressively deeper encodings, leading to expectations of correspondingly higher performance in the memory task. This expectation is consistently upheld under a variety of task conditions (Craik & Tulving, 1975). Memory for the meaning of an event consistently seems to exceed memory for its appearance and name. Craik and Tulving suggest that even "minimal semantic analyses will be more beneficial for memory than elaborate sensory analyses [p. 291]."

Our own work on comparing the relative effectiveness of the two types of features has been allied with the cuing paradigm (Bahrick, 1970; Thomson & Tulving, 1970). Although the results of this effort tend to support the inference of semantic superiority, they also indicate that this superiority is not inevitable. Mixed results are quite compatible with expectations based upon the selectivity and interactiveness assumptions allied with the sensory–semantic model. The memorability of an event is seen as complexly determined by a host of factors surrounding conditions of both encoding and retrieval.

The purpose of our first experiment was to compare directly rhymes and synonyms as retrieval cues (Nelson & Brooks, 1974). During study, 24 words were shown individually at a 2-sec rate, and following the last item, instructions for extralist cuing were read. For different groups of subjects these instructions indicated that rhymes or synonyms would now be shown and that each of these cues would aid in remembering one of the study words, or targets. Most importantly, the preexperimental strength of relation between cues and their targets was equated for rhymes and synonyms by the use of normative data, at both strong and weak levels. In addition, category size also was equated for the two types of cues. These norms were used to avoid confounding preexperimental relationships with type of cue. Semantic cues might have produced a higher level of recall, but it is crucial to be able to show that this higher level of recall occurred because of what was encoded during the experiment, not before (Bahrick, 1970). In other words, semantic cues might have produced higher recall because the associative relationships between the semantic cues and their targets were stronger to begin with, not because semantic information is inherently superior.

The results showed that recall was highest with strong cues, intermediate with weak cues, and lowest when no cues were provided (free recall). Rhyme and synonym cues were ordered in the same way and *did not differ*. Hence, when preexperimental relationships are carefully equated, sensory and semantic retrieval cues appeared to have equally effective redintegrative power. To a semantic agnostic, the implication that meaning might not be the sine qua non of memory was exciting. The paper was immediately shipped to the editor.

Almost as immediately, an extensive replication was undertaken with the same lists but with encoding conditions varied to control more directly sensory and semantic analyses of the stimuli (Nelson, Wheeler, Borden, & Brooks, 1974). In addition to manipulations of type and strength of cue, the cues were shown only during test as in the original experiment, or they were presented at study and again at test. The availability of the cue during study was expected to provide more specific sensory or semantic contexts, contexts that were expected to modify the encoding of the cue—target relationship (e.g., *TWIST MIST* versus *HAZE MIST*). Finally, the amount of encoding time was relatively short (1.2 sec) or relatively long (3.0 sec). All variables were manipulated between subjects, with the exception of strength.

The results were expected to conform to those of the initial experiment. They did, but with some important differences. Relative to free recall, reliable cuing effects were obtained for both rhyme and synonym cues, and independently of all other variables, strong were superior to weak cues. However, the similarity ended here. Variations of encoding conditions had no influence whatever upon the effectiveness of the rhyme cues. Regardless of study time or the presence of context cues, recall cued by rhymes produced about the same level of performance, with 67% of the targets remembered. By comparison, variations of encoding conditions substantially altered the effectiveness of the synonyms. When these cues were shown at test only, following the fast study rate, recall was at its lowest, 51%. This value increased to 62% as encoding time was lengthened. When synonym cues were shown at both study and again at test, these values increased from 67% to 79% as encoding time was lengthened. Thus, when contextual cues were absent during study, providing sensory information about the target was more likely to be helpful than the equal provision of semantic information. Under these conditions, rhymes were more effective than synonyms. However, the reverse appears to be true when contextual cues were present during encoding *and* encoding time was relatively long. In this situation, providing semantic information about the event was more beneficial, synonyms were more effective than rhymes. Given certain encoding and retrieval conditions, the greater effectiveness of semantic cues cannot be denied. For now, we attend the semantic church. However, sensory features can be effectively used to redintegrate previously encoded information, and as such these findings are consistent with much previous data (e.g., Brown & McNeill, 1966; Horowitz, White, & Atwood, 1968; Nelson, Fosselman, & Peebles, 1971).

The context interaction explanation. The findings associated with these cuing experiments are consistent with the fourth encoding assumption of the sensory−semantic model, with the idea that recall performance is directly affected by the interactive nature of the processing during study. When contextual cues are absent during encoding, specific sensory features are more likely to be functionally activated than specific semantic features, especially when processing time is very limited. Less encoding variability is associated with visual and phonemic features than with meaning features, not more (but see Martin, 1968). Under these conditions there are fewer options for encoding sensory features; they are more invariant. With this restriction, an extralist retrieval cue that unambiguously *reactivates* a specified portion of the sensory features of the target will be more successful than one that *activates* a portion of its semantic features, a specific set of attributes that may not have been processed during encoding. This view should not be construed as indicating that meaning is not activated at all. The emphasis here is on the conjoint study−test activation of specific features shared by both cue and target. Cue effectiveness is seen as the product of what was encoded during study and what specific information is provided by the retrieval cue at test (Tulving, Chapter 19, this volume). For example, given the target word *MIST* at study without contextual cues, the extralist cue _TWIST_ is more likely to redintegrate it than the extralist cue _HAZE_. In the rhyme cue, there is simply a greater degree of overlap of specifically activated features.

When contextual cues are present during study and there is sufficient time for interactive processing, then both sensory and semantic features of the individual cues and targets will be activated, including specific information shared by the two items. According to the selectivity assumptions of the sensory—semantic model, if the shared information is sensory in nature, then processing will be biased toward encoding these attributes. The "focal" cue—target encoding will be sensory. Although the semantic features of the cue and its target are activated, their semantic features do not share any obvious preexperimental relationship, and so most of the processing effort will be directed toward the obviously overlapping features, the sensory features. However, when the shared information is rhyme, the contextual cue does little more than recapitulate the sensory features of its target, virtually adding no unique information beyond that supplied during the processing of the target itself. Accordingly, the availability of the rhyme cue during study would not be expected to have much effect compared to showing it only at test. The cue is redundant in the features that it does share with its target, and in essence, the target remains relatively unmodified. As a consequence, any facilitating effect produced by providing a rhyme cue would seem to be primarily limited to the retrieval test itself and would help only because the cue serves to reinstate sensory attributes activated during study.

By way of contrast, if the shared information is semantic, processing will be biased toward encoding shared meaning attributes, and the "focal" cue—target encoding will be semantic. In this situation, the contextual cue interacts with and modifies the meaning of the target in terms of mutually shared semantic features. The cue indicates what particular meanings of the target among the many possible interpretations are most relevant. These particular meanings might have been activated when the target was presented in the absence of any contextual cue, but the activation of the same specific meanings inherent in a subsequently presented retrieval cue would seem to be less likely. Accordingly, presenting the semantic cue during study would be expected to have a substantial facilitating effect compared to showing it only at test. When the semantic cue is present in both phases, the same and shared meaning is more likely to be reactivated by the cue during test. In the example, the unique semantic information corresponding to "thin glassy vapor" is more likely to be reactivated if *MIST* is specifically encoded in the context of the cue _HAZE_.

One implication of the context interaction assumption is that semantic superiority is attributed to the context provided by the cue itself, not to the greater durability of the semantic code as initially suggested by Craik and Lockhart (1972). The two types of context cues should be equally effective over a retention interval that is at least as long as that usually required to test all list items. To test the durability hypothesis, Joe Wheeler, Dave Brooks, and I completely replicated the conditions involving the presentation of cues at study and test (i.e., Nelson, Wheeler, Borden, & Brooks, 1974). Retention was measured on an immediate test in one condition and after a 10-min filled delay in another condition. The subjects experiencing this delay solved long division and multiplication problems as rapidly and as accurately as possible. If semantic features are more durable over this interval, then a relatively smaller loss in the effectiveness of the synonym cues would be expected. The findings of the original cued-recall experiment were replicated on the immediate test, and at the delayed test, approximately 15% of the items were forgotten, a value that was evenly distributed over type of cue, encoding time, and strength. Thus, when preexperimental cue strength and category size are equated for rhyme and synonym cues, the rate of loss of sensory and semantic features appears to be equivalent. At least over an interval that is longer than that required to test retention for all list items, the superiority of the synonym cues canot be attributed to their relatively greater durability.

WHAT IS BEING ENCODED?

The model offered here suggests that both the sensory and the meaning features of *individual cues and targets* are activated regardless of whether the pairs are rhyme related or meaningfully related. However, the context provided by a rhyme cue and the context provided by a synonym cue differ substantially in how they influence the encoding of the cue−target *relationship*. The presence of a rhyme cue during study focuses processing upon the sensory relationship, but this cue does not seem to modify the encoding of the shared sensory features. The presence of an associatively or semantically related contextual cue focuses processing upon the meaning relationship and substantially modifies the nature of the cue−target encoding. The semantic cue acts to increase the likelihood that unique meaning characteristics shared by both the cue and its target will be activated. Semantic modification induces a more interactive and therefore a more distinctive cue−target encoding.

This context interaction explanation of rhyme−synonym differences emphasizes the importance of interactive encoding during study and the redintegrative role of the retrieval cue at test. This view is compatible with Tulving's encoding specificity principle (Tulving, Chapter 19, this volume) and is similar in many respects to the revised conception of levels of processing (Craik & Tulving, 1975; Fisher & Craik, 1977; Lockhart, Craik, & Jacoby, 1976). However, one important difference between these approaches is in the stress placed upon the exclusivity of the effects of the encoding operations in activating particular types of memory codes. Craik and Tulving (1975) imply that the nature of the encoding strategy or operations determines what gets stored. Questions directed to sensory features activate sensory codes, and questions directed to meaning features activate meaning codes. In contrast, the "focal" code assumption associated with the sensory–semantic conceptualization suggests that whereas the encoding operations can be focused on particular features, other attributes are processed and redintegrated into effective representations that influence performance.

Two cuing experiments were designed to examine this issue of what is encoded, one employing dual cues and one involving cue switches at the recall test. In the first experiment, the sensory–semantic model led to the expectation that context cues sharing both sensory and associative features with their targets should produce higher recall performance than cues sharing only a single attribute. For example, given that *GIRL* is encoded in a memory experiment, the retrieval cue *GLAMOUR* should be more effective in redintegrating its recall than the cue *DAINTY*. The normative strength of both cues is identical; but *GLAMOUR* shares both an associative and a first-letter relationship with the target, and therefore it provides additional unique information if no other target in the list begins with the letter *G*. To test this assumption Nelson and Borden (1977) varied the amount, the type, and the location of sharing. Cue–target pairs were associatively related and shared first letters, were only associatively related, or shared only first letters. Cues were presented only during test as extralist primes, or they were presented at study and again at test.

In essential agreement with earlier findings, having first-letter cues available during study had no effect relative to presenting them only at test (43% vs 39%), but the associative cues were much more effective if they were available during both phases (77% vs 49%). More importantly, dual cues were superior to single cues with each feature contributing independently and additively to recall. Percent correct recall in the cues-at-test-only condition was 67% for dual cues and 49% for associative cues. Comparable values for study–test conditions were 92% and 77%. These findings are consistent with the assumption that both sensory and meaning features are activated during encoding and that both types of features can act together to facilitate redintegration of target information. Thus, *GLAMOUR* is a better cue than *DAINTY* for recalling *GIRL* even when the subject's processing efforts are focused primarily if not only upon the associative relationship.

The second experiment was designed to examine the reverse possibility. For example, even though processing operations may be focused upon the shared sensory features of rhyme pairs, the meaning features of the individual cues and targets may also be activated. Hence, following the lead of Brooks (1974), John Walling and I designed a between-subjects cuing experiment in which subjects were given rhyme pairs or associatively related pairs during encoding, with retrieval cued by identical study cues, by extralist rhyme cues, or by extralist associative cues. Type of encoding was crossed with type of retrieval cue. In addition, these variables were crossed with the number of meanings possessed by the target. In one set of lists targets were nonhomographs, and in another, targets were homographs balanced so that each meaning was about equally likely in the absence of context.

Examples should clarify these manipulations. In the nonhomograph rhyme list, one of the study pairs was *TOWER FLOWER*, which was cued at test by *TOWER*, *SHOWER*, or *ROSE*. In the associative list, the comparable pair was *TULIP FLOWER*, cued by *TULIP*, *SHOWER*, or *ROSE*. In the homograph lists, one of the rhyme study pairs was *PECK DECK* cued by *PECK*, *SPECK*, or *CARDS*, with the corresponding associative pair being *BOAT DECK* cued by *BOAT*, *SPECK*, or *CARDS*. This variation in number of meanings was crucial, as different results were expected for nonhomographs and homographs in the associative shift conditions. Normative data were used to equate all types of cues and targets in terms of the strength of preexperimental relationships and in terms of category sizes. All pairs were shown at a 3-sec study rate, and all test trials were subject paced.

The most interesting aspect of this experiment is provided by the contrast in expectations derived from the sensory–semantic and the levels conceptualizations. Both predict that meaning cues will be superior to rhyme cues when the study and test cues are identical. Both ideas suggest that switching to an extralist rhyme cue should produce higher recall after a rhyme encoding than after an associative encoding, and both suggest that switching to an extralist associative cue will produce higher recall after an associative encoding, provided that the same meaning is cued at test as was processed during study. All of these expectations are based upon similar conceptions of the nature of the focal code during study and upon the idea that recall is dependent on reinstating the original encoding. However, the two views differ in conceptualizing the degree of control exerted by the nature of the encoding operations. In its most extreme form, the "levels" interpretation (Lockhart, Craik, & Jacoby, 1976) implies that only sensory information will be encoded for rhyme pairs. The sensory–semantic notion implies that the "focal" encoding will be sensory but that meaning features of the target also will be activated. Hence, the two approaches predict different results in the rhyme to associate shift condition for the nonhomograph as compared to the homograph lists. If the encoded representation established during study is only sensory, then recall in these conditions should be very low and equal. *TOWER FLOWER* at study followed by *ROSE* at test should produce the same low level of recall as *PECK DECK* followed by *CARDS*. However, if the meaning features of the target are activated at study, then recall should be less by half for homograph pairs. Since these items were balanced, the "boat" meaning of deck is just as likely to be activated as the "cards" meaning. The associatively related cue should reactivate the same meaning features only about half the time.

The findings of this experiment are displayed in Table 3.1. As reflected in these probabilities, all expectations based on the sensory—semantic model were confirmed, even the rhyme to associate shifts. Recall was essentially reduced by one-half, from 0.51 to 0.25, when the target in the rhyme pair had two equally probable meanings. These results are consistent with the paired-associate and the pictorial encoding findings described earlier in suggesting that there may be a considerable degree of independence between the specific kinds of encoding operations or strategies and the effective activation of features or codes corresponding to appearance, name, and significance. Even though processing is focused on sensory attributes, semantic information seems to be activated; and even though processing is focused upon semantic characteristics, sensory features appear to be functionally activated. The implication of these results is that a target item appearing within a rhyme pair is apparently processed just as "deeply" as a target item within an associatively related pair—just as "deeply" in the sense that target meaning is activated in both types of context. This result is important. The superiority of associative relative to rhyme cues when study and test cues are the same cannot be attributed to the activation of target meaning per se. It must be attributed to the greater interactive or elaborative encoding of the semantic *relationship* between the cue and its target.

TABLE 3.1
Probability of Correct Recall as a Function of Number of
Target Meanings, Types of Encoding Context, and
Type of Retrieval Cue.[a]

	Retrieval Conditions		
Target Meanings/Encoding Context	*Same Cue*	*Rhyme Shift*	*Associate Shift*
Nonhomograph targets			
Rhyme (*TOWER FLOWER*)	*TOWER* 0.70	*SHOWER* 0.48	*ROSE* 0.51
Associate (*TULIP FLOWER*)	*TULIP* 0.81	*SHOWER* 0.47	*ROSE* 0.60
Homograph targets			
Rhyme (*PECK DECK*)	*PECK* 0.65	*SPECK* 0.48	*CARDS* 0.25
Associate (*BOAT DECK*)	*BOAT* 0.78	*SPECK* 0.51	*CARDS* 0.21

[a]In several shift conditions, some subjects apparently experienced difficulty in attempting to remember which item was the cue and which was the target. When a lenient scoring criterion was used in which both target recall and cue intrusions were scored as correct, recall was affected only in the rhyme encoding-rhyme shift conditions, which averaged 0.68 after rescoring, and in the nonhomograph meaning shift condition, which averaged 0.70 after rescoring.

CONCLUSIONS

The sensory–semantic model described in this chapter is different from the original version of levels of processing (Craik & Lockhart, 1972) and from our own earlier formulation (Nelson, Wheeler, Borden, & Brooks, 1974). It is similar in many respects to Craik's revised conception (Craik & Tulving, 1975; Fisher & Craik, 1977; Moscovitch & Craik, 1976). Both approaches emphasize qualitative distinctions between sensory and semantic features; both views accept the notion that sensory feature processing precedes semantic analysis and that processing need not unfold in a lockstep fashion with antecedent features completely redintegrated before succeeding ones can be accessed. In addition, both approaches accept the notion that encoding operations can be directed toward specific types of features through variations in instructional sets, encoding contexts, materials, and tasks. Finally, each conceptualization is compatible with the idea that the retrieval cue serves to provide reconstructive access to information encoded during study, an idea that embraces Tulving's encoding specificity principle.

The sensory–semantic approach and the revised conceptualization of levels of processing clearly share a number of assumptions. However, there are at least two important differences. First, the sensory–semantic approach places much greater emphasis upon the importance and mnemonic effectiveness of activated sensory codes allied with words and pictures form a functionally effective with paired-associate and cuing paradigms. These procedures have shown that sensory codes allied with words and pictures from a functionally effective portion of the mnemonic representations activated under a variety of encoding conditions involving the presentation of discrete stimulus events. The sensory code linked with an individual word appears to have a characteristic serial organization reflecting the activation of both visual and phonemic features or of only phonemic features, depending on presentation mode. This code is tenacious in the sense that interference produced by sensory similarity—although seemingly limited to the retrieval test—is very difficult to eliminate by experimental means, by either focusing processing efforts on semantic or on imaginal attributes of the cues during study. In addition, with preexperimental strength and category size relationships controlled, sensory cues can be more effective than semantic cues as retrieval aids under certain task conditions. Moreover, these sensory codes can be equally persistent, at least over short intervals, and these sensory codes can combine additively with semantic retrieval cues in increasing recall performance. Finally, the sensory—semantic approach explicitly incorporates pictorial stimuli within its theoretical domain. The relative ease of remembering pictures in different tasks seems to be directly related to the effectiveness of sensory information provided by their visual features, by their appearance.

At the very least, sensory information activated for words and pictures cannot be summarily dismissed as unimportant, nonfunctional information that quickly decays or disappears as processing effort is directed toward other types of features. This conclusion does not imply that sensory information is somehow functionally superior to or even equivalent to semantic information encoded about a stimulus event, only that such information can be highly effective in its own right. The answer to the question concerning what types of information are mnemonically superior obviously will depend on the materials and the task conditions under which encoding and retrieval take place. Because of the interactive and distinctive nature of semantic information, memory performance for word pairs usually will be differentially facilitated by processing semantic types of features; but this superiority is not inevitable, occurring under all conditions, in all tasks, and for all subjects. Thus, the sensory–semantic conceptualization expressed here accepts the assumption that there are constraints operating upon the orders of processing various types of information; it accepts the basic idea of levels. Access to some types of features precedes access to other types of features. However, this approach does not accept the proposition that minimal semantic analysis will invariably produce higher recall performance than elaborate sensory analysis (Craik & Tulving, 1975). Trace retention is not primarily determined by the depth of analysis, with deeper encodings equivalent to semantic elaboration. Rather, trace retention is a function of the types of features encoded, of the distinctive, interactive, and unitary qualities of the encoding; and finally, it is a function of the characteristics of the retrieval cue used to provide reconstructive access to the encoding. Thus, the principles responsible for good retention espoused here are similar to those advocated by Craik, with one exception (Craik & Tulving, 1975; Moscovitch & Craik, 1976). The notion of distinctiveness is directly analogous to uniqueness, and the concept of interactiveness is related to the idea of congruity (Craik & Tulving, 1975; Moscovitch & Craik, 1976; Schulman, 1974). Interactiveness, as conceived in this chapter, refers both to compatibility with existing cognitive structures—e.g., the knowledge that chickens have feathers—and to the creation of new cognitive structures—e.g., to the representation created when a subject is told to generate an image of a chicken waving a flag. As such, interactiveness seems to be a broader term. The exception and the principal difference between the two positions surrounds the concept of depth itself, a concept that Craik seems to feel is a necessary addition to uniqueness and congruity (Moscovitch & Craik, 1976). The approach offered here suggests that this concept may be superfluous. The mechanisms of distinctiveness and interactiveness seem to be sufficient for explaining the superior memorability of semantically encoded events, when such superiority is evident.

The sensory–semantic conceptualization also differs from the levels orientation in the emphasis given to the exclusivity of effects produced by encoding strategies or operations applied to stimulus events (Craik & Tulving, 1975; Jenkins, 1974; Kolers, 1975). A common theme runs throughout the findings reviewed in this chapter. There seems to be a considerable degree of independence between specific encoding operations directed to words and pictures and the effective activation of features corresponding to appearance, name, and significance. Even though the mental activity of the learner may be directed toward processing semantic or imaginal features, sensory features seem to be consistently and effectively activated. Similarly, even though processing efforts may be concentrated upon encoding sensory features, semantic characteristics of the individual items making up the word pairs apparently are activated. Thus, whereas the nature of the mental activity of the learner may be directed by exigencies associated with instructional set, encoding context, and task— exigencies that influence the selective focus of the processing effort—other attributes of the stimuli seem to be consistently activated with consequent effects upon memory performance.

This activation of nonfocal attributes appears to be partially controlled by two factors. First, their activation seems to be influenced by habitual modes of semantic processing. For example, semantic features of the *individual words* making up a paired-associate pair or a cue–target pair seem to be activated under a wide range of encoding conditions. The second factor reflects constraints induced by the order of access to information, by what code is needed to perform the task, and by what other features must be processed prior to gaining access to that code. This constraint seems to be most clearly demonstrated when subjects learned to order pictures and words, a task that apparently is acquired most easily when the stimuli are consistently named (Nelson, Reed, & McEvoy, 1977a). Given that the focal code is *name* in this task, the relative order of access assumption implies that semantic similarity should disrupt sequential learning of the pictures to a greater extent than the words. Such was the case.

The findings reviewed here suggest that even when the mental activity of the learner is specifically directed to a particular type of feature inherent in the stimulus events, other types of information seem to be functionally activated. Of course, the processing of those nonfocal attributes represents some portion of the mental activity of the learner, and this activity is reflected in what is remembered about the stimulus events. The present view is entirely consistent with and sympathetic to the importance of what subjects *do* during encoding. However, the most extreme form of the mental operation approach is not consistent with the findings discussed in this chapter (cf. Jenkins, 1974; Kolers, 1975). Encoding operations directed toward semantic features do not result in *only* semantic processing, and encoding operations directed toward sensory features do not result in only sensory processing. Even though encoding operations may be focused on meaning or significance, appearance or name is often remembered; even though operations may emphasize appearance or name, significance is often activated.

ACKNOWLEDGMENTS

The research reported in this chapter was supported by National Institute of Mental Health Grant MH 16360. I am particularly indebted to Harold Hawkins, Dewey Rundus, John Walling, and Joseph Wheeler for their helpful comments on early drafts of this chapter and for their constant barrage of criticisms—criticisms that forced me to clarify, modify, and change many of my initial assumptions. To them I am grateful.

REFERENCES

Anderson, D. R., & Bower, G. H. *Human associative memory*. Washington, D.C.: Winston, 1973.

Arbuckle, T. Y., & Katz, W. A. Structure of memory traces following semantic and non-semantic orientation tasks in incidental learning. *Journal of Experimental Psychology: Human Learning and Memory*, 1976, *2*, 362–369.

Baddeley, A. D. Short-term memory for word sequences as a function of acoustic, semantic and formal similarity. *Quarterly Journal of Experimental Psychology*, 1966, *18*, 362–365.

Baddeley, A. D. Retrieval rules and semantic coding in short-term memory. *Psychological Bulletin*, 1972, *78*, 379–385.

Bahrick, H. P. Two-phase model for prompted recall. *Psychological Review*, 1970, *77*, 215–222.

Battig, W. F. Paired-associate learning. In T. R. Dixon & D. L. Horton (Eds.), *Verbal behavior and general behavior theory*. Englewood Cliffs, N.J.: Prentice–Hall, 1968.

Bencomo, A. A., & Daniel, T. C. Recognition latency for pictures and words as a function of encoded-feature similarity. *Journal of Experimental Psychology: Human Learning and Memory*, 1975, *104*, 119–125.

Bower, G. H. A multicomponent theory of the memory trace. In K. W. Spence & J. T. Spence (Eds.), *The psychology of learning and motivation* (Vol. 1). New York: Academic Press, 1967.

Brooks, D. H. The processing of word features in cued recall. Unpublished doctoral dissertation, University of South Florida, 1974.

Brown, R., & McNeill, D. The "tip of the tongue" phenomenon. *Journal of Verbal Learning and Verbal Behavior*, 1966, *5*, 325–337.

Bruce, D., & Murdock, B. B., Jr. Acoustic similarity effects on memory for paired-associates. *Journal of Verbal Learning and Verbal Behavior*, 1968, *7*, 627–631.

Bruner, R. W., & O'Dowd, D. A note on the informativeness of parts of words. *Language and Speech*, 1958, *1*, 98–101.

Craik, F. I. M., & Levy, B. A. Semantic and acoustic information in primary memory. *Journal of Experimental Psychology*, 1970, *80*, 77–82.

Craik, F. I. M., & Lockhart, R. S. Levels of processing: A framework for memory research. *Journal of Verbal Learning and Verbal Behavior*, 1972, *11*, 671–684.

Craik, F. I. M., & Tulving, E. Depth of processing and the retention of words in episodic memory. *Journal of Experimental Psychology: General*, 1975, *104*, 268–294.

Dempster, F. N., & Rohwer, W. D. Component analysis of the elaborative encoding effect in paired-associate learning. *Journal of Experimental Psychology*, 1974, *103*, 400–408.

Ellis, H. C., & Tatum, B. C. Stimulus encoding and the relationship between stimulus recognition and association formation. *Journal of Verbal Learning and Verbal Behavior*, 1973, *12*, 174–184.

Fisher, R. P., & Craik, F. I. M. The interaction between encoding and retrieval operations in cued recall. *Journal of Experimental Psychology: Human Learning and Memory*, 1977, *3*, 701−711.

Frost, N. Encoding and retrieval in visual memory tasks. *Journal of Experimental Psychology*, 1972, *95*, 317−326.

Gibson, E. J. Perceptual learning and the theory of word perception. *Cognitive Psychology*, 1971, *2*, 351−368.

Glanzer, M., Koppenaal, L., & Nelson, R. Effects of relations between words on short-term storage and long-term storage. *Journal of Verbal Learning and Verbal Behavior*, 1972, *11*, 403−416.

Hintzman, D. L. Articulatory coding in short-term memory. *Journal of Verbal Learning and Verbal Behavior*, 1967, *6*, 312−316.

Horowitz, L. M., & Prytulak, L. S. Redintegrative memory. *Psychological Review*. 1969, *76*, 519−531.

Horowitz, L. M., White, M. A., & Atwood, D. W. Word fragments as aids to recall: The organization of a word. *Journal of Experimental Psychology*, 1968, *76*, 219−226.

Hyde, T. S., & Jenkins, J. J. Recall for words as a function of semantic, graphic, and syntactic orienting tasks. *Journal of Verbal Learning and Verbal Behavior*, 1973, *12*, 471−480.

Jacoby, L. L. The role of mental contiguity in memory: Registration and retrieval effects. *Journal of Verbal Learning and Verbal Behavior*, 1974, *13*, 483−496.

Jenkins, J. J. Remember that old theory of memory? Well, forget it! *American Psychologist*, 1974, *29*, 785−795.

Johnson, M. G. A cognitive feature model of compound free associations. *Psychological Review*, 1970, *77*, 282−293.

Kendler, H. H., & Kendler, T. S. Vertical and horizontal processes in problem solving. *Psychological Review*, 1962, *69*, 1−16.

Kintsch, W., & Buschke, H. Homophones and synonyms in short-term memory. *Journal of Experimental Psychology*, 1969, *80*, 403−407.

Kleiman, G. M. Speech recoding in reading. *Journal of Verbal Learning and Verbal Behavior*, 1975, *14*, 323−340.

Kolers, P. A. Memorial consequences of automatized encoding. *Journal of Experimental Psychology: Human Learning and Memory*, 1975, *1*, 689−701.

Laurence, M. W. Role of homophones in transfer learning. *Journal of Experimental Psychology*, 1970, *86*, 1−7.

Lesgold, A. M., & Goldman, S. R. Encoding uniqueness and the imagery mnemonic in associative learning. *Journal of Verbal Learning and Verbal Behavior*, 1973, *12*, 193−202.

Lockhart, R. S., Craik, F. I. M., & Jacoby, L. Depth of processing, recognition, and recall. In J. Brown (Ed.), *Recall and recognition*. New York: John Wiley & Sons, 1976.

Martin, E. Relation between recognition and paired-associate learning. *Journal of Experimental Psychology*, 1967, *74*, 500−505.

Martin, E. Stimulus meaningfulness and paired-associate transfer: An encoding variability hypothesis. *Psychological Review*, 1968, *75*, 421−441.

Meyer, D. E., Schvaneveldt, R. W., & Ruddy, M. G. Functions of graphemic and phonemic codes in visual word recognition. *Memory & Cognition*, 1974, *2*, 309−322.

Moscovitch, M., & Craik, F. I. M. Depth of processing, retrieval cues and uniqueness of encoding as factors in recall. *Journal of Verbal Learning and Verbal Behavior*, 1976, *15*, 447−458.

Nelson, D. L. Paired-associate acquisition as a function of association value, degree and location of similarity. *Journal of Experimental Psychology*, 1968, *77*, 364−369.

Nelson, D. L. Information theory and stimulus encoding in free and serial recall: Ordinal position of formal similarity. *Journal of Experimental Psychology*, 1969, *80*, 537−541.

Nelson, D. L. Words as sets of features: The role of phonological attributes: In R. F. Thompson & J. F. Voss (Eds.), *Topics in learning and performance*. New York: Academic Press, 1972.

Nelson, D. L., Bercov, S., & Leslie, L. Ordinal positions of letters within words as concepts: Effect of assigning identical responses to words sharing letters in various ordinal positions. *Psychonomic Science*, 1970, *18*, 201−202.

Nelson, D. L., & Borden, R. C. Effect of "meaning" on the processing of the phonetic features of words. *Journal of Experimental Psychology*, 1973, *101*, 373−375.

Nelson, D. L., & Borden, R. C. Encoding and retrieval effects of dual sensory−semantic cues. *Memory & Cognition*, 1977, *5*, 457−461.

Nelson, D. L., & Brooks, D. H. Independence of phonetic and imaginal features. *Journal of Experimental Psychology*, 1973, *97*, 1−7. (a)

Nelson, D. L., & Brooks, D. H. Functional independence of pictures and verbal memory codes? *Journal of Experimental Psychology*, 1973, *98*, 44−48. (b)

Nelson, D. L., & Brooks, D. H. Relative effectiveness of rhymes and synonyms as retrieval cues. *Journal of Experimental Psychology*, 1974, *102*, 503−507.

Nelson, D. L., Brooks, D. H., & Borden, R. C. Sequential memory for pictures and the role of the verbal system. *Journal of Experimental Psychology*, 1973, *101*, 242−245.

Nelson, D. L., Brooks, D. H., & Borden, R. C. The effects of formal similarity: Phonetic, graphic or both? *Journal of Experimental Psychology*, 1974, *103*, 91−96.

Nelson, D. L., Brooks, D. H., & Fosselman, J. R. Words as sets of features: Processing phonological cues. *Journal of Experimental Psychology*, 1972, *92*, 305−312.

Nelson, D. L., Brooks, D. H., & Wheeler, J. W. Sensory and meaning features in stimulus recognition and associative retrieval. *Journal of Experimental Psychology: Human Learning and Memory*, 1975, *1*, 711−719.

Nelson, D. L., & Davis, M. J. Transfer and false recognition based on phonetic identities of words. *Journal of Experimental Psychology*, 1972, *92*, 347−353.

Nelson, D. L., Fosselman, J., & Peebles, J. Words as phonological sequences. *Journal of Experimental Psychology*, 1971, *87*, 361−366.

Nelson, D. L., & Reed, V. S. On the nature of pictorial encoding: A levels of processing analysis. *Journal of Experimental Psychology: Human Learning and Memory*, 1976, 2, 49−57.

Nelson, D. L., Reed, V. S., & McEvoy, C. L. Learning to order pictures and words: A model of sensory and semantic encoding. *Journal of Experimental Psychology: Human Learning and Memory*, 1977, *3*, 485−497. (a)

Nelson, D. L., Reed, V. S., & McEvoy, C. L. Encoding strategy and sensory and semantic interference. *Memory & Cognition*, 1977, *5*, 462−467. (b)

Nelson, D. L., Reed, V. S., & Walling, J. R. The pictorial superiority effect. *Journal of Experimental Psychology: Human Learning and Memory*, 1976, 2, 523−528.

Nelson, D. L., & Rowe, F. A. Information theory and stimulus encoding in paired-associate acquisition: Ordinal position of formal similarity. *Journal of Experimental Psychology*, 1969, *79*, 342−346.

Nelson, D. L., Wheeler, J. W., Jr., Borden, R. C., & Brooks, D. H. Levels of processing and cuing: Sensory vs meaning features. *Journal of Experimental Psychology*, 1974, *103*, 971−977.

Nelson, D. L., Wheeler, J. W., & Brooks, D. H. Meaning and the elimination of sensory interference. *Journal of Experimental Psychology: Human Learning and Memory*, 1976, 2, 95−102.

Nelson, T. O., & Rothbart, R. Acoustic savings for items forgotten from long-term memory. *Journal of Experimental Psychology*, 1972, *93*, 357−360.

Osgood, C. E. Toward a wedding of insufficiencies. In T. R. Dixon & D. L. Horton (Eds.), *Verbal behavior and general behavior theory*. Englewood Cliffs, N.J.: Prentice−Hall, 1968.

Paivio, A. *Imagery and verbal processes*. New York: Holt, Rinehart and Winston, Inc., 1971.

Paivio, A., & Csapo, K. Concrete-image and verbal memory codes. *Journal of Experimental Psychology*, 1969, *80*, 279−285.

Paivio, A., & Csapo, K. Picture superiority in free recall: Imagery or dual coding? *Cognitive Psychology*, 1973, *5*, 176−206.

Posner, M. I., & Warren, R. E. Traces, concepts, and conscious construction. In A. W. Melton & E. Martin (Eds.), *Coding processes in human memory*. Washington, D.C.: Winston, 1972.

Potter, M. C., & Faulconer, B. A. Time to understand pictures and words. *Nature*, 1975, *253*, 437–438.

Raser, G. A. False recognition as a function of encoding dimension and lag. *Journal of Experimental Psychology*, 1972, *93*, 333–337.

Rubenstein, H., Richter, M. L., & Kay, E. J. Pronounceability and the visual recognition of nonsense words. *Journal of Verbal Learning and Verbal Behavior*, 1975, *14*, 651–657.

Rumelhart, D. E., Lindsay, P. H., & Norman, D. A. A process model for long-term memory. In E. Tulving & W. Donaldson (Eds.), *Organization of memory*. New York: Academic Press, 1972.

Runquist, W. N. Formal intralist similarity in paired-associate learning. *Journal of Experimental Psychology*, 1968, *78*, 634–641.

Runquist, W. N. The assessment of discriminative encoding in memory for paired associates. *Memory & Cognition*, 1974, *2*, 472–478.

Runquist, W. N., & Evans, A. Stimulus recognition and associate coding. *Journal of Experimental Psychology*, 1972, *95*, 242–244.

Saltz, E. Compound stimuli in verbal learning: Cognitive and sensory differentiation versus stimulus selection. *Journal of Experimental Psychology*, 1963, *66*, 1–5.

Schulman, A. I. Memory for words recently classified. *Memory & Cognition*, 1974, *2*, 47–52.

Seymour, P. H. K. A model for reading, naming and comparison. *British Journal of Psychology*, 1973, *64*, 35–49.

Shulman, H. G. Encoding and retention of semantic and phonetic information in short-term memory. *Journal of Verbal Learning and Verbal Behavior*, 1970, *9*, 499–508.

Till, R. E., & Jenkins, J. J. The effects of cued orienting tasks on the free recall of words. *Journal of Verbal Learning and Verbal Behavior*, 1973, *12*, 489–498.

Thomson, D. M., & Tulving, E. Associative encoding and retrieval: Weak and strong cues. *Journal of Experimental Psychology*, 1970, *86*, 255–262.

Tulving, E. Ecphoric processes in recall and recognition. In J. Brown (Ed.), *Recall and recognition*. New York: John Wiley & Sons, 1976.

Tulving, E., & Thomson, D. M. Encoding specificity and retrieval processes in episodic memory. *Psychological Review*, 1973, *80*, 352–373.

Tulving, E., & Watkins, M. J. Structure of memory traces. *Psychological Review*, 1975, *82*, 261–275.

Tversky, B. G. Encoding processes in encoding and recall. *Cognitive Psychology*, 1973, *5*, 275–287.

Wheeler, J. W. Word organization as a function of age and reading skills. Unpublished doctoral dissertation, University of South Florida, 1978.

Wickelgren, W. A. Auditory or articulatory coding in verbal short-term memory. *Psychological Review*, 1969, *76*, 232–235.

Wickens, D. D., Ory, N. E., & Graf, S. A. Encoding by taxonomic and acoustic categories in long-term memory. *Journal of Experimental Psychology*, 1970, *84*, 462–469.

Wicker, F. W. On the locus of picture–word differences in paired-associate learning. *Journal of Verbal Learning and Verbal Behavior*, 1970, *9*, 52–57.

4

Remembering Events: Discussion of Papers by Jacoby and Craik, Battig, and Nelson

Robert S. Lockhart
University of Toronto

Each of the three papers given in this session provides a mixture of data and theory that reflects clearly the influence of the recent tradition that has given rise to the present workshop. This influence is evident not only in the kinds of experiments they describe but also and especially in their development of theoretical concepts that are predominantly perceptual in nature. I see this as progress, but I will argue that in none of these papers have the authors gone far enough and that in various ways they have failed to pursue the full implications of the original statement of Craik and Lockhart (1972).

The fundamental and unoriginal purpose of the 1972 paper was to stress the fact that the study of human memory is the study of an aspect of general cognitive functioning, especially of perceptual processes. Memory research was, and still is, too dominated by the traditions of verbal learning. The essence of this tradition is to present "items" to subjects along with instructions to "study" them and then to test the subject's memory for these items. The task of a theory of memory is then seen as that of providing an account of what a subject does when confronted with this peculiar set of circumstances. The tour de force of this tradition was the buffer model of Atkinson and Shiffrin, and one of its most attractive aspects was the careful distinction between control processes and the structural properties of the memory system. The continued popularity of this distinction is especially evident in Battig's account of variable processing.

WITHIN-INDIVIDUAL DIFFERENCES AND
VARIABLE PROCESSING

Battig draws attention to the ubiquity and magnitude of both within- and between-individual differences in strategies employed in the typical laboratory task. When a subject is confronted with a task such as free recall or a paragraph of text that he or she is asked to read and try to remember, subsequent performance will be governed by two classes of variables. The first concerns factors that influence the choice of control processes or what Battig refers to as problem-solving behavior. Should the subject rehearse? form images? use the mnemonic device learned in last week's introductory psychology lecture? weep from boredom? The second class of variables is the relative effectiveness of any particular control process relative to the nature of the material to be studied, the retention interval, the retrieval requirements, and the circumstances under which retrieval is to occur.

Now I would argue strongly that it is the latter set of factors that is the major concern of the memory theorist; the former is more properly the domain of the student of education, of individual differences, or of cognitive style. The problem is this: The factors that govern such control processes typically have little to do with the basic properties of the memory system, and moreover, they probably have little validity beyond the laboratory tasks and materials that generate them or the undergraduate population that employ them. I am therefore somewhat skeptical about the dominant role that Battig assigns to the study of strategy differences. It is true that his concern is largely with intra- rather than inter-individual differences, but the above comments are applicable to both. On the other hand, much of the actual research that Battig describes is not really the study of strategy differences at all but is something much more valuable. I am referring to the work that centers around the interesting notion that variable "modes of processing" may be intrinsically beneficial. The aim of these experiments is not to document the strategies that subjects choose to employ from one item or task to the next but rather to study the consequences of variable processing as such. The important point is that the processing is under experimental control; it is an independent rather than a dependent variable, and it is this fact that makes Battig's research of such great interest and places it within the domain that I have described as the proper concern of the memory theorist.

It was precisely to gain such control that Craik and Lockhart (1972) placed so much emphasis on the use of incidental orienting tasks and argued their virtue over the standard intentional instructions. The use of incidental orienting tasks has its own difficulties, some of which are raised by Nelson in his chapter, but their use does have the advantage of eliminating much of the strategy component of laboratory tasks; and if, like Battig, one wishes to study the importance of variable processing, they provide a valuable means of exerting a measure of experimental control over such variation.

THE ISSUE OF ECOLOGICAL VALIDITY

There is another advantage to the use of incidental orienting tasks, and this concerns the question of ecological validity that I have hinted at already. I consider this to be the single most important issue currently confronting students of human memory. It is one to which the general notions of levels of processing have considerable relevance and to which none of the papers in this session has given due attention.

Of course, the use of incidental orienting tasks in no way guarantees a high degree of ecological validity, but it does permit such considerations to play a major role in selecting and designing the orienting task themselves. Whatever other features they may possess, orienting tasks should tap those cognitive processes that are functionally important. Indeed, it is essential that they do so if the typical "levels" experiment is to avoid the fate of becoming a substantively autonomous paradigm in the manner of paired-associate learning or the much-studied Sternberg paradigm. Although resilient to this trend, it is possible to encounter people who claim to be "studying levels of processing." Nelson implicitly reflects the reality of this danger when, quite correctly, he points out that orienting tasks are not pure representations of different levels. That this point needs to be made (and it does) is a symptom of the possibility that certain orienting tasks (such as, "does it rhyme with. . . ?") will achieve the status of a "standard levels-of-processing paradigm" and that this paradigm will itself then become the object of study.

Strictly speaking, orienting tasks should never be selected to represent different levels of processing. They should be chosen on the grounds that they model (that is, capture the essential features of) an aspect of cognitive processing that is functionally important and that they have a high degree of ecological validity. The notion of levels of processing is a derivative one; it is a way of structuring and thus understanding the subsequent data.

I found all three papers in this session to be lacking in the extent to which their choice of orienting task was motivated by these considerations. Jacoby and Craik, for example, use an orienting task in which subjects must choose which of two words is more highly related to a focus word. Why this particular task? Their subsequent theoretical analysis is an interesting one, but what is it about discriminating the degree of relatedness that makes it interesting to the student of human memory?

Similar comments might be made about the papers of Battig and of Nelson. Battig's interest in variable processing seems to stem more from its prominence in the laboratory than from the obvious fact that for an organism functioning in its natural environment, incidental variation would be the rule rather than the exception. It is a trite and obvious but nonetheless true statement that no object or event can ever be perceived in the same way on two different occasions, and it is this fact that makes the study of variation so interesting. But it would be valuable to have a more thorough analysis of the nature and function of variation, an analysis that would provide a sounder basis for the meaningful selection of orienting tasks.

This consideration of ecological validity leads to a further problem raised by Battig. He, like most of us, is concerned with what he describes as the "radical shifts in research emphases, such that today's hot research topic may well be of little, if any, concern tomorrow [p. 23]." The difficulty is not only in the rapid change of fashion, however; it is also in the fact that there is little cumulative progress. As Newell (1973) has remarked, "Matters simply become muddier and muddier . . . far from providing the rungs of a ladder by which psychology gradually climbs to clarity [p. 288]."

The etiology of this Battig—Newell syndrome is largely the neglect of ecological validity and functional significance. Although I have heard it argued that the growing concern over ecological validity is itself just another passing fashion, the fact of the matter is that psychology is subject to fads and changing fashion precisely because of its failure to take these issues seriously. Psychology's only source of genuine stability is the external reality of the problems it tackles. If the problems are merely laboratory creations, then their perceived importance—even their existence—will depend on the current views and interests of their creators. A concern for "real problems" provides not only a yardstick against which progress can be measured but also an anchor that links ongoing research to a world that, unlike the laboratory, exists and functions independently of the psychological observer.

Of course, even with real problems, fashion and popularity may change. But this is unimportant if when interest returns to a given question, former periods of interest have left a valid data base on which to build. One of the neglected measures of a good theory or of a theoretical framework is the extent to which it directs research to collect data whose importance can outlast that of the theory itself. The key to such longevity, and the cure for the Battig—Newell syndrome, is to ensure that the phenomena being investigated are functionally significant and the experiments ecologically valid.

SENSORY CODES

It is clear that one of the focal points of criticism of Craik and Lockhart (1972) is that of sensory codes. Nelson's paper as well as several others in later sessions have seen this point as one at which the notions of levels of processing is most vulnerable.

In its simplest form, the original claim was that the trace of an event becomes unavailable at a rate that decreases as the depth of processing increases. The counterclaim is that all traces are born equal and given equal opportunity, one will be as resilient and available as another. The apparent superiority of memory for items processed to a semantic level is an instance of what Tulving has termed cue-dependent forgetting; given the appropriate retrieval environment, memory can be made independent of the level of initial encoding. Now there are two separate issues involved in this problem that are frequently confused but that should be kept distinct.

The first of these is the relationship between the encoding event and the retrieval requirements as defined by the experimenter. One of the perplexing aspects of the use of incidental orienting tasks is the difficulty one has in specifying a criterion that distinguishes the sublime from the ridiculous. It seems eminently sensible (my comments in the preceding section notwithstanding) and indeed quite interesting to do what Jacoby and Craik have done in having subjects decide which of two words is more highly related to a focus word and then to examine subsequent memory for these words as a function of the degree of difficulty of such a discrimination. It seems not unreasonable to ask if a target word rhymes with another word and then to test the subject's memory for such target words. These all seem plausible orienting tasks. But does it make sense to ask subjects if the words contain the letter *E* and then ask for the recall of the words? Possibly; but to move one step further, consider an orienting task that requires the subject to say whether or not the word has more than five letters or whether the word's last letter is composed entirely of straight lines. A point is reached where manifestly, subjects—in being required to remember *items*—are being asked to remember events that have never occurred. The subject may have perfect memory for all that has gone before and yet be quite unable to meet the requirements of the experimenter. The difficulty here is not the adequacy or otherwise of the retrieval cues, so-called, but in the relationship between the processing that constitutes the event that actually occurred and the item that the experimenter requires to be recalled. Now the real problem for the memory theorist is that there appears to be no clear line that divides the interesting from the trivial, and this dilemma suggests the need for some reconceptualization. Both Kolers and Bransford together with his colleagues at Vanderbilt have seen clearly the nature of this problem, and it is valuable to read their chapters with this perspective in mind.

The second issue is that of cue effectiveness, which has been a major topic of concern of a number of papers, especially that of Tulving, Chapter 19. It is important to distinguish this form of compatibility from that described in the preceding paragraph. We have just considered the possible incompatibility between the processing operations constituting the event that occurred and the ''item'' that the subject is required to recall. The problem of cue effectiveness, however, concerns the relationship between the retrieval context and either the event or the item to be recalled. Hence there are relationships amongst three elements to be considered—the event, the experimenter-defined item to be remembered, and the cue or context present at retrieval.

The importance of cue effectiveness has been extensively investigated. Nelson in his paper as well as others in this volume have shown that with suitable cuing conditions or encoding–cuing relationshps, the otherwise robust "levels effect" can be attenuated, totally eliminated, or in some cases even reversed. I should like to make three general comments on this kind of result.

1. Just as orienting tasks are not pure representations of different levels of processing (Nelson's third encoding assumption), neither are nominal retrieval cues pure representations of their putative cuing level. A rhyme cue should not be assumed to provide only phonemic information. Jacoby and Craik's notion of directed retrieval clearly allows for the possibility of transformation of the nominal retrieval cue, and Tulving's use of the term "copy cue" begs the entire question.

2. The distinction between sensory and semantic codes has in an important sense been drawn too sharply. There is a tendency to regard the sensory components of a word or a picture as a kind of detachable skin within which is the kernel of meaning but that is itself meaningless. Sensory and semantic features do not possess this simple additive relationship. The sensory codes are aspects of analyses of meaning. The distinctiveness and internal coherence (interactiveness, to use Nelson's expression) of these sensory codes do not exist independently of meaning. There are no raw sensory codes; such codes are aspects of coordinated, meaning-extracting operations. As Dewey puts it, "Sensory qualities are important. But they are intellectually significant only as consequences of acts intentionally performed" (Dewey, 1929, p. 112).

3. It follows from the above analysis that meaning should not be equated with verbal semantics; sound qualities and other nonverbal material may be processed in a manner that involves extensive analysis of meaning. Nelson's analysis of picture stimuli is a valuable contribution to this general point and represents a most promising approach to the study of nonverbal material.

Finally, in discussing sensory codes, it would seem important to consider the possible role of selective retroactive interference. Little attention has been paid in recent years to the differential effects attributable to the nature of the material or processing that fills the retention interval; yet in the case of sensory codes especially, one might expect such effects to be substantial. Nelson, for example, has very explicit encoding and retrieval assumptions, but little is said about the importance of what happens in between. To use Melton's (1963) term, there are no storage assumptions.

EPISODES AND MEANING

My final comments concern the status of the concept of episodic memory (or event memory, to use the philosopher Ayer's term) and its relevance to each of the three papers. The concept is important in the present context because of the strong emphasis on memory for sensory information and because I think none of these papers gives it sufficient attention.

Despite its ubiquity in the philosophical literature and Tulving's careful and detailed analysis, the concept of episodic memory and the distinction between it and semantic or "habit" memory has caused psychologists a great deal of difficulty. One reason for this state of affairs is the tendency to define episodic memory in terms of particular experimental paradigms and to identify it with a particular kind of question asked of memory. It is probably the case that any act of remembering past events invokes an interaction between episodic and semantic aspects, and to define the two systems in terms of particular paradigms or queries is to invite the kind of confusion described by Donald Norman in the new edition of *Memory and attention* (Norman, 1976, p. 189).

For example, a query such as "what did you eat for breakfast this morning?" appears to be a question entirely of the episodic system. (In fact it is Bertrand Russell's own example of "pure memory.") Yet much of this question might be answered correctly without any recollection of the actual experiences or action of this morning. For example, one may have no recollection of a highly auto-matized action such as adding sugar to one's coffee yet be perfectly confident that the action was performed, since one knows that if the sugar had not been added, the consequences of such an oversight would have been remembered. Thus the most episodic-type question might be answered from the semantic system. This is similar to the kind of gap filling that Bartlett discussed in a somewhat different context. Strictly speaking, then, episodic memory is memory for past responses, not memory for items or stimuli. A subject may *infer* that a given item was presented, but to *remember its being presented* is to recollect one's past responses. It is the difference between remembering that the Norman invasion of England occurred in 1066 and remembering the experience of being told that fact. Or it is the difference between remembering that the word *horse* was in the list and remembering its actual appearance on the screen.

Now I realize that this analysis raises a host of philosophical problems; but I shall blithely set them aside in order to get back to the three papers at hand. Consider Battig's multitrial experiments. If a subject recalls an item, is he or she remembering an episode (or several episodes), or has the subject learned a new fact (that *horse* was on the list)? The subject may be able to assert that the word was in the list either by reference to the episodes involving the item's presentation or by reference to a knowledge structure that involves no direct recollection of such episodes. Indeed, one can regard the acquisition of knowledge as precisely this process of information being stripped of its episodic aspects—a process of abstraction that leaves knowledge available for future use without the need to reconstruct the circumstances of its acquisition. If this is a valid way to regard multitrial free recall, it makes good sense that this process is facilitated by variation in context.

Another way of stating this analysis is to distinguish between the study of memory for ideas and memory for events. It is a distinction that should not be pushed too far, but it is of value in any discussion of how one should set about doing research. It influences the materials used and what is said to constitute correct remembering. If one is interested in memory for ideas, then one is concerned primarily with the content and structure of ideas. If one is interested in memory for events, then primary concern shifts to an analysis of the structure of temporal experience. Now in terms of this distinction, lists of isolated words have an ambiguous status, and this ambiguity is reflected to some degree in all three papers. It *is* true that since each word has a meaning, it can be thought of—in some limited sense—as representing an idea. But I must confess that if one is interested in memory for ideas, presenting lists of isolated words seems a strange and, I suspect, an unprofitable way to proceed.

It would seem, then, that word-list experiments might best be viewed as a means of studying memory for events. If this is so, then we should not be interested (as an end in itself) in how subjects come to remember words but rather in using words (or pictures) to bring about events over whose properties we can exert a measure of control.

It is in this context that I find interesting Jacoby and Craik's work on the role of discrimination difficulty. It is a promising line of research precisely because of its perceptual orientation and its focus on properties of the perceptual interaction. There is, of course, the constant danger of circularity in the use of terms such as *difficulty* and *distinctiveness* as explanatory constructs; but I think such terms have at least heuristic value, and conceptual clarification will follow in the light of experiments of this kind. Concepts such as Nelson's notion of "interaction" as well as Jacoby and Craik's emphasis on context and distinctiveness are valuable efforts to move from a language dominated by attempts to describe memory in terms of attributes of items to one that emphasizes properties of events.

But I think they should go further. What is needed is a more systematic language and a more complete set of concepts, appropriate to the description of *events* rather than items. We need a more perceptually oriented language to develop concepts of temporal boundaries and contours, temporal contrast, coherence, and the like. Such descriptions of events will provide the only sound basis for a theory of remembering or retrieving events and when accomplished will constitute the final break with the tradition of verbal learning. The research programs that underlie the three papers given in this session provide a data base that will play an important role in this endeavor as well as contributing some tentative steps toward this new theoretical language.

ACKNOWLEDGMENT

This work was supported by a Grant Number A0355 from the National Research Council of Canada.

REFERENCES

Craik, F. I. M. & Lockhart, R. S. Levels of processing: A framework for memory research. *Journal of Verbal Learning and Verbal Behavior,* 1972, *11,* 671–684.
Dewey, J. *The quest for certainty.* New York: Putnam's 1929.
Melton, A. W. Implications of short-term memory for a general theory of memory. *Journal of Verbal Learning and Verbal Behavior,* 1963, *2,* 1–21.
Newell, A. You can't play 20 questions with nature and win: Projective comments on the papers of this symposium. In W. G. Chase (Ed.), *Visual information processing.* New York: Academic Press, 1973.
Norman, D. A. *Memory and attention* (2nd ed.) New York: Wiley, 1976.

II

EXTENSIONS AND APPLICATIONS

5 Depth, Elaboration, and Distinctiveness

Michael W. Eysenck
Birkbeck College, University of London

1. INTRODUCTION

The levels-of-processing approach initially formulated by Craik and Lockhart (1972), and subsequently developed by Craik (1973; 1977), Craik and Tulving (1975), and Lockhart, Craik, and Jacoby (1976), has a number of desirable characteristics. Whereas most experimentation and theorizing on human memory suffers from the problem of paradigm specificity, Craik and Lockhart sought to identify general principles that would explain the retentivity of memory traces in any situation as a function of cognitive–perceptual operations.

A related aim of their original article was subsequently clarified by Lockhart and Craik (1978): "The underlying intent of that formulation was *not* to offer a theory of memory that was subject to direct empirical test in the hypothetico-deductive tradition. Rather, and as the subtitle of the paper stated, the major purpose was to present arguments in favor of a new framework for research [p. 171]." Their approach was designed to further our understanding rather than to make specific predictions.

It is probably true that psychologists attach undue importance to theories making predictions that are consistently confirmed, even if the predictions are trivial. Although there is merit in the notion that scientific method is characterized by the criterion of falsifiability (Popper, 1959), it is less sure that empirical "refutations" (Popper, 1963) require the abandonment of the relevant theory or hypothesis. For example, when Newton published his *Principia*, it was well known that it could not even explain the motion of the moon. Nevertheless, the successful predictions and enhanced understanding produced by Newtonian theory meant that it was retained essentially unchanged for several

89

decades. These issues are discussed at length in Lakatos and Musgrave (1970).

Even if understanding is preferred to prediction, there is nothing actually wrong with making and testing theoretical predictions. The major prediction from the levels approach—that retentivity should be a positive function of processing depth—has proved difficult to test because of the absence of an independent index of depth. As Eysenck (1978a) has pointed out, "In view of the vagueness with which depth is defined, there is the danger of using retention-test performance to provide information about the depth of processing, and then using the putative depth of processing to 'explain' the retention-test performance, a self-defeating exercise in circularity [p. 159]." It is possible that processing depth is related to processing effort. If so, then there are a number of measures of processing effort that might reflect depth of processing. Kahneman (1973) has suggested pupillary dilation and skin conductance as autonomic measures of effort and measures of spare capacity as behavioral indices of effort. Spare capacity can be measured by observing performance on a subsidiary task.

There is some indirect evidence that these measures may be of relevance. Johnston and Uhl (1976) used a dual-task paradigm in which subjects performed list study and a simple reaction-time task concurrently. Recall of the list words was inversely related to reaction-time performance, indicating that processing effort partially determines retention. Several investigators (e.g., Kleinsmith & Kaplan, 1963, 1964) have found that items eliciting a large galvanic skin response at presentation are better retained than other items after long retention intervals, a result explicable in terms of processing depth or effort. Unfortunately, very little (if any) work has considered in detail the potential applicability of effort measures to the Craik—Lockhart approach.

Other problems with the Craik—Lockhart formulation have been discussed at length by Eysenck (1977, 1978a, 1978b) and will only be mentioned *en passant*. For example, Craik and Lockhart favored a paradigm in which subjects perform various orienting tasks followed by an unanticipated retention test, due to the putative degree of control over the subject's processing afforded. However, there is much evidence (e.g., Nelson, Chapter 3, this volume) that subjects consistently engage in a considerable amount of processing extraneous to that necessitated by the orienting task. A more consequential problem is that the original formulation was not very explanatory; no explicit mechanisms indicating exactly *why* deep levels of processing should be better retained than shallow levels were proposed.

Weimer (1977) has pointed out that most current information-processing theories follow the Aristotelian tradition of viewing the mind as fundamentally sensory. With such theories, there is the intractable problem of explaining how perceptually derived traces can initiate and sustain effective action in the environment. The levels-of-analysis approach has little to offer with regard to this problem.

The main experimental finding of relevance to the levels-of-processing approach is that semantic encodings are usually considerably better retained than phonemic encodings (e.g., Craik, 1973; Hyde & Jenkins, 1969). Craik and Lockhart (1972) proposed in essence that the greater longevity of semantic than of phonemic information was due primarily to the greater depth of processing necessitated by semantic analysis. One of their major claims was that "trace persistence is a function of depth of analysis, with deeper levels of analysis associated with more elaborate, longer lasting, and stronger traces [p. 675]." It is now clear that the degree of empirical support for this hypothesis depends heavily on the nature of the retrieval environment (Bransford, Franks, Morris, & Stein, Chapter 15, this volume). Moreover, as Eysenck (1978b) has noted, although Craik and Lockhart argue in favor of the encoding specificity principle, "the hypothesis that deeper levels of analysis lead to strong traces is logically inconsistent with the encoding specificity principle, since the hypothesis contains no reference to the conditions of retrieval [p. 177]."

Subsequent experimentation has indicated that the spread or elaboration of encoding is an important factor. Craik and Tulving (1975) proposed that the data on depth of processing could be interpreted in terms of "the idea that memory performance depends on the elaborateness of the final encoding [p. 291]," although no very explicit mechanisms to explain why richness of elaboration should facilitate retention were adduced. Anderson and Reder (Chapter 18, this volume) have advanced a similar notion.

The importance of spread or elaboration of encoding at the semantic level was demonstrated by Klein and Saltz (1976). They used various semantic tasks, all of which required the subject to rate nouns in terms of semantic attribute dimensions (e.g., pleasant−unpleasant). Subsequent recall was better for words rated on two dimensions than for words rated on a single dimension.

A different but related interpretation of the retention-test superiority of deep to shallow encodings was offered by Lockhart et al. (1976). They proposed the following hypothesis: "Both recall and recognition are superior when 'deeper', 'richer', 'more semantic' traces are formed at input. . . . By the present view, the beneficial effect of depth of encoding is that deeper, richer encodings are also more distinctive and unique [p. 86]." Informal evidence of the importance of distinctiveness is available in the remake of the film *King Kong*. Some eight months after seeing the film, the author can remember the name of only one of the characters—namely, Dwan, the aspiring actress, who had changed her name from Dawn in order to make it more distinctive.

There is also more formal evidence to support the plausible notion that distinctiveness or uniqueness enhances retention. For example, Going and Read (1974) found that faces rated high in uniqueness relative to all the faces known to the subject were much better recognized than low-unique (*sic*) faces (71.7% versus 53.1%). Cohen and Carr (1975) had faces rated for distinctiveness relative to other faces in the presentation set and found that distinctiveness was positively related to recognition performance.

The hypothesis that processing depth strongly determines retention-test performance because deeper encodings are more distinctive was investigated by Jacoby (1974). In his study, pairs of related words were presented in a list under conditions that did or did not encourage simultaneous processing of the members of the pair (i.e., implicit contiguity). On the subsequent recall test, the first item of each pair was used as a cue for recall of the second-presented pair member. The subjects either processed the words phonemically or semantically on the presentation trial. It was argued that recall would be enhanced by implicit contiguity, provided that the context provided by implicit contiguity modified the resultant encoded trace. Since the phonemic encoding of a word is presumably essentially constant irrespective of context (i.e., nondistinctive), implicit contiguity should not affect phonemic encoding. On the other hand, semantic encoding is strongly affected by contextual factors, so that implicit contiguity would produce a distinctive encoding. As predicted, phonemic processing was associated with much lower levels of recall than semantic processing. More importantly, implicit contiguity only enhanced recall for semantically processed items. It is possible that implicit contiguity allowed for more thorough as well as or instead of more distinctive encoding at the semantic level.

Moscovitch and Craik (1976) pointed out that phonemic encodings tend to be nondistinctive because there is a relatively small number of phonemes in the English language. The result of this is that there is much overlap of encoded phonemic features among a list of words processed phonemically. On the other hand, the enormous variety of potential semantic encodings means that there is relatively little feature overlap among groups of semantically processed words. However, this may be an unfair comparison. On one hand, with the exception of homophones, all words in the English language possess unique combinations of phonemes; on the other hand, the number of semantic "primitives" is unknown.

Moscovitch and Craik showed their subjects a series of target words about which they had to answer either a phonemic or a semantic encoding question. Either each target word was associated with a different unique question, or sets of target words were associated with the same question. The questions were re-presented as retrieval cues on the subsequent recall test. The most important result was the large interaction between type of cue and depth of processing. In this interaction, semantically encoded information was much better recalled with unique cues than with shared cues because of the reduced distinctiveness with shared cues. Phonemically encoded words were poorly recalled irrespective of cue type, presumably because phonemic encodings are not distinctive even with unique cues.

The concept of distinctiveness requires some clarification at this point. A plausible distinctiveness hypothesis would assume that retention of an item presented in the experimental situation depends on: (a) the similarity of prior encodings of that item to the intraexperimental encoding; and (b) the number of such prior encodings. In general, distinctiveness of the intraexperimental encoding will vary inversely with both the similarity and number of prior encodings.

More specifically, the manner in which distinctiveness might affect recognition memory is shown in Fig. 5.1. In a typical recognition–memory experiment, subjects possess considerable preexperimentally acquired information about each word (circle A). Within the experimental situation, each word is encoded on the presentation trial (circle B) and on the test trial (circle C). It should be noted that the test-trial encoding potentially comprises four separate kinds of information:

1. information unique to the test-trial encoding;
2. information derived exclusively from preexperimental encodings;
3. information derived exclusively from the study-trial encoding;
4. information common to the preexperimental encodings and to the study-trial encoding.

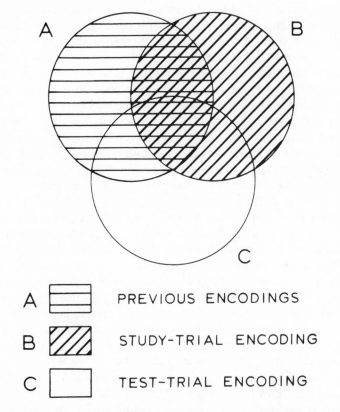

A ⊟ PREVIOUS ENCODINGS

B ▨ STUDY-TRIAL ENCODING

C ☐ TEST-TRIAL ENCODING

FIG. 5.1. Schematic representation of the basic ingredients of the distinctiveness hypothesis. Degree of elaboration of each encoding is represented in terms of circle size.

Tulving (1976) has argued that the main determinant of recognition-test performance is the extent of the overlap between the study-trial and the test-trial encodings. A distinctiveness hypothesis would propose that there is an important distinction between two kinds of overlap between study- and test-trial encodings. Overlapping information either contains information common to preexperimental encodings (nondistinctive overlap), or it does not (distinctive overlap). Recognition-test performance is assumed to depend far more on distinctive than on nondistinctive overlap. Although this hypothesis focuses primarily on distinctiveness as defined by the relationship between an item's current encoding and its prior encodings, distinctiveness also depends, of course, on the relationship between an item's encoding and the encodings of other list items.

Both empirically and theoretically, it is difficult to distinguish between elaboration of encoding and distinctiveness of encoding, and they are usually positively related. In terms of the representation in Fig. 5.1, however, the two factors can be seen to be conceptually distinct. A distinctive study-trial encoding would be represented by minimal overlap of the A (previous encodings) and B (study-trial encoding) circles. On the other hand, a rich or elaborate study-trial encoding would be represented by a large B (study-trial encoding) component. On most assumptions, elaborate encodings will tend to be more distinctive than nonelaborate encodings, but there is nothing inevitable about this tendency.

In spite of the conceptual distinction between distinctiveness and elaboration, it is often the case that distinctive stimuli are well remembered because they are more thoroughly processed than nondistinctive stimuli. Berlyne (1960) investigated those stimuli involving a conflict between what had been expected and what was actually presented and identified several collative properties of stimuli (e.g., novelty, incongruity, surprisingness, complexity) related to distinctiveness. Stimuli possessing these collative properties are more likely to be attended to (e.g., Berlyne & Ditkofsky, 1976) and are associated with greater phasic arousal than other stimuli. Kahneman (1973) has interpreted this finding as follows: "Novel and surprising stimuli which spontaneously attract attention also require a greater effort of processing than do more familiar stimuli. The surge of arousal that follows a novel stimulus represents, at least in part, a surge of mental effort [p. 4]." The von Restorff effect is probably explicable in such terms (Eysenck, 1972). Evidence for the notion that the distinctive stimulus receives a disproportionate amount of processing time is available in the typically poor retention of the item following the isolate (Wallace, 1965) and in Rundus's (1971) finding, using an overt rehearsal technique, that the isolated item received many more rehearsals than any other item. However, the Rundus finding may have been due to his explicit instructions to his subjects to be sure to remember the isolated item. Einstein, Pellegrino, Mondani, and Battig (1974) did not give their subjects any special instructions concerning memory for the isolated item and found no evidence at all that the isolate was rehearsed any more than the remaining items.

In sum, we have seen that there is a considerable problem in distinguishing among the closely related concepts of trace depth, trace elaboration, and trace distinctiveness. The experiments discussed hereafter investigated predictions that follow from the distinctiveness hypothesis. Previous work (e.g., Jacoby, 1974; Moscovitch & Craik, 1976) suggests that some of the memorial advantage of semantic over phonemic encodings may be due to the greater trace distinctiveness of the former, and this hypothesis is further explored. The distinctiveness hypothesis may also be relevant in the interpretation of the inverse relationship between word frequency and recognition–memory performance (cf. Gregg, 1976). Brown (1976) suggested that "the relative difficulty of recognizing a high-frequency word is commonly and plausibly attributed to its lower distinctiveness [p. 17]," and this hypothesis is also explored.

2.   EXPERIMENTATION

Experiment 1

Previous research by Jacoby (1974) and by Moscovitch and Craik (1976) has indicated that the retention of phonemic encodings is poor and is unaffected by attempted manipulations of trace distinctiveness, presumably because phonemic encodings are nondistinctive in all circumstances. Moscovitch and Craik concluded that phonemic encodings are necessarily poorly remembered: "Uniqueness is not enough; the fact that an item is unique in a set of items to be memorized, or even unique in the person's experience, is not sufficient to guarantee its memorability. The event must be discriminable and unique *semantically,* before retention is enhanced [p. 457]."

This experiment addresses the question as to whether or not manipulations of distinctiveness can influence the retention of phonemic encodings and, more particularly, whether or not distinctive phonemic encodings could show levels of retention comparable to those of semantic encodings. Distinctiveness was manipulated by means of the processing instructions given to the subjects. Nouns with irregular grapheme–phoneme correspondence were selected from the *Concise Oxford English dictionary.* Examples of such words are *denial, glove,* and *comb.* Ninety-six of these words were presented singly, and each of four tasks was performed on one-quarter of the words. Two tasks involved phonemic processing and were designed to differ in terms of their effects on phonemic trace distinctiveness. In the nondistinctive, phonemic typical condition, subjects were required to pronounce each word overtly with its usual pronunciation. In the distinctive, phonemic atypical condition, subjects had to pronounce each word as it would be pronounced if it had regular grapheme–phoneme correspondence (e.g., *glove* would be pronounced to rhyme with *cove*). The remaining two tasks involved semantic processing. In the nondistinctive, semantic typical condition, subjects were told to produce a descriptor (e.g., adjective) that typically modified each noun, whereas in the distinctive, semantic atypical condition, they were instructed to think of a descriptor that could be, but infrequently is, used as a modifier for each noun. In all four processing conditions, each word was presented for 0.5 seconds, and the subject responded overtly, stopping a timer. There were 20 subjects.

Word frequency was included as a further variable, because according to contemporary wisdom (e.g., Brown, 1976; Lockhart et al., 1976), the inverse relationship between word frequency and recognition−memory performance is due at least in part to the greater distinctiveness of encodings of rare than of common words. Half of the subjects received an almost immediate recall test, and the other half performed a recognition test. The subjects had not anticipated that there would be a retention test.

There were significant differences in processing times across the four instructional conditions (see Table 5.1). Semantic processing took much longer than phonemic processing, and atypical processing took significantly longer than typical processing with the semantic task. Word frequency did not affect processing time.

The most interesting results were obtained from recognition-test performance. As can be seen in Fig. 5.2, there was a highly significant interaction between depth of processing and processing typicality, $F (1,9) = 32.34$, $p < 0.001$. Although depth of processing had its customary effect on recognition performance where typical processing was involved, $F (1,18) = 76.69$, $p < 0.001$, there was no effect of processing depth where atypical processing was involved, $F (1,18) = 3.47$. This interaction can be interpreted by assuming that semantic levels of analysis typically produce more discriminable memory traces and thus better retention than phonemic levels of analysis. On this line of argument, the memorial advantage of semantic over phonemic encodings would be attenuated, provided it were possible to devise a phonemic processing task that produced distinctive traces. The results indicated that the phonemic atypical task that was utilized in the attempt to produce a more distinctive trace led to recognition−

TABLE 5.1
Processing Time as a Function of Processing Depth, Processing
Typicality, and Word Frequency. Times Are in Seconds, and
Standard Deviations Are in Parentheses (Exp. 1).

Word Frequency	Phonemic		Semantic	
	Typical	Atypical	Typical	Atypical
Common	0.74 (0.24)	1.52 (0.49)	2.79 (1.11)	4.77 (3.15)
Rare	0.82 (0.26)	1.51 (0.42)	3.11 (1.56)	5.13 (3.66)

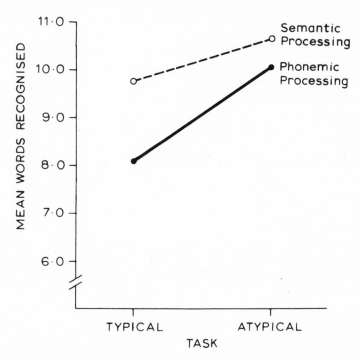

FIG. 5.2.   Recognition performance as a function of processing depth and processing typicality (Exp. 1).

memory performance that was comparable to that produced by semantic processing.

It has to be recognized that there is a scaling problem when comparing distinctiveness on two different dimensions. In the absence of an agreed metric, there is no way of equating distinctiveness of semantic and phonemic encodings. In connection with the above finding that there was a nonsignificant effect of processing typicality with semantic processing tasks, it might simply be the case that semantic processing did not differ in the semantic typical and semantic atypical tasks. This was investigated by means of independent ratings of the typicality of the words produced in these two tasks in relation to the target words, the ratings being done on a 5-point scale running from very typical (1) to very atypical (5). The mean rating across subjects was 3.88 for words produced in the semantic atypical condition and 2.18 for words produced in the semantic typical condition, t (9) = 12.14, p < 0.001.

The recognition data also produced a highly significant interaction between processing typicality and word frequency (see Fig. 5.3). Although there is some suggestion of a ceiling effect, the interaction indicates that there was the usual recognition superiority for rare words over common words with typical processing tasks, F (1,18) = 19.17, p < 0.001, but there was no word-frequency

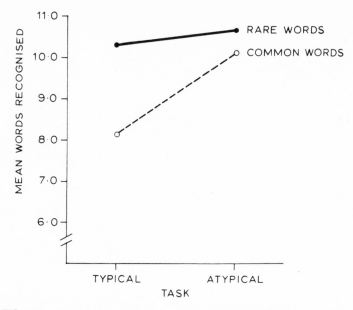

FIG. 5.3.   Recognition performance as a function of processing typicality and word frequency (Exp. 1).

effect with atypical processing tasks. Alternatively expressed, processing atypicality enhanced recognition for common words, presumably because typical processing produced a relatively nondistinctive trace; whereas processing atypicality had no effect on recognition memory for rare words, because such words are associated with distinctive encodings even with typical processing.

There was reasonable similarity between the pattern of results for recognition and for recall. In the recall data, the effect of processing depth was significant with typical processing, $F (1,18) = 16.14$, $p < 0.01$, but was not significant with atypical processing, $F < 1$. In addition, whereas common words were better recalled after atypical processing than after typical processing, processing typicality had no effect on the recall of rare words. Furthermore, the three-way interaction among word frequency, processing depth, and processing typicality was significant and is shown in Fig. 5.4. The effects of processing typicality were much greater for common words processed phonemically than for any other treatment condition. Theoretically, of course, common words in the phonemic typical condition would be associated with the least distinctive encodings and so would stand to gain the most from processing atypicality.

In general terms, the results of the first experiment are consistent with the distinctiveness hypothesis. With reference to Fig. 5.1, atypical processing instructions would be expected to reduce the overlap between the preexperimental and study-trial encodings and thus to enhance the distinctiveness of the

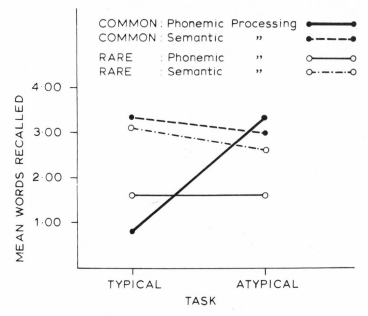

FIG. 5.4. Recall performance as a function of processing typicality, processing depth, and word frequency (Exp. 1).

study-trial encoding. If typical semantic processing produces minimal overlap, whereas typical phonemic processing produces substantial overlap, then the retention-enhancing effects of atypical processing should be more pronounced for phonemic encodings. Similarly, if rare words are usually encoded with much less overlap between preexperimental and study-trial encodings than common words, the distinctiveness- and retention-enhancing effects of atypical processing should be greater for common words. Both the recall and the recognition data supported these predictions.

There are some difficulties with the distinctiveness hypothesis, however. If rare words are more distinctively encoded than common words, and if trace distinctiveness is positively related to retention, then word frequency should be inversely related to both recall and recognition. In fact, the evidence obtained in this experiment and previously (see Gregg, 1976) indicates that whereas word frequency is inversely related to recognition, word frequency is either unrelated or positively related to recall. It has been suggested (e.g., Lockhart et al., 1976) that common words and rare words differ in terms of the thoroughness of the processing they receive. To the extent that the processing time measure used in this experiment is an approximate index of encoding thoroughness, this notion is inconsistent with the data, since there was no effect of word frequency on processing time. However, it may be noted that a word-frequency effect has often been found in naming tasks, with common words being named more rapidly than rare words (e.g., Forster & Chambers, 1973).

Experiment 2

The second experiment was intended to clarify the interpretation of the results of the first experiment. The experimental design was as before with five major exceptions:

1. Word frequency effects were not looked for.
2. Processing time in all tasks was equated at 10 seconds per item.
3. Processing time was not recorded.
4. Two additional tasks were used. (Phonemic both: Subjects had to perform both the phonemic typical and phonemic atypical tasks on each word. Semantic both: Subjects performed both the semantic typical and semantic atypical tasks on each word.)
5. For each word recalled or recognized, subjects indicated which of the six processing tasks had been used with that word on its study-trial presentation.

On the presentation trial there were 108 nouns with irregular grapheme — phoneme correspondence, 18 words being used in each of the six instructional conditions. When the subject finished his or her designated task on each word, he or she reiterated the required processing until the end of the 10-second period. An unexpected free-recall or recognition test followed 30 minutes after the conclusion of the presentation phase. There were 37 subjects.

It was decided to equate processing time in all conditions because of the confounding in the first experiment of instructional task and processing time. The extra processing tasks and the judgment on the retention test of the original processing task for each word recalled or recognized were included, since the higher levels of recall and recognition under the phonemic atypical condition than the phonemic typical condition in the first experiment might have been due to greater elaboration of encoding or more semantic processing in the former condition than in the latter. It was hoped that any such nonrequired processing might reduce judgmental accuracy of study-trial processing.

The recognition data indicated that there was a highly significant interaction between processing depth and processing typicality, $F(2,34) = 5.36, p < 0.01$. As in the first experiment, processing typicality had a highly significant effect on the phonemic tasks, $F(2.68) = 9.28, p < 0.001$, but had no effect on the semantic tasks. However, the same interaction was not significant for the recall data.

The extremely low levels of recall precluded any detailed consideration of the accuracy of processing-task judgments in free recall. Accordingly, the main emphasis will be on processing-task judgments for those items correctly recognized. Judgmental accuracy in terms of the percentage of each subject's judgments falling into the six judgmental categories is shown in Table 5.2. It can be seen that inaccurate judgments tended to retain information about the

TABLE 5.2
Judgmental Task Data as a Function of Initial Processing Task.
Figures Given Are Mean Percentages (Exp. 2).

| | Initial Processing Task | | | | | |
| | Semantic | | | Phonemic | | |
Guesses	Typical	Atypical	Both	Typical	Atypical	Both
Semantic typical	50.6	18.0	16.1	5.7	4.2	3.9
Semantic atypical	14.1	44.2	13.4	1.4	3.7	2.0
Semantic both	15.4	23.5	55.3	1.0	0.9	2.7
Phonemic typical	5.2	6.6	4.1	38.4	21.1	22.8
Phonemic atypical	7.7	4.8	7.2	26.3	43.6	34.2
Phonemic both	6.6	3.3	4.1	27.4	26.5	34.0

depth of processing. The data do not support the hypothesis that the superiority on the recognition test of the phonemic atypical condition over the other phonemic conditions was attributable to more extensive semantic or phonemic encoding in the phonemic atypical condition. A reasonable prediction from such a hypothesis is that a smaller percentage of accurate processing-task judgments would be obtained in the phonemic atypical than in the phonemic typical or phonemic both conditions. Analysis of the data revealed no significant overall difference in accuracy among the three phonemic conditions.

Interesting confirmation of the greater ease of access to phonemic atypical than to phonemic typical information was obtained from an analysis of the judgmental errors in the phonemic both condition. Of the 18 subjects given the recognition test, 14 selected the phonemic atypical category relatively more frequently than the phonemic typical category when making processing-task judgments on phonemic both items, three showed the opposite tendency, and one subject selected the two categories equally frequently (for the comparison, $p < 0.05$).

Experiment 3

The hypothesis that recognition–memory superiority of rare words over common words and of semantic encodings over phonemic encodings are both attributable in part to differences in trace distinctiveness was explored further in the third experiment. An appropriate method for reducing trace distinctiveness was used by Kinsbourne and George (1974). They presented their subjects with a series of to-be-learned words, some of which had been given a preexposure immediately prior to the learning task for ostensibly unrelated purposes. They found that preexposure substantially reduced subsequent recognition–memory performance, presumably because the additional encoding on the preexposure trial had the effect of reducing the distinctiveness of the learning-trial encoded traces. Somewhat surprisingly, Kinsbourne and George found that there was no differential effect of preexposure on recognition memory of rare and common words. As a result, they concluded as follows: "This result renders all accounts based on . . . supposedly great distinctiveness of rare words unnecessary [p. 68]."

In terms of the distinctiveness hypothesis, preexposure reduces recognition—memory performance to the extent that the preexposure encoding of a word overlaps its study-trial encoding. Since successive phonemic encodings of a word overlap far more than successive semantic encodings (Jacoby, 1974), it is predicted that the detrimental effects of preexposure will be greater for phonemic than for semantic encodings.

There are at least two related ways in which preexposure might exert differential effects on rare and common words:

1. Common words tend to have more dictionary meanings than rare words, and there is evidence (e.g., Reder, Anderson, & Bjork, 1974) that this is an important factor in determining memorability. The probability of considerable overlap between the preexposure and study-trial encodings will be greater for words having relatively few meanings—i.e., rare words—and thus the prediction is that preexposure should have more of an effect on rare words.

2. Although the overlap between the preexposure and study-trial encodings may be the most important determinant of the distinctiveness of the study-trial encoding, distinctiveness may also be partially determined by the number of preexperimental encodings of an item. Since, by definition, there have been considerably more preexperimental encodings of common than of rare words, common words may be nondistinctively encoded even in the absence of a peexposure encoding, whereas there will be little proactive interference from preexperimental encodings in the case of rare words. Again the prediction is that preexposure should have more of an effect on rare words, because the small number of prior encodings of rare words allows more scope for preexposure to reduce trace distinctiveness.

On either hypothesis, there should be a similar interaction between preexposure and word frequency. The fourth experiment attempted to decide between these two hypotheses.

The experimental design comprised four within-subject factors: processing depth (semantic vs. phonemic), processing typicality (typical vs. atypical), word frequency (rare vs. common), and preexposure (absent vs. present). In the preexposure phase of the experiment, subjects received 128 nouns with irregular grapheme—phoneme correspondence, processing 32 of them in accordance with each of the four instructional conditions used in both of the two previous experiments (phonemic typical, phonemic atypical, semantic typical, and semantic atypical). Half of the words used with each processing task were rare, and half were common. Processing time for each task was equated at 6 seconds per word. There were 15 subjects.

Ten minutes after the termination of the preexposure phase, there was the study trial. On the study trial, subjects also received 128 words (64 rare and 64 common) and performed each of the four processing tasks on 32 of the words. Half of the words in each processing condition had been presented during the preexposure, and half had not. Those words that were presented on both the preexposure and study trials were associated with the same processing task on both trials.

An unexpected recognition test followed some time after the end of the study trial. The subject's task was to select those words that had been presented during the study phase. On some pages of the recognition task, subjects had to discriminate between words presented on both the preexposure and study trials and those presented only on the study trial; on other pages, they had to discriminate between words presented only on the study trial and those not previously presented at all.

As Kinsbourne and George (1974) had found, preexposure produced a detrimental effect on recognition memory. However, more interesting was the fact that the predicted interaction between preexposure and word frequency was significant, F (1,14) = 7.64, p < 0.025 (see Fig. 5.5). Preexposure substantially reduced recognition performance for rare words, F (1,28) = 23.42, p < 0.001, but had no effect on the recognition of common words. The usual inverse relationship between word frequency and recognition memory was obtained under no preexposure conditions, F (1.28) = 32.92, p < 0.001, but was eliminated by preexposure.

The above interaction accords with expectation, but it is noteworthy that Kinsbourne and George (1974) failed to obtain a significant interaction between word frequency and preexposure. Although the precise reason for this discrepancy of results is unknown, Kinsbourne and George did utilize different tasks on the preexposure and study trials. In their study, subjects were asked to rate the concreteness of the presented words on the preexposure trial, whereas they were told to memorize the words on the study trial. Since the relationship between the processes involved in these two tasks is unknown, it is difficult to interpret their results. However, as can be seen in Fig. 5.5, the interaction was primarily attributable to performance with the phonemic processing tasks, whereas Kinsbourne and George used tasks of a more semantic nature.

The preexposure variable also interacted predictably with processing depth, F (1,14) = 27.83, p < 0.001 (see Fig. 5.5). Preexposure led to a marked reduction in recognition performance for phonemically processed words, F (1,28) = 37.71, p < 0.001, but did not affect retention of semantically processed words. It is assumed that the preexposure and study-trial encodings overlapped much more with phonemic than with semantic processing.

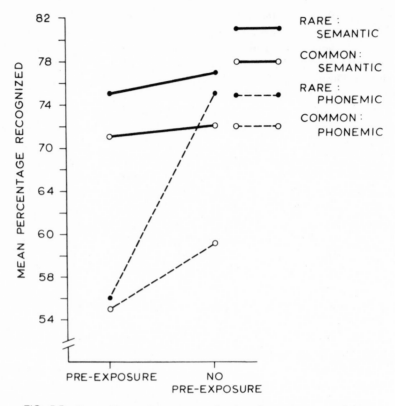

FIG. 5.5. Recognition performance as a function of preexposure, word frequency, and depth of processing (Exp. 3).

As had been found in the first experiment, processing typicality interacted with both processing depth and word frequency (see Fig. 5.6). In the interaction between processing depth and processing typicality, $F(1,14) = 8.76$, $p < 0.025$, processing typicality had a significant effect on phonemic but not on semantic tasks. The interaction between processing typicality and word frequency was marginally significant, $F(1,14) = 4.52$, $0.05 < p < 0.10$. Word frequency was only related to recognition memory under typical processing conditions.

The results of this experiment strongly support the hypothesis that differences in encoded distinctiveness are involved in depth and word-frequency effects in recognition memory. Encoded distinctiveness was manipulated by means of a task-instructional variable and by the presence or absence of preexposure of target words. Both variables interacted predictably with depth of processing and task typicality to produce recognition performance. However, the failure of semantic encodings to be affected either by task typicality or by preexposure is rather surprising. For example, semantic encodings of rare words should be more detrimentally affected by preexposure than semantic encodings of common

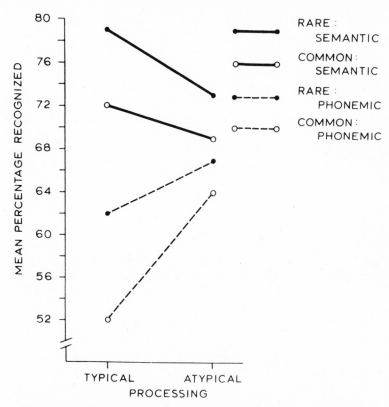

FIG. 5.6. Recognition performance as a function of typicality, word frequency, and processing depth (Exp. 3).

words. This prediction is consistent with theoretical notions proposed by Reder et al. (1974). They observed that word frequency correlates positively with number of dictionary meanings and argued that because of this, high-frequency words should be more vulnerable to the effects of shift in context. In two experiments, they reported this effect for recognition and cued recall. If there are fewer potential semantic encodings of rare than of common words, then the pre-exposure and study-trial semantic encodings of rare words should tend to be more similar than those of common words, with the result that preexposure would affect rare words more than common words. Since it is possible that the processing time of 6 seconds per item allowed the subjects to form rich and elaborate encodings that were resistant to preexposure, the processing time was reduced in the fourth experiment.

Experiment 4

In light of the above considerations, it was decided to investigate further the effects of preexposure on the semantic processing of rare and common words.

Subjects were told that there would be a retention test and that they were to attempt to process the words semantically. Subjects were presented with one word every 2 seconds. In order to clarify the question as to whether word frequency effects in recognition memory are due to frequency per se or to number of dictionary meanings, equal numbers of nouns were selected, belonging to each of the four following categories: common, few meanings; common, many meanings; rare, few meanings; rare, many meanings. Rare words had Thorndike–Lorge frequencies of 1 or 2 per million, and common words had frequencies of 50 and above per million. According to the Oxford English dictionary, the mean number of different dictionary meanings was 2.54 for words with few meanings and 4.79 for words with many meanings. Since there is evidence that word-frequency effects in recognition memory may be confounded by differences in concreteness (Gorman, 1961), in word length (Schulman, 1967), or in orthographic distinctiveness (Zechmeister, 1972), all the rare and common words used in the experiment had two syllables and were equated for concreteness and orthographic distinctiveness on the basis of a previous rating task performed by different subjects.

In order to investigate the word-frequency variable thoroughly, "unknown" words were also presented. These were two-syllable nouns with Thorndike–Lorge frequencies below 9 per 18 million that had been consistently rated in a previous study as having a completely unknown meaning. These words were divided into high and low orthographic distinctiveness groups on the basis of preliminary rating data.

On the preexposure trial, subjects received 144 words: 24 rare words with few meanings, 24 rare words with many meanings, 24 common words with few meanings, 24 common words with many meanings, 24 unknown words of high distinctiveness, and 24 unknown words of low distinctiveness. They were instructed to learn the words, processing them semantically if possible. The presentation rate was 1 word every 2 seconds.

Seven minutes after the termination of the preexposure trial came the study trial. On this trial, 144 words were presented, 72 of which had been presented on the preexposure trial (12 in each category). The instructions were the same as for the preexposure trial.

A recognition test was given 7 minutes after the end of the study trial. Subjects were asked to select those words presented on the study trial. On half the pages of the recognition test, subjects had to discriminate between words presented on both the preexposure and study trials and those presented only on the study trial. On the remaining pages, they had to discriminate between words presented only on the study trial and those not previously presented.

The major analysis was performed on the recognition data for common and rare words and comprised the three factors of word frequency, number of meanings, and preexposure. There was a significant effect of preexposure, $F(1,11) = 6.10$, $p < 0.05$, but no main effect of either word frequency or number of meanings. There were two interesting interactions shown in Fig. 5.7. The interaction between preexposure and word frequency was highly significant in the predicted direction, $F(1,11) = 11.00$, $p < 0.01$. Preexposure had a considerable effect on retention of rare words, $F(1,22) = 15.70$, but no effect at all on retention of common words. A finding of some interest is that with no preexposure, rare words were better recognized than common words, $F(1,22) = 5.99$, $p < 0.025$. This indicates that the usual inverse relationship between word

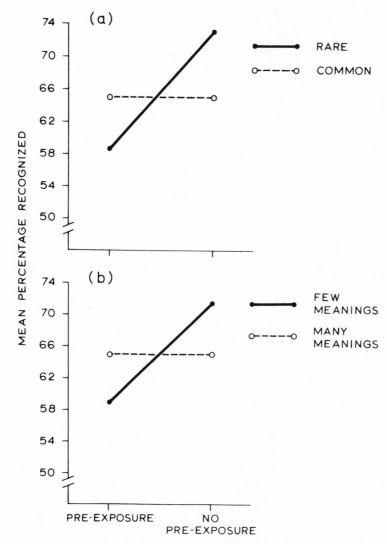

FIG. 5.7.   (a) Recognition performance as a function of preexposure and word frequency and (b) as a function of preexposure and number of meanings (Exp. 4).

frequency and recognition memory is not entirely due to differences in number of meanings, since this factor was controlled.

The interaction between preexposure and number of meanings, shown in Fig. 5.7, was also significant, F (1,11) = 4.85, $p < 0.05$. Preexposure reduced recognition performance for words with few meanings, F (1,22) = 4.69, $p < 0.05$, but had no effect on recognition for words with many meanings.

It was suggested previously that the distinctiveness of the study-trial encoding of rare words would be reduced more than that of common words by means of either or both of two related mechanisms. On one hand, it can be argued that the semantic encoding space is smaller for rare words than for common words, because rare words have fewer meanings than common words. It follows that the probability of substantial overlap between the preexposure and study-trial encodings is greater for rare than for common words. On the other hand, it could be argued that the important factor is the number of prior encodings of rare and common words. The greater the number of prior encodings, the higher will be the probability that the preexposure encoding will overlap completely with prior encodings and thus not reduce the distinctiveness of the study-trial encoding. Although both factors (i.e., number of meanings and number of prior encodings) operate in terms of their effects on the prior encoding A circle of Fig. 5.1, the evidence of this experiment indicates that the differential effect of preexposure on rare and common words is due to an amalgam of the two factors.

Analysis of the "unknown" word data indicated that unknown words of high distinctiveness were better remembered than those of low distinctiveness, F (1,11) = 6.94, $p < 0.05$, and there was a significant interaction between preexposure and distinctiveness. Distinctiveness was associated with good retention in the absence of preexposure, F (1,22) = 12.40, $p < 0.005$, but there was no effect of distinctiveness under preexposure conditions. It thus appears that the distinctiveness hypothesis has relevance to encodings of an almost entirely nonsemantic character.

Experiment 5

It is increasingly claimed that the same processes operate in recall and recognition. For example, Lockhart et al. (1976) argued as follows: "We believe that recall and recognition do not differ in any crucial way—they are different only in the sense that in recognition, re-presentation of the stimulus provides better information from which the initial encoding can be reconstructed [p. 85]." Indirect evidence in favor of this notion is available in the positive association between depth of processing and both recall and recognition performance (e.g., Craik, 1973) and the enhancing effects of trace distinctiveness on both recall and recognition obtained in Experiment 1. An interesting question is whether or not depth and distinctiveness affect recall and recognition in the same manner.

An appropriate paradigm to investigate this issue was used by Broadbent and

Broadbent (1975). In essence, they compared recognition for those items from a list that could not be recalled with recognition for all list items. Surprisingly, they found that the nonrecalled items showed no recognition disadvantage. However, the same processing instructions were used for all items. If subjects were required to process some items phonemically and some semantically, then the semantically processed items would tend to be recalled. Since semantically processed items are extremely well recognized, the elimination of these recalled items should reduce recognition performance.

On a similar line of argument, if some items are processed distinctively and others nondistinctively, then the distinctively encoded items will tend to be recalled. Since such items are well recognized, recognition memory should be reduced if the recalled items are not included in the analysis of the recognition data.

Subjects were presented with 90 words at the rate of 1 word every 3 seconds. All the words were nouns with irregular phoneme−grapheme correspondence. Each of the three tasks (phonemic typical, phonemic atypical, and semantic typical) was performed on 30 words and the subject responded overtly. The subjects were told that there would be a retention test. Immediately after presentation, the recall-first subjects were told to write down as many of the list words as possible in 5 minutes, and the recognition-only subjects spent an equivalent length of time cancelling letters on a sheet. Then all subjects were given a recognition test and were required to select 90 words from a total of 180 words. There were 12 subjects. In the subsequent analysis, recognition performance for recall-first subjects was considered only for those items that a subject had not managed to recall.

Preliminary analyses indicated that semantic typical processing was associated with significantly higher levels of recall, t (10) = 2.70, $p < 0.025$, and of recognition, t (11) = 4.35, $p < 0.001$, than was phonemic typical processing. Comparison of the phonemic atypical and phonemic typical tasks indicated that phonemic atypical processing produced slightly but nonsignificantly higher levels of recall and of recognition.

The main analyses involved the recognition data summarized in Table 5.3. If depth of processing affected recall and recognition performance in the same way, then recognition performance on the combined phonemic typical and semantic typical data should have been higher for recognition-only than for recall-first subjects. In fact, the difference was slightly but nonsignificantly in the opposite direction. The hypothesis that distinctiveness affects recall and recognition in similar fashion was also not confirmed, since recognition performance on the combined phonemic typical and phonemic atypical conditions was equivalent for recognition-only and recall-first subjects. Comparison of recognition performance under the recall-first and recognition-only conditions for each of the three processing tasks separately also produced nonsignificant results. It might have been expected that *within* each processing task it would be the more

TABLE 5.3
Recognition and Recall Data (Exp. 5).

(a) Percentage of Items Correctly Recognized

	Phonemic Typical	Phonemic Atypical	Semantic Typical
Recall first	68.5	73.6	84.6
Recognition only	62.2	67.8	78.3

	Phonemic Typical + Semantic Typical
Recall first	74.9
Recognition only	70.3

	Phonemic Typical + Phonemic Atypical
Recall first	70.6
Recognition only	65.0

(b) Mean Items Recalled

	Phonemic Typical	Phonemic Atypical	Semantic Typical
Recall first	4.3	6.0	9.7

thoroughly and/or distinctively encoded items that would be recalled, thus making recognition better under the recognition-only than under the recall-first condition.

Broadbent and Broadbent (1975) did a long series of experiments and came to the following conclusion: ''The findings of these experiments therefore, suggest most surprisingly, that non-recalled items are as easy to recognize as items drawn from a whole list; recall would, so far as this result is true, involve some difficulty quite extra and separate from that involved in recognition [p. 581].'' Obviously, such a conclusion can be drawn appropriately only provided that certain assumptions are true, of which the most important is that the traces of nonrecalled items are not strengthened or affected during the recall test. Without wanting to overinterpret the results of this small-scale experiment, it appears possible that depth of processing affects recall and recognition in rather different ways, and the same may be true of distinctiveness. In addition, of course, the results support those of Broadbent and Broadbent in finding that there is no special difficulty of recognition associated with nonrecalled items.

Though the data collected in the Broadbent–Broadbent paradigm are exploratory rather than definitive, there is other evidence that there is a rather low correlation between recall and recognition (e.g., Underwood, 1972). Tversky (1973) correlated recall and recognition scores for subjects and obtained a small positive correlation when the subjects were tested on recall first and then on recognition, but no correlation when the recognition test was given first. Paivio (1976) correlated recall and recognition for 72 items and found that the correlations were small and generally nonsignificant. Furthermore, when the data were factor analyzed and subjected to a Varimax rotation, memory scores from recall and recognition loaded on independent factors. If the processes involved in recall and recognition are in fact as dissimilar as implied by these findings, then this suggests that more attention should be paid to the possibility that retention-enhancing factors may operate differently in recall and recognition. Some speculative comments are offered in the next section.

3. CONCLUSIONS

The encoding specificity principle (e.g., Tulving & Thomson, 1973) proposes that recognition memory depends on the degree of overlap between the study-trial and test-trial encodings of any given item. There is now considerable experimental evidence (e.g., Thomson, 1972; Winograd & Conn, 1971) that recognition memory can be impaired by changes from study to test of the context in which an item is presented, presumably because such contextual changes reduce the similarity of the study- and test-trial encodings.

The distinctiveness hypothesis extends the encoding specificity principle by arguing that the most important factor in recognition memory is the extent to which the test-trial encoding contains information that is unique to the study-trial encoding. In the case of an item that is phonemically encoded at input and at test, there would appear to be substantial encoding overlap. However, recognition memory is poor for phonemic encodings, because the study-trial encoding is highly similar to previous phonemic encodings of the same word.

The above emphasis on the relationship between the study-trial and previous encodings of target items is similar to ideas put forward by Lockhart et al. (1976). They argued as follows:

When a particular pattern of encoding operations is induced by the test stimulus, *all* episodic traces of the pattern are contacted and help to constrain further reconstructive encoding of the stimulus. If there are many traces of the pattern, a "familiar" encoding will be achieved easily (since it is guided by many traces and thus easily encoded), but the stimulus will not elicit recognition of a *specific* previous instance (since many different contexts are competing for conscious awareness). If the pattern was unique or distinctive, however, only one or a few traces of such a pattern exist—now, if the retrieval information (the test stimulus) is specific enough, the previous trace will be contacted and the present encoding will contain contextual features from the initial encoding [p. 83].

One of the most important factors affecting recognition memory is word frequency. The experiments discussed previously lend support to the notion that rare words are more distinctively encoded than common words and that this is partially responsible for the superior levels of recognition associated with rare words. More specifically, the fact that rare words have fewer meanings on average than common words means that the overlap between the study- and test-trial encodings will tend to be greater for rare words, and the relative paucity of previous encodings of rare words means that there is less overlap between pre-experimental and study-trial encodings for rare words.

In terms of the distinctiveness hypothesis, the great advantage of semantic over phonemic encodings is due to the fact that the vastly greater variety of potential encodings of any given word at the semantic level means that the overlap between preexperimental and study-trial encodings is considerably less for semantic than for phonemic encodings. The experimental evidence discussed in the previous section supported various predictions from this hypothesis. In general terms, the probability that a semantic encoding will be distinctive is positively correlated with the degree of richness or elaboration of that encoding.

The original version of the distinctiveness hypothesis is in need of some revision. Although it is true that the greater the dissimilarity between the study-trial encoding and previous encodings of the same item, the greater the potential level of recognition, it is clear that the extent to which this potential is realized is dependent on the test-trial encoding context. Since a distinctive encoding is, by definition, highly specific to a given situation, such encodings may be thought of as "context bound." Any difference in the encoding context at study and at test may be expected to produce a more substantial reduction in recognition performance for distinctive than for nondistinctive encodings. For example, the first moon landing by man in July 1969 is a distinctive memory for most people, and yet *pari passu* there are few retrieval environments that cause recollection of that event.

Some evidence relevant to this hypothesis was obtained by Tulving and Thomson (1971) and by Thomson (1972). Tulving and Thomson presented a series of words for learning and told their subjects that it might facilitate subsequent recognition if they discovered the relationship between two words presented together. Of interest here, subjects were presented with some weakly associated pairs of words and some strongly associated pairs of words. It is reasonable to assume that strongly related words were encoded with the dominant sense of each word (i.e., nondistinctively), whereas with weakly associated words, at least one of the two words was encoded in terms of a less frequently used sense of the word (i.e., distinctively). On the recognition test, subjects had to decide whether or not each word had been presented before, but many words were tested in the context of another word. When words from weakly and strongly associated pairs were tested in the same context as at input, words from weakly associated pairs were slightly better recognized than those from strongly associated pairs (62% and 59% respectively). This effect was stronger in the Thomson study (61.5% and 55%, respectively). On the other hand, when the test context was different from the input context, words from weakly associated pairs tested in the presence of a strong associate were much less well recognized than words from strongly associated pairs tested in the presence of a weak associate (37% and 50%).

Other evidence also suggests that distinctive encodings can show either better or worse memory performance than nondistinctive encodings, dependent on the retrieval environment (see Jacoby & Craik, Chapter 1, this volume). In a recent study, I compared recognition memory for phonemic typical and phonemic atypical encodings as a function of retrieval context. Subjects were presented initially with pairs of words and asked to pronounce the second word so as to rhyme with the first. The second word was always a word having irregular phoneme−grapheme correspondence. Thus *glove* would receive a phonemic atypical encoding if presented in the pair *cove glove* and a phonemic typical encoding if presented in the pair *love glove*. On the subsequent recognition test, subjects had to make a judgment about each word separately. The second words of each pair were either paired with the same word as at input or with a new word biasing the alternative pronunciation of the second word. There was a significant interaction between initial processing condition and retention-test context (same vs. different). In this interaction, phonemic atypical encodings were unaffected by context change, $F (1,18) < 1$, whereas phonemic typical encodings were better recognized when context at test was the same as that used originally, $F (1,18) = 7.60, p < 0.05$.

It is not clear exactly why distinctive encodings are sometimes more affected than nondistinctive encodings by context changes and sometimes less affected. Presumably the extent to which the original encoding can be reconstructed on the basis of retention-test information is a relevant factor. A subject receiving *cove glove* at input and *love glove* at test can probably reconstruct the appropriate phonemic encoding of *glove* at test, since there are so few potential phonemic encodings of the word *glove*. On the other hand, the Tulving and Thomson (1971) finding that words from weakly associated pairs were poorly recognized in the different context of strong associates may have been due to the difficulty of reconstructing the appropriate nondominant semantic encoding under those conditions of testing.

In some respects, the distinctiveness hypothesis has a familiar ring about it: *Plus ça change, plus c'est la même chose*. For example, Gibson (1940) put forward a hypothesis asserting that "a major necessity of verbal learning is the establishment of *discrimination* among the items to be learned, and this process of discrimination is actually a fundamental part of what is called generally the learning process [p. 197]." One empirically confirmed prediction from this hypothesis is that retroactive interference is a function of the degree of similarity of original and interpolated tasks. Gibson also argued that differentiation or distinctiveness would be greater for more meaningful material, citing words and nonsense syllables as exemplars of more and less meaningful material, respectively. In more modern terminology, she proposed that stimulus items permitting semantic analysis would be more distinctively encoded (and thus better remembered) than stimulus items processed only at the phonemic and/or orthographic level.

One difference between contemporary approaches and many of the earlier ones is that there is now more emphasis placed on similarity relations among encodings of items rather than among the items per se. However, Woodworth (1938) pointed out that retroactive interference was affected both by similarity of *material* between the original and interpolated tasks and by similarity in the *operation* performed. By operation, Woodworth meant something approximating to type of processing.

It is of interest to note that interference theory has consistently stressed similarity relations among stimuli and responses in order to account for the phenomena of proactive and retroactive interference, and of course the embryonic distinctiveness hypothesis also emphasizes the importance of similarity relations to an understanding of memory. At this juncture, it is relevant to consider briefly the experimental paradigm utilized in Experiments 3 and 4. In those experiments, preexposure clearly constituted a potential source of proactive interference. Accordingly, a reasonable way of expressing one of the main findings is that semantic encodings are less susceptible to certain forms of proactive interference than are phonemic encodings. As a framework for future research, the following hypothesis suggests itself: *The usual memorial superiority of deep over shallow encodings is due to the fact that deep encodings are less susceptible to proactive and retroactive interference than are shallow encodings. This differential susceptibility to interference is in turn due to the greater trace distinctiveness usually associated with deep encodings.*

This may be an appropriate point to mention some of the problems with a distinctiveness hypothesis that will have to be faced shortly. The main difficulty is that there is no satisfactory independent index of trace distinctiveness. For example, consider a series of experiments involving pictures (Nelson, Chapter 3, this volume), in which it was found that phonemic similarity among the names of the objects depicted had a detrimental effect on memory performance in some tasks but not in others. Though we may be tempted to conclude that trace distinctiveness was affected by task demands, the argument rapidly becomes circular. With very simple stimuli, psychophysical methods allow us to examine the relationship between a psychological variable and its physical counterpart throughout the range of physical magnitudes. Such research has led to Stevens's power law, i.e., sensation magnitude is a power function of the physical magnitude (Stevens, 1961). Similarity relations among perceived sensation magnitudes of different physical stimuli might prove to be predictive of memory performance. With more complex, multidimensional stimuli, the problems of measuring distinctiveness are much greater. One possibility would be to measure response latencies in a same–different perceptual judgment task—the argument being that such judgments would be faster in the case of more distinctive stimuli.

A related problem is that an encoding can only be considered to be either distinctive or nondistinctive relative to some set of encodings, and an encoding that is distinctive with respect to one set of encodings may well be nondistinctive with respect to a second set of encodings. Since distinctiveness is relative rather than absolute, prediction can be difficult in many circumstances. For example, if one to-be-learned item is distinctively encoded on dimension A but not on dimension B, whereas a second item is distinctively encoded on dimension B but not on A, we cannot predict with confidence which item will be better retained.

Do depth and distinctiveness of encoding affect recall in the same way that they affect recognition? Experiment 5 provided modest evidence that they operate differently on recall and recognition. Underwood (1969) proposed a distinction between discriminative and retrieval attributes of memory and claimed that recall depended heavily on retrieval attributes whereas recognition relied on those attributes discriminating one memory trace from another. In terms of this distinction, distinctiveness is clearly a discriminative rather than a retrieval attribute. It is not certain that recall necessarily involves great reliance on discriminative attributes. For example, Bousfield and Rosner (1970) compared free and uninhibited recall of a list of ostensibly unrelated words. The instructions for uninhibited recall emphasized that the subject was to emit *any* words that came to mind even if he or she knew that they were nonlist words. There was an average of less than one intrusion error per trial with uninhibited recall, suggesting that recall sometimes lacks the conscious evaluation of item appropriateness that is characteristic of recognition.

This analysis suggests that distinctiveness per se may not be an important determinant of recall performance. At the very least, recall is usually considerably more affected than recognition by reconstructive problems, due to the exiguous information provided by the retrieval cues available for free recall. A similar position is argued by Jacoby and Craik (Chapter 1, this volume). The evidence indicates that rare words are more distinctively encoded than common words, and yet they are not better recalled. In similar fashion, the processing typicality variable was more strongly related to recognition than to recall performance in Experiments 1 and 2. The evidence suggests that recall depends on associations formed among list members. For example, Hall, Grossman, and Elwood (1976); Tversky (1973), and Broadbent and Broadbent (1975) all found that subjects expecting a recall test were more likely to form interrelations among list words than subjects expecting a recognition test, and it has also been found (e.g., Schwartz & Humphreys, 1974; Tversky, 1973) that recall performance is enhanced by interrelating the items within a list.

In sum, it is proposed that depth of processing facilitates recognition performance primarily by making the study-trial encoding dissimilar to previous encodings, i.e., by making it distinctive. Although there may be analogous effects of depth of processing on recall, depth also facilitates recall-test performance by increasing the number of interitem relationships that are formed, i.e., by producing greater elaboration of encoding.

ACKNOWLEDGMENTS

The author would like to express his appreciation and thanks to the Social Science Research Council for financial assistance (Grant HR 3801/2) during the preparation of this manuscript. Thanks are also due to Max Coltheart and Vernon Gregg for helpful suggestions and, in particular, to Christine Eysenck, who has made manifold valuable contributions to this work.

REFERENCES

Berlyne, D. E. *Conflict, arousal and curiosity*. London: McGraw–Hill, 1960.

Berlyne, D. E., & Ditkofsky, J. Effects of novelty and oddity on visual selective attention. *British Journal of Psychology*, 1976, 67, 175–180.

Bousfield, W. A., & Rosner, S. R. Free vs. uninhibited recall. *Psychonomic Science*, 1970, 20, 75–76.

Broadbent, D. E., & Broadbent, M. H. P. The recognition of words which cannot be recalled. In P. M. A. Rabbitt & S. Dornic (Eds.), *Attention and performance* (Vol. V). London: Academic Press, 1975.

Brown, J. An analysis of recognition and recall and of problems in their comparison. In J. Brown (Ed.), *Recall and recognition*. London: Wiley, 1976.

Cohen, M. E., & Carr, W. J. Facial recognition and the von Restorff effect. *Bulletin of the Psychonomic Society*, 1975, 6, 383–384.

Craik, F. I. M. A "levels of analysis" view of memory. In P. Pliner, L. Krames, & T. M. Alloway (Eds.), *Communication and affect: Language and thought*. London: Academic Press, 1973.

Craik, F. I. M. Depth of processing in recall and recognition. In S. Dornic & P. M. A. Rabbitt (Eds.), *Attention and performance* (Vol. VI). London: Academic Press, 1977.

Craik, F. I. M., & Lockhart, R. S. Levels of processing: A framework for memory research. *Journal of Verbal Learning and Verbal Behavior*, 1972, 11, 671–684.

Craik, F. I. M., & Tulving, E. Depth of processing and the retention of words in episodic memory. *Journal of Experimental Psychology: General*, 1975, 104, 268–294.

Einstein, G. O., Pellegrino, J. W., Mondani, M. S., & Battig, W. F. Free-recall performance as a function of overt rehearsal frequency. *Journal of Experimental Psychology*, 1974, 103, 440–449.

Eysenck, M. W. *Conditions modifying memory: The von Restorff and the 'release' effects*. Unpublished Ph.D. thesis, London University, 1972.

Eysenck, M. W. *Human memory: Theory, research, and individual differences*. London: Pergamon, 1977.

Eysenck, M. W. Levels of processing: A critique. *British Journal of Psychology*, 1978, 68, 157–169. (a)

Eysenck, M. W. Levels of processing: A reply to Lockhart and Craik. *British Journal of Psychology*, 1978, 69, 177–178. (b)

Forster, K. I., & Chambers, S. M. Lexical access and naming time. *Journal of Verbal Learning and Verbal Behavior*, 1973, 12, 627–635.

Gibson, E. J. A systematic application of the concepts of generalization and differentiation to verbal learning. *Psychological Review*, 1940, *47*, 196–229.

Going, M., & Read, J. D. Effects of uniqueness, sex of subject, and sex of photograph on facial recognition. *Perceptual and Motor Skills*, 1974, *39*, 109–110.

Gorman, A. M. Recognition memory for nouns as a function of abstractness and frequency. *Journal of Experimental Psychology*, 1961, *61*, 23–29.

Gregg, V. Word frequency, recognition and recall. In J. Brown (Ed.), *Recall and recognition*. London: Wiley, 1976.

Hall, J. W., Grossman, L. R., & Elwood, K. D. Differences in encoding for free recall vs. recognition. *Memory & Cognition*, 1976, *4*, 507–513.

Hyde, T. S., & Jenkins, J. J. The differential effects of incidental tasks on the organization of recall of a list of highly associated words. *Journal of Experimental Psychology*, 1969, *12*, 471–480.

Jacoby, L. L. The role of mental contiguity in memory: Registration and retrieval effects. *Journal of Verbal Learning and Verbal Behavior*, 1974, *13*, 483–496.

Johnston, W. A., & Uhl, C. N. The contributions of encoding effort and variability to the spacing effect in free recall. *Journal of Experimental Psychology: Human Learning and Memory*, 1976, *2*, 153–160.

Kahneman, D. *Attention and effort*. London: Prentice–Hall, 1973.

Kinsbourne, M., & George, J. The mechanism of the word-frequency effect on recognition memory. *Journal of Verbal Learning and Verbal Behavior*, 1974, *13*, 63–69.

Klein, K., & Saltz, E. Specifying the mechanisms in a levels-of-processing approach to memory. *Journal of Experimental Psychology: Human Learning and Memory*, 1976, *2*, 671–679.

Kleinsmith, L. J., & Kaplan, S. Paired-associate learning as a function of arousal and interpolated interval. *Journal of Experimental Psychology*, 1963, *65*, 190–193.

Kleinsmith, L. J., & Kaplan, S. Interaction of arousal and recall interval in nonsense syllable paired-associate learning. *Journal of Experimental Psychology*, 1964, *67*, 124–126.

Lakatos, I., & Musgrave, A. (Eds.). *Criticism and the growth of knowledge*. Cambridge: Cambridge University Press, 1970.

Lockhart, R. S., & Craik, F. I. M. Levels of processing: A critique. A reply. *British Journal of Psychology*, 1978, *68*, 170–177.

Lockhart, R. S., & Craik, F. I. M. Levels of processing: A reply to Eysenck. *British Journal of Psychology*, 1978, *68*, 171–175.

Moscovitch, M., & Craik, F. I. M. Depth of processing, retrieval cues, and uniqueness of encoding as factors in recall. *Journal of Verbal Learning and Verbal Behavior*, 1976, *15*, 447–458.

Paivio, A. Imagery in recall and recognition. In J. Brown (Ed.), *Recall and recognition*. London: Academic Press, 1976.

Popper, K. R. *The logic of scientific discovery*. London: Hutchinson, 1959.

Popper, K. R. *Conjectures and refutation*. London: Routledge and Kegan Paul, 1963.

Reder, L. M., Anderson, J. R., & Bjork, R. A. A semantic interpretation of encoding specificity. *Journal of Experimental Psychology*, 1974, *102*, 648–656.

Rundus, D. Analysis of rehearsal processes in free recall. *Journal of Experimental Psychology*, 1971, *89*, 63–77.

Schulman, A. I. Word length and rarity in recognition memory. *Psychonomic Science*, 1967, *9*, 211–212.

Schwartz, R. M., & Humphreys, M. S. Recognition and recall as a function of instructional manipulations of organization. *Journal of Experimental Psychology*, 1974, *102*, 517–519.

Stevens, S. S. The psychophysics of sensory functions. In W. A. Rosenblith (Ed.), *Sensory communication*. Cambridge, Mass.: MIT Press, 1961.

Thomson, D. M. Context effects in recognition memory. *Journal of Verbal Learning and Verbal Behavior*, 1972, *11*, 497–511.

Tulving, E. Ecphoric processes in recall and recognition. In J. Brown (Ed.), *Recall and recognition*. London: Academic Press, 1976.

Tulving, E., & Thomson, D. M. Retrieval processes in recognition memory: Effects of associative context. *Journal of Experimental Psychology*, 1971, *87*, 116–124.

Tulving, E., & Thomson, D. M. Encoding specificity and retrieval processes in episodic memory. *Psychological Review*, 1973, *80*, 352–373.

Tversky, B. Encoding processes in recognition and recall. *Cognitive Psychology*, 1973, *5*, 275–287.

Underwood, B. J. Attributes of memory. *Psychological Review*, 1969, *76*, 559–573.

Underwood, B. J. Are we overloading memory? In A. W. Melton & E. Martin (Eds.), *Coding processes in human memory*. London: Winston, 1972.

Wallace, W. P. Review of the historical, empirical, and theoretical status of the von Restorff phenomenon. *Psychological Bulletin*, 1965, *63*, 410–424.

Weimer, W. B. A conceptual framework for cognitive psychology: Motor theories of the mind. In R. Shaw & J. Bransford (Eds.), *Perceiving, acting, and knowing*. London: Wiley, 1977.

Winograd, E., & Conn, C. P. Evidence from recognition memory for specific encoding of unmodified homographs. *Journal of Verbal Learning and Verbal Behavior*, 1971, *10*, 702–706.

Woodworth, R. S. *Experimental psychology*. London: Methuen, 1938.

Zechmeister, E. B. Orthographic distinctiveness as a variable in word recognition. *American Journal of Psychology*, 1972, *85*, 425–430.

6 Amnesic Patients' Level of Processing

Laird S. Cermak
Psychology Service, Boston Veterans Administration Hospital
and
Aphasia Research Unit, Neurology Department
Boston University School of Medicine

The alcoholic Korsakoff patients' amnestic syndrome has been described in great detail during the last decade. Clinically, it is known that these patients have suffered severe subcortical brain damage primarily in the midline thalamic (n. medialis dorsalis) and limbic system (mamillary bodies) areas (Victor, Adams, & Collins, 1971). The precise cause of this brain damage is not known; however, the possibility exists that it may be a combination of poor nutrition, which results in a thiamine deficiency, and the toxic effects of alcohol acting on the central nervous system. These patients have been shown to demonstrate memory deficits in what has traditionally been called long-term memory as well as in short-term memory and even in sensory memory. Talland (1965) was one of the first to point out that these patients are totally incapable of learning and remembering new information, day−to−day events, current news, or even hospital personnel and procedures. In fact, the only information that seems to be available to these patients at·all is that which they learned prior to the onset of their disorder. In other words, they can still recall events from their childhood and early adulthood, including public events taking place some 30 to 40 years ago. However, nothing of current interest is known by these patients. They know neither the year, their age, the name of the president, nor even the name of the facility in which they reside.

Given that these patients seem so completely unable to learn new material, it occurred to us that they might provide an excellent testing ground for any theory of memory that is based upon the premise that retentive capability is in any way correlated with initial information processing ability. Since these patients have no real retentive ability, it could be asked whether or not they have an information-processing deficit of such a magnitude that it could account for their memory disorder. If it turned out that these patients did have such an information-processing deficit, then the relationship between processing level and retention level would receive support. If the patients did not have a processing disturbance, then such a direct relationship would have to be questioned; and indeed either a stage between "encoding" and retrieval might have to be proposed to account for these patients' deficit, or the deficit would have to be shown to be one purely of retrieval.

The possibility that these patients' memory disorder might be related to an impairment in the extent to which they process information during its presentation was first noted in a study by Cermak and Butters (1972) in which a list of eight words, consisting of two words from each of four categories (e.g., animals, vegetables, professions, and names), was read to the patients. Following the reading of this list, the patients were immediately asked to freely recall as many of the words as they could. Then, some time later, the patients were read a second, similarly constructed list of eight words. However, this time they were told prior to the reading of the list precisely what categories were going to be represented and were instructed that they would have to recall each word in response to its being prompted by a category cue. Under these conditions, chronic alcoholics with drinking histories that paralleled those of the Korsakoffs but who had not suffered brain damage, recalled more words under cued than under free recall. However, the Korsakoff patients actually retrieved fewer words under cued recall than they had under free recall. The Korsakoff patients could freely "spew out" the words immediately after the presentation of the list, but they could not give each word back under its appropriate category. It almost appeared as if they were retaining the material in an uncategorized state sufficient for immediate free recall but not for the more complex, cognitive manipulations required in cued recall. This immature processing of information reinforced the possibility that an impairment in analysis might be contributing to these patients' memory difficulties.

The above experiment used lists of words in which each item bore some semantic relationship to at least one other item in the list. When no obvious semantic characteristics exist within a list of words, it is well known that normal adult subjects generally impose some form of subjective organization upon the list (Tulving, 1962). They may, for instance, rehearse the material in chunks of three or more contiguous items; or they may rehearse items together that for some idiosyncratic reason seem, to them, to belong together. Rundus and Atkinson (1970) have developed a technique that allows one to observe this subjective organization in progress. Specifically, the subject is asked to rehearse aloud during list presentation, so the extent to which they chunk during rehearsal can be monitored. Rundus and Atkinson have found that normal adults generally rehearse not only the word presently before them, but several words previously presented in the list as well. However, Cermak, Naus, and Reale (1976) discovered that Korsakoff patients tend spontaneously to rehearse only one word at a time (see Fig. 6.1), that word being the one currently presented. This strategy results in the Korsakoffs actually rehearsing each individual word more frequently than either alcoholic or nonalcoholic controls (Fig. 6.2), but still retaining far fewer items than either control group (Fig. 6.3). This single-word strategy occurred even when the level of organizational saliency of the list (i.e., whether categories were represented in the list or whether it consisted only of unrelated words) was increased. Obviously, the Korsakoff patients were focusing on no more than one item in the list at a time. In fact, as we shall see, it turns out that they tend to focus on only one "feature" of each particular item—that feature being the phonemic characteristic of the item.

Evidence supporting this single phonemic feature strategy on the part of Korsakoff patients came initially in a study by Cermak, Butters, and Gerrein (1973), using an adaptation of Underwood's (1965) false recognition test. In their test, 60 words were shown to the patient at a rate of 1 word every 2 seconds.

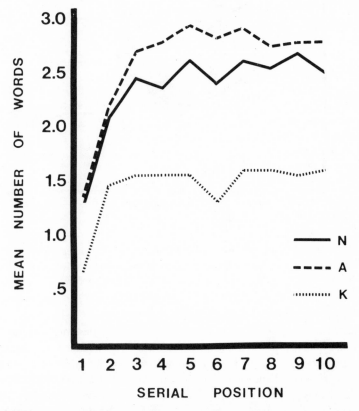

FIG. 6.1. The number of different items rehearsed per rehearsal set as a function of the serial position of the rehearsal set for Korsakoff patients (K), alcoholic controls (A), and normal controls (N). (From Cermak, Naus and Reale, 1976.)

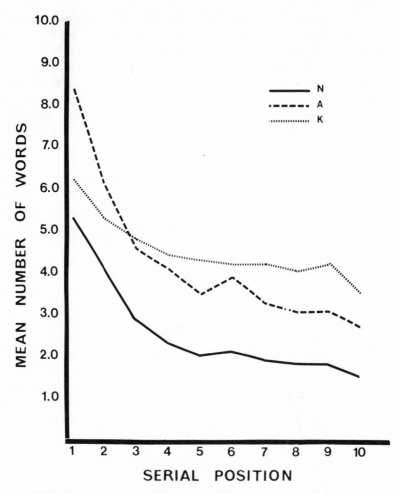

FIG. 6.2.   The total number of rehearsals of each word averaged across all rehearsal sets as a function of the serial position of the word for Korsakoff patients (K), alcoholic controls (A), and normal controls (N). (From Cermak, Naus, & Reale, 1976.)

The patient's task was to detect any repetitions of words that might occur in the list. The list actually did contain repetitions but also contained several homonyms (e.g., *bear* and *bare*), high associates (*table* and *chair*), and synonyms (*robber* and *thief*). Whenever the patient indicated that a homonym, an associate, or a synonym was a repetition, he was scored as having "falsely" recognized a word. The rationale for the experiment was that the more completely a patient analyzed the component features of each word, the less likely it would be that he would falsely recognize a homonym, associate, or synonym as being a "repeat." However, if his level of analysis were meager, i.e., if he restricted himself solely to an analysis of the phonemic features of the word, he might decide that a homonym was actually a repeat. It was also possible that he might indicate that an associate was a repeat, since the associate may have been implicitly elicited (to use Underwood's terminology) during the presentation of a prior word.

The outcome of the experiment was that Korsakoff patients falsely recognized more homonyms and associates than the controls while at the same time managing to identify nearly as many of the actual repetitions. They did not, however, make any more synonym or unrelated errors than normals. This suggests that the patients were probably relying heavily upon their phonemic analysis, coupled with a limited amount of elicited semantic analysis (as indicated by the fact that implicit associates could not be discriminated from explicit stimuli), to analyze each word. Thus, in this experiment the strategy of focusing primarily on the phonemic features of verbal information was in fact found to be a characteristic of Korsakoff's syndrome.

Further evidence that Korsakoff patients tend to focus upon the phonemic features of verbal information was provided in a later study by Cermak and Moreines (1976), employing a somewhat similar paradigm to the one just described, with one exception. In their task, certain features were supposed to be "detected" rather than "falsely" recognized. This test required that the patient listen to a list of words read at a constant rate and indicate when a word was repeated (repetition condition), or when a word rhymed with a previous word (phonemic condition), or when a word belonged to the same category as a preceding word (semantic condition). The patient did not have to indicate which previous word was the match, nor did he have to explain the rationale for his choice. All he had to do was to indicate when the target word occurred. Memory for the particular features was then monitored by plotting the number of correct choices as a function of the number of words intervening between the initial and probe members of each pair. Since no verbal response had to be made, Broca's aphasics (patients whose primary deficit consisted of an inability to use

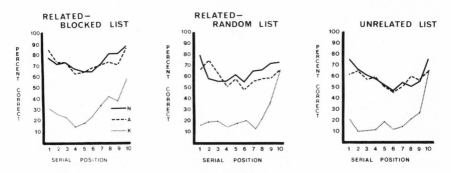

FIG. 6.3.   Percentage of words correctly recalled as a function of list type and serial position for Korsakoff patients (K), alcoholic controls (A), and normal controls (N). (From Cermak, Naus, & Reale, 1976.)

expressive language) were given this same task, so that comparisons between this group and the alcoholic Korsakoff groups could be made.

The results of this experiment (Fig. 6.4) were that the Korsakoff patients performed significantly worse than the normals on the Semantic Task and approximately the same as normals on all other tasks except where four items intervened during the Phonemic Task. This suggested that indeed Korsakoff patients may be capable of retaining verbal information in working memory on the basis of a phonemic code but that they suffer when the capacity of this system is exceeded or when they are asked to make semantic judgments based on this code. This finding has been more fully confirmed by a series of experiments using Wickens's modification of the distractor technique to which we now turn.

Wickens (1970) has repeatedly shown that proactive interference (PI) can be generated within the confines of the Brown—Peterson distractor paradigm simply by presenting material from the same class of information (e.g., all animals) on several consecutive trials. He has also demonstrated that this PI can be reduced through the introduction of material from a new class of information. This results in an increase in recall over that of the preceding trial. Wickens feels that this PI release phenomenon is a reflection of the subject's ability to analyze and store the new class of information on the basis of those semantic features that differentiate it from the prior material. On the basis of this rationale, it might be anticipated that Korsakoff patients would show a release of interference when the two classes of verbal material required only a very rudimentary categorization such as that which differentiates letters from numbers. However, they might not show a similar release when the categorization involved more abstract semantic discriminations such as differentiating taxonomic classes of animals from vegetables.

The first expectation was confirmed by Cermak, Butters, and Moreines (1974), who found that the alphanumeric-shift condition resulted in a PI release for the Korsakoff patients. In fact, the patients' recall performance on the release

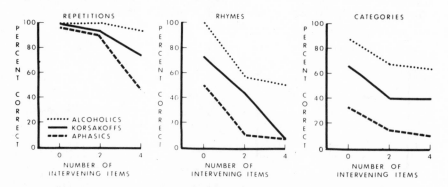

FIG. 6.4.   Percentage of target words correctly identified by each group on each of the three tasks as a function of the number of intervening words. (From Cermak, & Moreines, 1976.)

trial was just as high as their performance had been on the very first trial of the experiment. The second expectation was also fulfilled by the same investigators when they found no PI release for the taxonomic-shift condition. In fact, the Korsakoff patients performed at the same level following a shift in categories as they did when no switch in categories occurred. Apparently, Korsakoff patients are capable of detecting the difference between letters and numbers and of using this as a basis for differentiating them in memory but cannot do this for the more complex, semantically based, taxonomic categories. Since these results have been confirmed by Kinsbourne and Wood (1975) using similar materials, it appears that Korsakoff patients must perform an insufficient amount of semantic analysis on verbal material and thus are unable to remove the effects of interference in memory so that the material might be available for recall at the desired time.

Since the Korsakoff patients seem to rely so heavily upon their phonemic analysis to retain verbal information, it makes sense to assume that they might be more susceptible than normals to the effects of any phonemic interference that occurred during a retention interval. To test this assumption, DeLuca, Cermak, and Butters (1976) used yet another modification of the distractor technique— one in which the nature of the distractor task, rather than the nature of the to-be-remembered stimuli, was varied. In one condition of their experiment the patients were asked to perform a note-tracking task (nonverbal distraction); in a second condition they were asked to shadow consonant trigrams presented through headphones (acoustic distraction); and in a third they were told to scan a page of words looking for those that belonged to a given target category (semantic distraction). It was discovered (Fig. 6.5) that the Korsakoff patients' retention of words was interfered with by shadowing consonant trigrams, but this task did not interfere with the controls' retention. This implies that the Korsakoffs must have been relying much too heavily upon their phonemic analysis of the words. Nonverbal distraction (note tracking) did not interfere with either group's verbal retention, whereas the semantic distraction interfered with both groups' retention. Since this latter type of distraction was related phonemically as well as semantically to the memoranda, it very nearly destroyed the Korsakoff patients' memory trace.

In a follow-up investigation, Cermak, Reale, and DeLuca (1977) discovered that alcoholic Korsakoff patients could actually retain verbal material for up to 40 seconds when no distraction at all occurred (Fig. 6.6). Thus, the phonemic analysis that Korsakoffs perform on verbal material must be sufficient to provide a recirculatory mechanism that they can use to retain the material as long as no distraction prevents this rehearsal. However, as soon as verbal distraction does occur, this same verbal material can be seen to dissipate quite rapidly across retention intervals varying from 5 to 40 seconds (Fig. 6.6). Evidently, these patients' phonemic recirculatory mechanism is capable of strengthening their memory trace sufficiently to permit immediate retrieval, but the trace loses strength rapidly once verbal interference is interjected.

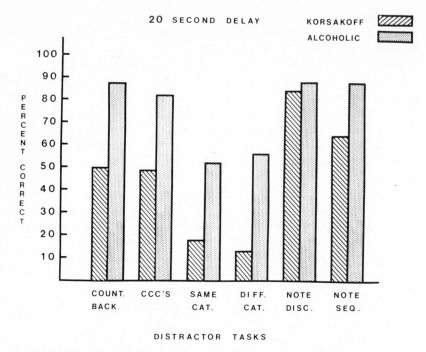

FIG. 6.5. Percentage of correct responses following two acoustic distraction tasks (counting backward, repeating CCCs), two semantic distraction tasks (scanning for same category words, scanning for different category words), and two nonverbal distraction tasks (note discrimination, note sequencing). (From DeLuca, Cermak, & Butters, 1976.)

This latter study also demonstrated an interesting characteristic of alcoholic Korsakoff patients' nonverbal retention, because—unlike their verbal retention—their nonverbal memory for randomly generated nonsense forms dissipated over time (0—40 secs) even when no distraction occurred (Fig. 6.6). It was almost as if these patients did not possess a mechanism for the rehearsal of nonverbal material in a manner similar to that which they possess for rehearsal of verbal material. One would suspect that normals might use some form of imagery to retain nonverbal materials, so it would have to be hypothesized that Korsakoff patients do not spontaneously employ this technique. Cermak, Reale, and DeLuca (1977) also found that nonverbal distraction causes Korsakoff patients' retention of nonverbal materials to dissipate immediately (Fig. 6.6) rather than gradually as had been the case for verbal retention in the face of verbal distraction. Apparently, then, both verbal and nonverbal retention are impaired in Korsakoff patients but for somewhat different reasons. In the case of verbal retention, their dependence on a relatively low level of analysis results in a weak recirculatory mechanism that is easily disrupted by interference from similar material. In the case of nonverbal retention, no real development of a recirculatory mechanism occurs; thus, memory impairments occur with or without distraction.

The experiments that we have just been describing help to delineate some of the factors underlying alcoholic Korsakoff patients' extensive difficulties in learning and remembering new information. Lately, however, yet another factor that may contribute to these patients' overall memory disorder has been demonstrated by Cermak, Reale, and Baker (1978), who have been investigating the nature of alcoholic Korsakoffs' semantic memory. As is well known, Tulving (1972) pointed out that verbal memory might conveniently be divided into two components, which he labeled *episodic* and *semantic*. He has defined episodic memory as memory for specific, personally experienced events, whereas

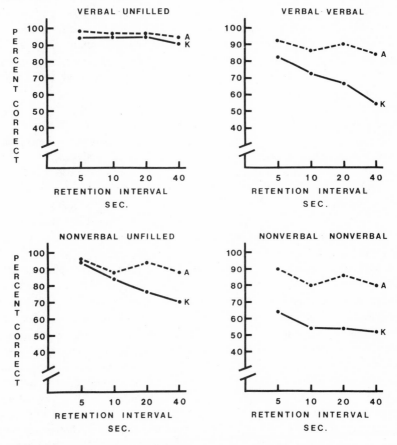

FIG. 6.6. Percentage of correct responses on two verbal recognition tasks (one with and one without distraction) and two nonverbal recognition tasks (one with and one without distraction). (From Cermak, Reale, & DeLuca, 1977.)

memory for general principles, associations, rules, etc. he defined as semantic memory. By now the reader must realize that Korsakoff patients' episodic memory is quite impaired; however, whether or not their semantic memory is impaired and whether or not this interacts with or in any way parallels their deficits in episodic memory has not yet been mentioned.

It was precisely to investigate these possibilities that a modification of the semantic memory search procedure originally devised by Freedman and Loftus (1971) was developed for use with Korsakoff patients. This procedure involved presenting a category name followed by a single letter (e.g., fruit − A) to the patient, who was asked to produce as quickly as possible a word belonging to this particular category and beginning with this particular letter. Actually, two analyses of search speed were made: one based upon category searches with single letter cues as just described and the other making a similar search given a category paired with a descriptive adjective (e.g., fruit − red). These two different types of search were introduced, because Collins and Loftus (1975) had hypothesized the existence of two "types" of semantic memory that could be differentially tapped by these two different types of cues. One semantic network that they felt to be organized along the lines of phonemic or orthographic similarity was termed the "lexicon"; the other, organized on the basis of semantic similarities between properties of words, they called "conceptual" semantic memory. The single-letter search was thus designed to assess organization of the "lexicon," whereas the adjective search assessed "conceptual" semantic memory organization. In the actual experimental procedure, each patient's response time was measured by means of a voice key apparatus activated by the presentation of the slide and terminated by the patient's response.

The results were that the Korsakoff patients' search of lexical semantic memory was somewhat slower than normals, but it was not significantly slower. On the other hand, their search of conceptual semantic memory was dramatically and significantly slower than normals. In fact, these patients required on the average 1 full second longer than did normals to search their conceptual semantic memory. This outcome—i.e. that Korsakoffs' search of their conceptual, semantically organized memory is impaired whereas search of their phonemically based lexicon is not impaired—parallels in many respects impairments in these same patients' episodic memory. Episodically, we have seen that Korsakoff patients' analysis and episodic retention of material on the basis of its semantic characteristics is significantly impaired whereas their analysis and retention of phonemic features is only slightly and not significantly impaired (Cermak, 1977; Cermak & Moreines, 1976). Now we can see that retrieval from semantic memory is also impaired when based solely on the semantic (conceptual) features of verbal information but not impaired when it is based primarily on the nonsemantic (lexical) features.

Such parallelism naturally raises the possibility that Korsakoff patients' semantically based episodic impairments might actually be a consequence of their semantic memory impairments. Episodic semantic analysis of incoming information might depend in part on comparing each new item to old items of information drawn from conceptual semantic memory. An impaired search through conceptual semantic memory might make such comparisons difficult for the Korsakoff patients, and fewer semantic comparisons will be made. As a consequence of this reduced search, a lower level of analysis will be performed on the new material. Since the patients appear to possess a nearly normal lexical search speed, a more normal level of phonemic analysis of new information can be performed by the Korsakoffs. Consequently, a more normal level of retention occurs when it can be based on that level of analysis.

Of course, it is also possible that the speed of any given semantic search might depend to some extent on episodic memory. Loftus (1973a, 1973b) reported this possibility and showed that when two consecutive category searches occurred from within the same category, albeit with differing letter cues, the search speed during the second instance is faster than would ordinarily be expected. Apparently the previous trial's activation of that particular category (an episodic event) acts to "prime" the second search of that category. Loftus reported that this primed activation decreases quickly as soon as two or more intervening items occur between same-category searches. Based on the fact that Korsakoff patients' episodic memory is impaired, it was hypothesized that they would probably show no priming effect or at least less so than the controls, since the effect seems to depend on retention of a previous trial. In order to assess this notion, the category—single-letter task was again given to a group of Korsakoff patients (Cermak, Reale, & Baker, 1978). The basic procedure was the same as just described, the only difference being that categories—paired with different single letters—were repeated within a test session. These same-category trials were separated by either 0, 1, 2, or 3 intervening trials containing items from categories other than the critical repeated category.

The outcome of this task was that the Korsakoff patients evidenced absolutely no activation of their lexical semantic memory even when the category was "primed" by the immediately prior trial. The improvement in search speed that occurred for the control patients was simply not present for Korsakoff patients. Apparently the "episode" of having just previously searched that particular category was already lost by the time it was probed again—even when the probe occurred on two adjacent trials. This implies that the "preactivation" described by Collins and Loftus (1975) is nothing more than just normal memory for a recently completed search.

Interestingly enough, the results of this experiment also imply that preactivation of the lexicon must necessarily involve some form of interaction or communication with conceptual memory, because—were the search merely phonemic—the Korsakoffs would be expected to remember the product of that search (the episode) almost as well as normals (see Cermak & Moreines, 1976). However, since preactivation does not occur, it must be that "meaning" has to be retained in order to preactivate the lexicon. In summary, then, and as a consequence of all these various hypothesized interactions, it must be concluded that an intact conceptual memory is necessary for encoding to occur on a semantic level in episodic memory—which, in turn, is a necessary condition for any preactivation of lexical memory.

At this point it can be said with some degree of confidence that alcoholic Korsakoff patients' entire information-processing system must be deficient. It is apparent that they analyze each individual item of information to a lesser extent than normals, that they contrast each item with other information in permanent memory less readily than normals, and that they use inappropriate strategies for rehearsal and chunking of information. All these factors must be contributing to their overall anterograde memory deficit. The next obvious question to ask is whether or not techniques designed to improve processing will lead to improved retention in Korsakoff patients.

The technique that we chose to use was one recently devised by Craik and Tulving (1975) and used extensively by Jenkins (Hyde & Jenkins, 1973; Till & Jenkins, 1973; Walsh & Jenkins, 1973). This procedure attempted to direct the patient's analysis of incoming information so that he would be "forced" to analyze the semantic features of the information rather than just the phonemic features. The patient was not told that he would have to remember anything; rather, he was simply instructed to analyze each word on the basis of the particular feature of that word that was dictated by the nature of the question asked about the word. The rationale was that the higher the level of analysis the individual was required to perform on a word, the greater would be the probability that he would remember the word on an unexpected recognition test. Questions were chosen so as to necessitate processing on either a shallow, orthographic level (e.g., a question about the word's physical appearance such as "Is it written in upper-case letters?"); an intermediate, phonemic level (e.g., "Does the word rhyme with ___?"); or a higher, semantic level (e.g., "Does the word fit in the sentence: ___ ___ ___?"). For each question, the patient was required to respond either "yes" or "no" by pressing the appropriate response key. After the entire series of questions was finished, the patient was given a recognition test to see how many words he could recognize as having appeared in the series.

In the actual experiment (Cermak & Reale, 1978), each patient was asked to answer 60 questions, including 20 sentence, 20 rhyme, and 20 case questions, divided evenly into "yes" and "no" responses. The unexpected recognition task given at the end of the questioning session consisted of a typewritten sheet containing 180 words: the 60 list words plus 120 unrelated filler nouns. It was discovered that Korsakoff patients could respond to the questions without error and at a nearly normal rate (Fig. 6.7), but their recognition performance fell far below normal on all but the case words (Fig. 6.8). This was largely due to the fact that the Korsakoff patients recognized no more semantically or phonemically analyzed words than they did those that had been analyzed on a structural level.

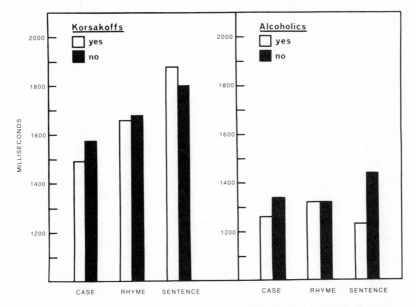

FIG. 6.7.   Initial decision latency (msecs) for Korsakoff and alcoholic control patients as a function of the type of question asked about the word (Exp. 1).

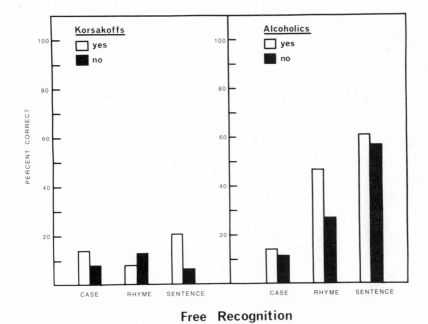

Free Recognition

FIG. 6.8.   Proportion of words correctly recognized by Korsakoff and alcoholic control patients as a function of the initial task (Exp. 1).

It appeared as if no greater benefit to later retention accrued for the words that were analyzed at the ''deeper'' levels than had accrued for words analyzed at ''shallow'' levels. It was possible, however, that the nature of the recognition task had produced these results by so overwhelming the patients that they merely scanned the list briefly, circled a few words, and gave up. So, in order to obviate this situation, a new recognition list, consisting of 60 groupings of 3 words each with 1 word always being correct, was used in a later experiment.

The same materials, questions, and procedure were used as in the preceding experiment; but the 180 words appearing on the recognition test were now presented in groups of 3s (2 filler words and a target item), and the patient was instructed to circle 1 word from each of the 60 triads. For those Korsakoff patients who participated in the prior experiment, a different question regarding each word was asked in the present experiment. This was done even though no patient remembered having ever performed this type of task before, and they would not of course have remembered that an unexpected recognition test was going to occur.

Figures 6.9 and 6.10 show that the results of this experiment very nearly duplicated those of the previous experiment despite the change in recognition procedure. Instructions to perform semantic analysis did not result in greater retention than did lower levels of processing for the Korsakoff patients. It was decided at this point that perhaps the sentence questions that had been used in

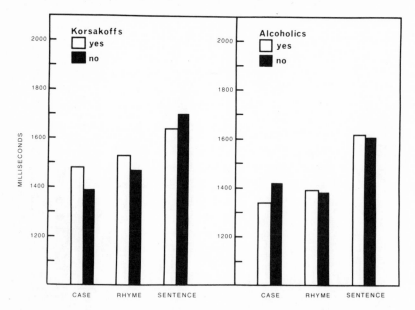

FIG. 6.9.   Initial decision latency (msecs) for Korsakoff and alcoholic control patients as a function of the type of question asked about the word (Exp. 2). (From Cermak & Reale, © 1978 by the American Psychological Association. Reprinted by permission.)

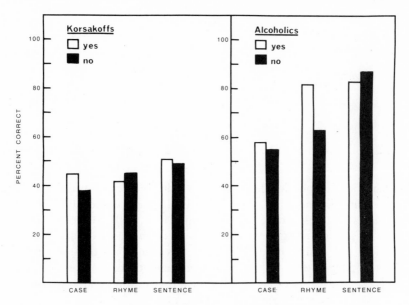

Forced-Choice Recognition

FIG. 6.10.   Proportion of words correctly recognized by Korsakoff and alcoholic control patients as a function of the initial task (Exp. 2). (From Cermak & Reale, © 1978 by the American Psychological Association. Reprinted by permission.)

the first two experiments did not provide enough structure (see also Jacoby & Craik, Chapter 1, this volume; and Eysenck, Chapter 5, this volume) for the Korsakoff patients to utilize in storing and retrieving the words. Consequently, it was decided to use two other forms of semantic query: One form depicted the category of the test word; the other asked a specific question that could only be answered by the test word.

Fifty-six words were chosen in such a way that four different types of questions could be asked of each. Two questions were of the same variety as those used in the preceding experiments—namely, sentence and rhyme questions. The other two were directed more specifically toward defining the target words. One question was of the type, "Is this a ___?", where the blank was filled with the name of a category. The other question asked was, "Does this ___ have ___?", where the first blank was again the name of a category but where the second blank included a defining characteristic of the word. Examples of these questions, which we called "Category" and "Specific Marker" questions, are give in Table 6.1. It was felt that category questions might define the words more fully than sentence questions and that specific marker questions might yet further define the words.

The form of recognition task that was used was again the forced-choice recognition task. Words were arranged in groups of 3 with each triad containing 1 correct and 2 incorrect words making a total of 56 triads. The results (Figs. 6.11

TABLE 6.1
Examples of Additional Questions and Answers Used in Experiment 3

Type of Question	Example of Question Type	"Yes" Answer	"No" Answer
Category	Is this a flower?	rose	chair
Specific marker	Does this animal have stripes?	zebra	lion

and 6.12) again replicated those of the preceding two experiments. The Korsakoff patients responded somewhat more slowly than the alcoholic controls, but their pattern of responding was the same (Fig. 6.10). However, again the Korsakoff patients recognized far fewer words than did the alcoholics under all conditions with no differences in recognition as a function of question type for the Korsakoff patients (Fig. 6.11). On the other hand, the controls recognized more marker, sentence, and category words than rhyme words and marginally more marker words than sentence or category words.

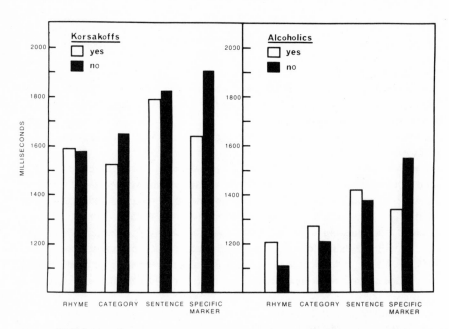

FIG. 6.11. Initial decision latency (msecs) for Korsakoff and alcholic control patients as a function of the type of question asked about the word (Exp. 3). (From Cermak & Reale, © 1978 by the American Psychological Association. Reprinted by permission.)

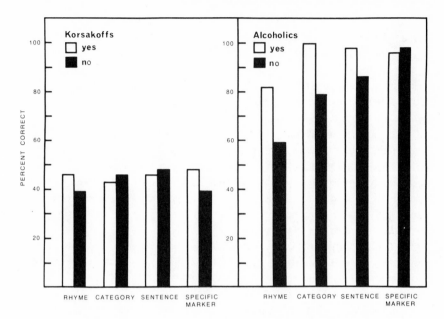

FIG. 6.12.   Proportion of words correctly recognized by Korsakoff and alcoholic control patients as a function of the initial task (Exp. 3). (From Cermak & Reale, © 1978 by the American Psychological Association. Reprinted by permission.)

Despite the fact that the questions used in this experiment had been designed to direct the patient toward specific semantic characteristics of the words, no improvement in retention over and above that produced by phonemic analysis occurred for the Korsakoff patients. Thus, it simply had to be concluded that even when these patients are forced to encode in a specific manner and to circle an appropriate number of responses, their probability of retaining semantically analyzed information is no better than their retention of information analyzed on the basis of ordinarily less robust features within the confines of this paradigm. It became obvious that if an "effect" of semantic analysis were to be demonstrated with Korsakoff patients, the basic paradigm would have to be modified considerably. Therefore what we did was to break the list down into several short lists, each followed by a recognition trial. The experiment differed from the basic task in that the patients were no longer given the 60 words and questions in a continuous order followed by a 180-word recognition test. Instead, they were asked just 12 questions about 12 words, followed by a 36-word "free" recognition test. This procedure was repeated 5 times until all of the 60 words had been queried and tested for recognition. Each of the 12-item lists contained 4 words queried by a case question, 4 queried by a rhyme question, and 4 by a sentence question. In addition, 2 "yes" and 2 "no" questions were asked within each of these 3 conditions. This manipulation put the alcoholic controls' performance at ceiling for all levels of analysis. However, since the usual "pattern" of recognition responses was now so well documented, the test was still conducted and reported as a within-subject design using only the Korsakoff patients.

Figure 6.13 depicts the reaction-time results using this procedure with Korsakoff patients. The figure combines the results from all five response-time and recognition subtests given to the patients. An analysis of variance performed on the time required to respond to each question revealed a significant difference between question types, and in addition there was now a significant question type by response type interaction. Figure 6.13 also shows the results of performance on all five recognition tests combined. Here a significant effect between question types finally occurred for the Korsakoff patients, since at last they recognized significantly more sentence words than either rhyme or case words and marginally more rhyme than case words.

The results of this final experiment have somewhat redeemed our rationale for using the Craik and Tulving procedure to study the relationship between information analysis and retention, for it demonstrated that Korsakoff patients' retention of at least a brief list of material can be affected by the level of analysis they perform on each word. Under these conditions of abbreviated-list reten-

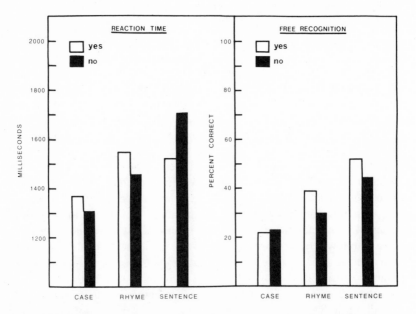

FIG. 6.13.   Initial decision latency (msecs) and proportion of words correctly recognized by Korsakoff patients as a function of the type of question asked about the word (Exp. 4). (From Cermak & Reale, © 1978 by the American Psychological Association. Reprinted by permission.)

tion, the differential effects of physical, phonemic, and semantic analysis can be seen to have the same relative effect for Korsakoff patients as they do for normals. This strengthens our contention that differential levels of analysis can "produce" differential probabilities of retrieval, for it must have been the type of analysis demanded by the instructions that was responsible for the improvement. Had no improvement occurred or had it occurred equally for all levels of analysis, then the "production" hypothesis would not have received any support. However, the results of the final experiment are in agreement with this hypothesis of a relationship between level of analysis and probability of retrieval.

It must also be pointed out that the Korsakoff patients' speed of analysis following different types of query was consistently performed in a normal pattern. Semantic analyses always took longer than phonemic, which in turn took longer than physical. The only instance in which the Korsakoff patients took significantly longer to analyze the words than the controls was in the experiment in which categorical comparisons were required. However, this finding is consistent with Cermak, Reale, and Baker's (1978) demonstration that Korsakoff patients are impaired in the rate at which they can search "conceptual" semantic memory. It could be, as was suggested earlier, that their impairment in speed of analyzing categorical features is a reflection of their impairment in search speed through this type of semantic memory.

In summary, it appears that Korsakoff patients' recognition memory for verbal information can be affected by the level to which they process that information at least under some conditions. This in turn lends support to previous contentions (e.g., Cermak, 1977; Cermak & Moreines, 1976) that Korsakoff patients' anterograde amnesia stems at least in part from a preference not to perform semantic analyses of to-be-retained verbal information. Had we not been able to demonstrate under any circumstances that instructions to perform semantic analysis improved these patients' retentive abilities, then we would have had to discontinue proposing that deficiencies in informational analysis account, in part, for these patients' memory deficits. However, since instructions did improve retention, such a hypothesis does remain tenable and deserves further investigation.

One direction that seems reasonable to explore would be the assessment of the interaction between level of processing and level of retrieval cue. This has been suggested within several of the other chapters in this volume (e.g. Jacoby & Craik, Bransford et al., Tulving, and Jenkins, Chapters 1, 15, 19, and 20) as a viable means of determining more precisely how well each type of analysis is performed and retained. By giving instructions and encoding cues at input and output, conditions become equalized; and we might better establish whether the patient is actually better equipped to analyze phonemically or whether, as we have proposed, he simply relies upon such analyses as a matter of strategy. This research, which is currently in progress, promises to open a new area in the exploration of the relationship between information processing and amnesia.

ACKNOWLEDGMENTS

The research included in this report was supported in part by a NIAAA Grant AA-00187 to Boston University School of Medicine and by the Medical Research Service of the Veterans Administration.

REFERENCES

Cermak, L. S. The contribution of a "processing" deficit to alcoholic Korsakoff patients' memory disorder. In I. M. Birnbaum & E. S. Parker (Eds.), *Alcohol and memory*, Hillsdale, N.J.: Lawrence Erlbaum Associates, 1977.

Cermak, L. S., & Butters, N. The role of interference and encoding in the short-term memory deficits of Korsakoff patients. *Neuropsychologia*, 1972, *10*, 89–96.

Cermak, L. S., Butters, N., & Gerrein, J. The extent of the verbal encoding ability of Korsakoff patients. *Neuropsychologia*, 1973, *11*, 85–94.

Cermak, L. S., Butters, N., & Moreines, J. Some analyses of the verbal encoding deficit of alcoholic Korsakoff patients. *Brain and Language*, 1974, *1*, 141–150.

Cermak, L. S., & Moreines, J. Verbal retention deficits in aphasic and amnesic patients. *Brain and Language*, 1976, *3*, 16–27.

Cermak, L. S., Naus, M. J., & Reale, L. Rehearsal and organizational strategies of alcoholic Korsakoff patients. *Brain and Language*, 1976, *3*, 375–385.

Cermak, L. S., & Reale, L. Depth of processing and retention of words by alcoholic Korsakoff patients. *Journal of Experimental Psychology: Human Learning and Memory*, 1978, *4*, 165–174.

Cermak, L. S., Reale, L., & Baker, E. Alcoholic Korsakoff patients' retrieval from semantic memory. *Brain and Language*, 1978, *5*, 215–226.

Cermak, L. S., Reale, L., & DeLuca, D. Korsakoff patients' nonverbal vs. verbal memory: Effects of interference and mediation on rate of information loss. *Neuropsychologia*, 1977, *15*, 303–310.

Collins, A. M., & Loftus, E. F. A spreading-activation theory of semantic processing. *Psychological Review*, 1975, *82*, 407–428.

Craik, F. I. M., & Tulving, E. Depth of processing and retention of words in episodic memory. *Journal of Experimental Psychology, General*, 1975, *104*, 268–294.

DeLuca, D., Cermak, L. S., & Butters, N. The differential effects of semantic, acoustic and nonverbal distraction on Korsakoff patients' verbal retention performance. *International Journal of Neurosciences*, 1976, *6*, 279–284.

Freedman, J. C., & Loftus, E. F. Retrieval of words from long-term memory. *Journal of Verbal Learning and Verbal Behavior*, 1971, *10*, 107–115.

Hyde, T. S., & Jenkins, J. J. Recall for words as a function of semantic, graphic and syntactic orienting tasks. *Journal of Verbal Learning and Verbal Behavior*, 1973, *12*, 471–480.

Kinsbourne, M., & Wood, F. Short-term memory processes and the amnesic syndrome. In D. Deutsch & A. J. Deutsch (Eds.), *Short term memory*. New York: Academic Press, 1975.

Loftus, E. F. *How to catch a zebra in semantic memory*. Paper presented at the *Minnesota Conference on Cognition, Knowledge and Adaptation, Minneapolis, 1973. (a)*

Loftus, E. F. Activation of semantic memory. *American Journal of Psychology*, 1973, *86*, 331–337. (b)

Rundus, D., & Atkinson, R. C. Rehearsal processes in free recall: A procedure for direct observation. *Journal of Verbal Learning and Verbal Behavior*, 1970, *9*, 99–105.

Talland, G. *Deranged Memory*. New York: Academic Press, 1965.

Till, R. E., & Jenkins, J. J. The effects of cued orienting tasks on free recall of words. *Journal of Verbal Learning and Verbal Behavior*, 1973, *12*, 489–498.

Tulving, E. Subjective organization in free recall of "unrelated" words. *Psychological Review*, 1962, *69*, 344–354.

Tulving, E. Episodic and semantic memory. In E. Tulving & W. Donaldson (eds.), *Organization of memory*. New York: Academic Press, 1972.

Underwood, B. J. False recognition by implicit verbal responses. *Journal of Experimental Psychology*, 1965, *70*, 122–129.

Victor, M., Adams, R. D., & Collins, G. H. *The Wernicke–Korsakoff syndrome*. Philadelphia: F. A. Davis, 1971.

Walsh, D. A., & Jenkins, J. J. Effects of orienting tasks on free recall in incidental learning: "Difficulty," "effort," and "process" explanations. *Journal of Verbal Learning and Verbal Behavior*, 1973, *12*, 481–488.

Wickens, D. D. Encoding categories of words: An empirical approach to meaning. *Psychological Review*, 1970, *77*, 1–15.

7 Broader Methods and Narrower Theories for Memory Research: Comments on the Papers by Eysenck and Cermak

Harry P. Bahrick
Ohio Wesleyan University

The papers by Eysenck and Cermak in this volume make significant substantive contributions and at the same time provide an opportunity for the discussion of methodological issues that affect the development of psychological knowledge. This discussion focuses on methodological issues and deals with substantive questions in relation to methodology.

GENERAL METHODOLOGICAL CONSTRAINTS OF MEMORY RESEARCH

The first 70 years of memory research produced much information about the conditions under which individual associations are weakened, and the last 20 years have yielded information about encoding, storage, and retrieval processes of episodic memory. Neither the early analytic approach nor the more recent cognitive approach have yielded generalizations regarding the acquisition, maintenance, or loss of complex knowledge systems that constitute the so-called semantic content of memory. It is the semantic content of memory that constitutes the primary product of education and of professional and vocational training. Since psychological research has concerned itself primarily with the episodic content, the ecological impact of memory research has been minor, and this fact has been widely recognized (Kintsch, 1974; Tulving, 1972). In contrast, the ecological impact of research concerned with the *learning* process has been far greater. For example, the research of Thorndike and others on the acquisition and transfer of skill and Skinnerian programming and behavior modification techniques have significantly influenced educational practices and training

141

procedures for many years. It is a primary thesis of this discussion that broader based methods and more empirically oriented theories are needed before memory research can yield comparable benefits.

Present methods of memory research focus on laboratory investigations with college students as subjects. Much of this research is designed to document or refute global theories related to cognitive models of memory. In most instances, laboratory research is limited to short acquisition periods and short retention intervals. In contrast, the semantic content of memory is acquired and maintained over extended periods. In order for psychological research to produce information that can answer questions regarding the long-term retention of knowledge, it will be necessary to deal with a realistic data base, and such a data base cannot be generated by relying exclusively on material learned in the laboratory. I do not advocate the abandonment of the laboratory—rather, the use of a wider range of methods including large-scale ecological investigations. Such research requires the acceptance of trade-offs between loss of control over variables that determine the acquisition and rehearsal of the material to be retained, and the gain of information concerning long-term retention of content acquired over extended time periods in real-life situations.

The restriction of memory research to material learned in the laboratory can be understood historically as the only strategy that could gain acceptance for psychology in the social climate of the 19th-century scientific community. The attainment of scientific status is no longer a crucial issue, and the availability of the high-speed computer has made it possible to assess interactions among a large number of variables in settings far more complex than the laboratory. As a result, the traditional single-variable experiment is no longer the best, or only, way of investigating memory. Assessing the effects of several uncontrolled variables yields information not available by holding key variables constant. Anderson and Reder (1974) have recognized the importance of taking advantage of this methodological option in the study of semantic memory. This writer has previously shown (Bahrick, Bahrick, & Wittlinger, 1975) that a cross-sectional approach can be used to study memory over very long time periods if the approach is combined with adjustments of dependent variables by means of multiple regression estimates. This approach makes it possible to study memory in semistructured, real-life settings, which permit estimates, but not control, of variables defining level of acquisition and rehearsal of learned material.

The broadened methodology advocated here must also include data from clinical and developmental investigations (see comments by Brown, Chapter 11, and by Naus and Halasz, Chapter 12, in this volume). The work reported in this volume by Cermak, Chapter 6, illustrates how investigations of defective memory systems make significant contributions to knowledge of the memory system. Clinical studies such as those reported by Cermak offer the particularly valuable opportunity to examine interactions of the episodic and semantic content of memory. The need for such information is emphasized by several contributors to this volume.

EMPIRICAL VS. THEORETICAL RESEARCH EMPHASIS

In accordance with reinforcement theory, psychologists modify their habits of theory construction as a function of the consequences, but the level of processing is not always deep enough to assure a lasting impact. The hypothetico−deductive approach to theory of the 1940s showed that research guided by the intent to prove or disprove global principles was wasteful. It engendered long series of experiments that failed to accomplish their purpose. The latent learning controversy, for example, inspired nearly 50 experiments, and yet the question of whether learning occurs without reinforcement was not answered. The results of these studies established empirical relations between task and procedural variables on one hand and performance variables on the other, but these benefits could have been obtained far more economically if the experiments had been designed for that purpose. Skinner and others argued for hypothesis-free research designed to investigate interactions among variables. Concentration on such research promised to reduce the burden of spurious experimenter effects and of other wasteful by-products of investigations designed by experimenters who were determined to prove a point. The impact of this empirical trend has diminished during the last decade as investigators revived earlier interest in cognitive processes, and a reading of current memory literature brings back echoes of the 1940s. It is clear that this writer agrees with Eysenck's statement in this volume: "Psychologists attach undue importance to theories making predictions that are consistently confirmed [p. 89]."

The levels-of-processing framework for research has provided welcome relief from this trend, and many of the contributions to this volume do not suffer from the problem of paradigm specificity. The argument advanced here is not that investigators renounce conceptualization of how the memory system functions; rather that the thrust of research be directed at determining interactions among variables in a greater variety of tasks and situations; that cognitive conceptualizations be limited explicitly to tasks and materials under investigation; and that more global conceptualizations of the memory system be delayed until interactions among variables can be compared for a greater variety of tasks. At that time, global principles are more likely to reflect inductive rather than deductive considerations, and this may reduce the wastefulness of research inspired by the determination to prove or disprove the validity of overambitious generalizations. The Lachmans in this volume (Chapter 9) support the point that global theories, reminiscent of the neobehaviorist age, are insensitive to data; and Postman (1976) in a recent review also advocates an analytic approach, with separate study of various classes of memory tasks prior to the emergence of general theory.

Even a casual consideration of the great diversity of situations under which information is retrieved from the memory store supports the need for a task-specific approach to theory. A person who recites the alphabet, identifies a suspect in court, tries to remember where he left a misplaced article, describes the details of a home he has visited, or tries to recall past presidents of the United States may use retrieval strategies that differ widely in accordance with the demands of each task. Furthermore, one is likely to change retrieval strategies several times in the performance of a single task, upon finding that a given strategy fails to yield additional information and if one has reason to believe that additional information is in store. What is needed is a greater awareness of the flexibility of human retrieval strategies and, based upon this awareness, an exploration of a variety of strategies and a determination of boundary conditions within which each strategy is likely to be used.

RELATIONS AMONG FOUR COMMONLY USED MEMORY TASKS

This discussion focuses on certain similarities and differences among four commonly used memory tasks. Two of the tasks are recognition tasks; the distinction between recognizing newly learned items vs. previously known items is discussed. The other two tasks are recall tasks; the distinction between free- and cued-recall tasks is reviewed. These topics have been selected, because they are particularly relevant to an evaluation of the distinctiveness hypothesis discussed by Eysenck, Chapter 5, and by Jacoby and Craik, Chapter 1, in this volume; because they illustrate the need for a task-specific emphasis in the development of theory; and because certain aspects of the relations among these tasks have been overlooked in past discussions.

Familiar vs. Unfamiliar Target Items in Recognition Tasks

In a recognition test, the subject must perform certain discriminations in regard to items that are presented. How well the subject can do this depends on characteristics of the items and on the information the subject brings to bear on the required discrimination. If the target items are well known to the subject, e.g., common English words, the subject would not be challenged by a task that requires the discrimination of these items from a list of nonwords. This discrimination can be based on information stored in semantic memory, and performance would be quite independent of the contextual cues present at the time of retrieval. Recognition tasks using familiar material, therefore, usually require subjects to make context-related discriminations rather than discriminations of target items based on class characteristics. The typical procedure is to present a list of words and to require the subject to discriminate these words from other words that are not presented on the list or that are presented on a different list. The required recognition decision, then, is not based on characteristics of the target items per se but on associations of the target item with some aspect of the episodic context in which the items were presented. This type of task has provided the basis for most recent memory research. Tagging models, e.g., Bower (1967) and Underwood (1969), as well as investigations of encoding specificity (Tulving & Thomson, 1973) have made extensive use of such recognition data.

The required discrimination is usually different in tasks in which subjects have no preexperimental familiarity with the target items. If the target items are drawings of objects, or photographs of people not known to the subject, or words in an unfamiliar language, the recognition test usually requires the subject to discriminate the target items from foils belonging to the same class as the target items but not previously presented. The subject can base the required recognition decision primarily on item characteristics, and context associations become much less important. The learning process focuses on item characteristics, and the discrimination can be based on relative familiarity with the item, with little regard to the specific context in which the item was encoded.

In terms of the distinction between episodic and semantic memory, familiar material is part of the semantic memory content. This means that many previous encodings of the material have occurred, and identification of previously exposed material on a recognition test must be based upon a unique episodic trace tying the material to the encoding context. Unfamiliar material, however, is not part of the semantic memory content; no previous encodings of target items exist, and identification of such items on a recognition test can be based upon a judgment of familiarity without regard to the specifics of the encoding context. The possibility of basing recognition decisions on familiarity of items has been discussed by others (e.g., Atkinson, Herrmann, & Wescourt, 1974; Craik & Jacoby, 1975), but more attention must be given to the circumstances under which recognition decisions are based upon item familiarity vs. contextual clues. Watkins, Ho, and Tulving (1976) demonstrated that recognition of unfamiliar faces could be slightly improved if a second face that was paired with the target face during training was also paired with the target on the recognition test. To achieve this context effect, it was necessary to establish a prior set for differentiating correctly paired from incorrectly paired pictures. Bower and Karlin (1974), who did not establish a prior set for attending to context, failed to obtain significant context effects for the recognition of unfamiliar material. The Watkins, Ho, and Tulving study shows that context effects can be obtained for the recognition of unfamiliar material if subjects are trained to attend to the context. The study does not demonstrate that context effects are an important aspect of what is being learned in recognition tasks using previously unfamiliar material.

The Distinctiveness Hypothesis in Relation to Familiar and Unfamiliar Material

Research concerned with encoding specificity as well as the research reported by Eysenck in this volume in regard to distinctiveness have focused on interactions of the encoding and the retrieval environment. It would appear that these interactions play an important role in recognition performance when familiar target items are used and a comparatively trivial role in recognition tasks in which unfamiliar target items are used. Eysenck has shown that the *amount* of overlap of the encoding and retrieval context is less predictive of performance than the degree of distinctiveness of the overlap. He has shown further that the predictions apply not only to distinctiveness of the overlap of the external encoding and retrieval environments, but that distinctiveness of the elaborations created by the subjects' responses are equally decisive. Both of these conclusions represent significant extensions and modifications of earlier conceptualizations derived from the principle of encoding specificity.

Data recently collected in the Ohio Wesleyan University laboratory with a bilingual word list support the distinctiveness hypothesis for the recognition of familiar material. The list of 15 English and 15 equally common Spanish words was shown individually in random order to 16 bilingual subjects. Eight of the subjects were Venezuelans who had spent approximately 1 year in the United States. The other 8 were American students who had spent about 1 year in Spain. Following a brief filler task, the subjects took a recognition test in which each of the 30 words was shown in both English and Spanish and subjects had to identify the 30 originally exposed words. Analysis of recognition errors shows that subjects make over twice as many recognition errors for words presented in their stronger language as for words presented in their weaker language (4.1 vs. 1.9 errors per subject). American students are more accurate in recognizing words shown in Spanish, and Venezuelans are more accurate in recognizing English words. This finding supports Eysenck's generalization: With familiar material, recognition is facilitated by the degree of distinctiveness of the overlap between the encoding and retrieval environment. For the above data, the *amount* of overlap between the encoding and retrieval environment was the same for English and Spanish words, but the degree of distinctiveness of the overlap was greater for the less commonly used language.

Interactions of Distinctiveness with Subject Characteristics

The above example illustrates that the distinctiveness of overlap is not just a function of the characteristics of the encoding and retrieval environment but also a function of the subjects' past experience. The operational referent for the term *distinctiveness* must be some dimensional analysis of similarity. The literature of the first half of this century has dealt extensively with the concept of similarity in regard to phenomena of generalization, transfer, and retention. One outcome of this research is the distinction between primary or sensory similarity—inherent in stimulus characteristics—and secondary or mediated similarity—dependent on the past experience of the subject. Thus, the semantic similarity of words is a significant variable in predicting generalization gradients in conditioning but only if the relevant semantic knowledge can be assumed for the subject. Similarly, distinctiveness of the overlap of the encoding and retrieval context is a joint function of task characteristics that the experimenter can manipulate and of the entire previous encoding history of the subject. Such individual difference variables are particularly likely to affect performance in memory experiments in which distinctiveness is manipulated by varying instructions regarding encoding strategies, elaboration, etc.

Free- and Cued-Recall Tasks in the Study of Retrieval Processes

This section focuses on the importance of the distinction between effortless vs. effortful retrieval. Shiffrin and Atkinson (1969), Posner (1973), and others have emphasized such a distinction, but it has been overlooked frequently in the discussion of theoretical issues. The distinction refers to the fact that one is able to access some of the information in memory without a time-consuming search, whereas other information can be retrieved only on the basis of such a search. William James (1907) compared memory search to rummaging one's house for a lost object. ''In both cases we visit what seems to us the probable neighborhood of that which we miss [p. 290].'' James based his views on those of James Mill who described the process in the following way:

> I meet an old acquaintance whose name I do not remember, and wish to recollect. I run over a number of names, in hopes that some of them may be associated with the idea of the individual. I think of all the circumstances in which I have seen him engaged; the time when I knew him, the persons along with whom I knew him, the things he did. . . . If I chance upon any idea with which the name is associated, then immediately I have the recollection; if not, my pursuit of it is vain [p. 289].

More recent conceptualizations of memory search have taken the form of generation–recognition models according to which recall is the product of a two-stage process. The target item must be among those generated in the first stage, and once generated as a possible candidate, it must be correctly recognized in the second stage.

A number of such models have been proposed, and one by the present author (Bahrick, 1970) has been cited as an explicit account of generation—recognition processes (Tulving, 1976; Tulving & Thomson, 1973). Tulving and his associates (Thomson & Tulving, 1970) labeled this conceptualization of retrieval processes the continuity view and have contrasted it with the encoding specificity view. According to the latter, retrieval cues can be effective only if they were encoded at the time of presentation of a target item. In reviewing the relevant evidence, Tulving and his associates (Tulving, 1976; Tulving & Thomson, 1973) fail to distinguish between recall that is based on search and recall that is effortless and immediate. Bahrick's model was never intended to apply to the recall of all information from the memory store; rather, it is explicitly limited to the retrieval of information not accessible to free recall. The lead sentence of the abstract (Bahrick, 1970) of the formal statement of the model reads: "The model described deals with free recall failures of previously learned responses [p. 215]," and the text similarly elaborates: "The general situation dealt with by this model is one in which free recall has failed to produce a previously learned response [p. 215]." This boundary condition is also stressed in later publications (Bahrick, 1971) in relation to interpreting the findings of Thomson and Tulving (1970). No one has ever seriously suggested, for example, that recalling the name of one's wife involves generating a series of female names and selecting the correct name after having rejected several erroneously generated candidates. Much information of both an episodic and semantic type is recalled without effort and without a time-consuming search. Tests of retrieval theory must take account of this important distinction and determine boundary conditions that delimit the use of various strategies. Tests of theory that ignore stated boundary conditions are not likely to be profitable.

It is not contended here that conventional free-recall tests establish a dependable dichotomy between information that is directly accessed, i.e., retrieved without effort, and information that is accessed through a generation— recognition or other type of search process. *Some* of the information obtained on free-recall tests may well be the product of elaborate search processes, and this is especially likely if generous time limits are allowed for free recall (Williams & Norman, 1976). Thus an individual who has difficulty in recalling a name, but who remembers some features of the name, may go through generation— recognition search processes and may ultimately include the product of such a search in his or her free-recall protocol. The point is that tests of the generation— recognition model (Bahrick, 1970) must be limited to free-recall failures, since free-recall successes are presumed to include much directly accessed information.

There is another advantage to examining cued-recall performance under conditions that exclude target items accessed in free recall. The separation permits a comparison of the effectiveness of episodically and semantically organized search under a variety of circumstances. Episodic encoding will yield not only directly accessed free-recall content but also indirectly accessed products of a generative search. Thus a subject who recalls that *spinach* was one of the words on a list he or she was asked to learn and that there were also other vegetables on the list is likely to give the directly accessed response first, and then add other responses he or she may recover on the basis of a generation— recognition search. This search is self-initiated and based on episodic information: "There were other vegetables on that list." The search under conditions of cued recall is initiated on the basis of a cue supplied by the experimenter. If no prior free-recall test is given, it is impossible to determine what portion of the information retrieved on the basis of the cue could also have been retrieved without the cue. By separating the recall content attributable to subject-initiated search from the additional recall attributable to experimenter-initiated search, it becomes possible to compare the contribution of episodically based search with the contribution of a search based upon semantic knowledge in which only the final acceptance decision rests on episodic memory. These relative contributions may differ greatly depending on the orienting task, the material learned, and other parameters; and relevant findings may yield better understanding of retrieval processes under a variety of circumstances.

The Distinctiveness Hypothesis in Relation to Free and Cued Recall

It was argued earlier that the degree of contextual encoding varies depending on the nature of the task and the material learned, and that the distinctiveness hypothesis is likely to be relevant only if contextual associations are central to the subject's task. Applying the same reasoning to recall tasks, distinctiveness of the overlap of the encoding and retrieval environments would affect both free and cued recall but in different ways. For cued recall (exclusive of the free-recall component), distinctiveness would be expected to influence the recognition phase of the search process but not the generative phase (Bahrick, 1970). The generative process itself is assumed to be governed by hierarchies of associations that form part of semantic memory and are largely independent of the retrieval context. The initiation of the generative process is based upon a cue supplied by the experimenter, not upon a response made by the subject in the retrieval context. Thus a subject who failed to list any vegetables in free recall of a word list is given the cue *vegetable* by the experimenter and generates a list of vegetables. One may presume the subject to be uninfluenced by distinctiveness of the target−context association until he or she generates a correct target item. At this point, distinctiveness should favor recognition of the target item.

The situation is more complex in free recall. Several of the contributors to this volume (Hagen, Brown, and Naus and Halasz, Chapters 13, 11, and 12) conclude that recall, more than recognition, depends on active processing at the time of encoding. As pointed out earlier, the encoding processes provide the basis not only for direct access but also for subject-initiated search processes. The type of encoding, in turn, is determined by the orienting task. Distinctiveness of the encoding−retrieval context plays a role in the effectiveness of retrieval, but the role is subordinate to the general type of encoding activity established by the orienting task. Thus subjects improve recall when they are instructed to form distinctive visual images related to a word list, but the distinctiveness may have less effect than the use of visual images per se. The orienting task determines whether subjects will use semantic, graphic, visual, acoustic, or other organizing activities. Although it is now clear (Kolers, Chapter 17, in this volume) that semantic processing does not necessarily yield retention superior to graphemic processing, the type of processing as well as the distinctiveness of the overlap affect recall. Recognition performance is also affected by the type of orienting task, but the relative effect is greater for recall (Tulving, 1976). This differential effect of orienting tasks on recall vs. recognition should be enhanced if the comparison is based upon mutually exclusive components, i.e., recalled target items vs. nonrecalled but recognized target items. The relation between recall and recognition performance is discussed more generally in the last section of this paper.

Interactions of Subject Characteristics with Free- vs. Cued-Recall Performance

Data that reveal differential facilitation and impairment of cued- vs. free-recall performance make it particularly evident that separate analysis of these two types of tasks can contribute much toward understanding memory retrieval. Cermak and his associates (Cermak & Butters, 1972) collected such data, and Cermak has reviewed the results in this volume (Chapter 6). Cermak and Butters report, for example, that the usual superiority of cued- over free-recall performance is reversed in Korsakoff patients. This reversal may reflect differential impairment of generative search processes and effortless free recall. The generative processes require effortful, systematic utilization of information in semantic memory, whereas much of the immediate episodic content of free recall can be accessed without such effort. This interpretation agrees with Cermak's suggestion (Chapter 6) that the patients retained material ''in an uncategorized state, sufficient for immediate free recall, but not for the more complex, cognitive manipulations required in cued recall [p. 120].''

Failure of Korsakoff patients to benefit from taxonomic changes of material in a PI release task (Cermak, Butterş, & Moreines, 1974) provides further evidence that distinctiveness as a predictive variable in retention must be viewed as an interaction of task characteristics and subject characteristics. Tversky (1977) discusses such interaction phenomena as a general aspect of the diagnosticity principle, and Jenkins (Chapter 20 in this volume) deals with them as one of the major determinants of retrieval. Distinctiveness of material affects retrieval only if it leads to distinctive encoding operations, and whether or not encoding operations are distinctive depends on the information available to the subject and other individual difference variables.

Recall and Recognition Tasks—Difficulty Level and Intercorrelation

Much has been written about conceptualization of recall and recognition processes. This section deals primarily with conditions that determine the relative performance levels of the two types of tasks and the circumstances under which recall and recognition performance exhibit different amounts of correlation.

It has been found in most instances that recognition performance is superior to recall performance of the same target items; however, exceptions to this generalization have been noted for some time (Bahrick & Bahrick, 1964; Bruce & Cofer, 1967). The degree of superiority of recognition performance to recall performance varies as a function of the orienting task, but this relationship has received little systematic attention. Tasks that require active rehearsal and organization, e.g., those using traditional memorizing instructions, generally yield high recall/recognition ratios (e.g., Bahrick, 1974; Postman & Rau, 1957). In contrast, incidental learning tasks, or orienting tasks that do not directly instruct the subject to rehearse or organize the material, yield much lower recall/recognition ratios (e.g., Bahrick et al., 1975, Craik & Lockhart, 1972; Schulman, 1974). This finding is in keeping with the view expressed by several contributors to this volume (Brown, Naus and Halasz) that recognition performance reflects relatively passive emitted processes, greatly influenced by stimulus exposure, but relatively less dependent on active processing and organizing strategies. In contrast, recall performance is relatively unaffected by stimulus exposure per se and depends much more on active processing. Instructions to organize and rehearse greatly enhance recall without creating comparable benefits for recognition, and this leads to relatively high recall/recognition ratios (Estes & DaPolito, 1967).

Whereas recognition performance is relatively unaffected by rehearsal instructions, it is greatly affected by the discriminations required on the recognition test. These discriminations become more difficult if target items and foils are more similar, or if cues that formed the basis of the discrimination during training are withheld during testing. The usual superiority of recognition performance to recall performance can be reversed if the recognition task requires finer discriminations between targets and foils than the discriminations necessary for the recall task, or if significant cues available for recall are withheld for the recognition test.

Consider as an example a paired-associate task in which subjects are instructed to learn the names of individuals shown in portraits. If the recognition task requires the subject to match portraits and names, performance will generally be better than performance on a recall task in which the subject must retrieve each name as the corresponding portrait is presented (Bahrick, 1974). However, if the recognition task were to change so that the subject is presented with portraits of identical twins as foils on the matching task, the proportion of names correctly matched might well be lower than the proportion of names correctly recalled when each target portrait is shown individually. In the example given, the recall task requires that each target portrait be discriminated from the other target portraits, whereas the matching task using portraits of twins as foils requires a much finer degree of discrimination. The increased difficulty of target discrimination may more than offset the requirement of name retrieval of the recall task, bringing about the reversal of the usual recall/recognition difficulty.

Tulving and his associates (Tulving & Wiseman, 1975; Watkins, 1974; Wiseman & Tulving, 1975) have shown that the reversal may also be obtained if the recognition context is changed from the encoding to the retrieval situation, thus depriving subjects of cues important in discriminating foils from targets on the recognition test. This leads to a large number of recognition failures of recallable responses for tasks in which context associations are an important part of what is learned. The effect is observed for high-frequency words but not low-frequency words (Postman, 1975; Reder, Anderson, & Bjork, 1974).

The phenomenon of recognition failure of recallable responses can be considered generally as a consequence of the relative difficulty level of the recall and recognition task and of the degree of correlation between the two tasks. If success on the two tasks is *uncorrelated*, the proportion or recognition failures of recallable responses is obtained simply by multiplying the proportion of recognition failures by the proportion of recall successes. Thus, if 0.20 of target items are failed in a recognition test and 0.40 are passed on a recall test, $0.20 \times 0.40 = 0.08$ of all targets will be recognition failures and recall successes. If performance on the two tasks is maximally correlated, there will be no failures on the easier of the tasks paired with successes on the more difficult task, and the proportion of successes on the easier task paired with failures on the more difficult task is given by the difference in the proportion of successes on the two tasks. Thus if the correlation is maximal and 0.60 target items are recognized and 0.40 are recalled, there will be no items that are recalled but not also recognized, and 0.20 of all items will be recognized but not recalled. Thus the phenomenon of recognition failure of recallable responses occurs with highest probability when the correlation between the two tasks is low and when the recognition task is difficult in relation to the recall task. The circumstances under which the recognition task will be more difficult than the recall task have already been discussed, and the remaining discussion deals with circumstances under which different correlations between the tasks are to be expected.

One may conceive of correlation in terms of the proportion of elements common to the phenomena in question. Viewed in this manner. recall and recognition performance are likely to correlate maximally in tasks that impose common processes on both types of performance and minimally in tasks that impose divergent processes.

Previous discussion has stressed the greater importance of organizational processes in recall compared to recognition. Since organizational processes are not shared by the two tasks, it would follow that recall and recognition performance would correlate less in tasks that require much organization and more in tasks that permit only minimal organization. Examples of tasks permitting minimal organization are traditional paired-associate tasks, particularly those using meaningless material. The opportunities for organization are minimized in such tasks by changing the presentation sequence of the pairs on each presentation trial, thus altering list context, and by using material that is relatively impoverished in regard to prior semantic relations. In such tasks, very high correlations are obtained between recognition and recall performance. Conditional probability of matching success, given anticipation or cued-recall success, is very high (Bahrick, 1974), and this reflects the fact that the tasks share common requirements in regard to stimulus discrimination and response discrimination. The additional retrieval of the response term required in the anticipation or recall task is the only element not shared by the matching task. However, retrieval must be based primarily on the association between the stimulus and the response, and this same association also provides the basis of correct matching. Memory research during the first half of this century relied primarily upon the study of such paired-associate tasks, and as a result, single trace strength theories were plausible. According to such theories, recall and recognition differed only in regard to the strength of the required association, i.e., recall required a higher threshold than recognition (Bahrick, 1965; Postman, Jenkins, & Postman, 1948). These theories became untenable when other tasks permitting a much wider range of organizational processes were introduced to the psychological laboratory. The use of meaningful material and the presentation of material in other than paired-associate form demonstrated that recall was influenced by a variety of conditions that had less influence or the opposite influence on recognition (Kintsch, 1970). Such data invalidated single trace strength theories. The foregoing example illustrates how the adequacy of theory depends on the range of tasks under investigation. The history of experimental psychology offers many other examples of theories based upon evidence obtained under highly restrictive conditions. The inadequacies of such generalizations become apparent when the range of observations is extended. This history lends support to the appeal made in this discussion for the examination of a wider range of memory tasks and for the explicit restriction of theory to task-specific generalizations.

The correlation between recall and recognition performance is reduced not only in tasks that present opportunities for organizational strategies but also in tasks that impose discrimination requirements on recognition irrelevant to the recall task. Thus Bahrick and Boucher (1968) found no correlation between the ability to recall the names of objects previously shown as pictures and the ability to identify the pictures on recognition tests in which the foils were other pictures of the same type of object. The recognition test required discriminations of the idiosyncratic characteristics of the drawing; the recall test required only the discrimination of the class characteristics of the object shown in the drawing, and retention of these respective characteristics was uncorrelated.

The preceding discussion shows that the recognition failure of recallable responses is a phenomenon that reflects the relative difficulty level of the two tasks and the correlation between the tasks. Relative performance is generally superior on recognition tasks, particularly when subjects do not organize or rehearse. Recall may be superior to recognition when the recognition test requires discriminations not necessary for recall or when cues available for recall are withheld or altered in recognition tests. The correlation between the tasks is very high when the task restricts organizational activities, when the required discriminations are comparable, and when traditional memorizing instructions are given. The correlation is low if the required discriminations differ, if retrieval cues are changed, or if the task entails extensive organization. Viewed from this perspective, the phenomenon of recognition failure of recallable responses is task specific and does not provide a basis for eliminating generation–recognition search as a strategy in situations where direct access has failed.

The phenomenon of recall failure of recognizable responses has received scant attention from investigators, although it has theoretical importance and occurs with much higher frequency than the phenomenon of recognition failure of recallable responses. Recall failures of recognizable responses provide an unexploited opportunity for investigating unretrievable information stored in memory. This is particularly true in tasks that require comparable discriminations and provide the same cues for the recall and recognition tests. Several unpublished studies in the Ohio Wesleyan laboratory indicate that under these circumstances, orienting tasks that impose different levels of processing and that have a large effect on recall performance have no effect on the portion of information that can be recognized but not recalled. This evidence supports the view expressed by Brown, Naus and Halasz, and others in this volume that recognition performance in contrast to recall is relatively less dependent on active processing and organizing. Investigations that fail to exclude the recallable portion of recognition memory do not provide adequate tests for this position.

CONCLUDING COMMENTS

Research of the last few years has demonstrated that the retrieval of episodic information is greatly affected by overlap of the encoding and retrieval context. Evidence reviewed in this volume by Eysenck (Chapter 5) and others shows that distinctiveness of the overlapping context is more significant to retrieval than the amount of overlap per se and that distinctiveness reflects the stimulus situation as well as the encoding operations of the subject.

This discussion has stressed that the role of context in episodic retrieval depends on the retention task and the type of material encoded. Context effects are most important in free recall and recognition of material familiar to the subject but are comparatively unimportant in the recognition of material unfamiliar to the subject prior to the experiment. Context effects are more important in free recall than in cued recall, but because of overlap, this difference is not apparent unless the comparison is based on cued recall exclusive of material retrieved in free recall.

It is argued that the emphasis of future research should not be directed at proving or disproving the general validity of retrieval principles such as encoding specificity, distinctiveness, or continuity. Rather, what is needed is a systematic comparison of results in a greater variety of tasks in which critical variables are manipulated or allowed to vary. On the basis of such comparisons, boundary conditions can be established for groups of tasks for which common results are obtained. Generalizations established on this basis are more likely to do justice to the great flexibility of retrieval strategies, and ultimately, models of retrieval developed on this basis will give a more realistic account of the capabilities and options of the memory system.

ACKNOWLEDGMENT

Preparation of this report was made possible by Public Health Service Research Grant HD00926-16.

REFERENCES

Anderson, J. R., & Reder, L. M. Negative judgments in and about semantic memory. *Journal of Verbal Learning and Verbal Behavior*, 1974, *13*, 664−681.

Atkinson, R. C., Herrmann, D. J., & Wescourt, K. T. Search processes in recognition memory. In R. L. Solso (Ed.), *Theories in cognitive psychology: The Loyola Symposium.* Washington, D.C.: Winston, 1974.

Bahrick, H. P. The ebb of retention. *Psychological Review*, 1965, *72*, 60−73.

Bahrick, H. P. Two-phase model for prompted recall. *Psychological Review*, 1970, *77*, 215−222.

Bahrick, H. P. Accessibility and availability of retrieval cues in the retention of a categorized list. *Journal of Experimental Psychology*, 1971, *89*, 117−125.

Bahrick, H. P. The anatomy of free recall. *Memory & Cognition*, 1974, *2*, 484−490.

Bahrick, H. P., & Bahrick, P. O. A re-examination of the interrelations among measures of retention. *Quarterly Journal of Experimental Psychology*, 1964, *16*, 318−324.

Bahrick, H. P., Bahrick, P. O., & Wittlinger, R. P. Fifty years of memory for names and faces: A cross-sectional approach. *Journal of Experimental Psychology: General*, 1975, *104*, No. 1. 54−75.

Bahrick, H. P. & Boucher, B. Retention of visual and verbal codes of the same stimuli. *Journal of Experimental Psychology*, 1968, *78*, 417−422.

Bower, G. H. Multicomponent theory of the memory trace. In K. W. Spence & J. T. Spence (Eds.), *The psychology of learning and motivation.* New York: Academic Press, 1967.

Bower, G. H., & Karlin, M. B. Depth of processing pictures of faces and recognition memory. *Journal of Experimental Psychology*, 1974, *103*, 751−757.

Bruce, D. & Cofer, C. N. An examination of recognition and free recall as measures of acquisition and long-term retention. *Journal of Experimental Psychology*, 1967, *75*, 283−289.

Cermak, L. S., & Butters, N. The role of interference and encoding in the short-term memory deficits of Korsakoff patients. *Neuropsychologia*, 1972, *10*, 89−96.

Cermak, L. S., Butters, N., & Moreines, J. Some analyses of the verbal encoding deficit of alcoholic Korsakoff patients. *Brain and Language*, 1974, *1*, 141–150.

Cermak, L. S., Naus, M. J., & Reale, L. Rehearsal and organizational strategies of alcoholic Korsakoff patients. *Brain and Language*, 1976, *3*, 375–385.

Craik, F. I. M., & Jacoby, L. L. A process view of short-term retention. In F. Restle (Ed.), *Cognitive theory* (Vol. 1). Hillsdale, N.J.: Lawrence Erlbaum Associates, 1975.

Craik, F. I. M., & Lockhart, R. S. Levels of processing: A framework for memory research. *Journal of Verbal Learning and Verbal Behavior*, 1972, *11*, 671–684.

Estes, W. K., & DaPolito, F. Independent variation of information storage and retrieval processes in paired-associate learning. *Journal of Experimental Psychology*, 1967, *75*, 18–26.

James, W. *Psychology*. New York: Holt, 1907.

Kintsch, W. *Learning, memory and conceptual processes*. New York: Wiley, 1970.

Kintsch, W. *The representation of meaning in memory*. Hillsdale, N.J.: Lawrence Erlbaum Associates, 1974.

Posner, M. I. *Cognition: An introduction*. Glenview, Ill.: Scott Foresman, 1973.

Postman, L. Tests of the generality of the principle of encoding specificity. *Memory & Cognition*, 1975, *3*, 663–672.

Postman, L. Interference theory revisited. In J. Brown (Ed.), *Recall and recognition*. London: Wiley, 1976.

Postman, L. W., Jenkins, O. L., & Postman, D. L. An experimental comparison of active recall and recognition. *American Journal of Psychology*, 1948, *61*, 511–520.

Postman, L., & Rau, L. Retention as a function of the method of measurement. *University of California Publications in Psychology*, 1957, *8*, 217–270.

Reder, L. M., Anderson, J. R., & Bjork, R. A. A semantic interpretation of encoding specificity. *Journal of Experimental Psychology*, 1974, *102*, 648–656.

Schulman, A. I. Memory for words recently classified. *Memory & Cognition*, 1974, *2*, 47–52.

Shiffrin, R. M., & Atkinson, R. C. Storage and retrieval processes in long-term memory. *Psychological Review*, 1969, *76*, 179–193.

Thomson, D. M., & Tulving, E. Associative encoding and retrieval: Weak and strong cues. *Journal of Experimental Psychology*, 1970, *86*, 255–262.

Tulving, E. Episodic and semantic memory. In E. Tulving & W. Donaldson (Eds.), *Organization of memory*. New York: Academic Press, 1972.

Tulving, E. Ecphoric processes in recall and recognition. In J. Brown (Ed.), *Recall and recognition*. London: Wiley, 1976.

Tulving, E., & Thomson, D. M. Encoding specificity and retrieval processes in episodic memory. *Psychological Review*, 1973, *80*, 5, 352–373.

Tulving, E., & Wiseman, S. Relation between recognition and recognition failure of recallable words. *Bulletin of the Psychonomic Society*, 1975, *6*, 79–82.

Tversky, A. Features of similarity. *Psychological Review*, 1977, *84*, 327–352.

Underwood, B. J. Attributes of memory. *Psychological Review*, 1969, *76*, 559–573.

Watkins, M. J. When is recall spectacularly higher than recognition? *Journal of Experimental Psychology*, 1974, *102*, 161–163.

Watkins, M. J., Ho, E., & Tulving, E. Context effects in recognition memory for faces. *Journal of Verbal Learning and Verbal Behavior*, 1976, *15*, 505–517.

Williams, M. D., & Norman, A. *Some characteristics of retrieval from very long-term memory*. Paper presented at the meeting of the Psychonomic Society, St. Louis, November 1976.

Wiseman, S., & Tulving, E. A test of confusion theory of encoding specificity. *Journal of Verbal Learning and Verbal Behavior*, 1975, *14*, 370–381.

III LANGUAGE PROCESSES

8 Levels of Language and Levels of Process

Charles A. Perfetti
University of Pittsburgh

The levels-of-processing framework (Craik & Lockhart, 1972) originally appeared to assert the memory principle that as far as semantics is concerned, more is better. Manipulations of processing depth typically contrasted some semantic activity with some nonsemantic activity involving the same linguistic forms. Despite the potential embedding of linguistic levels within a framework that emphasizes the value of semantic processing over superficial linguistic processing, there has been little contact between concepts of levels of language and depth of processing. Such separation is not surprising, given the general disenchantment with attempts to describe cognitive processes by reference to linguistic structures.

However, at least some cognitions concerning language do seem to have something to do with levels of language. In particular, there are two levels of language themes that are developed in this paper. The first is that specific levels of language structure are of cognitive interest provided: (1) that they are defined over a single language unit, and (2) that cognitions of interest are not arbitrarily restricted to the comprehension of linguistic messages. The second is that levels of language processing can be understood in terms of attentional selection and that deeper, more opaque semantic levels (one level in particular) are selected for attention under normal conditions of discourse. In this connection, it is suggested that something other than processing time or orienting task is critical for achieving "deeper" levels and more durable memories.

LEVELS OF A SENTENCE

One way to deal with levels of language and levels of process would be to reason as follows: In natural language understanding, units of language are processed

159

incompletely as other components of a message—components from different as well as the same levels—press their demands for attention. Comprehension than is seen as complex interactions among levels, as identification of *units* of one level are partly guided by the interpretation of *units* at other levels. Accordingly, this reasoning would suggest that detailed processing analyses are the proper means for refining vague notions about levels of language processing.

Although there is much value in this approach, it may be premature. Furthermore, it may be misleading and unnecessary for a more modest purpose. If units of language are kept separate from levels of language, a different approach is possible. The advantage is that we can begin with a unit that is an intuitive and theoretical primitive and explore the levels of cognition that involve this unit. Consider the following sentence as an utterance:

(1) *The old man blocked his path.*

At what "level" will this or any sentence be processed? This question is nearly nonsense, although not quite. We can ask directly not about its level of processing but about its level of analysis.

It will turn out that there are seven linguistic levels that can be analyzed for this simple sentence. Some of these share wide agreement linguistically, others not; but in all cases they are internally consistent and can be independently motivated. They also provide information appropriate to specific question types.

The possibilities of a linguistic levels analysis can be seen by reference to a particular sentence, example (1) given earlier. Seven levels are proposed below and summarized in Table 8.1. The levels are partly hierarchical in structure, but there is no corresponding processing assumption. They are hierarchical in so far as at least some levels can include the information of the previous levels.

Level 1: Prelinguistic

Acoustic properties of stress and pitch are functional in communication and encodable in memory. The defining characteristic of a prosodic level is that changing acoustic *patterns* are involved; intonation rises or falls, and stress patterns are perceived as relative acoustic energy distribution over a phrase (Trager & Smith, 1951). This level does not include information on segmental phonemes. However, broad acoustic energy bands associated with vowel sounds may be included.

Encoding tasks. If a listener is asked to mimic vowel sounds only, even though this is explicitly a phonemic task, Level 1 is engaged. The important feature is that the orienting task not emphasize accurate repetition of consonant-vowel segments rather than acoustic features. In this example, producing *ðiy ow æ a i æ* would be Level 1, and so in fact would humming (see Table 8.1). Theoretically, the analysis at this level can be based on one of several systems

TABLE 8.1
Summary Table of Seven Levels of Sentence-Utterance Structure
Partly Ordered by Opaqueness

Level	Information to Be Represented	Example	Charcteristic Memories
Normally transparent		The old man blocked his path.	
1. Prelinguistic	acoustic patterns, intonation contours, stress sequences	2 3 2 2 2 3[–] mm + mm + mm + mm + mm + mm	vocal quality (e.g., voice intensity or pitch)
2. Phonological	phonemic segments; hierarchically includes suprasegmentals of 1	/ðiy owld mæn blakt hiz paeθ/	phoneme sequences (e.g., consonant-vowel sequences)
3. Syntactic	superficial constituents; hierarchically includes 2	S(NP(The(old man)))(VP(blocked (his path)))	constituent sequences (e.g., verbatim phrases)
Normally opaque			
4. Propositional	basic semantic relations	CAUSE (Agent: X(PLACE (Instrument: Z, Object: O, Location: Path of Y)))	local semantic relations (e.g., actions, states)
Sometimes opaque, often transparent			
5. Referential	identification of referential constituents	$\exists X[(X,man) \cdot (X,old)]$ $\exists Y[Y, male]$	references (e.g., names, places)
6. Thematic	thematic; role of referential constituents	a) The old man (blocked an intruder's path) b) Siegfried (had his path blocked by an old man)	connections with text (e.g., themes)
7. Functional	intentions, motivations, deleted and generalized propositions	a) A confrontation existed b) Siegfried faced possible injury	connections with text and nontext knowledge (e.g., scripts)

that use one or more parameters of pitch, juncture, and intonation; e.g., Trager and Smith (1951) use four levels of stress and three of pitch. It has been demonstrated (Lieberman, 1967) that physical cues to these perceptual phenomena may not be sufficient. However, it is the perceptual phenomena that are of interest: A listener with minimal knowledge of a language can encode a tonal structure and reproduce it. One extrapolation of the Lieberman (1967) experiment, in which trained linguists performed stress and pitch analysis, is that to the extent that physical cues are present, a listener may be more accurate in a language he or she doesn't know. In a familiar language, acoustic perceptions are heavily influenced by syntactic knowledge.

Level 2: Phonological

The phonological level is the level of encoded speech. (In English and most languages, this means consonant–vowel combinations, not simple vowel sounds.) Level 1 will not be sufficient to distinguish *The old man blocked his path* from any other utterance with the same nonphonetic acoustic patterns. However, the phonological level does include those acoustic features of Level 1 that are phonological (suprasegmentals), and thus Level 1 and Level 2 are potentially hierarchical. Our example sentence is represented:

(2) /ðiy owld mæn blakt hiz pæ θ/

Encoding phonologically. It is my impression that this is a naturally occurring level only if it also contains the nonsegmental phonemic information of juncture and stress of Level 1. The encoding task might be verbatim repetition or imitation of an utterance, but memory in such cases is strongly affected by syntactic structure. Phoneme discriminations or syllabic comparisons of orally presented nonsense "words" may be more suitable perceptual encoding tasks. Real words naturally include nonphonemic levels, whereas nonwords potentially separate a phonemic level from semantic and syntactic levels.

Level 3: Syntactic

A syntactic level is restricted to superficial structures. It is that level at which a speaker judges a sentence to be grammatical, and it can be the level for some perceptual analysis. It is potentially hierarchical to Level 2 in representation, with the addition of morphemic structures: *S(NP((ðiy)((owld)(mæn)))(VP((blak)(ed))(NP((hiz)(pæθ))))*. As an indication of abstractness phonemic notation can be dropped at this level to produce (3).

(3) *S(NP (the (old man)))(VP (blocked (his path)))*

Encoding tasks. Judgments of grammaticality are the paradigm case of the syntactic level. Although there appears to be wide variation in individual abilities at engaging just this level, it must be a genuine level for linguists to have adopted the methodology of grammatical judgments. Though it may be difficult to decide whether a sentence such as (4) is anomalous or ungrammatical, that does not diminish the persuasiveness of easy cases such as (5) and (6), which are grammatical and ungrammatical, respectively.

(4) *Your rock believes in astrology.*

(5) *Everyone knew McDonald would quit.*

(6) *Knew quit that McDonald would everyone.*

There may be other "orienting" tasks that can engage primarily the syntactic level but only rarely in pure form. Skilled proofreading of manuscripts may do this, and so may memorizing formulae and sentence lists, although memory tasks generally reach a semantic level.

Level 4: Propositional (Relational)

Semantic levels are descriptions of the relations among arguments and predicates, or descriptions of relations among syntactic constituents in deep structure. The choice of these descriptions is a matter of metatheoretical preferences, and their shared aspect of relational structures is more important here than possible differences. A semantic terminology has the advantage of transparency. It reveals structural relations without mapping of syntactic descriptions onto a range of possible semantic interpretations. Hence our example is represented as a first approximation as:

(7) *(X caused some obstacle to be placed in the path of Y)* which can be made more abstract to indicate structural relations

(8) *CAUSE (Agent: X(PLACE (Instrument: Z, Object: O, Location: Path of Y)))*

This analysis reveals both how much structure is implicit in the sentence and how much indentification is lacking. To say that someone blocked someone's path is ambiguous in two ways, only one of which is represented by the analysis. However, it is indeterminant in at least five ways, as revealed by the semantic analysis.

    i. X is not identified.

   ii. Y is not identified.

  iii. Z is not identified.

  iv. O is not identified.

   v. The manner of PLACE is not specified.

X is indexed in the original sentence as "the old man." However, following the convention of predicate calculus and its linguistic adaptation by McCawley (1970), it is preferable to allow only relational structures to be represented at this level. Arguments, or variables, are indexed and identified by separate referential structures. Note, however, that even without this convention, Y is not identified but merely indexed by a pronoun. The proposal of separate referential indexing has the advantage that it treats *The old man* and *him* in the same way, with neither as specified as it may be.

More interesting is the indeterminancy of O and Z. These can only be indexed and not referenced. In fact X, Z, and O may all have the same identity. Had this possibility been specified syntactically, then we would have had only X and Y as variables, and the structure would have represented X as an agent and object with no instrument. However, the indeterminacy of the instrument allows the readings (9) and (10).

   (9) *The old man placed a log in the path of Y.*

   (10) *The old man enticed someone to place an obstruction in the path of Y.*
In the case of (10) the instrument is unknown in principle and could include the unidentified Y. The representation includes these indeterminacies and thus is quite revealing in showing lacunae that are not ordinarily noticed.[1]

Encoding tasks.   There are some linguistic intuition tasks that engage this level, but they are seldom used. For example, *If X blocked the path of Y, then someone blocked the path of Y,* is a logical implication from the example sentence, and a subject who decides its truth in entailment terms is performing an abstract semantic relation task. One can also detect contradictions of the example, such as (11), and certain types of paraphrases, such as (12).

   (11) *The old man blocked X's path, but nobody blocked X's path.*

   (12) *His path was obstructed by the old man.*
In general, those properties that propositions assume—truth or falsity, analyticity, contradiction, entailment—are the properties of semantic relation, and persons are engaging this level when they make such judgments. Of course, this sort of pure semantic encoding is as rare among everyday language users as are syntactic judgments. Moreover, it is unlikely that this level is isolated in ordinary language comprehension and production. The observation that semantic properties are what we remember is not one for this level.[2] Rather, it is a claim that semantic and referential information, as defined in the next level, are remembered.

Level 5: Referential

At the next level, the semantic descriptions plus the referential constituents are given. For the example, the information $X = old\ man$, $Y = ?[male]$ is added to

---

[1]Van Dijk (1977) has pointed out how commonplace such lacunae are in texts and has argued that many are the result of systematic deletions of text bases, predictable from discourse conventions.

[2]Of course there is evidence that memory for relations outlasts memory for individual words (Fillenbaum, 1973; Sachs, 1967). However, such evidence is a matter of showing that people remember that X did it to Y rather than vice versa. What is necessary is to show that memory for someone did it to someone persists over memory for X did something (but I can't remember what).

the relational descriptions of Level 4. Although these identification constituents may seem trivial in the present example, they are quite revealing in general, as examples with ambiguous quantifier scopes attest.[3] The linguistic advantage of separating relational structures from identity constituents was first stressed by James McCawley (1968, 1970), and it is a level well motivated by predicate calculus as well (e.g., Reichenbach, 1947).[4]

Encoding tasks. In natural conditions of language understanding, Level 5 may be reached with Level 4. The encoding of relations and identities go together. However, they are separable under some conditions, and memories for semantic relations and referential identities often seem to have different fates. Remembering that a conversation was *about X* or that a lecture was *about Y* and forgetting what was asserted about *X* or *Y* seems a fairly common occurrence, at least intuitively. Likewise, it must also happen that we remember that someone *scolded, questioned,* or *frightened* someone else without remembering who and whom. Tasks that encourage encoding references would certainly include conscious referring situations, such as ratings of concreteness, or image production.[5] Studies of imagery in which subjects are instructed to imagine the two nouns in interaction (Bower, 1972) are examples of referential encoding in a context that promotes relational encoding. A question to represent this level would have the form "who (what) was involved/described/referred to?" The answer to the example is "some old man" and "some unspecified male being."

Level 6: Thematic

Levels 4 and 5 are the heart of semantic interpretation, because they provide the semantic relations and the references entering the relations. Thematic information will add to basic semantic interpretation a sense of discourse value. One discourse feature that affects sentence interpretation is the given-new distinction of Halliday (1967, 1970). The following sentences illustrate this (by now) well-known principle.

---

[3]For example, the sentence *Everybody is loved by someone* results from two possible propositions: *There is an X such that X has the property of loving each Y*, and *There are X's and Y's such that each Y is loved by at least one X*. The identity or referential constituents are clearly nontrivial here; i.e., they assert the identity of the indexes involved in the relational assertion, thus disambiguating it.

[4]For example, in propositional functions, an existential operator asserts the "existence" of some "thing" that has the property asserted by some separate operand. $(\exists X)\ (fX)$ asserts the existence of some X that has the property of $f(X)$. This is analogous to asserting, in our example, that there is some X that has the property of being an old man.

[5]High retention of word lists follows tasks that focus on referential encodings, such as rating of "goodness" (Hyde & Jenkins, 1973), and tasks that focus on semantic features, such as producing synonyms (Elias & Perfetti, 1973). However, I am not aware of evidence on separating reference and structure in sentences, although relevant data are present in any study of sentence or text recall in which recall of verbs and nouns can be distinguished.

(13) *John read* THE NUN'S TALE.

(14) THE NUN'S TALE *was read by John.*

(15) *It was John who read* THE NUN'S TALE.

(16) *It was* THE NUN'S TALE *that John read.*

(13) (perhaps) and (16) (certainly) tend to focus on THE NUN'S TALE as the new information and presuppose *John* as the given information. (14) and (15) focus on John as new and presuppose THE NUN'S TALE as given. Of the four sentences, (13) is characteristic of an ordinary active voice sentence in being relatively weak with respect to any given-new distinction. In fact, such sentences linguistically should be considered unmarked with respect to the distinction, as either subject or object may receive focus. (There is even some psychological evidence for this assumption from Hornby, 1974.)

However compelling three out of these four examples are, it is possible that this feature of language is somewhat overrated. First, note that of the four sentences, the one that most fails to mark given-new is the most common of the four forms. Furthermore, there seems little reason to assume that sentences typically focus on one or the other nouns of a sentence. Indeed the construction of any plausible discourse context for our example makes this clear:

(17) *Siegfried saw an old man.*

The old man blocked his path.

(18) *An old man encountered the young hero.*

The old man blocked his path.

In neither case does the final sentence introduce new information concerning X and Y; it is the relationship between X and Y, the semantic structure, that is new. It is likely that such "given-new" structures are at least as common as those attributing information value to the nouns. Indeed the entire distinction is somewhat misleading if more realistic discourse structures are imagined, as the following extended examples illustrate.

(19) There was an old man who lived in the dark woods. He liked being alone with the forest and he resented intruders who occasionally came through. One day, an adventurous young man named Siegfried wandered off the main road and through the dark woods. He became curious as he came upon a trail hidden by thick bushes. He followed the trail with great excitement until he caught a glimpse of a bearded figure out of the corner of his eye. Suddenly, he was forced to stop in his tracks. *The old man blocked his path.*

(20) There was an old man who lived in the dark woods. He liked being alone with the forest and he resented intruders who occasionally came through. One day, an adventurous young man named Siegfried wandered off the main road and through the dark woods. The old man spotted the intruder and followed him at a distance. He thought about how serene the silence of the forest was and how much more he could trust the deer and the bear that visited him than a stranger. Suddenly he decided to rid himself of the intruder. *The old man blocked his path.*

These texts illustrate the principle that it is common for a sentence to presuppose both references and assert a new relationship. However, some concept of focus does seem to apply. The first discourse (19) seems to be mainly about young Siegfried, and the second seems to be mainly about the unnamed old man. This impression is verified by counting the number of propositions containing the two references. This relative propositional structure has been termed *thematization* (Perfetti & Goldman, 1974). This example should make it clear that notions of theme in terms of the first-occurring element of a sentence (Halliday, 1967, 1970) are of limited generality, because *The old man* is the first element in each case. However, such thematic properties marked by sentence structures as (16) and passives tells us that these structures are marked in that they focus attention on the object, whereas ordinarily focus is determined solely by discourse structure. Notice, in support of this claim, that whereas the two discourses (19 and 20) equally well take the active sentence, only (19), which thematizes the object, permits the object focus of the passive:

(21) *His path was blocked by the old man.*

Of course, thematization is not the only discourse value assumed by sentence elements. The feature of "topic," when defined as the initial surface structure noun phrase (Hockett, 1958), is also a discourse feature of sentences. *Foregrounding* (Chafe, 1972) then refers to the presumed activation of memory structures necessary for sentence interpretation and thus is the interface between theme and topic. In particular, topic constraints are imposed by theme and foreground by the principles:

i. Topicalization is determined by thematization except when overridden by momentary foregrounding, *ceteris paribus*.
ii. Topicalization is unconstrained (free) when thematization and momentary foregrounding do not coincide, *ceteris paribus*.

Other aspects of discourse and their influence on sentence interpretation undoubtedly are important. Some of these belong to Level 7, others are non-systematic, and some can be considered as special cases of the discourse already considered.

Encoding tasks. If the foregoing argument is essentially correct, then encoding an unmarked sentence, such as our example (1), thematically is either impossible or arbitrary until discourse context is provided. However, in the case of marked sentences, there is ample evidence that topical structures are discerned and differentially processed (Hornby, 1974; Olson & Filby, 1972). With or without discourse contexts, one might propose that requiring a person to indicate the "most important" sentence element, or some similar instruction, would be thematic encoding. However, this is unnecessary except in isolated sentences and not meaningful except in marked sentences. By contrast, instructions to "comprehend" discourse seem to involve this level of encoding. Nothing special is needed. Understanding connected discourse is thematic encoding that hierarchically includes Levels 4, 5, and 6 as a matter of necessity.

Level 7: Functional

What remains after we have interpreted the semantic relations, referential identities, and thematic features?—much that is unsystematic and perhaps some that is systematic. What's left to know in the example can be seen most easily by posing these questions:

(22) *Why did the old man block his path?*

(23) *Why are you telling me that the old man blocked his path?*

(24) *What was the consequence of his path being blocked by the old man?*

Not included is a question such as (25),

(25) *How did the old man block him?*

It is true that (25) seems as contextual as the "why" questions; i.e., it is not answered by the sentence itself. The justification for this apparently arbitrary exclusion is that *how* questions are asked by the (implicit) semantic structure, which contains an instrumental argument. (Notice that there is not an instrumental answer in the structure, only an instrumental question.)

Whether contextual messages of this sort can be assigned to a well-defined level is difficult to say. One obvious candidate for organizing this contextual information is Searle's (1969) speech acts (see also Austin, 1962). However, speech acts seem to require social contexts and even social roles as means of relating sentences to utterance "force." They are of no obvious help in organizing language features of discourse, although some conventionalized knowledge will have to be represented in any case. Neither is anything gained by imagining that the text author and reader are analogous to a speaker and hearer whose communications carry interactions testable by various nonlinguistic (felicity) considerations.

Instead, this level, termed *functional* with some reluctance, is one of deleted text propositions having to do in this case with the narrator's perspective. But the deletions are (potentially) systematic and knowable to the text comprehender. Van Dijk (1977; van Dijk & Kintsch, 1977) has pointed out the systematic deletions that are possible and perhaps obligatory in narration.

Encoding tasks. As with Level 6, discourse comprehension naturally includes this level, although a strong claim about inevitably attaining this functional level is probably not warranted. If some possible information is excluded, then encoding at this level is encouraged by questions of *why*. Also, instructing people to summarize texts (van Dijk & Kintsch, 1977) can recover information at this level. However, it seems unlikely that any procedure will tap this level to the exclusion of others. Since this level can be defined by relations among propositions, it is at the boundary of a sentence levels analysis. Indeed, it is clear that the game is up at this point and no further claim to coherence can be made.

How Many Are Enough?

These seven levels actually represent penurious leveling. It is possible to propose many more. Note, for example, that there is no phonetic level, an omission particularly grievous from some linguistic points of view. Nor is there a syllable level or a phrase level or a speech−act level. These and more are applicable to analyzing utterances for some purposes. J. M. Carroll and T. G. Bever (1976) have listed twelve levels constituting a list they regard "by no means complete."[6]

However, such lists are incomplete, because they are not defined over a single unit. By contrast, focusing on the sentence-as-utterance provides single units that are minimal discourse objects as well as the units for linguistic semantic analysis. The number of levels at which a sentence can be "understood" is not indefinitely large. For example, a level of morphemic analysis is subsumed by syntactic level and semantic levels in so far as it provides the units for such analysis.

There is an important distinction to be made between unit and level. Units are necessary for analysis. To analyze the syntactic structure of sentences, morphemes or words must serve as units. A step down, the analysis of sound structure of words or morphemes requires units of phonemes or phones. A step up, the analysis of discourse requires propositions as units. The general principle is that units of analysis are from one level lower than the structures to be analyzed. This question of unit of analysis approaches infinite regression, however. Furthermore, it is not necessarily helpful to speak of units of analysis in language processing without being more specific.

For example, there has been considerable interest in the unit of analysis in speech perception. The perceptual nonreality of the phoneme was apparently established by Savin and Bever (1970), who argued that the unit was at least as large as the syllable. The evidence that established this claim was the experimental result that detecting syllable targets was faster than detecting phoneme targets in a list of syllables. However, it turned out, thanks to McNeill and Lindig (1973), that detection latencies for targets defined by linguistic levels varied with the match between the unit of the target and the units of the search list. In a list of phonemes, the unit with the shortest detection times was the phoneme; in a list of syllables, the fastest unit was the syllable and similarly for lists of words and short sentences. McNeill and Lindig (1973) thus were able to

---

[6]Linguistic theories outside of transformational grammar have made use of levels. Halliday's (1967, 1970) systemic grammar is a network of grammatical class relations, with levels such as phrase, clause, sentence; Pike's (1964) tagmemics and Lamb's stratificational grammar make use of levels. Lamb (1966) suggested that English and some other languages have six "strata," while assuming that four levels were minimally required by a language.

show that the speech unit question was not being answered by identifying larger and larger basic units.

This example illustrates the problem of postulating linguistic levels as processing levels. It is not that the linguistic levels are not "psychologically real." It is that no single one is "the unit" of perceptual analysis. In fact, all the levels described here are real in a specific sense: A speaker of the language can direct his or her attention to a given level and ignore other levels, *relatively* speaking. This is not a perceptual hypothesis, nor is it a memory hypothesis. It is properly a hypothesis of what has come to be called, perhaps regrettably, metalinguistic awareness.[7] It is, in other words, possible to make judgments about or otherwise attend to some level of language to the momentary (relative) exclusion of other levels. There is no reason to doubt the significance (or "reality") of these types of cognitions. Indeed, the "reality" of these cognitions at least in part enable the discovery, description, and understanding of linguistic levels.

TRANSPARENT AND OPAQUE PROCESSING LEVELS

So far I have suggested seven levels of language that define structures over a sentence and have proposed a specific psychological reality for these levels; namely, that they represent features of language that can be the object of attention, thus yielding linguistic awareness. There are (at least) two ways to minimally elaborate this perspective on language awareness.[8]

Transparent levels. One way to understand levels of language in language awareness is to assume that attention in language is ordinarily focused on meaning. Form is transparent, meaning opaque. Hence, during ordinary listening or reading we are aware of superficial forms only incidentally. We can become aware of forms easily enough for special purposes. For example, reading difficult handwriting can bring grapheme identification to a conscious level. If the style is awkward, if there seems to be a word missing, the syntactic level pushes into consciousness. The same effect may result from trying to understand one's native

---

[7]The term may be misleading because it unnecessarily implies another layer of cognition. What is really involved is simply linguistic awareness, i.e., consciousness of linguistic forms as forms. It is the formal aspects of language that are normally not in consciousness. Awareness is simply exercising formal intuitions about language.

[8]Although there is not yet a specification of awareness that cuts across levels of language, linguistic awareness has been an object of research in language development (de Villiers & de Villiers, 1974; Gleitman, Gleitman, & Shipley, 1972). It appears that the expression of linguistic intuitions is not an easy matter for young children at the syntactic level (Gleitman et al., 1972) or the phonemic level (Liberman, Shankweiler, Fischer, & Carter, 1974; Rosner, 1974). Neither are syntactic-level intuitions easily articulated by all adults (Gleitman & Gleitman, 1970).

language spoken by a nonfluent foreigner. Polanyi (1958) illustrates the transparency of language form in this way:

> My correspondence arrives at my breakfast table in various languages, but my son understands only English. Having just finished reading a letter, I may wish to pass it on to him, but must check myself and look again to see in what language it was written. I am vividly aware of the meaning conveyed by the letter, yet know nothing whatever of its words. I have attended to them closely but only for what they mean and not for what they are as objects. If my understanding of the text were halting, or its expressions or its spelling were faulty, its words would arrest my attention. They would become slightly opaque and prevent my thought from passing through them unhindered to the things they signify [p. 57].

One can withhold unreserved acceptance of this introspective account of bilingual processing without doubting the essential truth—that ordinarily meaning is opaque and the levels of language involving semantic relations (4, 5, 6, and 7 here) are the focus of attention, whereas superficial levels are transparent. Awareness should be more commonplace for semantic levels than for non-semantic levels.

However, it may not be a simple matter of opacity increasing as levels of language become "more semantic." In Table 8.1, all the nonsemantic levels (1−3) are designated as transparent, but not all semantic levels (4−7) are opaque. These designations are certainly tentative and probably incorrect. However, as a first approximation, it is assumed that Levels 5, 6, and 7 can be made transparent more readily than Level 4. The propositional level is normally opaque. It usually requires attention to meaning relations in order to understand discourse. However, for referential, thematic, and functional levels it is possible that transparency is often achieved. For example, as a conversation about a third person proceeds, the initial opaqueness of the reference gives way to an easy transparency. We know now that we are talking about a specific person, and although attributions, states, and actions continue to be the focus of comprehension, identifying the X that is the subject and object of the various predicates has become transparent. So too with thematic levels and functional levels. As a thematic structure develops, it can be used without effort in constructing new representations. If Level 7 relies on conventional knowledge, as I assume it does, then activation of an appropriate schema in the course of a discourse should aid in comprehension. However, during parts of a discourse, especially at the beginning, we may be conscious of not knowing which of several schemata to apply. This would be attention demanding or opaque.

Control and selective attention.   A related way to elaborate the notion of awareness of language levels is to suggest that it is a question of allocating attention. Allocating attention is a matter of controlled processing, limited in time and limited by capacity. This view of attention is an active rather than passive one, as would seem necessary to understand the levels of language we are discussing. Thus, of the various theories of attention that have been proposed, one allowing selectional control of input features (Shiffrin & Schneider, 1977) may be particularly suitable.[9]

The levels of language are available to conscious perception, and the relevant control processes are accessible. According to Shiffrin and Schneider (1977), accessible control processes are those that can be initiated or modified by instruction, in contrast to *veiled* control processes that are more difficult to manipulate with instruction. Thus, comparison of items in STM is an example of a *veiled* control process, whereas an alphabetic search of STM is an accessible control process.

Control processes of this sort have not been discussed in connection with levels of language. (In fact, the feeling that a homunculus is needed to run the controls has caused control processes to receive only scant attention in lower level memory tasks.) However, there are certain properties of control processes that highlight their applicability to language levels:

1. Control processes are attention-demanding, limited-capacity processes.
2. Because the control processes for language levels are the accessible type, they are quickly initiated and modified for given tasks.
3. Control processes by implication of (1) are carried out sequentially, not in parallel. Attentional selectivity is a pointer to one or the other level of language at any given moment, i. e., whatever level is currently used in controlled processing.

Controlled processing and automatic processing can go on in parallel, according to the Shiffrin and Schneider (1977) theory. For language levels, I assume that attentional selectivity is operating at any given moment on exactly one level. Other levels are processed automatically, if at all. Automatic processes have properties complementary to controlled processing:

1. They are not demanding of attention because they do not depend on capacity limitations.
2. They are not easily learned and are not easily modified by instructions.
3. They can be done in parallel.
4. They are not easily inspected in consciousness.

If one is trying to detect the highest pitch in an utterance or a song lyric,

---

[9]Other theories of attention can be applied to this problem (Broadbent, 1958; Deutsch & Deutsch, 1963; Neisser, 1967). The issue that divides theories of attention is the point in processing at which unattended information is ignored. The advantage of Shiffrin and Schneider (1977) is the distinction between automatic processing and controlled selection.

attentional selection is on acoustic features. Correspondingly, if syntactic judgments are being made, then attentional selection is for the syntactic level, and other levels can be processed to the extent that automatic processing at other levels is possible. Semantic attributes may be processed in certain situations by well-practiced language users.

This brings us to an important feature of levels of processing in language awareness: Some levels are more likely to be automatic than others. Since only those levels that are automatic can be processed while attention is selected for a different level, there will be some asymmetries in the levels with respect to what gets processed. For example, there is reason to suppose that phonological analysis is automatic. This does not mean that phonological information is easy to remember; in fact, automatic processing should lead to poor retention unless there is also controlled processing (Shiffrin & Schneider, 1977). It means that it can be done without disrupting other processing. (Ordinary information-processing tasks may not reveal this easily, because other levels depend on a phonological code in STM.) Thus, a subject attending to syntax will automatically process phonology. But a subject attending to phonology will not necessarily automatically process syntax. This asymmetry is not simply because recognizing syntax presupposes recognizing phonology but not vice versa. Indeed, it is reasonable to suppose that identification of morphemes and identification of phrase constituents goes on in alternation: part identification of morphemes, part identification (prediction) of phrases, then further morpheme identification, etc. Instead the problem is that automatic processing is restricted to overlearned, i.e., highly familiar and predictable, input patterns. Any given phoneme fits this restriction; any given syntactic structure may not.

Hierarchical levels. This begins to look like a bottom-up theory, so it is timely to make explicit an assumption. Any given level of language assumes the analysis at the next lowest level, but not vice versa. This makes it a hierarchy of language levels, each level including the analysis of the next lowest level. This is not a processing claim, but a logical one. There is ample opportunity for top-down processes. In fact, the evidence of McNeill and Lindig (1973) suggests that identification of units is top down or bottom up, *depending* on the size match between units. The assumption of the hierarchy and the asymmetry of dependencies clearly implies that some levels will (potentially) become automatic more easily than others.[10]

---

[10]If this assumption is general enough, it has significance for process interactions in cognition. It implies that lower level skills are prime candidates for the training to a level of automaticity. Higher level skills will be less trainable to automatic levels of processing. Thus, although complex skills such as reading are indeed interactions of higher and lower level processes, it is the lower level processes that the individual must master to high (automatic) levels in order to become skilled. Alan Lesgold and I have made this argument in varying degrees of elaboration (Lesgold & Perfetti, 1977; Perfetti & Lesgold, 1977; in press).

Levels and Memory

The original levels-of-processing paper by Craik and Lockhart (1972) was concerned primarily with memory. Their proposal was that depth of processing provided a framework for investigating memory. The aspect of their theory that received most attention was that semantic processing was deeper than non-semantic processing and hence led to a more durable memory trace.

It is natural to expect that levels of language correspond to depth of processing and thereby to retention: Memory for language will be a function of levels of language, with semantic levels resulting in more permanent memories than nonsemantic levels. However, the difficulty of independently defining level of processing exists no less for language than for other processes. Is it possible to define depth of processing by reference to time of processing, or kind of processing, or anything at all? The answer must be sought in terms of processing quality, not processing time. Furthermore, it may not be just a question of orienting task or quality of encoding.

It has generally been assumed that the identification of processing level is a matter of encoding task. Semantic encoding is achieved by a semantic orienting task (generating synonyms, categorizing words); formal encodings are achieved by "formal" orienting tasks (generating rhymes, searching for letter patterns, etc.). However, orienting tasks are simply devices to bring about different levels of processing that actually are observable within a single encoding task. The problem is that typically different orienting tasks force attention to different aspects of the input. Some aspects of the input may be more suitable for memory tasks, regardless of processing depth. For example, Craik and Tulving (1975) encouraged category (semantic) encoding by asking subjects to answer questions such as "Is the word a type of fish?" One type of formal encoding was encouraged by the question "Is the word in capital letters?" and another type by "Does the word rhyme with weight?" Such questions are successful in bringing about a certain level of encoding. But they are also likely to bring about "orientation" for those features that turn out to be more retrievable at the time of the test. This may be simply another way of saying that long-term memories are mainly semantic. But the question is whether this is all there is to levels of processing: Long-term memory is a process of retrieving semantic attributes from stored inputs; thus, anything that is semantically encoded shows superior memory. Further understanding of a phenomenon described in this way seems remote. We will be hard pressed to compare the value of the features of one level with the value of those features of another level for a task that seems defined by reference to just one level. The analogy to the McNeill and Lindig (1973) analysis of perceptual units in speech is useful: Will a semantic-category encoding be superior to rhyme encoding if the subject is asked to test whether a certain syllable has been presented? The critical aspect may be the match between the encoding and the test. (This issue is also addressed in the papers by

Bransford, Franks, Morris, and Stein (Chapter 15) and by Tulving (Chapter 19) in the present volume.)

This is not a problem for the levels-of-processing framework if we understand processing to be a qualitative contextual encoding. The context part of the encoding can come from the orienting task. However, in the case of language, there is a more interesting means of context–trace encoding. It's again the transparency of language, a transparency people have learned through uncountable (nonlaboratory) hours of verbal experience. The assumption of transparency is that lower levels of language are normally processed automatically and that the higher levels are normally attended. In general, memory for linguistic events should be directly related to the degree of controlled attention-demanding processing and inversely related to the degree of automatic processing. Memory for higher levels should be superior independently of (1) processing time and (2) orienting task.

Two Experiments

The foregoing account is helpful for interpreting a couple of experiments carried out for other purposes. The first experiment demonstrates that at the word level, even longer processing time on a semantic task is not sufficient for higher memory when processing tends "automatically" to engage the semantic level. The second experiment demonstrates that not only is memory not dependent on processing time, it is not dependent on orienting task.

Experiment 1. Semantic and "nonsemantic" visual search. In this experiment, we were interested, among other things, in the relationship between two decision levels in visual word search and recognition memory for nontarget items from the search task. In the word-level task, children had to decide whether a visual display of 1, 3, 5, and 7 words contained a particular target word that remained constant over 32 trials. In the category-level task, they had to decide whether a display contained a particular target category (e.g., animal).

An "incidental" forced-choice recognition memory test followed each search task. It consisted of nontarget items from the search task paired with foils of equal frequency and the same initial letter. The data, summarized in Table 8.2, were quite striking. Decision times were longer for the category level search task, as one would expect. However, recognition memory was unaffected by the task. This is particularly surprising in view of the fact that semantic judgments were both at a higher level and required more processing time. One explanation is that in the word-level search, lower level graphic and phonemic features were attended and were sufficient for memory. The other possibility is that semantic information at the categorical level is relatively transparent for single-word units, at least for skilled readers. If so, transparency and opaqueness are not independent of units. The suggestion is that meaning is relatively transparent at a

TABLE 8.2
Processing Times and Recognition Memory for Two Search Tasks[a]

	Search Task	
	Word Level	*Category Level*
Above-average readers		
Mean RT	1.62	1.82
Proportion correct recognition	0.77	0.73
Below-average readers		
Mean RT	2.14	3.05
Proportion correct recognition	0.55	0.55

[a]From Perfetti & Bell, in preparation.

word-at-a-time level, even though it is relatively opaque at a word-combination (sentence) level.

Experiment 2: Discourse context and word memory. A second experiment is more informative for the role of orienting tasks and processing time in determining level of processing. The main problem of this experiment concerned the effects of discourse context on single-word decoding and memory of children of varying reading skill.

In one condition, single words appeared in isolation on a screen and the subject's vocalization latency was recorded. In a second condition, single words appeared in the manner described, except that a discourse context was provided. The subject heard a story over headphones, and a tone occasionally directed his or her attention to the screen. When the word appeared, the subject said it as quickly as possible, as in the isolated condition. There was a third condition, in which the context was a short list of unrelated words. A second experiment involved the same task, with context being provided through reading rather than through listening. Finally, for both experiments, a recognition test was given to each subject consisting of the words vocalized in the various conditions, plus foils. Care was taken to match all words to be vocalized on initial letter, initial phoneme, printed frequency, and appropriate word length.

For present purposes, the important features of the experiment are these:

1. Level of processing and time of processing are empirically separable. The vocalization latency measure for each word provides the time of processing. (The words automatically disappeared with initial vocalization.)

2. Level of processing is independent of orientation task. The orientation task was identical across conditions: The subject was told to say the word that appeared on the screen as quickly as possible.

The data from the isolated and discourse conditions of this experiment are shown in Table 8.3. The main result for levels of processing is that time of processing was negatively related to memory. The most compelling comparison is for below-average readers, whose mean processing time in the reading experiment was about 250 milliseconds longer for the isolated condition. However, their probability of recognizing a processed word was about 0.19 lower in the isolated condition than in the discourse condition. This within-individual comparison is mirrored by a between-individual comparison. Those subjects who processed words faster (the above-average readers) recognized more words than subjects who processed words slower. This pattern of results holds for listening as well as reading.

Processing quality.   The results of this experiment are incompatible with the idea that memory is a function of processing time and with the possibility that depth of processing can be identified with processing time, thus supporting the points made by Craik and Tulving (1975). However, they go further in showing that depth of processing effects can be obtained without explicitly different encoding tasks. Of course, one might claim that the discourse context tacitly promotes an encoding task different from the isolated, no-context conditions. Although this may be so, it begs the question of how task demands serve to control encoding and makes the notion of orienting task, as an experimental manipulation, much too broad.

An alternative can be suggested. Control processes of attentional selection, in the sense discussed previously, are responsive to language structures. The

TABLE 8.3
Processing Time and Recognition Memory
for Isolated Vocalized Words
(Reading Experiment)[a]

	Context Condition	
Group	Isolated	Discourse
Low skill		
Mean V. L.	1096	775
d′	0.675	1.171
High skill		
Mean V. L.	695	662
d′	0.789	1.319

[a]Vocalization latencies (V. L.) are for words correctly produced only. When the occasional errors of low-skill readers are included, the mean V.L.s of that group are 1,120 and 867 for isolated and discourse conditions, respectively. d′ is based on the group average percent "old" responses to targets and foils, rather than individual d′ values. Data are from Perfetti, Goldman, & Hogaboam, in preparation.

transparent forms of language are (relatively) automatically processed under conditions of natural language understanding. Semantic processes involving several levels (4 through 7) are the focus of attentional selection when people are listening or reading as they were in the second experiment. Those features of meaning are part of the text representation that is constructed and will serve reasonably well in a recognition test for words. However, conditions of memory tests may match conditions of comprehension to varying degrees. In fact, memory for single words following discourse should not be so good as memory for propositions. The point made by McNeill and Lindig (1973) for perception of speech can be extended to memory for language. When subjects are given the task of reading words in isolation, there is some shift from attentional selection to lower level features and a concomitant reduction of semantic features. It is not the case that semantic features at the word level are not processed in such a condition. There is reason to suppose that this semantic level can attain some degree of attention-free processing and that the semantic attributes are encoded and used for memory search at test time. However, the encoding is not sufficiently rich with respect to the semantic levels defined over a sentence. They include no propositional, thematic, or contextual interpretive information of the sort discussed in the first part of this paper. In a memory test, the subject reads the word *milk*, which he or she has vocalized, and has some semantic features and some lower level features available, but the subject lacks a large number that are naturally available through discourse. Even though the word itself has occurred only once in a discourse, it enters into other structural relations at levels above the propositional.

This principle can be generalized beyond single words. Perfetti and Goldman (1974) found that recall of a sentence was higher when it was part of a paragraph than when it was in isolation. There are no processing time data in that case; but it is sensible to believe, as in the experiment reported here, that greater context produces less processing time unless the subject is explicitly required to make context judgments during encoding (Dooling, 1972; Mistler—Lachman, 1972). It is parsimonious to treat the sentence-memory effect of Perfetti and Goldman (1974) and the word-memory effect reported here within the same framework as explicit depth-of-processing experiments that manipulate instructions. There is nothing special about deep processing of language. It is a "natural" mode for ordinary language. The structure is in the discourse, and it is not a matter of processing time but of control of attention that may be partly determined by structural properties of discourse.

CONCLUSION AND SUMMARY

The foregoing sketch of sentence levels and processing is necessarily general, and detailed processing descriptions are notably absent. The most interesting proposal may be that levels of a sentence do not increase uniformly in opaqueness. The propositional level is particularly opaque, whereas higher semantic levels are often transparent and lower levels are typically transparent.

A second conclusion is that the cognitions that tap levels of language in their "purest" forms are found in tasks of language awareness, not in memory. Memory tasks will necessarily include information from more than one level and, more importantly, will bias toward semantic levels. Conscious control of attention on a particular level reveals the levels most directly, although they can be seen in comprehension and memory situations in interesting ways.

However, there seem to be empirical constraints on levels of comprehension and memory:

1. Levels are not reached simply as a function of processing time.

2. For single word units, some encoding tasks automatically select attention for a semantic level, effectively making it opaque.

3. In other encoding situations, particularly involving normal discourse, attention may be selected for higher semantic levels, effectively making word meaning transparent. Memory is a function of encoding context rather than task orientation.

Attentional selection (control processes) is the means for contacting normally opaque levels, and automatic (attention-free) processes are the means for contacting normally transparent levels. It remains to be seen how these processes are acquired by individuals and activated by discourse conditions.

ACKNOWLEDGMENTS

I am grateful to Thomas Scovel for some useful linguistic discussions and to Laura Bell, Susan Goldman, and Thomas Hogaboam for collaboration in the experiments that are described.

REFERENCES

Austin, J. L. *How to do things with words*. Oxford: Oxford University Press, 1962.

Bower, G. H. Mental imagery and associative learning. In L. W. Gregg (Ed.), *Cognition in learning and memory*. New York: Wiley, 1972.

Broadbent, D. E. *Perception and communication*. London: Pergamon Press, 1958.

Carroll, J. M., & Bever, T. G. Sentence comprehension: A case study in the relation of knowledge and perception. In E. C. Carterette & M. P. Friedman (Eds.), *Handbook of perception* (Vol. 7). New York: Academic Press, 1976.

Chafe, W. L. Discourse structure and human knowledge. In J. B. Carroll & R. U. Freedle (Eds.), *Language comprehension and the acquisition of knowledge*. Washington: V. H. Winston & Sons, 1972.

Craik, F. I. M., & Lockhart, R. S. Levels of processing: A framework for memory research. *Journal of Verbal Learning and Verbal Behavior*, 1972, *11*, 671−684.

Craik, F. I. M., & Tulving, E. Depth of processing and the retention of words in episodic memory. *Journal of Experimental Psychology, General*, 1975, *1*, 268−294.

Deutsch, J. A., & Deutsch, D. Attention: Some theoretical considerations. *Psychological Review*, 1963, *70*, 80−90.

de Villiers, J. G., & de Villiers, P. A. Competence and performance in child language: Are children really competent to judge? *Journal of Child Language*, 1974, *1*, 11−22.

Dooling, D. J. Some context effects in the speeded comprehension of sentences. *Journal of Experimental Psychology*, 1972, *93*, 56−62.

Elias, C., & Perfetti, C. A. Encoding task and recognition memory: The importance of semantic encoding. *Journal of Experimental Psychology*, 1973, *99*, 151−156.

Fillenbaum, S. *Syntactic factors in memory*. The Hague: Mouton Publishers, 1973.

Gleitman, L. R., & Gleitman, H. *Phrase and paraphrase: Some innovative uses of language*. New York: W. W. Norton Co., Inc., 1970.

Gleitman, L. R., Gleitman, H., & Shipley, E. The emergence of the child as grammarian. *Cognition*, 1972, *1*, 137−164.

Halliday, M. A. K. Notes on transitivity and theme in English: II. *Journal of Linguistics*, 1967, *3*, 199−244.

Halliday, M. A. K. Clause types and structural function. In J. Lyons (Ed.), *New horizons in linguistics*. Baltimore, Md.: Penguin Books, 1970.

Hockett, C. F. *A course in modern linguistics*. New York: Macmillan, 1958.

Hornby, P. Surface structure and presupposition. *Journal of Verbal Learning and Verbal Behavior*, 1974, *13*, 530−538.

Hyde, T. S., & Jenkins, J. J. Recall for words as a function of semantic, graphic, and syntactic orienting tasks. *Journal of Verbal Learning and Verbal Behavior*, 1973, *12*, 471−480.

Lamb, S. M. *Outline of stratificational grammar*. Washington, D.C.: Georgetown University Press, 1966.

Lesgold, A. M., & Perfetti, C. A. *The development of discourse processing skill: Levels of analysis*. Paper presented at the Society for Research in Child Development, New Orleans, March 1977.

Liberman, I. Y., Shankweiler, D., Fischer, F. W., & Carter, B. Explicit syllable and phoneme segmentation in the young child. *Journal of Experimental Child Psychology*, 1974, *18*, 201−212.

Lieberman, P. *Intonation and perception in language*. Cambridge, Mass.: MIT Press, 1967.

McCawley, J. D. The role of semantics in grammar. In E. Bach & R. R. Harms (Eds.), *Universals in linguistic theory*. New York: Holt, Rinehart and Winston, Inc., 1968.

McCawley, J. D. Where do noun phrases come from? (Unpublished revised version of paper.) In R. Jacobs & P. S. Rosenbaum (Eds.), *Readings in English transformation grammar*. Waltham, Mass.: Ginn & Co., 1970.

McNeill, D., & Lindig, K. The perceptual reality of phonemes, syllables, words and sentences. *Journal of Verbal Learning and Verbal Behavior*, 1973, *12*, 419−430.

Mistler−Lachman, J. L. Levels of sentence comprehension in processing of normal and ambiguous sentences. *Journal of Verbal Learning and Verbal Behavior*, 1972, *11*, 614−623.

Neisser, U. *Cognitive psychology*. Englewood Cliffs, N.J.: Prentice−Hall, 1967.

Olson, D., & Filby, N. On comprehension of active and passive sentences. *Cognitive psychology*, 1972, *3*, 361−381.

Perfetti, C. A., & Bell, L. Semantic, lexical and graphemic search by skilled and less-skilled young readers. In preparation.

Perfetti, C. A., & Goldman, S. Thematization and sentence retrieval. *Journal of Verbal Learning and Verbal Behavior*, 1974, *13*, 70−79.

Perfetti, C. A., Goldman, S. R., & Hogaboam, T. W. Word identification in context and reading skill. In preparation.

Perfetti, C. A., & Lesgold, A. M. Discourse comprehension and sources of individual differences. In P. Carpenter & M. Just (Eds.), *Cognitive processes in comprehension*. Hillsdale, N.J.: Lawrence Erlbaum Associates, 1977.

Perfetti, C. A., & Lesgold, A. M. Coding and comprehension in skilled reading. In L. B. Resnick & P. Weaver (Eds.), *Theory and practice of early reading*. Hillsdale, N.J.: Lawrence Erlbaum Associates, in press.

Pike, K. L. On systems of grammatical structure. *Proceedings of the Ninth International Congress of Linguistics, Cambridge, Massachusetts, 1962*. The Hague: Mouton, 1964.

Polanyi, M. *Personal knowledge: Towards a post-critical philosophy*. New York: Harper and Row, 1958.

Reichenbach, H. *Elements of symbolic logic*. New York: Macmillan, Co., 1947.

Rosner, J. Auditory analysis training with prereaders. *The Reading Teacher*, 1974, *27*, 379–384.

Sachs, J. S. Recognition memory for semantic and syntactic aspects of connected discourse. *Perception & Psychophysics*, 1967, *2*, 437–442.

Savin, H. B., & Bever, T. G. The nonperceptual reality of the phoneme. *Journal of Verbal Learning and Verbal Behavior*, 1970, *9*, 295–302.

Searle, J. *Speech acts: An essay in the philosophy of language*. New York: Cambridge University Press, 1969.

Shiffrin, R. M., & Schneider, W. Controlled and automatic human information processing: II. Perceptual learning, automatic attending, and a general theory. *Psychological Review*, 1977, *84*, 127–190.

Trager, G. L., & Smith, H. L., Jr. An outline of English structure. *Studies in linguistics, occasional papers, 1951*. Reprinted Washington, D.C.: American Council of Learned Societies, 1957.

van Dijk, T. A. Macro-structures and cognition. In P. Carpenter & M. Just (Eds.), *Cognitive processes in comprehension*. Hillsdale, N.J.: Lawrence Erlbaum Associates, 1977.

van Dijk, T. A., & Kintsch, W. Cognitive psychology and discourse. Recalling and summarizing stories. In W. U. Dressler (Ed.), *Trends in text linguistics*. New York and Berlin: De Gruyter, 1977.

9 Comprehension and Cognition: A State of the Art Inquiry

Janet L. Lachman and Roy Lachman
University of Houston

The theme of this conference is levels of processing, and we have been asked to discuss its possible relation to language comprehension. This is a difficult assignment, because the concept of processing levels has figured only minimally in language comprehension research and theory. There are several reasons for this lack of contact.

The "levels" concept (Craik & Lockhart, 1972) was proposed not as theory but as metatheory. It was intended as an alternative metaphor to the multistore models that figured so prominently in the short-term memory research of the 1960s. But psycholinguistics has operated for the most part outside the context of multistore models. Several multi*stage* models have been proposed (Clark & Chase, 1972; Glucksberg, Trabasso, & Wald, 1973; Olson & Filby, 1972; Trabasso, Rollins, & Shaughnessy, 1971), but these have been specific to the sentence–picture verification task.

Second, short-term memory and psycholinguistic researchers deal with memory in fundamentally different ways. Short-term memory studies have typically focused on correspondences between stimulus and recall, whereas in certain ways psycholinguistic experiments have concerned noncorrespondences. In the usual short-term memory study, the researcher measures people's ability to reproduce the stimulus exactly. Recall of items *similar* to the stimuli is seldom interesting in its own right; in fact, materials are ordinarily used that lend themselves as little as possible to such constructive activity on the subject's part. The reverse trend obtains in psycholinguistics, where comprehension has never

This chapter is based in part on Chapters 11 and 12 of R. Lachman, J. L. Lachman, and E. C. Butterfield. *Cognitive psychology and information processing: An introduction*. Hillsdale, N.J.: Lawrence Erlbaum Associates, in press.

been equated with exact recall. When a subject in a psycholinguistic experiment reproduces a sentence exactly, this is often considered to mask comprehension processes rather than to reveal them. Comprehension is viewed as changing the input somehow. Transformations, recodings, inferences, and integrations— these are the issues that motivate most studies of language processing. Small wonder then that psycholinguists have displayed minimal interest in the factor of processing levels, which influences the ability to render an exact reproduction of input units.

This difference in interests relates to the distinction Tulving (1972) has made between semantic and episodic memory. Language researchers have been relatively uninterested in episodic memory; to the extent that memory engages them, it is of a generally semantic sort. Levels of processing, in contrast, was introduced in the context of an episodic memory task (Craik, 1973), and it has proved difficult to extend beyond the laboratory paradigm in which it originated. The general structure of the task does not adapt readily to psycholinguistic questions; all but the "deepest" orienting tasks require subjects to deal with linguistic stimuli in ways that are quite unlike normal language comprehension. Thus, levels of processing seem to end just about where comprehension begins.

This observation accords with that of several conference participants, who have noted that "depth" of processing has often appeared synonymous with *semanticity* of processing. Orienting tasks that are considered to engender "deep" processing seem to require people to attend to the meaning of stimuli, whereas those that are "shallow" encourage subjects to treat the stimuli more as objects of a nonsymbolic sort. But anything that can fairly be called "comprehension" is semantically saturated; comprehension is as semantic as it can be. It does not make sense to order comprehension tasks, or performances, by semanticity. This does not mean, of course, that they cannot be ordered; they can even be ordered on a dimension called "depth" or "levels" (Mistler–Lachman, 1972, 1974). However, it is not clear what relationship, if any, obtains between this dimension and the one involved in levels-of-processing research and the theoretical analysis such research supports.

Charles Perfetti (Chapter 8, this volume) has offered a creative analysis of one way that "levels" might be used to dimensionalize various aspects of the comprehension process. His approach seems to emphasize levels as *automaticity,* a usage that is also reflected in the papers of Brown (Chapter 11) and Naus and Halasz (Chapter 12). We do not attempt to improve upon Perfetti's analysis here. Instead, we take this opportunity to examine the state of the art in information-processing approaches to language comprehension. This is a timely moment for such examination. On some issues, at least, there is broad consensus. Some new approaches are taking shape, with aspirations as formidable as the difficulties they face. At the same time, some sources of dissatisfaction exist, and some changes in the general information-processing framework may soon become necessary. How fundamental these changes may be is considered at the end of

the paper. We also consider points of contact between the research in comprehension and the concept of levels, though it must be said in advance that the
relationships tend to be relatively peripheral.

Much of what we say comes from two chapters on comprehension in our
forthcoming textbook on cognitive psychology (Lachman, Lachman, & Butterfield, in press). In this book, we have taken a consensual methodological approach to our discipline, making a deliberate effort to characterize what is
common to the work of "information-processing psychologists." We have
attempted to identify their shared pretheoretical ideas, intellectual antecedents,
and central analogies, as well as the more familiarly mentioned commitment to
scientific verification methods. We have constructed a case that these elements—
which Kuhn (1963) has collectively called a "paradigm" and Holton (1976) has
identified with "themata"—can substantially account for the class of assumptions and approaches that most members of the group would consider congenial.
Before it became fashionable to seek one's "roots," we found it necessary to
trace intellectual family trees of various lines of work. Figure 9.1 shows our

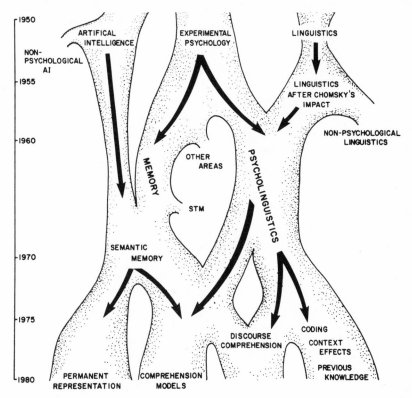

FIG. 9.1.   Roots: Intellectual antecedents of various areas of information-
processing psychology.

version of the sources of influence on today's research and thinking about the comprehension process; the contemporary areas discussed in this paper are at the lower edge of the figure. All these areas are at home within the information-processing approach. In our textbook, we have attempted to detail the major characteristics of this approach, of which there are very many. Probably the most conspicuous is the effort to exploit commonalities between information-processing machines and human information processors to extend our knowledge of human cognition. This effort accounts for the fact that information-processing models are sometimes called "computer metaphor models" (e.g., Brown, Chapter 11 this volume); however, we have identified two separate deployments of the so-called computer metaphor, of which only one is truly metaphorical (Lachman, Lachman & Butterfield, in press).

Within information-processing psychology, there seem to be two major sources of interest in comprehension. We have called them "mainstream psycholinguistics" and "global models." Mainstream psycholinguistics is a continuation of the psycholinguistic tradition of the 1960s. Global models constitute an extension of the work on semantic memory motivated by experimental psychology, artificial intelligence, and linguistics. The concerns of the two groups are rather different. In this paper, we first characterize the issues of interest in mainstream psycholinguistics. These primarily concern the form and content of semantically analyzed linguistic inputs. Then we describe the main issues facing the global modelers. Following this review, we consider the possible points of contact between the literature on comprehension and the issues associated with levels of processing. Finally, we take up criticisms of large-scale comprehension theory and relate these to the broad metatheoretical context in which complex theoretical statements are made and evaluated.

PART I: MAINSTREAM PSYCHOLINGUISTICS

Mainstream psycholinguistics has evolved in an orderly way from the work done in the 1960s on syntax. However, the issues have changed substantially between then and now. Empirical outcomes contributed importantly to the change. The experimental effect of syntactic variables, though reliable, proved easy to override with pragmatic and semantic factors (Gough, 1966; Olson & Filby, 1972; Wason, 1965). Psycholinguists' early preoccupation with syntax has given way to an interest in the extralinguistic factors that determine linguistic information processing. This trend has entailed a break with linguistics. Fifteen years ago, Katz and Fodor (1963) argued that no serious theory of semantics could account for extralinguistic factors such as context and world knowledge, and many psychologists conceded reluctant agreement. Today, however, it is probably the majority view that no serious psychological theory of the comprehension process can fail to take account of extralinguistic factors. Interestingly, linguistics itself is increasingly semantic in orientation and has become less monolithic since Chomsky's position has come under attack. In this context, psycholinguistics has shed its "follower" relationship to linguistics and has developed a character of its own.

Nevertheless, many traditions remain that reflect the extent of linguistic influence in the early life of the field. Despite a happy trend toward increasing research on discourse and narratives, most psycholinguistic studies continue the tradition of using the isolated sentence as the unit of analysis. Most contemporary psycholinguistic research on comprehension concerns an entity that we have called the *synthesized code*. Figure 9.2B illustrates the relation of the synthesized code to a number of other language-processing activities; it is the representation of the input available to the comprehender after the semantic content of a message has been extracted. We coined the term *synthesized code* to distinguish this particular representation from the permanent representation of knowledge that absorbs theorists of semantic memory. The synthesized code may be hardy, but it is still transient. In Tulving's (1972) terms, it is still part of the episodic memory system. This does not mean, however, that studies of the synthesized code necessarily belong in the same domain as studies of episodic memory. The difference is that psycholinguists are interested primarily in the formation of the code, which is heavily influenced by semantic memory processes, and the way in which it differs from the literal stimulus. Episodic memory studies tend to focus at least as much on retention of input codes, which

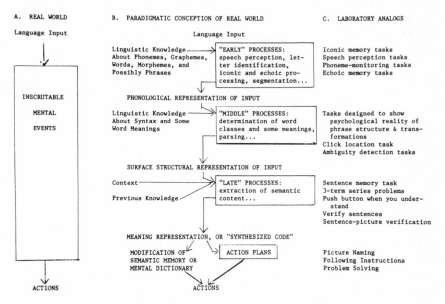

FIG. 9.2.   What we know for sure, hypothetical conception, and laboratory analogues of the comprehension process.

is measured by the subject's ability to produce or identify an exact copy of the input stimulus.

Several comments are in order about Fig. 9.2. Panel A is all we know with any confidence. Panel B is an information-processing-style effort to organize the emptiness of Panel A into researchable components, and Panel C lists some of the laboratory analogs of the various components that have been proposed. Panel B may or may not describe the modal view of the language-comprehension process, but it certainly captures some popular intuitions. "Early" processing events, including speech perception and segmentation, yield a phonological representation of the input (which presumably has some analogue in reading). The phonological representation, or its visual analogue, supplies input to "middle" processes concerned with structure. Word classes, and probably some word meanings, are ascertained, and sentence constituents are isolated. The activities result in a surface structural representation of the input message that in turn is semantically processed to extract meaning. Semantic processing (about which we know virtually nothing) ends with a semantically analyzed representation of the input; it is this representation that we have called the *synthesized code*. The synthesized code, in its turn, can impact permanent memory structures and effect additions or changes in permanent memory content; or it can give rise to action plans terminating in overt behavioral responses.

It might at first seem logical to identify the early, middle, and late processes of Panel B with levels of processing, and a superficial relationship may indeed exist. However, such an identification would require the assumption that the orienting tasks in "levels" studies serve to truncate comprehension processes, rather like sidelining freight cars partway to their destination. It seems likelier that the orienting tasks result not in partial processing for comprehension but in complete processing for some noncomprehension treatment of stimulus items. "Levels" effects may result from the extent to which these treatments approximate the facile, automatic comprehension processes with which nature has equipped the human species and to which that force has undoubtedly linked human memory capacities.

Panel B is not without difficulties. It is based on at least some empirical data; studies by Green (1975), Layton and Simpson (1975), and Sachs (1967) support certain aspects of it. However, it is supposed to be a flowchart and therefore unidirectional; and a distressing amount of retroaction seems to be possible among its major components. But in spite of its problems, Panel B does illustrate some common assumptions about the comprehension process; and it serves our present purpose of identifying the focus of much psycholinguistic research, the synthesized code. The chart conveys the information-processing assumption that a linguistic input must be continuously represented during comprehension but recoded for each subsystem that operates upon it. The synthesized code is the name we have given to one of these recodings, namely the one that follows semantic analysis or meaning extraction. Psycholinguistic research has addressed two questions of interest about the synthesized code. First, what is its form? Second, what are the factors that determine its content?

The Form of the Synthesized Code

Several characteristics of the synthesized code are important in identifying its form. First, the semantic content of the code can be recalled in paraphrase even when surface structures have been lost. Second, it does not require continued focal attention for its maintenance. Third, the synthesized code is likely to be in a form compatible with permanent memory. Conclusions about the form of the synthesized code, therefore, have implications for permanent memory structure. Two candidates for the form of the code have received substantial research attention: linguistic/propositional and imaginal formats.

A major assumption of linguistic/propositional theory is that the synthesized code can be represented by a string of languagelike symbols. Clark's (1969, 1974) theories nicely illustrate the operation of this assumption, which he coupled with a process model to explain three-term-series problem solution (Clark, 1969) and sentence−picture verification (Clark, 1974; Clark & Chase, 1972). The problem in the latter task has been to find a common format by which the knowledge expressed in a sentence and that conveyed by a picture could be represented for comparison. The format Clark adopted resembled the propositional forms of mathematical logic. Although Clark's own interests have moved on, a descendant of his theory is that of Carpenter and Just (1975). They also utilize logicallike propositions to represent the information extracted from both sentences and pictures, incorporating this representational format in a process model of the sentence−picture verification task.

An alternative view regarding the form of the synthesized code is that it is perceptually based. The best-known representative of this position is A. U. Paivio, who has suggested that at least some sentences are represented as images (Begg & Paivio, 1969). This position, called dual-coding theory, asserts that concrete sentences are represented as both images and verbal codes, whereas abstract sentences are represented by verbal codes alone. Begg and Paivio (1969) supported this argument in an experiment using a variation of Sachs's (1967) recognition−memory technique. Meaning changes were detected more often in concrete sentences, whereas wording changes were detected more often in abstract sentences. Dual-coding theory has produced quite a number of experiments, many challenging Begg and Paivio's methodology. The basic criticism has been that abstract sentences are initially harder to understand. This was the case in Begg and Paivio's experiment (Johnson, Bransford, Nyberg, & Cleary, 1972; Moeser, 1974; Pezdek & Royer, 1974) and is apparently true in general (Holmes & Langford, 1976). This fact may be a valid criticism of Begg and Paivio's interpretation, but in and of itself it is an empirical fact to be explained. Since concreteness and rated imageability facilitate comprehension, the subjective experience of imagery and the comprehension process cannot be totally unrelated. Other experimenters as well have found evidence that imagery plays a role in comprehension (Jorgensen & Kintsch, 1973; Thorndyke, 1975). Thus, although dual-coding theory may or may not be the correct interpretation of its role, imagery or some perceptually related factor cannot be dismissed as a factor in understanding language. The same general conclusion (both in the context of language and episodic memory for nonsentential verbal units) is suggested by the persistence of perceptual information in situations where task demands do not require it (e.g., Kolers, Chapter 17, this volume; Nelson, Chapter 3, this volume).

Imagery and propositional formats may appear to be direct competitors for the form of the synthesized code. In fact, they are not, since they have rather different epistemological status. Propositions generally serve as notational formalisms in which any theoretical content, including images, may in principle be expressed. Images are not notational. They generally are proffered as inferences or rationalizations from data. Pylyshyn (1973) has challenged the suitability of images for this role, whereas Kosslyn and Pomerantz (1977) have argued that he is wrong. Appropriateness aside, many psychologists have found the concept of imagery a useful one (e.g., Bower, 1972; Bugelski, 1970; Paivio, 1971). The implicit role images have played for these theorists is as a conceptual entity that accounts for their own subjective experiences as well as the reports and behavior of their subjects. Images do not therefore compete with propositions as *the* form of the synthesized code. However, both imagery theorists and propositional theorists would agree that the question of the code's form is an important one and that the information in the input must be represented in some format or other. Both therefore would be challenged by proponents of "direct perception" (Gibson, 1966; Shaw & Bransford, 1977), who would argue that representation is unnecessary to explain extraction of meaning from perception—including, presumably, linguistic stimuli. We have more to say on this issue later. For the time being, the question is not whether the synthesized code is "really" an image or a proposition. The question of interest is why the subjective experience of imagery is so closely tied to objective measures of comprehensibility.

The Content of the Synthesized Code

Several lines of work in mainstream psycholinguistics deal with the content of the synthesized code, particularly research on constructive processes, presupposi- tions, word meanings, and nonliteral comprehension. All these areas converge with striking clarity and unanimity on one conclusion: The knowledge a person has after processing a sentence cannot be characterized solely by reference to the literal content of the sentence. Constructive processes are ubiquitous in com- prehension, a claim that is supported more or less directly by scores of studies in the contemporary literature.

The most popular technique for demonstrating the constructive nature of com-prehension processes has been the sentence recognition—memory experiment. Bransford and Franks's (1971) now classic study used this technique to show that separately presented sentences "fuse" into a single, integrated semantic repre-sentation. Barclay (1973) made a very similar point; his sentences described ordered arrays. A number of studies (Bransford, Barclay, & Franks, 1972; Harris, 1974; Johnson, Bransford, & Solomon, 1973; Schweller, Brewer, & Dahl, 1976) have found high false-alarm rates to recognition distracters containing plausible inferences from presented sentences. If we assume that the subject interrogates the synthesized code in a recognition test, we must conclude that his or her previous knowledge and the inferences it supported figured in the initial formulation of that code. Interestingly, very similar work has been done using pictures as stimuli (Baggett, 1975; Jenkins, 1977) with entirely comparable results.

Linguistic presuppositions give rise to a special kind of inference. A sentence such as *Professor Craik has stopped assaulting students* presupposes that Pro-fessor Craik did at one time assault students, and it asserts that he has now ceased this nefarious practice. Hornby (1974) has shown that factual errors in pre-supposed information are less easily detected than those in asserted information. In other words, it would be easier to reject the example sentence above if Pro-fessor Craik still assaults students than it would be if he had never done so. This observation suggests that the normal comprehension strategy is to assume or infer that presupposed information is true. If in fact it is false, reasoning pro-cesses other than those normally invoked in comprehension may be necessary. Hornby's work is supported by Loftus's (Loftus, 1975; Loftus & Zanni, 1975), in which people's recall of a fast-moving visual event is influenced by the wording of questions asked immediately after the event. Whether correct or not, "facts" presupposed by the questions tend later to be recalled as true of the event itself. Presumably, Loftus's subjects "recall" not the visual experience but an inference they made from someone else's characterization of the event. This, incidentally, may be an interesting example of linguistically originated content appearing subjectively as a visual image.

So far, it might seem that constructive processes merely follow literal inter-pretations, appending something to literal meanings. However, a group of cued-recall studies suggest that literal meaning may itself depend on constructive processes and extralinguistic knowledge. These studies (Anderson & Ortony, 1975; Barclay, Bransford, Franks, McCarrell, & Nitsch, 1974; Johnson, Doll, Bransford, & Lapinski, 1974) have primarily concerned word meaning and have adopted the logic of studies on encoding specificity (see, e.g., Tulving, Chapter 19, this volume). Although a word has many nuances of meaning, only some appear to be encoded. Only those that are encoded constitute highly effective retrieval cues. When a word is embedded in a sentence, which aspects are actually encoded appears to depend on the total meaning of the sentence; this in turn depends on a comprehender's knowledge of the world. Here is another challenge to theorists of comprehension. How can the words in a sentence determine the sentence's meaning at the same time the sentence determines the meaning of its constituent words? It is clear that this constitutes a problem for theories of word meaning and therefore any more encompassing comprehension theory. We return to this matter in connection with the global models.

Finally, it is possible for a comprehender to transcend literal meaning entirely. As comprehenders, we have known this for a long time, but as psychologists we have only just discovered it. Fillenbaum (1974) asked his subjects to paraphrase peculiar sentences such as *Don't print that or I won't sue you.* Despite explicit instructions not to improve on the sentences, Fillenbaum's subjects normalized them anyway—in many cases apparently without realizing it. Clark and Lucy (1975) studied conversationally conveyed requests such as *Must you do that?* and found that people had no difficulty in responding to the conveyed rather than the literal meaning of such requests.

Following up the Clark and Lucy (1975) experiment, Clark and Haviland (Clark, 1978; Clark & Haviland, 1977; Haviland & Clark, 1974) have begun to formulate a theory of conversational comprehension, which requires attention to the role of both speaker and listener. Both are conceived as parties to a sort of contract, called the *given-new contract,* which makes available to the listener a particular comprehension strategy called the *given-new strategy.* The strategy involves isolating that part of the message the speaker thinks the listener already knows and seeking a node in memory corresponding to that information. The new information is integrated with the already-known information, and if the product is implausible in context, the comprehender checks to see if a plausible nonliteral interpretation exists. The theory is still in its infancy, but it does a very fine job of integrating much of the literature on constructive processes, inference, presuppositions, and nonliteral comprehension. It is easily the most comprehensive theory ever to emerge from mainstream psycholinguistics.

Finally, a rather new line of work on narratives and discourses, like the single-sentence research, emphasizes the importance of previous knowledge in the comprehension process. One kind of previous knowledge is *structural*. People may know the structures of well-formed stories and rely on these to help them identify the structural components of passages as they read. Several investigators (Rumelhart, 1975; Thorndyke, 1975, 1977; van Dijk, 1976) are attempting to develop "grammars" for text—rules by which discourse constituents are isolated. And Kintsch (1974, 1976), about whom we presently say more, is attempting to develop a theory of the propositions that inhere explicitly and implicitly in passages. A second kind of knowledge is *thematic*. People's previous knowledge, activated by a title or topic, can impose order and structure on otherwise chaotic language (Bransford & Johnson, 1972; Dooling & Lachman, 1971). Themes also influence people's recognition and recall of the individual words in a passage (Pompi & Lachman, 1967). Studies of thematic knowledge pick up a tradition begun by Bartlett (1932), who used the concept of *schemata* to designate previous knowledge that shapes comprehension and memory for novel discourses. The schema is a useful and powerful concept; however, it must be invoked with care. As Brown (Chapter 11, this volume) has noted, the notion does lend itself to indiscriminate application and can be used to cover previous knowledge of everything from pencils to life-styles. And the process by which schemata might be formed is in need of specification. Nevertheless, the potential utility of the concept is attested by the fact that schemata are being rediscovered not only in psychology but in other disciplines as well. In artificial intelligence, they go under such names as *scripts* (Schank, 1972) and *frames* (Minsky, 1975). In anthropology, they are being used in ethnology in ways that may prove far more viable than componential analysis for getting at meaning (Agar, 1973; Metzger & Williams, 1963).

To summarize the current state of mainstream psycholinguistics, then, most research concerns the form and content of the entity we have named the synthesized code. Although it can be conveniently represented propositionally, there appear to be perceptual dimensions to its form that are not well understood. With regard to the content of the code, there is wide agreement that previous knowledge is heavily implicated, and a number of demonstrations support this consensus. It remains to be seen what psycholinguistics will do with this fundamental insight. Hopefully, the mechanisms by which previous knowledge is brought to the comprehension process can be studied in advance of understanding how previous knowledge is structured and maintained. This latter understanding may take centuries.

A group that is working on the formidable task of characterizing previous knowledge, and its relationship to new linguistic inputs, are the global modelers. Many of these theorists come from a somewhat different tradition than mainstream psycholinguistics. Their work clearly illustrates the difficulty and complexity of characterizing the previous knowledge a comprehender brings to the comprehension process. Let us now consider some of the issues global modelers face in their efforts.

PART II: GLOBAL MODELS

Global modelers are distinguished by the scope of the processes they wish to model. All are responsive to the research just described, recognizing that comprehension of individual language units such as sentences cannot be characterized independently of the knowledge background of the comprehender. Therefore, global models are designed to account for the process whereby new sentences (or passages) relate to what is already in permanent memory. Their scope is broader than that of psycholinguistic theories, which generally deal with the synthesized code, and are silent about structural aspects of permanent memory. Global models are also broader than theories of semantic memory (e.g., Collins & Quillian, 1970; Smith, Shoben, & Rips, 1974), whose authors have limited themselves to problems they consider tractable and whose support has come largely from data in the subject–predicate verification task.

The first global models were developed in artificial intelligence (Quillian, 1968; Winograd, 1972). However, the first such model whose authors were primarily identified with experimental psychology was HAM (Anderson & Bower, 1973). The others we include in our category are the models of Schank (1972, 1975), Kintsch (1974, 1976), the LNR group (Norman & Rumelhart, 1975; Rumelhart, Lindsay, & Norman, 1972), Frederiksen (1975), Anderson (1976), and Miller and Johnson–Laird (1976). No well-specified inclusion rule generated this list, which we view as a "fuzzy set" whose members differ in degree of similarity to a prototype. As is common, no single exemplar matches our prototype. The prototypical theory contains a propositional system for representing word meanings, the larger class of concepts, and the relationships among concepts. It has a parsing device and control systems. It is partly implemented as a computer simulation, can answer questions intelligently, and processes sentences in the context of natural-language discourse. It has generated some empirical research and is responsive to at least some extant data. Our personal prototype also utilizes network notation, though yours may not. As you can see, none of the exemplars has all these characteristics. Nevertheless, they have something in common that led us to consider them in the same category— probably the ultimate necessity of modeling the entire comprehension process and the permanent memory that supports it.

Most of the global models are book length, containing a forbidding amount of detail. With respect to these details, the models are almost completely non-comparable. Even at a less detailed level, it is difficult to compare and contrast the models, because they differ widely in emphasis, degree of development, and direction of development. What is absolutely central to one model, exquisitely detailed, and lovingly researched, may be dismissed, left to the future, or treated as a minor assumption by others. Nevertheless, commonalities exist in terms of the motivations, central assumptions, and strategies of the modelers; and certain major issues face them all at an early stage.

With respect to motivation, most of the global modelers are committed to sufficiency, which in this context means that they want their models to do justice to the range of things people actually *do,* particularly with language. The majority of the global modelers have a common conceptual antecedent in Quillian's Teachable Language Comprehender, and most continue to incorporate ideas from artificial intelligence as well as linguistics, philosophy, and experimental psychology. Most have adopted the rather similar strategy of first attempting to define the type and range of information in the permanent memory, then trying to develop a system that is capable of encoding and representing that information. The next step is the development of interface systems—the mechanisms by which the permanent memory interacts with the environment. The modelers all assume that permanent information is stored in a representational system and that incoming information makes contact with that system.

The greatest attention at present is devoted to developing adequate theoretical representational systems. The modelers agree that a representational system is needed, and they generally agree about what must be represented. Most of the modelers' attention, therefore, is directed at two issues that immediately arise in the context of the representational problem: First, how is world knowledge represented? Second, how are word meanings represented?

Formal Representation of World Knowledge

Three major requirements seem to have motivated the global modelers in the construction of systems for representing world knowledge. First, the system must be sufficient—capable of representing the range of things human beings actually know. Second, it must support efficient search and retrieval, given an immense amount of material to store. There seems to be general agreement (Bower, 1975; Frijda, 1972) that human memory is content-addressable; however, there is less agreement on the units that supply the locative information. Third, the system must be capable of efficient, high-speed inference. Some of the global models are, in addition, capable of accretion; some can be extended to work across different natural languages; and some are able to convert simple ideas into complex ones. Despite these impressive accomplishments, however, none has emerged as a major unifying theoretical force, as the theories of Hull and Chomsky did in their time. This may result from their newness, from problems intrinsic to the models, or from the increasing diversity of the field as a whole.

Several of the global models are described in network notation. The nodes and links of a network lend readability and flexibility to the theory and permit retrieval through the mechanism of spreading activation of nodes adjacent to the one corresponding to an input. Use of this notation does not itself have theoretical force, of course, although it can generate genuine theoretical issues such as the types of links and nodes admitted by the theory, strength values assigned to links, and so on.

All the global models feature propositional representation. The propositions used reflect the influence of Fillmore's case grammar, propositional logic, and predicate calculus. Propositions are attractive because they constitute an entity that can stand in a type-token relationship to surface structures, thereby accounting for the obvious fact of paraphrase. Further, they can capture ''gist'' independently of specific words, as people have been shown to do (Bransford, Barclay, & Franks, 1972; Pompi & Lachman, 1967; Sachs, 1967). However, propositional representation is not problem-free. For one thing, the formal aspects of propositional notation come from mathematical logic, where propositions were intended to represent only a subset of the ideas that could be expressed in natural language. Formation rules, also part of the formal systems, served to define well-formed propositions. In the context of comprehension theory, however, the requirement of sufficiency obviates the function of the formation rules, since any idea that can be expressed in natural language must be considered well formed in a system that is sufficient for representing human knowledge. Kintsch has recently acknowledged the informal and intuitive nature of his formation rules (Kintsch & van Dijk, 1975), but he is not alone. None of the other global modelers can specify their formation rules precisely, either. The propositional theories of Clark (1974) and of Carpenter and Just (1975) have been criticized for the excessive flexibility such intuitive representations afford. Tanenhaus, Carroll, and Bever (1976) have pointed out that alternative propositional representations exist for a particular surface structure, and the theorists have no way of specifying antecedently which will predict the language performance of an experimental subject. This criticism applies to any theorist who adopts the theoretical representation of propositional logic or predicate calculus without explicit rules of formation. It remains to be seen whether the global modelers will solve this fundamental problem. In view of the newness of the models, many thorny problems are naturally to be expected; it is too soon to judge whether more stability of form can be introduced into the proposition without losing its potential for richness of content.

The Representation of Word Meaning

Since all the modelers are concerned with language processing, all must have some way of representing the meaning of words. Most consider the surface properties of words—phonemic and graphemic features—of rather peripheral interest. And of course all the modelers reject the notion of reference as a complete characterization of word meanings. The theorist's task, then, is to characterize the abstract conceptual entities to which words presumably direct comprehenders. Two related problems affect the effort to characterize the internal lexicon. First, word meaning is volatile. As several previously mentioned experiments have shown, linguistic context appears to determine which of the nuances of a word's meaning is activated in the course of comprehension (Anderson & Ortony, 1975; Barclay et al., 1974; Johnson et al., 1974). The question is, should all the nuances that might potentially constitute part of the meaning of a word in some particular usage be stored as an integral part of the word's meaning? There are convincing arguments in the negative. In a powerful critique of Katz and Fodor's (1963) semantic theory, Bolinger (1965) demonstrated how intractable such a dictionary would be. The opposite extreme is to include only those meaning components that are always present. However, Richard Anderson and his colleagues (Anderson, Pichert, Goetz, Schallert, Stevens, & Trollip, 1976) have cited convincing examples of words whose "core" meaning is, if not nonexistent, at least very difficult to characterize. To represent only core meanings may for some words be to represent no meaning at all, which of course will not do; people know what words mean. A range of solutions exists between representing only meanings that are always present and all meanings that are ever present; which solution is the most satisfactory remains to be resolved.

A second problem concerns the need for semantic primitives, and on this issue the modelers clearly differ. Most of the modelers would agree that some words can be defined in terms of more primitive meaning components. *Sell,* for example, involves the notions of *exchange for money.* But further decomposition is possible into transfers of possession of money and some other commodity, voluntarily and permanently, and so on. The amount of decomposition possible may be limited only by the imaginations of linguists and philosophers. The disagreement is not that some of this *can* be done but how much of it comprehenders actually do, and therefore how much of it ought to inhere in the dictionaries of one's model. On the one extreme are Schank (1972, 1976b) and Norman and Rumelhart (1975), who are attempting to break most or all surface verbs into one or more meaning components. At the other extreme are Anderson (1976) and Kintsch (1974), who work with the words themselves, sidestepping for the moment the matter of how they are to be defined in the representational system's dictionary. Kintsch argues that people can, upon demand, engage in semantic decomposition; but under what circumstances they do so and how much they do is a matter that will not be resolved by fiat. The problem of word meaning is one that has confronted all the global modelers and been satisfactorily resolved by none. It remains as a central issue with which information-processing theories of comprehension must wrestle.

The Interface Problem

Whatever the representational structures in a global model are, there must be some way for a natural-language utterance to make contact with them. There must also be a way for the system to express its knowledge in comprehensible natural-language utterances. As yet, there has not been a great deal of empirical attention to these interfacing mechanisms on the global modelers' part. In contrast, it appears that most mainstream psycholinguistic research concerns the interface problem on the input side. It may be that relatively well-specified theories of synthesized-code content (such as Clark's may eventually become) will be adopted, or modified by global theories as interfaces.

Summary

The major issues confronting global models, then, are the twin representational problems: How are word meanings represented, and how is permanent knowledge represented? In addition, there are issues concerning the mechanisms by which inputs contact previous knowledge, how inferences are made, and how knowledge is expressed in sentential form.

Global models have not been accorded universal adulation. There are several reasons for the mixed reception they have received. One is the simple fact that they are overwhelming—book length, replete with detail, often containing idiosyncratic notation, and rapidly changing. Their scope may be sufficiently reminiscent of the neobehaviorist age of theory to activate some of the metatheoretical biases that accompanied rejection of behavioristic psychology. These are relatively pragmatic reasons; however, various global models have also been criticized on more principled grounds. The criticisms are not specific to the current crop of models but extend to any comprehension theory that can do justice to the "Inscrutable Mental Events" of Fig. 9.2A.

We take up these criticisms when we evaluate the state of the art in the study of comprehension. For the moment, let us consider what points of contact there may be between the literature we have reviewed and the various interpretations that have been made of "levels of processing."

PART III: LANGUAGE COMPREHENSION AND LEVELS OF PROCESSING

Tulving (Chapter 19, this volume) has interpreted "levels" studies as a special case of encoding specificity, and we have mentioned studies (e.g., Anderson & Ortony, 1975) that interpret word meanings in a similar light. Encoding specificity studies and those concerned with word meaning differ in their degree of concern with retrieval processes; but both share the view that contextual factors determine what aspects of the literal stimulus are actually encoded and therefore available for access during retrieval.

Several contributors (Anderson & Reder, Chapter 18, this volume; Bransford, Franks, Morris, & Stein, Chapter 15, this volume; Jacoby & Craik, Chapter 1, this volume) have espoused the view that "levels" might best be viewed as elaboration of processing. Such a treatment of levels comports well with network models of semantic memory that work by means of spreading activation, such as ACT (Anderson, 1976). Anderson and Reder have shown how elaboration in ACT might function to enhance retrievability.

It is not clear what relationship obtains between the early, middle, and late processes of Fig. 9.2B and levels of processing. One relationship is clearly not to be assumed, however. "Shallow" must not be equated with "early" and "deep" with "late." This would turn levels of processing into a multistage model of just the type it was intended to replace. Panel B is strictly a description of input processes, whereas "levels" cannot be separated from the subsequent retrievability of inputs. This fact makes it very hard to relate the "levels" of levels of processing to the hypothetical component processes of Panel B.

Although language research and levels of processing are difficult to relate in specific ways, in a broader sense one relationship is clear: Both are permeated by the problem of representation. We have described the issues surrounding the form and content of the synthesized code, which is fundamentally concerned with how new inputs are represented. We have presented the two aspects of the representation problem that currently confront the global models—representing permanent knowledge and word meaning. In many of the papers presented at this conference, the fundamental question concerns what the subject in a typical episodic memory experiment encodes and subsequently retrieves. "Encoding," of course, implies "representing" something that can later be interrogated and more or less accurately reproduced. The common concern of language comprehension and episodic memory researchers with representation reflects their shared commitment to central assumptions of information-processing psychology. Thus, although the theoretical relationship between episodic memory and language comprehension is currently obscure, the pretheoretical ideas that guide research in both domains are fully compatible.

PART IV: EVALUATION OF RESEARCH AND THEORY IN LANGUAGE COMPREHENSION

Reviewers of the Kintsch (Schank, 1976a) and LNR (Chi, 1976) global models have asserted that there is little or no relationship between data and theory. HAM and ACT have been similarly attacked, in the lobbies if not in the literature. This criticism is worth discussing in detail, for it is likely to be said of any theory of comprehension that is broad enough to account for any substantial amount of extralaboratory language behavior. Any nonsimplistic account of the language-comprehension process will be similar to Fig. 9.2B in that it will contain a veritable zoo of hypothetical structures and processes. These will be expressed in one or another formalism, whose logico–mathematical forms may be viewed as reflecting mental structures and mechanisms. "Relation of theory to experiment" is basically a matter of how to test these inferred entities experimentally— an issue that must eventually confront all psychologists for whom theories of the language comprehension process are important. This almost surely includes the vast majority of scholars cited in this paper, whether mainstream psycholinguist or global modeler, whether empirically or theoretically oriented, whether an advocate of propositional or imaginal theory. Since the global models are the first comprehensive language theories since Skinner's—and he chose not to regard his speculative mechanisms as "entities"—the problem has lain dormant for a while. The appearance of several comprehensive theories and the promise of more brings the issue once again to center stage. How are the hypothetical micro-processes of multicomponent theory related to observable behavior? What kind of experiment constitutes a satisfactory empirical test?

Prudent theorists are usually obscure on these points, because they usually do not know what ontological claims to make for their inferred mechanisms nor what would constitute empirical corroboration. This problem is neither new nor unique to psychology. Competent scholars still disagree on how to evaluate hypothetical mechanisms and inferred structures by means of observable events. Anderson (1976) has taken a strong stand on this issue in his introduction to ACT, concluding that it is impossible to uniquely identify internal processes and structures. Let us place the issue of inferred entities in a broader perspective, because it arises in any science that deals with complex systems.

The atom of contemporary quantum theory and the molecule of turn-of-the-century physical chemistry have been reified to strong ontological claims about the subvisible microscopic structure of material things. At the end of the 19th century, the ontological status of atoms and molecules was no more secure than that of our links, nodes, and propositions. In fact, such hypothetical particles stood at the center of a long and bitter controversy that had forced the scientific giants of the middle and late 19th century into opposite, warring camps. It is instructive to consider the evidentiary basis on which the controversy was resolved and the way cleared for the reification of atoms and molecules. In 1905, Einstein developed a theory explaining the phenomenon of Brownian motion, a theory that was subsequently supported by the experiments of Perrin. The theory entailed a concrete mechanical conception of individual molecular agitation and is said to have reestablished the reality of molecules and atoms as material particles (Polanyi, 1964, p. 144). Two aspects of this event in physical science are important from our present viewpoint. First, during half a century of debate on the molecular hypothesis, it was never clear what kind of evidence would ultimately support an ontological claim for molecules and atoms. Brownian motion was not new; the phenomenon had been known for a long time. But no one knew that it would figure in the resolution of the debate over the reality of subvisible particles. It was nothing directly aimed at that issue that finally resolved it. Einstein's theory and the subsequent experiments were undertaken to explain Brownian motion. The theory assumed the existence of subvisible particles; and its success as a theory swept its assumptions in with it. A second important point about the Einsteinian resolution is that the theory, and the experiments that supported it, were not decisive in and of themselves. The end of the controversy reflected a collective heuristic judgment that, in the context of the cumulative data and theory of almost 50 years, Einstein's work supported an ontological claim.

In psychology, we are in no better position than the physical scientists of the last century to know in advance what kind of experimental evidence will ultimately appear decisive in supporting (or rejecting) ontological claims for our theoretical entities. We are therefore not able to make definitive statements about how well the global models relate to experimentation. Global comprehension theories, like their counterparts in other fields, will not be confirmed directly by experiment. Heuristic judgments by information-processing psychologists will eventually consign them to prosperity or oblivion. Some may survive; some will certainly fall. Experimental outcomes will weigh in the judgments, but so will formal adequacy, sufficiency, plausibility, and other values—with different practitioners assigning different weights to the various factors. Theory choice is not a totally canonical process; accounts that describe it as such are reconstructions or idealizations of what actually happens. This is not to say that the process is frivolous, random, or unscientific. It is only to say that a preponderance of evidence of an antecedently unspecifiable sort is responsible for the conclusions of a science, although the conclusions of individual scientists may be reached somewhat differently. Weizenbaum (1976) has recently gone as far as to conclude that all scientific claims, even those based directly on mathematics and formal logic, are fundamentally acts of persuasion. This conclusion may sit badly with some of our colleagues; however, it is consistent with some well-thought-out views of the scientific enterprise. We cannot but agree with the conclusion. Parenthetically, we might notice that levels of processing made a significant impact on the field in this regard. Although the levels approach itself has not gained a strong foothold, its originators (Craik & Lockhart, 1972) argued persuasively that an alternative to multistore models was needed. The central role of such models has been greatly diminished as a result of such argumentation, though no "definitive experimental proof" has ever been, or ever can be, offered.

The next question is, how likely is it that the global models or their descendants will become widely accepted as adequate accounts of the comprehension process? An answer to this question requires both a consideration of the state of development of the models themselves and an assessment of the well-being of the information-processing assumptions with which they are so closely identified.

The global models are still in a very early stage of development—so early that they might better be termed "experiments in conceptualization." They may be testing the limits of the information-processing approach to cognition. Information processing provides a framework of assumptions, a set of concepts, a language, and central analogies within which testable hypotheses can be formulated. The global modelers have trained their sights on the central issues of human psychology that have been waiting around for centuries for someone to develop adequate conceptual tools to grapple with them. By trying to formulate theories of these issues within the information-processing paradigm, the global modelers may reveal whether our approach has at last supplied these tools. In a sense, this reverses the usual direction of the relationship between the themata of a scientific community and its research problems. Normally, pretheoretical ideas suggest problem areas. "Buffer" storage, such as iconic and echoic memories, capacity limitations, control processes, and many issues from the memory literature are examples of problems suggested by central information-processing analogies. The issues addressed by the global models contrast sharply with these. They are not the province of any particular approach; they are the timeless questions humans have asked about their own minds. The questions have meaning to everyone, not only to those schooled in the extant experimental literature; but it is not altogether obvious how our information-processing paradigm constrains our attempts to research them. The global modelers seem to be attempting to force an answer. If none is forthcoming, the rise of the global models may sow the seeds of the next revolution. We do not mean to say that the modelers themselves define their activities this way; quite the contrary—we should expect that many would be surprised at our characterization. Nevertheless, this will be one outcome of their collective effort.

Obviously, if the information-processing approach is abandoned, the current group of global models will very likely become obsolete with it. Despite some setbacks, we do not sense deep enough dissatisfaction with information-processing psychology to anticipate its incipient demise. However, two developments in the field seem likely to prove important to the future of information processing: One is the call for increasing links with biology, and the other is a quite fundamental challenge to the central concept of representation.

Information-processing psychology typically parallels human cognition to aspects of nonliving systems. Such parallels have been drawn with communication devices (Miller, 1951), the mathematical theory of communication (Garner, 1962, 1974; Shannon, 1948), control theory (Powers, 1973), finite theory of automata (Hunt, 1971; Suppes & Rottmayer, 1974), artificial intelligence programs (Newell & Simon, 1972; Schank, 1972, 1975), and an entire class of computer programming analogies (e.g., Atkinson & Shiffrin, 1968; Haber, 1969). These sources of hypotheses about human intellectual functioning contrast sharply with those of our behaviorist predecessors, whose theories of learning relied on assumed parallels between humans and other species. Since the information-processing revolution, biology has been a rather unfashionable source of ideas about cognitive processes. Efforts to relate cognitive processes to human neurology have been regarded as naively premature. The phylogeny of the species, except insofar as it presumably rendered cognitive processes efficient and self-regulating, has been thoroughly ignored. Ontogeny, or developmental psychology, appears to be viewed as something of a camp follower—drawing on the ideas developed in the study of adult cognition but doing little to shape those ideas.

This aspect of the information-processing approach has been criticized by several groups. For example, some developmental psychologists complain that the paradigm's preoccupation with system architecture leads to an underestimation of the importance of growth and change (see, e.g., Brown, Chapter 11, this volume). Ecological psychologists (e.g., Shaw & Bransford, 1977) object to the mechanistic aspect of the models, suggesting that fundamental aspects of human cognition derive from a meaningful and dynamic interaction between organism and environment. Since information-processing models tend not to characterize the environment, in the view of such theorists something essential is sure to be missing from these models.

It is possible that the critics have a point and that our preference for analogies with nonliving systems has deprived us of potential insights and sources of constraint on our theories. For example, psycholinguistics expended a great deal of effort on the "psychological reality" of various aspects of transformational grammar. Many of the questions that were asked and expensively researched entirely ignored the matter of what language was designed to do for its users. The ideal speaker–hearer was conceived as a kind of code-breaking automaton equipped only with language knowledge—a complete grammar and dictionary. This view, which was explicit in the semantic prototheory of Katz and Fodor (1963), left unclear why the ideal speaker–hearer might wish to break the code and precluded him or her from interpreting pidgin language, baby talk, metaphorical language, and incorrect syntax. The ability to interpret such aberrant forms seems incidental to one who considers the heart of language use to be the breaking of well-formed codes. But if one views the heart of language use to be the conveyance of largely shared ideas, such abilities become central and correct grammatical structures appear rather unessential. The deduction of mental structures from the study of correct grammatical structures then appears somewhat misguided; and in fact, psycholinguists have turned their recent attention largely to semantic issues.

Interestingly, however, the effort to capture semantic content is still guided by analogies with inanimate systems. The propositional forms that have been adopted by the global models come from logical systems implementable as automata. A central problem for the modelers, as we have said, is to extend these systems to encompass all the ideas that humans can encode, even though the systems were only designed to describe the logically consistent ones. An account of all human conceptualization may require theories of inconsistent logic. Such theories might require much closer attention to the possible function of reasoning, inference, and world knowledge in the phylogeny of the species. Consistent logic may be a by-product rather than a central aspect of human beings' way of knowing—which must have arisen in a context where philosophical ruminations had less survival value than pragmatically useful cognitive skills.

The developmentalist's complaint that information-processing approaches are insensitive to ontogenetic issues may also have more than a grain of truth. Whatever the adult cognitive system is like, it emerged in some orderly fashion from that of a child. Constraints on possible cognitive organization in adulthood therefore exist from ontogenesis. The system may literally be organized in just such a way as to foster growth and change; alternatively, it may not. But if it is, we will be a long time discovering this fact with our usual habits of thought about mental structures.

These criticisms seem to come together under a general call for more active incorporation of biological considerations than has been our custom in our theorizing about cognition. Such a call is not a fundamental challenge to the information-processing approach, however; it might even be considered an extension of it. Posner (1975a, 1975b), who is clearly a sympathetic insider, suggests that the time is ripe to integrate neurology into our cognitive theories. Such a widening of the information-processing approach could be undertaken without strain on the basic assumptions, pretheoretical ideas, analogies, and methods currently in use.

There is, however, one challenge to the approach that is indeed fundamental, in that it strikes at the very heart of information-processing approaches to cognition. This is the assertion by proponents of "direct perception" that the concept of representation is wrong (Shaw & Bransford, 1977). We have shown how central representation is to information-processing views of the language comprehension process. It is equally central to information-processing views of pattern recognition and memory, which like the language comprehension literature, consider the important questions to involve matching of input data to previously stored data. Many of the questions that are currently the focus of much research effort in memory, attention, pattern recognition, and language make little sense without the notion of representation. Many researchers find Haber's (1969) account thoroughly congenial:

> Information-processing analysis attempts to look for correlations between contents of the stimulus and contents of the responses measured at various times after the stimulation begins. By examining these correlations some notions can be gained of the properties of the flow of information in the nervous system, especially regarding the content of that information at any given point. . . .
>
> What is assumed is that if the appropriate operations could be devised, it should be possible to sample and examine the contents of stimulation at every point in time, and at every level in the nervous system, [p. 2].

The "contents of stimulation" must, of course, be a representation—perhaps continuously recoded—of the stimulus information. To the extent that Haber's account is descriptive of the assumptions and goals of information-processing researchers, then, the challenge to representation is a strike at the heart of the paradigm.

How successful it will be can only be guessed at this time. The theorists who argue that representation is unnecessary offer an alternative, ecological approach that has been most extensively developed in the area of perception (Gibson 1966, 1977). However, the approach does not extend to memory in any simple and straightforward fashion; it will take considerable effort to show how it can guide memory researchers in formulating theories and experiments. It is very hard to think about remembering without postulating something that spans the time between an experience and a memory for that experience. That "something" is currently considered to be a representation. The ecological approach may well impact the kind of properties we assign to the representation, and perhaps it will guide us in thinking about what kinds of things people are capable of representing. But it will be an uphill climb to convince the field that the whole concept of representation must go.

The climb would be less steep if there were widespread dissatisfaction with the conceptual apparatus of information processing. We have argued that theories are validated consensually, not canonically; the claim can be made even more strongly for the conceptual guides inherent in paradigms or themata. An alternative approach, even a good one, will be much less likely to gain a foothold if the practitioners of the science are satisfied with the progress that has been made and are optimistic about the future. Approaches fall as much from the weight of repeated failure as from the availability of worthwhile alternatives. Problems that are manifestly important prove unapproachable or unresolvable; a central kind of experiment consistently comes out wrong; "trivial" experimental variations consistently reverse experimental outcomes; theory does not develop. Were these problems widespread in information-processing psychology, the field would be full of "shoppers" looking for new approaches. As it happens, however, normal science in cognition appears to be moving smoothly along. There is no accumulation of experimental dead ends to suggest that we are asking our questions the wrong way. Researchers are not at a loss to find plausible information-processing models to explain their results. The assumption that human cognition has important correspondences with computational systems has served well; it is extremely rich and its full potential remains to be tapped. We therefore do not expect profound changes in approach for some time to come. However, we do think the ecological approach may contribute importantly to the direction information processing will take. We can make good use of reminders from its proponents that the human cognitive system developed in the context of natural selection and that it evolved interactively with an environment, many of whose properties are known or knowable. This perspective may, in turn, lead to a greater interest in using what is known about child development to guide theories of adult cognition.

In the relatively brief space alloted us, we have touched on many issues that are central to the scientific study of cognition, which includes language and memory as well as a number of other topics. Much of the treatment has been briefer than we would have liked; however, we shall have more to say on these matters.

REFERENCES

Agar, M. *Ripping and running*. New York: Academic Press, 1973.

Anderson, J. R. *Language, memory, and thought*. Hillsdale, N.J.: Lawrence Erlbaum Associates, 1976.

Anderson, J. R., & Bower, G. H. *Human associative memory*. Washington, D.C.: V. H. Winston & Sons, 1973.

Anderson, R. C., & Ortony, A. On putting apples into bottles—a problem of polysemy. *Cognitive Psychology,* 1975, *7,* 167–180.

Anderson, R. C., Pichert, J. W., Goetz, E. T., Schallert, D. L., Stevens, K. V., & Trollip, S. R. Instantiation of general terms. *Journal of Verbal Learning and Verbal Behavior,* 1976, *15,* 667–679.

Atkinson, R. C., & Shiffrin, R. M. Human memory: A proposed system and its control processes. In K. W. Spence & J. T. Spence (Eds.), *Advances in the psychology of learning and motivation research and theory* (Vol. II). New York: Academic Press, 1968.

Baggett, P. Memory for explicit and implicit information in picture stories. *Journal of Verbal Learning and Verbal Behavior,* 1975, *14,* 538–548.

Barclay, J. R. The role of comprehension in remembering sentences. *Cognitive Psychology,* 1973, *4,* 229–254.

Barclay, J. R., Bransford, J. D., Franks, J. J., McCarrell, N. S., & Nitsch, K. Comprehension and semantic flexibility. *Journal of Verbal Learning and Verbal Behavior,* 1974, *13,* 471–481.

Bartlett, F. C. *Remembering: An experimental and social study.* Cambridge: Cambridge University Press, 1932.

Begg, I., & Paivio, A. U. Concreteness and imagery in sentence meaning. *Journal of Verbal Learning and Verbal Behavior,* 1969, *8,* 821–827.

Bolinger, D. W. The atomization of meaning. *Language,* 1965, *41,* 555–573.

Bower, G. H. Mental imagery and associative learning. In L. W. Gregg (Ed.), *Cognition in learning and memory.* New York: John Wiley & Sons, Inc., 1972.

Bower, G. H. Cognitive psychology: An introduction. In W. K. Estes (Ed.), *Handbook of learning and cognitive processes.* Hillsdale, N.J.: Lawrence Erlbaum Associates, 1975.

Bransford, J. D., Barclay, J. R., & Franks, J. J. Sentence memory: A constructive versus interpretive approach. *Cognitive Psychology,* 1972, *3,* 193–209.

Bransford, J. D., & Franks, J. W. The abstraction of linguistic ideas. *Cognitive Psychology,* 1971, *2,* 331–350.

Bransford, J. D., & Johnson, M. K. Contextual prerequisites for understanding: Some investigations of comprehension and recall. *Journal of Verbal Learning and Verbal Behavior,* 1972, *11,* 717–726.

Bugelski, B. R. Words and things and images. *American Psychologist,* 1970, *25,* 1002–1012.

Carpenter, P. A., & Just, M. A. Sentence comprehension: A psycholinguistic processing model of verification. *Psychological Review,* 1975, V. 82, *1,* 45–73.

Chi, T. H. The representation of knowledge. *Contemporary Psychology,* 1976, *21,* 784–785.

Clark, H. H. Linguistic processes in deductive reasoning. *Psychological Review,* 1969, V. 72, *4,* 387–404.

Clark, H. H. Semantics and comprehension. In T. A. Sebeok (Ed.), *Current trends in linguistics, V. 12: Linguistics and adjacent arts and sciences.* The Hague: Mouton Publishers, 1974.

Clark, H. H. Inferring what is meant. In a forthcoming book edited by W. J. M. Levelt and G. B. F. d'Arcais, 1978.

Clark, H. H., & Chase, W. G. On the process of comparing sentences against pictures. *Cognitive Psychology,* 1972, *3,* 472–517.

Clark, H. H., & Haviland, S. E. Comprehension and the given-new contract. In R. O. Freedle (Ed.), *Discourse, production, and comprehension.* Norwood, N.J.: Ablex Publishing, 1977.

Clark, H. H., & Lucy, P. Understanding what is meant from what is said: A study in conversationally conveyed requests. *Journal of Verbal Learning and Verbal Behavior,* 1975, *14,* 56–72.

Collins, A. M., & Quillian, M. R. Does category size affect categorization time? *Journal of Verbal Learning and Verbal Behavior,* 1970, *9,* 432–438.

Craik, F. I. M. A "levels of analysis" view of memory. In P. Pliner, L. Krames, & T. M. Alloway (Eds.), *Communication and affect: language and thought.* New York: Academic Press, 1973.

Craik, F. I. M., & Lockhart, R. S. Levels of processing: A framework for memory research. *Journal of Verbal Learning and Verbal Behavior*, 1972, *11*, 671–684.

Dooling, D. J., & Lachman, R. Effects of comprehension on retention of prose. *Journal of Experimental Psychology*, 1971, *88*, 216–222.

Fillenbaum, S. Pragmatic normalization: Further results for some conjunctive and disjunctive sentences. *Journal of Experimental Psychology*, 1974, V. 102, *4*, 574–578.

Frederiksen, C. H. Representing logical and semantic structure of knowledge acquired from discourse. *Cognitive Psychology*, 1975, *7*, 371–458.

Frijda, N. H. Simulation of human long-term memory. *Psychological Bulletin*, 1972, *77*, 1–31.

Garner, W. R. *Uncertainty and structure as psychological concepts*. New York: Wiley, 1962.

Garner, W. R. *The processing of information and structure*. Hillsdale, N.J.: Lawrence Erlbaum Associates, 1974.

Gibson, J. J. *The senses considered as perceptual systems*. Boston: Houghton–Mifflin Co., 1966.

Gibson, J. J. The theory of affordances. In R. Shaw & J. Bransford (Eds.), *Perceiving, acting and knowing: Toward an ecological psychology*. Hillsdale, N.J.: Lawrence Erlbaum Associates, 1977.

Glucksberg, S., Trabasso, T., & Wald, J. Linguistic structures and mental operations. *Cognitive Psychology*, 1973, *5*, 338–370.

Gough, P. B. The verification of sentences: The effects of delay of evidence and sentence length. *Journal of Verbal Learning and Verbal Behavior*, 1966, *5*, 492–496.

Green, D. W. The effects of task on the representation of sentences. *Journal of Verbal Learning and Verbal Behavior*, 1975, *14*, 275–283.

Haber, R. N. *Information-processing approaches to visual perception*. New York: Holt, Rinehart & Winston, 1969.

Harris, R. J. Memory and comprehension of implications and inferences of complex sentences. *Journal of Verbal Learning and Verbal Behavior*, 1974, *13*, 626–637.

Haviland, S. E., & Clark, H. H. What's new? Acquiring new information as a process in comprehension. *Journal of Verbal Learning and Verbal Behavior*, 1974, *13*, 512–521.

Holmes, V. M., & Langford, J. Comprehension and recall of abstract and concrete sentences. *Journal of Verbal Learning and Verbal Behavior*, 1976, *5*, 559–566.

Holton, G. On the role of themata in scientific thought. *Science*, 1976, *188*, 328–334.

Hornby, P. A. Surface structure and presupposition. *Journal of Verbal Learning and Verbal Behavior*, 1974, *13*, 530–538.

Hunt, E. What kind of computer is man? *Cognitive Psychology*, 1971, *2*, 57–98.

Jenkins, J. J. *Constructive processes in memory for pictures*. Colloquium at the University of Houston, February 1977.

Johnson, M. K., Bransford, J. D., Nyberg, S. E., & Cleary, J. J. Comprehension factors in interpreting memory for abstract and concrete sentences. *Journal of Verbal Learning and Verbal Behavior*, 1972, *11*, 451–454.

Johnson, M. K., Bransford, J. D., & Solomon, S. K. Memory for tacit implications of sentences. *Journal of Experimental Psychology*, 1973, *98*, 203–205.

Johnson, M. K., Doll, T. J., Bransford, J. D., & Lapinski, R. H. Context effects in sentence memory. *Journal of Experimental Psychology*, 1974, *103*, 358–360.

Jorgensen, C. C., & Kintsch, W. The role of imagery in the evaluation of sentences. *Cognitive Psychology*, 1973, *4*, 110–116.

Katz, J. J., & Fodor, J. A. The structure of a semantic theory. *Language*, 1963, *39*, 170–210.

Kintsch, W. *The representation of meaning in memory*. Hillsdale, N.J.: Lawrence Erlbaum Associates, 1974.

Kintsch, W. Memory for prose. In C. N. Cofer (Ed.), *The structure of human memory*. San Francisco: W. H. Freeman and Company, 1976.

Kintsch, W., & van Dijk, T. A. Comment on rappelle et on resume des histoires. *Langage*, 1975, *9*, 98–116.

Kosslyn, S. M., & Pomerantz, J. R. Imagery, propositions, and the form of internal representations. *Cognitive Psychology*, 1977, *9*, 52−76.

Kuhn, T. *The structure of scientific revolutions*. Chicago: University of Chicago Press, 1963.

Lachman, R., Lachman, J. L., & Butterfield, E. C. *Cognitive psychology and information processing: An introduction*. Hillsdale, N.J.: Lawrence Erlbaum Associates, (in press).

Layton, P., & Simpson, A. J. Surface and deep structure in sentence comprehension. *Journal of Verbal Learning and Verbal Behavior*, 1975, *14*, 658−664.

Loftus, E. F. Leading questions and the eyewitness report. *Cognitive Psychology*, 1975, *7*, 560−572.

Loftus, E. F., & Zanni, G. Eyewitness testimony: The influence of the wording of a question. *Bulletin of the Psychonomic Society*, 1975, *5*, 86−88.

Metzger, D., & Williams, G. E. A formal ethnographic analysis of Tenajapa Ladino. *American Anthropologist*, 1963, *65*, 1072−1101.

Miller, G. A. *Language and communication*. New York: McGraw−Hill, 1951.

Miller, G. A., & Johnson−Laird, P. N. *Language and perception*. Cambridge, Mass.: Harvard University Press, 1976.

Minsky, M. A framework for representing knowledge. In P. Winston (Ed.), *The psychology of computer vision*. New York: McGraw−Hill, 1975.

Mistler−Lachman, J. Levels of comprehension in processing of normal and ambiguous sentences. *Journal of Verbal Learning and Verbal Behavior*, 1972, *11*, 614−623.

Mistler−Lachman, J. Levels of comprehension and sentence memory. *Journal of Verbal Learning and Verbal Behavior*, 1974, *13*, 98−106.

Moeser, S. D. Memory for meaning and wording in concrete and abstract sentences. *Journal of Verbal Learning and Verbal Behavior*, 1974, *13*, 682−697.

Newell, A. & Simon, H. *Human problem solving*. Englewood Cliffs, N.J.: Prentice-Hall, 1972.

Norman, D. A., & Rumelhart, D. E. *Explorations in cognition*. San Francisco: W. H. Freeman, 1975.

Olson, D. R., & Filby, N. On the comprehension of active and passive sentences. *Cognitive Psychology*, 1972, *3*, 361−381.

Paivio, A. *Imagery and verbal processes*. New York: Holt, Rinehart & Winston, 1971.

Pezdek, K., & Royer, J. M. The role of comprehension in learning concrete and abstract sentences. *Journal of Verbal Learning and Verbal Behavior*, 1974, *13*, 551−558.

Polanyi, M. *Personal knowledge*. New York: Harper & Row (Torchbook Edition), 1964.

Pompi, K. F., & Lachman, R. Surrogate processes in short-term retention of connected discourse. *Journal of Experimental Psychology*, 1967, *75*, 143−150.

Posner, M. I. Psychobiology of attention. In M. Gazzaniga & C. Clakemore (Eds.), *Handbook of psychobiology*. New York: Academic Press, 1975. (a)

Posner, M. I. The temporal course of pattern recognition in the human brain. In G. F. Inbar (Ed.), *Signal analysis and pattern recognition in biomedical engineering*. New York: Halsted Press, 1975. (b)

Powers, W. T. *Behavior: The control of perception*. Chicago: Aldine Publishing Co., 1973.

Pylyshyn, Z. W. What the mind's eye tells the mind's brain: A critique of mental imagery. *Psychological Bulletin*, 1973, *80*, 1−24.

Quillian, M. R. Semantic memory. In M. Minsky (Ed.), *Semantic information processing*, Cambridge, Mass.: MIT Press, 198.

Rumelhart, D. E. Notes on a schema for stories. In D. G. Bobrow & A. M. Collins (Eds.), *Representations and understanding: Studies in cognitive science*. New York: Academic Press, 1975.

Rumelhart, D. E., Lindsay, P. H., & Norman, D. A. A process model for long-term memory. In E. Tulving & W. Donaldson (Eds.), *Organization of memory*. New York: Academic Press, 1972.

Sachs, J. S. Recognition memory for syntactic and semantic aspects of connected discourse. *Perception & Psychophysics*, 1967, *2*, 437−442.

Schank, R. C. Conceptual dependency: A theory of natural language understanding. *Cognitive Psychology*, 1972, *3*, 552−631.

Schank, R. C. *Conceptual information processing*. New York: American Elsevier Publishing Co., Inc., 1975.

Schank, R. C. Memory representation. *Contemporary Psychology*, 1976, *21*, 326−328. (a)

Schank, R. C. The role of memory in language processing. In C. N. Cofer (Ed.), *The structure of human memory*. San Francisco: W. H. Freeman & Company, 1976. (b)

Schweller, K. G., Brewer, W. F., & Dahl, D. Memory for illocutionary forces and perlocutionary effects of utterances. *Journal of Verbal Learning and Verbal Behavior*, 1976, *15*, 325−337.

Shannon, C. E. A mathematical theory of communication. *Bell System Technical Journal*, 1948, *27*, 379−423, 623−656.

Shaw, R., & Bransford, J. Introduction: Psychological approaches to the problem of knowledge. In R. Shaw & J. Bransford (Eds.), *Perceiving, acting and knowing: Toward an ecological psychology*. Hillsdale, N.J.: Lawrence Erlbaum Associates, 1977.

Smith, E. E., Shoben, E. J., & Rips, L. J. Structure and process in semantic memory: A featural model for semantic decisions. *Psychological Review*, 1974, *81*, 214−241.

Suppes, P. & Rottmayer, W. Automata. In E. Carterette & M. Friedman (Eds.), *Handbook of Perception* (Vol. 1). New York: Academic Press, 1974.

Tanenhaus, M. K., Carroll, J. M., & Bever, T. G. Sentence−picture verification models as theories of sentence comprehension: A critique of Carpenter and Just. *Psychological Review*, 1976, *83*, 310−317.

Thorndyke, P. W. Conceptual complexity and imagery in comprehension and memory. *Journal of Verbal Learning and Verbal Behavior*, 1975, *14*, 359−369.

Thorndyke, P. W. Cognitive structures in comprehension and memory of narrative discourse. *Cognitive Psychology*, 1977, *9*, 77−110.

Trabasso, T., Rollins, H., & Shaughnessy, E. Storage and verification stages in processing concepts. *Cognitive Psychology*, 1971, *2*, 239−289.

Tulving, E. Episodic and semantic memory. In E. Tulving & W. Donaldson (Eds.), *Organization of memory*. New York: Academic Press, 1972.

van Dijk, T. A. *Complex semantic information-processing*. Paper contributed to the Workshop on Linguistics and Information Science, Stockholm, Sweden, May 1976.

Wason, P. The contexts of plausible denial. *Journal of Verbal Learning and Verbal Behavior*, 1965, *2*, 7−11.

Weizenbaum, J. *Computer power and human reason: From judgment to calculation*. San Francisco: W. H. Freeman & Co., 1976.

Winograd, T. *Understanding natural language*. New York: Academic Press, 1972.

10 Levels of Processing Language Material: Discussion of the Papers by Lachman and Lachman and Perfetti

Walter Kintsch
University of Colorado

The two papers under discussion here cover an extremely wide range. But they start out from a common core—the application of levels-of-processing models beyond list learning to problems of sentence and text memory. I focus upon this point here, specifically upon Fig. 9.2 of Lachman and Lachman and Table 8.1 of Perfetti, and the problems and questions that such analyses present. Since I talk mostly about the problems later on, let me at the outset say how promising I believe these approaches to be: If one wants to study levels of processing, it is particularly interesting to do so in the context of sentences and text, for the simple reason that the problem is so much richer in this context. The higher levels of analyses that are prominent in the aforementioned tables simply do not exist if one restricts oneself to list-learning paradigms.

Figure 10.1 shows a description of the processing stages involved in reading a text that I proposed some time ago, which closely parallels the Lachman and Perfetti analyses (Kintsch, 1975). The question immediately arises, of course—which table is right or which is most closely right? The Lachmans' table, as well as my own, were offered as convenient illustrations and pedagogical devices, without claims that our list of processing stages was complete and sufficient. For instance, I don't suppose the Lachmans would object very much if the process they labeled "speech perception" were decomposed into such subprocesses as segment classification, phone synthesis, phoneme synthesis, word candidate generation, etc. Perfetti's analysis, on the other hand, is considerably more ambitious. He argues that by adopting a fixed unit of analysis—the sentence, in his case—it becomes possible to identify a complete and sufficient sequence of processing stages. It is a good try, but I remain unconvinced. Neither the proposed separation between levels nor the definitions of the levels themselves,

211

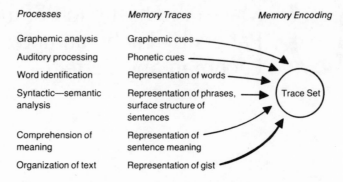

FIG. 10.1.   An outline of stages of comprehension in reading, the memory traces arising from these processes, and their selection for encoding in memory. The thickness of the arrows indicates the likelihood that particular types of memory traces will be encoded in memory for long-term retention under standard reading conditions. (From Kintsch, 1977).

as offered by Perfetti, appear very satisfactory to me. The acoustic—phonological distinction is surely tenuous. And I think he misinterprets Lieberman's results: They do not "demonstrate that the physical cues for the perceptual phenomena are not sufficient [p. 162]"; they merely show that a particular theoretical representation of the physical cues—the spectrogram—is insufficient. Perhaps there are alternative representations (Fourier analysis/something as yet unknown?) that would work better! Perfetti's Levels 3, 4, and 5 are equally problematic. Not all linguists feel that a separate syntactic level can be justified, and even fewer psychologists are of that opinion. The separation of referential and propositional level seems quite arbitrary at this point. What is good for the predicate calculus is not necessarily relevant psychologically. Of course, all semantic representation must somehow contain both relational and referential information. In my work on text analysis, for instance, the latter has always played an important part as the new arguments in a text base (e.g., Kintsch, Kozminsky, Streby, McKoon, & Keenan, 1975); but until it is demonstrated that something is to be gained by treating these as a separate level, I would just as well do without this additional complexity.

As we go to Levels 6 and 7, Perfetti's definitions appear to suffer from the fact that he has never made up his mind whether pragmatic factors do or do not have a place in his analyses. His decision to restrict himself to sentences as his unit of analysis now gets in the way; he needs to talk here about macrostructures and speech acts—that is, pragmatic aspects—but without a shift in the unit of analysis, this can't be done.

Thus, I see little reason to prefer Perfetti's seven levels to the Lachmans' or my own vagueness. Some kind of analysis into qualitatively different processing stages appears necessary, however. Anderson and Reder, in Chapter 18, want to substitute a uniform propositional representation for the qualitative distinctions implied here. Where I like to talk about verbal, semantic, graphemic, phonemic cues and so on, they mimic these qualitative riches with propositions alone. No doubt this is possible and no doubt that it is more parsimonious—but the alternative is much less strained. In any case, this point does not deserve serious discussion, since it is not empirically decidable and therefore is merely a question of personal preference.

I am also unwilling to enter into long arguments of whether procedures are remembered or traces are remembered. Surely people remember processes, as Kolers maintains in Chapter 17. But to say that one remembers a process or procedure implies that the process leaves some kind of trace behind. Until someone shows me an operational distinction between "remembering processes" and "remembering the traces of processes," I see no need to take the distinction seriously.

Another presently popular dichotomy, that between procedural and declarative representations of knowledge, appears equally problematic, at least when considered as mutually exclusive alternatives. Anderson, though not the inventor of that distinction, has become its defender, so let me discuss his arguments (Anderson, 1976; Anderson & Reder, Chapter 18, this volume). First he says declarative knowledge is all−or−none—one either knows that something is true or doesn't—whereas procedural knowledge may be partial. But we are not concerned with truth or falsity but with the representation of knowledge itself, and a proposition may just as well be partially known as a procedure! For instance, one may know only the predicate of a proposition and forget its arguments or know only the general class of the argument rather than a specific concept. His second argument is a version of the first—that declarative knowledge is acquired all−or−none by assertion ("something is true") whereas procedures must be learned through practice the hard way. Again, we are not so much concerned with the truth of something but with the nature of that something, and that may require a long and gradual learning process. Finally, Anderson claims that declarative knowledge is verbally communicated whereas procedural knowledge cannot be described and must be demonstrated. But pictures, graphs, and maps (declarative knowledge) may be very hard to describe verbally, whereas there are at least some procedures that are quite well communicated verbally, as the continued popularity of cookbooks demonstrates. Therefore, instead of setting up a lot of dichotomies and pseudodichotomies (another one is the verbal-imagery controversy, well discussed in the Lachmans' chapter), we should agree that both declarative and procedural representations have their uses; formally, these two representations are equivalent, and psychologically, they are a matter of taste.

If we accept some kind of open-ended sequence of processing levels, with the specific one being quite context- and task-specific, we then must be very careful not to confuse this logical sequence with a psychological model—that is, a processing sequence or a stage hierarchy. Perfetti has elaborated this point. He points out that the processes in Fig. 10.1 are not necessarily sequential and hierarchical. One might think of each process as a dimension in a multidimensional space, with a particular encoding episode being specified by high or low values on several of these dimensions but perhaps unspecified on some irrevelant one (e.g., "organization of text" in a list-learning experiment or "auditory analyses" in a study concerned with text processing). The value on each dimension would be the amount of activity at this encoding level; e.g., in a typical reading context, most activity occurs at the highest comprehension levels—gist comprehension—and therefore, most of the memorial consequences would be expected at that level (indicated in Fig. 10.1 by the heavy arrow). When I read French, however, most of the activity is at the word—and—syntax level, so that after painstakingly translating a whole article, I on occasion find that I don't know what I have read.

Figure 10.1 therefore has the status of a task analysis. Although this is a necessary first step for a psychologist, we of course cannot stop here. What kind of processing model can we devise? In the original Craik and Lockhart (1972) paper, a sequential, bottom-up processing model was proposed where the processing stops as soon as the required level is reached. That is, if the task required only analyses at a certain level, the processes up to that level were engaged whereas higher levels were idle (Craik & Lockhart, 1972). As the contributions by these authors in the present volume indicate (Chapters 1, 4, and 22), this model has now been abandoned for a variety of reasons; and one emphasizing differential weighting of levels has been substituted. The question— whether the processing is sequential or not—is left open.

A number of psychologists (among them, Kintsch, 1975) have speculated that the processes in Fig. 10.1 operate in parallel. At each level of analysis, a whole set of analyzers, rules, inference generators, productions, demons, and the like are continuously evaluated against the data base. A high degree of interaction occurs among levels; the goal of the system is not to complete processing at each level but to obtain an output at a specified level. Hence, for example, a syntactic parser might only rarely complete its processing when an easy text is being read and the goal is gist comprehension.

This is of course not the place to specify the details of such a model (nor would I be able to do so), but I would like to briefly respond to the question of why I think such a model is necessary and then to look at a number of problems that arise in the construction of such a model.

A CASE FOR PARALLEL PROCESSING

The main reason for considering a parallel processing model lies in the repeated demonstrations that even in tasks that do not require a semantic analysis, there is a parallel access to the semantic domain prior to response generation. I shall only mention two well-known results. The first is Meyer and Schvaneveldt's (1971) finding that subjects responded faster that two-letter strings were words when the two words were associatively related. The second is Allport's (1978) demonstration of a recognition bias for "drown herself (stabbed herself)" after subjects had listened to "That night she killed herself" on the attended channel in a dichotic listening task with "water (knife)" on the unattended. For more results of that nature and a systematic discussion, see Chapter 14 by Treisman in the present volume. Here, I would like to discuss briefly a result with similar implications recently obtained by Masson and Sala at the University of Colorado (1978).

Masson and Sala worked in the context of Kolers's work (e.g., Chapter 17 in the present volume). Like Kolers, they wanted to show that memory is a function of the encoding and retrieval operations, and they employed the experimental techniques developed by Kolers. Unlike Kolers, however, they considered not only perceptual operations but also semantic operations. For this purpose, they supplemented Kolers's basic experimental design in two ways. They had subjects read sentences in either normal or inverted typography and later gave them a recognition test. Their design combined four factors orthogonally: (1) inverted or normal type at the time of study, (2) inverted or normal type at the time of testing, (3) verbatim reproductions or paraphrases at the time of testing, and (4) task demands during encoding. Subjects either read the sentences aloud or were asked to provide a sentence continuing the one they were reading in a meaningful way. Masson and Sala argued that reading aloud does not ensure sufficient semantic processing, whereas the sentence-continuation task forces subjects to process the sentences at a relatively deep semantic level. The verbatim−versus−paraphrase manipulation was included to detect the extent to which subjects were relying on semantic rather than perceptual cues on the recognition test.

Thus, after reading a set of 85 sentences, subjects were given a recognition deck consisting of verbatim reproductions of some study sentences, paraphrases of others, and distractor sentences, for a total of 107 sentences. For each sentence, subjects responded whether it was one they had read before and if so, whether the type was the same. From the rich results of this study, I mention only the two that are most relevant to the present discussion. First, consider the recognition performance for the sentences as a function of the four experimental variables, as measured by the d' statistic (with performance on semantically different distractors providing estimates of the false-alarm rate). Oversimplifying, we can say that neither typeface at the time of test nor the verbatim−paraphrase variable made much difference, whereas the factors of typeface at study time and task demands interacted in an interesting way. When the subjects read normal sentences, they remembered them much better when processing them at a deep semantic level (the sentence continuation condition, $d' = 2.49$) than when the processing was merely superficial (reading aloud, $d' = 1.86$). However, when inverted sentences were studied, it made no difference what the additional task demands were: d' was 2.75 for the sentence-continuation task and 2.67 for the read-aloud task. Note that if we consider the read-aloud results alone, they replicate the typical Kolers finding of better memory for inverted sentences. However, the interaction obtained here between typeface and depth of semantic processing implies that the better memory for inverted sentences in the reading-aloud task cannot be attributed merely to the greater amount of perceptual processing that these sentences had experienced, because sentence continuation for inverted sentences are always processed at a deep semantic level. Normal sentences can be read aloud without deep semantic processing (and are, as a consequence, relatively poorly recognized, as is usual for auto-matically processed material; see Shiffrin & Schneider, 1977). Inverted sen-tences, however, require *both* an excessive amount of bottom-up perceptual processing and top-down semantic processing! Phenomenologically, reading inverted sentences, for me at least, is a guessing game; on the basis of some deciphered visual features and the sentence context, plausible words are gen-erated. Of course, in a sense reading is always like this; but reading normal texts is a highly automatic performance, and only when the automatic encoding processes are disturbed can this process be observed in more detail.

Thus, Masson and Sala support Kolers's contention that what is processed is remembered, but they supplement his results by showing that the processes involved in reading inverted type are not merely perceptual but just as much semantic. A consideration of the savings in reading time when sentences were reread at the recognition test without changes in the typeface supports this argument nicely, for savings were just as great for paraphrases as for verbatim copies of the sentences. For inverted sentences, 16 sec were saved when the sentence was reread verbatim and 15 sec when a paraphrase was read instead. For normal sentences, the savings were much less, of course, but again identical for verbatim sentences and paraphrases (both less than 1 sec, data from Experiment 2).

I have discussed Masson and Sala's work at some length here, because it serves well to relate Kolers's work with our concerns and provides a strong and clear argument for the kind of highly interactive, parallel levels-of-processing model advocated here. Of course, advocating such a model is rather less than having one, and the problems that one encounters in constructing it are serious ones. In equal parts, they appear to be theoretical puzzles and simple ignorance about some empirical questions. I discuss a few of these problems not in order to offer solutions but to pose questions.

PROBLEMS WITH PARALLEL PROCESSORS

If one distinguishes qualitatively separate levels of analysis, how is the output of these separate analyzers interrelated so as to form a unitized memory episode?

Specifically, how does the system know that a given set of perceptual cues (or procedures) and a given set of semantic cues (or procedures, again) are part of the same or different memory units? There are various possibilities to achieve this synthesis, e.g., via pointers or tags. Perhaps it is useful to consider a memory episode as a point in a multidimensional space, or a set of cues, as implied in Fig. 10.1 and elaborated in Kintsch (1974, Chapter 4).

A more serious problem is what is best called Selz's Problem. Selz (1922) pointed out a dilemma encountered by all parallel processing models in the context of the "constellation theory" of James and others (for discussions, see Mandler & Mandler, 1964; and Kintsch, 1974). The problem is simply that it is usually assumed that a lot of analyses operating in parallel will reinforce each other and thereby automatically arrive at the correct solution. To use Selz's example, suppose one must decide whether *occupation* is the superordinate of *farmer*; the constellation theory holds that this task activates all superordinates (among them *occupation*) as well as all associations of *farmer*, which results in the double activation of the *farmer−occupation* association and thereby in the correct response. But there are other superordinates (e.g., *artisan*) also associated with *farmer* (a coordinate term), which would be strengthened in the same way—but which *never* occur in response to *farmer* when the task is to supply the superordinate. A process of automatic strengthening of associations would, however, predict such intrusions. Selz argues therefore for a structured system, with knowledge patterns ("Komplexe") in place of unlabeled associations. Similarly, parallel processing models of the type considered here cannot simply trust that the correct output will be selected through the simultaneous interplay of analyzers at many different levels. Well-defined knowledge structures together with some processes of hypothesis-testing within these structures might be able to overcome these difficulties, but await their detailed explication.

According to the present levels-of-processing view, information is selected in different amounts from different levels, depending on task demands. However, selection does not proceed equally at all levels. Not all levels of analysis are under attentional control, and selection is possible from some but not others. Some proceed automatically (and are therefore poorly remembered). Perfetti provides a good discussion of this problem in terms of transparency and opaqueness (though I would rather talk about "attention demanding" than "opaque" and save the literature from a new-fashioned word).

Once traces have been selected from a level, does their forgetting rate depend on the level? More specifically, are the higher level traces (i.e., the ones at the bottom of Fig. 10.1) forgotten more slowly than the lower, more sensory levels? The issue is by no means settled, with Anderson and Reder (Chapter 18, this volume) arguing against differential forgetting rates. I had previously suggested that all those traces that are successfully encoded in a memory episode remain in long-term memory, though the memory episode as a whole becomes subject to retrieval difficulties. On the other hand, for the traces that did not enter long-term memory, the evidence available at that time suggested differential forgetting rates, with faster loss of sensory rather than semantic attributes (Kintsch, 1975). Experimental data that provide a strong test of this model are currently not available, however.

It is difficult to collect such data because of the complex interactions that obtain between encoding and testing conditions. If a test emphasizes information at one level and another test information at a different level, divergent results may be obtained. Performance is a joint function of encoding and retrieval processes—as was repeatedly stressed at this meeting, e.g., in the contributions of Bransford, Franks, Morris, and Stein (Chapter 15) and Tulving (Chapter 19). For instance, rather different conclusions may be reached when memory for a sentence is tested requiring verbatim reproduction or merely gist reproduction. A recent study by Bates, Masling, and Kintsch (1978) concerned recognition memory for statements from a television play. Specifically, subjects watched an episode from a popular soap opera and were then tested for their memory. One of the questions investigated in this study concerned the effects of marking in sentences. Three types of marked—unmarked sentence pairs were used. In one case, the marked sentence contained a name where its unmarked pair had merely a pronoun, e.g.: "You mean they have taken Rachel (her) to the hospital?" The second sentence type was concerned with ellipsis: "We are doing everything we can to make sure she regains consciousness (she does), Eta." In the final marked—unmarked pair, a social role and name were interchanged: "I wanted to get the letter done while his wife (Rachel) was out of the office." Distractor items were constructed by inserting plausible but wrong characters or actions into these sentences, e.g., by letting Eta go to the hospital or out of the office or letting her "keep the baby" rather than "regain consciousness." When verbatim recognition memory was tested, performance was significantly better on the marked than on the unmarked sentences; the more specific marked sentences were better retained (performance corrected for guessing was 0.40 for marked and 0.19 for unmarked sentences, respectively). However, if gist rather than verbatim memory was measured, this difference disappeared (0.66 versus 0.67). For gist memory, it does not matter how we refer to someone as long as comprehension is assured. Thus, the level we have chosen for our testing and measurement operations can also be reflected in the nature of the results we obtain.

CONCEPTUAL LEVELS OF ANALYSES IN TEXT PROCESSING

I end this discussion with a plea for the study of higher level of analyses. Actually, the Lachmans and Perfetti have already argued for this good cause, and I merely join them. It is clear from this conference that (a) the promise offered by such study is exciting, and (b) very little of it has so far been fulfilled. At the semantic and pragmatic levels lie some important research questions as well as our hopes for applications for this type of work. By sticking too closely to our familiar, much-tested laboratory paradigms, we throw away some of the strongest levels effects that we could study. Bransford has pointed out that truly spectacular levels effects are obtainable if we include pragmatic levels of processing in our experiments: The sentence "Bill bought a red car" is surely more memorable when it is processed semantically (e.g., by having the subject generate a continuation) than when it is not (e.g., by having him count the number of "r's" in it); but it is even more deeply processed and better remembered when I hear it in a conversation, knowing Bill and his circumstances.

What do I mean by "more deeply processed" in the foregoing sentence? I am referring to the role that inferences play in comprehension and memory for text. It is a truism that we do not comprehend and remember merely what is directly mentioned in a text. The role of a text is rather to serve as a stimulus for the construction of a complex edifice in the reader's mind; a representation of the text itself is part of that edifice, but other parts are added from the reader's store of knowledge about the topic under discussion. By contacting the reader's "apperceptive mass," the text may grow into a new structure that is part textual, part inferential. Such a structure *may* be developed in comprehension, but exactly how many inferences are in fact produced—and which ones—under a given set of experimental conditions is so far a poorly understood question. It is, however, a question of first importance if progress is to be made in the area of text comprehension. As Bransford has stressed at these meetings, the problem of learning is not so much learning inputs, but learning from inputs.

Others have also recognized the importance of this problem, including the Lachmans and Perfetti in their present contributions (e.g., Perfetti's discussion of the "old man" example). Experimental demonstrations of the psychological reality of inferences in comprehension also exist by now in abundance (for examples, see the discussion in Kintsch, 1977). We need, however, to go beyond this stage of demonstrations and discussions and develop a more detailed understanding of the processes involved in making inferences from texts. In this respect, psychological understanding is still most primitive, though attempts are being made in various quarters to overcome these limitations. I briefly outline one of these (Kintsch & van Dijk, 1978), to indicate the kind of thing that can be achieved in this area.

We started by narrowing down the general problem of how inferences are made from text to the study of inferential processes in summarizing certain kinds of well-structured texts (e.g., stories, psychological research reports). Our model starts with the semantic (i.e., propositional) representation of a text, neglecting the processes necessary to produce this representation. Its first concern is with the coherence of this semantic text representation; it specifies *how many* inferences are required to establish a coherent text base and *where* in the text these inferences must occur, but it does not specify *how* they occur nor their precise nature, beyond some general constraints. Even so, it could be shown that these processes have significant consequences for the readability of a text (Kintsch & Vipond, 1978).

The status of inferences that occur during comprehension is quite interesting from a levels-of-processing standpoint. Such inferences are represented in memory only at a propositional level, whereas statements directly derived from the text are multiply represented at sensory−linguistic levels as well as the propositional one. At least this is the case shortly after reading a text; after some delay filled with further reading, the interference at the sensory and word levels builds up to such a degree that the memory traces at these levels become less accessible so that the difference between inferences and explicitly presented statements disappears in some tasks. This is the case, for instance, in verification tasks: If one asks a reader to verify an explicitly presented statement shortly after reading, it takes less time to do than when the reader verifies an inference; after 20 minutes of intervening reading, however, this difference disappears, and explicit and implicit statements are verified equally fast (e.g., Keenan & Kintsch, 1974; the verification data reported by Anderson & Reder in Chapter 18 in this volume can readily be interpreted in the same way). The same holds true when a text is presented pictorially (via cartoons) rather than verbally (Baggett, 1975). However, the equal verification times after a delay for explicit and implicit statements do not mean that the surface cues for the explicit statement have been lost; Baggett showed that people still can recognize quite well whether or not they have seen a particular cartoon, but recognizing that they have *not* seen a picture that fits into the story (i.e., one that they would call "true" in a verification task) takes a long time, longer in fact than the "true" response in a verification task. Hence, the surface traces are still there but are so weak that they are of no more help in the verification task.

In comprehending a text, we are concerned not only with local comprehension but also with a more global, "gist" comprehension. Our model attempts to specify precisely the operations involved in comprehending the "gist" of a text. This is done by describing operators, called macro-operators, that transform the original propositional text base into a derived text base, which we call the macrostructure of the text. The macrostructure is also propositional (containing macropropositions) and is hierarchical; that is, macro-operators may be applied to macropropositions, generating higher order macropropositions. The function of the macro-operators is to summarize the text (e.g., by deletion or generalization of irrelevant or redundant material). The macrostructure of a text, therefore, corresponds to the intuitive notion of gist. Macro-operators are not, however, applied deterministically but are used in different ways depending on the control structure of the process, which in turn is derived from the reader's goals and knowledge base. The only such control structure we have studied so far is the story schema, used to summarize stories.

Thus, in our model, the memory of a text consists of a propositional representation of its meaning (the microstructure), plus the inferences necessary to assure the coherence of this propositional network, and the various levels of the macrostructure. Note that there is no such thing as "the" macrostructure of a text; but different readers with different knowledge bases and different goals will apply the macro-operators differently, producing a family of possible macro-structures for any given text.

The model then includes a production component to describe how the memory structures just outlined are used to generate outputs, specifically free-recall protocols and summaries. We have described three types of output operations. The first is reproduction: Any proposition still retrievable in memory may be reproduced, whether it is a macro or microproposition. (Note that propositions "deleted" from the macrostructure are not thereby erased from memory; they still may be retained as micropropositions!) Secondly, there are the recon-struction processes—namely addition of relevant detail, particularization, and specification of normal components, conditions, or consequences of action sequences. These are used to generate additional material to complement what was actually remembered (i.e., reproduced). Normally this material is correct, in the sense that it consists of contextually plausible inferences, but sometimes "errors" are introduced into a protocol in this way. Finally, a process of generating metastatements has been described—that is, statements that are neither reproduced nor reconstructed from the content of the text but that are about the text or about the process of remembering itself.

When a subject is asked to recall a story, all these production processes are operative, and of course the output that is generated is again under the control of the story schema, just as the original encoding was. When the subject is asked to summarize the story, instead of recalling it, he or she reproduces mostly macropropositions with less reliance upon micropropositions and reconstructions.

The model outlined here can be used to classify experimental protocols (recall or summaries) in terms of the probable origin of the statements they contain; i.e., whether they are reproductions of micropropositions, reproductions of macro-propositions (note that these are a particular kind of inference), reconstructions (another king of inference), or metastatements. We hope that thereby a more detailed study of inference processes in text comprehension will become possible. I have outlined this model here in order to show that the "higher" processes involved in comprehension (i.e., the ones at the bottom of Fig. 10.1) are open to serious investigation and should no longer be neglected but also to make a further point—namely, how model-dependent this kind of work is. Before one can do much empirically with a response as complex as the recall protocol from a story, we need to have a very detailed model of the processes involved in generating that protocol. Without such a model, we just don't know where to look—which aspect of our data is significant and which is not. Of course, the model that we use is mostly guesswork at first; but we hope that we can collect the kind of data with this model—data interaction that will result in a well-founded scientific theory, in much the same way as the erstwhile Baron Münchhausen pulled himself out of a swamp by his own hair.

REFERENCES

Allport, D. A. Conscious and unconscious cognition. In L. G. Nilsson (Ed.), *Perspectives on memory research*. Hillsdale, N.J.: Lawrence Erlbaum Associates, 1978.

Anderson, J. R. *Language, memory and thought*. Hillsdale, N.J.: Lawrence Erlbaum Associates, 1976.

Baggett, P. Memory for explicit and implicit information in picture stories. *Journal of Verbal Learning and Verbal Behavior*, 1975, *14*, 538–548.

Bates, E., Masling, M., & Kintsch, W. Aspects of memory for dialogue. Journal of Experimental Psychology: Human Learning and Memory, 1978, 4, 187–197.

Craik, F. I. M., & Lockhart, R. S. Levels of processing: A framework for memory research. *Journal of Verbal Learning and Verbal Behavior*, 1972, *11*, 671–684.

Keenan, J. M. & Kintsch, W. The identification of explicitly and implicitly presented information. In W. Kintsch, *The representation of meaning in memory*. Hillsdale, N.J.: Lawrence Erlbaum Associates, 1974. Pp. 153–165.

Kintsch, W. *The representation of meaning in memory*. Hillsdale, N.J.: Lawrence Erlbaum Associates, 1974.

Kintsch, W. Memory representations of text. In R. L. Solso (Ed.), *Information processing and cognition*. Hillsdale, N.J.: Lawrence Erlbaum Associates, 1975.

Kintsch, W. *Memory and cognition*. New York: Wiley, 1977.

Kintsch, W., Kozminsky, E., Streby, W. J., McKoon, G., & Keenan, J. M. Comprehension and recall of text as a function of content variables. *Journal of Verbal Learning and Verbal Behavior*, 1975, *14*, 196–214.

Kintsch, W., & van Dijk, T. A. Towards a model of that comprehension and production. *Psychological Review*, 1978, *85*, 363–394.

Kintsch, W., & Vipond, D. Reading comprehension and readability in educational practice and psychological theory. In L. G. Nilsson (Ed.), *Perspectives on memory research*. Hillsdale, N.J.: Lawrence Erlbaum Associates, 1978.

Mandler, J. M., & Mandler, G. *Thinking: From association to Gestalt*. New York: Wiley, 1964.

Masson, M. E. J., & Sala, L. S. Interactive processes in sentence comprehension and recognition. *Cognitive Psychology*, 1978, 10, 244–270.

Meyer, D. E., & Schvaneveldt, R. W. Facilitation in recognizing pairs of words: Evidence of a dependence between retrieval operations. *Journal of Experimental Psychology*, 1971, *90*, 227–234.

Selz, O. *Zur Psychologie des produktiven Denkens and Irrtums*. Bonn: Cohen, 1922.

Shiffrin, M. R., & Schneider, W. Controlled and automatic human information processing: II. Perceptual learning, automatic attending, and a general theory. *Psychological Review*, 1977, *84*, 27–190.

IV DEVELOPMENTAL ISSUES

11 Theories of Memory and the Problems of Development: Activity, Growth, and Knowledge

Ann L. Brown
University of Illinois

I. INTRODUCTION

This chapter consists of two parts. In the first section, I examine briefly, from a developmental perspective, the major theoretical positions dominating the literature on adult cognition. Two questions are considered: First, how compatible are the theories with the notion that thinking systems develop within living environments? Second, what are the implicit or explicit assumptions of the theories concerning the quintessential developmental problem of growth?

In the second section I consider the general class of levels-of-processing models. These frameworks, unlike other theories of adult cognition, have been widely adopted by developmentalists. I argue that developmental theories are particularly compatible with such models, because they are themselves variants of levels-of-processing approaches. Both emphasize three major issues: the importance of involuntary memory, the activity of the subject and the goal of that activity, and ''headfitting''—i.e., the compatibility between what is known and what can be known. To illustrate, I compare current levels-of-processing models and similar developmental theories, notably European structuralism as represented by Piaget and Soviet dialecticism as represented by Leont'ev, Vygotsky, and Zinchenko. The European tradition and the emergence of levels-of-processing frameworks converged to assert a powerful influence on developmental studies of cognition. Throughout the chapter I have attempted to demonstrate where developmental data are particularly relevant for an issue of concern for adult theories and where adult models can guide the theory construction of developmentalists. To date, however, the dominant approach to human cognition has been teleological, and there is an implicit acceptance that human thought processes reach a steady state, i.e., become static and immutable at maturity. I argue here that a consideration of ontogenetic factors would increase our understanding not only of the child but of the adult thinker.

II. THEORIES OF COGNITION AND THE PROBLEM OF GROWTH

The dialogue between developmental psychology and adult cognition has been less than a vital force in the evolution of either discipline; why this lack of communication? At the trivial level, it is true that the adherents often fail to follow each other's literatures, an oversight that is inevitable given the information overload resulting from the proliferation of research outlets. I have been reduced to treating the task of following current controversy in adult cognition as a semantic shadowing task; I only divert my full attention to the relatively unattended channel when a topic of particular personal salience is raised.

In general, developmental psychologists have shown a lamentable insensitivity to the need for theory-guided research, perhaps due to the origins of the discipline, rooted as they are in clinical and educational practice. As such it is not uncommon to encounter developmental cognitive psychologists who are not only unaware of major trends in adult cognition but are also oblivious to the need for such awareness. By the same token, cognitive psychologists often fail to consider pertinent developmental data even when such data could provide the optimal test for a question of interest. Cross-fertilization among the disciplines could be of help to both.

At a more fundamental level, the crucial issues for a developmentalist—i.e., change and growth—have not in the past been major concerns of adult models. In fact, adult models share major problems that are most apparent when the topic of cognitive growth is considered. It is precisely because of these characteristic weaknesses that developmental psychologists seeking theories have often looked elsewhere for guidance. In the next section I illustrate this point with a cursory examination of the main trends in adult cognition. The concentration is on how the models speak to developmental concerns and how developmental data can be used to investigate some crucial issues for the models.

A. Information-Processing Models: The Computer Metaphor

Craik and Lockhart's (1972) original paper was primarily motivated by a reaction to the then-dominant metaphor of adult cognition—the computer. I do not wish to reiterate their well-known criticisms here; instead I would like to add a further complaint arising from a developmental perspective. Computer-metaphor models concentrate on the flow of information in and between the major architectural structures of the system (STM, LTM, etc.). The primary issues are when, where, and how, rather than what information is processed. The principal structures of the system are fixed; they do not grow, neither do they function in dynamic interaction with a meaningful environment. Shaw and Bransford (1977) characterized the systems as "mechanistic," "purposeless," and "passive." A system that cannot grow or show adaptive modification to a changing environment is a strange metaphor for human thought processes, which are constantly changing over the life span of the individual and the sociocultural evolution of the race (Kvale, 1975; Riegel, 1975). This is the major criticism of such models raised by ecological psychologists; for example, Shaw and Bransford (1977) who believe that a "man-machine analogy becomes a hindrance rather than an aid to the psychological theory when it derails our thinking about how living creatures gather and act upon knowledge in dynamic natural contexts. Such questions can in no way be reduced to questions of how information is represented, stored, or retrieved from storage by static devices in artificially controlled experiments [p. 4–5]."

Notwithstanding these obvious limitations for a field devoted to understanding cognitive growth, theory-oriented developmental psychologists did adopt the prevailing metaphor with some success but also with many attendant problems that can serve to illustrate some limitations to the original model.

First the modal model of this type makes a sharp distinction between structure and process. This distinction has not gone unchallenged even within the domain of adult cognition (Winograd, 1975). As Newell (1972) has pointed out, what we regard as structure and what we regard as process are very much a function of the theoretical viewpoint we adopt. But this is even more troublesome for developmentalists, for what we regard as structural must undergo change if by structure we mean some limitation imposed by the impoverished state of the child's knowledge base (Brown, 1975; Chi, 1978).

A more specific type of structural limitation has been suggested by the computer models; it is more akin to the notion of channel capacity. If children do poorly on a rote-recall task, one might ask whether this is because of some capacity limitation, defined in terms of presence or absence of a major system, amount of space within one of the systems, or rate of decay. The notion that immature learners do suffer from some form of limited memory capacity is a dominant one (Chi, 1976), and it is only recently that a series of ingenious developmental studies (Chi, 1976; Huttenlocher & Burke, 1976) has come to grips with the difficulties in distinguishing between the "capacity" limitations of the immature that are structural or procedural. In summary of this work, there appears to be no compelling data to suggest that capacity differences, defined by presence or absence of an architectural system (e.g., STM), amount of space in one of the architectural units (e.g., the number of slots in STM), or in terms of durability of information in these systems, differentiates the child from the adult thinker (Belmont, 1972; Belmont & Butterfield, 1969; Brown, 1974; Chi, 1976; Wickelgren, 1975). What does hamper the inexperienced is the paucity of strategic processes available to the system and the debilitating effect of an impoverished knowledge base (Brown, in press a). The studies of Chi concerned with STM limitations and iconic memory in children illustrate the complexity of separating out process and structure, an illustration that is no less informative to the student of adult cognition.

Chi's (1976, 1978) theory is a good example of an information-processing developmental model that emphasizes the problems of an impoverished knowledge base. Long-term memory is seen as the repository of rules, strategies, and operations that can be used to make more efficient use of a limited capacity system; young children have not yet acquired these routines. In addition, Chi believes that the child's knowledge base is deficient in at least three ways: (a) the amount of information it contains, (b) the organization and internal coherence of that information, and (c) the number of available routes by which it can be reached. These differences impose several limitations on the child's information-processing abilities, even in such simple situations as reading information from the icon or maintaining information in STM (Chi, 1975, 1976). Such basic cognitive processes as ease of retrievability, and speed of encoding, naming, and recognition are all influenced by restrictions imposed by an impoverished knowledge base.

Although models such as Chi's provide some insight into what might develop within an information-processing framework, there are still some interesting difficulties when one tries to account for qualitative rather than quantitative growth. How does the system become rich, rather than impoverished, if by that we mean more than a mere accumulation of facts? How does the organization and internal cohesion of information change qualitatively with age? What is meant by the number of routes by which information is reached? Others have noted the problems with basic memory metaphors (Bransford & Franks, 1976; Neisser, 1967) with their emphasis on searching in discrete locations. If we really believe in an accumulation of facts, which become increasingly accessible by means of well-trodden routes, we must face fundamental problems when it comes to dealing with questions such as how such a system can recognize novelty (Höffding, 1891; Neisser, 1967) and why experts do not take longer to "access" their known facts than novices (Bransford, Nitsch, & Franks, 1977; Smith, Adams & Schorr, in press).

B. The Episodic–Semantic Distinction

One of the most influential distinctions to be made in the area of memory in recent years is that between semantic and episodic memory (Tulving, 1972). But the terms have come to mean different things to different people, and it is not at all clear that they produce either an exhaustive or exclusive classification. The confusion that has followed the idiosyncratic and varying usage of the terms has been dealt with elsewhere (Nelson & Brown, in press). Here I consider briefly the distinction in connection with how thinking systems grow.

In view of the controversy concerning terminology, I will state explicitly my use of the terms. The term *episodic* is used to refer to a form of memory input leading both to remembered autobiographical events (Tulving, 1972)—e.g., what happened on one's fifth birthday—and to the formation of generalized event structures, or scripts (Nelson, 1977; Schank, 1975)—e.g., what you expect to happen in a restaurant, at a store, etc. Both Schank (1975) and Nelson (1977) conceive of these generalized event structures as important components of an underlying conceptual memory, and as the most important component for the young child. The term *semantic* memory is reserved for the storing of information about words and concepts represented in the language, i.e., the strictly linguistic (lexical or semantic).

There has been a tendency in current developmental research to classify all of the child's real-world knowledge as semantic knowledge (Brown, 1975; see also Naus & Halasz, Chapter 12, this volume), thereby avoiding the central question of how semantic structures develop from episodic experience. For example, there is an increasing body of literature concerned with the very young child's memory for nonlinguistic information such as spatial layouts (Siegel & White, 1975), spatial locations (Acredolo, Pick, & Olsen, 1975; Harris, 1973), and actions (Foellinger & Trabasso, 1977). But these types of memories are neither "semantic" nor "episodic" as these terms have previously been defined. Clearly one of the major developmental questions, especially in the preschool period, is how such nonverbal memory relates to verbal memory, as well as vice versa. Labeling both types of representation *semantic* obscures rather than illuminates the problem.

The crucial developmental question has been raised and dropped by most theorists concerned with some variant of the episodic–semantic distinction. For example, Tulving (1972) stated that "relatively little is known about the role that the perceptual system and episodic memory play in the storage of information into semantic memory. Problems of acquisition of semantic information, and problems of modification of existing semantic structures, have not yet been studied by students of semantic memory . . . [p. 393]." This statement emphasizes the uncertain relation between semantic and episodic memory and the role of experience in the formation of both. Earlier, Posner and Warren (1972) were concerned with how automatic structures (semantic memory) are derivable from traces (episodic experience), but they too dropped the question. Similarly, Kintsch asked how does "general knowledge (semantic memory) develop on the basis of particular experiences (episodic memory)" although he notes "this question need not concern us here [Kintsch, 1974, p. 79]." Kintsch was also sensitive to the fact that nonverbal representation of knowledge must exist, for he states (1974):

It is unlikely that all knowledge can be represented in the same way. Propositional knowledge, which will be our sole concern, is primarily verbal, though it is possible to represent nonverbal information by such means as well. . . . On the other hand, analog representation of knowledge may underlie sensorimotor memory. The decision to neglect nonpropositional knowledge here by no means implies a judgment that only verbal sources of knowledge are worth considering for the psychologist. It merely reflects the state of the art today [p. 15].

This recurrent problem has especial importance for the developmental psychologist who must ask: How does the memory system of the young child encode and reconcile nonverbal and verbal sources of knowledge? How does the latter emerge from the former? Nelson's (1977) attempts to deal with this issue are of great importance for developmental theory, and the adult models themselves could be enriched by a consideration of the developmental issue.

C. Semantic Memory Models

Semantic memory models are currently fashionable and controversial (Collins & Loftus, 1975). I do not wish to enter this arena but do consider the models as they relate to the problem of growth. An excellent discussion of growth and semantic models can be found in several recent papers of Bransford and his colleagues (Bransford & Franks, 1976; Bransford & Nitsch, 1977; Bransford, Nitsch, & Franks, 1977), and therefore I touch only on the main points.

The main controversy engrossing semantic memory modelers concerns the nature of the organization in LTM, whether this is characterized as sets of features (Smith, Shoben, & Rips, 1974) or networks of relationships (Collins & Loftus, 1975). The main game played by the participants is some variant of a verification task. Subjects are required to verify that a canary has skin, or is yellow. The latter, they do more quickly; why? Whatever theory is espoused, a basic tenet is that the ease of verification can be accounted for by making assumptions concerning the preexisting structure of already-acquired information.

Bransford, Nitsch, and Franks (1977) wrote:

Theories of semantic memory therefore attempt to account for knowing solely on the basis of the structure of already acquired information. So-called "process" models of semantic memory are involved with elucidating how one uses *already stored* information to retrieve facts, make comparisons, etc. However these notions of "process" are not equivalent to the processes involved in the development of knowing. From the present perspective, the important processes involve knowing how to do something to *go beyond* what one knows right now [ms. p. 34].

The major development forays in this area have been studies showing that children have networks similar to adults (Nelson & Kosslyn, 1975) but again without consideration of how these structures arose or developed.

Although it would be simplistic to deny that an important aspect of understanding involves the relationship between what is now to be understood and what is already known, Bransford and his colleagues are certainly right in emphasizing that it is at least equally important to consider how novelty is comprehended. Novelty cannot simply be understood as a recombination of already available information, and this is nowhere more apparent than when one considers the problem of development. Children are universal novices; they must cope with novelty constantly. Semantic memory models cannot help us answer the problem of growth, for they have not been primarily concerned with the issue of how the system becomes a network, or feature repository, or how there develops a structure through which spreading activation can spread. This problem is isomorphic with the previously mentioned question of how an abstract decontextualized system of knowledge evolves from the personal episodic experience of the child (Nelson, 1977; Nelson & Brown, in press). The virtual equation of understanding with contacting previous knowledge must bring such models face to face with the problems of growth, novelty, and preformism, problems that present difficulties for all psychological theories.

D. Schema Theories of Knowing

Schema theories of human thought have been popular at least since Kant's (1787) *Critique of pure reason*; they have never been totally in abeyance, although in the heyday of radical behaviorism they lurked predominantly under the cover of the "soft" areas of developmental (Piaget, 1928) and social (Allport & Postman, 1945; Bartlett, 1932) psychology.

It is probably true that some version of a schema theory is the dominant metaphor of current cognitive psychologists; at least it is a very healthy contender for that position, vying only with the competing information-processing computer metaphor. Computer metaphors themselves have begun to incorporate schemalike entities into their conceptualization. Minsky's (1975) frame notion, which has been favored by workers in the Artificial Intelligence field (Charniak, 1975; Winograd, 1975), and Schank's scripts and plans are basically schemata notions (Schank & Abelson, 1975). The LNR group has not been entirely uninfluenced by AI, and they have also developed theories of schemata-driven cognition (Bobrow & Norman, 1975; Norman, 1975; Rumelhart & Ortony, 1977).

The defining features of schema theories are somewhat difficult to specify. The use of the term *schema* is widespread, vague, and not always overladen with meaning. One of my favorite games is to remove the word *schema* from a paper written in schematese and look for changes in meaning. Take, for example, the sentence "preexisting knowledge schemata function to orient people to interpret a message in a certain way." Where is the loss of clarity in removing the word *schemata*? It is somewhat surprising to find that there rarely is a loss of meaning following such ablation tactics. The foregoing sentence was one of my own, by the way, and I had already been through the paper eradicating superfluous schemata. To be fair, many of the more recent theories are far more precise in their use of the term (Rumelhart & Ortony, 1977), but there is still an abundance of needless schematese in contemporary cognitive psychology.

The major scaffolding of schema theories seems to be some version of the Piagetian assimilation and accommodation interaction or the reflection—refraction transactions of Soviet dialectic theories (Wozniak, 1975). Assimilation is the function by which the events of the world are incorporated into preexisting knowledge structures, whereas accomodation is the process by which the existing knowledge structures are modified in accordance with novel events. By the reciprocal influence of input on preexisting concepts and extant knowledge on input, the thinker comes to know his or her world. There are nontrivial problems associated with both terms. Recent theorists have taken divergent opinions on the issue, ranging from those who have few problems with assimilation but question how accommodation occurs (Anderson, 1977), those who accept accommodation but express concerns with assimilation (Neisser, 1976a), and those who appear to be disconcerted by both (Turvey, 1977). One cannot legitimately consider assimilation without accommodation or vice versa, as they are twin mechanisms in a dynamic transaction. But I will try to give the flavor of objections to both processes, as if they could be separated. In keeping with the focus of this chapter, I concentrate on issues of critical interest to the basic developmental questions: growth and change.

A major criticism of schema theories in adult cognition is that they are basically assimilation models. Mechanisms that permit acquisition and articulation of schemata are not specified in sufficient detail to afford an adequate developmental perspective. How are existing conceptions modified in the face of inconsistent input? How do such theories deal with novelty? To say that "learning may be dealt with by supposing that when a radically new input is encountered a [new schema] without variables is constructed" (Rumelhart & Ortony, 1977, p. 125) does not tell us either how we know it is a new input or how we construct a new schema. Similarly it is undoubtedly true that much schema growth can be accounted for by the twin processes of schema generalization and schema specification (Rumelhart & Ortony, 1977), but the theory is quite vague concerning the mechanisms and contexts that would permit such development.

The problem of growth is not only of gradual extension and refinement of schemata, but an adequate theory must be able to account for major changes in perspective (Anderson, 1977) or paradigmatic shifts of theory or world view (Kuhn, 1970). It must also deal with emotionally based resistance to such major cognitive reorganization, for it is true that inconsistencies and counterexamples are often assimilated into schemata to which a person is heavily committed, as Abelson's (1973) Cold Warrior example can illustrate. Accommodation is not the necessary result of inconsistent input. What then would constitute necessary or sufficient conditions for a schema shift, or major accommodation, to occur? How does our preexisting knowledge change as a function of experience? by gradual extension? by dynamic shifts in perspectives? (For a detailed discussion of this point, see Anderson, 1977.)

There are those for whom the problems of accommodation are relatively trivial, for one must first account for assimilation. Gibsonian-attuned theorists find the latter to be the more problematic concept. Assimilation presupposes at least two interrelated assumptions that render the concept implausible for Gibsonians and embarrassing for schema theorists whose consciousness has been raised by this school (Neisser, 1976a). First, one can know only by reference to prior knowledge. Closely linked to this problem is the age-old one of preformism, or radical nativism; i.e., the organism must come prewired with a set of schemata; some knowledge about the world must be present from the very beginning.

The problem of preformism has been dealt with in depth by Shaw and Bransford (1977). No one really questions that phylogenetic attunement of some kind must preset an organism to interact with its environment. Radical empiricism is no longer a viable tenet, for most contemporary theories accept some form of genetic attunement, some primitive universals, even though there is considerable discussion concerning what these might be.

The notion that assimilation involves epistemic mediation of some form is also a theoretically controversial one (Turvey, 1977). Gibsonians, as direct though critical realists, believe that everything we can perceive we perceive directly and there is no problem for such theories of input change or internal representation. Schema theorists, on the other hand, do invoke some epistemic mediation. Truly constructive theories are awkwardly autistic; if we truly construct our world, and we all construct it on the basis of our unique configuration of individual experience, it would be difficult to account for how accurately we perceive our world and how constant is the pattern of major ontogenetic change. Neisser (1976a) reaches a form of compromise in that he assumes that perceiving does not change the world, it changes the perceiver; so that information in the world is only significant, indeed can only be picked up, if there is a developmental format ready to accept it. For a full discussion of these differences, the reader is referred to Neisser (1976a), Bransford, Franks, Morris, and Stein (Chapter 15, this volume), and Shaw and Bransford (1977).

Thus a major problem with assimilation theories is the now familiar argument that it is only possible to understand current input by reference to preexisting structures. This is as problematic for schema theories as for any other. And it is exacerbated by the tendency of some schema theorists to maintain the terminology of a memory metaphor by referring to schemata as if they were knowledge structures stored in the head. Schemata have slots into which things fit; frames often read very much like static places to put things in. But if this is so, then one could only know by rifling through available schemata until one finds a suitable fit; or one could invoke a notion of content-addressable schemata! This is one of the common pitfalls that schema theories wish to avoid. Experience does not result in the formation of an inner replica of an event in the head, but it functions more by altering or tuning the organism in such a way that it will see all subsequently related events in a new light. Reconstituted schema theories (Neisser, 1976a) do go part of the way in avoiding the content-address-able problem by this notion of tuning, which is the result of the dynamic, reciprocal relation between the current cognitive–perceptual situation and the significant information in the environment (Bransford et al., 1977). Schemata are not filed in a library system in the mind. As Neisser points out (1976a), "someone who has a currently inactive schema should not be thought of as an owner of a particular kind of mental property. He is just an organism with a particular potentiality. His inactive schema are not objects but aspects of the structure of his nervous system [p. 62]." Similarly, Bransford's notion of experience setting the stage (Bransford & Franks, 1976) for grasping the significance of an event is a tuning notion that has much in common with the Gibsonian concepts of the mutual compatibility between the organism's effec-tivities (goal-directed functions that reflect its potential actions) and the environ-mental affordances. There are major differences, to be sure, between the Gibsonian ecological theories and even reconstituted schema theories (Neisser, 1976a), and these differences center on the problem of epistemic mediation (Turvey, 1977). But there is a convergence on the important issue that remains the mutual compatibility of the organism and its naturally evolving environ-mental niche.

In summary, the fundamental problems facing schema theories are the same as those that must eventually be confronted by any adequate psychological model. They must be able to deal with such issues as: With what preexisting structures must the nascent organism come equipped? how do these structures undergo change with age and experience? how does the organism go beyond its current state of knowing? how are the perceptual and cognitive systems preattuned by experience? in short, how do we account for cognitive growth? One of the major influences of the ecological theories (Shaw & Bransford, 1977; Turvey, 1977) is that they force us to address just these issues, even if they cannot yet resolve them.

E. Developmental Theories

In the last stop in this quick tour of theories of cognition and the concept of growth, I now consider briefly developmental theories, lumped together into one uneasy category. It is a natural step to go from a consideration of schema theories to the developmental literature, as most of the dominant theories of cognitive development are based on some schemalike construct. This is true of European (Binet & Henri, 1894; Piaget, 1971), Soviet (Riegel, 1975; Wozniak, 1975), and

American (Werner, 1948) psychology, in some guise or another. It would, of course, be impossible to give even a thumbnail description of the viable developmental models; and in keeping with the main focus of this section of the paper, I concentrate only on how developmental models cope with growth. One might imagine that a consideration of theories specifically addressed to growing organisms might provide some answers not found in adult models. A concern with growth should be a defining feature of a theory of cognitive development. Unfortunately, this is not so; developmental theories have also been adept at avoiding the basic issue of growth by describing what develops rather than concentrating on how growth occurs. Indeed, just as a major problem with adult models is that they are generally silent on the issue of how thinking systems grow or change, so too, a major objection to many developmental models is that at best they provide a description of the stages or states of development but they cannot account for the transformations that lead to growth (Nelson, 1977). There is considerable disagreement surrounding even such basic issues as whether cognitive growth is a continuous process that proceeds slowly and gradually or whether it consists of a set of abrupt, stagelike leaps (Flavell, 1971; Toussaint, 1974).

To illustrate how developmental models have difficulty with the concept of growth, I use a somewhat extreme example. At a recent conference concerned with intelligence, Klahr (1976) presented a simulation of children's performance on Piagetian conservation problems. But in order to successfully model this development, Klahr would need to build into his system some accommodation-like process. In short, to model growth, one must understand it. Neisser, as the discussant of the paper, pointed out that this is exactly what systems like Klahr's cannot do, for we do not yet understand the processes of growth. According to Neisser (1976b), the system proposed by Klahr:

> . . . does not undergo accommodation; it does not learn. Klahr agrees that the issue of self-modification is central to the conception of intelligence, but neither his own system nor any of those reviewed by him meet this issue successfully. For better or worse my [Neisser's] 1963 claim that Artificial Intelligence has not modeled cognitive development remains valid. There is a reason for this. The development of human intelligence occurs in a real environment with coherent properties of its own. Many of these properties vary greatly from one situation to another; others remain invariant at a deeper level. As long as programs do not represent this *environment* systematically, in at least some of its complexity, they cannot represent cognitive growth either. [pp. 143–144].

Thus for Neisser, as well as for ecological theorists (Shaw & Bransford, 1977), the minimum unit of analysis must be the activity of the organism in its natural environmental niche.

It is perhaps not too surprising that Klahr could not successfully capture the essence of accommodation in a computer simulation. But how successful, in this regard, has been the pivotal developmental model, Piagetian theory. I have a sneaking suspicion that Piaget's theory is a gigantic projective test and that it is possible to find there what one is looking for—surely a confirmation of Piaget's basic tenet. What follows is my interpretation of the essence of the theory. Piaget's theory rests on his changing notion of equilibration, which is seen by some to be a homeostatic mechanism (Riegel, 1975). The organism is constantly seeking balance and stability. Every interaction with the environment precipitates a compensating equilibration activity consisting of both an assimilative and accommodative function. The end state of these reciprocal forces is balance. A problem here is that such a homeostatic notion would serve to maintain a child at a given level of development, and one major issue has been how Piaget extracts himself from the dilemma of providing a basically homeostatic model of account for growth.

Piaget is not insensitive to this issue as some of his critics would have us believe (Riegel, 1974), and in his more recent writings he has introduced the homeorhetic (Pufall, 1977) processes of physical and reflective abstraction (Piaget, 1970, 1971). These are not easy concepts to come to grips with, and luckily, for my purposes here, it is sufficient to point out that the major questions that Piaget is attempting to answer in his more recent work focus on the problem of growth. Indeed, Riegel (1974) has characterized Piaget's own development as one of three stages—the functional, the structural, and now the transformational periods.

Thus, it would seem that even developmental theories have not yet arrived at a satisfactory conception of change and growth; as with adult theories, the tendency is to fall back on an accumulation notion sometimes accompanied by reference to some unspecified qualitative reorganization at some unspecified critical stages. In defense of such theories, however, it should be said that they do address the issue; it is a constant concern; it is the focal point where theoretical controversy centers. For example, the stage vs. continuous growth controversy (Flavell, 1971), which dominated the 1960s, centered on the problem of growth. In the 1970s, another theoretical controversy has arisen—although not everyone would believe it to be a controversy (Youniss, 1974)—between Piagetian "structuralism" and Soviet dialecticism as espoused by its American adherents (Riegel, 1975; Wozniak, 1975). This controversy was nicely illustrated by the football analogy introduced by Gardner (1973) and extended by Riegel (1974). In order to illustrate the methods of structural analysis used by Lévi–Strauss to examine rituals and orgies of primitive societies, Gardner subjected American football to a similar analysis. There is structure in the field, the rules of the game, and the strategies of performance. The action is characterized by a sequence of sudden quick actions, each leading to a new structural state where the action appears to be temporarily frozen. Riegel believes this analogy is suitable for capturing the essence of a structural theory of growth like Piaget's early conceptions. By contrast, Riegel believes that dialectic theories, such as his own, can best be characterized by analogy to soccer, a game of ceaseless action that depends on continuous interactions between the individual members and the transaction between the members of opposing teams. Soccer, like dialectic theory, is a game of continuous motion; football, like structural theory, is one of sudden activity producing stable states. The analogy has flaws certainly, but it does illustrate that one of the current controversies in developmental theory—dialecticism vs. Piagetian structuralism—is rooted in the notions of growth and change. Whether or not these theoretical metaphors lead to a concrete increase in our understanding of human growth, they at least sensitize us to a major problem for psychological theory.

Although space limitations must restrict my treatment of most aspects of the dialectic approach to human growth, I would like to add one point. Another criticism leveled against Piagetian theory by the dialectic school is that it concentrates on biological maturation and individual interactions with objects in the world; the impression is that these forces play the primary role in development. By contrast, Riegel (1975) and his adherents stress the Soviet position that development is largely the result of sociohistorical influences. I believe the difference is only one of emphasis and the value of both theories is the concentration on the individual, the environment, and the mutual compatibility between the two. Together with many recent calls for an "ecological psychology" (Brown, 1977, in press a; Brown & DeLoache, in press; Bruner, 1972; Cole & Scribner, 1977; Neisser, 1976a, 1976b; Shaw & Bransford, 1977), the two major global developmental theories lay stress on the essential importance of considering ontogenetic and phylogenetic adaptation as adaptation to dynamic natural contexts. Human thought is naturally evolving, and although this undoubtedly complicates the issue, psychologists eventually must consider adaptation in reference to the particular sociohistorical context in which the organism has evolved and must survive.

I would like to end this section with another quote from Neisser. "No theory that fails to acknowledge the possibility of development can be taken seriously as an account of human cognition" (Neisser, 1976a, p. 62). As yet, neither the major adult or developmental models can satisfactorily account for growth other than by postulating a gradual accumulation of facts, accompanied by some unspecified qualitative reorganization and restructuring. We are, however, beginning to see frameworks in which to couch the question, particularly Bransford and Nitsch's (1977) abduction schema, Neisser's (1976a) updated schema theory, Piaget's (1971) inchoate notions of reflective abstraction, and the ecological theories of Turvey and Shaw, (Shaw & Bransford, 1977; Turvey, 1977). The main point of this section was not, unfortunately, to provide new insights into the problem of growth but to illustrate that attention to issues of growth and change should be an essential factor in the formation of our conceptions about human thought.

III.   LEVELS OF PROCESSING AND
DEVELOPMENTAL PSYCHOLOGY

To have progressed this far in the paper without mentioning levels-of-processing (LOP) models might seem somewhat perverse, given the theme of the volume, but the participants were encouraged to consider alternative viewpoints. In the preceding section, I dealt mainly with reasons why developmental psychologists and those concerned with adult cognition do not generally cross-fertilize each other's theory construction. In this section I emphasize why it is that LOP frameworks are the major exception to this rule. From their very inception, the LOP frameworks have been adopted and incorporated into the developmental literature. Why should this be so? What distinguishes LOP models from other adult models, so that they are particularly compatible with developmental approaches? They certainly do not deal satisfactorily with the issue of growth, relying as they do on the typical gradual incremental notion. They bypass the thorny problem of assimilation—accommodation with statements such as "highly familiar, meaningful stimuli are compatible *by definition* [emphasis mine] with existing cognitive structures" (Craik & Lockhart, 1972, p. 676). Although they helped us avoid some of the less fruitful blind alleys of the container metaphors (Brown & DeLoache, in press), they still maintain much of the terminology of general memory metaphors (Bransford & Franks, 1976). Why then have LOP frameworks been so readily adopted by developmental theorists?

I have described the major impact of LOP frameworks in previous papers (Brown, 1974, 1975), and Naus and Halasz (Chapter 12, this volume) also give an excellent in-depth review of the literature; I do not want to reiterate much of this discussion. I argue here that the compatibility between LOP approaches and developmental psychology is due to the fact that developmental models have always been predominantly LOP frameworks. Both emphasize three (not independent) main points: (a) the concept of *voluntary* versus *involuntary* memory; (b) the idea that it is the *activity* of the subject that determines what is remembered; and (c) *headfitting* (Brown, 1975; Jenkins, 1971, 1974), nicely captured in Jenkins's quote (1971): "the head remembers what it does [p. 285]". These three points are the major issues that guide empirical work in developmental psychology, whether the orientation is European (Binet & Henri, 1894; Piaget, 1970), American (Brown, 1975), or Russian (Istomina, 1975; Vygotsky, 1962; Yendovitskaya, 1971).

A. Voluntary vs. Involuntary Memory

1. *Voluntary and deliberate learning.*   A primary distinction made by Soviet developmental psychologists is that between voluntary and involuntary memory. This is roughly equivalent to the LOP distinction between incidental

and intentional learning. Voluntary or intentional learning refers to the standard situation in laboratory memory tests (and schools), where the subject is specifically requested to invoke all efforts to retain the material. Under such circumstances, adults deploy a remarkable array of ingenious mnemonics, even when faced with the most impoverished stimuli or artificial laboratory tasks (Reitman, 1970); indeed, it is extremely difficult to interfere with this ingenuity. There is, however, ample evidence that young children do not spontaneously employ a variety of strategic methods until the onset of the grade-school years and that they continue to refine and extend their repertoire as they mature. Along with the gradual emergence and refinement of specific memorial strategies, the child's knowledge and control of these processes also develop as he or she is faced increasingly with more demanding situations. Children learn to evaluate realistically the task demands (Brown, 1978a, 1978b), their memory ability (Brown, Campione, & Murphy, 1977; Brown & Lawton, 1977; Flavell, Friedrichs, & Hoyt, 1970), and the interaction of their abilities and the task (Brown & Barclay, 1976). The development of knowledge about memory—metamemory (Brown, 1975, 1977, in press a; Brown & DeLoache, in press; Campione & Brown, 1977; Flavell & Wellman, 1977)—has only recently received attention; however, such knowledge and beliefs concerning one's own memory processes must play a vital role in determining if strategies and plans will be adopted and if appropriate plans will be used. Without such introspective knowledge, it would be difficult if not impossible to select an appropriate strategy at the onset of a task and to change or modify that strategy in the face of its success of failure.

To illustrate the development of knowledge and control of deliberate strategies for learning, I will briefly describe some ongoing research from my laboratory concerned with acquiring information from prose passages (Brown & Smiley, 1977; in press). Our subject population has ranged from preschoolers as young as 3 years of age to college students, and the stories are adapted to suit the different age groups. We find two main consistencies across age: With or without conscious intent to do so, subjects extract the main theme of a story and ignore trivia. Even the youngest child's recall favors the essential action sequences of the story. In addition, children are misled in their comprehension of stories by the same snares that trap adults (Brown, Smiley, Day, Townsend, & Lawton, 1977). Led to believe certain "facts" concerning a main character or the location of an action, facts that never appear in the original story, children disambiguate and elaborate in the same way as adults (Anderson & Reder, Chapter 18, this volume). They falsely recognize theme-congruent distractors in recognition tests and introduce importations from their preexisting knowledge when recalling. Furthermore, they have difficulty distinguishing between their own elaborations and the actual story content.

There are some interesting developmental trends, however, that follow from the increasingly strategic nature of the older child's study habits. As children mature, they become able to identify the essential organizing features and crucial elements of texts (Brown & Smiley, 1977; in press). Thanks to this foreknowledge, they make better use of extended study time. If given an extra period for study, children from seventh grade up improve their recall considerably for important elements of text; recall of less important details does not improve. Children below seventh grade do not usually show such effective use of additional study time; their recall improves, if at all, evenly across all levels of importance. As a result, older students' recall protocols following study include all the essential elements and little trivia. Younger children's recall, though still favoring important elements, has many such elements missing.

The older students benefit from increased study time as a direct result of their strategic intervention, which in turn rests on their ability to predict ahead of time what are important elements of the text. Younger students, not so prescient, cannot be expected to distribute extra time intelligently; they do not concentrate on only the important elements, since they do not know in advance what they are. To substantiate this hypothesis, consider the overt study actions of the subjects—in particular, the physical records they provided, notes and underlining of texts. A certain proportion of children from fifth grade and up spontaneously underlined or took notes during study. At all ages, the physical records of spontaneous subjects favored the important elements; i.e., the notes or underlined sections concentrated on elements of the text previously rated as crucial to the theme.

Students induced to adopt one of these strategies did not show a similar sensitivity to importance; they took notes or underlined more randomly. Some of the very young children underlined almost all the text when told to underline! Although the efficiency of physical record keeping in induced subjects did improve with age, it never reached the standard set by spontaneous users of the strategy. Furthermore, the recall scores of spontaneous producers were much superior. Even the few fifth graders who spontaneously underlined showed an adultlike pattern and used extra study to differentially improve their recall of important elements. The relationship between spontaneous strategy use and effective recall was clear for all ages.

This brief summary of some ongoing research illustrates what I believe to be a repetitive pattern in cognitive development. What develops with age and experience is often increasing strategic control over an early emerging process. For example, even young children extract the essential gist of a story if they are not misled by red herrings, such as artificially increased salience of nonessential detail. With increasing experience with such tasks, children acquire this propensity and gradually refine their control over these strategies. Using their knowledge about elements of texts, their knowledge concerning how to study, and the interface of these two factors, older students can become much more efficient when processing information presented in texts. A similar developmental pattern can be found in many other deliberate (voluntary) learning situations (Brown, 1974, 1975).

2. *Involuntary memory or incidental learning.* Involuntary memory is roughly the equivalent of incidental learning in the LOP framework, and indeed both the Soviet and American schools distinguish between two main types of involuntary memory. The first is the product of a deliberate learning task, for the subject is involved in a learning problem during which he or she is exposed to material that is irrelevant to the task as specified by the learning instructions. This is a Type II incidental learning situation, according to Postman's (1964) nomenclature. Both American and Soviet (Smirnov & Zinchenko, 1969; Vygotsky, 1962; Zinchenko, 1962) developmental psychologists have found the same pattern in children. As they mature, they increasingly attend to informative and ignore irrelevant aspects of a learning situation.

The second type of incidental learning situation, the Type I task (Postman, 1964), has generated the most interest within the LOP models. Here the subject is exposed to the stimulus material but is given no explicit instructions to learn; the subject interacts with the material for purposes other than the intent to learn. Under these circumstances, adults (Craik & Lockhart, 1972) as well as children (Istomina, 1975; Murphy & Brown, 1975; Smirnov & Zinchenko, 1969) retain more information if the orienting instructions are sufficient to induce deep, meaningful processing. The paradigm is of particular interest to developmentalists, because a specific developmental prediction can be made. As young children are not noted for the production of effective strategies in response to instructions to learn, children performing a favorable orienting task should do

TABLE 11.1
Proportion Correct Recall by Intentional and
Incidental Learners: Preschool Children.

Condition	Study 1[a]	Study 2[a]	Study 3[b]
Intentional learning	0.33	0.22	0.44
Semantic orienting tasks			
Categorize	0.49	0.41	0.64
Buying items at store	0.51	–	–
Nice-Nasty	–	0.38	–
Formal orienting tasks			
Sound	0.29	–	–
Color	0.24	0.18	–

[a]Adapted from Murphy & Brown (1975).
[b]Adapted from Zinchenko (1962).

better than those under instructions to attempt deliberate learning with no mention of what strategy they might adopt. Again, both Soviet (Vygotsky, 1962; Zinchenko, 1962) and American (Murphy & Brown, 1975) developmental psychologists have confirmed this prediction. In Table 11.1 we present some representative data. Although the absolute level of recall varies, as do the experimental procedures, the same pattern is observed. Intentional learners do less well than those performing any of a variety of semantic orienting tasks. Indeed, they perform at approximately the same level as children performing formal orienting tasks such as identifying the color of objects or initial sounds of words.

We have further evidence from our laboratory that it is the deployment of strategies suitable to the task that induces effective learning. Thieman (1976), in an unpublished doctoral dissertation, divided his intentional learners (adults) into subgroups depending on the strategy they reported using. These data are shown in Table 11.2. When one considers the combined mean for all intentional learners, they appear to be performing as well as in the most effective semantic orienting conditions, a typical finding in the literature. However, when one considers the intentional learners, as a function of the strategy they adopt, the more ingenious tend to perform better than subjects in the best semantic orienting conditions, and the less ingenious tend to perform as poorly as on the worst semantic orienting task and, indeed, as poorly as in the formal orienting conditions. These data, taken together with the developmental literature, provide strong support for the hypothesis that intentional learning instructions are only

TABLE 11.2
Mean Proportion Correct Recall of Intentional Learners
as a Function of Strategy (Adapted from Thieman, 1976).

Group	Strategy	Experiments		
		1	2	3
Intentional learners	(a) Stories, sentences, or scenes	0.67	0.59	0.46
	(b) Interitem associates or categories	0.36	0.48	0.45
	(c) Rote rehearsal	0.30	0.37	0.34
	Total	0.44	0.48	0.42
Incidental learners[a]	(a) Semantic orientation	0.33-0.46	0.38-0.49	0.44-0.51
	(b) Formal orientation	–	0.30-0.35	0.31

[a]The incidental learners are included for comparative reasons. The orienting tasks varied widely across studies. Included here is the range between the least and most effective conditions.

effective to the degree that they induce suitable strategies. Instructions to learn per se seem to be irrelevant.

As a final example of the interesting interaction of age by voluntary – involuntary memory conditions, I have chosen one of the original studies conducted with the paradigm by Zinchencko in approximately 1940 (see Wertsch, 1977, for translation). This is a particularly interesting study, not only because its early emergence reinforces a cyclical notion of history (all the elements of our current incidental – intentional studies are there) but also because it provides some evidence of an interaction between orienting activity and the nature of the material to be processed, a basic LOP notion. Adult and child subjects were given sets of four words, each consisting of a target item (e.g., *house*) and three associates called logical (e.g., *building*), concrete (e.g., *window*), or no meaningful connection (*fish*). These are the only examples given, so it is difficult to specify what a logical or concrete connection is exactly. However, from the example it looks like they are dealing with taxonomic-superordinate versus thematic categories (Overcast, Murphy, Smiley, & Brown, 1975). For adult subjects there were three incidental orienting tasks: Underline the word in each set with (a) a logical connection, (b) a concrete connection, and (c) with no meaningful connection to the target. The data for immediate (surprise) free recall are given in Table 11.3. There is an interaction between type of material and orienting activity. For subjects seeking logical connections, logical connections are recalled than concrete ones, which in turn are recalled better than the unrelated items. Variations in orienting instruction, however, modify this somewhat, for subjects seeking concrete connections remember slightly more concrete words than logical ones. Note also that the subjects in the no-connection group dramatically improve their recall of no-connection words. The interaction of material with orienting instruction is an interesting one that is repeated in the data from further groups of adults who performed the same orienting task together with instructions to learn the specific words they underline. The degree of retention is a function of both the type of material and the orienting task of the subject.

The developmental data, also included in Table 11.3, are incomplete and a little confusing. The pattern for young school children is reasonably clear. Incidental orienting instructions, if anything, produce better recall than intentional learning situations, even when the same activity was engaged in by both groups. For older children, the pattern is more complex. In the incidental condition, the same pattern of results is found (with lower overall recall scores) for both adults and children, an interaction of orienting activity and stimulus type. In the intentional condition, however, a different pattern emerged. Zinchenko describes these middle-school children as just at the stage when they had gained considerable control of mnemonics of rote recall, which they applied diligently. But they had great difficulty initially remembering any of the unrelated words; as a result, they devoted considerable extra effort in the

TABLE 11.3
From P. I. Zinchenko, *Involuntary Memory* (1962)
College Student Data.

Orienting Condition	Incidental			Intentional		
Instructions	Logical	Concrete	None	Logical	Concrete	None
Material						
Logical	7.0	5.9	5.2	7.1	5.2	4.8
Concrete	4.7	5.2	4.5	4.1	5.4	4.4
None	1.8	2.0	3.2	1.5	1.6	3.4
Old School Children						
Logical	5.7		4.1	8.3		2.8
Concrete	3.6		3.7	4.2		2.3
None	0.4		2.9	0.5		6.2
Young School Children						
Logical	5.4			4.0		
Concrete	2.6			2.4		
None	1.1			1.0		

intentional condition when asked to remember the unrelated words. Subsequently, they dramatically improved recall of unrelated words at the expense of the logical and concrete connections. This is a complicated study, and its results can only be explained by recourse to much post hoc speculation (a clean replication would be welcomed); however, it does show that the interaction between strategies and material is an interesting one.

B. Activity and the Goal of Actions

Activity, referred to variously as mental operations or mental activity, is a central issue for LOP frameworks. Craik and Tulving summarized the literature in 1975: "All these studies conform to the new look in memory research in that the stress is on mental operations; items are remembered not as presented stimuli acting on the organism, but as components of mental activity. Subjects remember not what was out there but what they did during encoding [p. 292]."

In its first version this "new" focus on activity involved a somewhat simplistic conception of good and bad operations that could be performed by the learner. For example, it was easy to infer from the original descriptions of orienting activities that semantic ones were good and formal ones were bad.

There are at least two problems with the invited inference. First it suggests a neat dichotomy between the types of tasks, and second it ignores the necessary relationship between a processing activity and the goal at hand.

Consider first the dichotomy notion. Semantic-orienting tasks were thought to be those that required the subject to consider the meaning of stimuli, whereas formal tasks did not require a consideration of meaning. Although the division of orienting tasks based on the presence or absence of a requirement to consider meaning has a good deal of intuitive appeal, this view is not without its difficulties. First is the problem of determining an appropriate point of division between semantic and nonsemantic tasks, for several of the tasks selected appear to fall into a virtual no-man's-land. One difficulty of categorizing some tasks is that they can be performed in several ways; so the tasks themselves are neither semantic nor nonsemantic, but the operations carried out to perform the tasks can be based on either type of strategy. For example, determining the part of speech of words may be performed either by paying attention to the morphology or phonology of the words or by considering their meanings. This is not to imply that the two levels of decision are mutually exclusive, but differences in emphasis may explain why Hyde and Jenkins (1973) consider this a nonsemantic task, whereas Eagle and Leiter (1964) and Mandler and Worden (1973) consider it a semantic task. In short, a more reasonable assessment of the type of operations that can be performed by the learner is that they form a continuum in terms of the degree of semantic analysis that must be undertaken (Thieman, 1976).

A further problem related to the classification of tasks or underlying processes as semantic or nonsemantic on the basis of recall performance is the often-cited circular and post hoc nature of this reasoning. Roughly, the argument states that since semantic or deep processing results in efficient retention, then if an orienting task produces high retention in incidental learning, it must have entailed semantic processing. But how strongly should the argument aligning memory and meaningful analysis be made? The strongest position holds that semantic processing is both a necessary and sufficient condition for good memory. This view is expressed by Craik and Tulving (1975), who state ''it seems clear that attention to the word's meaning is a necessary prerequisite of good retention [p. 269],'' and that ''it now becomes possible to entertain the hypothesis that optimal processing of individual words, qua individual words, is sufficient to support good recall [p. 270].'' An equally extreme alternative position would be that semantic analysis is neither necessary nor sufficient for good memory, but the efficiency of retention is attributable to some other factor, such as the development of effective retrieval cues, that may be semantically or nonsemantically related to the presented material.

A compromise between the two positions seems to have been reached (Tulving, Chapter 19, this volume); i.e., recall of a large number of unrelated items will be unsuccessful, regardless of whether the meaning of each item has been considered, unless there exists some systematic retrieval mechanisms for reinstating those items at recall. Experiments by Craik and Tulving (1975), Schulman (1975), and Moscovitch and Craik (1976) also provide strong evidence that under certain circumstances semantic analysis is insufficient to ensure high recall unless the products of this semantic analysis form a "coherent, integrated unit" that can serve as an effective redintegrative cue at recall (Horowitz & Prytulak, 1969). The compatibility of encoding and retrieval environments has been discussed at length by other contributors to this volume (Tulving, Chapter 19; Bransford et al., Chapter 15).

The controversy concerning encoding–retrieval compatibility was a reaction to the early attempts of LOP adherents to classify activity irrespective of the goal of that activity. Postman (1975) suggested that there is a significant distinction to be drawn between *deep* processing and optimal processing; but optimal can only be defined in the context of the particular goal of the processing. Optimal processing must be whatever is most effective in the total context of the subject's goal-directed activity; for it is the purposive nature of activities that guides the selection of information (Cassirer, 1946). Seen in this light, it should not matter where on the formal–semantic dimension an encoding activity might fall; the crucial variable would be the compatibility of the activity with the task demands, task demands that include retrieval as well as acquisition restraints. Bransford and his colleagues (Bransford et al., Chapter 15, this volume; Morris, Bransford, & Franks, 1977) report an experiment in support of this position, for under certain conditions a typical formal task—rhyming—can be superior to a typical semantic task—fitting words into sentences. The trick was that the "retention" test required the subjects to make use of rhyme-relevant information. The main point is that it is only in the context of what the subject is doing that one can meaningfully speak of optimal activity. This statement is also a fair representation of one of the basic tenets of the Soviet theory of activity (Leont'ev, 1974; Wertsch, 1977; Zinchenko, 1962)—that actions, operations, and activities are always purposive; they do not occur in a vacuum; they occur in the context of some meaningful goal.

One of the main difficulties of giving a quick sketch of the Soviet theory of activity is confusion concerning their nomenclature, and I am sure that real devotees will find much to quarrel with in my usage of terms. The Soviets make quite subtle distinctions between terms such as *activities, actions, acts, operations, motives, means,* and *goals.* For this reason it is often difficult to follow their discourse, and I suspect that the problem is exacerbated because the terms, so subtly defined originally, are sometimes used interchangeably by translators. A detailed review of the theories can be found elsewhere (Meacham, 1977; Wertsch, 1977); here I give my translation of the major positions, changing the terms when necessary to be consistent.

The most difficult term is *activity* itself. *Activities* are defined as molar processes by which we "transform objects into subjective forms and make objective the more subjective aspects of personality (cf. assimilation and accommodation in Piaget's theory). Thus activities structure the relationship of the individual to his material and social world, and it is through his activities that the individual is able to understand or give meaning to his external world" (Meacham, 1977, p. 276). Thus the term *activity* is used to refer to the assimilation–accommodation interaction of man and the external world. But it is also used to refer to the current social pursuit the individual is engaged in. At each stage of development, a particular form of activity becomes dominant; that is, it is the *"leading" activity* of that stage of ontogenesis. It is within the context of the leading activity that the major reorganizations of mental processes will occur. For example, it is within the context of manipulating objects and developing means of direct emotional communication, the leading activities of infancy, that the very young child comes to know the world and to structure that knowledge. Although the sequence of leading activities will be modified by the particular environment in which the individual must function, the "normal" progression described by the Soviets for modern development in schooled societies is manipulation of objects and direct emotional communication, followed by play, then school-related learning and interpersonal communication, and finally career-related learning activities (Elkonin, 1972; Kussman, 1976). For example, it is a typical Soviet-inspired statement that the leading activity of schools is the development of decontextualized skills of deliberate learning (Brown, in press a).

Activities, whether leading or otherwise, serve to motivate certain specific *actions* (sometimes confusingly called *acts*), which are directed toward a conscious goal. A goal-directed action can be performed by means of various *operations* depending on the particular task demand. Even these operations might have subparts, sometimes called *acts*, associated with them. To interject some well-needed concrete examples, consider the case of a child during a play activity of constructing a toy boat, going to get a list of items needed for that construction. The *leading activity* of early childhood is play. The specific goal-directed *action* the child is currently engaged in is building the boat. One *operation* he must perform in order to carry out this action is remembering the list of items he must fetch, and an *act* of remembering might be rehearsal. Note that the operation of remembering here is subordinated to the action of building a toy; it is not the goal in itself. In another context, remembering could be the goal. For example, consider an older child in a school situation who is directed to learn a vocabulary list. Here the *leading activity* of middle childhood is school-related learning; the specific goal-directed *action* is rote remembering; an *operation* that might be used to accomplish this could be rehearsal. Note two things: Rehearsal, for example, out of context, cannot be designated an act, an operation, or an action. It can only be defined in terms of its place within the total activity of the child in context. Second, note that in both examples, remembering is more or less deliberate; but in the second it is the goal itself, whereas in the first it is subordinated to the goal of building a toy. Finally, it should be emphasized that the voluntary−involuntary distinction as well as the definition of an activity can only be made in the context of a purposive goal-directed pursuit.

Although the terminology of the Russian literature may be less than helpful, the basic philosophy is simple and entirely compatible with the position that the subjects' activities are optimal only in the sense that they are tailored to some goal in a purposive sequence. Activities are purposive, goal-directed, and occur in natural contexts. The theory has much in common with that of transfer-appropriate processing developed by Bransford and his colleagues (Chapter 15, this volume).

Before leaving the Soviet theory of activity, there is one implication that has particular relevance for developmentalists but also might be informative for those who deal with adult subjects. The Soviet position that one cannot divorce an activity from its purpose and that activities take place in natural contexts is beginning to have an important influence on the way developmental psychologists conduct their investigations. Developmental psychology as an experimental science is a relatively new area of specialization in American psychology. Initial forays in this field were very much influenced by experimental psychology, which until the 1960s meant animal experimentation. The early questions were borrowed from the animal literature, and children were set to solve such gripping problems as two-choice discrimination learning tasks and "run" for many trials until they reached criterion—or refused to cooperate. The experimental situation was also adapted from animal laboratories; a large number of studies in the 1960s actually used a modified Wisconsin General Test Apparatus—a form of cage developed by Harlow for testing monkeys. That children were also enclosed in boxes was presumably a safeguard to protect the purity of the experimental demands, for I assume children in the 1960s were not rabid and, therefore, the physical protection of the experimenter could not have been a prime motivation. To complete the child-as-animal metaphor, it was a typical practice to place stimuli over reward wells, which were baited (with M&Ms, the developmentalist's lab chow). All social or verbal interactions with the child were minimized, and any suggestion of a purpose for the activity was reduced to the plea to the child to "come play my game."

Children were notoriously unreliable accomplices; the variability in their data suggested perversity rather than compliance. Even if they reached solution, they were too temperamental to maintain a criterion run. Note that the descriptive language used, the experimental setup, and the tasks were all inspired by the animal metaphor. Children usually outperformed animals, but they still performed abysmally; and the resultant view of young children was negative; they were not producers, not strategic, did not mediate, did not transfer rules, etc. (Brown & DeLoache, in press).

With the wide dissemination of the Russian developmental literature, American psychologists have begun to consider children's competencies in more naturalistic situations. Observational and clinical methods are being combined with experimentation in an innovative way, and it is becoming commonplace for developmental psychologists to at least pay lip service to the need to evaluate a child's potential in a meaningful situation. Soviet psychologists have always conducted their developmental inquiries in this manner. For example, Istomina (1975), in a study conducted in the early 1940s, examined how children would go about remembering a five-item list. Americans will tell you that under normal laboratory learning instructions, one can expect about two items from cooperative 3-year-olds. But one of the most interesting features of Istomina's experiment was a comparison between children's memory for lists of words in the relatively standard list-learning situation vs. their memory for comparable lists embedded in a meaningful (to the child) activity of buying items at a store. Istomina's reasoning for contrasting these two conditions was the standard Soviet contention that "the development of retention and recall as internal, purposeful acts takes place initially as part of a broader, articulated, and meaningful activity (since it is only within the context of such activity that the specific acts of remembering and recall have any meaning for a child) [pp. 8−9]." This hypothesis was confirmed as recall was clearly superior in the game situation; for younger children, recall was twice as good when buying items at a store than in a typical rote-learning situation.

Istomina not only recorded the objective data produced in each condition; she also observed the activities of the children as they undertook the task, thus providing a rich clinical picture of the developing skills. To extract some examples: Three-year-old Valerik barely waited for the list of items to be read before rushing off to the store. The 3-year-old's view of the game seems to be limited to assuming the role of going to the store and returning with items but does not seem to include the notion of bringing back the specific items on the list. Four-year-old Igor listened attentively to the shopping list and then tried to carry out his errand as quickly as possible. He even seemed to try to avoid distraction, refusing to stop and talk when on his way to the store. Very few 4-year-olds showed more specific mnemonic behaviors, but between 4 and 5 a qualitative shift seemed to occur, and all the older subjects seemed to make active attempts to remember. Some 5- and 6-year-olds actively rehearsed; they were often observed moving their lips, repeating the words over to themselves as the experimenter read them and as they walked to the store. Many of the older children seemed to be monitoring their own memory states and even checking themselves to determine how well they would remember. Some children were even seen testing themselves on the way to the store. Finally, the oldest children (6 to 7 years old) displayed quite sophisticated strategies of trying to form logical connections between the items on their lists, often rearranging the order of the words based on their meaning.

Istomina's (1975) work is fascinating not just for the information it provides about young children's memory processes but also for the methodological point it emphasizes. The best situation in which to study very early memory development is in a natural context in which the child is likely to understand the task and be motivated to perform it. Young children's performance on laboratory tasks is often markedly inferior to their performance in a game setting. Although this variable is crucially important when studying very young children, the same general point is applicable to other ages as well. Subjects of any age, even adults, are likely to perform better in a meaningful task in which they are actively engaged. Mental acts occur in living contexts, and, to reiterate a previous theme of this paper, the minimum unit of analysis must be the operations performed by an individual in context (Neisser, 1976a). This is an extremely important point for developmentalists who must consider intelligent behavior of children in terms of the naturally occurring contexts of early childhood (Brown, 1975, 1978a) or divergent cultures (Brown, 1977, in press a; Cole & Scribner, 1975). But the message might have some import for theories of adult cognition, particularly varieties such as LOP models, with their explicit concern with the influence of activities on levels of knowing.

C. Headfitting

The final point of compatibility between developmental psychology and LOP frameworks is a concern for headfitting (Brown, 1975; Jenkins, 1971, 1974). Again, I have dealt with this topic elsewhere (Brown, 1975), and Naus and Halasz (Chapter 12, this volume) have a detailed overview of the problem. Here I restrict myself to three points: headfitting as a source of error variance; headfitting for instructional purposes; and headfitting and the problem of meaning.

First, what do I mean by headfitting? The basic premise is that there is an intimate relation between what is known and what can be known, and because we must come to know more with increasing age and experience, there must be a close correspondence between what a child can understand at any point in life and his or her concurrent cognitive status. The typical position of both adult and developmental constructivists is that meaning does not reside in the world; it is constructed from the interaction between the current state of knowledge and that which is to be known. As we have seen, there are philosophical problems with this position (Sections, II. D. and E.) that I will not reiterate here. But the very concept of meaning for those of a constructivist persuasion is one of headfitting. LOP frameworks have always incorporated a headfitting notion, reflected in terms such as "compatibility (of material) with the analyzing structures." In more recent statements of the LOP approach (Lockhart, Craik, & Jacoby, 1975), the proponents become more explicitly embroiled in the problem as they address the question of "automatic" encoding for material highly compatible with the preexisting contents of the head.

How have developmental psychologists been concerned with the headfitting issue? Experimental psychologists often operate as if they wished to control for it, e.g., they regard developmental variations in knowledge as a source of extraneous variability. For example, in standard memory tasks they attempt to ensure that even their youngest subjects are familiar with the stimuli, at least to the level that they can name them. If a name is not readily given by a small participant, the experimenter generously provides one and then operates as if stimulus familiarity were equated across ages (see Chi, 1978, for a full treatment of this problem). That familiarity may involve more than access or even speed of access to the name code is rarely considered. After this "control", variations in performance across ages are then attributed to factors other than variations in knowledge, e.g., capacity limitations or strategy deficits (Chi, 1976).

A more enlightened way that developmental psychologists have expressed concern with the headfitting problem has been in their treatment of instruction. If one wishes to instruct children to perform in a way they previously could not, the most intelligent way to proceed is to find out where their heads are at initially. Developmental psychologists interested in instruction have typically indulged in detailed task analyses that map the progression of the children as they move toward adultlike understanding. Such task analyses provide detailed specifications of feasible rules for solution, and systematic error patterns are used to diagnose the children's pretraining competencies, areas of weakness, etc., so that instructional routines can be tailored to fit the diagnosees (Siegler, 1976).

It is a widespread assumption of developmental psychologists of quite divergent theoretical viewpoints that the distance between the child's existing knowledge and the new information he or she must acquire is a critical determinant of how successful training will be (Brown, 1975; Inhelder, Sinclair, & Bovet, 1974; Piaget, 1971; Siegler, 1976). Near training, i.e., training aimed at just one level above a child's starting knowledge, is far more successful than far training, aimed at least two levels beyond the child's understanding (Siegler, 1976). Thus, it is a critical concern for those involved in instruction to detail the stages through which the learner must pass. And the map between the child's current understanding and the instructional routine is a critical determinant of what instruction will be introduced—a practical headfitting problem.

The third headfitting issue is the "task by head" interaction stressed by many developmental theorists. A task is easy or hard, material is comprehensible or not, to the extent that it maps onto the peexisting knowledge and preferences of the learners. Extreme versions of this approach suggest that if material is highly compatible, understanding will be "automatic" (Brown, 1975; Jenkins, 1974) and that both comprehension and memory are born of meaning (Piaget & Inhelder, 1973). One way that the developmental literature has been influenced by this position is that there has been a shift toward studying such phenomena as semantic integration, inferential reasoning, etc. in the context of meaningful materials such as prose passages. It is as if turning to prose is by itself a reflection of concern for meaning. As Jenkins (1974) pointed out in his seminal treatment of the psychologist's definition of meaning, what one regards as meaningful is very much a matter of historical press. In their time, those concerned with memory for words looked askance at retrogressive advocates of the nonsense syllable. Now it is trendy to berate those who look at words or even sentences, for meaning is carried in larger chunks of texts. But if meaning is not in the material but in the compatibility of the subject's level of understanding and the nature of the material, then changing stimulus types does not necessarily help or hinder the basic question. Even for the learner attempting to acquire nonsense syllables, the basic unit of analysis is the relationship of prior knowledge, current activity, and the material. Both LOP frameworks and developmental theories that espouse a headfitting notion must somehow deal with the problem of meaning, where meaning is defined as one of task and subject compatibility.

The ultimate demonstration of the headfitting notion is one that should be readily found in the developmental literature. Ideally, little thinkers lacking some basic knowledge should be hindered in their comprehension of any information that presupposes the existence of that prior knowledge. Though this is undoubtedly true, it has proved difficult to demonstrate the phenomenon neatly within well-controlled experiments. The main thrust of the Piagetian work on the development of memory has been to demonstrate the close alliance of preexisting knowledge and memory (Piaget & Inhelder, 1973). These experiments have not been totally successful.

Another ploy is to show that experimentally induced preexisting knowledge determines what is understood. Although this has been successfully demonstrated with both children (Brown, Smiley, Day, Townsend, & Lawton, 1977) and adults (Anderson & Pichert, 1977), no interesting developmental trends have been identified; for example, even the younger children disambiguated vague or misleading sections of text in a manner congruent with their preexisting expectations. Indeed it is not necessary in the standard Bartlett prose-recall situation to manipulate age as well as preexisting knowledge. Inducing adults to take different perspectives before reading a passage is an ideal way of demonstrating that comprehension is an interaction of expectations and actual textual materials (Anderson & Pichert, 1977; Bower, 1977). Thus, whereas we have ample anecdotal evidence that the younger reader's comprehension is affected by a limited knowledge base—e.g., reports that children read stories in terms of the concrete action sequences rather than the deeper allegorical meaning (Brown, in press b)—we do not have a great deal of neat experimental evidence of the ideal type—little heads leading to little understanding.

What we do have is the inverse of the ideal finding, and it is just as pertinent to my argument; indeed, it may be more so because it is so dramatic. In a recent series of studies, Chi (1978) has been investigating the memory and metamemory performance of skilled chess players, an honorable psychological pursuit dating back at least to Binet (1894). Chi's twist is that in her sample of players, knowledge is orthogonal to age. In general the children are the experts whereas the adults are the novices. It is the experts who outperform the novices both in terms of actual memory performance and in predicting in advance how well they will perform—a nice example of the headfitting notion. It is not how old your head is but how much it has experienced in a particular cognitive domain.

SUMMARY

In view of the traditional separation of developmental theories from current adult models, the widespread adoption of LOP frameworks is particularly noteworthy. I have suggested here that the essential compatibiity of LOP models and developmental interests follows from a shared concern with three main issues: involuntary memory, activity, and headfitting. Developmental data are often particularly apt demonstrations of the main tenets of the LOP frameworks, and LOP models provide a language and a viewpoint through which the issues of interest for developmentalists can be reinterpreted.

Another theme of this chapter is that thinking systems are naturally evolving and theories of cognition must eventually consider how their model of man came about. The teleological position has been fruitful in guiding research, but it is not surprising that any theory that can account for only a limited subset of adult behavior on a set of severely constrained tasks may have difficulty dealing with the questions of growth and change. A consideration of the phylogenetic and ontogenetic forces that shape the evolution of thought might lead to a richer understanding of how humans come to know the significant information of their environment.

ACKNOWLEDGMENTS

The preparation of this manuscript was supported in part by Grants HD 06864, HD 05951, and a Research Career Development Award HD 00111, from the National Institutes of Child Health and Human Development and in part by the Reading Center grants MS-NIE-C-400-76-0116. I would like to thank Joseph C. Campione for his comments on an earlier version of this manuscript and Richard Anderson, John Bransford, Katherine Nelson, Rand Spiro, Thoman Thieman, and James Wertsch for discussions that led to my interest in the topic. Of course, responsibility for the final contents is entirely my own, and the people with whom I have discussed these issues should not be blamed for any misinterpretations.

REFERENCES

Abelson, R. P. The structure of belief systems. In R. C. Schank & K. M. Colby (Eds.), *Computer models of thought and language*. San Francisco: Freeman, 1973.
Acredolo, L. P., Pick, H. L., Jr., & Olsen, M. G. Environmental differentiation and familiarity as

determinants of children's memory for spatial location. *Developmental Psychology*, 1975, *11*, 495—501.

Allport, G. W., & Postman, L. J. The basic psychology of rumor. *Transactions of the New York Academy of Science*. Series II, 1945, *8*, 61—81.

Anderson, R. C. The notion of schemata and the education enterprise. In R. C. Anderson, R. J. Spiro, & W. E. Montague (Eds.), *Schooling and the acquisition of knowledge*. Hillsdale, N.J.: Lawrence Erlbaum Associates, 1977.

Anderson, R. C., & Pichert, J. W. *Recall of previously unrecallable information following a shift in perspective* (Tech. Rep. No. 14). Urbana, Illinois: University of Illinois, Center for the Study of Reading, April 1977.

Bartlett, F. C. *Remembering: A study in experimental and social psychology*. Cambridge: Cambridge University Press, 1932.

Belmont, J. M. Relation of age and intelligence to short-term color memory. *Child Development*, 1972, *43*, 19—29.

Belmont, J. M., & Butterfield, E. C. The relation of short-term memory to development and intelligence. In L. P. Lipsitt & H. W. Reese (Eds.), *Advances in child development and behavior* (Vol. 4). New York: Academic Press, 1969.

Binet, A. *Psychologie des grands calculateur et joueurs d'echess*. Paris: Hachette, 1894.

Binet, A., & Henri, V. La memoire des phrases (memoire des idées). *L'année Psychologique*, 1894, *1*, 24—59.

Bobrow, D. G., & Norman, D. A. Some principles of memory schemata. In D. G. Bobrow & A. M. Collins (Eds.), *Representation and understanding: Studies in cognitive science*. New York: Academic Press, 1975.

Bower, G. *Memory for prose*. Paper presented at the meeting of the Western Psychological Association, Seattle, Washington, April 1977.

Bransford, J. D., & Franks, J. J. Toward a framework for understanding learning. In G. Bower (Ed.), *The psychology of learning and motivation* (Vol. 10). New York: Academic Press, 1976.

Bransford, J. D., & Nitsch, K. E. Coming to understand things we could not previously understand. Unpublished manuscript, Vanderbilt University, 1977.

Bransford, J. D., Nitsch, K. E., & Franks, J. J. Schooling and the facilitation of knowing. In R. C. Anderson, R. J. Spiro, & W. E. Montague (Eds.), *Schooling and the acquisition of knowledge*. Hillsdale, N.J.: Lawrence Erlbaum Associates, 1977.

Brown, A. L. The role of strategic behavior in retardate memory. In N. R. Ellis (Ed.), *International review of research in mental retardation* (Vol. 1). New York: Academic Press, 1974.

Brown, A. L. The development of memory: Knowing, knowing about knowing, and knowing how to know. In H. W. Reese (Ed.), *Advances in child development and behavior* (Vol. 10). New York: Academic Press, 1975.

Brown, A. L. Development, schooling and the acquisition of knowledge about knowledge. In R. C. Anderson, R. J. Spiro, & W. E. Montague (Eds.), *Schooling and the acquisition of knowledge*. Hillsdale, N.J.: Lawrence Erlbaum Associates, 1977.

Brown, A. L. Knowing when, where, and how to remember: A problem of metacognition. In R. Glaser (Ed.), *Advances in instructional psychology*. Hillsdale, N.J.: Lawrence Erlbaum Associates, 1978, in press. (a)

Brown, A. L. Metacognitive development and reading. In R. J. Spiro, B. Bruce, and W. F. Brewer (Eds.), *Theoretical issues in reading comprehension*. Hillsdale, N.J.: Lawrence Erlbaum Associates, 1978, in press. (b)

Brown, A. L., & Barclay, C. R. The effects of training specific mnemonics on the metamnemonic efficiency of retarded children. *Child Development*, 1976, *47*, 71—80.

Brown, A. L., Campione, J. C., & Murphy, M. D. Maintenance and generalization of trained metamnemonic awareness in educable retarded children. *Journal of Experimental Child Psychology*, 1977, 24, 191—211.

Brown, A. L., & DeLoache, J. S. Skills, plans and self-regulation. In R. Siegler (Ed.), *Carnegie—Mellon symposium on cognition*. Hillsdale, N.J.: Lawrence Erlbaum Associates, 1978, in press.

Brown, A. L. & Lawton, S. C. The feeling of knowing experience in educable retarded children. *Developmental Psychology*, 1977, *13*, 364−370.

Brown, A. L., & Smiley, S. S. Rating the importance of structural units of prose passages: A problem of metacognitive development. *Child Development*, 1977, *48*, 1−8.

Brown, A. L., & Smiley, S. S. The development of strategies for studying prose passages. Child Development, 1978, in press.

Brown, A. L., Smiley, S. S., Day, J. D., Townsend, M. A. R., & Lawton, S. C. Intrusion of a thematic idea in children's comprehension and retention of stories. *Child Development*, 1977, *48*, 1454−1466.

Bruner, J. S. Nature and uses of immaturity. *American Psychologist*, 1972, *27*, 687−708.

Campione, J. C., & Brown, A. L. Memory and matamemory development in educable retarded children. In R. V. Kail, Jr., & J. W. Hagen (Eds.), *Perspectives on the development of memory and cognition*. Hillsdale, N.J.: Lawrence Erlbaum Associates, 1977.

Cassirer, E. *Language and myth*. New York: Dover Publications, 1946.

Charniak, E. Organization and inference in a frame-like system of common sense knowledge. In *Proceedings of theoretical issues in natural language procesing: An interdisciplinary workshop*. Cambridge, Mass.: Bolt, Beranek & Newman, Inc., 1975.

Chi, M. T. H. *The development of short-term memory capacity*. Unpublished doctoral dissertation, Carnegie−Mellon University, 1975.

Chi, M. T. H. Short-term memory limitations in children: Capacity or processing deficits? *Memory & Cognition*, 1976, *4*(5), 559−572.

Chi, M. T. H. Knowledge structure and memory development. In R. Siegler (Ed.), *Carnegie—Mellon symposium on cognition*. Hillsdale, N.J.: Lawrence Erlbaum Associates, 1978, in press.

Cole, M., & Scribner, S. Theorizing about socialization of cognition. *Ethos*, 1975, *3*, 249−268.

Cole, M., & Scribner, S. Cross-cultural studies of memory and cognition. In R. V. Kail, Jr., & J. W. Hagen (Eds.), *Perspectives on the development of memory and cognition*. Hillsdale, N.J.: Lawrence Erlbaum Associates, 1977.

Collins, A. M., & Loftus, E. F. A spreading-activation theory of semantic processing. *Psychological Review*, 1975, *82*, 407−428.

Craik, F. I. M., & Lockhart, R. S. Levels of processing: A framework for memory research. *Journal of Verbal Learning and Verbal Behavior*, 1972, *11*, 671−684.

Craik, F. I. M., & Tulving, E. Depth of processing and the retention of words in episodic memory. *Journal of Experimental Psychology*, 1975, *104*, 268−294.

Eagle, M., & Leiter, E. Recall and recognition in intentional and incidental learning. *Journal of Experimental Psychology*, 1964, *68*, 58−63.

Elkonin, D. B. Toward the problem of stages in the mental development of the child. *Soviet Psychology*, 1972, *10*, 225−251.

Flavell, J. H. Stage-related properties of cognitive development. *Cognitive Psychology*, 1971, *2*, 421−453.

Flavell, J. H., Friedrichs, A. G., & Hoyt, J. D. Developmental changes in memorization processes. *Cognitive Psychology*, 1970, *1*, 324−340.

Flavell, J. H., & Wellman, H. M. Metamemory. In R. V. Kail, Jr., & J. W. Hagen (Eds.), *Perspectives on the development of memory and cognition*. Hillsdale, N.J.: Lawrence Erlbaum Associates, 1977.

Foellinger, D. B., & Trabasso, T. Seeing, hearing and doing: A developmental study of memory for actions. *Child Development*, 1977, 48, 1482−1489.

Gardner, H. *The quest for mind: Piaget, Lévi−Strauss and the structuralist movement*. New York: Alfred Knopf, 1973.

Hagen, J. W. Strategies for remembering. In S. Farnham−Diggory (Ed.), *Information processing in children*. New York; Academic Press, 1972.

Harris, P. L. Perseverative errors in search by young infants. *Child Development*, 1973, *44*, 28−33.

Höffding, H. *Outlines of psychology*. New York: Macmillan, 1891.

Horowitz, L. M., & Pryrulak, P. Redintegrative memory. *Psychological Review* 1969, *76*, 519−531.

Huttenlocher, J., & Burke, D. Why does memory span increase with age? *Cognitive Psychology*, 1976, *8*, 1−31.

Hyde, T. S., & Jenkins, J. J. Recall for words as a function of semantic, graphic, and syntactic orienting tasks. *Journal of Verbal Learning and Verbal Behavior*, 1973, *12*, 471−480.

Inhelder, B., Sinclair, H., & Bovet, M. Learning and the development of cognition. Cambridge, Mass.: Harvard University Press, 1974.

Istomina, Z. M. The development of voluntary memory in preschool-age children. *Soviet Psychology*, Summer 1975, *13*(4), 5−64.

Jenkins, J. J. Second discussant's comments: What's left to say? *Human Development*, 1971, *14*, 279−286.

Jenkins, J. J. Remember that old theory of memory? Well, forget it! *American Psychologist*, 1974, *29*, 785−795.

Kant, E. *Critique of pure reason* (1st ed., 1781; 2nd ed., 1787; trans. N. Kemp Smith). London: McMillan & Company, 1963.

Kintsch, W. *The representation of meaning in memory*. Hillsdale, N.J.: Lawrence Erlbaum Associates, 1974.

Klahr, D. Steps towards the simulation of intellectual development. In L. Resnick (Ed.), *Intelligence*. Hillsdale, N.J.: Lawrence Erlbaum Associates, 1976.

Kuhn, T. S. *The structure of scientific revolutions*. Chicago: University of Chicago Press, 1970.

Kussman, T. The Soviet concept of development. In K. F. Riegel & J. A. Meacham (Eds.), *The developing individual in a changing world* (Vol. 1: Historical and cultural issues). The Hague: Mouton, 1976.

Kvale, S. Memory and dialectics: Some reflections on Ebbinghaus and Mao Tse-tung. *Human Development*, 1975, *18*, 205−222.

Leont'ev, A. N. The problem of activity in psychology. *Soviet Psychology*, 1974, *13*, 4−33.

Lockhart, R. S., Craik, F. I. M., & Jacoby, L. L. Depth of processing in recognition and recall: Some aspects of a general memory system. In J. Brown (Ed.), *Recognition and recall*. London: Wiley, 1975.

Mandler, G., & Worden, P. E. Semantic processing without permanent storage. *Journal of Experimental Psychology*, 1973, *100*, 277−283.

Meacham, J. A. Soviet investigations of memory development. In R. V. Kail, Jr., & J. W. Hagen (Eds.), *Perspectives on the development of memory and cognition*. Hillsdale, N.J.: Lawrence Erlbaum Associates, 1977.

Minsky, M. A framework for representing knowledge. In P. H. Winston (Ed.), *The psychology of computer vision*. New York: McGraw−Hill, 1975.

Morris, C. D., Bransford, J. D., & Franks, J. J. Levels of processing versus transfer appropriate processing. *Journal of Verbal Learning and Verbal Behavior*, 1977, *16*, 519−533.

Moscovitch, M., & Craik, F. I. M. Depth of processing, retrieval cues, and uniqueness of encoding as factors in recall. *Journal of Verbal Learning and Verbal Behavior*, 1976, *15*, 447−458.

Murphy, M. D., & Brown, A. L. Incidental learning in preschool children as a function of level of cognitive analysis. *Journal of Experimental Child Psychology*, 1975, *19*, 509−523.

Neisser, U. *Cognitive psychology*. Englewood Cliffs, N.J.: Prentice−Hall, 1967.

Neisser, U. *Cognition and reality*. San Francisco: W. H. Freeman, 1976. (a)

Neisser, U. General, academic and artificial intelligence. In L. Resnick (Ed.), *Intelligence*. Hillsdale, N.J.: Lawrence Erlbaum Associates, 1976. (b)

Nelson, K. Cognitive development and the acquisition of concepts. In R. C. Anderson, R. J.

Spiro, & W. E. Montague (Eds.), *Schooling and the acquisition of knowledge*. Hillsdale, N.J.: Lawrence Erlbaum Associates, 1977.

Nelson, K., & Brown, A. L. The semantic—episodic distinction in memory development. In P. Ornstein (Ed.), *Memory development*. Hillsdale, N.J.: Lawrence Erlbaum Associates, in press.

Nelson, K., & Kosslyn, S. Semantic retrieval in children and adults. *Developmental Psychology*, 1975, *11*, 807—813.

Newell, A. A note on process—structure distinctions in developmental psychology. In S. Farnham—Diggory (Ed.), *Information processing in children*. New York: Academic Press, 1972.

Norman, D. A. *Resources and schemas replace stages of processing*. Paper presented at the Sixteenth Annual Meeting, Psychonomic Society, Denver, Colorado, November 1975.

Overcast, T. D., Murphy, M. D., Smiley, S. S., & Brown, A. L. The effects of instruction on recall and recognition of categorized lists in the elderly. *Bulletin of the Psychonomic Society*, 1975, *5*, 339—341.

Piaget, J. *The child's conception of the world*. New York: Harcourt Brace, 1928.

Piaget, J. *The child and reality: Problems of genetic psychology*. New York: Grossman Publications, 1970.

Piaget, J. *Biology and knowledge*. Edinburgh: Edinburgh University Press, 1971.

Piaget, J., & Inhelder, B. *Memory and intelligence*. New York: Basic Books, 1973.

Posner, M., & Warren, P. Traces, concepts and conscious constructions. In A. W. Melton & E. Martin (Eds). *Coding processes in human memory*. New York: Winston & Sons 1972.

Postman, L. Short-term memory and incidental learning. In A. W. Melton (Ed.), *Categories of human learning*. New York: Academic Press, 1964.

Postman, L. Verbal learning and memory. *Annual Review of Psychology*, 1975, *26*, 291—335.

Pufall, P. B. The development of thought: On perceiving and knowing. In R. Shaw & J. Bransford (Eds.), *Perceiving, acting and knowing*. Hillsdale, N.J.: Lawrence Erlbaum Associates, 1977.

Reitman, W. What does it take to remember? In Norman (Ed.), *Models of human memory*. New York: Academic Press, 1970.

Riegel, K. F. The structure of the structuralists. *Contemporary Psychology*, 1974, *19*, 811—813.

Riegel, K. F. Structure and transformation in modern intellectual history. In K. F. Riegel & G. C. Rosenwald (Eds.), *Structure and transformation: Developmental and historical aspects*. New York: Wiley, 1975.

Rumelhart, D., & Ortony, A. The representation of knowledge in memory. In R. C. Anderson, R. J. Spiro, & W. E. Montague (Eds.), *Schooling and the acquisition of knowledge*. Hillsdale, N.J.: Lawrence Erlbaum Associates, 1977.

Schank, R. C. The structure of episodes in memory. In D. G. Bobrow & A. M. Collins (Eds.), *Representation and understanding*. New York: Academic Press, 1975.

Schank, R. C. & Abelson, R. P. Scripts, plans and knowledge. In *Advance Papers of the Fourth International Joint Conference on Artificial Intelligence*. Tbilisi, Georgia, USSR, 1975.

Schulman, A. I. Encoding processes and the memorability of events. In A. Kennedy & A. Wilkes (Eds.), *Studies in long-term memory*. New York: Wiley, 1975.

Shaw, R., & Bransford, J. D. Introduction: Psychological approaches to the problem of knowledge. In R. Shaw & J. D. Bransford (Eds.), *Perceiving, acting and knowing*. Hillsdale, N.J.: Lawrence Erlbaum Associates, 1977.

Siegel, A. W., & White, S. H. The development of spatial representations of large-scale environments. In H. W. Reese (Ed.), *Advances in child development and behavior* (Vol. 10). New York: Academic Press, 1975.

Siegler, R. S. Three aspects of cognitive development. *Cognitive Psychology*, 1976, *8*, 481—520.

Smirnov, A. A., & Zinchenko, P. I. Problems in the psychology of memory. In M. Cole & I. Maltzman (Eds.), *A handbook of contemporary Soviet psychology*. New York: Basic Books, 1969.

Smith, E. E., Adams, N., & Schorr, D. Fact retrieval and the paradox of interference. *Cognitive Psychology*, 1978, in press.

Smith, E. E., Shoben, E. J., & Rips, L. J. Structure and process in semantic memory: A featural model for semantic decisions. *Psychological Review*, 1974, *81*, 214–241.

Thieman, T. J. *What's so deep about deep processing: A critical analysis of the relation between incidental orienting tasks and retention*. Unpublished doctoral dissertation, University of Illinois, 1976.

Toussaint, N. A. An analysis of synchrony between concrete-operational tasks in terms of structure and performance demands. *Child Development*, 1974, *45*, 992–1001.

Tulving, E. Episodic and semantic memory. In E. Tulving & W. Donaldson (Eds.), *Organization of memory*. New York: Academic Press, 1972.

Turvey, M. T. Contrasting orientations to the theory of visual information processing. *Psychological Review*, 1977, *84*, 67–89.

Vygotsky, L. S. *Thought and language*. Cambridge: M.I.T. Press, 1962.

Werner, H. *Comparative psychology of mental development*. Chicago: Follett, 1948.

Wertsch, J. V. *The concept of activity in Soviet psychology*. Unpublished manuscript, Northwestern University, 1977.

Wickelgren, W. A. Age and storage dynamics in continuous recognition memory. *Developmental Psychology*, 1975, *11*(2), 165–169.

Winograd, T. Frame representations and the declarative/procedural controversy. In D. G. Bobrow & A. Collins (Eds.), *Representation and understanding: Studies in cognitive science*. New York: Academic Press, 1975.

Wozniak, R. H. Dialecticism and structuralism: The philosophical foundation of Soviet psychology and Piagetian cognitive developmental theory. In K. F. Riegel & G. C. Rosenwald (Eds.), *Structure and transformations: Developmental and historical aspects*. New York: Wiley, 1975.

Yendovitskaya, T. V. Development of memory. In A. V. Saparozhets & D. B. Elkonin (Eds.), *The psychology of preschool children*. Cambridge: M.I.T., Press, 1971.

Youniss, J. Operations and everyday thinking: A commentary on "dialectical operations." *Human Development*, 1974, *17*, 386–391.

Zinchenko, P. I. Involuntary memory and the goal-directed nature of activity. In P. I. Zinchenko (Ed.), *Involuntary memory*. Moscow: Academy of Pedagogical Science Press, 1962.

12 Developmental Perspectives on Cognitive Processing and Semantic Memory Structure[1]

Mary J. Naus and Frank G. Halasz
Haverford College

The developmental literature offers a unique perspective for understanding the memory system and how it operates. Whereas studies of adult memory investigate a relatively unchanging system by focusing on asymptotic memory performance, studies of age-related differences in memory investigate the characteristics of a dynamic, evolving memory system. The relatively invariant set of relationships among the various components of the adult memory system make it difficult to isolate the functions of these components and their interrelationships. However, in an evolving memory system the various components and their interrelationships change with time, allowing for a more complete analysis of the individual components and how they work together. Examination of memory performance at several developmental levels allows a comparison of the relationships among the various components in differing configurations and thus clarifies both the operation of each component and the functional relations among them. In this way a developmental perspective provides an additional dimension of memory performance, leading to a richer data base from which to understand memory functioning.

The importance of a dynamic, evolutionary perspective can be seen in the clarification that developmental data provide for a number of critical issues in current models of memory. For example, short-term memory phenomena have been interpreted within a multistore framework (e.g., Atkinson & Shiffrin, 1968,

---

[1]Although this paper refers to a "developmental" perspective, it should be pointed out that only a limited developmental range of preschool to college age is included. Although this reflects the current state of developmental psychology, it is unfortunate that more is not known about memory in infants and the aged. This would certainly contribute to an understanding of a broader range of memory phenomena.

1971) as reflecting a structural component or memory store which has a limited capacity and from which information decays rapidly over time. In contrast, the levels-of-processing approach of Craik and his colleagues (Craik & Jacoby, 1975; Craik & Lockhart, 1972; Lockhart, Craik & Jacoby, 1976) conceptualizes the same set of phenomena in terms of the type of processing that information undergoes within a limited capacity cognitive processor. Investigations of short-term memory performance in adults have provided little information to distinguish between the structural and process approaches. Few procedures have been developed that directly investigate possible structures of short-term memory independently of the processes operating within those structures.

An investigation of age-related differences in performance in immediate memory tasks leads to a better understanding of the operation of the structure and/or processes in short-term memory phenomena. Studies of age-related changes in short-term memory capacity using memory-span tasks (e.g., Brener, 1940; Crannell & Parrish, 1957; Gates & Taylor, 1925; Hurlock & Newmark, 1931), serial probed recall tasks (e.g., Atkinson, Hansen, & Bernbach, 1964; Siegel & Allik, 1973), and recognition under limited exposure tasks (e.g., Haith, Morrison, Sheingold, & Mindes, 1970) all indicate that young children show a short-term memory capacity deficit in comparison to adults. Although there are some differences between paradigms, in general the short-term memory capacity of adults is reported to be twice that of preschool children. In a recent review of this literature, Chi (1976) found little evidence to suggest that this difference in performance results from age-related changes in such structural parameters of short-term store as capacity or rate of information loss. Rather, the majority of studies suggest that developmental differences in short-term memory result from an inefficiency in young children's use and acquisition of memory processes such as rehearsal, grouping, and recoding. (See Chi, 1976, for a detailed discussion of these arguments.) These developmental studies suggest that the major age-related changes in short-term memory tasks involve differences in the way in which information is processed, rather than developmental changes in the characteristics of a particular memory store. These developmental findings further indicate that the critical determinants of short-term memory performance in adults are likely to be the characteristics of the processing of stimulus information, rather than the structural characteristics of a short-term store.

In addition to clarifying the relationship between structural and processing components of the memory system, as illustrated in the foregoing example, a developmental perspective can also help to isolate different aspects of memory processing that may be confounded in adult investigations. For example, recent research on verbal rehearsal has attempted to determine which aspects of this process are responsible for improved recall performance. Using an overt rehearsal procedure in which college-age subjects practiced the to-be-remembered words aloud as they were presented, Rundus (1971; Rundus & Atkinson, 1970) found that rehearsal frequency was directly related to memory performance, with those items that were rehearsed more often having a higher probability of recall. However, developmental investigations of rehearsal processing (e.g., Cuvo, 1975; Ornstein, Naus, & Liberty, 1975) suggest that rehearsal frequency and content are confounded in the adult memory data. By adapting Rundus's overt rehearsal procedure for use with children of different ages, Ornstein et al. (1975) were able to investigate rehearsal frequency and content independently. Under these circumstances the content of rehearsal, not the quantity, was directly associated with improved recall. Third graders actually rehearsed the to-be-remembered items more than the older children (sixth and eighth graders), and yet their recall was poorer. However, rehearsal content, defined as the number of different items the children practice together as each word in the list is presented, was found to vary directly with age. That is, the third graders who recalled less were found to rehearse each to-be-remembered item in relative isolation, whereas the superior recall of the older children was associated with a "richer" rehearsal style in which each to-be-remembered item was practiced with many other items in the list. Although experimental procedures can be developed to isolate the effects of various aspects of rehearsal processing in adults (e.g., Craik & Watkins, 1973; Jacoby & Bartz, 1972; Woodward, Bjork, & Jongeward, 1973), these procedures often involve complicated instructional or training conditions that do not allow the analysis of spontaneous memory processing. Thus, a developmental perspective allows the isolation of the components of memory processing which are often obscured or confounded in adult data.

These two examples illustrate the unique contribution that a developmental perspective can provide for the understanding of memory performance. The present chapter outlines two modifications that a developmental perspective suggests in the levels-of-processing memory framework. Although emphasis is placed upon a consideration of the levels-of-processing conceptualization of memory, the arguments presented here also apply to the more traditional multistore models. (See Naus, Ornstein, & Hoving, 1978, for a comparison of the multistore and levels-of-processing models from a developmental point of view.) The first modification that a developmental perspective suggests is a distinction between two categories of memory processes—deliberate strategies and automatic processes. Both Soviet (Smirnov & Zinchenko, 1969; Yendo-vitskaya, 1971) and American (Brown, 1975) developmental psychologists have differentiated between two types of memory tasks, which reflect these two different types of memory processing. Very different developmental patterns in memory performance have been found in these two types of tasks. Whereas clear developmental differences are observed in tasks involving the use of deliberate, mnemonic strategies that are purposely instigated to attain a specific memory goal, few age-related changes have been found in tasks where memory is the nonpurposeful product of the child's interaction with a meaningful environment. These two differing developmental patterns suggest that the memory processing involved in the two types of tasks represent independent components of the memory system. Thus, the developmental literature indicates that the levels-of-processing model must differentiate between these two types of processing.

The second modification suggests that models of memory must focus on semantic memory and the mechanism by which its structure and contents can be altered through experience with environmental stimuli. Both Piaget's investigation of the relation between intelligence and memory (Piaget & Inhelder, 1973) and the more recent investigations of developmental differences in constructive memory (e.g., Barclay & Reid, 1974; Paris, 1975) suggest that the way in which information is processed in memory is highly dependent on the structure and contents of the information stored in semantic memory. Since the structure and contents of semantic memory are continually changing with age, memory processing cannot be studied in isolation but must be considered as operating within the semantic memory structures. This approach is currently incorporated within the levels-of-processing framework. However, developmental work further suggests that a mechanism for the modification of the semantic memory system due to experience must be included in any memory model. The present chapter presents the data and arguments that support the importance of including these two modifications in the levels-of-processing framework.

MEMORY PROCESSING

Brown (1975) has recently proposed a distinction between deliberate and involuntary memory tasks. This distinction is based on the Soviet developmental psychologists' (Smirnov & Zinchenko, 1969; Yendovitskaya, 1971) differentiation between those tasks in which memory is the primary goal and those in which memory is subordinate to the completion of meaningful activity. Deliberate memory tasks are those that involve the use of mnemonic strategies. These tasks typically involve a voluntary plan purposely adopted by the subject to improve memory performance in a particular situation or to obtain a specific memory goal. In contrast, involuntary memory tasks are considered to be those in which memory is the unplanned product of a person's continuous interaction with a meaningful environment. Thus, involuntary memory results from comprehending or understanding a situation, rather than from a deliberate plan to remember.

Although Brown's distinction originally consisted of a taxonomy of memory tasks, its major emphasis can be incorporated within the levels-of-processing framework as a process distinction. The characteristics that form the basis for this distinction are summarized in Table 12.1. In a recent discussion of the levels-of-processing framework, Lockhart et al. (1976) proposed that when a

TABLE 12.1
Characteristics of Memory Processing

Deliberate	Automatic
voluntary, planful	involuntary, unplanned
generated by the subject in response to specific task demands	elicited by environmental stimuli and the contents of semantic memory
may or may not be conscious	unconscious
requires attention	typically does not require attention
developmental trends demonstrated by production deficiencies and related to metamemory	few developmental trends

stimulus is highly compatible with a particular level of semantic analysis, it may be impossible to prevent processing from occurring at that level. For example, the Stroop effect demonstrates a situation in which subjects automatically process the semantic aspects of a stimulus even though this processing may interfere with optimal task performance. The present conceptualization suggests that these "automatic" processes are those that operate in Brown's involuntary memory tasks. If a stimulus is highly compatible with existing semantic memory structures, i.e., if it has meaning for the subject, it will be processed automatically with the need for planful intervention. This automatic processing is thus considered to be "stimulus-driven" in the sense that particular processes are involuntarily *elicited* by the properties of the stimulus and the existing semantic memory structures. Further, once initiated, automatic processing typically continues until those analyses with which the stimulus is compatible have been completed. Thus, for example, geometric patterns are typically only analyzed at a structural level, whereas words in the subject's vocabulary are automatically processed to a deeper, semantic level. In contrast, if a stimulus is not compatible with current memory structures, i.e., if it has little meaning for the subject, then deliberate, strategic processing must be employed to elaborate and encode the stimulus in order to increase the probability that the stimulus can be successfully retrieved. Deliberate memory strategies are task-dependent plans of action which the subject *generates* to deal with the absence of inherent meaning in the stimulus. Therefore, whereas automatic processes are sensitive to changes in the properties of the stimulus and the characteristics of the subject's semantic memory structures, deliberate memory strategies are less stimulus bound and more determined by the task demands and the subject's understanding of his or her abilities to meet these demands. Whereas deliberate and automatic processing are viewed as independent components of the memory system, performance in any given task typically represents an interaction of both types of processing. In some tasks it may be that the use of a particular deliberate strategy modifies or overrules the automatic processing typically elicited by the stimulus. In other tasks, memory processing may consist of a mixture of automatically elicited operations and deliberately imposed strategies. Nevertheless, a developmental perspective suggests that these two types of memory processing are operationally independent.

The developmental patterns of these two types of processing are quite different and can be used to differentiate between them. Deliberate processing begins as conscious, planful mnemonic activity designed to accomplish a given task. Through practice and repetition, these mnemonic strategies become maximally efficient, requiring fewer analyses and a minimum of processing to accomplish the same task. In contrast, the development of automatic processes proceeds in conjunction with the development of the structure and contents of semantic memory. Since automatic processes are determined by the properties of the stimulus in relation to semantic memory structures, changes in semantic memory involve corresponding changes in the available automatic processes. It should be clear that automatic processes do not develop from deliberate processes but rather that these two types follow independent developmental courses and that they operate in functionally distinct ways. Thus, within the levels-of-processing framework, Brown's distinction between automatic and deliberate memory can be viewed as the difference between processing stimuli that are meaningful, in the sense that they are compatible with semantic memory, and processing less meaningful stimuli that require deliberate remembering plans.

Deliberate memory strategies.   It has been claimed that if a mnemonic strategy is required to efficiently perform some task, developmental differences will be evident in that task (Flavell, 1970); however, if no such strategy is required, there will be relatively few developmental trends (Brown, 1973, 1974). Most of the developmental memory work in the past 15 years has investigated precisely these age-related differences in the successful use of deliberate memory strategies. In general, the data indicate that the efficient use of deliberate strategies emerges over a period of years, with children developing a working, flexible repertoire of mnemonic strategies by age 11 or 12.

Since memory strategies are defined as deliberate plans of action (or constellations of processes) generated by the subject to obtain a specific mnemonic goal, the major theoretical question involves specifying those factors which determine the application of a particular strategy in a given task. An examination of the developmental trends in how children come to employ the most efficient strategy in any given situation helps to isolate these factors. The development of any given mnemonic strategy can be seen as progressing from total absence of the strategy (mediational deficiency) to the ability to use the strategy when instructed to do so (production deficiency), to the spontaneous generation of the strategy in the appropriate task—first with inefficient implementation (production inefficiency) and then, with sufficient practice, in a maximally efficient manner (optimal production). Mediational deficiency represents the total inability of the child to employ a particular mnemonic strategy to improve memory performance. Even if the child is shown how to execute the strategy, he or she cannot use it to facilitate remembering. Production deficiency refers to that stage in the development of a particular strategy when the child fails to spontaneously generate a given strategy in the appropriate situation but can, if instructed, use that strategy to facilitate memory performance. Children may fail to spontaneously generate a particular strategy because they may not realize that the task requires the use of that strategy, or because it is in competition with a less efficient but better learned strategy. Production inefficiency, a term originally suggested by Flavell and his co-workers (Corsini, Pick, & Flavell, 1968), refers to that stage where children attempt to spontaneously use a particular strategy but, due to some developmentally related limitation in their facility with the strategy, do so ineptly. The final stage in the effective use of a deliberate memory strategy involves the spontaneous implementation of the strategy in an efficient fashion in the appropriate situations.

These developmental trends suggest that the failure to successfully employ a particular mnemonic strategy may sometimes result because that strategy is incompatible with existing semantic memory structures, leading to a mediational deficiency. However, these trends do not suggest an explanation for the absence of the spontaneous use of a particular strategy, given that the strategy mediates improved memory performance. Recent investigations of the development of metamemory, i.e., a person's knowledge of the operation of his or her memory system, are an attempt to examine the mechanisms leading to these production deficiencies (e.g., Flavell & Wellman, 1978; Kreutzer, Leonard, & Flavell, 1975). The failure of a child to use a particular strategy may reflect a lack of knowledge either about his or her own memory capabilities, the requirements of the task at hand, and/or the potential strategies that could efficiently meet these task demands. An examination of production deficiencies in memory performance, together with children's understanding of the operation of their memory and the task, may facilitate an understanding of the effective employment of deliberate memory strategies in a given task. Since the developmental literature investigating memory strategies is large and has been adequately reviewed elsewhere (e.g., Hagen, Jongeward, & Kail, 1975; Ornstein, 1977), the present discussion is designed only to illustrate developmental trends found in the successful application of memory strategies.

Age-related differences in verbal rehearsal have been shown to be a critical determinant of developmental changes in recall performance in deliberate memory tasks (Belmont & Butterfield, 1971; Garrity, 1975; Kingsley & Hagen, 1969; Ornstein & Naus, 1978). Recent use of overt rehearsal techniques has allowed an in-depth analysis of the development of the appropriate use of efficient rehearsal strategies (Cuvo, 1975; Kellas, McCauley, & McFarland, 1975; Ornstein et al (1975). Ornstein et al., for example, examined children's rehearsal techniques during the acquisition of a free recall list of unrelated items. Third-, sixth-, and eighth-grade children were asked to rehearse aloud during the presentation of each to-be-remembered word. In addition, control groups at each age were given standard free-recall instructions. Recall data for both the overt and covert control subjects paralleled those typically observed in this task (e.g., Cole, Frankel, & Sharp, 1971), with age-related changes in recall occurring in the prerecency portions of the serial position curves. The recall data for the overt subjects are presented in Panel A of Fig. 12.1. Analysis of the children's rehearsal protocols indicated that rehearsal frequency, summarized in Panel B of Fig. 12.1, was not systematically related to recall performance. However, the composition of the rehearsal sets (i.e., the rehearsal recorded as each stimulus word was presented) was quite different among the three age groups. The third graders tended to rehearse each item as it was presented either alone (e.g., *cat, cat, cat, cat*) or in minimal combination with other items (e.g., *cat, dog, cat, cat*). In contrast to this "rote" repetition, the rehearsal of the older children was more active, with several words being intermixed in each rehearsal set (e.g., *cat, iron, man, desk*). These age-related differences in rehearsal are summarized in Panel C of Fig. 12.1. A comparison of Panels A and C indicates that the age-related differences in rehearsal content correspond directly to developmental differences in recall. Similar rehearsal and recall patterns were also observed for the younger and older children with categorized word lists. Thus, younger children do not spontaneously employ active rehearsal strategies when studying word lists, whereas older children do.

Although third graders do not spontaneously employ active learning strategies in deliberate memory tasks such as free recall, they can do so when instructed. Naus, Ornstein, and Aivano (1977), for example, instructed third and sixth

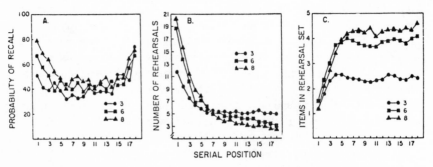

FIG. 12.1.   The probability of recall (Panel A), number of rehearsals (Panel B), and number of different items in each rehearsal set (Panel C) as a function of serial position for third, sixth, and eighth graders. (From P. A. Ornstein, M. J. Naus, & C. Liberty, 1975.)

graders to use identical active rehearsal strategies in which three unique items were rehearsed as each to-be-remembered word was presented. Since this instructed rehearsal strategy is similar to that spontaneously employed by older children (Ornstein et al., 1975), no change in the sixth graders' recall performance was expected. For the third graders, the spontaneous use of passive rehearsal in the Ornstein et al. (1975) study was thought to reflect a production deficiency, and thus, instructed use of the three-item, active rehearsal strategy was expected to lead to improved recall. As predicted, Naus et al. (1977) found no change in the recall performance of the sixth graders, whereas recall of the third graders improved, approaching that of the older children. Similarly, in a second training study, Ornstein, Naus, & Stone (1977) found that the memory performance of second graders improved when they were instructed to use an active rehearsal strategy. Furthermore, when these second graders were presented with a new list of words to learn in a transfer task, they continued to rehearse in an active fashion, although they were not required to do so. Recall for these transfer lists approximated the recall of older children who spontaneously employed active rehearsal.

These overt rehearsal studies of Naus, Ornstein, and their colleagues demonstrate the developmental sequence associated with the acquisition of an active rehearsal strategy. Although young children (second and third graders) are able to employ an active rehearsal strategy to improve their recall when instructed to do so, they do not typically use this strategy spontaneously.[2] However, although these studies characterize the developmental trend of efficient strategy employment, they do not identify those factors that determine efficient strategy use. Recent investigations have begun to isolate these factors through an examination of those age-related changes in metamemory knowledge that are associated with the development of active rehearsal strategies.

Kreutzer et al.'s (1975) investigation of metamemory established a developmental trend in children's ability to recognize and articulate that purposeful strategies such as verbal rehearsal are required in order to efficiently memorize lists of items. When kindergarten, first, third, and fifth graders were asked how they would learn a list of categorized pictures, few of the younger children thought of something planful to do, whereas most of the third and fifth graders suggested some kind of verbal rehearsal or grouping strategy. Although this work suggests a developmental trend in children's understanding of the importance of using mnemonic strategies in deliberate memory tasks, it does not differentiate between more and less effective strategies such as active and passive

---

[2]Further studies have suggested that third-grade girls may be in a transitional period between production deficiency and spontaneous use of active rehearsal. When Naus et al. (1977) simplified the free-recall task by decreasing the presentation rate from 5 to 10 seconds per item, third-grade girls were able to spontaneously use active rehearsal, and their recall performance approached the level of the sixth graders who spontaneously rehearsed actively under both presentation rates.

rehearsal. The recent work of Naus and Dennig (in preparation) involved testing nursery school, second, and fifth graders on both their metamemory knowledge and their memory performance in a free recall, overt rehearsal task. Developmental trends in rehearsal and recall replicated previous findings (Naus et al., 1977; Ornstein & Naus, 1978; Ornstein et al., 1975; Ornstein et al., 1977). Metamemory was tested using a forced-choice procedure, an example of which is provided in Table 12.2. The ordering of each child's preferences among a series of alternatives was determined by examining their forced choices for each possible pair of alternatives. Preference orderings that did not show transitivity

TABLE 12.2
Examples of Interview Questions Using Forced-Choice
Testing Procedure for a Metamemory Study

(a)   If you were trying to learn a list of words, which is the best way to practice them?

_____ To study each word alone, just a few times, like
          apple, apple, apple
          barn, barn, barn
          table, table, table

_____ To study each word alone, many times, like
          apple, apple, apple, apple, apple, apple, apple
          barn, barn, barn, barn, barn, barn, barn
          table, table, table, table, table, table, table

(b)   If you were trying to learn a list of words, which is the best way to practice them?

_____ To study each word in a group with other words, like
          apple, barn, table
          apple, barn, table
          apple, barn, table

_____ To study each word alone, just a few times, like
          apple, apple, apple
          barn, barn, barn
          table, table, table

(c)   If you were trying to learn a list of words, which is the best way to practice them?

_____ To study each word alone, many times, like
          apple, apple, apple, apple, apple, apple, apple
          barn, barn, barn, barn, barn, barn, barn
          table, table, table, table, table, table, table

_____ To study each word in a group with other words, like
          apple, barn, table
          apple, barn, table
          apple, barn, table

(From M. J. Naus & L. Dennig, in preparation.)

were excluded from the data analyses. The metamemory question illustrated in Table 12.2 examined children's judgments of the relative efficiency of several possible rehearsal strategies involved in learning a free recall list: passive rehearsal with three repetitions of each item (*apple, apple, apple*); passive rehearsal with seven repetitions of each item (*apple, apple, apple, apple, apple, apple, apple*); and active rehearsal (*apple, barn, table*). Children of all ages judged passive rehearsal with three repetitions to be the most inefficient rehearsal strategy. Whereas nursery school and second graders judged the passive rehearsal strategy with seven repetitions as the most efficient, fifth graders selected the active rehearsal strategy as most effective. Therefore, children's awareness of the facilitating effect of active rehearsal seems to develop in correspondence with their ability to spontaneously use this strategy effectively in free recall tasks.

The older children's increased sensitivity to the demands of a rehearsal task might result from an increasing awareness of the demands of memory tasks and/or their own memory capabilities. Naus and Dennig (in preparation), for example, investigated the development of children's knowledge of the importance of organization in deliberate memory tasks. Children were asked to judge the relative ease of memorizing a list of items that were either semantically related (categorized), accoustically related (rhyming), or not related at all. Whereas the nursery-school and second-grade children chose acoustically related lists, fifth graders selected semantically related lists as being easiest to learn. Kreutzer et al. (1975) also demonstrated a similar developmental pattern in children's knowledge of the importance of organization in list learning. They asked children to predict whether it would be easier to learn a list of word pairs where the pairs were opposites (e.g., *boy—girl*) or where the pairs consisted of an arbitrary association between a person and an action (e.g., *Mary—walk*). Kindergarten children predicted arbitrary pairs would be easier to learn, whereas first graders chose the two types of pairs with equal frequency, and third and fifth graders predicted that the opposites would be easier. A study by Tenney (1975) showed a similar developmental trend. When asked to generate lists that would be easy to remember, kindergarten children produced lists indistinguishable from their free association protocols, whereas sixth graders generated categorized lists. Similar findings have also been reported by Moynahan (1973) and Salatas and Flavell (1976a). These studies indicate that older children have an increasing awareness of the operation of organization in mnemonic tasks.

A similar developmental trend has been found in studies investigating children's knowledge of their own memory capabilities (Flavell, 1977; Flavell, Friedrichs, & Hoyt, 1970; Flavell & Wellman, 1978; Levin, Yussen, DeRose, & Pressley, in press; Markman, in press; Naus & Dennig, in preparation; Yussen & Levy, 1975). For example, both Naus and Dennig (in preparation) and Yussen and Levy (1975) found that older children were significantly more accurate in predicting their short-term memory capacity than younger children, who consistently tended to overestimate their memory capacity. Thus, there are developmental trends in children's knowledge of the operation of their memory in free-recall, overt rehearsal tasks, which coincide with the developmental trends in children's ability to spontaneously use active rehearsal effectively. Recent developmental work has also suggested the possibility of a similar correspondence between the development of successful retrieval strategies (e.g., Kobasigawa, 1974) and relevant metamemory knowledge (e.g., Flavell, 1977; Naus & Dennig, in preparation; Salatas & Flavell, 1976b; Wellman, 1977; Yussen & Levy, 1977).

These investigations of deliberate memory indicate a clear developmental trend in the successful employment of efficient memory strategies, which seems to be directly related to corresponding changes in children's knowledge of their own memory capabilities and the requirements of particular memory tasks. By the age of about 11 to 12 years, children are able to spontaneously use effective storage and retrieval strategies, at least in simple laboratory tasks, and seem to have a corresponding metamemory knowledge of the operation of these processes. Although at present, research on the development of metamemory is just beginning and existing data do not indicate that changes in metamemory knowledge lead to changes in the implementation of mnemonic strategies, the development of metamemory and deliberate memory processes seem highly interdependent. These data also suggest that the effective implementation of memory strategies in adults may be determined by subjects' comprehension of their memory capabilities, the task demands, and the possible strategies that are available to meet those demands.[3]

Automatic memory processes.   Although deliberate memory strategies have been extensively investigated in the developmental literature, little attention has been devoted to defining and investigating other types of memory processing (Naus, Ornstein, & Hoving, 1978). The class of automatic processes suggested here and by Brown (1975) represents an attempt to deal with processing that is non-strategic in that it does not involve a purposeful plan of action directed toward some specific memory goal. Rather, automatic processes refer to those involuntary processes that operate when a person is interacting with a meaningful environment. When a stimulus has meaning for a subject, it automatically

---

[3]The relationship between metamemory and memory behavior is just beginning to be investigated (Flavell, 1977; Naus & Dennig, in preparation). Although the present argument suggests developmental changes in metamemory as a possible explanation for age-related differences in performance in deliberate memory tasks, it is recognized that the relationship between metamemory and memory behavior is extremely complicated and not always causal. Flavell (1977) has suggested that the interaction may be reciprocal, with changes in metamemory leading to changes in memory behavior and vice versa. It is certainly recognized in the context of the present paper that developmental changes in deliberate memory processing affect metamemory by mediating changes in semantic memory structure.

elicits in semantic memory those encoding and elaboration analyses with which it is highly compatible. Automatic processes are highly dependent on the structure and contents of semantic memory as well as on the properties of the environmental stimuli and, therefore, are sensitive to changes in these factors. Developmental trends in automatic processing, then, reflect changes in semantic memory and its relation to processing, rather than changes in the successful application of appropriate mnemonic strategies in a given memory task. The major theoretical question of interest in investigations of automatic processes is the interrelation between semantic memory and memory processing. This orientation is consistent with the levels-of-processing approach, which views the processing of stimulus information as operating within the cognitive structures of semantic memory. Although existing data are inadequate to clarify this relationship, developmental investigations of constructive memory and incidental learning can help to specify the operation of automatic processing.

Investigations of semantic integration and inferencing in constructive memory studies indicate that encoding and elaboration of meaningful material is an automatic process that occurs in children as young as 4 years old (Barclay & Reid, 1974; Bartlett, 1932; Bransford & Franks, 1971; Brown, 1976; Brown & Murphy, 1975; Paris, 1975; Paris & Carter, 1973; Paris & Upton, 1974). These studies of constructive memory are based upon a view in which rather than being considered simply a snapshot of events filed in memory at storage and faithfully retrieved at recall, memory is thought of as a construction of an internal interpretation of the stimulus by the subject. This cognitive construction consists of selecting relevant information from incoming stimuli as well as elaborating this information on the basis of stored semantic knowledge. Similarly, the process of retrieval from memory is seen as an active reconstruction process in which the remembered material is constructed from information available in semantic memory and in the recall environment. In Bartlett's (1932) terms, memory involves "going beyond the information given" and actively embellishing stimulus information. In the present view, this elaboration and integration of environmental stimuli in conjunction with semantic memory is viewed as an automatic process.

Empirical investigations of constructive memory in both adults and children have centered on the study of semantic integration. These studies have shown that rather than remembering individual stimuli from a group of semantically related pictures or sentences, subjects tend to abstract semantic relationships from the stimuli and integrate these relationships in memory (e.g., Bransford & Franks, 1971; Brown, 1976; Franks & Bransford, 1971; Paris, 1975; Posnansky & Neumann, 1976). In adults, Bransford and Franks (1971) have shown that subjects most confidently recognize sentences or pictures that have not actually been previously seen but which represent a thematic integration of the previously presented stimuli. Similar results have been shown in children by Paris (1975; Paris & Carter, 1973; Paris & Mahoney, 1974) and Barclay and Reid (1974). In the Paris studies, for example, children in grades 2 and 5 were presented three sentences—two of which were premises from which certain inferences could logically be drawn while the third was an irrelevant filler item. (For example: *The bird is in the cage* [premise]. *The cage is under the table* [premise]. *The bird is yellow* [filler].) The children were then tested for recognition of the presented sentences using a variety of distractor sentences, including negations of the premise sentences as well as inferences that either could or could not logically be derived from the premises. (For example: *The bird is in the cage* [true premise]. *The cage is over the table* [false premise]. *The bird is under the table* [logical inference]. *The bird is on top of the table* [illogical inference].) The results, which are summarized in Fig. 12.2, showed a very high false-alarm rate for logical inferences; that is, the children incorrectly responded "old" to logical inferences just about as often as they correctly responded "old" to actual premises. This finding was not the result of generally poor memory, since rejection of both false premises and illogical inferences was fairly accurate. These results suggest that like adults, children as young as 7 years old integrate the semantic relationships among sentences and store general abstract descriptions rather than the verbatim stimuli. In a similar vein, Barclay and Reid (1974) presented children with sets of sentences in which the test sentence was either a full passive sentence including an actor, a truncated passive sentence where the actor was introduced in a later sentence, or a truncated passive sentence where

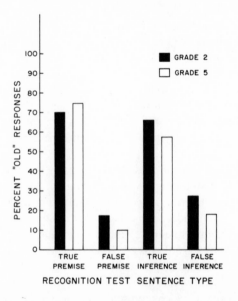

FIG. 12.2.   Percentage of "old" responses as a function of recognition test sentence type for second and fifth graders. (From S. G. Paris, 1975, based on S. G. Paris & A. Y. Carter, 1973.)

the actor was never introduced. The results of a test requiring verbatim recall showed that the truncated passives where an actor was supplied tended to be recalled as full passive or active sentences. Where no actor was supplied, recall remained in truncated passive form. Clearly, the introduction of an actor allowed a thematic integration that altered the verbatim recall of the sentences.

Semantic integration in the foregoing tasks seems to be automatic. Both of these tasks required verbatim memory for the sentences. Nevertheless, the subjects semantically integrated the stimuli even though this led to poorer memory performance. Brown and Murphy (1975) have demonstrated the power of these automatic integration processes in children as young as 4 years old. They presented preschool children with a series of pictures that either depicted a logical narrative sequence or a random series of events. In addition, there was a scrambled condition in which the logical narrative was presented out of sequence. The subject was required to reconstruct the exact sequence of pictures after a lag of 0 to 5 intervening sets of stimuli. As illustrated in Fig. 12.3, performance remained constant over lag for the logically ordered sets but decreased as a function of lag for the random sets. This result was interpreted as indicating that subjects were able to use inferential reasoning to reconstruct the logically ordered sequences after relatively long lags, whereas they were unable to do this in recalling random sets where no organization was present. The most interesting result, however, was that performance on the scrambled sets was worse than that on random sets, decreasing with lag at a more rapid rate. This last finding indicates that the imposition of order onto stimulus materials is an automatic process that cannot be prevented even if the task demands ignoring implicit order in the stimuli. The poor performance in the scrambled conditions points to the power of automatic constructive processes in memory performance.

In both the Paris (1975; Paris & Carter, 1973) and Barclay and Reid (1974) experiments, no significant developmental trends in semantic integration were found. Paris (1975) has suggested that perhaps developmental trends are not observed in the semantic integration of sentences, since the ability to integrate and make inferences might improve in correspondence with the ability to discriminate and remember when such inferences have actually been made. Thus, when verbatim memory is required, false alarms to logical inferences should not increase with age. In response to this insensitivity of the semantic integration paradigm to developmental trends, Paris (1975; Paris & Upton, 1974) began to study inferencing in narrative passages. In these studies kindergarten through fifth-grade children were read a short story of approximately eight sentences and were then asked questions about their understanding of words and relationships in this story. A typical story and its corresponding test questions are presented in Table 12.3. The questions tested both explicit, verbatim recall and implicit, inferential recall. The inferential questions involved either lexical inferences concerned with the meanings of particular words or contextual inferences concerned with the semantic integration of several sentences. As

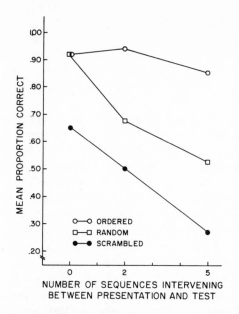

FIG. 12.3. Mean proportion of sequences reconstructed in the presented order as a function of the number of stimulus sequences intervening between initial presentation and test for the ordered, random, and scrambled sequences of pictures. (From A. L. Brown & M. D. Murphy, 1975.)

illustrated in Fig. 12.4, the results showed that both inferential and verbatim recall increased with age. Although lexical inferences were slightly easier than contextual inferences, both showed similar developmental trends. Initially it was unclear whether these developmental trends were due to an increase in inferencing capabilities with age or simply reflected an increase in memory capacity for the older children. However, by considering responses to verbatim questions as an indication of memory capacity, Paris (1975) was able to control for memory capacity differences and show that the ability to inference increases substantially with age. Additional work by Paris and Lindauer (1976) supports this contention. Thus, the increase in children's ability to remember stories seems to reflect an increase in both memory capacity and the tendency to use implicit information in the story to provide the basis for integrating and inferencing from the story's explicit content.

In the present view of automatic processing, these developmental differences in inferencing ability are associated with age-related changes in the structure and contents of semantic memory. Developmental changes in semantic memory that might lead to age-related differences in the inferencing process include not only increases in children's general knowledge about the world but also changes in their understanding of the relationship among stimuli and their selection of the stimulus features to be encoded. Unfortunately, although there is general agreement that between the ages of 5 and 11 children's general knowledge of the world increases, these developmental changes and their relationship to inferencing ability have yet to be demonstrated empirically.

Although the work on constructive memory just presented deals with simple inferences that occur involuntarily as a product of the comprehension of meaningful stimuli, it is certainly possible for subjects to use inferences as a strategic memory activity in certain tasks. In fact, Paris and his colleagues (Paris, 1975; Paris & Lindauer, 1976) suggest that some of the developmental trends in children's tendency to inference might be due to such strategic intervention. Investigations of incidental memory in children of different ages provides an opportunity to investigate the development of automatic processes independent of strategic intervention by the subject. Most of the developmental work in incidental memory has focused upon paradigms that test memory of presented information which is irrelevant to a central learning task (Type II paradigms in Postman's 1964 distinction) (Druker & Hagen, 1969; Hagen, 1967, 1972; Hagen & Sabo, 1967; Hale & Piper, 1973, 1974). However, these tasks are not directly relevant to the present discussion, since the learning of irrelevant material does not necessarily involve the interaction of the child with a meaningful stimulus. In contrast, a few recent developmental studies (e.g., Geis & Hall, 1976; Murphy & Brown, 1975; Smirnov & Zinchenko, 1969; Yendovitskaya,

TABLE 12.3
Stimulus Materials for an Investigation
of Children's Comprehension of Prose Materials

Stimulus Story

Linda was playing with her new doll in front of her big red house. Suddenly she heard a strange sound coming from under the porch. It was the flapping of wings. Linda wanted to help so much, but she did not know what to do. She ran inside the house and grabbed a shoe box from the closet. Then Linda looked inside her desk until she found eight sheets of yellow paper. She cut up the paper into little pieces and put them in the bottom of the box. Linda gently picked up the helpless creature and took it with her. Her teacher knew what to do.

Test Questions

Question	Type	Correct Response
Was Linda's doll new?	Premise	Yes
Did Linda grab a match box?	Premise	No
Did Linda like to take care of animals?	Inference–Contextual	Yes
Did Linda take what she found to the police station?	Inference–Contextual	No
Did Linda use a pair of scissors?	Inference–Lexical	Yes
Did Linda find a frog?	Inference–Lexical	No

(From S. G. Paris, 1975, based on S. G. Paris & L. R. Upton, 1974.)

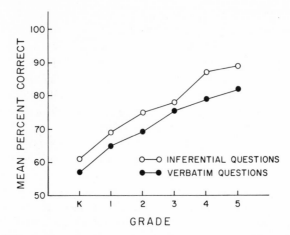

FIG. 12.4.   Mean percentage of correct responses on verbatim and inferential questions as a function of grade. (From S. G. Paris, 1975, based on S. G. Paris & L. R. Upton, 1974.)

1971) have investigated incidental memory in paradigms in which children are forced to process the stimulus material without being given specific instructions to remember it (Type I paradigms in Postman's 1964 distinction). By varying the type of cognitive processing that is required of the subject, these studies allow the investigation of automatic processing independent of concurrent strategic processing.

Murphy and Brown (1975) investigated incidental memory in 4-year-olds by comparing their recall performance in several task conditions. Each child learned two lists of pictures—one under specific instructions to memorize the list for free recall and the other under one of two types of incidental memory instructions. For some of the subjects, these incidental memory instructions can be characterized as a semantic categorization task involving classifying the stimulus pictures, whereas for the remaining children these instructions involved a formal orienting task in which subjects either simply labeled or noted the dominant color of the stimuli. The results showed no difference in recall between the free-recall instruction conditions and the incidental memory conditions with formal orienting instructions. However, recall was greater in the incidental memory conditions in which children received the semantic categorization instructions. In general, 4-year-olds did not engage in strategic processing under free recall instructions, leading to a low level of recall performance in the free recall conditions. The equivalent performance between the formal-orienting, incidental-instruction conditions and the free recall conditions indicates that merely attending to stimuli does not mediate memory. However, the greater recall performance in the semantic categorization incidental conditions than in the free recall conditions demonstrates that semantic processing, regardless of any intention to remember, is sufficient to facilitate remembering. These results suggest that instructions to remember are not necessary to elicit appropriate memory activities and that nonstrategic comprehension of the stimulus in the absence of the intention to remember is sufficient to yield adequate memory performance. Further evidence for the absence of developmental trends in the operation of automatic processes in incidental memory tasks has recently been provided by Geis and Hall (1976). First, third and fifth graders each showed greater recall of words after semantic orienting activities than after either acoustic or orthographic orienting activities.

In summary, this work on constructive memory and incidental learning demonstrates that many of the important operations of memory are in fact carried out by nonstrategic, automatic processes that result from the interaction of environmental stimuli with semantic memory structures. These studies have indicated that semantic integration, inferencing, and sequential reorganization are automatic processes elicited by appropriate, meaningful stimuli even under circumstances where these processes lead to poorer task performance. The work in incidental memory has shown that this nonstrategic, semantic processing is sufficient to mediate adequate memory performance. Furthermore, the absence of developmental trends in these incidental memory studies suggests that these automatic processes are a critical component of memory processing even in very young children. Within the present view, the developmental differences found in the studies on inferencing from narrative prose can be interpreted as resulting from either developmental changes in semantic memory that facilitate the inferencing process, or age-related changes in the implementation of inferencing as a strategic process to facilitate memory. Unfortunately, although these developmental studies demonstrate the importance of automatic processing in memory, they do little to clarify the nature of the relation between this processing and the structure of semantic memory. Nevertheless, this work indicates that the development of automatic processing follows a very different pattern from that of deliberate processing. These separate developmental patterns provide strong support for the consideration of these two types of processes as independent components of the memory system within the levels-of-processing framework.[4]

---

[4]A similar distinction between automatic and controlled (strategic) processing has recently been made in the human perception and performance literature by Shiffrin and Schneider (1977). They demonstrated that in a rapid, multi-frame visual detection task two very distinct letter detection processes can be elicited. Under conditions where the set of target items was well-defined automatic detection processes which did not require attention, could not be strategically controlled, were not capacity limited, operated in parallel, and were dependent upon well-learned associations in long-term memory were observed. In contrast, when target and distractor items were intermixed across trials a strategically controlled, limited capacity, serial search process was seen. A similar distinction between limited capacity, strategically controlled processes and unlimited capacity, automatic processes has also been suggested by Posner and Snyder (1975) and by LaBerge and Samuels (1974). While these conceptualizations are complimentary to the automatic/strategic distinction suggested in the present paper, the developmental literature further suggests that automatic processing may operate throughout the memory system rather than simply in low-level perceptual tasks as demonstrated in the human performance literature.

SEMANTIC MEMORY

Perhaps the most critical contribution of the levels-of-processing framework is its emphasis on semantic memory as the center of the cognitive system. Within this view, memory processing can be seen as occurring within the context of a person's general knowledge of the world. In this conceptualization, the contents of semantic memory both affect and are affected by memory processing. The theoretical questions of interest involve not only the effect of semantic structure on the processing and remembering of new stimulus information but also the mechanism by which current experience comes to be included in a person's general knowledge about the world. Only by employing a developmental perspective involving a dynamic, evolutionary view of memory can these two aspects of the relation between semantic memory and memory processing be adequately clarified.

What is remembered is determined by what is already known.   As a developmental perspective suggests, memory processing must be considered within the context of a person's existing memory system. The depth to which information is processed is a function of both the demands of the task and the degree of compatibility between environmental stimuli and the structure of semantic memory. Any significant change in semantic memory structures, either in the adult or the growing child, will result in a corresponding change in the way in which new stimulus information is processed and remembered. According to this argument, what is remembered is determined by what is already known. It is not surprising that much of the research investigating memory performance in adults, all of whom share similar stable semantic structures (at least for the materials typically tested in the laboratory), has not focused upon investigating memory processing as a function of a dynamic semantic memory system. Within the adult population, any differences between input stimuli and output protocols can best be accounted for by the assumption that the stimulus is being altered by an unchanging characteristic of the memory system. However, investigations of age-related patterns in memory performance have been forced to examine changes in memory processing within the context of a developing semantic knowledge base. Several lines of developmental research demonstrate and elaborate the point of view that memorization is an active, constructive process that is based upon, i.e., determined by, the nature of current knowledge (Paris, 1975; Piaget & Inhelder, 1973).

Piaget's work on the nature of intelligence and logical thinking in children is perhaps the best example of the role of semantic structure in memory processing. In this work, intelligence is conceptualized as consisting of both a child's world knowledge and the procedures through which environmental stimuli are cognitively processed. This view of intelligence is very similar to the current conceptualization of semantic memory. Piaget views the development of intelligence as an invariant sequence of mental stages, each one characterized by a particular constellation of cognitive structures or schemata that incorporate the child's knowledge about the world. The critical component of Piaget's theory is that a stimulus only has significance or meaning to the extent that there is a cognitive structure which permits its assimilation; the child processes information by assimilating incoming stimuli into the current cognitive schemata. A child's current constellation of schemata (i.e., his or her operational stage) determines how information is processed, what problems are solvable, what is understood, and what interpretation is given to incoming stimuli.

Piaget and Inhelder (1973; Inhelder, 1969) have applied this notion of cognitive development to memory. Memory and intelligence are seen as inseparably interrelated; what is remembered in any given situation is viewed as determined by the current constellation of schemata. Memory is seen as a store of information that has been encoded by a process of assimilation, and therefore, its content and structure reflect the child's schemata through which knowledge is assimilated. Based on this orientation, Piaget and Inhelder derived two predictions about the memory behavior of children. First, and least surprising, is the hypothesis that what children remember depends on their basic understanding of the situation or task at hand. Second, and more controversial, is the prediction that if children's underlying cognitive structures undergo a critical reorganization during the retention of a memory trace, the memory *per se* will be altered and in some cases actually improved. It is unclear whether this improvement occurs through a change in the actual trace during retention of is a result of constructive/reconstructive processes occurring through the new operational schemata at retrieval.

Piaget and Inhelder (1973) and others (Inhelder, 1969; Liben, 1978) have performed a number of studies to test these two predictions. Each study involves the examination of children's ability to remember some situation or series of objects as a function of their level of cognitive development. Furthermore, a given child's memory for a situation is examined over time and correlated with changes in his or her level of cognitive development that have occurred during the retention interval. In one study (Inhelder, 1969), children of various ages were shown a serial configuration of sticks arranged in length from shortest to longest. After a retention period of 1 week, recall was tested by requiring the child to draw the original configuration. The recall drawings differed according to age— progressing from a simple series of sticks all of the same length at age 3 or 4, to a variety of combinations of sticks of various lengths but without the serial order of the original configuration at 5 years old, and finally, to the correct serial configuration at age 6 or 7. In addition, 74% of the children asked to recall the configuration again after 6 to 8 months showed an improvement in their memory performance.

Similar results have been found in studies involving such concepts as the effects of gravity on water levels, causal relations, and numerical/spatial corre-spondences. Piaget and Inhelder (Inhelder, 1969) suggest that these results indicate that memory is not a simple residue of perception but rather an inter-pretation of the perceived stimulus that has been assimilated by the schemata of the child. During the interval between the two recall sessions, the schemata evolve, leading to a change in the use of the memory trace. The schemata at any stage provide the code for memory, and at each stage the memory trace is processed in accordance with the constraints of this semantic structure. This work, together with that of Paris and his colleagues (Paris, 1975; Paris & Carter, 1973; Paris & Upton, 1974), clearly illustrates that any model of memory must incorporate the view that memory is an active, constructive process that operates on the basis of the current knowledge and semantic organization of the individual. Thus, in a literal sense, what is remembered is determined by what is already known.

By what processes does semantic memory change?   Unfortunately, the prop-osition that semantic memory determines what is remembered does not tell us much about the nature of semantic memory—what it is, how it is organized, or how it changes. Although at present developmental psychology contributes little to an understanding of the structure of semantic memory, it does point to the importance of determining the processes by which semantic memory changes, i.e., the processes by which new information is learned. Although little empirical work directly addresses this question, a theoretical consideration of the de-velopment of memory requires the formulation of a mechanism through which experiences modify semantic memory and also places certain constraints on the nature of this mechanism. The levels-of-processing framework provides an orientation in which this mechanism can be specified.

Most current approaches to the question of how semantic memory changes are stated in terms of Tulving's (1972) distinction between episodic and semantic memory. Episodic memory is seen as the memory of specific occurrences or events stored in terms of a temporal—autobiographical reference. In contrast, semantic memory is seen as the organized, structured, symbolic representation of one's knowledge about the world and the procedures for manipulating those symbols. Although much of the work investigating semantic memory in both adults (e.g., Bransford & Franks, 1971) and children (e.g., Barclay & Reid, 1974; Paris, 1975) has studied verbal material, semantic memory refers to nonlinguistic, as well as linguistic, information that is organized along any nonautobiographical dimension. As diagramed in Panel A of Fig. 12.5, the levels-of-processing framework as proposed by Lockhart et al. (1976) incor-porates a strong version of this distinction. Incoming information is processed in semantic memory, and the result of this processing is entered as a new trace in episodic memory. These two stores are for all practical purposes considered separate but interacting components of memory. In keeping with Tulving's distinction, the question of what causes a change in semantic memory is often rephrased: How do episodic traces become semantic structures? Within the current levels-of-processing framework, then, some mechanism or process must be proposed through which information in episodic memory adds to or reorganizes semantic memory. However, such a process has not been proposed, and it is hard to imagine what it would be like. The absence of such a process points to the need for a reexamination of the episodic−semantic memory distinction.

The distinction between episodic and semantic memory has not been strictly maintained in the present formulation of the levels of processing framework. There are several places in which there is inconsistency in the application of this distinction. Episodic memories are seen as by-products of semantic encoding. Some of this encoding may involve very high levels of abstraction, stripping all contextual information from incoming stimuli and elaborating it in a highly semantic manner. However, the by-product of this processing is an episodic trace. Thus, in some sense, episodic memory contains highly structured, abstract information that is primarily semantic in nature. This point would be inconsequential, however, if this semantic organization was never used in retrieving or processing information. However, Lockhart et al. specify two retrieval processes from episodic memory, only one of which—search—can be said to operate on an unstructured memory. In contrast, in the process of reconstruction, retrieval is based on feedback from relevant memory traces, and this process must depend on some sort of structure. Feedback is received from those episodic traces that are relevant to the current reconstruction, a process which seems remarkably close to content-addressability. For a process like reconstruction to work, episodic memory must have some structure that allows the locating of correct feedback traces. Thus, the episodic−semantic distinction in the current levels-of-processing framework is somewhat blurred; episodic memory seems to contain and use structured information, an attribute usually reserved for semantic memory.

The ambiguity of this distinction suggests that the episodic−semantic dimension may not be dichotomous. Rather, long-term memory can be viewed as a unitary structure with a single set of principles of organization and operation. Storage and retrieval may consist of a continuous dimension that proceeds from what is now called episodic, i.e., contextual and autobiographical, to what is now considered semantic, i.e., structured and abstract. Any stored information can be viewed as lying somewhere along this dimension, containing some mixture of unstructured-contextual and symbolic-abstract information. How a given piece of information is stored will determine which storage and retrieval processes will be effective in dealing with that memory trace.

With this unitary memory, the levels framework becomes a closed loop, as is diagramed in Panel B of Fig. 12.5. Incoming information is processed within the single memory. Processing is predominantly semantic, but the possibility

A: DICHOTOMOUS MEMORY SYSTEM

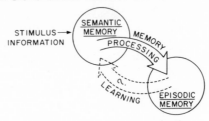

B: UNITARY MEMORY SYSTEM

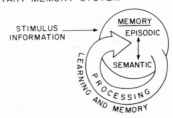

FIG. 12.5.   The interrelationship of semantic memory, episodic memory, and memory processing in the dichotomous (Panel A) and unitary (Panel B) memory systems.

remains that episodic traces could affect this processing. The end product of processing is a memory trace that is entered into the single memory. How the new trace is processed determines where along the episodic—semantic dimension it will be stored. Information that is processed to a deep semantic level or processed extensively in any domain will most probably be stripped of all contextual information during encoding and enter into the system as a semantic trace that cannot be retrieved "episodically." In contrast, information processed less extensively and retaining its contextual information will not be semantically organized when entered into memory and thus will have to be retrieved by an episodic search. Those stimuli that are processed to an intermediate level will be available to a variety of semantic or episodic processes.

In this formulation, semantic memory is a developing structure. Each time a stimulus is encoded to some semantic level, either an old trace is strengthened, or—if the encoding results in some new semantic information—a new semantic trace results. Thus, semantic memory builds upon itself; incoming stimuli are interpreted on the basis of current semantic structure and, in turn, change that structure if a new interpretation results. This formulation of a unitary memory is motivated by the need for a parsimonious explanation within the levels-of-processing framework for the evolving characteristics of semantic memory. Clearly, learning does occur, and radical shifts in the structure and contents of semantic memory are common during memory development. Rather than introduce an entirely new set of processes mapping episodic into semantic memory, it is far more parsimonious to postulate a single set of processes responsible for both learning (the acquisition of new semantic traces) and memory (the acquisition of new episodic traces). Moreover, it is also more plausible to assume that learning occurs as a result of interactive processing of environmental stimuli within semantic memory rather than to view it as the result of some transfer process that occurs "after the fact." Thus, the development of memory with age results directly from the semantic processing of information during children's continuous interaction with environmental stimuli.

This formulation of a unitary memory also helps to clarify some of the confusion caused by the dichotomous distinction between episodic and semantic memory as to the operation of memory in tasks that seem to fall somewhere between the two memory types. For example, list learning tasks where the subject imposes some organization on the material have been considered to be episodic, since they represent the learning of no new semantic information but rather involve memory pertaining to a particular context. However, the subject is applying order to these lists and in fact is using this structure to facilitate recall. It is difficult to know how to classify this type of procedure in a dichotomous memory categorization. No system that functionally or conceptually separates semantic and episodic memory could easily explain typical performance in list learning tasks. Rather than being purely episodic, list learning procedures involve a mixture of semantic and episodic processing and, hence, have something in common both with memorizing a table of random numbers and making inferences from narrative passages. Thus, the unitary memory concept within the levels-of-processing framework provides not only a powerful conceptualization of the dynamic, developmental characteristics of semantic memory but also a clarification of memory processing in the adult.

Both the investigations of developmental changes in memory processing as a function of changes in semantic memory and the theoretical consideration of the processes by which semantic memory develops suggest that any model of memory must incorporate a dynamic view of the memory system in which the contents and structures of memory are functionally interdependent with memory processing. Not only does the configuration of semantic memory determine the characteristics of memory processing, but a developmental perspective suggests that memory processing is the critical mechanism by which the structure and contents of semantic memory evolve.

SUMMARY AND CONCLUSIONS

The unique perspective offered by investigations of a developing memory system suggests a number of important contributions for understanding the operation of the memory system in both children and adults. The present paper describes two of the most critical contributions provided by this perspective. The developmental work on memory strategies suggests that a distinction must be made between deliberate and automatic memory processes. These two types of memory processing have very different characteristics. Deliberate memory processes are planful patterns of action selected by the subject in order to attain some specific mnemonic goal. In contrast, automatic processes are involuntary operations elicited by environmental stimuli in conjunction with semantic memory during the subject's interaction with a meaningful environment. The differing developmental patterns observed for these two types of processing suggest that they are independent components of the memory system. Examination of the developmental patterns of verbal rehearsal demonstrates the increasing ability of children to effectively employ these mnemonic strategies in appropriate situations. The increases in processing efficiency correspond to developmental changes in children's metamemory regarding both their own memory capabilities and the demands of memory tasks. In contrast, investigations of the development of automatic processes in inferencing, semantic integration, and incidental memory show few age-related changes in the operation of processing meaningful stimuli. Those developmental changes in automatic processing that are observed seem to be due either to changes in semantic memory that affect automatic processing or to an increase in children's ability to employ strategic processes in addition to automatic processes in certain tasks.

A developmental perspective further suggests that memory processing must be considered as operating within the context of a person's existing semantic memory. This perspective suggests both that semantic memory plays an important role in determining memory processing and that this processing is a critical mechanism by which the structure and contents of semantic memory evolve. The proposition that what is remembered is determined by what is already known is suggested by the work of Piaget on the relation between memory and intelligence and that of Paris and others on constructive memory. Theoretical consideration of the episodic−semantic memory distinction suggests that the mechanism by which memory develops and learning occurs is the processing of meaningful stimuli within the cognitive structures of semantic memory.

This developmental perspective is consistent with the levels-of-processing framework, since both of the viewpoints stress the interrelationship between memory processing and semantic memory. However, developmental work suggests modifications that must be made in the levels-of-processing conceptualization of semantic memory, memory processing, and the relationship between them. First, the levels-of-processing framework must provide for automatic and deliberate processing as independent components of the cognitive system. Second, a mechanism should be specified by which semantic memory changes through experience with environmental stimuli. This mechanism is best viewed as operating within a unitary memory system in which information is stored along a dimension of organization ranging from temporal—autobiographical (episodic) to highly structured and abstract (semantic). These two modifications represent an initial attempt to provide for a more dynamic, evolutionary conceptualization of memory within the level-of-processing framework. The viewpoint that the memory system is continually developing through its interations with a meaningful environment is critical not only for the understanding of the significant changes in memory performance that occur as children develop but also for a clarification of the processes of learning and memory that operate in the more stable memory system of adults. Thus, any complete model of memory must be based upon a dynamic, evolutionary orientation to memory processing and structure.

REFERENCES

Atkinson, R. C., Hansen, D. N., & Bernbach, H. A. Short-term memory with young children. *Psychonomic Science,* 1964, *1,* 255–256.

Atkinson, R. C., & Shiffrin, R. M. Human memory: A proposed system and its control processes. In K. W. Spence & J. T. Spence (Eds.), *The psychology of learning and motivation* (Vol. II). New York: Academic Press, 1968.

Atkinson, R. C., & Shiffrin, R. M. The control of short-term memory. *Scientific American,* August 1971, 82–90.

Barclay, J. R., & Reid, M. Semantic integration in children's recall of discourse. *Developmental Psychology,* 1974, *10,* 277–281.

Bartlett, F. C. *Remembering: A study in experimental and social psychology.* Cambridge, England: Cambridge University Press, 1932.

Belmont, J. M., & Butterfield, E. C. Learning strategies as determinants of memory deficiencies. *Cognitive Psychology,* 1971, *2,* 411–420.

Bransford, J. D., & Franks, J. J. The abstraction of linguistic ideas. *Cognitive Psychology,* 1971, *2,* 331–350.

Brener, R. An experimental investigation of memory span. *Journal of Experimental Psychology,* 1940, *26,* 467–482.

Brown, A. L. Judgments of recency for long sequences of pictures: The absence of a developmental trend. *Journal of Experimental Child Psychology,* 1973, *15,* 473–481.

Brown, A. L. The role of strategic behavior in retardate memory. In N. R. Ellis (Ed.), *International review of research in mental retardation* (Vol. 7). New York: Academic Press, 1974.

Brown, A. L. The development of memory: Knowing, knowing about knowing, and knowing how to know. In H. W. Reese (Ed.), *Advances in child development and behavior* (Vol. 10). New York: Academic Press, 1975.

Brown, A. L. Semantic integration in children's reconstruction of narrative sequences. *Cognitive Psychology,* 1976, *8,* 247–262.

Brown, A. L., & Murphy, M. D. Reconstruction of arbitrary versus logical sequences by preschool children. *Journal of Experimental Child Psychology,* 1975, *20,* 307–326.

Chi, M. T. Short-term memory limitations in children: Capacity or processing deficits? *Memory & Cognition,* 1976, *4,* 559–572.

Cole, M., Frankel, F., & Sharp, D. Development of free recall learning in children. *Developmental Psychology,* 1971, *4,* 109–123.

Corsini, D. A., Pick, A. D., & Flavell, J. H. Production of non-verbal mediators in young children. *Child Development,* 1968, *39,* 53–58.

Craik, F. I. M., & Jacoby, L. L. A process view of short-term retention. In F. Restle, R. M. Shiffrin, N. J. Castellan, H. R. Lindman, & D. B. Pisoni (Eds.), *Cognitive theory* (Vol. 1). Hillsdale, N.J.: Lawrence Erlbaum Associates, 1975.

Craik, F. I. M., & Lockhart, R. S. Levels of processing: A framework for memory research. *Journal of Verbal Learning and Verbal Behavior,* 1972, *11,* 671–684.

Craik, F. I. M., & Watkins, M. J. The role of rehearsal in short-term memory. *Journal of Verbal Learning and Verbal Behavior,* 1973, *12,* 599–607.

Crannell, C. W., & Parrish, J. M. A comprehension of immediate memory span for digits, letters, and words. *Journal of Psychology,* 1957, *44,* 319–327.

Cuvo, A. J. Developmental differences in rehearsal and free recall. *Journal of Experimental Child Psychology,* 1975, *19,* 265–278.

Druker, J. F., & Hagen, J. W. Developmental trends in processing of task-relevant and task-irrelevant information. *Child Development,* 1969, *40,* 371–382.

Flavell, J. H. Developmental studies of mediated memory. In H. W. Reese & L. P. Lipsitt (Eds.), *Advances in child development and behavior* (Vol. 5). New York: Academic Press, 1970.

Flavell, J. H. *Metacognitive development.* Paper presented at NATO Advanced Study Institute on Structural/Process Theories of Complex Human Behavior, Alberta, Canada, June 1977.

Flavell, J. H., Friedrichs, A. G., & Hoyt, J. D. Developmental changes in memorization processes. *Cognitive Psychology,* 1970, *1,* 324–340.

Flavell, J. H., & Wellman, H. M. Metamemory. In R. V. Kail & J. W. Hagen (Eds.), *Memory in cognitive development.* Hillsdale, N.J.: Lawrence Erlbaum Associates, 1978.

Franks, J. J., & Bransford, J. D. Abstraction of visual patterns. *Journal of Experimental Psychology,* 1971, *90,* 65–74.

Garrity, L. I. An electromyographical study of subvocal speech and recall in preschool children. *Developmental Psychology,* 1975, *11,* 274–281.

Gates, H. I., & Taylor, G. A. An experimental study of the nature of improvement resulting from practice in a mental function. *Journal of Educational Psychology,* 1925, *16,* 583–592.

Geis, M. F., & Hal, D. M. Encoding and incidental memory in children. *Journa of Experimental Psychology,* 1976, *22,* 58–66.

Hagen, J. W. The effect of distraction on selective attention. *Child Development,* 1967, *38,* 685–694.

Hagen, J. W. Strategies for remembering. In S. Farnham–Diggory (Ed.), *Information processing in children.* New York: Academic Press, 1972.

Hagen, J. W., Jongeward, R. H., & Kail, R. V. Cognitive perspectives on the development of memory. In H. W. Reese (Ed.), *Advances in child development and behavior* (Vol. 10). New York: Academic Press, 1975.

Hagen J. W., & Sabo, R. A. A developmental study of selective attention. *Merrill–Palmer Quarterly,* 1967, *13,* 159–176.

Haith, M. M., Morrison, F. J., Sheingold, K., & Mindes, P. Short-term memory for visual information in children and adults. *Journal of Experimental Child Psychology,* 1970, *9,* 454–469.

Hale, G. A., & Piper, R. A. Developmental trends in children's incidental learning: Some critical stimulus differences. *Developmental Psychology,* 1973, *8,* 327–335.

Hale, G. A., & Piper, R. A. Effect of pictorial integration on children's incidental learning. *Developmental Psychology,* 1974, *10,* 847–851.

Hurlock, E. B., & Newmark, E. D. The memory span of preschool children. *Journal of Genetic Psychology,* 1931, *39,* 157–173.

Inhelder, B. Memory and intelligence in the child. In D. Elkind & J. H. Flavell (Eds.), *Studies in cognitive development.* New York: Oxford University Press, 1969.

Jacoby, L. L., & Bartz, W. A. Encoding processes and the negative recency effect. *Journal of Verbal Learning and Verbal Behavior*, 1972, *11*, 561–565.

Kellas, G., McCauley, C., & McFarland, C. E. Developmental aspects of storage and retrieval. *Journal of Experimental Child Psychology*, 1975, *19*, 51–62.

Kingsley, P. R., & Hagen, J. W. Induced versus spontaneous rehearsal in short-term memory in nursery school children. *Developmental Psychology*, 1969, *1*, 40–46.

Kobasigawa, A. Utilization of retrieval cues by children in recall. *Child Development*, 1974, *45*, 127–134.

Kreutzer, M. A., Leonard, C., & Flavell, J. H. An interview study of children's knowledge about memory. *Monographs of the Society for Research in Child Development*, 1975, *40*, (1, Serial No. 159).

Levin, J. R., Yussen, S. R., DeRose, T. M., & Pressley, G. M. Developmental changes in as-' sessing recall and recognition memory capacity. *Developmental Psychology*, in press.

Liben, L. S. Piagetian investigations of the development of memory. In R. V. Kail & J. W. Hagen (Eds.), *Memory in cognitive development*. Hillsdale, N.J.: Lawrence Erlbaum Associates, 1978.

LaBerge, D. & Samuels, S. J. Toward a theory of automatic information processing in reading. *Cognitive Psychology*, 1974, *6*, 293–323.

Lockhart, R. S., Craik, F. I. M., & Jacoby, L. L. Depth of processing, recognition and recall. In J. Brown (Ed.), *Recognition and recall*. New York: John Wiley & Sons, 1976.

Markman, E. M. Realizing that you don't understand: A preliminary investigation. *Child Development*, in press.

Moynahan, E. D. The development of knowledge concerning the effect of categorization upon free recall. *Child Development*, 1973, *44*, 238–246.

Murphy, M. D., & Brown, A. L. Incidental learning in preschool children as a function of level of cognitive analysis. *Journal of Experimental Child Psychology*, 1975, *19*, 509–523.

Naus, M. J., & Dennig, L. Developmental changes in metamemory knowledge and memory performance. In preparation, 1977.

Naus, M. J., Ornstein, P. A., & Aivano, S. Developmental changes in memory: The effects of processing time and rehearsal instructions. *Journal of Experimental Child Psychology*, 1977, *23*, 237–251.

Naus, M. J., Ornstein, P. A., & Hoving, K. L. Developmental implications of multistore and depth of processing models of memory. In P. A. Ornstein (Ed.), *Memory development in children*. Hillsdale, N.J.: Lawrence Erlbaum Associates, 1978.

Ornstein, P. A., Memory development in children. In R. Liebert, R. Paulos, & G. Marmor (Eds.), *Developmental psychology* (2nd ed.). Englewood Cliffs, N.J.: Prentice–Hall, 1977.

Ornstein, P. A., & Naus, M. J. Rehearsal processes in children's memory. In P. A. Ornstein (ed.), *Memory Development in children*. Hillsdale, N.J.: Lawrence Erlbaum Associates, 1978.

Ornstein, P. A., Naus, M. J., & Liberty, C. Rehearsal and organizational processes in children's memory. *Child Development*, 1975, *46*, 818–830.

Ornstein, P. A., Naus, M. J., & Stone, B. P. Rehearsal training and developmental differences in memory. *Developmental Psychology*, 1977, *13*, 15–24.

Paris, S. G. Integration and inference in children's comprehension and memory. In F. Restle, R. M. Shiffrin, J. Castellan, H. Lindman, & D. Pisoni (Eds.), *Cognitive theory* (Vol. 1). Hillsdale, N.J.: Lawrence Erlbaum Associates, 1975.

Paris, S. G., & Carter, A. Y. Semantic and constructive aspects of sentence memory in children. *Developmental Psychology*, 1973, *9*, 109–113.

Paris, S. G., & Lindauer, B. K. The role of inference in children's comprehension and memory for sentences. *Cognitive Psychology*, 1976, *8*, 217–227.

Paris, S. G., & Mahoney, G. J. Cognitive integration in children's memory for sentences and pictures. *Child Development*, 1974, *45*, 633–642.

Paris, S. G., & Upton, L. R. *The construction and retention of linguistic inferences by children*. Paper presented at the Western Psychological Association Meeting, Chicago, May 1974.

Piaget, J., & Inhelder, B. *Memory and intelligence*. New York: Basic Books, 1973.

Posnansky, C. J., & Neumann, P. G. The abstraction of visual prototypes by children. *Journal of Experimental Child Psychology*, 1976, *21*, 367–377.

Posner, M. I. & Snyder, C. R. Facilitation and inhibition in the processing of signals. In P. M. A. Rabbitt & S. Dornic (Eds.), *Attention and Performance V*. New York: Academic Press, 1975.

Postman, L. Short-term memory and incidental learning. In A. W. Melton (Ed.), *Categories of human learning*. New York: Academic Press, 1964.

Rundus, D. Analysis of rehearsal processes in free recall. *Journal of Experimental Psychology*, 1971, *89*, 63–77.

Rundus, D., & Atkinson, R. C. Rehearsal processes in free recall: A procedure for direct observation. *Journal of Verbal Learning and Verbal Behavior*, 1970, *9*, 99–105.

Salatas, H., & Flavell, J. H. Behavioral and metamnemonic indicators of strategic behaviors under remember instructions in the first grade. *Child Development*, 1976, *47*, 81–89. (a)

Salatas, H., & Flavell, J. H. Retrieval of recently learned information: Development of strategies and control skills. *Child Development*, 1976, *47*, 941–948. (b)

Shiffrin, R. M., & Schneider, W. Controlled and automatic human information processing: II. Perceptual learning, automatic attending, and a general theory. *Psychological Review*, 1977, *84*, 127–190.

Siegel, A., & Allik, J. P. A developmental study of visual and auditory short-term memory. *Journal of Verbal Learning and Verbal Behavior*, 1973, *12*, 409–418.

Smirnov, A. A., & Zinchenko, P. I. Problems in the psychology of memory. In M. Cole & I Maltzman (Eds.), *A handbook of contemporary Soviet psychology*. New York: Basic Books, 1969.

Tenney, Y. V. The child's conception of organization and recall. *Journal of Experimental Child Psychology*, 1975, *19*, 100–114.

Tulving, E. Episodic and semantic memory. In E. Tulving & W. Donaldson (Eds.), *Organization of memory*. New York: Academic Press, 1972.

Wellman, H. M. Tip of the tongue and feeling of knowing experiences: A developmental study of memory monitoring. *Child Development*, 1977, *48*, 13–21.

Woodward, A. E., Bjork, R. A., & Jongeward, R. H. Recall and recognition as a function of primary rehearsal. *Journal of Verbal Learning and Verbal Behavior*, 1973, *12*, 608–617.

Yendovitskaya, T. V. Development of memory. In A. V. Zaporozhets & D. B. Elkonin (Eds.), *The psychology of preschool children*. Cambridge, Massachusetts: MIT Press, 1971.

Yussen, S. R., & Levy, V. M. Developmental changes in predicting one's own span of short-term memory. *Journal of Experimental Child Psychology*, 1975, *19*, 502–508.

Yussen, S. R., & Levy, V. M. Developmental changes in knowledge about different retrieval problems. *Developmental Psychology*, 1977, *13*, 114–120.

13

Development and Models of Memory: Comments on the Papers by Brown and Naus and Halasz

John William Hagen
University of Michigan

Although the development of memory in children has been a topic of study for almost a century, only during the past decade or so has memory development been systematically investigated and viewed within a broader theoretical perspective—namely the information-processing model (Hagen, Jongeward, & Kail, 1975). Early researchers such as Hunter (1913) made phylogenetic as well as developmental comparisons in memory via the *delayed reaction* technique. Differential psychologists who invented the intelligence test quickly found that measures of memory were well suited to discriminating among children on the basis of their chronological age, and the measures they used included both rote tasks, such as digit span, and semantic memory, such as recall of stories (Anastasi, 1968). Clinical psychologists found that memory deficits were associated with various diagnostic categories in children. "The fact that memory does follow a predictable developmental course has led to its utility in the formulation of a wide variety of measuring instruments. Yet, the attempt to understand how and why these developmental changes occur in memory is quite recent" (Hagen, Jongeward, & Kail, 1975, p. 59).

In the two chapters preceding this one, the reader has learned something of the wealth of information resulting from this recent concern with understanding the development of memory processes. Before discussing these chapters, I shall present briefly an overview of the range of topics that have been included in this study. In a recent volume on memory and cognitive development edited by Robert Kail and myself (Kail & Hagen, 1977), the first section is devoted to the development of basic memory processes. The eight chapters include these topics: encoding, rehearsal, imagery, constructive processes, organizational factors, retrieval strategies, memory as viewed by Russian investigators, and finally, metamemorial processes. In the second section, on memory as related to other aspects of cognitive development, the six chapters cover the following: memory and logical thought, Piagetian investigations, cross-cultural studies, memory in retardates, the role of instruction, and memory as related to the educational process. It is evident, then, that the amount of research generated by the wave of interest in children's memorial abilities is impressive. One might ask, has the work been grounded in sound theoretical constructs, and have the important advances in memory achieved by those studying adults been taken into account in this developmental work? These questions cannot be answered now, but one should keep them in mind while reading this volume. Then, perhaps, we shall be in a better position to evaluate the importance of the work of developmentalists and its impact on the field.

Many important issues are raised in Chapter 12 by Naus and Halasz. It is clear that although there is not consensus as to the reasons behind developmental differences, there is certainly impressive evidence for their existence! In discussing the distinction between memory tasks involving deliberate strategies as compared to those in which automatic processes seem to dominate, Naus and Halasz argue that two types of processing seem to be involved. For the former type of task, clear developmental differences are observed, whereas for the latter, few age-related changes have been found. I am not so sure, however, that this distinction is as neat and clear as it appears to be.

Strategies are said to be employed deliberately, at least in their initial usage, and may later become "automated." Strategies vary from the very simple, such as naming aloud stimuli as they are presented, to the extremely complex, which may involve rules, elaborate encoding and retrieval mnemonic devices, information already in storage, and various other components. Some of these strategies have been found to be functional at some developmental levels though not at others (e.g., Hagen, 1972). That many of these strategies appear to become well practiced and hence more automatic with continued usage and/or development is reasonable. The very simple ones may be used automatically from the beginning; certainly the naming of pictures seems to be an almost irresistible behavior at a certain point in the young child's development. This practice will facilitate recall of recency items in a serial-recall task, and the improvement is constant across a wide age span. More complex strategies, such as cumulatively rehearsing primacy items in this task, involve many components. Skill in these component tasks must be available as well as the ability to integrate them into a smooth strategy before the strategy will prove beneficial in solving a given task. A study by Ornstein, Naus, and Liberty (1975) illustrates this point. Not until the eighth grade did children reveal the active strategy of combining words into sets for rehearsal.

Two recent studies are cited by Naus and Halasz in which instructions in use of strategies for rehearsal were successfully employed with second- and third-grade children. Not all studies have been successful at this age level, though. In several studies, we have taught children to use cumulative rehearsal in serial recall with success (e.g., Kingsley & Hagen, 1969). However, we then taught our induced strategy with and without a correction technique (Hagen, Hargrave, & Ross, 1973). For first and second graders, recall was facilitated only when their errors were corrected during the actual rehearsing. It is not surprising, then, that these children did not continue to use rehearsal spontaneously in subsequent recall tasks. Older children, who spontaneously and successfully employ this strategy with no prompts or correction, quite obviously have some other abilities at their disposal as well, one of which must include some form of self-correction. It is the converging of the mastery of the component parts that makes successful use of strategies possible. Some of these may come about automatically and some deliberately, and in their integration and employment, no doubt some conscious effort is required. I agree that studies of metamemory have proved valuable in trying to establish the emergence of awareness here.

The second type of task was identified as being dominated by automatic processes. Here, the individual is interacting with a meaningful environment. Although I do not believe that the material the individual encounters in tasks involving strategies is meaningless, I shall not elaborate upon this point here. At any rate, it seems obvious that much information a person encounters is so immediately meaningful, or useful, or just interesting that it is processed and retained for just those reasons. Here, semantic memory is presented as the key to successful performance.

Yet it is apparent that preverbal children and animals do have impressive memories, and one usually assumes that their processing occurs automatically without resorting to deliberate use of strategies. Hence, a lot of what is included in the automatic memory of meaningful information must not rely, at least not exclusively, on the *semantic* structure and contents of the organism. Obviously, the genes provide a memory structure for the organism's survival. Piaget provides an account of how in the infant's day-to-day encounters with the environment, increasingly sophisticated use is made of these given structures. Semantic abilities come in considerably later than the mastery of many important tasks and the emergence of automatic memory of interesting and apparently meaningful events. Most studies of semantic integration and constructive memory do not even look at children under 4 years old (e.g., see Chapter 12, this volume, by Naus & Halasz). What we should say here, I propose, is that when semantic knowledge is sufficiently well developed, it begins to be involved in those cognitive constructions that begin very early, certainly in the infancy period, and that occur spontaneously as part of the organism's interactions with its environment. It is difficult for me to imagine that these early memory processes do not involve construction of some sort or at some level.

What are the developmental changes that seem to occur once the child has sufficient semantic structure and knowledge to facilitate memory? Expansion of one's general knowledge level seems to be an obvious factor, but it is very difficult (perhaps impossible) to demonstrate this effect empirically. Inferential ability seems also to be included, and Naus and Halasz point out that whereas simple inferences are no doubt automatically employed, more complex ones appear to involve strategies (e.g., see Paris & Lindauer, 1977). Here, Naus and Halasz propose that incidental memory paradigms of the Type I variety (Postman, 1964) allow us to look at automatic processes independent of the strategic intervention of the child and reveal the unique role of semantic processing.

Let's consider these studies in some detail. Murphy and Brown (1975), as already described in Brown's chapter, used several different orienting tasks with 4-year-old children. Retention was higher for tasks requiring comprehension than for those requiring orienting to specific features, such as color. Further, comprehension or semantic categorization instructions led to better recall than did an intentional baseline condition. In the age range from first to fifth grade, Geis and Hall (1976) found best recall for words following semantic orientation as compared to either acoustic or orthographic orienting activities. However, the orienting tasks chosen here may not have been well suited to the children's current knowledge or skills.

In a study aimed at controlling for possible differences in task difficulty level, Catherine Sophian and I (Sophian & Hagen, in press) compared a formal orienting task based on colors of pictures with a semantic task based on category membership of objects depicted. Children at the preschool and kindergarten levels were included. Pictures were sorted into groups, either according to color or to category. As an index of depth of processing, sorting times were recorded. The retrieval phase of this task also included an experimental manipulation. Although encoding strategies may be controlled in an incidental orienting task, the retrieval phase may well involve strategies. In fact, retrieval skills seem to occur very early in memory development (Ritter, Kaprove, Fitch, & Flavell, 1973). If information is stored in equivalent amounts but in different ways following different orienting tasks, recall may reveal differences in accessibility to this information rather than differences in actual availability. Cues might well minimize or eliminate differences in accessibility. Thus, any differences found under conditions of cued recall are more likely to be the result of differences in availability of information in memory.

Following the encoding specificity hypothesis of Tulving and Thomson (1973), cues were matched to initial orienting activity. Four conditions resulted: Color cues were paired with either color or semantic category orienting tasks, and category cues were paired with one or the other of the orienting tasks. Murphy and Brown (1975) used only category cues and found that these resulted in improved performance for the categorization orienting task only. In this study, the effects of both cuing conditions can be observed.

The task was introduced as a picture game. A total of 18 pictures and 3 different categories were used. For the color condition, pictures were sorted into red, blue, and yellow groups. For the category condition, they were sorted into clothes, furniture, or vehicles. Each child made two sortings, one by color and one by category. About 1 minute after sorting, the child was asked to recall all the pictures s/he could from either set. When s/he could recall no more, the two cued-recall tests were administered, one in which color cues were used and the other presenting category cues. The child was asked to name *all* the pictures, not just the ones s/he could not recall previously. The three cues of each type were presented in a fixed order.

Consider the findings for sorting times first. Color sorts were completed significantly faster than category sorts, and there was no interaction with age level. These differences were large, in a ratio of almost 2 to 1.

For free recall, both the age level and the type of sorting condition resulted in significant differences. Older children recalled more items than younger, and recall was better for category-sorted than for color-sorted items. Age by sort type was significant (at $p < 0.10$), with older children's differences between sort types being larger than younger children's. The differences between lists were significant for older but not for young children's recall. Hence the expected developmental change in effectiveness of the two types of orienting tasks was found.

For cued recall, older children recalled more items than did younger children, and more category-sorted than color-sorted items were recalled. The age by sort type interaction was not significant (in fact, $F < 1$), supporting the notion that accessibility may play a role in the interaction that was found in the free-recall responses. Both younger and older children recalled more of the category-sorted than the color-sorted items under cuing conditions. Hence, more information seems to have been stored for category as compared to color sorting, but younger children did not retrieve this information until retrieval cues were provided. Not only did category cuing produce better recall than color cuing; the color cuing resulted in lower performance than was found for free recall, consistent with an earlier finding reported by Moely (1974).

A significant sort type × cue type interaction was also found. The difference between color- and category-cued recall was greater for category-sorted than for color-sorted items. Some support, then, was found for the encoding specificity hypothesis.

In a second experiment, the relation of storage to retrieval factors was investigated. A *recognition* procedure was used to minimize the role of retrieval. If the different types of sorting tasks result in differences in amount of information stored in memory, the results of recognition measures should parallel those found with free recall. Again, preschool and kindergarten children were tested. The stimuli were similar to those of the first experiment, but four categories and four colors were now used. Two sets of eight pictures were used for the sorting tasks, and each set contained only two colors and two categories, so that entirely different colors and categories appeared in the two sets. Sixteen additional items were used as distractors in the recognition test. The orienting task was administered in a very similar fashion to the procedure of the first study. Following sorting, there was a 2-minute delay, followed by presentation of the recognition task.

Sorting times were obtained, and this time older children sorted more quickly than did younger children. Color sorts were completed more quickly than were category sorts, and the difference in time required for category as compared to color sorts was greater for younger than for older children. Because the sorting task was easier in this study than in the first, since there were only eight pictures to be sorted into two instead of three categories, it is difficult to compare latencies in the two studies or to interpret the differences.

Now consider "hits" in the recognition data. No effects for age or condition were found. Hence, it appears that the differences found in the first study may be due to differences in retrieval rather than storage processes. For the correct "rejections" of new items in recognition, the age effect again was not significant.

To summarize the major findings of the two studies—for the older children, free recall was better following a semantic orienting task than following a formal orienting task, whereas this effect was found for both younger and older children in cued recall. For recognition, however, neither group of children showed a difference due to type of orienting task.

Whereas the sorting tasks provide for involuntary memory at acquisition, the memory test is a voluntary one. Deliberate mnemonic strategies may well be used for retrieval. The recognition test may provide a measure of involuntary memory, since it appears to be a relatively automatic function within memory (Perlmutter & Lange, 1978). If age or task differences are not found for recognition measures, the view that involuntary memory processes do not change as a function of age *or* depth of processing is supported.

Although comparable amounts of information appear to have been stored by both the younger and older children in these studies, apparently the older children used retrieval strategies more effectively than did the younger. Further, the strategies were better suited to the categorical than to the color organization. Retrieval cues seem to have facilitated the use of categorical search strategies, whereas color cues did not elicit effective retrieval strategies. Finally, category cues were useful for the younger and older children, indicating that they had available appropriate search strategies.

The sorting time differences in these studies are not as neat as we had hoped. Perhaps performance factors other than depth of processing come into play in tasks such as this. An independent measure of depth of processing is needed in this type of research. At any rate, I am in agreement with the view that the distinction between voluntary and involuntary memory is important, as is the distinction between acquisition and retrieval processes. It seems clear that voluntary memory strategies do play a role in age differences found in recall in the Type I incidental paradigm. The position of both Brown (1975) and Hagen, Jongeward, and Kail (1975), that age-related improvements in memory come about through the emergence of an increasing repertoire of deliberate strategies, receives further support from this work.

Naus and Halasz (as well as Brown) propose that the episodic—semantic distinction may not represent a dichotomy and then postulate "unitary memory" as an alternative. Their following argument, that certain memory tasks such as list learning are really "a mixture of semantic and episodic processing [p. 283]," is the precise one I had planned to make. To restate a position I have taken before, many of the tasks used by developmentalists and usually considered episodic are, in fact, closely related to many of the tasks children are given in school and in other settings and are certainly far from meaningless to the children. It seems that Naus and Halasz have now left behind one of the neat distinctions laid down early in their paper. The argument for a unitary concept of memory of course fits in with the levels-of-processing model and thus helps to bring some unity to a major theme of this conference. However, although the dichotomy for episodic versus semantic memory may actually be a continuum, it is still possible that more than one memory system exists and that information at one end of this continuum is typically handled by one system, whereas information at the other end is better processed by another system, and information in the middle may go to either or both of the coexisting memory systems. Data for this argument are of course lacking, and the model lacks elegance.

I shall now turn briefly to a consideration of the work using the Type 2 incidental paradigm, since Ann Brown's studies on the development of "constructing the gist" seem more related to this type of study than to the Type 1 incidental paradigm, and because I have contributed more than my fair share of the work on memory development using this paradigm. The question is really one of selectivity in recall when more information is presented than the individual can process. Whereas Brown has used recall of prose passages, recall of pictures, geometric shapes, or colors has been studied in the work of my colleagues and myself. Our major finding is that in the age range from approximately 6 years through the teenage years, recall of central, or task-set, information increases regularly with increasing age level, whereas recall of incidental or task-irrelevant information shows a slight increase during the grade-school years and then levels off by 10 to 12 years and often declines thereafter (for a review of studies, see Hagen & Hale, 1973).

Brown has found that recall of prose material increases with age across approximately the same age span and further, that even at the youngest ages, children are able to pick out for recall the important elements in the messages. Brown argues that extracting the meaning from messages depends on both the current input and the cognitive perceptual environment, which is determined in part by preexisting knowledge schemata. In one study (Brown & Smiley, 1977), the evidence for intrusions based on information provided is impressive. No age trends, across grades 2 through 6, were found, as was the trend in this series of studies. What *is* developing here, according to Brown, is volitional control of naturally occurring tendencies, permitting more flexible and efficient gathering of information. This control process sounds very similar to what we have described as the developmental process responsible for increasing selection of central over incidental information, thereby leading to more efficient processing within a limited capacity system (Hagen & Hale, 1973). In the study of what Brown and Smiley (1977) call metacognition, it was found that third graders made no reliable distinctions between what was important and what wasn't in the story ratings; fifth graders were able to isolate only the most important levels; seventh graders were able to separate low, medium, and high levels of importance; and college students made the finest distinctions of all. This developmental trend seems to fit well with the central—incidental age trends from our work.

Brown also explored study strategies in college students and in fifth grade, junior, and senior high school students. It was found that deliberate study strategies, under intentional memory instructions, led to enhanced recall of important units of information in stories. Further, an *unfilled* delay led to especially large improvements of recall of important elements for college students. The developmental data showed that fifth graders did not improve in recall with extra study time, whereas junior-high age students did. The increased efficiency in recall found here with the provision of study time is similar to that found by Hagen and Kail (1973), except the effect occurred at an earlier age in our simpler serial-recall task. We also found that a filled delay led to a decrement in recall for 10-year-olds, bringing their level of performance to that of children 3 years younger. This finding led to our concluding that all of the improvement in memory in this task between 7 and 10 years of age is due to the use of rehearsal strategies. The similarity in findings for these two very different types of memory tasks is encouraging for the generality of the developmental model of strategy acquisition that both Brown and I have advocated.

The findings reported by Brown on the use of spontaneous versus induced strategies, here underlining or taking notes, are also illuminating. The superiority of the spontaneous, as contrasted to induced, employment of these strategies on subsequent recall has both theoretical as well as practical implications. At least some fifth graders underlined spontaneously, and they showed an adultlike pattern in their studying. Others, who were prompted, improved their overall recall but appeared to use less selectivity in emphasizing important as compared to less important elements of the text. This situation seems to be an instance where an attempt to accelerate the course of development actually leads to less efficient processing of information to be recalled than would occur normally.

Before concluding, I shall mention briefly some findings from a recent study of ours (Hagen & Zukier, 1977). In the Type 2 paradigm, the element of surprise is important in the assessment of incidental learning. Our task was administered in its usual form to 8- and 11-year-old children. The expected age difference was found for central recall, whereas incidental recall did not differ for the two groups. Then the central task was administered a second time. Even though no instructions were given, the children should anticipate that another incidental measure for recall would follow. This time, recall of central information declined at both age levels, whereas recall of incidental information increased, and now 11-year-olds performed significantly better than the 8-year-old children on incidental recall. This is the first time we have obtained such a finding. Apparently, the older children took advantage of the implicit set that "incidental" items would be needed later. They adjusted their task strategies more efficiently to the task requirements than the younger children. Here, as in Brown's story-recall tasks, children seem to show increasing sensitivity with increasing age to subtle cues in the task as well as in the context in which it is presented.

In Brown's work as well as my own, there is good evidence that with development, children become increasingly proficient in selecting out the important from the less important information. The course of this development is gradual, as changes are found from the preschool years into young adulthood. The nature of the material and the task affects the developmental patterns as well. However, the convergence from these research programs leads to renewed optimism. Our models are certainly compatible with a "process-oriented" approach to the study of memory. Now we must push the models further to see where there are compatibilities or incompatibilities with the models evolved from research on adults.

REFERENCES

Anastasi, A. *Psychological testing*. New York: Macmillan, 1968.

Brown, A. The development of memory: Knowing, knowing about knowing, and knowing how to know. In H. Reese (Ed.), *Advances in child development and behavior* (Vol. 10). New York: Academic Press, 1975.

Brown, A. L., & Smiley, S. S. Rating the importance of structural units of prose passages: A problem of metacognitive development. *Child Development*, 1977, *48*, 1–8.

Geis, M. F., & Hall, D. M. Encoding and incidental memory in children. *Journal of Experimental Child Psychology*, 1976, *22*, 58–66.

Hagen, J. W. Strategies for remembering. In S. Farnham–Diggory (Ed.), *Information processing in children*. New York: Academic Press, 1972.

Hagen, J. W., & Hale, G. A. The development of attention in children. In A. Pick (Ed.), *Minnesota Symposia on child psychology* (Vol. 7). Minneapolis: University of Minnesota Press, 1973.

Hagen, J. W., Hargrave, S., & Ross, W. Prompting and rehearsal in short-term memory. *Child Development*, 1973, *44*, 201–204.

Hagen, J. W., Jongeward, R. H., Jr., & Kail, R. V., Jr. Cognitive perspectives on the development of memory. In H. Reese (Ed.), *Advances in child development and behavior* (Vol. 10). New York: Academic Press, 1975.

Hagen, J. W., & Kail, R. V. Facilitation and distraction in short-term memory. *Child Development*, 1973, *44*, 831–836.

Hagen, J. W., & Zukier, H. *Mode of interference, set and selective attention.* Paper presented at the biennial meetings of the Society for Research in Child Development, New Orleans, March 17–20, 1977.

Hunter, W. S. The delayed reaction in animals and children. *Behavior Monographs*, 1913, *2*, (no. 1), 1–86.

Kail, R. V., Jr., & Hagen, J. W. (Eds.). *Perspectives on the development of memory and cognition.* Hillsdale, N.J.: Lawrence Erlbaum Associates, 1977.

Kingsley, P. R., & Hagen, J. W. Induced versus spontaneous rehearsal in short-term memory in nursery school children. *Developmental Psychology*, 1969, *1*, 40–46.

Moely, B. E. *Facilitation of young children's recall through the use of nomeaningful recall cues.* Paper presented at the annual meeting of the American Psychological Association, New Orleans, September 1974.

Murphy, M. D., & Brown, A. L. Incidental learning in preschool children as a function of level of cognitive analysis. *Journal of Experimental Child Psychology*, 1975, *19*, 509–523.

Ornstein, P. A., Naus, M. J., & Liberty, C. Rehearsal and organizational processes in children's memory. *Child Development*, 1975, *46*, 818–830.

Paris, S. G., & Lindauer, B. K. Constructive aspects of children's comprehension and memory. In R. V. Kail, Jr., & J. W. Hagen (Eds.), *Perspectives on the development of memory and cognition.* Hillsdale, N.J.: Lawrence Erlbaum Associates, 1977.

Perlmutter, M., & Lange, G. A developmental analysis of recall–recognition distinctions. In P. A. Ornstein (Ed.), *Memory development in children.* Hillsdale, N.J.: Lawrence Erlbaum Associates, 1978.

Postman, L. Short-term memory and incidental learning. In A. Melton (Ed.), *Categories of human learning.* New York: Academic Press, 1964.

Ritter, K., Kaprove, B. H., Fitch, J. P., & Flavell, J. H. The development of retrieval strategies in young children. *Cognitive Psychology*, 1973, *5*, 310–321.

Sophian, C., & Hagen, J. W. Involuntary memory and the development of retrieval skills in young children. *Journal of experimental child psychology,* in press.

Tulving, E., & Thomson, D. M. Encoding specificity and retrieval processes in episodic memory. *Psychological Review*, 1973, *80*, 352–373.

V PERCEIVING, ACTING, AND KNOWING

14 The Psychological Reality of Levels of Processing

Anne Treisman[1]
University of Oxford

One of the central questions in memory research since Craik and Lockhart's seminal paper in 1972 has been how far the level of perceptual processing that an item receives determines its survival in memory. Many experiments have suggested that the "deeper" or the more "semantic" the analysis an item receives, the longer lived its trace will be. Craik and Lockhart offered a coherent and plausible conceptual framework incorporating this generalization, which was to replace the then fashionable, structural, two-store theory of short- and long-term memory. Their proposals bore fruit in a proliferation of further experiments designed to test the relationship between depth and retention in more detail. Most gave results consistent with the predictions, and some uncovered new and interesting facts. More recently, however, a certain uneasiness has begun to spread among memory theorists, and alternative accounts in terms of encoding specificity, transfer-appropriate processing, trace distinctiveness, spread, or elaboration have been offered (see, for example, chapters in this book: by Tulving, 19; by Bransford, Franks, Morris, & Stein, 15; by Nelson, 3; and by Lockhart, 4).

I should like to suggest another reason for uneasiness, not so much with the central postulate of the theory—that depth of processing predicts retention—but with the inadequate perceptual foundations of the concept of "depth." If the ways of inferring particular processing levels during perception are misguided, the theory relating them to memory cannot be adequately explored or tested. This seems unfortunate and justifies an attempt to analyze the perceptual aspects more carefully.

Three main questions seem relevant. The first is the general question of how

---

[1]Now at the University of British Columbia.

one can empirically test the psychological reality and the organization of processing levels during perception. This is the main concern of this chapter. The other two questions relate to memory and ask: whether any similar methods can demonstrate the existence of hierarchical levels of representation in memory and explore their characteristic storage and retrieval properties; and whether perception can be more directly linked to memory by the evidence already available, if we analyze the likely nature of the perceptual processing induced by the particular orienting tasks typically chosen in memory research. Their role has often in fact been unclear. They were originally assumed to control the initial perceptual processing of the stimulus, to arrest it at an early stage, or to encourage it toward a late stage. However, as Craik and Tulving (1975) point out, this relation of task to temporal ordering is by no means guaranteed. Some supposedly "early"-level orienting tasks may actually act late in the sequential order of processing. For example, counting syllables could follow rather than precede word identification and access to meaning. The final section of this chapter briefly comments on these links to memory research.

What could "depth" actually measure? Is it related to the sequential order of the processing stages through which a stimulus is analyzed? Or to the temporal order in which different representations of that stimulus become available? Or to the sheer amount of processing? Or to its degree of semanticity? Or is depth logically defined, quite independently of psychological processing, in terms of the level of abstraction or of complexity of the units of description? If all these measures coincide, we are in the happy position of being able to use them interchangeably; however, people have tended to assume this without offering much evidence for it. Thus, before attempting to investigate levels of processing, we need to clarify their definition.

There seem to be two main senses in which the term has been used, which do not necessarily yield the same candidates for "leveldom." First, a level can be defined objectively as a particular description of the input, contrasting with other possible descriptions in the elements and relationships of which it is composed, but mappable into these other possible descriptions in a systematic, rule-governed fashion. We can then ask whether any one or more of these possible descriptive levels has "psychological reality" as a representation that exists in the mind and that can be separately accessed or manipulated, either introspectively or by some empirical task. Second, and more commonly, a level is treated as the output available from a particular stage of processing in a temporal sequence of operations initiated by the stimulus and resulting in perception. An example may illustrate this distinction and show that quite different hierarchies could both have "psychological reality," but in different senses. If we accepted the hypothesis that an early stage in the visual processing of shape is a Fourier analysis of spatial frequencies, a description in terms of power spectrum, phase relations, and so on would form one level in the psychological hierarchy of processing stages. However, it would not invalidate a descriptive or intro-spective decomposition of complex shapes into elements such as lines, curves, and angles; nor would it rule out the possibility that such a description also has psychological reality, not in this case as an early processing stage, but perhaps, for example, as a set of elements to which we can selectively attend either before or after the complete shape has been identified. Thus the very fact that we (as people rather than psychologists) can describe shapes as constructions of local features gives these some psychological reality.

If levels are taken to be stages of processing, further questions arise about the organization of the hierarchy: Is it sequentially ordered, so that the output from one stage must be the input to the next, or is it simply temporally ordered, perhaps because limited processing resources must be transferred serially from one level to the next? Is the order fixed or flexible? Is it bottom-up or top-down? Can some levels be bypassed, and can processing be stopped short, responses triggered, and information stored before the final level is reached? What determines which levels can access conscious awareness? Memory theorists using the concept of levels have often assumed a fixed, bottom-up, sequential hierarchy of processing stages with optional stopping, controllable by task instructions and with direct access from any level to memory and to conscious awareness. All these assumptions could be correct, but each one can be challenged.

The type of empirical evidence supporting the psychological reality of par-ticular processing levels depends on which definition is used—sequentially ordered processing stages or alternative descriptive representations. Depth is equivalent to lateness in a temporally ordered sequence; but to abstractness, complexity, or semanticity in a timeless hierarchy of representations. If the analysis of a stimulus proceeds from the whole to its parts, for example, would processing of parts be considered "deeper" than processing of wholes, or the reverse? The predictions from the theory for memory will be correspondingly unclear.

The description, "top-down" analysis, has itself been used in different senses. In the literal sense, it implies that the first thing registered about a stimulus is its highest level structure and that this can then be analyzed (if necessary) into its elements at progressively lower levels. However, the term is also used in a weaker sense to cover cases in which the subject has advance information or expectancies about what he or she will see or hear; these expectancies are defined at the highest level and are then used to prime or selectively to lower thresholds for those lower level components that would support that particular highest level hypothesis. Thus in the strongest sense, it is the registration of the stimulus itself that starts at the top of the hierarchy; in the weaker sense, it is an internal hypothesis that can—by top-down facilitation or inhibition—bias bottom-up registration of the stimulus.

I. CONSCIOUS REPORTS AS EVIDENCE FOR LEVELS OF PROCESSING

If we can introspectively access a particular representation of a stimulus, we can argue that by definition, it has *psychological reality* in one sense of the term. However, the converse is certainly untrue. We are quite unable consciously to compare the order of arrival of a single click at the left and the right ear; yet the difference is clearly registered, since it gives rise to perception of a particular spatial direction of the source. The methods that rely on conscious access are usually applied only to levels that there is good reason to suppose are accessible to introspection; no one would attempt, for example, to ask subjects to introspect about their retinal images or basilar membranes. However, even in cases where levels are normally available to subjective experience, there are difficulties. One is that certain factors appear to prevent subjective awareness without also "knocking out" the level in question. For example, brain damage may appear to remove a level of processing in the sense that patients can no longer report awareness of its output, and yet by using forced-choice or indirect measures, one can show that the information is still being processed. A striking example is the "blind-sight" described by Weiskrantz (1974) in a patient with occipital damage; although subjectively blind to half the visual field, he could accurately "guess" whether a cross or circle was being presented in his hemianopic field. He might be basing his discrimination on some representation other than the one normally used, or it might be the normal one that has lost its control of conscious awareness.

With normal people and either subthreshold or unattended stimuli, there is evidence for subliminal analysis at levels that with attended or above-threshold stimuli are normally accompanied by awareness. Corteen and Dunn's finding (1974) that shock-associated city names in an unattended message could trigger autonomic responses, but not a simple instrumental response, shows this dissociation very clearly. It is a fascinating problem—what, in fact, determines whether a particular level is consciously accessible? We appear normally to be aware of those elements or structures that are currently determining our choice of voluntary action (Shallice, 1972), but the blind-sight patient, many Freudian anecdotes, and recent experiments reviewed by Nisbett and Wilson (1977) show that this association is not a necessary one.

Less obviously, the correlation between the *order* of introspective availability and the order of processing is equally open to question. It could be the case that processing always continues through to the final level and that earlier levels, although they are real stages of processing, cannot be directly accessed and must be reconstructed. One example, which has been used as evidence for top-down processing, is the phonemic restoration described by Warren and Warren (1970), in which a totally deleted speech sound (which has been replaced by a cough or other extraneous noise) is clearly "heard." Its identity may even be determined by a phrase that occurs slightly later in time. Here a phrase or sentence seems to be understood before the identity of each component sound is determined. However, this is a case in which we should distinguish perceptual processing from the synthesis of a conscious percept. The result is compatible with early identification of some phonological patterns, followed by sentence interpretation, followed in turn by the creation *from* this interpretation of a complete subjective image or representation of the inferred phonological input. The synthesis of what we "hear" in conscious awareness appears to be a top-down process; processing of the physical input need not be. While the nature of consciousness and its connection to processing levels in perception are so uncertain, it seems vital to use converging evidence from other behavioral paradigms.

The remainder of this paper reviews some of these "indirect" methods to tap the existence and temporal ordering of possible levels. A wide variety of different methods has been used to support claims for the "psychological reality" of particular levels of processing. These differ: (a) in the way in which they attempt to access the levels in question; and (b) in the definition of the "psychological reality" they can claim to support. Some support only the weakest claim for the simple "existence" of a level; some support claims about the temporal order in which representations at two levels are formed; and finally, some support a claim that two levels are sequentially ordered, so that the output from one is the input for the next. Levels must exist if they form part of a temporal or sequential hierarchy of processing stages, but the converse is not the case. They could be logically "nested" (Neisser, 1976) and simultaneously or directly accessible in any order required. I give a few examples of methods from which people have made these different claims, attempt briefly to discuss the validity of the underlying assumptions, and compare the conclusions that can be drawn from results in each case. The research cited serves to illustrate the methods and inferences rather than to provide clear answers to the question raised, since a far more comprehensive review would be needed before firm conclusions can be drawn. (A fuller review of perceptual research on levels of processing is in preparation.)

II. SEQUENTIAL ORDERING OF LEVELS

1. High-Level Structures Formed by Modulation of Elements at Lower Levels

This offers probably the most incontrovertible evidence for sequential organization. It occurs when the units at one level are defined by the spatial or temporal patterning of lower level entities. For example, a circular area filled with vertical lines may be surrounded by a background filled with horizontal lines of the same length, width, and spatial frequency. Perception of the circle then depends on detection of the difference in orientation and of its spatial boundaries. Notice that if there were no surrounding horizontal lines, it would be unclear whether the orientation of the lines in the circular area had been processed before the shape of the circle, since the low-level input for perception of the circle could equally well have been the difference in average intensity or simply the presence of contour regardless of orientation.

There are many other examples where the visual shape of a boundary can be defined by discontinuities in elements at what must therefore be a lower level; differences in the binocular disparity of otherwise identical elements (Julesz, 1971)—in their speed of movement, in their color or spatial frequency, even differences in the simple features of shape such as curved versus straight lines (Olson & Attneave, 1970)—can all mediate figure–ground segregation and must all therefore be detected before the shapes that their boundaries define. On the other hand, differences in the direction of rotary movement or differences at the semantic level, for example between words and nonsense, cannot function in this way (Julesz, 1971), and neither can differences in the spatial arrangements of lines (Beck, 1966), nor in the particular combinations of properties such as color and shape or curves, lines, and angles (see my research described in Section V). Not all examples of higher level structures resulting from patterning at a lower level depend on figure-ground segregation. Another compelling illustration is the emergence of form from coordinated patterns of moving lights demonstrated by Johanssen (1973). The most dramatic example is his walking human being, perceived in the dark from the movement of light sources attached to each major joint.

Julesz (1971) suggests that the inverse argument can also be used to order levels of processing. Thus if structure at one level can disrupt perception of structure at another level, the former must precede the latter. For example, detection of symmetry or recognition of words in a monocular pattern of otherwise random dots can be disrupted by stereoscopic perception of a competing pattern. Julesz infers that stereopsis therefore precedes the recognition of monocular shapes. The logic here seems to me more questionable. It depends on the assumption that if some change of conditions prevents conscious access to a particular property or structure, that property is no longer being processed. Although possible, this explanation does not seem a necessary one. It could be that the binocular representation is formed later than the monocular one and prevents our becoming aware of its existence. To take an extreme analogy, we would not deny the existence of separate activity in red and green cones at a peripheral level, simply because what we consciously perceive when presented with a mixture of red and green wavelengths is yellow.

It is true that in all the examples I gave where higher level structures were formed by the patterning of lower level elements, the lower level mediating elements did remain perceptible in their own right. Binocular disparity is not registered as such, but the resultant stereoscopic depth impression is, of course, visible. It would be interesting to know whether there are other conditions where the high-level modulation can be perceived without its low-level medium being consciously accessible. Notice, however, that the inference of sequential organization does not depend on the availability of the lower level components. It is logically entailed by the definition of the high-level structures that we do perceive.

2. Equivalence and Interchangeability of Elements

a. *Equivalence.*   There are cases in which we can vary the specific form of potential lower level components, leaving their category unchanged. Upper- and lowercase versions of the same letter would be one example. If we can show that recognition of higher level units is no more impaired by irrelevant physical variation among their elements than is recognition of the elements themselves, we can infer that the two levels are sequentially ordered. Thus if recognition of words composed of mixed-case letters shows no more impairment than recognition of mixed-case letters, we can infer that words must be recognized on the basis of categorical decisions about their component letters. On the other hand, if the words are more impaired, it would suggest that they are directly recognized as such or built from different word-specific features rather than letters. In fact, the decrement in performance is usually small, ranging from 0% in visual search and reading prose aloud (Smith, 1969; Smith, Lott, & Cronnell, 1969) to about 15% under difficult tachistoscopic conditions (Coltheart & Freeman, 1974). The small drop in performance could be due either to subjects finding it easier to use a single ''program'' to identify letters within words than to switch between two, or to ambiguous fragments being wrongly given a same-case interpretation more often when words are expected than when random letters are. McClelland (1976) found that the word-superiority effect in reporting letters in words, pseudowords, or unrelated letter strings was still present even in mixed-case displays. This seems strong evidence that identified letters constitute the data for word identification.

A similar argument can be made if we present component elements to separate input channels and find that they are reconstructed perceptually into the normal units at the next hypothesized level. Day (1968) found that separate phonemes simultaneously presented could be taken from each ear and combined to form words. Studdert–Kennedy and Shankweiler (1970) showed that the same could occur for distinctive features, and Rand (1974) showed it even for the acoustic cues to distinctive features. The equivalence method thus seems a useful source of evidence for sequentially ordering pairs of levels.

b. *Interchangeability.*   A related test is to see whether ''illusory conjunctions'' are formed under conditions of time pressure. If units at one level are composed from different combinations of lower level units, wrong combinations could potentially be formed, interchanging elements that are simultaneously presented. Although such illusions are rare, they do occur. For example, Efron and Yund's subjects (1974) sometimes heard the pitch of a tone in one ear at the intensity of a tone simultaneously presented to the other ear. Lawrence (1971) found that subjects, who were set to search for a word in uppercase letters in a rapidly presented series of visual words, sometimes reported clearly seeing in uppercase letters the word that followed the target, although it had been presented in lowercase. Treisman, Sykes, and Gelade (1977) found a high proportion of errors of this kind in a same−different matching task in which subjects wrongly recombined shapes and colors or features of schematic faces (see Section V of this chapter). The occurrence of such illusory conjunctions of elements implies that the elements are first registered as separable components at one level and only then combined or miscombined to form more complex representations at the next level.

III.   TEMPORAL ORDERING OF LEVELS

We turn now to examples of methods that test a somewhat weaker hypothesis, namely that two levels are serially ordered in time although not necessarily logically ordered in a sequence in which the output from one forms the input to the next.

1. Additive Effects on Reaction Time

Sternberg (1969) proposed what is probably the most important and best-known method of inferring the existence of processing stages from the finding of additive effects of two or more variables on choice reaction times. If (and this proviso will not always be met) the levels we are interested in testing correspond to independent as well as serially ordered stages of processing, this method offers a powerful tool for inferring their existence. It does not directly tell us the identity or the temporal order of the levels it implies; nor does it relate them in a logical sequence. However, their nature, order, and logical sequence can often be inferred from the nature of the variables that affect them.

The method has been applied to a number of tasks that potentially involve different levels of processing. Sternberg (1967) found that after practice in a classification task, the effect of stimulus degradation is independent of the effect of number of targets. This allows the inference that at least two independent levels are involved, one at which the test stimulus is still in a sensory form subject to visual interference and another at which it has been coded into a more categorical form for comparison with the set of memorized targets. Sekuler and

Nash (1972) found that size difference and orientation produced additive effects on response times in matching rectangles. Their results may be used to separate a stage at which rotation invariance is achieved from a stage at which sizes are normalized, suggesting that the two operations are independent.

Meyer, Schvaneveldt, and Ruddy (1975) found an interaction of stimulus degradation and semantic priming in a lexical decision task and concluded that both affect the same early level of processing, probably the visual encoding stage. However, this conclusion illustrates one of the problems with the additive method: Interactions are in general less easily interpreted than additive effects. Evidence of additivity, provided that the variance is small, gives strong support for the existence of two stages, but interactions could arise in a number of different ways. They could result from processing within a single stage. However, they could also result from interacting parallel stages or from a choice between alternative second stages contingent on the outcome of processing at the first stage. Or finally, an experimental manipulation could affect not only the duration of a stage but also the quality of its output. Moreover, varying the factors used to probe separate stages may in fact change the nature of these stages as well as their duration (Pachella, 1974). Subjects could adopt one strategy under one condition and a different strategy under another condition. The method is therefore less informative when interactions are found than when it reveals additivity. However, additive effects have now been demonstrated in many important contexts and do offer positive and quite compelling evidence for serially ordered levels of processing.

2. Input Channels

Another way in which we may be able to infer the separate existence and temporal ordering of particular levels is to pinpoint two candidate levels as occurring one before and one after two input channels converge (e.g., the two eyes, the two ears, ear and eye). This ensures that the two levels are both separable and temporally ordered. For example, Treisman and Davies (1973) used vision and hearing as input channels and compared within-modality with between-modality division of attention. Possible candidate levels were descriptively defined, and different conditions required processing at one or another of these levels. Thus in one condition, subjects were to monitor two messages for a target syllable, and in the other condition, they were to monitor them for any animal's name. The two messages were presented either in the same modality (vision or hearing) or in different modalities. If syllables are analyzed before the modalities converge onto a common linguistic system and semantic categories only after convergence, one might expect messages in the same modality to interfere with each other at both levels, whereas messages in different modalities interfered only at the semantic level. We did not in fact find the predicted interaction between presentation modalities and monitoring levels. This suggests that syllables as well as meaning may be identified only after the visual and auditory channels converge, perhaps after lexical access of the words that contain them.

A parallel can be drawn between this experiment and those on visual masking by Turvey (1973). He showed that monoptic presentation led to masking both by random dots and by a pattern mask, whereas dichoptic presentation produced interference only by the pattern mask. This suggests two levels of processing— one preceding binocular convergence at which brightness and contrast are processed and one succeeding it at which pattern features are extracted.

3. Detection Latencies

The simple task of target detection, where the targets are defined at different levels of a descriptive hierarchy, initially appears to provide direct evidence for a temporal sequence of levels. The assumption is that the earlier the level at which the target is identified, the faster it will be detected. For example, if phonemes are registered earlier than words or syllables, they should give shorter detection latencies. Savin and Bever (1970) found the reverse to be the case and inferred that syllables are identified directly, that they can then be decomposed into phonemes if the task requires it, but that the phoneme string is not normally an independent level of representation in speech perception. A similar rationale was suggested by Posner and Mitchell (1967) as one possible interpretation of their results in a "same−different" matching task: If physical codes are formed before name codes, they should be compared faster, and the difference in latencies for name and visual matching might indicate the time to convert one representation into another.

However, there is a difficulty in using these methods to infer ordered levels of processing. They depend on the assumption that other aspects of the task are the same for targets defined at each level. This is not necessarily the case; for example, a phonemic representation could be formed as a necessary stage before the word level is reached and yet be much slower to trigger an instrumental response (since this is a very unfamiliar task) and/or much less accessible (or not directly accessible at all) to conscious awareness. The visual matching task involves two operations whose durations need not covary; the stimuli must be both encoded and then compared with each other. Physical representations of letters could (indeed must) be formed before their names are retrieved, and yet it could be the case that comparing these physical codes is slower than comparing their names. Thus differences in access time (Savin and Bever) or in comparison time (Posner and Mitchell) could either add to, subtract from, or completely cancel out differences in the time at which the different levels are reached in the perceptual processing sequence.

Posner and Mitchell noted also that differences in response times to tasks requiring different levels of processing can by themselves support only differences in the time at which processing at each level is completed. Without further evidence, they would be compatible with either parallel or serial onset of processing at each level. As we shall see, this is probably true also of the last method I discuss for temporally ordering levels.

4. Directional Facilitation or Interference

The claim here is that if variations in the structures or relations defined at one level can facilitate or interfere with tasks that require processing at another level, the former must be analyzed before the latter. The examples I have chosen depend on selective facilitation; but similar use can be made of interference paradigms, and similar problems arise (see, for example Wood, 1975; and Pomerantz & Sager, 1975).

A recent experiment by Banks and Prinzmetal (1976) suggests that Gestalt grouping and segregation may precede letter identification. They found that a forced-choice decision, whether a target was an F or a T, was improved when the nontargets (hybrid $F-T$'s) formed a Gestalt group and the target was perceptually isolated, even though this was achieved by adding more nontargets to the display. Bregman and Rudnicky (1975) showed similar ''unmasking'' for a temporal order judgment of two tones embedded in other tones when their neighbors were perceptually (not physically) separated from them by the addition of more tones with which they grouped.

Some of the best-known examples in which selective facilitation of one level by another has been claimed are those that challenge the belief that processing is bottom-up. For example, Weisstein and Harris (1974) found improved identification of a line segment when it was embedded in a ''good,'' apparently three-dimensional figure (an ''object''), rather than a flat rearrangement of the parts of the same figure. However, before concluding that processing of objects is top-down, it is important to note that the line segments were even better identified when presented alone than in ''objects,'' suggesting that the ''object'' context reduced the interference from extraneous lines rather than improving detection of the target lines alone. Weisstein and Harris suggest three possible explanations of their result:

1. Objects are recognized holistically rather than as conjunctions of features (top-down processing in my strongest sense).
2. Objects activate more complex feature detectors as well as simple ones, and this redundancy increases accuracy (parallel processing or bottom-up with delayed decision).
3. There are recurrent loops rather than a fixed serial hierarchy, so that higher level structure can enhance the sensitivity of particular feature detectors (the weaker sense of top-down analysis in which priming rather than stimulus analysis is top-down).

A further example of top-down facilitation avoids these alternative interpretations and suggests that the category of alphanumeric symbols may be available before their identity. Jonides and Gleitman (1972) found that search for '0' was faster in a context of letters when it was defined as "zero" and faster in a context of digits when it was defined as the letter '*O*' than it was with the opposite pairings of background and target definition. Since the stimuli were identical, it is difficult to attribute these differences to anything but the difference in category.

On the other hand, we need also to ask the converse question, whether knowing the specific identity of the target can facilitate search for a category. Is searching for a *K* in digits easier than searching for any letter in digits? If facilitation is present in both directions, it cannot be used as evidence for a serial temporal ordering; instead, it would suggest either parallel access or exhaustive processing, with decisions taken only after stimuli have formed a representation at all the levels in question. Brand (1971), in fact, found that many subjects were no faster at searching for a specified single letter or digit than at searching for any letter or digit, provided that the background items belonged to a different category. Thus the category facilitation effect does appear to be asymmetric. It is therefore stronger evidence for a serial order at least of completion times, with category labels becoming accessible earlier than letter or digit names. It does not, however, distinguish parallel from serial onset of processing at these levels.

A number of problems arise in inferring processing order from asymmetries of facilitation or interference. To summarize, these are:

1. Apparent effects from another level could also in some cases be mediated by relationships within the level being tested. Thus letter strings that form words also form more predictable sequences at the letter level.

2. The facilitation or interference cannot always be attributed unequivocally to the perceptual encoding stage. They may affect temporary storage or a late construction for subjective experience rather than initial extraction of the information on which this will be based.

3. Asymmetries of facilitation or interference may result from parallel processing with either different completion times or differences between levels in their potential for benefiting or impairing performance.

4. Finally, there is the possibility that we are "compulsive encoders" (Teichner & Krebs, 1974); in other words, that we run right through the perceptual hierarchy before selecting our responses.

These difficulties mean that evidence for directional facilitation or interference will be, at most, consistent with a particular processing order rather than demonstrating it unequivocally. On the other hand, *selective* interference or facilitation of a particular level independently of others can offer evidence for its psychological reality and independent existence. I discussed it in this section rather than the next, because it can at least *suggest* a particular temporal ordering, which may then be checked using other converging methods.

IV.   EVIDENCE FOR THE EXISTENCE OF LEVELS

The evidence in this last section supports only the existence of particular levels in perceptual processing. However, since it is possible that a fixed sequential or temporal ordering is the exception rather than the rule, it may be as important to determine the existence and separability of levels as to attempt to order them. What further evidence could support the existence of levels without assuming any necessary pattern of access? If we alter a task in such a way as to tap a supposedly different level, we expect some qualitative changes in performance to emerge. There are many forms these might take, several of which I have already discussed in previous sections. Examples are a change in the form of interference or in the source of priming or expectancy. There are also some further differences, not previously discussed, that may give new support to the existence of separate levels.

1. Categorical Perception

One such difference might be a change from continuous to "categorical" perception. This has been very fully discussed (e.g., by Liberman, Cooper, Shankweiler, & Studdert−Kennedy, 1967; and by Wood, 1975) as evidence for a special speech processor. The argument is that when subjects hear a sound that they perceive as speech, their discrimination is determined by, and therefore no better than, their ability to categorize the sounds as particular phonemes; whereas for nonspeech perception, discrimination is typically much better than categorization. Some doubts have recently arisen about tying this change to the speech versus nonspeech levels, since categorical perception also appears with some musical sounds (Cutting & Rosner, 1974), is not always present with speech sounds (particularly vowels), and can be shown to some extent by monkeys as well as men (Morse & Snowdon, 1975). However, the fact that the same differences between pairs of sounds can be perceived either categorically or not, depending on their auditory context or on the temporal direction in which they are played (Mattingly, Liberman, Syrdal, & Halwes, 1971) or on the way the task is defined (Pisoni & Lazarus, 1974), is more consistent with an interpretation in terms of levels than with any account that ties the categorical/noncategorical distinction to particular classes of sounds.

2. Passive Versus Active Processing

A second qualitative difference that might index a difference in levels is the contrast between "passive" and "active" analysis (e.g., Neisser, 1967). A task defined on elements at one level may be unaffected by prior information or expectancy, whereas one defined at another level shows large effects of probability, precuing, context, and so on. The passive−to−active change is normally assumed to correlate with early versus late levels, presumably because priming is assumed to come from top-down, with decreasing likelihood of reaching the lowest levels. This assumption is not logically necessary, although there is in fact probably more evidence suggesting purely passive processing of features and properties, with any effects of set occurring at decision or response, than there is for more complex stimuli. For instance, Harris and Haber (1963) conclude from their attempts to bias perception of particular properties like shape, color, and number that any positive effects can be attributed entirely to encoding for memory.

Broadbent (1977) has drawn the distinction between "passive" and "active" processing somewhat differently. Although both can be affected by prior probabilities, the mechanism by which this occurs is different in the two cases. In passive processing, criteria may be permanently lowered in favor of frequent combinations of features and elements. However, in active processing, the subject forms hypotheses and then tests them by selecting only a subset of the possible sensory data, those that could confirm the hypothesis. Broadbent attributes the word-frequency effect to the passive process and the effects of verbal context and word emotionality to active testing. Becker (1976) orders these two stages in a sequential model of perception in which passive registration precedes and suggests hypotheses for active testing. Here the stages do not yet correspond to hierarchical levels. However, Broadbent relates Becker's suggestion to one by Navon (1977) that equates the passive stage with global analysis and the active with local or detailed analysis. What is particularly interesting is Broadbent's demonstration that the difference between passive and active testing interacts with the type of stimulus degradation that is most effective; high-frequency masks remove or reduce the effects of letter context and emotionality, whereas low-frequency masks reduce the word-frequency effect. These selective effects would be consistent with the idea that different properties of words, the global and the local, are analyzed at different levels and that only the latter can be modified by active selection of subsets of features to be tested in the light of the immediate context or of subjective importance or emotionality.

These various examples of different empirical approaches to the problem of levels of processing are selected from a much wider range. They illustrate some of the conceptual difficulties that arise in making theoretical inferences from the data and emphasize the importance of using converging evidence from several different paradigms. However, they do give considerable support at least for the psychological "existence" of different levels of representation.

V. RESEARCH ON FEATURES AND THEIR INTEGRATION INTO COMPLEX PERCEPTS

Before making some final comments on implications for perceptual and memory theories, I will outline some current research of my own, using a variety of tasks whose results appear both to distinguish and order two levels of representation. They illustrate some further types of evidence not discussed in the previous review and show how consistent conclusions, both across a variety of paradigms and using a variety of stimuli, can strengthen our confidence in a hypothesis that any one paradigm on its own would leave plausible but only weakly supported. Finally, they suggest a particular type of forgetting that involves loss of higher level rather than lower level information about the items presented. The two hypothesised levels with which I have been concerned are: (1) a level at which separable features or dimensions are registered independently of each other and spatially in parallel; and (2) a level at which these separate components are integrated into the complex multidimensional percepts of which we are normally aware.

Since another main aim was to relate these levels to a new hypothesis about selective attention, the story will probably gain coherence if I first outline the rationale determining my choice of experiment. My starting point was the evidence, both physiological and psychological, that at least some features and properties are registered by relatively independent "channels" or "analyzers." Garner's (1974) criteria for separability offer some ways of distinguishing which physical dimensions also form independent perceptual dimensions and which form compound or integral dimensions, unitized patterns. My concern was with the separable features and properties, more specifically with the question of how these are integrated perceptually into the correct combinations rather than into what might be called "illusory conjunctions" (e.g., a green X when a red X and a green O were presented). The hypothesis I proposed was that we normally avoid such errors by using focal attention and scanning different locations serially (Treisman, Sykes, & Gelade, 1977). Whatever features or properties are registered within the same central "fixation" of attention are combined to form a single percept. Simple features or dimensions can be registered in parallel without focal attention, since no risk of illusory conjunctions arises with these. More complex stimuli may also be processed in parallel, provided that their component parts or properties are registered integrally, whether by innate neural detectors or because practice and overlearning have led to "unitization" (Laberge, 1975).

If this suggestion is correct, it predicts some qualitative differences in perceptual performance for features and for conjunctions.

1. In a visual search task, targets defined by a single property or part should be detected in parallel, but targets defined by conjunctions should require serial search through the display. Thus a qualitative difference in the type of processing would suggest the existence of two separable levels.

2. Texture segregation, which is normally assumed to be a preattentive process, should be possible on the basis of simple or unitized features, but not on the basis of conjunctions. This could therefore order the two levels in relation to the grouping operation, one preceding and one succeeding it.

3. Identifying a conjunction necessarily requires us to locate it spatially, whereas identifying a feature may not. It is possible, therefore, that a stage at which accurate position information is accessed could act at another "landmark" ordering the two levels.

4. Errors in both perceptual and memory tasks, when performed under time pressure or divided-attention conditions, could take the form of illusory conjunctions, interchanging features of the stimuli presented to form new combinations at the conjunction level. This interchangeability of elements at one level when combining at the next level offers further support for their separate existence and for a particular sequential ordering.

This is a preliminary exploration, and I chose simple examples of stimuli to work with (colored shapes, letters, and schematic faces). If clear conclusions emerge, it may be possible to use them in analyzing more complex examples of possible feature–conjunction relations.

1. Visual Search

a. *Properties.*   In the first experiment, we used colored shapes and defined the target either by two disjunctive properties ("blue" or S) or by a conjunction of properties ("a green T"). The nontargets were identical in the two conditions and consisted of equal numbers of green X's and brown T's. Thus the "blue" or S targets could each be detected on the basis of a single feature, color or curvature, whereas the green T could only be distinguished from the nontargets by the conjunction of its two properties in a single item. In both conditions, however, two features were relevant. Half the displays contained a single target and the other half none. Subjects classified them on this basis as quickly as they could. The number of items in the display varied randomly across trials—either 1, 5, 15, or 30. The results showed almost no effect of display size on positive responses to the single-feature targets (a slope of 3 msec per item and significant departures from linearity) and a strictly linear increase in search time with display size for the conjunction targets (a slope of 29 msec per item). This was not due to poorer discriminability of the conjunction target in the usual sense, since in the single-item display, it was actually classified 14 msec faster than the disjunctive targets. Thus its difficulty arose only when more than one item was present and the risk of illusory conjunctions became possible. The linear increase in search time in this condition suggests serial processing, as predicted by the hypothesis that focal attention is necessary when features must be correctly integrated. The dramatic difference in performance between the two conditions strongly suggests a change of processing level.

Shiffrin and Schneider (1977) recently suggested that search typically changes from serial to parallel scanning with practice, once a constant mapping of stimuli to classification responses has become overlearned. It therefore seemed important to test whether this occurs with conjunctions as well; if it did, my suggestion would be that a single-feature analyzer had been set up for the conjunction of properties that were previously detected only by the two-level process of checking the co-occurrence of activation in two separate feature detectors. We ran two of the six subjects for 13 sessions on the same conjunction search. We found some decrease in the slope of search time against display size for these two subjects, changing from 41 msec to 27 msec per item; but this decrease occurred almost entirely in the first three blocks, and there was little change beyond that. The functions stayed extremely linear throughout the 13 days with no hint of a change to parallel processing. Thus, if unitization and automatic detection can develop for conjunctions of properties, it must require appreciably greater amounts of practice than our subjects were given.

b. *Parts.*   Beck and Ambler (1973) have shown that discrimination of T from T is unimpaired when attention must be spatially distributed rather than focused on one item, whereas discrimination of T and L is greatly impaired when the number of items presented is increased, although no harder when focal attention is possible. This might be because T and T differ in a single feature (line orientation), whereas T and L differ only in the spatial arrangement or conjunction of their parts (vertical and horizontal lines). It is of interest to see whether conjunctions do pose a problem in letter search or whether letters are such familiar stimuli that they have become unitized and can be detected in parallel. This is an important question, since much recent evidence suggests that categorical or highly practiced alphanumeric targets can be detected in parallel (Brand, 1971; Jonides & Gleitman, 1972; Schneider & Shiffrin, 1977). On my hypothesis, focal attention and serial scanning should be necessary only if we use sets of letters whose parts are interchangeable so that they risk forming illusory conjunctions. Single features could serve to distinguish within sets of letters where such illusory conjunctions are impossible. We tested four sets of letters to see whether search times vary primrily with target to nontarget similarity or with the risk of conjunction errors. We compared search for T in a background of I's and Z's and R in a background of P's and Q's (both possible illusory conjunctions) with search for T in a background of I's and Y's and R in a background of P's and B's (where Y and B are more similar to the targets T and R than are Z and Q). The increases in search time with display size were both steeper and more linear for the conjunction sets than for the more similar control sets. This supports the theory and extends it to highly familiar stimuli and to features defined as local elements of complex shapes in addition to different dimensions.

2. Texture Segregation

Linear reaction-time functions are not unequivocal proof of serial processing but could be produced by a parallel system with limited capacity and exponentially distributed processing times (Townsend, 1971). It would therefore be helpful to look for other paradigms to test the hypothesis that discrimination between conjunctions requires focal attention to one item at a time. One such prediction is that texture segregation should not be possible on the basis of conjunctions of features. Beck (1966) and Olson and Attneave (1970) have shown that textures segregate much better on the basis of line orientation than on the basis of line arrangements. Julesz (1975) has proposed a powerful, general theory of texture perception based on the claim that only first- or second-order statistics can be detected at this level of processing. Julesz's hypothesis is about the properties of the display that allow texture segregation, whereas mine is about the properties of the perceptual system that allow or disallow it. In other words, I try to predict whether texture segregation will be possible from the results of other physiological or psychological experiments suggesting whether the the features in question are registered integrally or separably.

The experiments on texture segregation clearly indicate that segregation can occur on the basis of either a color difference (red O's and N's versus blue O's and N's) or a shape difference (red and blue O's versus red and blue N's), but not on the basis of a conjunction of these properties (red O's and blue N's versus red N's and blue O's). We also tested segregation based on conjunctions of parts rather than properties, using letters as stimuli. In one experiment, we compared segregation of P's and Q's versus R's and O's with segregation of F's and Q's versus E's and O's. These pairs should be equally similar, since P and R are no more confusable than E and F. However, with PQ/RO there are no unique features on either side of the boundary, and illusory conjunctions could potentially transform one pair into the other. With FQ/EO, on the other hand, there is at least one unique feature (the diagonal line of the Q) which could distinguish one side of the boundary from the other. Thus texture segregation should occur with FQ/EO but not with PQ/RO. Again the results were consistent with this prediction.

3. Spatial Localization of Features and Conjunctions

Here we tested a stronger prediction in the sense that it is more counterintuitive. Detection without localization should be impossible for conjunctions if we must focus attention on the particular location each occupies in order to identify it correctly. However, the theory allows the possibility (although it does not require it) that features and properties could be detected without at the same time being located spatially. Thus there could be a level at which they are "free-floating," unrelated to each other and only loosely localized spatially. (Some idea of the main areas they occupy is necessary for texture segregation, but this need apply only to the boundaries of homogeneous groups of elements, not to individual elements within or outside the groups.) Locating a feature certainly does not involve a random serial search; we can rapidly find the position of a red item in a display. However, the theory allows the possibility that this could be done after its presence is detected rather than at the same time and that it might take a measurable additional time. I have carried out two different experiments to explore this possibility.

a. *Precued locations.* Since we know from the visual search results that we can detect a single feature in parallel across a display, we should gain little advantage from precuing its location. For conjunctions, we predict a large advantage from precuing, since this would eliminate the need for serial search and allow attention to be focused in advance on the correct location. Furthermore, if it is possible to detect a single feature *before* locating it, it might actually be more difficult if we are forced to specify its location, e.g., to respond to it only if it is in the cued location. We tested both single features (colors and shapes) and conjunctions (colored shapes) in two different conditions. In the noncued condition, subjects responded "yes" if the target was present anywhere in the display (a circular arrangement of 12 items) and "no" if it was not. In the precued condition, they responded "yes" if the target was in the precued location (cued by a 50-msec exposure of an external line pointing at one of the 12 locations 100 msec before the display) and "no" if it was either in a noncued location (half the negative trials) or not present at all (the other half of the negative trials). There was never more than one target present. We found that precuing the location made the positive responses 164 msec faster in the conjunction condition, as predicted; and again as predicted, it actually made them 41 msec slower in the single-feature conditions, even though the cards were identical in the precued and noncued conditions. The negatives with no target present showed a 366-msec advantage for precuing with conjunctions and no significant difference with the single features. In the single-feature conditions, the negatives with a target in a noncued location close to the cued location were 51 msec slower than those with no irrelevant target, showing some interference with the negative response, a failure of selective attention. This interference was not present in the conjunction condition, suggesting that attention is more efficiently focused at this level than at the single-feature level. The increased latency on the precued positives in the single-feature condition cannot be explained by interference from irrelevant targets, since none was presented on positive trials; it seems therefore to reflect the additional operation of locating the target once it has been detected, an operation that is not required in the noncued condition. This gives some support to the notion of a level at which features are registered but are in some sense free-floating, and it allows the possibility of the illusory conjunctions I conjured up as the risk to be counteracted by the mechanisms of focal attention.

b. *Interdependence of identity and location.* This experiment tests the same aspect of the theory in a different way. If conjunctions cannot be formed without locating their features, there should be a clear dependency between the probability of identifying which of two conjunction targets was presented on a given trial and the probability of identifying where it was presented. However, for single features, there need be no such dependency; in fact, identification could be quite independent of localization, although some degree of positive correlation might result simply from fluctuations across trials in the subject's overall efficiency. In this experiment, we measured accuracy rather than latency. It was divided into two parts: In the first, an exposure duration for the display (followed by a mask) was determined for each subject at which he or she reached about 80% accuracy in forced-choice reporting which of two possible targets was presented. In the conjunction condition, these were pink X's or blue O's, and the nontargets were pink O's or blue X's. In the single-feature condition, the targets were orange or H and the nontargets were again pink O's and blue X's. (The orange targets were either X's or O's, and the H was either pink or blue, but these additional features were irrelevant to the task.) In the second part of the experiment, with the same exposure duration, the subject had to report both the identity of the target and its location in the array of two lines of six items (of which only the inner eight positions could contain a target). No extra response delay was introduced in reporting location as well as identity, since the response consisted of writing the identity of the target in the appropriate cell of a given 4×2 matrix. The results, corrected for guessing, showed that the conditional probability of reporting location correctly, given that the target was correctly identified, was 0.8 for the conjunction targets and only 0.3 for the single features. The exposure duration required for 80% correct identification was much longer for the conjunctions than for the single features (as expected from the change from parallel to serial processing). What is interesting is that the rapid parallel processing of features that allowed their identity to be accessed apparently did not also provide accurate spatial information.

4. Memory for Conjunctions

The final experiment (Treisman, 1977) involves memory as well as perception. It suggests that a similar serial focusing of attention may be required when we retrieve conjunctions from memory. It also offers evidence that even after conjunctions have been registered perceptually, they may return to their free-floating state in memory, that forgetting in one of its forms may dissolve the glue that integrates features into the correct complex wholes. Subjects were given a "same–different" matching task in which they had to decide whether either of two display stimuli exactly matched either of two memorized targets. We used colored letters again and also schematic faces whose eyes and mouths could vary interchangeably. In both cases, we found that subjects made many false-positive conjunction errors (up to one-third) when the targets and display were identical in features but differed in their combination (e.g., blue X and red O in the display were judged the same as blue O and red X as targets). This occurs almost as often with simultaneous presentation (25%) as with successive presentation and is good evidence for a sequential ordering of the feature and conjunction levels. As I argued earlier, if elements at one level can recombine to form wrong conjunctions at the next, they must first be independently registered. The pattern of latencies suggested three additive stages in which the subject first checked all four items in parallel for the presence of a matching feature, then focused serially on display locations containing a matching feature, and finally—and only if necessary—focused serially on the memorized targets. The tentative suggestions were that serial "focusing" on memorized as well as on stimulus items is necessary when conjunctions are relevant and that focusing on a memory may be more difficult than focusing on a display location.

This program of research is clearly still in its early stages and could well be building a house of cards. However, it does so far offer converging evidence that there is a pair of identifiable levels, the second level serially combining parts or properties that have been detected at the first level by independent analyzers operating spatially in parallel. The features detected at the first stage are initially free-floating but can be rapidly located, perhaps by a fast homing-in operation. Their presence can then be used to control the sequence of focal scanning for conjunctions.

These features would also mediate texture segregation and grouping of figure from ground. They would therefore allow the possibility that attention could be focused on a spatially homogeneous group rather than exclusively on individual items. Thus grouping by color or shape of the nontarget in a conjunction search could dramatically increase the speed of target detection. For example, if all the red O's were on the left and all the blue X's were on the right, a red X would probably be found as quickly with a large as with a small display. I would explain this by suggesting that the focus of attention is narrowed only to the extent necessary to exclude illusory conjunctions (e.g., to half the display in the example above). Within the focus of attention, processing will be parallel; only successive "fixations" of attention will be serial. This hypothesis has not yet been tested but predicts that the number of spatially distinct groups of homogeneous items will determine the latency of search rather than the number of items as such. However, there must be clear limits to the spatial complexity of the area on which attention can be focused, since it would otherwise have segregated all the items of the target color in our randomly mixed conjunction displays and allowed subjects to check in parallel for the target shape. The rule might be, for example, that the focal area must always be bounded by convex edges. Alternatively, it might be that Gestalt qualities (such as good continuation, symmetry, etc.) determine the groups to which attention can be selectively directed (Kahneman, 1973; Kahneman & Henik, 1977).

GENERAL CONCLUSIONS

Do any generalizations emerge about methodology or about possible perceptual hierarchies, and are there any implications for the levels-of-processing approach to memory?

a. *Methodology.*   A number of morals have emerged as people have had second thoughts about ways of inferring levels. Among them are the following:

1. Do not assume that all levels can be directly accessed introspectively or for voluntary responses.
2. Do not assume that the order of introspective access need reflect the order of perceptual processing. Conscious access may be more closely related to the order of usefulness in everyday life.
3. Do not assume that processing can optionally be stopped at any given level.
4. Do not assume that levels must be traversed in a fixed order, or once only.
5. Do distinguish, if possible, between sequential ordering and temporal completion differences, since the latter are consistent with parallel onset of processing.
6. Do also distinguish between top-down priming and top-down analysis.
7. Finally, do not equate failure to discover a single invariant hierarchy with failure to show anything of interest; a task-related flexible, interactive system can be empirically explored, often with the same methods that were designed to prove a rigid ordering.

However, converging evidence from different methods in one situation and diverging evidence from the same method in different situations may be needed before we can gain any coherent understanding of the available strategies and of the structures that constrain their use.

b. *Levels of processing.*   Since my aim was more to classify and assess methods than to propose a complete theory of perception, the material reviewed could not lead to a comprehensive account of perceptual levels. In shape or object recognition, there is evidence for the reality of a feature to conjunction mapping, which suggests a new interpretation of selective attention. Within the language system, it may be possible to separate the acoustic or visual feature levels, the visual level or spoken syllable levels, and the word levels, although there is less evidence for independence within the lexical−syntactic−semantic system. The various forms of top-down travel and parallel entry allow the possibility of incomplete and highly selective analysis at lower levels. We should note, however, that we are in fact quite sensitive to many kinds of ''error'' or unlikely details when these are physically clear in the stimulus. Warren and Warren's (1970) deleted phoneme had to be masked by a cough to prevent its absence being noted and to allow the synthesis of a plausible replacement. Thus we should be cautious before inferring from our enormous skill at using context in degraded or noisy conditions that we make an equally sketchy sensory analysis of the physical input where it is clearly discriminable. To give flesh to (or to bury) these painfully skeletal conclusions could occupy us for some time to come.

c. *Memory.*   Finally, I will touch briefly on questions that relate processing levels to memory. Firstly, is memory, like perception, hierarchically organized, holding information at many levels; or are items normally stored as unitary representations at one level only? Secondly, can the principles and examples outlined in the review of perceptual methods be applied to the particular orienting tasks typically used in memory research, in order to throw any light on the relation between perceptual processing and memory?

A hierarchical perceptual system requires two distinct forms of storage: one for the sensory data still waiting to be processed and the other for the decisions taken at each level. If the levels are sequentially ordered, sensory data are strictly needed only at the first, and decisions could be discarded at each level as soon as the next has been reached. However, this would preclude any possibility of rechecking the analysis, and it would also prevent subsequent response to lower level structures and perceptual learning from their use. There are therefore good reasons, even with a fixed sequence of levels, for storing both data and decisions at levels other than the highest one reached.

The distinction between storage of sensory data, about which decisions may subsequently be taken, and storage of the decisions themselves may be important in interpreting the results of some memory research on levels of processing. Many experiments on sensory storage, both visual and auditory, have shown rapid loss over time (e.g., Glucksberg & Cowen, 1970; Sperling, 1960). Now sensory data are usually assumed to be stored and available only at a low level of perceptual processing; this is true by definition in a sequential hierarchy and true empirically in most studies of sensory storage, since a restriction to simple physical dimensions has been one of the characteristics defining storage as sensory rather than categorized. This correlation found in the research paradigms so far explored, between storage of data rather than decisions and low rather than high levels of the hierarchy, may not be a necessary one; decisions can also be taken and stored about low-level properties. However, if it is a general rule that data are lost more rapidly than decisions, the conclusion that low levels give poorer recall could be due in part to this possible confounding between the paradigms to study "low" levels of processing and the paradigms to study sensory as opposed to categorical memory.

How can we discover whether memory is hierarchically organized and whether different levels of representation entail different storage or retrieval characteristics? Many of the methods that suggest a sequential ordering or simply the existence of levels in perception can also be applied to memory. There is no space to indicate more than a few possible parallels with the perceptual research. One example already given is that elements can be interchanged to produce incorrect conjunctions in recall as well as in perception. My experiment illustrated this for faces and for colored shapes. This finding conflicts with the more usual conclusion that higher levels survive better than lower ones and illustrates how one form of forgetting can result from slippage in the reverse direction, *down* the hierarchy, with loss of conjunctions and retention of features.

Selective facilitation or interference can act on memory traces as well as during perception. Thus similar manipulations could probe whether information is stored hierarchically or whether a single level of representation is typically selected. It may be possible to link different kinds of interference with particular memory paradigms. One interesting example where perception and memory converge is the suffix effect, in which interference varies with the physical but not the semantic characteristics of the items (Morton, Crowder, & Prussin, 1971). It appears that physical but not semantic grouping during perception determines the way in which items are "packaged" for and retrieved from short-term memory. The reduction in interference with a change of location or voice quality in the suffix relative to the list cannot be attributed to a failure to register the item perceptually. Subjects would certainly notice if its identity changed, e.g., from "zero" to "nought." It appears that perceptual segregation also produces segregation within short-term memory, whereas semantic segregation does not. On the other hand, similarity at the semantic level does increase the proactive interference that builds up across trials. A shift in semantic category produces greater release from P.I. (proactive interference) than a shift in physical category (Wickens, 1970). It would be interesting to distinguish three alternative possibilities: (1) that longer term semantic effects are superimposed on the perceptual grouping effects; or (2) that perceptual groupings disappear after higher level processing; or (3) that some semantic memory paradigms simply bypass the physical grouping stage by using a different route through the perceptual hierarchy. For example, Kahneman and Henik (1977) showed strong effects of perceptual grouping on interitem dependencies in the immediate recall of letters. Their paradigm might be modified to require semantic classification of words formed within or across perceptual groups of letters; one could thus explore the possible interactions between physical segregation and segregation by word or meaning as they change over time in memory.

Many of the methodological pitfalls associated with perceptual theorizing will apply also to memory. For example, accessibility to consciousness need not reliably index the amount stored at different levels. Eagle, Wolitzky, and Klein (1966) found that semantic content in an ambiguous picture can be registered and reflected later in spontaneously generated stories without being either consciously seen or accessible for voluntary recall. Potter (1976) found that a 200-msec exposure will suffice for any picture in a rapid sequence to be accurately matched to a brief and general verbal description, but not for each picture to be subsequently recognized. Although target detection does not prove that all the nontarget pictures reached an equal level of semantic coding, it suggests that reaching the semantic level may not guarantee storage in memory. Thus one advantage of semantic orienting tasks may be that they allow "consolidation" whereas the structural tasks prevent it.

One of the main advantages of semantic over physical coding may reflect easier, more efficient retrieval rather than more adequate storage. One interesting possibility is that there are differences in the optimal method of accessing information stored at different levels. The information that we normally need to *recall* is usually about object identities, abstract or semantic properties of events rather than their particular embodiments. This is the type of information that we mentally manipulate in solving problems, planning our actions, making decisions, and communicating with others. There are also conditions that require us to store more specific, concrete, physical information, but they seldom require *recall*. They involve either recognition, as when we identify places, objects, people, or voices; or transfer of skills, as when we improve in reading, riding a bicycle, and so on. These requirements certainly necessitate retention of physical or early-level representations, but only in a way that allows matching, priming, or revival of previously registered stimuli. Thus in order to test memory for early levels of processing, it might be necessary to use indirect measures like savings, interference, recognition, or any other paradigm that reveals effects of past experience through a changed state of memory, without also requiring voluntary recall of that information.

There is some evidence consistent with this suggestion. For example, Kolers (see Chapter 17) showed that the skill of reading a specific form of inverted or rotated words was retained over long intervals and that recognition of both content and physical embodiment of the sentences could remain above chance, even across intervals as long as 32 days. Similarly, Nelson (Chapter 3) uses the indirect evidence of interference from physical features with the recall of paired associates to prove that graphemic and phonemic levels of representation do persist in memory over much longer intervals than their direct recall would suggest. Thus it is conceivable that the usual better recall of semantic representations and abstracted prototypes is largely a matter of habit, of what has generally proved the most useful level to retrieve.

In memory research, then, as in perception, there is evidence for separate levels of representation, hierarchically interrelated. Not all are equally accessible when tested in any given paradigm. However, the evidence for consistent differences across paradigms in the storage time or availability of particular levels is much less clear. There may be a parallel with perception in the fact that lower levels are less easily retrieved by direct recall, just as they are less easily available in perceptual tasks to either introspection or to control responses.

The second question concerned the evidence for a direct causal link between perception and memory. To establish a causal relation rather than simply a parallel between perceptual levels and memory requires two steps: We must first analyze, for any given orienting task, which levels are processed perceptually and in what order; only then can we look for the effects on survival time or retrieval order. Unfortunately, little systematic evidence is yet available on the perceptual processing required by the orienting tasks most commonly used in memory research. One example of an "early"-level task has been monitoring for the presence of a particular letter. Although letters may be identified before words (as suggested by the case-alternation results), it is unlikely that this monitoring task can arrest perception at a prelexical or presemantic level. Letter search can, for example, be facilitated by familiarity of the context (Krueger, 1970, 1975). The words or meaning must therefore be registered at some stage before the response is made. Monitoring for phonemes impairs immediate recall no more than monitoring for semantic targets of equal difficulty (Treisman & Tuxworth, 1974). Thus again, it is very unlikely that perception is arrested at the phonological level by the phoneme-monitoring task. However, delayed recall *is* more impaired by phoneme than by semantic monitoring. This suggests that the long-term retrievability of words depends not simply on the perception of their meaning, but on the degree of attention this level receives in the limited time available.

An important experiment by Green (1975) offers more direct evidence about the level of representation available to subjects immediately after listening to a sentence in two different orienting tasks. In one condition, subjects were asked to recall the sentence verbatim, and in another condition to generate a continuation of the sentence; however, on a proportion of trials, in both conditions, they were given instead a probe word to be classified as present in the sentence or not present. The relevant trials were the negatives in which the probe word resembled a sentence word either phonologically or semantically. Green found an interaction between the type of probe and the orienting task such that a probe that sounded similar to a word in the sentence was harder to reject if subjects were expecting rote recall, and a synonym was harder to reject if they were expecting to continue the sentence. Here Green successfully uses selective interference to distinguish two levels of representation in memory and, more important, to link them to different orienting tasks.

In general, it seems unlikely that the orienting tasks commonly used restrict processing exclusively to one level. A possible exception may be paradigms that overload subjects and force them to store data in a sensory form. The more typical results may simply reflect a correlation between the level that receives most attention during perception and the level that remains most directly accessible in memory by voluntary recall. However, it is also true that the stronger hypotheses have not been adequately tested. Real differences in storage may exist as well as differences in accessibility, and they may be determined by the levels of perceptual processing involved. To demonstrate this convincingly will be more difficult than it seemed initially and will require converging evidence from different analytic methods. The extent to which our memory of an event reflects the path we followed in perceiving it still seems an important question to explore.

ACKNOWLEDGMENT

This research was supported by the Medical Research Council and the chapter was completed at the Center for Advanced Study in the Behavioral Sciences, Stanford, California.

REFERENCES

Banks, W. P., & Prinzmetal, W. Configurational effects in visual information processing. *Perception & Psychophysics*, 1976, *19*, 361–367.

Beck, J. Effect of orientation and of shape similarity on perceptual grouping. *Perception & Psychophysics*, 1966, *1*, 300–302.

Beck, J., & Ambler, B. The effects of concentrated and distributed attention on peripheral acuity. *Perception & Psychophysics*, 1973, *14*, 225–230.

Becker, C. A. Allocation of attention during visual word recognition. *Journal of Experimental Psychology: Human Perception and Performance*, 1976, *2*, 556–566.

Brand, J. Classification without identification in visual search. *Quarterly Journal of Experimental Psychology*, 1971, *23*, 178–186.

Bregman, A. S., & Rudnicky, A. I. Auditory segregation: Stream or streams? *Journal of Experimental Psychology: Human Perception and Performance*, 1975, *1*, 263–267.

Broadbent, D. E. The hidden pre-attentive processes. *American Psychologist*, 1977, *32*, 109–118.

Coltheart, M., & Freeman, R. Case alternation impairs word identification. *Bulletin of the Psychonomic Society*, 1974, *3*, 102–104.

Corteen, R. S., & Dunn, D. Shock-associated words in a nonattended message: A test for momentary awareness. *Journal of Experimental Psychology*, 1974, *102*, 1143–1144.

Craik, F. I. M., & Lockhart, R. S. Levels of processing: A framework for memory research. *Journal of Verbal Learning and Verbal Behavior*, 1972, *11*, 671–684.

Craik, F. I. M., & Tulving, E. Depth of processing and the retention of words in episodic memory. *Journal of Experimental Psychology: General*, 1975, *104*, 268–294.

Cutting, J. E., & Rosner, B. S. Categories and boundaries in speech and music. *Perception & Psychophysics*, 1974, *16*, 564–570.

Day, R. S. Fusion in dichotic listening (Doctoral dissertation, Stanford University, 1968). *Dissertation Abstracts International*, 1969, *29*, 2649B.

Eagle, M., Wolitzky, D. L., & Klein, G. S. Imagery: Effect of a concealed figure in a stimulus. *Science*, 1966, *15*, 837–839.

Efron, R., & Yund, E. W. Dichotic competition of simultaneous tone bursts of different frequency: I. Dissociation of pitch from lateralization and loudness. *Neuropsychologia*, 1974, *12*, 249–256.

Garner, W. R. *The processing of information and structure*. Hillsdale, N.J.: Lawrence Erlbaum Associates, 1974.

Glucksberg, S., & Cowen, G. N., Jr. Memory for non-attended auditory material. *Cognitive Psychology*, 1970, *1*, 149–156.

Green, D. W. The effect of task on the representation of sentences. *Journal of Verbal Learning and Verbal Behavior*, 1975, *14*, 275–283.

Harris, C. S., & Haber, R. W. Selective attention and coding in visual perception. *Journal of Experimental Psychology*, 1963, *65*, 328–333.

Johanssen, G. Visual perception of biological motion and a model for its analysis. *Perception & Psychophysics*, 1973, *14*, 201–211.

Jonides, J., & Gleitman, H. A conceptual category effect in visual search. *Perception & Psychophysics*, 1972, *12*, 457–460.

Julesz, B. *Foundations of Cyclopean perception*. Chicago: University of Chicago Press, 1971.

Julesz, B. Experiments in the visual perception of texture. *Scientific American*, 1975, *232* (4), 34–43.

Kahneman, D. *Attention and effort*. Englewood Cliffs, N.J.: Prentice-Hall, 1973.

Kahneman, D., & Henik, A. Effects of visual grouping on immediate recall. In S. Dornic (Ed.), *Attention and performance VI*. Hillsdale, N.J.: Lawrence Erlbaum Associates, 1977.

Krueger, L. E. Search time in a redundant visual display. *Journal of Experimental Psychology*, 1970, *83*, 391–399.

Krueger, L. E. Familiarity effects in visual information processing. *Psychological Bulletin*, 1975, *82*, 949–974.

Laberge, D. Acquisition of automatic processing in perceptual and associative learning. In P. M. A. Rabbitt & S. Dornic (Eds.), *Attention and performance V*. New York: Academic Press, 1975.

Lawrence, D. H. Two studies of visual search for targets with controlled rates of presentation. *Perception & Psychophysics*, 1971, *10*, 85–89.

Liberman, A. M., Cooper, F., Shankweiler, D. P., & Studdert–Kennedy, M. Perception of the speech code. *Psychological Review*, 1967, *74*, 431–461.

Mattingly, I. G., Liberman, A. M., Syrdal, A. K., & Halwes, T. Discrimination in speech and nonspeech modes. *Cognitive Psychology*, 1971, *2*, 131–157.

McClelland, J. L. Preliminary letter identification in the perception of words and non-words. *Journal of Experimental Psychology: Human Perception and Performance*, 1976, *2*, 80–91.

Meyer, D. E., Schvaneveldt, R. W., & Ruddy, M. G. Loci of contextual effects on visual word recognition. In P. M. A. Rabbitt & S. Dornic (Eds.), *Attention and performance V*. London: Academic Press, 1975.

Morse, P. A., & Snowdon. C. T. An investigation of categorical speech discrimination by rhesus monkeys. *Perception & Psychophysics*, 1975, *17*, 9–16.

Morton, J., Crowder, R. G., & Prussin, H. A. Experiments with the stimulus suffix effect. *Journal of Experimental Psychology*, 1971, *91*, 169–190.

Navon, D. Forest before trees: The precedence of global features in visual information. *Cognitive Psychology*, 1977, *9*, 353−383.

Neisser, U. *Cognitive psychology*. Englewood Cliffs, N.J.: Prentice−Hall, 1967.

Neisser, U. *Cognition and reality*. San Francisco: W. H. Freeman, 1976.

Nisbett, R. E., & Wilson, T. D. Telling more than we can know: Verbal reports on mental processes. *Psychological Review*, 1977, *84*, 231−259.

Olson, R. K., & Attneave, F. What variables produce similarity grouping? *American Journal of Psychology*, 1970, *33*, 1−21.

Pachella, R. G. The interpretation of reaction time in information-processing research. In B. Kantowitz (Ed.), *Human information processing: Tutorials in performance and cognition*. Hillsdale, N.J.: Lawrence Erlbaum Associates, 1974.

Pisoni, D. B., & Lazarus, T. H. Categorical and non-categorical modes of speech perception along the voicing continuum. *Journal of the Accoustical Society of America*, 1974, *55*, 328−333.

Pomerantz, J. R., & Sager, L. C. Asymmetric integrality with dimensions of visual pattern. *Perception & Psychophysics*, 1975, *18*, 460−466.

Posner, M. I., & Mitchell, R. F. Chronometric analysis of classification. *Psychological Review*, 1967, *74*, 392−409.

Potter, M. C. Short-term conceptual memory for pictures. *Journal of Experimental Psychology: Human Learning and Memory*, 1976, *2*, 509−522.

Rand, T. C. Dichotic release from masking for speech. *Journal of the Acoustical Society of America*, 1974, *55*, 678−680.

Savin, H. B., & Bever, T. G. The nonperceptual reality of the phoneme. *Journal of Verbal Learning and Verbal Behavior*, 1970, *9*, 259−302.

Schneider, W., & Shiffrin, R. M. Controlled and automatic human information processing: I. Detection, search and attention. *Psychological Review*, 1977, *84*, 1−66.

Sekuler, R. W., & Nash, D. Speed of size scaling in human vision. *Psychonomic Science*, 1972, *27*, 93−94.

Shallice, T. Dual functions of consciousness. *Psychological Review*, 1972, *79*, 383−393.

Shiffrin, R. M., & Schneider, W. Controlled and automatic human information processing: II. Perceptual learning, automatic attending and a general theory. *Psychological Review*, 1977, *84*, 127−190.

Smith, F. Familiarity of configuration vs. discriminability of features in the visual identification of words. *Psychonomic Science*, 1969, *14*, 261−262.

Smith, F., Lott, D., & Cronnell, B. The effect of type size and case alternation on word identification. *American Journal of Psychology*, 1969, *82*, 248−253.

Sperling, B. The information available in brief visual presentations. *Psychological Monographs*, 1960, *74*, (Whole No. 498).

Sternberg, S. Two operations in character recognition: Some evidence from reaction-time measurements. *Perception & Psychophysics*, 1967, *2*, 43−53.

Sternberg, S. The discovery of processing stages: Extensions of Donder's method. In W. G. Koster (Ed.), *Attention and performance II*. Amsterdam: North Holland, 1969.

Studdert−Kennedy, M., & Shankweiler, D. P. Hemispheric specialisation for speech. *Journal of the Acoustical Society of America*, 1970, *48*, 579−594.

Teichner, W. H., & Krebs, M. J. Laws of visual choice reaction time. *Psychological Review*, 1974, *81*, 75−98.

Townsend, J. T. A note on the identifiability of parallel and serial processes. *Perception & Psychophysics*, 1971, *10*, 161−163.

Treisman, A. M. Focused attention in the perception and retrieval of multidimensional stimuli. *Perception & Psychophysics*, 1977, *22*, 1−11.

Treisman, A. M., & Davies, A. Divided attention to ear and eye. In S. Kornblum (Ed.), *Attention and performance IV*. London: Academic Press, 1973.

Treisman, A. M., Sykes, M., & Gelade, G. Selective attention and stimulus integration. In S. Dornic (Ed.), *Attention and performance VI*. Hillsdale, N.J.: Lawrence Erlbaum Associates, 1977.

Treisman, A. M., & Tuxworth, J. Immediate and delayed recall of sentences after perceptual processing at different levels. *Journal of Verbal Learning and Verbal Behavior*, 1974, *13*, 38–44.

Turvey, M. T. On peripheral and central processes in vision: Inferences for an information-processing analysis of masking with patterned stimuli. *Psychological Review*, 1973, *80*, 1–52.

Warren, R. M., & Warren, R. P. Auditory illusions and confusions. *Scientific American*, 1970, *223*, 30–36.

Weiskrantz, L. Visual capacity in the hemianopic field following a restricted occipital ablation. *Brain*, 1974, *97*, 709–728.

Weisstein, N., & Harris, C. S. Visual detection of line segments: An object-superiority effect. *Science*, 1974, *186*, 752–755.

Wickens, D. D. Encoding categories of words: An empirical approach to meaning. *Psychological Review*, 1970, *77*, 1–15.

Wood, C. C. Auditory and phonetic levels of processing in speech perception: Neurophysiological and information-processing analyses. *Journal of Experimental Psychology: Human Perception and Performance*, 1975, *1*, 3–21.

15

Some General Constraints on Learning and Memory Research

J. D. Bransford, J. J. Franks,
C. D. Morris, and B. S. Stein[1]
Vanderbilt University

It seems safe to assume that no one at the present conference purports to have a complete theory of memory. At the same time, most participants would presumably agree that a great deal of information about memory is currently known. As theorists, we face the challenge of utilizing what is already known in a manner that permits further conceptual development and growth.

Frequently, what is already known simply takes the form of a list of phenomena, variables, etc. Newell (1973) discusses problems with this type of approach; further development becomes equivalent to the construction of larger and larger lists of what is known. An alternate approach is to ask whether currently available information places constraints on the types of questions to be pursued further. Can we begin to differentiate meaningful questions from those that appear less fruitful? The present chapter attempts to identify some general constraints that seem applicable to learning and memory research.

In overview, the present chapter explores questions regarding learning and memory. Almost all studies of memory involve some type of learning or acquisition conditions. They also involve particular types of experimenter-defined criteria at time of test. A major focus of the first section of the present chapter is on acquisition−test relationships. The importance of such relationships seems intuitively obvious, yet their implications are rarely fully explored. For example, contrary to proponents of the levels-of-processing framework (e.g., Craik & Lockhart, 1972; Craik & Tulving, 1975; Lockhart, Craik, & Jacoby, 1976), we argue that the value or "goodness" of particular acquisition activities can be defined only in relation to the nature of the testing context (see also Tulving,

---

[1]All four authors made equal contributions to the present paper; the sequence of authors merely reflects an alphabetical ordering.

Chapter 19, this volume). This relativistic assumption places constraints on the types of claims that seem reasonable. For example, a statement like "deeper, semantic processing produces better memory than shallow, more superficial processing" contains no reference to the nature of the testing context. As such, it illustrates the type of statement we wish to avoid.

The second section of the present chapter discusses relationships between particular to-be-learned inputs and the sets of skills and knowledge currently available to the learner. The ease of acquiring and utilizing particular types of information must be defined relative to the learner's available knowledge and skills. At first glance, this statement may appear to merely paraphrase the levels-of-processing claim that deeper processing leads to better memory. Thus, an "expert" in some area (e.g., chess; see Chase & Simon, 1973; de Groot, 1965) may exhibit better memory performance than a novice, because the former has more knowledge and hence can process appropriate inputs at a "deeper" level. We argue that this usage of the term *deeper* is different from that employed by most proponents of the levels-of-processing framework.

The third section of the paper involves an examination of the concept of "elaboration" as it relates to memory. Our purpose is to illustrate how the general types of constraints developed in the first two sections can clarify the nature of elaboration as a hypothetical memory process.

Section IV extends the application of these constraints beyond the domain of remembering into the more general domains of transfer and learning. In this section the encoding specificity principle as developed by Tulving (Chapter 19, the present volume) is compared to the viewpoint we have termed transfer-appropriate processing (Morris, Bransford, & Franks, 1977). Transfer-appropriate processing is a cover term for a system of general constraints on learning and memory research that we begin developing in the present chapter. We argue that this viewpoint is more general in its applicability than the encoding specificity principle.

I.   RELATIONS BETWEEN ACQUISITION ACTIVITIES AND TYPES OF TESTS

The argument made in the present section is that the "goodness" of particular acquisition activities can be defined only in relation to particular testing contexts. Furthermore, we propose that the potential range of "testing contexts" must be broader than those that simply measure subjects' abilities to remember the precise inputs presented during acquisition. A major reason for learning something is that one can *transfer* to new situations; for example, one can now understand events he or she could not previously understand or can understand "old" events in new and more adequate ways (See Bransford & Franks, 1976; Bransford & Nitsch, in press). From the present perspective, measures of remembering constitute only a subset of potential transfer situations. Indeed, it has been suggested (e.g., Bransford & Franks, 1976) that acquisition activities that facilitate certain types of transfer may not affect or may even *debilitate* one's ability to remember the precise inputs experienced during acquisition. Four types of studies are presented in support of the arguments just summarized.

Investigations of Learning and Subsequent White-Noise Detection

Hannigan (1976) investigated the degree to which certain acquisition experiences facilitate subsequent transfer. Her major test of transfer measured subjects' abilities to detect "novel but appropriate" (relative to what was learned) sentences embedded in white noise. Hannigan's assumption was that certain types of acquisition experiences would help subjects learn "what to listen for" when attempting to detect white noise embedded sentences that were related to their previous learning experiences. She further reasoned that these skills would not necessarily be reflected by measures of recognition memory alone (without white-noise detection) for the sentences experienced during acquisition.

Hannigan compared the effects of three different types of acquisition conditions to a group of *Baseline* subjects who received no acquisition but simply attempted to identify each of the white-noise-embedded test sentences. Table 15.1 illustrates samples of the acquisition inputs presented to the *No-Framework* and *Framework* groups. Both groups heard the same set of acquisition sentences (70 in all). The *No-Framework* subjects simply heard the list of sentences and rated them for "ease of comprehension." The *Framework* subjects heard the same set of acquisition sentences. However, they were first told that the task was to learn about "survival on a previously inhabited but now deserted island." They were therefore asked to rate the comprehensibility of each sentence in terms of the "survival" framework as well as one of each of seven subcategories of survival (some are illustraed in Table 15.1). The subjects in the third acquisition condition (*Framework After*) received the same set of inputs as those in the *No-Framework* condition. However, following acquisition but before the white-noise-detection task, these subjects were told about the survival framework plus the subcategories. They were then given the white-noise-detection test.

Hannigan's results indicate that only subjects in the *Framework* group were able to detect "novel but appropriate" white-noise-embedded sentences significantly better than *Baseline* subjects. These results have been replicated and extended by Lee (1977). Subsequent studies by Hannigan (1976) suggest that measures of recognition memory (without white noise) reveal only slight differences between *Framework* and *No Framework* subjects (note: ceiling effects were not a problem). In short, assumptions about the value of particular acquisition experiences must be defined in relation to the types of testing contexts. Furthermore, situations requiring that subjects recreate the exact inputs presented during acquisition are only a subset of the transfer situations that one may ultimately wish to perform.

TABLE 15.1
Example Sentences from Hannigan (1976).

No-Framework Condition:

The man set up housekeeping in the airplane.
The man threw the curtain over the metal bar.
The man propped the door against the rock wall.
The man thrashed the leaves with his cane.
The man put the chair at the base of the tree.
The man piled the bricks under the oak.
The man opened his briefcase.
The man turned the bell upside down.
The man made a sack out of the sheet.

Framework Condition:

Obtaining a Shelter:

The man set up housekeeping in the airplane.
The man threw the curtain over the metal bar.
The man propped the door against the rock wall.

Reaching for Food on a Branch Above One's Head:

The man thrashed the leaves with his cane.
The man put the chair at the base of the tree.
The man piled the bricks under the oak.

A Container for Carrying Food:

The man opened his briefcase.
The man turned the bell upside down.
The man made a sack out of the sheet.

Investigations of Semantic Versus Rhyme Processing

A series of studies by Morris, Bransford, and Franks (1977) further illustrates the importance of focusing on acquisition–test relationships. A major impetus for these studies derives from experiments conducted by Craik and Tulving (1975).

Craik and Tulving (1975) varied levels of processing (structural, rhyme, or semantic) for a set of acquisition words and then tested recognition memory for those acquisition inputs. Results indicated that semantic processing resulted in better recognition performance than did the more "superficial" (i.e., structural, rhyme) acquisition modes. Morris et al. (1977) repeated Craik and Tulving's (1975) basic procedure using rhyme–versus semantic-orienting tasks and replicated Craik and Tulving's results.

However, consider the nature of the recognition tests used in the previously discussed studies. They tested for recognition of the nominal stimuli, but did they adequately access what was learned given a rhyme-acquisition mode? Many studies (e.g., Bransford & Franks, 1971, 1973) suggest that people are more likely to acquire and remember the abstract invariants characterizing a total set of aquisition stimuli than they are to recognize the precise inputs experienced during acquisition. It seems highly possible that acquisition activities like rhyme processing may also facilitate the acquisition of certain abstractly defined sound patterns. Subjects' abilities to remember the precise acquisition *exemplars* of those abstract patterns may nevertheless be relatively poor.

Morris et al. (1977) tested the latter possibility by presenting half of their subjects with a rhyme-oriented recognition test. The targets on this test were items that rhymed with the initial acquisition items but had never occurred during acquisition. Given this latter test, results indicated that rhyme processing during acquisition produced significantly better performance than semantic processing. This pattern persisted even when subjects received a 24-hour delay between acquisition and test (see Morris et al. for more details and discussion). In short, "superficial" levels of processing led to more adequate performance given certain types of memory tests.

Investigations of Orthographic-Case Versus Semantic Processing

Experiments by Stein (in press) provide further evidence for a relativistic approach to questions regarding the value or "goodness" of particular types of acquisition activities. His subjects were presented with encoding trials that focused their attention on either case (i.e., orthographic) properties or semantic properties of the to-be-learned target words. In the semantic encoding condition, subjects had to determine if each visually presented target word fit appropriately into a sentence frame. In the case encoding trials, subjects had to determine if each target word had a particular letter capitalized. Each subject received a mixed list of these encoding trials followed by a recognition test for the target items exactly as they were presented (with one letter capitalized). Two types of recognition tests were employed.

One group of subjects received a test that required them to discriminate the target item in the context of foils that represented different words that had the same letter capitalized in a similar lexical configuration (semantically oriented test). Another group of subjects received a test that required them to discriminate the target item in the context of foils that represented the same word but with a different letter capitalized (case-oriented test). An interaction between test type and acquisition mode was obtained. Target items encoded in a semantic mode were recognized better than those encoded in a case mode when a semantically oriented recognition test was given. However, when a case-oriented recognition test was given, target items encoded in a case mode were recognized better than those encoded semantically. These results are illustrated in Table 15.2.

TABLE 15.2
Mean Proportion Scores (Experiment 2).[a]

Acquisition Mode	Case-Oriented Test	Semantically Oriented Test
Semantic – Yes	0.284	0.951
Case – Yes	0.528	0.771
Semantic – No	0.292	0.916
Case – No	0.368	0.743

[a]From Stein, in press.

Investigations of Acquisition–Test Relations Within the Semantic Domain

As part of a larger investigation, Morris (in press) demonstrated the importance of examining the relations between acquisition activities and types of test situations when the variables involved all fall within the semantic domain. In simplified form, during acquisition, Morris presented to-be-learned words in either of two semantic contexts (see also Baker & Santa, 1977). One type of acquisition context consisted of presenting items within sentence frames that expressed normatively typical events involving the objects represented by the target words. For example, for a target word *Truck,* a normative context would be "The *TRUCK* was driven down the street." A second type of acquisition context involved sentence frames that expressed relatively novel or atypical events involving the target item. For the target *Truck,* for example, a novel context would be "The *TRUCK* was parked on top of the school."

Morris's design actually involved a number of different test conditions, but for present purposes two general types of test contexts are important. These two test contexts consisted of presenting target items in *new* sentence frames where the new sentence frame was either: (1) the same as the original type of acquisition context; or (2) different from the original context. That is, targets that appeared in normative contexts during acquisition were tested either in new normative contexts (same condition) or in new novel or atypical contexts (different condition). Likewise, targets occurring originally in novel, atypical contexts were tested in either new atypical contexts (same condition) or in new normative contexts (different condition). The new sentence frames chosen as the testing contexts were chosen so that they were *not* paraphrases of the original acquisition sentences. For instance, given the example acquisition sentence frames for *Truck* mentioned above, a new normative testing context would be "The *TRUCK* carried the heavy load," whereas a new atypical testing context would be "The *TRUCK* floated down the river." The subjects' task during test was to respond "yes" or "no" to whether they recognized the target word as having occurred during acquisition.

The pattern of results obtained by Morris nicely supports the present section's arguments for the importance of taking into account acquisition—test relations. The basic finding was that targets presented in test frames that were of the same type as the original acquisition frames (i.e., normative—normative and atypical—atypical acquisition—test combinations) resulted in better target recognition than those conditions where the test frame differed from the acquisition contexts (i.e., the normative—atypical and atypical—normative combinations). In addition, Morris found that the level of recognition performance was approximately equal for the two kinds of same acquisition—test combinations and likewise for the two kinds of different acquisition—test combinations. Overall the results indicate that even for variables like normativity versus novelty—which both fall within the domain of semantic processes—the nature of the conclusions one draws concerning the effects of such variables on memory must take into account the nature of the relations between types of acquisition activities and the types of testing conditions.

Summary of Section I

To summarize, the previously discussed experiments illustrate that statements about the value of particular acquisition activities must include reference to the nature of the testing contexts. This orientation questions assumptions underlying the levels-of-processing framework—for example, that deeper processing leads to better memory than shallower levels of processing. Morris et al. suggest that it might be helpful to replace the concept of levels of processing with one emphasizing *transfer—appropriate processing*. The latter concept focuses attention on relationships between acquisition and test situations. Furthermore, the concept of transfer-appropriate processing does not assume that certain traces are less adequate or durable than others simply because they involved more superficial levels of processing. Indeed, there is considerable evidence that seemingly superficial aspects of encoded inputs can be well retained (e.g., Arbuckle & Katz, 1976; Craik & Kirsner, 1974; Kirsner, 1973; Kolers, Chapter 17, this volume). Overall, the concept of transfer-appropriate processing suggests that superficial levels of processing may sometimes be better than deeper levels of processing for carrying out subsequent cognitive acts.

II. RELATIONS BETWEEN TO-BE-LEARNED INPUTS AND THE LEARNERS' CURRENT KNOWLEDGE AND SKILLS

The data presented in the previous section illustrate the importance of focusing on acquisition—test relationships. The major purpose of the present section is to argue that relationships between to-be-learned inputs and the current state of the learner's skills and knowledge must also be taken into account.

The importance of focusing on relations between particular inputs and the current state of learners' skills and knowledge is revealed by more detailed examination of data from Morris et al. (1977) and Stein (in press). Their data reflect the following pattern: Despite acquisition–test interactions, semantic processing–semantic test conditions result in better performance than either rhyme processing–rhyme test or case processing–case test. Fisher and Craik (1977) report similar patterns of data. They conclude that the superiority of semantic acquisition–semantic test conditions supports the "depth-of-processing" position. According to these authors, relations between acquisition activities and testing contexts may constitute one factor influencing memory, but the hypothesis that semantic processing leads to better memory than nonsemantic processing is assumed to constitute an additional factor. Our position is that the afore-mentioned patterns of data do not reflect the inherent superiority of semantic over nonsemantic processing activities. Instead, we propose that these patterns reflect particular types of relationships between to-be-learned inputs and the current state of the learner's knowledge and skills. The following inter-related arguments are offered in support of this claim.

First, we suggest that the aforementioned superiority of semantic acquisition—semantic test conditions does not constitute an invariant pattern that will hold over all experimental conditions. Indeed, data presented at the present conference (Nelson, Chapter 3, this volume) illustrate conditions under which rhyme acquisition–rhyme test produces performance that is at least equal to semantic acquisition–semantic test. We further predict that situations can be found where rhyme–rhyme conditions (for example) will be superior to semantic–semantic conditions. At present, the latter statement remains as a promissory note. Nevertheless, it performs the function of clarifying potentially different predictions that can help separate "levels of processing" from the present approach.

The second argument against the Fisher and Craik (1977) position involves the role of "expertise" in learning and remembering. For example, Morris et al. (1977) suggest that experienced poets and experts in linguistic dialects, speech perception, etc. may be as efficient at remembering certain types of auditory information as they are at remembering semantically processed information. Similarly, Stein (in press) discusses how the current state of a learner's skills and knowledge can affect the ability to learn and remember particular inputs. An important implication is that most subjects *usually* process items semantically (e.g., they focus on meaning rather than orthography), but semantic processing is not *inherently* superior to more "superficial" levels of processing. As Jenkins (1974) has suggested, an emphasis on the skills and knowledge available to particular learners is not necessarily equivalent to the "levels-of-processing" approach proposed by Craik and Lockhart (1972) and colleagues. The nature of those differences is more fully discussed in the third argument presented hereafter.

As noted in the overview of this chapter, it seems easy to assume that hypotheses about depth of processing are equivalent to those emphasizing the importance of input–learner relationships. The availability of appropriate skills and knowledge seemingly can simply be viewed as a prerequisite for permitting "deeper" processing of the acquisition inputs. Our position is that the latter usage of "depth" is different from that utilized by most proponents of the levels-of-processing view.

Figure 15.1 illustrates two different uses of the term *deeper* processing. Most proponents of the levels-of-processing framework have equated "deep" processing with "semantic" processing. The act of focusing on the *meaning* of inputs (e.g., a word) is assumed to involve semantic (i.e., deep) processing. Focusing on how a word sounds, how it is written, etc. is assumed to involve more superficial levels of processing. In short, "semantic" processing is assumed to covary with the concept of depth. This is illustrated on the vertical dimension of Fig. 15.1.

Figure 15.1 also illustrates an alternative to the assumption that "depth" covaries with "semanticity." This alternative reflects the position adopted here. Given certain knowledge, skills, and purposes, inputs can be meaningful *without* being processed at a "semantic" level. Consider an utterance like "Altitude precedes window" (cf. Bransford, Nitsch, & Franks, 1977). Most people orient toward the meaning of each word and hence have difficulty comprehending the sentence. However, if one realizes that the statement refers to the ordering of words on an alphabetic scale, attention to the spelling patterns of the first and last words (i.e., *a* precedes *w*) facilitates understanding. In short, attention to the

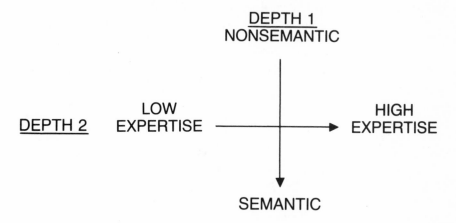

FIG. 15.1.   Two uses of the term *depth*.

semantic aspects of inputs is not necessarily equivalent to the problem of making inputs meaningful. Furthermore, information like brush strokes (on a painting), the sounds of people's voices, handwriting patterns, chess configurations, etc. can become more meaningful as one develops certain types of skills and knowledge (e.g., see Bransford, Nitsch, & Franks, 1977). Note, however, that this type of development is represented along the horizontal (i.e., degree of expertise) rather than vertical (i.e., semantic versus nonsemantic) component of Fig. 15.1.

Summary of Section II

The discussion has emphasized that memory is strongly affected by relations between inputs and the knowledge and skills currently available to learners. However, this position is not equivalent to a view that assumes that appropriate knowledge permits deeper, more semantic levels of processing. From the present perspective, "semanticity" vs. "nonsemanticity" is different from the problem of input–knowledge compatibilities. Statements like "Altitude precedes window" are comprehensible only if one attends to the "nonsemantic" aspects of *altitude* and *window*. In short, the utilization of past knowledge to make inputs *meaningful* is not equivalent to processing their *semantic meanings* (see also Bransford & Johnson, 1973; Bransford & McCarrell, 1975).

A potential advantage of the present emphasis on input–knowledge relationships is that it discourages the assumption that references to the "semanticity" of acquisition processing is sufficient to explain memory performance. A statement like "semantic acquisition–semantic tests are better because of the superiority of semantic processing" does little to further our understanding of learning and memory. By the same token, it is not sufficient to simply assume that memory is a function of the compatibility of input–knowledge relationships. An adequate theory of learning and memory must explain *how* relevant knowledge (whether "semantic" or "nonsemantic") can facilitate one's ability to perform subsequent acts of knowing and remembering. At the same time, such a theory must acknowledge the arguments from the preceeding section; namely that the value of particular acquisition activities is relative to particular testing contexts. Aspects of this problem are discussed in Section III.

III.   TOWARD A MERGING OF GENERAL CONSTRAINTS

Previous data and arguments suggest some general constraints on statements about the nature of learning and memory. First, one cannot make meaningful claims about the value of particular acquisition activities without considering the nature of the testing context. Second, claims about the value of certain types of acquisition–test relationships (e.g., semantic acquisition–semantic test versus nonsemantic — nonsemantic conditions) must include reference to relationships between the to-be-acquired knowledge and skills (e.g., recognizing the orthographic structure of inputs) and the current cognitive state of the learner. As Jenkins (Chapter 20, this volume) notes, every experimental task involves this total set of relationships. They form a context of constraints for conceptualizing patterns of memory results.

The purpose of the present section is to further illustrate the notion of a context of constraints by examining a commonly held assumption; namely, that memory is facilitated by elaboration (e.g., Anderson & Reder, Chapter 18, this volume; Craik & Tulving, 1975; Lockhart, Craik, & Jacoby, 1976). We assume that elaboration is effective only under certain conditions. The search for these conditions involves a search for the broader context of constraints that govern the effectiveness of elaboration. The arguments are elaborated next.

Consider a situation where performance, given semantic acquisition — semantic tests, is strongly influenced by the manner in which the learner's available knowledge is utilized as well as the nature of the testing context. Experiments by Stein (1977) represent a case in point. He presented subjects with a list of 24 acquisition statements (e.g., *A bumper is like a statue; A crab is like a pliers*) that provided frameworks for relating 24 pairs of target words (e.g., *bumper, statue*). One group of subjects was told to rate the statements as good or poor similes. The second group was instructed to compare the target words in each statement with respect to their hardness — softness. The simile-encoding instructions presumably allowed subjects to use their available knowledge and skills to uniquely differentiate the word pair episodes from one another by utilizing a different kind of information in each relationship. In contrast, the "hardness" encoding instructions severely constrained the kind of information or knowledge the subjects could use to uniquely specify each of the word pairs. Note that both types of tasks require a semantic level of analysis; subjects have to assess the meaning of the target words in order to make accurate ratings. Nevertheless, the "hard—soft" task should result in less precise encoded information concerning the individual pairs.

Results indicated that Stein's encoding manipulations had powerful effects on subjects' abilities to recall the second member of each word pair (given the first word as a cue) and to recognize correct word pairs. For example, cued-recall performance for Group I was 59% compared to 21% cued recall for Group II. When results were scored for the subset of acquisition items where subjects said the pair was a good simile (Group I) or was the same on a hardness — softness dimension (Group II), cued-recall performance was 78% for Group I and 36% for Group II. Further experiments by Stein (1977) showed that the encoding manipulations affected only the ability to recreate information about word pairings. Tests of individual item recognition and free recall (scored in terms of number of individual items recalled) revealed no differences between Groups I and II.

Consider how the concept of elaboration might be used to account for the results of Stein's experiment. For subjects in the simile condition, a statement like *A crab is like a pliers* may be elaborated by noting that both are relatively hard objects, have "pincher" or "grasping" potentials, etc. In contrast, subjects in the "hard—soft" condition may only note that both objects are hard. The superiority of Stein's simile-encoding conditions might therefore be attributed to the greater degree of elaboration that occurred at acquisition. Given this position, it is important to note that particular types of elaboration are differentially effective, depending on the subsequent testing environment. For example, subjects in Stein's "hard—soft" condition performed as well as those in the simile condition on *individual word* recognition and recall.

Experiments by Wilson and Bransford (in preparation) provide further evidence for differential effects of elaboration as a function of test situations. All subjects were first exposed to a list of to-be-remembered words and induced to process them semantically. They were then exposed to a second list of words, and different groups were provided with the following orienting tasks for this list: (1) syllable counting; (2) pleasant—unpleasant ratings; (3) intentional learning; (4) recognition instructions. The last-named task simply asked subjects to recognize which of the words on List II were "old" (i.e., had occurred on the first list) and which were "new." Note that some of the words on the second list had actually occurred on the first list; the other words had not. Furthermore, all subjects received the same words on their second list. Only their orienting tasks varied.

Following exposure to the second list, all subjects received an unexpected task: Recall all the words from List II. The question of major interest involved recall of the new items on List II as a function of orienting task. More particularly, how well would subjects in the "recognition" condition do in this task? Presumably, performance on this type of recognition task involves *semantic* processing (e.g., Light & Carter—Sobell, 1970). Nevertheless, subjects performing a recognition task might be expected to engage in a minimal amount of elaboration. What effect would this have on the recall task?

Table 15.3 presents recall data for the new List II items. Subjects performing the "recognition" orienting task performed more poorly than all other groups. Other subsets of subjects were tested on their ability to *recognize* rather than recall the new List II items. Under these conditions, subjects who performed the "recognition" orienting task did as well as the other groups.

The experiments by Stein (1977) and Wilson and Bransford (in preparation) can be interpreted as supporting the importance of "elaboration." However, they also demonstrate that particular types of elaboration are differentially effective depending on the subsequent tasks one wishes to perform (see also Bransford, Nitsch, & Franks, 1977). These results raise questions about the conditions under which elaboration is effective. This issue is more fully discussed next.

TABLE 15.3
Recall Given Various Orienting Tasks.[a]

Orienting Task	New Words Recalled (20 Possible)
Recognition	0.55
Syllable counting	1.75
Pleasantness rating	4.80
Intentional	5.50

[a]From Wilson & Bransford (in preparation).

The experiments by Stein (1977) and Wilson and Bransford (in preparation) suggest that elaboration is especially important for preserving information about relations among items (e.g., performing cued- or free-recall tasks). Note, however, that previous discussion of relation-preserving elaborations has emphasized only the *number* or *quantity* of connections. Thus, it was assumed that subjects in Stein's simile group could have elaborated a statement like *A crab is like a pliers* in terms of "hardness", "pincherness," etc. In contrast, subjects in the hard−soft condition presumably elaborated only in terms of "hardness." Greater numbers of connections between two items might be assumed to improve memory because of the increase in redundancy. We question the adequacy of this "quantity of elaborations" view. Our argument involves two parts.

Consider first an experiment by Bransford, McCarrell, Franks, and Nitsch (1977). They presented subjects with a list of 12 animal similes like *A whale is like a rabbit; A horse is like a spider; A gnat is like a bull;* etc. Following acquisition, subjects were presented with the subject nouns and asked to recall the object nouns. Subjects averaged less than 4 of 12 items correct. A second group of subjects heard similes involving the same set of animals, but the animals were re-paired. For example, they heard *A whale is like an elephant; A horse is like a zebra; A gnat is like a mosquito;* etc. Under these conditions, cued recall averaged 11.5 of 12 items correct. These results could be interpreted in terms of a "quantity-of-elaboration" position. Thus, one might assume that *A horse is like a zebra* can. be elaborated in more ways than *A horse is like a spiker*. Our reason for mentioning this first study is simply to illustrate that similes composed entirely of animals are not *necessarily* difficult to learn.

The crucial aspect of our argument involves a second experiment. The purpose was to devise a condition where a *larger number* of elaborations resulted in poorer cued recall than a condition permitting only minimal elaborative connections per simile. We tried to control subjects' elaborations by explicitly providing elaborative connections for each simile and by presenting the acquisition lists rapidly. Of course, it is impossible to guarantee exact control over subjects' elaborations. We simply did the best we could.

Table 15.4 illustrates nouns and elaborative connections for similes used in the experiment. The "minimal-elaboration" list included "A whale is like a sky-scraper because they are both large"; "A mosquito is like a doctor because they both draw blood"; etc. The "multiple-elaboration" list included "A whale is like a deer because they both eat, move and sleep"; A mosquito is like a raccoon because they both have head, legs, jaws"; etc. An inspection of these two lists (see Table 15.4) suggests the obvious outcome: The minimal-elaboration list produced almost perfect cued-recall performance. Subjects receiving the second list averaged only a few answers correct.

Although not conclusive, these results suggest that the mere quantity of elaboration is not sufficient to permit adequate remembering. Instead, elaboration appears to be effective only given a broader context of constraints. These constraints seem to include the provision that effective acts of elaboration are those that permit a relatively unique respecification of invariant relationships expressed during acquisition. For example, in order to recall what went with "robin," subjects receiving the minimal-elaboration list report recreating the idea of "redness," which then helped them recreate "stoplight" rather than "car," "hot dog," etc. In contrast, subjects receiving the multiple-elaboration list had difficulty even recreating the properties originally mentioned in conjunction with "robin" (e.g., bones, lungs, muscles). However, even if they had been presented with these properties at the time of test, it seems clear that such cues would provide insufficient constraints for respecifying the other members of the simile (i.e., "bear"). Given the acquisition list for the multiple-elaboration condition, elaborations like "bones, lungs, and muscles" (for "robin" — "bear") fail to help people differentiate between "robin—bear," "robin—

TABLE 15.4
Two Types of Elaboration Conditions.

Minimal Elaboration	Multiple Elaboration
whale—skyscraper (large)	whale—deer (eat, move, sleep)
mosquito—doctor (draw blood)	mosquito—raccoon (head, legs, jaws)
robin—stoplight (red)	robin—bear (bones, lungs, muscles)
lamb—blanket (wool)	lamb—snake (breathe, exist, eventually die)
bee—electric razor (buss)	bee—sunfish (eyes, body, mouth)
worm—hot dog (long)	worm—cat (need oxygen, food, appropriate temperature)
elephant—car (trunks)	elephant—wasp (run, hide, make noise)
turtle—soldier (shells)	turtle—dog (walk, swallow, need water)
rabbit—jackhammer (bounce up and down)	rabbit—moose (fur, stomach, ears)
lion—stomach (growl)	lion—seal (skin, heart, nose)
lobster—pliers (pinch)	lobster—frog (reproduce, swim, catch prey)
mouse—door hinge (squeak)	mouse—horse (brain, throat, hair)

deer,'' and other acquisition pairings. In short, a larger number of ''nondiffer-entiating'' elaborations is not necessarily as effective as a smaller number of elaborations that permit a unique respecification of particular invariants encoded during the acquisition task.

Summary of Section III

Discussion has focused on the concept of elaboration. The purpose has been to search for a context of constraints within which effective elaboration occurs. Some of the constraints that determine the effectiveness of elaboration involve the acquisition—test relations and input—available-knowledge relations as discussed in the first two sections of this paper. The experiments by Stein and by Wilson and Bransford demonstrate the importance of the relation between acquisition activities and type of test situations. The elaboration induced by a particular acquisition task can vary in its effectiveness depending on the nature of the test situation (e.g., recall versus recognition).

Stein's work also illustrates constraints on elaboration due to the relation between the to-be-learned input and the learner's available knowledge. Consider Stein's cued-recall results. Presumably, subjects in the ''hard—soft'' condition were limited in the effectiveness of their elaboration due to their lack of a ''hard—soft'' dimension. This was reflected in relatively poor recall. One might expect that the effectiveness of the subjects' elaborations could be enhanced by further learning experiences that provided a more adequate knowledge for differentiating degrees and subaspects of the ''hard—soft'' dimension. However, as indicated by the animal-pair experiments (Table 15.4), any enhanced effectiveness of elaboration due to a more developed knowledge cannot simply be attributed to subjects' abilities to elaborate quantitatively more connections. The overall acquisition—test relations in the animal-pair work put a premium on the uniqueness of relations between items and not on quantity of connections. Thus, both considerations of acquisition—test relations and input—available-knowledge relations seems to constrain the nature of the statements that can be made regarding the effectiveness of elaboration as a memory variable.

The present section's relatively brief excursion into the importance of general constraints for clarifying the effects of elaboration is not, of course, a complete development of a theory of elaborative processes. We have not attempted to cover all the factors that are involved in the various situations and results that have been discussed in terms of elaborative processes. Much more clarification is needed. However, our purpose was more limited. What we hope we have illustrated are some cases where considerations of more general constraints can begin clarifying the varying conditions of effectiveness for hypothetical learning and memory processes such as elaboration.

Before proceeding to Section IV, a brief aside seems to be appropriate regarding the concept of ''uniqueness'' as mentioned in this section. It is important to note that the problem of "uniqueness" being discussed involves *relations among* acquisition inputs, types of tests, and the current knowledge of the subject. Frequently, "uniqueness" is discussed as if it is a property of the inputs per se. For example, experiments by Goldstein and Chance (1971) show that subjects' recognition of particular snowflake patterns is quite poor, despite the fact that each individual snowflake is unique. From the present perspective, the subjects lacked the general knowledge and skills necessary to uniquely encode the individual snowflakes and hence differentiate them from the foil items (other snowflakes). Of course, the degree of differentiation necessary depends on the nature of subsequent tests to be performed. If asked to distinguish a snowflake from foils like triangles, horses, faces, etc., subjects would be expected to perform flawlessly. They can therefore encode the patterns at some level of precision, but not at a level sufficient to distinguish target from foil snowflake patterns. To perform the latter task would presumably involve considerable perceptual learning of snowflake patterns, just as the ability to detect subtle differences in wines involves a refinement of particular types of perceptual skills (e.g., Gibson & Gibson, 1955). This problem of refining one's general skills and knowledge is discussed in Section IV.

IV.   SOME GENERAL CONSTRAINTS ON THE GROWTH OF KNOWLEDGE AND SKILLS

The present section focuses on constraints governing the growth of general skills and knowledge (see also Brown, Chapter 11, this volume; Naus & Halasz, Chapter 12, this volume). We have argued that relations among acquisition activities and tests as well as to-be-learned inputs and the learner's skills and knowledge place constraints on theoretical statements regarding learning and memory. Our concept of "transfer-appropriate processing" is designed to highlight these constraints. In essence, the latter concept assumes that the value of particular acquisition activities must be defined relative to particular testing contexts as well as the current state of the learner's skills and knowledge. At this level, our orientation seems equivalent to Tulving's (Chapter 19, this volume) concept of encoding specificity. The purpose of the present section is to distinguish encoding specificity from the concept of transfer-appropriate processing. The major difference involves the types of learning and memory phenomena that the two positions address.

Most of our previous discussion has focused on the problem of *remembering* previously experienced episodes. It is this problem that is the major focus of the encoding specificity principle. However, we do not equate the general problem of learning with the ability to remember previous experiences. The problem of refining one's general knowledge and skills is not necessarily equivalent to the problem of learning inputs so that they can later be retrieved. Instead, growth involves *learning from* experiences in ways that facilitate subsequent transfer. For example, subjects in the *No-Framework* and *Framework-After* conditions in the previously discussed experiments by Hannigan (1976) and Lee (1977) were able to learn the inputs. However, only subjects in the *Framework* condition were able to *learn from* the inputs in a manner that permitted them to deal with novel examples. What is involved in learning from experiences in a manner that facilitates growth and development? How do we come to understand events that we could not previously understand or to understand old events in new and more adequate ways?

The present issue might be clarified by considering an analogy to the classic Guthrie and Horton (1946) experiments involving cats in a puzzle box. Through a series of trials, cats were repeatedly placed in the same puzzle box. Over trials, the cats became more and more constrained in their responses to the point of exhibiting extremely stereotyped escape responses. Contrast the situation imposed by Guthrie and Horton with a hypothetical condition in which cats are exposed to a wide variety of meaningful (for the cats) escape situations (for example, by varying the puzzle boxes over trials). With increasing experience in variable conditions, one might expect that the cats should become more and more flexibly adept at escaping from new situations. The stereotyped situation is an analogue of most remembering experiments, where the situations and tasks are designed to lead to recreation of previous episodes as accurately as possible. The flexible situation is an analogue of the issue presently being considered, where the goal is to learn to know and act in more adequate ways.

Consider the preceding examples from the perspective of current orientations toward memory, in particular, the principle of encoding specificity (Tulving, Chapter 19, this volume). Tulving argues that memory performance is a joint function of the information encoded at acquisition and the information available at retrieval. Fundamentally, Tulving is concerned with the phenomena of memory, and the encoding specificity principle is oriented toward problems of remembering. The stereotyped response patterns of the cats just mentioned can be discussed within the scope of the encoding specificity principle. The successive trials in the same box can be considered to be a situation that develops increasing overlap between the information encoded (over trials) and the information available for retrieval (at the next trial). The stereotype of response is analogous to very precise remembering, as would be expected on the basis of encoding specificity.

What about the cats exposed to variable situations and the hypothetical increase in their adaptive flexibility when exposed to new situations? We feel that this situation falls outside the usual scope of phenomena addressed by the encoding specificity principle. This situation involves problems of adaptive learning and flexible transfer rather than problems of remembering. The remainder of this section examines the problem of learning from experiences in a manner that permits the growth of flexibly usable knowledge and skills. This problem is examined from the perspective of the general acquisition–test and input–available-knowledge constraints as discussed in the first two sections of the paper. Our purpose is to illustrate that these general constraints have applicability to a broader range of phenomena than just remembering.

The general point we argue is that the acquisition–test relations and input–available-knowledge relations that are optimal for retrieval of previously experienced episodes (i.e., remembering) are not necessarily the same as those optimal for *further refinement* or development of what is already known. Note that a notion of "optimality" also underlies the principle of encoding specificity, although this view is primarily oriented toward remembering. As Tulving states (this volume) " . . . we can say that the probability of successful retrieval of the target event is, when other factors are held constant, a monotonically increasing function of the degree of similarity, or overlap, between information stored and information present at the retrieval [p. 408]."

The present development involves examination of a series of experiments by Nitsch (1977). These experiments employ a series of study and test trials rather than a single acquisition trial followed by a test (which seems to be the more typical procedure in current memory research). Our discussion of general constraints due to acquisition–test relations thus involves sequences of acquisition–test trials and assumes that test experiences themselves contribute to what subjects learn in these situations. Note that the earlier discussion of the development of stereotypy in cats' responses made a similar assumption.

As an initial illustration of our argument, imagine the task of acquiring a set of six new concepts (cf. Nitsch, 1977). Examples might be "crinch" (to offend someone by performing an inappropriate act) and "minge" (to gang up on a person or thing). College students have no trouble understanding these definitions at some level. However, it is possible to gain a much more precise understanding of these concepts. To do so requires a refinement of what one currently understands.

Note that one could receive a number of study trials where the previously experienced definitions were presented and the task was to retrieve the appropriate concept labels. Presentation of the definitions constitutes a respecification of information encoded at acquisition, and subjects can readily learn to use these definitions as retrieval cues for the concept labels (Nitsch, 1977). However, this type of encoding–test relationship does little to help subjects refine their understanding of the concepts. For example, adequate comprehension of the concepts should be reflected in subjects' abilities to identify novel examples of the concepts. Nitsch's (1977) data show that subjects receiving acquisition experiences like those just noted do relatively poorly on this type of transfer task. The acquisition–test relations involved in the aforementioned procedure are adequate for a particular kind of memory test (i.e., retrieval of the concept labels) but are inadequate for a transfer test requiring identification of novel examples. What type of acquisition—test relations would be more optimal for this latter transfer test?

An effective method for helping people further clarify their current level of understanding is to provide examples. Examples can clarify one's understanding of definitions, which in turn constrain the manner in which one understands the examples. Through this *reciprocal* influence of definitions on examples and examples on definitions, one can come to understand in new and more adequate ways (e.g., see Bransford & Franks, 1976; Bransford & Nitsch, 1977, for further discussion). The following discussion further illustrates this argument by considering various uses of examples across a series of study—test trials.

Consider the encoding specificity assumption that accuracy of remembering is a function of degree of overlap between information stored from encoding and information present at retrieval. For example, an acquisition trial involving presentation of six concept names (e.g., *crinch*), definitions (e.g., to offend someone by performing an inappropriate act), and examples (e.g., "The diner failed to leave a tip") can be viewed as forming initial "encoding contexts." Presentation of a retrieval cue like *The diner failed to leave a tip* would define a testing context that overlaps considerably with the initial encoding. According to the principle of encoding specificity, this should provide a better retrieval cue for "crinch" than a cue like *The cowboy did not remove his hat when he went into church*. We agree. Note, however, that the "learning" criterion here is accuracy of retrieving an aspect of a previously encoded episode (e.g., crinch). Given a set of to-be-learned concepts and a series of study—test trials, this learning criterion should be reflected by the number of trials necessary for subjects to achieve perfect scores in cued recall.

An emphasis on the problem of refining one's current level of understanding (e.g., of the concept of "crinch") provides a different perspective on the afore-mentioned situation. A series of test trials using the same cues (e.g., *The diner failed to leave a tip*) will permit accuracy in retrieving the label *crinch*. On the other hand, this series of test trials may do little to help subjects *further clarify* their current understanding of concepts like crinch. In contrast, assume that each test trial involves the presentation of a *different* example of each concept. Given that subjects can relate the test examples to the appropriate concept either on their own or via appropriate feedback, the examples will further clarify current information about the concept, which will in turn constrain their interpretations of the examples. (Note that this "Given . . . " implicitly invokes the input—available-knowledge constraint considered in Section II. This point is discussed later.) Through this reciprocal influence of example on concept and concept on example, subjects can refine their abilities to understand. This increased understanding should be reflected in their abilities to recognize novel examples of concepts. By the same token, subjects in this second condition should experience more difficulty during initial study—test trials than those repeatedly receiving retrieval cues that reinstate the initially encoded information (e.g., where a cue like *The diner failed to leave a tip* is the cue for "crinch" across the total set of study–test trials). This expectation is congruent with the encoding specificity principle, since in comparison with the same example condition, the use of different examples over trials will minimize the overlap between information available at retrieval and previously encoded information. However, the ability to retrieve a concept name or definition (for example) is no guarantee that subjects understand the to-be-learned concepts in a manner sufficient to perform well on subsequent transfer tests (e.g., to recognize novel examples of the concepts). In short, acquisition–test relations that facilitate accuracy of retrieval are not necessarily equivalent to those that permit the types of refinements in understanding that facilitate subsequent transfer. Recent experiments by Nitsch (1977) support the arguments just presented.

Table 15.5 (cf. Nitsch, 1977) illustrates two sets of examples that could be presented for the concept *crinch*. One set, the "same-context examples," involves a restricted contextual domain for each concept (i.e., all "crinch" examples involve waitresses in restaurants). In contrast, the "varied-context examples" involve a variety of contextual domains for each concept to be learned.

Imagine a situation where subjects are initially introduced to concept definitions plus some examples. On subsequent trials, they are presented with examples and asked to retrieve the correct concept (e.g., *crinch, minge*). As already noted, a situation involving a high degree of encoding–test overlap would involve the presentation of a particular acquisition example for each concept and then a representation of these same examples as retrieval cues (e.g., for the concept name) for a number of study–test trials. An intermediate degree of encoding–test overlap would involve varying the particular examples across

TABLE 15.5
Two Sets of Examples for "Crinch."[a]

Same-Context Examples

The diner failed to leave a tip.
The man argued about the prices of the menu.
The customer deliberately knocked the ketchup on the floor.
The man complained because the waitress was too slow.

Varied-Context Examples

The cowboy did not remove his hat when he went into church.
The spectator at the dog races jumped up on his seat and blocked the view of the people seated behind him.
The customer flicked cigarette ashes on the new refinished antique chest.
The man complained because the waitress was too slow.

---

[a]From Nitsch (1977).

study—test trials, but keeping the general context invariant for all examples of each concept. This is illustrated by the "same-context" examples in Table 15.5. In the "varied-context" condition, each successive example of a concept occurs in a different contextual setting. This condition represents a relatively lower degree of encoding—test overlap across study—test trials than does the "same-context" condition.

Nitsch (1977) did not explicitly investigate the "high encoding—test overlap" involving the same example for each concept over trials. Nevertheless, her data for the "same-context" versus "varied-context" conditions (see Table 15.5) support the arguments made (see also Battig, Chapter 2, this volume). Greater degrees of encoding—test overlap (Nitsch's "same-context" condition) led to more efficient initial learning, where "learning" refers to the accuracy of retrieving appropriate concept labels. However, once Nitsch's subjects from both conditions had reached an initial acquisition criterion, those in the "varied-context" condition performed much more accurately on the transfer test (including the ability to recognize novel examples of concepts in *new contexts* of application). The encoding specificity principle therefore appears to characterize factors influencing one's abilities to recreate previously experienced episodes. However, it doesn't address the problem of characterizing encoding—test relationships that facilitate refinements in understanding. Thus, high degrees of encoding—test overlap may facilitate accuracy of retrieving previously experienced episodes. However, the same degrees of encoding—test overlap are not necessarily most beneficial for helping one learn to understand in new and more adequate ways.

Note, however, that acquisition—test conditions optimal for subsequent transfer are not simply the converse of those that facilitate precise retrieval. A test situation that is too far removed from the learner's knowledge base will result in confusion rather than contributing to adaptive growth. Nitsch's studies were designed so that subjects at all phases of the experiments had sufficient available knowledge to at least minimally comprehend the examples and relate them to the appropriate concept labels. Thus, in addition to relations between acquisition and test activities, the relation between inputs and learners' available skills and knowledge places general constraints on processes of growth.

If growth is a function of input—knowledge as well as acquisition—test relationships, one should be able to consider both types of constraints simultaneously. An example is provided by a further experiment by Nitsch (1977). Her goal was to design a series of acquisition—test experiences that facilitate initial learning *as well as* transfer to novel examples. She did this by designing a "hybrid" procedure that divided the acquisition process into two parts. Nitsch first exposed subjects to study—test trials involving same-context examples. The purpose was to take advantage of the findings from the previous experiments that showed that given the average subject's available knowledge, same-context examples facilitated initial learning of the concepts. Once subjects had acquired a firm, contextualized basis for understanding the concepts (i.e., had refined their available knowledge), she exposed them to new varied-context examples. These subjects were not only easily able to deal with varied acquisition items, but exhibited extremely flexible transfer as well.

Summary of Section IV

The discussion in this section has focused on the importance of general constraints that apply to a broader range of phenomena than merely the processes involved in remembering. We have argued that constraints like acquisition−test relations and input−available-knowledge relations can also aid in clarifying learning and transfer processes and the relation between these phenomena and memory phenomena. Most of the discussion has been concerned with illustrating how various types of acquisition activities (e.g., Nitsch's same-context versus variable-context conditions) can be differentially effective in promoting later performance on different types of test situations (e.g., remembering versus further refinement of one's knowledge). In general, it was indicated that the kinds of acquisition−test relations that effectively facilitate learning and transfer to new situations are not necessarily equivalent to those that optimize remembering of previously encoded episodes. An experience (e.g., a test) that maximally overlaps with previous encodings may do little to help further refine one's current level of understanding. However, relations between new inputs and the learner's available skills and knowledge also place constraints on growth (e.g., Nitsch's "hybrid" acquisition procedure).

The encoding specificity principle has been proposed as an orientation that emphasizes the importance of considering the relations between acquisition activities and test situations. Our present position agrees with the encoding specificity principle as a fruitful general constraint that can aid in clarifying research on remembering. However, from a broader perspective in which tests of remembering are only a subset of the possible domain of transfer tasks, we see encoding specificity as a specialized form of the more general view that we have termed "transfer-appropriate processing." Transfer-appropriate processing refers to the framework of general constraints on learning and memory research that the present paper begins to develop. Nitsch's hybrid procedure utilizing "same-context" followed by "varied-context" acquisition examples represents an attempt to optimize initial learning as well as subsequent transfer. It involved attention to relations among acquisition and tests as well as among particular inputs and the momentary state of the learners' knowledge and skills.

If the afore-mentioned sets of relations form a context of constraint governing growth and development, one might examine other research domains and expect to find patterns of acquisition that are similar to those illustrated by Nitsch's hybrid condition. Recent research on language acquisition represents a case in point. For example, there is evidence that children first demonstrate the ability to understand and produce particular concepts and sentences in highly specific situations (e.g., Bloom 1974; Bloom, Hood, & Lightbown, 1974; Chapman, 1977; Nelson, 1977). Furthermore, there is evidence that newly acquired linguistic constructions take place in the context of highly familiar content words (especially verbs) that provide a basis for new development (e.g., Bloom, Hood & Lightbown, 1974). The search for abstract constraints that characterize general patterns of growth and development appears to be an important one for theorists of learning and memory to pursue.

ACKNOWLEDGMENT

This paper was supported in part by NSF Grant # BNS77-077248 to J. D. Bransford and J. J. Franks.

REFERENCES

Arbuckle, T. Y., & Katz, W. A. Structure of memory traces following semantic and nonsemantic orientation tasks in incidental learning. *Journal of Experimental Psychology: Human Learning and Memory*, 1976, 2, 362–369.

Baker, L., & Santa, J. Semantic Integration and Context. *Memory and Cognition*, 1977, 5, 151–154.

Bloom, L. Talking, understanding, and thinking. In R. L. Schiefelbusch & C. L. Lloyd (Eds.), *Language perspectives: Acquisition, retardation, and intervention*. Baltimore: University Park Press, 1974.

Bloom, L., Hood, L., & Lightbown, P. Imitation in language development: If, when, and why. *Cognitive Psychology*, 1974, 6, 380–420.

Bransford, J. D., & Franks, J. J. The abstraction of linguistic ideas. *Cognitive Psychology*, 1971, 2, 331–350.

Bransford, J. D., & Franks, J. J. The abstraction of linguistic ideas: A review. *Cognition: International Journal of Cognitive Psychology*, 1973, 1, 211–249.

Bransford, J. D., & Franks, J. J. Toward a framework for understanding learning. In G. H. Bower (Ed.), *The psychology of learning and motivation*. New York: Academic Press, 1976.

Bransford, J. D., & Johnson, M. K. Consideration of some problems of comprehension. In W. Chase (Ed.), *Visual information processing*. New York: Academic Press, 1973.

Bransford, J. D., & McCarrell, N. W. A sketch of a cognitive approach to comprehension: Some thoughts about understanding what it means to comprehend. In W. Weimer & D. Palermo (Eds.), *Cognition and the symbolic processes*. Hillsdale, N.J.: Lawrence Erlbaum Associates, 1975.

Bransford, J. D., McCarrell, N. S., Franks, J. J., & Nitsch, K. E. Toward unexplaining memory. In R. E. Shaw & J. D. Bransford (Eds.), *Perceiving, acting and knowing: Toward an ecological psychology*. Hillsdale, N.J.: Lawrence Erlbaum Associates, 1977.

Bransford, J. D., & Nitsch, K. E. Coming to understand things we could not previously understand. In J. F. Kavanagh & W. P. Strange (Eds.), *Speech and language in the laboratory, school, and clinic*. Cambridge, Mass.: MIT Press, in press.

Bransford, J. D., Nitsch, K. E., & Franks, J. J. Schooling and the facilitation of knowing. In R. C. Anderson, R. J. Spiro, & W. E. Montague (Eds.), *Schooling and the acquisition of knowledge*. Hillsdale, N.J.: Lawrence Erlbaum Associates, 1977.

Chapman, R. Comprehension strategies in children. In J. F. Kavanagh & W. Strange (Eds.), *Speech and language in the laboratory, school, and clinic*. Cambridge, Mass.: M.I.T. Press, in press.

Chase, W. G., & Simon, H. A. The mind's eye in chess. In W. G. Chase (Ed.), *Visual information processing*. New York: Academic Press, 1973.

Craik, F. I. M., & Kirsner, K. The effect of a speaker's voice on word recognition. *Quarterly Journal of Experimental Psychology*, 1974, *26*, 274–284.

Craik, F. I. M., & Lockhart, R. S. Levels of processing: A framework for memory research. *Journal of Verbal Learning and Verbal Behavior*, 1972, *11*, 671–684.

Craik, F. I. M., & Tulving, E. Depth of processing and the retention of words in episodic memory. *Journal of Experimental Psychology: General*, 1975, *104*, 268–294.

de Groot, A. B. *Thought and choice in chess*. The Hague: Mouton, 1965.

Fisher, R. P., & Craik, F. I. M. The interaction between encoding and retrieval operations in cued recall. *Journal of Experimental Psychology: Human Learning and Memory*, 1977, *3*, 701–711.

Gibson, J. J., & Gibson, E. J. Perceptual learning: Differentiation or enrichment? *Psychological Review*, 1955, *62*, 32–41.

Goldstein, A. G., & Chance, J. E. Visual recognition memory for complex configurations. *Perception & Psychophysics*, 1971, *9*, 237–241.

Guthrie, E. R., & Horton, G. P. *Cats in a puzzle box*. New York: Holt, 1946.

Hannigan, M. L. *The effects of frameworks on sentence perception and memory*. Unpublished doctoral dissertation, Vanderbilt University, 1976.

Jenkins, J. J. Can we have a theory of meaningful memory? In R. L. Solso (Ed.), Theories in cognitive psychology: The Loyola Symposium. Hillsdale, N.J.: Lawrence Erlbaum Associates, 1974.

Kirsner, K. An analysis of the visual component in recognition memory for verbal stimuli. *Memory & Cognition*, 1973, *1*, 449–453.

Lee, T. S. *The effects of specific memory and frameworks on sentence perception*. Unpublished manuscript, Vanderbilt University, 1977.

Light, L. L., & Carter–Sobell, L. Effects of changed semantic context on recognition memory. *Journal of Verbal Learning and Verbal Behavior*, 1970, *9*, 1–11.

Lockhart, R. S., Craik, F. I. M., & Jacoby, L. L. Depth of processing, recognition and recall. In J. Brown (Ed.), *Recognition and recall*. London: Wiley, 1976.

Morris, C. D. Transfer appropriate processing between different encoding dimensions. Ph.D. dissertation, Vanderbilt University, 1977.

Morris, C. D., Bransford, J. D., & Franks, J. J. Levels of processing versus transfer appropriate processing. *Journal of Verbal Learning and Verbal Behavior*, 1977, *16*, 519–533.

Nelson, K. Cognitive development and the acquisition of concepts. In R. C. Anderson, R. J. Spiro, & W. E. Montague (Eds.), *Schooling and the acquisition of knowledge*. Hillsdale, N.J.: Lawrence Erlbaum Associates, 1977.

Newell, A. You can't play 20 questions with nature and win. In W. G. Chase (Ed.), *Visual information processing*. New York: Academic Press, 1973.

Nitsch, K. E. *Structuring decontextualized forms of knowledge*. Ph.D. dissertation, Vanderbilt University, 1977.

Stein, B. S. *Depth of processing reexamined: The effects of the precision of encoding and test appropriateness*. Journal of Verbal Learning and Verbal Behavior, in press.

Stein, B. S. The effects of cue–target uniqueness on cued-recall performance. *Memory & Cognition*, 1977, *5*, 319–322.

16

Levels of Processing and Levels of Explanation: Discussion of the Papers by Treisman and Bransford, Franks, Morris, and Stein

Alan Baddeley
Medical Research Council, Applied Psychology Unit,
Cambridge, England

Perhaps the most striking characteristic of the two papers I have been invited to discuss is their range. Although the theme in each case is broadly that of the relationship between levels of processing and perception, they range from Anne Treisman's analysis of the use of the concept of levels in recent studies of perception and pattern recognition to the application of processing models to the development of an understanding of learning. It is clear that the two papers represent fundamentally different approaches, and I would like in this brief discussion to highlight some of these differences.

I would like to begin by considering the aims implicit in the original formulation of the levels-of-processing approach, to say a little about how these have developed over recent years, and to describe some misgivings about this development. Craik and Lockhart's original (1972) paper involved explanations at two rather different levels. On one hand it proposed a general principle, that deeper processing led to better retention, whereas on the other it attempted to support this through the specification of a number of more detailed processes, such as the various coding and retrieval strategies assumed to be responsible for both positive and negative recency effects in free recall. Any adequate explanation of human memory would clearly require both general principles and specific processes, and the attempt of the original Craik and Lockhart approach to operate at both levels represent one of its more attractive features. Unfortunately, however, in recent years the balance seems to have shifted towards paying more and more attention to a search for global principles and less and less to processes and mechanisms. This probably stems from the tendency of recent experimental work in the levels-of-processing tradition to ignore the primary memory component of the original framework in favor of experiments on the role of

355

coding in long-term memory. Indeed this tendency is so marked that Craik and Lockhart are often presented as having a unitary rather than a dichotomous view of memory (e.g., Postman 1975). My impression from the present workshop is that this trend is becoming even stronger, with levels of processing moving close to such concepts as the encoding specificity principle and to a reliance on such plausible but vague concepts as "distinctiveness" and "elaboration."

Consider, for example, the concept of distinctiveness. It has a strong resemblance to the concept of similarity, which formed the workhorse of nearly all attempts to explain human learning and memory emanating from the sterile functionalist approach that dominated American studies of human learning for so many years. Clearly, similarity is an important concept, and as such it implies that discriminability also is important. It is, however, likely to prove rather slippery, since it is far from obvious exactly how one would measure the discriminability of a set of memory traces. That in itself is not of course an objection to the concept, but I must admit to a sneaking fear that the sticky problem of measuring discriminability may be shelved while continuing to use discriminability as an explanatory "principle." This is what appears to have happened in the case of the encoding specificity hypothesis, which—having run into a number of difficulties in its original relatively clearly specified form—has been elevated into an untestable "principle." (See Baddeley, 1976, pp. 292– 299 for a further discussion of this.) I am, then, somewhat prejudiced against the search for "principles," particularly when these bear a close resemblance to the "principles" that dominated verbal learning in the 1940s and 50s. However, it is possible that I am being unduly pessimistic.

Underlying Craik and Lockhart's original levels-of-processing paper was an approach to perception that was perhaps represented most clearly by the work of Anne Treisman. The approach assumed a hierarchical sequence of information-processing stages, and it was this hierarchy that Craik and Lockhart suggested was associated with memory-trace durability. It is therefore particularly appropriate to have Treisman's very scholarly account of the subsequent development of the concept of levels within the general area of perception and pattern recognition. It is very clear from her account that the original concept of a chain of successive stages is a gross oversimplification. Clearly, a range of stages and processes has been identified; but their interrelationship is far from simple, and in most cases the necessary experiments to explore their interaction have not been adequately carried out. She does, however, make a strong case for the continued fruitfulness of the attempt to understand the underlying processes, despite their complexity. Her own work on memory for conjunctions is particularly intriguing and suggests some interesting parallels with the old and knotty problem of item and order information in STM.

I would like to supplement Anne Treisman's systematic survey with one further illustration taken from an elegant series of experiments by Marcel (Marcel, 1976; Marcel & Patterson, in press) on the tachistoscopic perception of individual words. Subjects were required to read words that were presented briefly and followed by a masking pattern. On a number of occasions, Marcel noticed that subjects produced intrusions that were semantically related to the appropriate word but that were visually quite dissimilar (e.g., *king* for *queen; red* for *yellow*), suggesting that semantic information was available and was overriding the influence of the visual stimulus. A second experiment explored this further, using a technique pioneered by Wickens, Shearer, and Eggemeier (1971) in which a word is presented, followed by a pattern mask, which in turn is followed by a two-alternative forced-choice test. This requires the subject to select which of two words is most similar to the original, either orthographically in one case or semantically in another. In a third condition, the subject was simply required to say whether or not a word had been presented. For each of these procedures, the delay between the presentation of the word and onset of the mask was systematically reduced. When this delay was long, performance on all three criteria was perfect; as the mask was moved systematically closer to the word, a point appeared in each case where performance dropped to a chance level, indicating that information of that type was no longer available to the subject. Contrary to what one might intuitively expect, Marcel found that the first type of information to become unavailable was that of whether or not any word had been present, followed by evidence on its visual properties, and finally by evidence of its semantic characteristics. In short, at a point where subjects were guessing at a chance level as to whether or not a word occurred, they were nevertheless showing clear evidence that they had processed it semantically.

Although this pattern of results was on the whole very clear, there was a subgroup of subjects who, very reasonably, were reluctant to make "guesses" about the meaning of a word that they felt was not there. This type of subject tended not to show the effect. A third experiment was therefore carried out in which this problem was avoided by using the lexical decision task. This requires the subject to decide whether a string of letters constitutes an English word or not and has been shown by Meyer, Schvaneveldt, and Ruddy (1975) to be sensitive to semantic priming. Hence, a subject will be faster at deciding that a word such as *butter* is a real word if it has been immediately preceded by a semantically related word, *bread*. This technique was modified by masking the priming word and then looking for evidence of semantic processing in the time taken to respond to the subsequent associate. Note that this allows the semantic processing of the masked word to be reflected, but does not require the subject to report its characteristics directly. In this third study, it was found that semantic priming was unaffected by masking, despite the fact that the subject's ability to judge whether or not a priming word had been presented was at chance level.

What are the implications of these results? They do not of course show that semantic information can be accessed independent of visual information, but they do imply that a conscious percept is not necessary for the semantic processing of verbal material. In this respect, they complement a wide range of studies on patients who have become dyslexic as a result of brain damange and who may be capable of understanding the meaning of a word while being quite unable to process it phonologically (Marshall & Newcombe, 1973; Patterson & Marcel, 1977); Shallice & Warrington, 1975). As such, these results are inconsistent with the simple sequential view of perception implied by the original Craik and Lockhart paper, whereby an attentional primary memory system transforms information from a simple visual form through a phonological code into a semantic interpretation. It implies that phonemic coding may occur at a *later* stage than the apparently deeper "semantic coding," a conclusion also reached by a number of recent studies on phonological coding in reading (Baddeley, in press; Kleiman, 1975).

In conclusion, it is becoming increasingly clear that the processes underlying perception and pattern recognition are not adequately represented by a simple hierarchy of sequential stages. The system is clearly a much richer and more interactive one than that assumed by the original concept of levels of processing. However, as Anne Treisman points out and illustrates with her own work, the problems are difficult, but by no means intractable, and their implications for the understanding of human memory continue to be crucial.

Whereas Treisman's paper is concerned with demonstrating that a single fixed sequence of levels can no longer account for the data in the area of perception, Bransford and his colleagues demonstrate a parallel series of shortcomings when the concept is applied to learning. They first point out that the claim that deeper processing leads to greater memory-trace durability was based on a series of experiments that used a very limited range of techniques for measuring retention. They go on to show that method of testing is crucial; apparently, "shallow" processing based on the phonemic characteristics of material or the case of the constituent letters may lead to better retention than semantic processing, given an appropriate test procedure. Consequently, an adequate account of human memory must specify not only the method of encoding, but also the procedures whereby learning is subsequently tested. A third crucial factor is the expertise of the learner, which again is not specified in the original levels-of-processing framework. Bransford, Franks, Morris, and Stein are clearly sympathetic to some of the later developments in levels of processing and also provide evidence for the importance of elaboration, particularly for learning the relations between material. However, they point out very clearly that quantity of elaboration is less crucial than the uniqueness of the specified relationship. Their concept of transfer-appropriate processing has some similarities with Tulvings' encoding specificity principle in emphasizing the importance of matching the conditions at retrieval to those operating during initial learning. However, transfer-appropriate processing seems to be a much broader concept, which is concerned not only with the recollection of specific episodes but also with generalization and understanding.

Bransford et al.'s paper is particularly welcome, because it manages to combine a series of ingenious and cogent experiments on current theoretical issues with a broad approach to human learning and memory that seems to offer some promise of developing into a usable theory of human learning having applications outside the narrow confines of the laboratory. I must confess, however, that I am a little worried at the concept of transfer-appropriate processing; it has a very real strength in suggesting that one should look hard at the way in which one tests for learning; and in the hands of Bransford and his colleagues, it has clearly produced a range of exciting new experimental techniques and some real theoretical progress. However, there is more than a suggestion of circularity about it. How does one know what kind of processing is appropriate for what kind of transfer? One hopes that a series of general principles will emerge, but there is a danger that in less skillful hands, the concept of transfer-appropriate processing may turn into a pretext for generating an interminable series of "suck it and see" experiments involving the endless permutation of processing and retrieval strategies. However, it has clearly not had this effect on John Bransford, so let us hope that it will provide an equally stimulating and productive concept for the rest of us.

Where then does this leave levels of processing? My overall impression is that the original concept has been overtaken by events. The concept of levels has proved to be an oversimplification. The processes suggested in the original paper have shown little development, although the general concept that memory and information processing are two sides of the same coin will, I think, continue to be fruitful. Although it was not featured in the present workshop to any very great extent, I myself believe that closer analysis of the underlying processes is both tractable and fruitful. For example, I myself find that a "working-memory" concept, not too dissimilar from Craik and Lockhart's "primary memory," provides a useful tool for examining a range of cognitive behavior from reasoning (Hitch & Baddeley, 1976) to reading (Baddeley, in press) and arithmetic (Hitch, 1977). I am personally less optimistic about the search for general principles of memory. In particular, I worry about both the testability and usefulness of some of the concepts that seem to be replacing levels. I can only hope that my fears will prove unfounded.

REFERENCES

Baddeley, A. D. *The psychology of memory.* New York: Basic Books, 1976.

Baddeley, A. D. Working memory and reading. In P. A. Kolers, M. E. Wrolstad, & H. Bouma (Eds.), *The proceedings of the conference on the processing of visible language, Eindhoven, 1978.* City: Publisher, in press.

Craik, F. I. M., & Lockhart, R. S. Levels of processing: A framework for memory research. *Journal of Verbal Learning and Verbal Behavior,* 1972, *11*, 671–684.

Hitch, G. J. Mental arithmetic: Short-term storage and information processing in a cognitive skill. In A. M. Lesgold, J. W. Pellegrino, J. W. Fokkema, & R. Glaser (Eds.), *Cognitive psychology and instruction.* New York: Plenum, in press.

Hitch, G. J., & Baddeley, A. D. Verbal reasoning and working memory. *Quarterly Journal of Experimental Psychology,* 1976, *28,* 603–621.

Kleiman, G. M. Speech recoding in reading. *Journal of Verbal Learning and Verbal Behavior,* 1975, *24,* 323–339.

Marcel, A. J. *Unconscious reading: Experiments on people who do not know that they are reading.* Paper presented to the British Association for the Advancement of Science, Lancaster, 1976.

Marcel, A. J., & Patterson, K. E. Word recognition and production: Reciprocity in clinical and normal studies. In J. Requin (Ed.), *Attention and performance VII.* Hillsdale, N.J.: Lawrence Erlbaum Associates, in press.

Marshall, J. C., & Newcombe, F. Patterns of paralexia: A psycholinguistic approach. *Journal of Psycholinguistic Research,* 1973, *2,* 175–199.

Meyer, D. E., Schvaneveldt, R. W., & Ruddy, M. G. Loci of contextual effects of visual word recognition. In P. M. A. Rabbitt & S. Dornic (Eds.), *Attention and performance V.* New York: Academic Press, 1975.

Patterson, K. E., & Marcel, A. J. Aphasia, dyslexia and the phonological coding of written words. *Quarterly Journal of Experimental Psychology,* 1977, *29,* 307–318.

Postman, L. Verbal learning and memory. *Annual Review of Psychology,* 1975, *26,* 291–335.

Shallice, T., & Warrington, E. K. Word recognition in a phonemic dyslexic patient. *Quarterly Journal of Experimental Psychology,* 1975, *27,* 187–199.

Wickens, D. D., Shearer, W., & Eggemeier, T. *Prerecognition processing of meaningful verbal materials: An approach to successive multiple encoding.* Paper presented to the Midwestern Psychological Association, Detroit, 1971.

VI

THEORETICAL
ALTERNATIVES

17

A Pattern-Analyzing Basis of Recognition

Paul A. Kolers
University of Toronto

The dominating notion underlying the levels-of-processing proposal of Craik and Lockhart (1972) is that the properties of a message or "word event" are extracted in a sequence of analytical operations. These are sometimes spoken of in terms of levels (yielding the metaphor of "depth of processing") and sometimes in terms of domains. Others more qualified than I as students of memory have described the virtues of this view, compared to the previously popular stage theories of memory. In the earlier view, memory was thought of as a number of places, usually defined by the number of items each contained or the duration of time for which items could be recalled—primary and secondary; or short-, medium-, and long-term, and so on. The superficial features of object appearance were said to be in short-term or primary memory, whereas more meaningful properties were in long-term or secondary memory, extracted from the superficial appearance usually by means of a linguistic encoding. How the smell of a flower, the sound of a quartet, or other nonlinguistic experiences were recognized and recalled was often a problem for those theories.

The levels-of-processing metaphor rejected the proposal of kinds of memory and substituted for it the idea of kinds of analysis, but in other respects it retained the fundamentally serial nature of the preceding model. Indeed the very idea of *levels* was that properties of a stimulus fell into a natural hierarchy or could be ordered, that the more superficial properties were extracted first and more profound properties were extracted later as the representation of the stimulus "flowed through" the nervous system. Hence the levels notion is still a serial-processing theory of the inflow of information, structurally identical in certain important respects to the previous theory of place, with kind of analysis substituted for kind of memory. The idea has been acknowledged to be inadequate as a theory of memory on several grounds (Craik & Tulving, 1975). In current views, the idea of levels has been modified out of all recognition, and the notion of parellelism that I suggested previously (Kolers, 1973) has been substituted. The new version is largely a theory that assumes that remembering occurs by virtue of the list of features that the person has made of the object to be remembered, including not only features of name and occasion, but also the list of analytical operations that the person directed at the stimulus; I show later why I believe that this is not a helpful advance.

About the time that Craik and Lockhart were developing their ideas, I became interested in aspects of word and sentence recognition as part of the problem of understanding how reading goes forward (Kolers, 1970). In the cause of the work, I was forced to reconsider some earlier research I had carried out on the roles of semantic and graphemic analysis in word recognition (Kolers, 1966a, 1966b). This led me to a series of experiments whose conclusions are in some ways similar to and in other ways quite different from the levels-of-processing notion. The similarity is largely in the emphasis on analysis and operations rather than on place as the basis of memory; the differences are many. I first review some of the experiments and then describe some of their implications.

CLASSIFYING SENTENCES

The experiments have all been carried out using spatially transformed text, examples of which are illustrated in Fig. 17.1. I used these texts because I wanted to work with skilled readers of English and with natural language stimuli that were not, however, wholly familiar. Normal text is processed so readily by the skilled reader as to make it quite difficult for the experimenter to discern the constituents of the reading process. Spatially transformed text preserves all of the properties of normal text except its graphemic familiarity. Making the material graphemically unfamiliar elicits some interesting aspects of performance.

The main question concerns the nature of reading. The standard wisdom holds that reading, like listening, goes forward by means of a two-stage process: In reading, an initial apprehension of the printed matter is held in some sort of iconic memory, short-term store, or the like for a brief interval; then its semantic features are extracted, recoded, and stored. I have referred to this as the pearl-in-the-oyster theory: The system works its way through the difficulties of the external wrappings to get to the pearl of meaning, discards the wrappings, and retains the pearl. The stored representation might be a feature list, a "deep-structure" or similar propositional abstraction, or an image or other pictorial transformation.

It is easy to show that this sort of two-stage theory is incomplete. People sometimes remember where on a page they have read something, the language in which they read it, the color of the book's binding, or other contingencies of

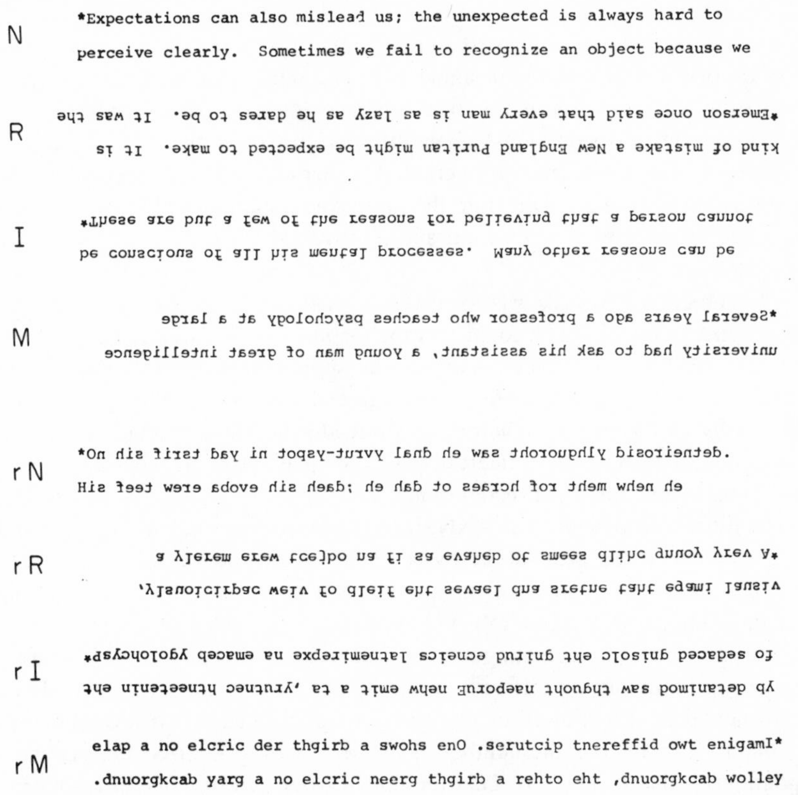

N   *Expectations can also mislead us; the unexpected is always hard to
    perceive clearly. Sometimes we fail to recognize an object because we

R   *Emerson once said that every man is as lazy as he dares to be. It was the
    kind of mistake a New England Puritan might be expected to make. It is

I   *There are but a few of the reasons for believing that a person cannot
    be conscious of all his mental processes. Many other reasons can be

M   *Several years ago a professor who teaches psychology at a large
    university had to ask his assistant, a young man of great intelligence

r N *On his first day in introductory laboratory he was thoroughly disoriented.
    His feet were sore from his dash; he had to wear test his

r R *A very young draft sees it as an obvious of sheer gritty youngster a
    visual image that leaves the eager and stares that seems immaturely,

r I *psychology's amaze na latemperate sotong during the unto seades
    the tenth youth ca a emit te hew burdouen thought was detaining by

r M *Imagine two different pictures. One shows a bright red circle on a pale
    yellow background, the other a bright green circle on a gray background.

FIG. 17.1.   Some examples of spatially transformed text. (From Kolers, 1974.)

appearance that, according to the theory, should not be in long-term memory (Kolers, 1974a). An explicit test of the role of graphemic encoding was carried out in an experiment in which college students first read some sentences and then read them and some others, indicating on the second reading which sentences were reread and which were new. Typography was an important variable in the design (Kolers & Ostry, 1974).

On the first reading, 30 sentences appeared in normal orientation (N) and another 30 appeared inverted (I), illustrated in Fig. 17.1. All the sentences were taken from a single book, sampled from many different pages of text. The reading was carried out under instruction to read aloud as accurately and rapidly as was possible; time and errors were recorded. A variable interval of time after this first reading, the subjects read a second deck of sentences—the 60 read previously and another 60 for the first time. The 60 reread sentences appeared, however, half in their original typography and half in the opposite typography. For example, 15 of the 30 that appeared originally in normal orientation (N) reappeared in that same orientation and are designated NN; the other 15 appeared the second time in the inverted orientation and are designated NI. Similarly for the sentences that were inverted initially (I): Fifteen reappeared in the same inverted orientation and are designated II; the other 15 reappeared in normal orientation, IN. Thus the words of a sentence could appear either in the same orientation on two occasions or in different orientations on each, and the orientation could be normal or inverted. Another 60 sentences appeared as lures on the second reading, taken from the same paragraphs as the others; they were presented 30 in normal orientation and 30 inverted. Figure 17.2 illustrates the paradigm.

The subject's first task was to read the sentences in the first deck aloud as rapidly and accurately as he could. For the second deck, the task was augmented, and after reading each sentence aloud, the subject placed it into one of three piles: a sentence read for the first time, a reread sentence appearing in the same typography as on the first reading, or a reread sentence appearing in the other typography. The question of interest was the degree to which typography made a difference in encoding and recognition.

The four kinds of sentences—NN, II, NI, and IN—are equivalent as semantic objects. Thus, if the pearl-in-the-oyster theory were correct, they should each produce equivalent degrees of recognition at the semantic level, other things remaining equal. The degree to which recognition depended on typography was assessed for intervals separating reading and recognition that ranged from a few minutes up to 32 days, a different group of subjects tested at each interval. The experimental design allowed us to decompose performance into several factors.

One assessment was the number of old sentences recognized irrespective of typography—that is, put into *either* the *same-typography* or *different-typography* category—compared to the number of new sentences put into those categories, d'(all). This level of analysis (recognition of the words of the sentence) was

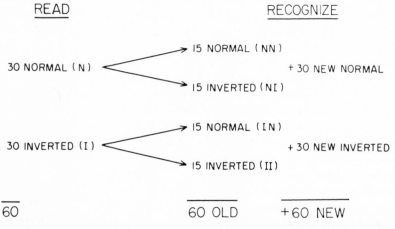

FIG. 17.2.   Structure of study and test decks in classification experiment.

carried out also in respect to sentence pairing: the number of NN sentences put into either of the old piles, the number of II sentences put there, and so on—evaluated in each case against the number of new sentences in normal or in inverted orientation put into those piles, d'(sem). In a third measure, correct recognition of a sentence was made contingent on correct recognition of its words in their proper typography—the NN and II sentences only in the *same-typography* category and the NI and IN sentences only in the *different-typography* category, the hits evaluated in each case against the new sentences in normal or in inverted orientation in the corresponding piles. The measure was called d'(new), regrettably; it would have been better called d'(typog), or d'(sent), or something similar. The final analysis evaluated memory of the sentences as pictorial objects. Sentences correctly recognized as old but misplaced in the *same-typography* pile were used as errors against which the sentences properly placed in the *different-typography* category were evaluated. This effort to get at some eidetic, imagistic, or otherwise pictorial representation of the sentences was called d'(old), although d'(photog) would be a better name.

The four evaluations of d' are summarized in Fig. 17.3, which shows them as composites taken across the various sentence pairings. The trend of the scores is similar, except that d'(old) tends to fall off a little more quickly than the others. The exceptional decline in performance at Day 1 may be an artifact of subject sampling.

As the data of Fig. 17.3 are composite, Figs. 17.4, 17.5, and 17.6 reveal their components. In Fig. 17.4 the values of d'(sem) are shown for each of the sentence pairings; in Fig. 17.5 the values are shown for d'(new), recognition of a sentence in its correct typography; and in Fig. 17.6 the two contrasts are shown for the pictorial memory of sentences whose words had been recognized. Three points can be brought out. The first is that information about typography, a superficial property of words, was encoded and retained for at least 32 days after reading, as shown by the values of d'(new) in Fig. 17.5. Although I am not an expert in memory theory, I do believe that 32 days exceeds the limits usually assigned to short-term memory! The second point is that the various sentence pairings do not produce equivalent results. II sentences were usually recognized best, IN next, followed by NN and NI. This finding holds even when the only question asked was whether the sentence was recognized as a semantic object, as a set of words, as shown by the values of d'(sem) in Fig. 17.4. The third point is that the result was not achieved through reference to some iconic or pictorial representation of the sentence as a set of marks on a surface, as shown by the equal values of d'(old) in Fig. 17.6. Hence typography enters into the encoding of the sentences and affects the likelihood of subsequent recognition, the less familiar typography inducing greater success in recognition; but it does not enter in as a picture of the sentences.

How should this be accounted for? The conjecture that comes to many minds is based on the observation that the inverted sentences are unfamiliar in

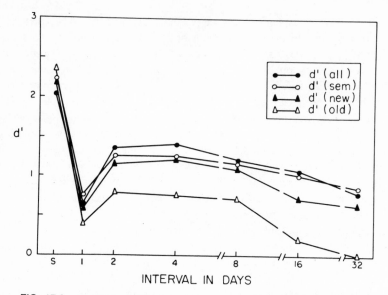

FIG. 17.3. Composite results for various levels of analysis. The symbol "S" on the abscissa designates subjects tested with the *Recognize* deck on the same day as the *Read* deck. (From Kolers and Ostry, 1974.)

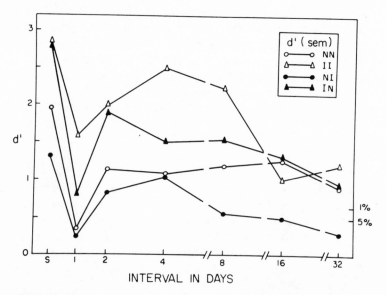

FIG. 17.4. Results at the semantic level as a function of typography and interval. (From Kolers and Ostry, 1974.)

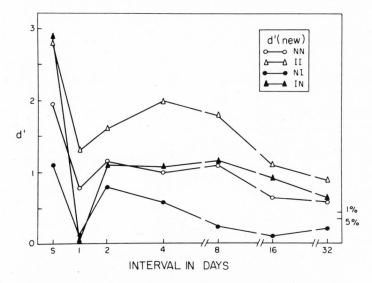

FIG. 17.5.   Results for *d'*(new) as a function of interval between initial reading and recognition test. (From Kolers and Ostry, 1974.)

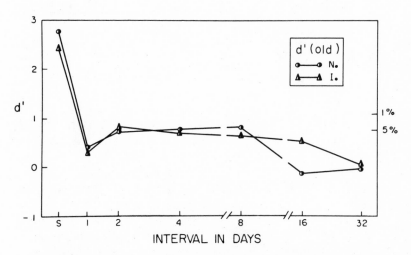

FIG. 17.6.   Results for *d'*(old) as a function of the interval between reading and recognition. (From Kolers and Ostry, 1974.)

appearance; hence, it is suggested, the subjects remembered that certain sentences were difficult to read, took longer than the normally oriented sentences, or appeared in an unfamiliar orientation; that is, the subjects remembered facts about the sentences they had read and meeting those sentences again, recognized them by virtue of remembering those facts. This hypothesis was tested with an experiment in which two kinds of unfamiliar and difficult orientation were used, along with normally oriented sentences (Kolers, 1974b).

The experiment was developed with the same logic as the foregoing. The two difficult transformations are illustrated in Fig. 17.1 as I—the inverted texts already used—and rR. Thirty sentences were prepared in each of the three orientations—N, I, and rR—as the reading deck; one-third of the sentences in each orientation were transformed to the other two for the recognition deck, and 30 other sentences in each orientation were added as lures. The design is illustrated in Fig. 17.7. (It should be appreciated that both in the preceding and in this experiment, the lures were taken from the very same paragraphs as the target sentences, hence were similar to the target sentences in subject, theme, style, and the like.)

The hypothesis that attributes superior performance with transformed sentences to difficulty, orientation, or other properties coded as tags or features of the sentences, would expect both inverted (I) and reversed-rotated (rR) sentences to be recognized more readily than normal (N) sentences. It must assume in addition that inverted and reversed-rotated sentences would be confused with each other, for they are both inverted, difficult, take relatively longer to read, and so on. (Of course one could add still other features to the list that conjecture

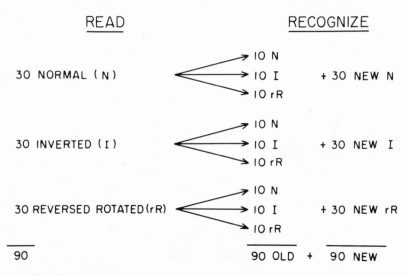

FIG. 17.7.   Structure of study and test decks with three typographies. (From Kolers, 1974.)

might have the reader using to distinguish the transformed sentences from normal ones and to discriminate among transformations. But adding features creates little advantage for encoding; rather it loads up with "footnotes" the reader's representation of the target, and adding enough footnotes about features would limit recall of the target items themselves [Kolers, 1965].)

The transformed sentences were recognized more frequently than the normally oriented sentences, as conjecture anticipated; in addition, the transformed sentences were distinguished from each other, and only rarely were rR and I sentences confused, however. The results of the test are shown in Table 17.1, where one may see that the values of d' are consistently higher for sentences initially in rR or in I than for sentences initially in N; moreover, the combinations of rR and I, as in IrR, or rRI, also yielded large values of d'. Hence the idea that difficulty by itself, or time, or lists of facts about the sentences account for the superior performance of II and IN in the first tests seems to be questioned. By conjecture, it was more a matter of what the readers were doing *to* the sentences than what they were encoding *about* them that accounted for the superior performance. What they were doing to them, by conjecture still, was analyzing them more, and they achieved superior recognition of the transformed sentences by repeating their analyses.

SPEED OF READING

Classification tests are not the strongest sort of evidence, however, for one never know certainly what a subject is doing to arrive at the classification that he or she does put forward. Hence a more direct measure of pattern analysis was sought as a way of getting another view of the role of analysis of the stimulus as integral to achieving its recognition. For the purpose, a long list of sentences was created—some in inverted orientation, others in normal orientation (Kolers, 1975b). In the test, the reader read a sentence twice; the second time, the words always appeared in inverted orientation. The first time, they were sometimes inverted, sometimes normal. A variable number of other sentences intervened between the two readings, the lag. The reader's task was to read each sentence aloud as rapidly and accurately as he or she could; time and errors were recorded. The measure of interest was the time to read an inverted sentence taken as a function of the appearance of the words on their first encounter. If only the semantic component were important to memory as measured by savings in reading speed, then a first encounter with a sentence should have about the same influence on its later reading, whether the first encounter was in normal orientation or in inverted orientation. The reason is that the sentences in the various orientations were equivalent as semantic objects. But if typographic analysis were part of the representation of a sentence, then practice at reading a sentence in one orientation should variably affect its subsequent reading,

TABLE 17.1
Hit Rate and d' for Sentence Pairs.

					Pairing					
	NN	*NI*	*NrR*	*II*	*IN*	*IrR*	*rRrR*	*rRN*	*rRI*	*SE_{DM}**
d' (sem)	1.72	1.42	1.64	2.87	2.49	3.09	3.10	2.57	2.50	0.22
d' (new)	1.94	1.29	1.34	2.30	2.24	2.20	2.70	2.21	2.19	0.28
d' (old)	2.19	0.79	0.86	1.81	1.28	1.12	1.79	1.08	1.35	0.31

*Standard error of the difference between means.

depending on the typography of the two appearances. Figure 17.8 shows in the bottommost curve the time taken to read normally oriented sentences, about 0.1 min (= 6 sec) on average; and in the topmost curve the time taken to read an inverted sentence on its first appearance, 0.6 min (= 36 sec). The sentences are shown for the first reading at the lag values they appeared at for the second reading; the notation designates sentences normal in orientation on their first reading and inverted on their second reading (NI), or inverted on both readings (II), and the numbers 1 and 2 designate first or second reading.

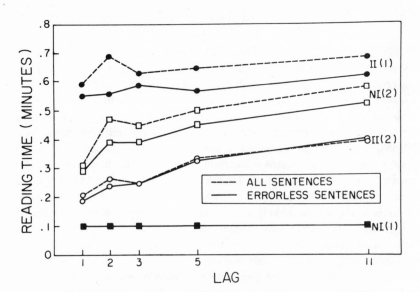

FIG. 17.8.   Time taken to read sentences. II(1): Inverted sentence on the first encounter; II(2): Same inverted sentence on second encounter; NI(1): Normally oriented sentence; NI(2): Same sentence but inverted on second encounter. Dashed lines are total reading time; solid lines are errorless time. (From Kolers, 1975.)

The times for normally oriented and inverted sentences on their first reading establish temporal bounds on performance; the time for a normally oriented sentence is an optimum, and the time for an inverted sentence on its first reading is an upper limit. The transfer scores lie between these values and are different from each other. The time to read an inverted sentence was longer when its words had been read previously in normal orientation—NI(2)—than when its words had been read in the same typography—II(2). Hence the facilitation of reading was not in the words alone, but in the words as visual patterns; not in the words as semantic objects only, but as graphemic objects as well. To assess these claims in another way, the test was repeated with bilingual readers.

French–English bilingual subjects participated in a similar experiment, but one in which sentences in French and in normal orientation were among those read on a first encounter and their translation into English and in inverted orientation was tested in a second encounter. This condition was added to that of the preceding experiment, but to reduce the length of the experiment, fewer lags were tested. The results are shown in Fig. 17.9; first reading of a normally oriented sentence either in French or in English—NI(1) or FI(1)—took about 0.1 min; first reading of an inverted sentence in English—II(1)—took about 0.8 min; and the other three tests lie between. When an inverted sentence in English followed soon after its normally oriented French version (lags of 1 or 3), a notable facilitation occurred, FI(2): The inverted English sentence was read in less time than were inverted sentences read for the first time—II(1). The effect dissipated at longer lags, and the time for FI(2) approached the time for II(1). When the same words were read in normal orientation in English before being read in inverted orientation, even more facilitation was found—NI(2). As semantic objects in some propositional or deep-structural sense, a sentence in English and its translation in French are equivalent; but behaviorally the influence of the sentences is different: Surface structure affects reading speed. Hence it is now no surprise that the greatest facilitation occurred on rereading the same words in the same typography—II(2).

The influence of the semantic component was tested in still a third way. Using the same design as the foregoing, but substituting an auditory condition in place of the French, some sentences were read aloud to the subjects as a first encounter, and the subjects read the sentences only on the second encounter. That is, auditory input of the very words to be read was provided for some sentences. As shown in Fig. 17.10, this group of subjects took about 0.1 min to read a normally oriented sentence and about 0.55 min to read an inverted sentence for the first time. Reading a sentence whose words they had just heard via a tape recording—AI(2)—took longer than reading a sentence whose words they had seen in normal orientation—NI(2); and this in turn took longer than reading a sentence in the same typography—II(2). In sum, the semantic component provided some transfer—FI(2) and AI(2); but not as much as the very words to be read, even in an alternate orientation—NI(2); and this in turn

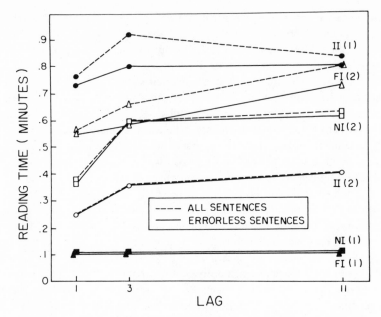

FIG. 17.9.   Time taken to read sentences with differential practice. FI(1): First
reading of a sentence in French; FI(2): Time to read its geometrically inverted
translation in English. Other legends the same as Fig. 17.8. (From Kolers, 1975.)

provided less transfer than the very words in the very orientation—II(2). Thus
the semantic component is weaker than the lexical, and the lexical is weaker than
the typographic, making it a reasonable conjecture that the pattern-analyzing
operations or procedures form part of the representation of the sentence. The
more nearly one can recover the procedures on a second encounter, the greater
the facilitation of performance. Moreover, contrary to the assertions of stagewise
or inflow theories, we found a strong influence of the semantic component upon
analysis of the graphemic—FI(2). By conjecture, it is the procedures themselves
rather than their product that provides the basis of the facilitation, the analytical
operations rather than their semantic result.

The influence of procedure is alluded to, albeit tangentially, in still another
aspect of the data of the classification tests described earlier (Fig. 17.3). Those
data were analyzed according to the procedures of Signal Detection Theory
(TSD), as already mentioned. According to those procedures, data can be
described in a 2 × 2 table, an old or a new stimulus classified as old or new
(Table 17.2). Previously presented (*old*) sentences that are classified as such by
the subject are called "hits," and those classified as "new" are called
"misses"; sentences presented for the first time (*new*) that are called "old" are
"false alarms," and when called "new" are "correct rejections." Hence there
are two kinds of correct answer in the table—hits and correct rejections. These

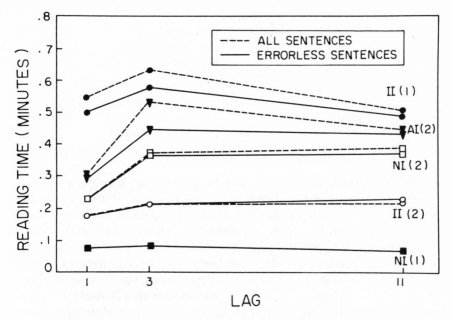

FIG. 17.10.   Time taken to read sentences with intermodal practice. AI(2):
Time taken to read an inverted English sentence that had been heard but not read
previously. Other legends as in Fig. 17.8. (From Kolers, 1975.)

rates were plotted separately, as in Fig. 17.11, each point on the abscissa
representing a different group of subjects. Quite different trends mark the two
curves: The hit rate declines with an increase in time between initial reading and
test, but the rate for correct rejections remains high and nearly flat. The results
show that the subjects forgot or lost track of the sentences they had read (hits),
but always recognized previously unread sentences as such (correct rejections);
they forgot what they had known, but knew what they did not know. This result
was not based on adoption of a higher criterion with passing time; the values of
beta were low and fairly similar across the groups of subjects. It would seem to
me to be quite difficult for most theories of memory to accommodate the ready
"recognition" of nonevents; a theory of recognition based on reinstitution of
procedures may be more successful.

SKILLED READING

What some of the procedures might be was sought in still other tests—only one
aspect of which will be brought out—relating to procedural as distinguished
from semantic representation. In the study, eight college students learned to read
inverted text, reading 160 pages in all, no more than 10 pages per day for a

TABLE 17.2
Structure of Signal Detection Data.

| | Response | |
Stimulus	Old	New
Old	Hit	Miss
New	False alarm	Correct rejection

number of days (Kolers, 1975a). The normal learning curve that plots time against trials is often hyperbolic; taking the logarithm of time against the logarithm of trials yields a straight line. Figure 17.12 plots the time scores for the eight subjects individually on logarithmic coordinates, each plotted point representing time to read one page. The slowest subject took about 30 min to read the first inverted page—HY—the fastest took about 10 min—EI. (Increments of 0.3 on the log scale produce doublings on an arithmetic scale, 0.3, 0.6, 0.9, . . . 1.8 representing 2, 4, 8, . . . 64, respectively.) Normal text, a few pages of which were spotted through the test days, was read with increasing speed by subject RH, more slowly at the end than inverted text by BR. When all 8 data points were averaged per page (mean curves), the first page of inverted

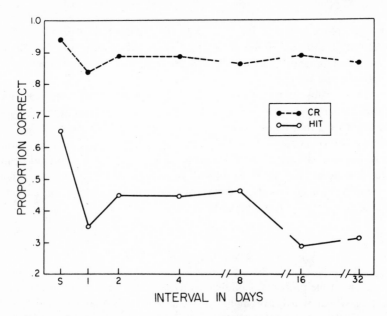

FIG. 17.11. Comparison of hit rates and correct rejections in the typography-contingent recognition of sentences. (From Kolers and Ostry, 1974.)

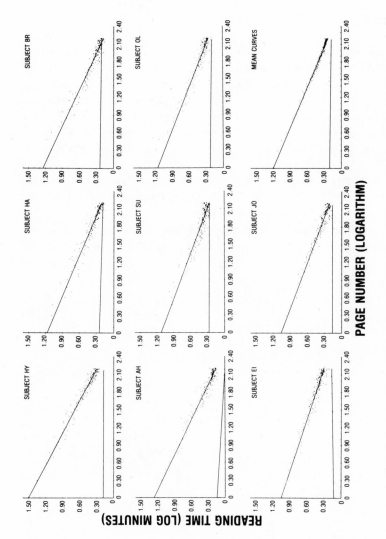

FIG. 17.12. Reading time as a function of practice. (Inclined lines are for inverted text, the flatter lines for normal text. Data for eight subjects individually [one observation per plotted point] and their average [mean curves].) Variations in size of the plotted points are distortions in printing. (From Kolers, © 1976, by the American Psychological Association. Reprinted by permission.)

text required about 15 min and the 160th about 1.7 min, a rather remarkable rate of gain in performance, compared to about 1.5 min for normal text. Let this be called Phase 1 of the experiment.

About a year later, six of the eight subjects were recovered for additional testing. They read 98 pages of inverted text, Phase 2 (Kolers, 1976). Performance on the second round revealed a substantial savings in pattern-analyzing skills, illustrated in Fig. 17.13. On this second round, however, half of the pages were taken from the set read for Phase 1; the other half were from the same books but were new pages. Figure 17.14 shows the least-squares line through the data points and indicates pages read for the first time with strokes and the reread pages with dots. There are more strokes above the line and more dots below the line; reread pages were read more quickly than pages read for the first time. An analysis of variance yielded an index of the difference in time—that is, yielded for each subject a number that described the relative difference in speed between once-read and twice-read pages; this number provided one measure of performance.

What is the basis of the facilitation? Is it skill or is it memory for contents, procedures or products? It cannot be merely memory for the content of the pages, because the readers would have to read the pages before they knew their contents and so could not then be helped in their speed of reading. Perhaps, alternatively, the readers recognized phrases here and there, snippets of sentences whose

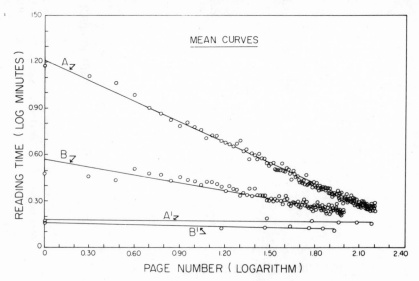

FIG. 17.13. Results for the same six readers in two tests more than a year apart. (The inclined lines A and B are for reading inverted text, the lines nearly parallel to the abscissa, A' and B,' are for normally oriented text. Lines A and A' are for pages read earlier, lines B and B' are for the pages of this experiment.) (From Kolers, © 1976, by the American Psychological Association. Reprinted by permission.)

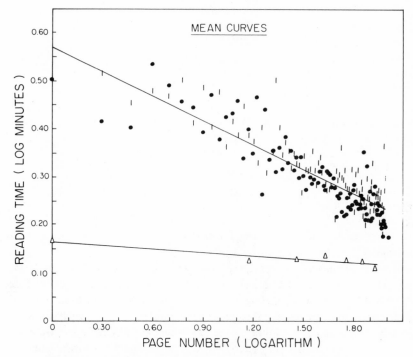

FIG. 17.14.   Composite results for six readers in Experiment 1.(Strokes are for
pages read once, filled symbols are for pages reread after 13 to 15 months.) (From
Kolers, © 1976, by the American Psychological Association. Reprinted by permission.)

reading went faster than other parts. Phase 3 of the experiment questions both of
these alternatives.

The day after finishing Phase 2, the subjects returned for Phase 3, to classify
168 pages: 49 read in Phase 1 and Phase 2 (*Both*), 49 read only in Phase 2
(*Recent*), 49 read only in Phase 1 (*Old*), and 21 taken from the same sources as
the others but not read previously (*New*). The results are shown in Table 17.3:
About 93% of the pages read only in Phase 2 (*Recent*) and about 95% of the pages
read in both Phase 1 and Phase 2 (*Both*) were recognized as read before, although
the occasion of reading was not always judged accurately; about 65% of the
pages read only in Phase 1 were recognized as read before (*Old*); and 66% of the
pages never read before were recognized as such (*New*). Overall, pages read in
Phase 2 (*Recent* and *Both*) were confused with each other but were not usually
confused with *Old* or *New*, and pages read only in Phase 1 (*Old*) or never read
before (*New*) were often confused with each other but not with pages read in
Phase 2. The opportunity to analyze the data according to TSD was blocked by
the fact that the three independent measures of d' were statistically different, so
chi-squared tests were used instead.

As the 4 × 4 table was significant for each subject, the data were analyzed

Table 17.3
Composite Results on Classifying Passages.

Stimulus	Both	Recent	Old	New
		Response		
Both	0.49	0.29	0.17	0.05
Recent	0.30	0.55	0.08	0.07
Old	0.06	0.03	0.56	0.35
New	0.00	0.04	0.30	0.66
Sum	0.85	0.91	1.11	1.13

(From Kolers, © 1976, by the American Psychological Association. Reprinted
by permission.)

with other features in mind: a test for discrimination of recency (*Recent* versus
the others), for frequency (*Both* versus the others) and for familiarity (*New*
versus the others). (Two of these tests were independent; the third adds
circumstantial evidence.) The facts of greatest interest are summarized in Table
17.4, showing the chi-squared values for each subject. It is easy to see that little
consistency marks the results. Recognition based on familiarity may be unassociated with recognition based on frequency or recency, and vice versa. Moreover,
the index of reading efficiency ("coefficient") is also minimally associated with
the results of the test of judgment. In fact the subject who scored highest on the
test of familiarity scored lowest in difference in time between once-read and
twice-read pages (BR); and the subject who scored highest on the latter scored
poorly on the former (AH). In this we have the answer to the question of whether
the superior reading of reread pages in due to memory for their contents or
facilitation of some procedure; I think the latter is clearly the implicated answer.
The fact that the various attributes of recognition—familiarity, recency, frequency, and reading speed—are not well-correlated, that judgments *about* pages

Table 17.4
Scores on Tests of Reading Speed and Classification.

Test	EI	JO	OL	HY	AH	BR
			Reader			
Familiarity (old–new)	7.46*	5.03	2.82	0.30	1.02*	6.80
Recency (old–recent)	31.25	21.15*	37.88	40.40	16.75	34.56
Frequency (recent–both)	4.24*	0.04	0.06*	16.35	1.10*	11.80
Coefficient (old–new)	−0.029	−0.024	−0.024	−0.021	−0.035	−0.015

*Discrimination in the wrong direction.

(From Kolers, © 1976, by the American Psychological Association. Reprinted
by permission.)

are not necessarily well correlated with performance *on* pages, suggests many things about memory and the nature of the memory trace, perhaps even calling the notion of trace into question.

SOME IMPLICATIONS

Templates are the standard description of representation; the templates may be pictorial as in an image or icon, or linguistic as in a proposition or formula. Template theories are usually adequate to deal with recognition of discrete objects or facts. But consider the data of Fig. 17.13, where we find that there is a systematic increase in speed of performance with practice. Such changes in performance are obviously due in some way to memory, whatever memory may be; yet it is not clear how template theory would accommodate such performances that are expressions of skill rather than of fact. (When is it "perception?" when is it "learning"? when is it "memory"? Data of this kind may be used to illustrate the imprecision that underlies the naming of cognitive functions.) In this case, representation of performance skills must change with their exercise; yet the performance skills illustrated are recognitive operations directed at textual material. There is a point to be made here regarding the basis of memory.

The findings I have reviewed support the commonplace observation that we remember remarkable amounts of trivia and not merely the messages that experimenters send us; or, perhaps, to put it another way—what is "message" and what is "trivium" is a matter of concern to some aspects of our nervous system, but not to those parts engaged in analyzing and indexing stimulus complexes. We may remember not only what we read, but where on the page we read it, the color of the book's binding, whether it was in one language or another, and perhaps the weather at the time of reading and the lighting level of the room—along, perhaps, with the name, sex, and appearance of the experimenter. Moreover, we may even recognize the typography. Our nervous system encodes remarkable amounts of detail regarding events, and whether that detail is considered to be irrelevant or not, its encoding requires an accounting. The simplest view is of course that we identify or isolate events and list their features.

Feature-list theories are forms of template theory, in the sense of template as a fixed record. The difficulty with feature lists as an account of perception and memory is of course that a proper specification of any object produces an infinite list of features, and usually we lack the time and may even lack the cognitive resources to create or process infinite lists of anything. We can usually tell any two objects apart at a glance; there is no obvious way that feature-list theories can account for such performance. And even if we modify feature-list theory to make it selective, we are in some difficulty. Suppose that we say we encode the familiar or distinguishing features of an object. This statement may be true but is inadequate, because we have first to encode the object before we can know which of its features distinguish it; there has to be a data base for the selection procedures to operate on. We have first to acquire the cup in memory before we can remember that it has such a nick or such a pattern or such a color or whatever. In a word, features and feature lists are the results of encoding but cannot (on logical groups alone) be the means by which encoding is first carried out.

An alternative that I have suggested (Kolers & Ostry, 1974) is that the reader applies many different analytical operations to a sample, all that he or she knows how to; and the more operations applied, the more of the stimulus that is acquired—hence the greater the subsequent opportunities for recognition. On the occurrence of some stimulus, all of the ways that the nervous system has available for operating upon it are brought to bear as purpose, motivation, and time allow. Rather than in the serial order that levels theory first proposed, the various kinds of analysis interact, the person's many skills aiding each other in a manner rich in feedback (Kolers & Perkins, 1975). A sentence that required extensive graphemic analysis might in fact be recognized better than another that required less graphemic analysis merely by virtue of the analysis required. And this seems to violate intuition.

One might think that a sentence that required extensive graphemic analysis would be remembered less well than another on which the reader needed to use resources only at the semantic level. The reverse is found, however: Sentences requiring extensive graphemic analysis—II and IN—are recognized better than sentences that require less—NN and NI (Figs. 17.4 and 17.5). This result would seem to conflict with the assertion of Craik and Tulving (1975). On their view, memory is a feature list of analyses carried out, and certain levels of analysis are intrinsically less capable of carrying the burden of memory than are others; for example, "a minimal semantic analysis is more beneficial for memory than an elaborate structural analysis [p. 291]," which is patently not true. In fact, Craik and Tulving have created arbitrary distinctions between kinds of encoding. They assume that the semantic is deepest, structural less deep, and that different kinds of operations are associated with those arbitrary divisions (pp. 289–291). It is not clear why a list of the operations carried out would be any more useful than any other list, however, unless of course a list of the operations carried out were something like: "I read the word *a* in such circumstances and then the word *b* and then the word *c*" and so on.

Words, like many other objects, are seen in many aspects; in all the aspects that their reader can command in the time available—graphemic, syntactic, semantic, temporal, locative, etymological, contextual, and so on. No one aspect is deeper or richer than another, save as purpose and need make it so. The semantic is richer or deeper than the graphemic only insofar as customary usage of language is directed as its reference or suggestion; change of skill or of purpose can change the importance and richness of a category of description. The various aspects named, moreover, are not fixed properties of the words so much as endowments projected onto them by the trained perceiver; hence they derive their importance largely from the occasion of usage, not from their structure or the properties of the light. What is structural on one occasion and for one reader may be semantic for another, and even the same reader may emphasize different aspects of a signal at different times. The notion of level of processing seems to confuse level of analysis or of description of the stimulus with level of processing in the nervous system; we can say much about the former, less about the latter. In this respect, however, the view described here argues against the standard inflow or serial-processing theories, substituting notions of interaction and interplay among skills. Skills with the semantic aspect of a message may aid the decoding of difficult graphemes; skills with graphemic factors may shape semantic interpretations; and other skills contribute their own influences, also, not all of which need be conscious. Indeed, it seems appropriate to hold that everything we know how to do can influence what we do, in a continuous way.

In the views I have been trying to work out, recognition is not due to a list of operations that memory keeps a record of, but goes forward by a reinstitution of operations at a later time of those engaged in earlier. How the operations are selected, whether they achieve organization, and what indexes a match are problems that have not yet been fully studied. A related question has to do with their change.

On the present view, every encounter with a stimulus elicits a different analysis from every other, up to some limiting value, for the selection and application of analytical operations becomes more efficient. In other words, recognition is achieved by virtue of the correlation between the operations carried out on two encounters with a stimulus event. The more similar the operations, the readier the recognition. But as nothing ever repeats itself exactly, recognition is based on the transfer of skills across occasions and *partial* correlation. If the operations that are activated are themselves the record of the stimulus, then as the operations change, the representation of the stimulus also changes; there is no permanent trace of an object, nor even a fixed trace, but skill-developed and occasion-dependent representations. Acquisition of skill is associated with refinement and precision of the component operations; recognition is associated with the transfer of skills across occasions. If the representations change, one wonders what interpretation to give to the notion of "memory." Remembering as activity or procedure implicates change, but the historical notion of memory is of fixity. Bartlett (1932), in emphasizing activity, may in fact not have gone far enough.

A FINAL NOTE

In most experiments on reading and memory, the experimenter presents material that is semantically novel but graphemically transparent. The reader than analyzes, figures out, or interprets the material to get at its semantic content, and memory for semantic content is usually found to be richer or better than memory for the graphemics. This finding has encouraged many students to the claim that only the semantic content is retained for long intervals and that the semantic provides a deeper or richer level of analysis and representation than the graphemic. By turning things around a bit to leave the semantic content in its usual form while making the graphemics more opaque, I have achieved the opposite result: Graphemic analysis produced a deeper and richer representation of sentences as measured by number, accuracy, and speed of recognition. The conclusion thus seems to be that the semantic is not necessarily a deeper or richer or more elaborate level of processing by virtue of its kind or nature. The semantic is usually remembered better, not because it is semantic, but because its acquisition requires particular analysis; the graphemic is usually lost, not because it is graphemic, but because its acquisition requires little analysis, at least by the skilled reader. What is remembered better is what was analyzed more; the analytical operations themselves, their extent and complexity, account for performance. The typical results of levels-of-processing experiments that favor semantic analysis seem to be at least partly due to the specific stimuli used and the specific task presented to the subject, and not to be necessary facts of memory.

REFERENCES

Bartlett, F. C. *Remembering*. Cambridge: Cambridge University Press, 1932.

Craik, F. I. M., & Lockhart, R. S. Levels of processing: A framework for memory research. *Journal of Verbal Learning and Verbal Behavior*, 1972, *11*, 671–684.

Craik, F. I. M., & Tulving, E. Depth of processing and retention of words in episodic memory. *Journal of Experimental Psychology: General*, 1975, *104*, 268–294.

Kolers, P. A. Bilingualism and bicodalism. *Language and Speech*, 1965, *8*, 122–126.

Kolers, P. A. Interlingual facilitation of short-term memory. *Journal of Verbal Learning and Verbal Behavior*, 1966, *5*, 314–319. (a)

Kolers, P. A. Reading and talking bilingually. *American Journal of Psychology*, 1966, *79*, 357–376. (b)

Kolers, P. A. Three stages of reading. In H. Levin & J. Williams (Eds.), *Basic studies on reading*. New York: Basic Books, 1970.

Kolers, P. A. Some modes of representation. In P. Pliner, L. Krames, & T. Alloway (Eds.), *Communication and affect: Language and speech*. New York: Academic Press, 1973.

Kolers, P. A. Remembering trivia. *Language and Speech*, 1974, *17*, 324–336. (a)

Kolers, P. A. Two kinds of recognition. *Canadian Journal of Psychology*, 1974, *28*, 51–61. (b)

Kolers, P. A. Memorial consequences of automatized encoding. *Journal of Experimental Psychology: Human Learning and Memory*, 1975, *1*, 689–701. (a)

Kolers, P. A. Specificity of operations in sentence recognition. *Cognitive Psychology*, 1975, *7*, 289–306. (b)

Kolers, P. A. Reading a year later. *Journal of Experimental Psychology: Human Learning and Memory*, 1976, *2*, 554–565.

Kolers, P. A., & Ostry, D. J. Time course of loss of information regarding pattern analyzing operations. *Journal of Verbal Learning and Verbal Behavior*, 1974, *13*, 599–612.

Kolers, P. A., & Perkins, D. N. Spatial and ordinal components of form perception and literacy. *Cognitive Psychology*, 1975, *7*, 228–267.

18 An Elaborative Processing Explanation of Depth of Processing

John R. Anderson
Lynne M. Reder
Carnegie–Mellon University

The purpose of this paper is to discuss a theoretical view that we think accounts for the results that have been organized under the rubric of "depth of processing" (to be called DOP). We argue that the variation in memory with DOP is a result of the number of elaborations subjects produce while studying the material, that these elaborations establish more redundant encodings of the to-be-remembered information, and that elaboration is what is critical, especially for long-term retention. Because extent of elaboration is the critical variable, a better spatial metaphor for the DOP phenomena might be "breadth of processing." We argue that depth of processing is as important to prose material as it is to the verbal learning material with which DOP is most commonly studied. With prose, elaborations take on another dimension of importance: They prove to be critical to the comprehension of the material. We make these points about elaboration, DOP, and prose processing with linguistic examples and interpretations of empirical results.

What Mechanism Underlies DOP?

At one level, the term *depth of processing* just summarizes an intuitive viewpoint about what makes for good memory: One can ask subjects to perform various orienting tasks while processing material. One can consult one's intuitions as to which orienting tasks demand "deeper processing." The prediction is that subjects engaged in what seem to be deeper processing tasks will perform better. There exist no explicit rules, however, for measuring the "depth" of a task. It is not clear how well subjective intuitions about depth will hold over a randomly selected set of orienting tasks in terms of predicting memory performance.

Nonetheless, this intuitive rule has worked thus far in predicting which tasks will produce superior performance.[1] The typical contrast (e.g., Hyde & Jenkins, 1973) is one that pits a phonemic judgment against a semantic judgment where the latter clearly seems to require deeper processing and seems to produce better memory. Of course, this intuitive rule of thumb, even if it is a good predictor, is inherently unsatisfactory. It is a matter of considerable frustration that where intuition seems to do so well, it is so hard to provide a succinct theoretical analysis of the mechanisms underlying the phenomenon.

It would be inaccurate to imply that the depth of processing metaphor has not been translated into theoretical proposals. A number of theorists (e.g., Craik & Lockhart, 1972; Craik & Tulving, 1975; Kintsch, 1975; Wickelgren, 1973) have advocated that processing information at various depths results in different types of traces being left in memory. For instance, Kintsch proposes that propositional traces have much slower decay rates that lexical traces. A similar notion has been offered by Wickelgren (1973), who suggests that propositional traces decay less rapidly because they suffer less interference from other memory traces.

Although these assumptions can explain a number of phenomena associated with depth of processing, there are a number of phenomena that cannot be so explained. For instance, the advantage of elaborative instructions for sentential material (e.g., Bobrow & Bower, 1969) cannot be explained by different traces, nor can the advantage of an elaborative context on larger units of prose (e.g., Bransford & Johnson, 1973). Presumably, the subjects in these experiments, under all conditions, are leaving propositional traces in memory. Yet, elaborative instructions leave "more deeply processed" propositional traces, and these seem more memorable.

The Elaboration Hypothesis

We hypothesize that manipulations designed to affect what has been referred to as *depth* of processing are having their effect by changing the *number* and *type* of elaborations stored. We believe that subjects typically store much more than the input presented in the memory situation. Consider the following transcript collected by Anderson (1972) from a subject as she went through 10 words of a larger free-recall list. This is her second pass through the list. The word following each number indicates the word being studied. Following it is a transcription of the subject's remarks. Each underlined word in the transcription is a word that was in the set of 40 to-be-recalled words:

---

[1]T. O. Nelson (1977) has recently written a paper criticizing the concept of depth of processing. One of the things he questioned was the degree to which there was interrater reliability as to the depth of a task. He proposed 13 tasks to be rated. As a curiosity, we took to independently rating these tasks, excluding 2 tasks whose descriptions were ambiguous. The correlation between our rank order ratings was .974.

1. garrison—*garrison, lieutenant, dignitary*
2. dignitary—*crown* queen, oh . . . *dignitary*
3. vulture—*vulture* . . . bird, there was a bird *present* . . . *vulture*, bird . . . garrison
4. disk—*disk* . . . *disk*, record, *disk*, can't remember statue
5. crown—*crown* queen, the *dignitary* visits the *crown* queen, the *lieutenant is in the garrison*
6. bowl—*bowl* . . . *bowl* of flowers . . . the *dignitary* visits the *crown* queen, and gives her a *bowl* of flowers
7. present—I am *present*, I also am a *student*, I think . . . *student*
8. student—*student*, I am *present*, I also am a *student* . . . the *dignitary* is also a *student* philosopher
9. dragon—oh, I forgot all the fairy tales . . . *goose, dragon*, mother *goose* fairy tales
10. kitchen—*kitchen*, still the mother, the *widowed* mother [p. 374]

This subject was given no special instructions; she was just asked to say out loud what she was thinking about during study. She is not an atypical subject. Moreover, we believe that the protocols just reflect the tip of the elaborative iceberg. From our introspections, it became apparent to us that the ideas and elaborations that occur during a memory experiment are generated at a rate that is too rapid to report verbally.

There is probably a purpose for the large amount of elaboration that is generated. We speculate that the rich elaboration affects memory performance. That is, we take the depth-of-processing results as an indication of a function and a consequence of the elaborative process—improved memory for material elaborated.

There are two critical questions that need to be addressed in making this theoretical proposal concrete. First, why should amount of elaboration affect memory performance? Second, why should amount of elaboration vary with depth of processing?

To answer these questions, it is necessary to articulate our view of the nature of the representation of information in a memory task. We assume that long-term memory is a network of interconnected propositions and that when a subject goes through an experiment, the subject adds propositions to this memory network. At a minimum, the subject adds propositions encoding the memory items. So, given the paired-associate "dog–chair" the subject would encode the proposition: "In the context of the experiment, I learned that *chair* was the response for the stimulus *dog*." Typically, of course, the subject encodes much more than this minimum. Frequently, this additional elaboration will be about the meaning of the words rather than the words per se.

Any particular encoded proposition is fragile. There is a significant chance that the subject will not be able to activate that proposition at test. So, if a person's memory for the item rested on the minimum proposition, poor memory would be the result. However, if the subject encoded multiple propositions that were partially redundant with the to-be-remembered information, he or she would have a much better chance of recalling it at time of test. For instance, suppose the subject gave the following semantic elaboration of the pair, "dog–chair":

> *Elaboration (a).*   The dog loved his masters. He also loved to sit on the chairs. His masters had a beautiful black velvet chair. One day he climbed on it. He left his white hairs all over the chair. His masters were upset by this. They scolded him.

Suppose the subject would not recall at test the original pair but could recall some elaboration from memory such as, "The dog climbed on the chair." Then, cued with "dog," the subject would have a good chance of guessing "chair" as a response. The probability of selecting "chair" over other items in the proposition would depend on such things as a knowledge of the statistics of list construction (e.g., noting that all responses were nouns), having the word tagged as a response, and the amount of elaboration of this concept versus alternatives like "climb."

It is interesting to note that we are making a commitment to a reconstructive[2] interpretation of memory like that advocated by Bartlett (1932) and Neisser (1967). The basic idea is that a memory episode is encoded as a set of propositions. This set can vary in its richness and redundancy. At time of recall, only a subset of these propositions will be activated. The richer the original set, the richer will be the subset. Memory for any particular proposition will depend on the subjects' ability to reconstruct it from those propositions that are active. This ability will in turn depend on the richness of the original set and hence on the amount of elaboration made at study.

Having now dealt with the question of why elaborations help recall, we turn to the question of why richness of elaboration should vary with depth of processing. Why should subjects be unable to form as rich an elaboration of peripheral information as of semantic information? For instance, consider our "dog–chair" example. Why could subjects not form to themselves the following elaboration about the pair as typographic objects?

> *Elaboration (b).*   The word *dog* is in the book. The word *dog* is also known to be above the word *chair*. The book has the word *chair* printed in large red letters. On one page, the word *dog* is larger than the word *chair*. The word *dog* has its green letters printed beside the word *chair*. The book tells about this. The book illustrates the word *dog*.

---

[2]The reconstructive position was one that has been criticized by Anderson and Bower (1973). The Anderson and Bower criticisms were largely directed at interpretations of certain empirical data by reconstructionists. Although these criticisms are valid, we feel that the phenomena of depth of processing and comprehension of connected discourse demand elaborative and reconstructive processes. So, though the first author may quibble about the data and reasoning used to argue for the reconstructive position, we do agree with the general conclusion.

This elaboration has an interesting property vis-à-vis the semantic elaboration illustrated earlier. They are basically isomorphic with respect to the graph structure of the propositions interconnecting them. This is illustrated in Figure 18.1, which sets forth schematically the structure of interconnections among the propositions. So, with respect to redundancy of connections, there is no necessary difference between orthographic and semantic processing. However, there are three observations to be made about Elaboration (a) versus Elaboration (b):

1. There is an enormous difference in the ease of generating the two types of elaborations. Semantic elaborations seem to come to mind without problem, whereas generating orthographic elaborations is like pulling teeth.

2. Even if differences in ease of generating the elaborations were removed by giving subjects (a) or (b) to study, subjects would still be likely to do better on (a) than (b). The reason for this is that it is easier to further elaborate on (a) than (b).

3. Even if the experimenter could manage to have the subject encode *only* elaboration (a) or *only* elaboration (b), there would still be an advantage for (a). This is because one's reconstructive processes are better able to interpret the ''semantic'' remnants at delay.

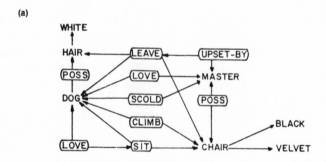

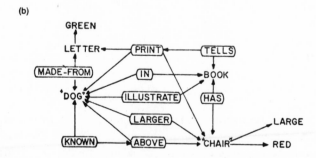

FIG. 18.1.   A graph structure illustrating the connectivity among concepts in (a) the semantic elaboration and (b) the typographical elaboration. From Anderson (1976).

We realize that the foregoing remarks presuppose some empirical evidence about the superiority of elaborations like (a) to elaborations like (b), and in fact, we do not have such evidence. However, we regard that result as so obvious that we have not been motivated to perform the experiment.

A critical assumption in our theory is that subjects are better able to *make* certain types of elaborations at study and are better able to *interpret* certain types of elaborations at test. A person is better at elaborating that type of information with which she or he has had the most experience. This is because one's elaborative abilities are a function of the availability of mental procedures to make elaborations, and these procedures do not come into existence except through practice. For two points of view as to the detailed nature of these elaborative procedures, see Anderson (1976) and Reder (1976; in press). We do not have to go into such technical detail here to make our points. It should be noted, however, that the type and extent of elaborations are the product of our real-world experience with concrete objects such as pets and furniture. A member of a non-Western culture would produce elaborations very different from those in (a) given earlier and might be no better able to elaborate the statement: "The dog is on the chair" than the statement: "The word *dog* is next to the word *chair*." It is also conceivable that by suitable experience and practice, a person could become facile at generating typographical elaborations as well as semantic elaborations of pets.

It is not the depth of processing per se that is important, but one's prior practice at making elaborations about various types of information and practice at interpreting the previously stored elaborations. The "better" processing is that which generates *more* elaborations of the input that can be interpreted at retrieval. For most people, semantic elaborations are easy to generate and facilitate recall. For a mnemonist, however, other kinds of elaborations might be more useful. An astronomer can extensively elaborate star patterns, whereas most people cannot. The instructions that can produce rich elaboration and the materials that can be richly elaborated must be defined with respect to the processor. The most critical determinant of retention is the number of elaborations. Holding "quality" of elaborations (i.e., whether they are deep or shallow) constant, the "quantity" of elaborations will predict recall; manipulating "quality" (to the extent this can be measured) while holding "quantity" constant should not be as good a predictor.

Elaboration and Other Theoretical Viewpoints

To review and expand upon our theoretical position: We assume information is encoded in a network of propositions interconnecting concepts. A subject encodes a to-be-remembered event by adding further propositions to the network. In a memory test, the subject is cued with a probe that gives him or her direct access to some concepts in memory. From these concepts, the subject must retrieve enough propositions encoding the event to permit recall. Our analysis is focused on the process by which a subject searches out from a concept node to try to retrieve the correct propositions. Connected to such a node will be a set of n irrelevant propositions encoding information unrelated to the memory episode and a set of m relevant propositions encoding the memory episode. We view the relevant propositions as highly redundant. That is, the subject need only retrieve a few of these m propositions to enable recall. There are two important variables affecting recall—n and m. The n irrelevant propositions provide interference—as this number increases, memory performance should deteriorate, because it will be harder to find the relevant information. For a review of evidence relevant to this interference prediction, see Anderson (1976, Chap. 8). We will return to the effect of n later. The m relevant propositions provide redundant encoding of the information—as this number increases, memory performance will improve. We see elaborations as affecting this redundancy factor.

Note that this analysis replaces the qualitative concept—depth of processing—with a quantitative concept—number of elaborations. We claim that people are better able to elaborate certain kinds of information than others and that "deep," semantic information tends to be more conducive to elaboration than "shallow," phonemic information. However, the degree of "depth" is not a function of semanticity per se, but rather is a function of the extent of past experience with the information. Thus, we speculate that a phonetician would find the phonetic level very helpful. Also, within the semantic level, we expect to see large variations depending on the amount of experience with that topic.

We agree with Fisher and Craik's (1977) conclusion that certain types of information are inherently easier to remember than others and find ourselves in disagreement with the extremely relativistic positions put forth by Bransford, Franks, Morris, and Stein (Chapter 15, this volume) and Tulving (Chapter 19, this volume). No doubt, if one encodes semantic information, one will be ill-prepared for a phonetic test and vice versa, but it still can be meaningful to inquire, within the context of a theoretical framework, which type of information is more easily encoded. For instance, even though two different input devices are encoding different information into a computer memory, it makes sense to ask which is encoding more information (as measured within an information-theoretic framework) and why.

We would like to consider one class of explanations of depth of processing that seemed especially popular at this conference. This kind of explanation states that a deeply processed item suffers less interference (Wickelgren, 1973), or is more distinctive (Eysenck, Chapter 5; Nelson, Chapter 3, this volume), or is more differentiated from other items (Bransford, et al., Chapter 15, this volume). These various explanations are at different stages of articulation and are probably not identical, but they all seem to hinge on the idea that the target memory must stand out from an interfering background of other memories.

These "interference—distinctiveness" interpretations have often been applied to the semantic—phonemic difference. It is argued that there are relatively few phonemic features but an abundance of semantic features. Therefore, phonemic features have occurred in more contexts and are subject to greater interference from past knowledge. This explanation seems unsatisfactory, because the assumption of a greater vocabulary of semantic primitives is not well motivated. One could propose a semantic vocabulary of 0's and 1's or a richer phonemic vocabulary. A common problem with these explanations is that a given memory trace is said to be more distinctive than another trace if memory for the first is better; i.e., the explanation tends to be circular.

Earlier we alluded to "the effect of the size of n"—the number of irrelevant propositions emanating from a concept node. The larger n, the greater the interference when looking for a relevant proposition. The need for elaboration of a proposition is less when there is less interference. We believe many of the claims made about distinctiveness can be thought of as differential interference. The results of Eysenck (Chapter 5, this volume) and Nelson (Chapter 3, this volume) are quite consistent with the interference view. However, to show that there is an important effect of interference is not to show that there is not an effect of the other variable in our model, viz., the amount of elaboration. We were forced to this second variable, because it seems clear that there are many phenomena that cannot be accounted for by interference.

Consider the two "dog—chair" paragraphs mentioned earlier. Certainly both are quite distinctive, but the semantic paragraph seems guaranteed to lead to better memory. An even more cogent argument for the insufficiency of the distinctiveness account comes from a memory experiment by Goldstein and Chance (1971), where the materials were pictures of faces and of snowflakes. Both types of stimuli were quite distinctive and discriminable. If anything, the features that define snowflakes are more unique and suffer less interference from other knowledge. However, memory for the faces is much better, presumably because subjects are able to attribute meaning to these stimuli (i.e., elaborate upon the stimuli). The more meaningful the stimuli, the greater the propensity to generate elaborations.

Memory for pictorial material is a particularly good domain to make the case for elaboration. Pictures are so rich in details that distinctiveness per se would seem unimportant. Bower and Karlin (1974) demonstrated better memory for faces processed under a "deep" orienting task (judgments of likability) than when processed under a "shallow" task (judgments of sex). Similarly, Bower, Karlin, and Dueck (1975) demonstrated that subjects' memory for droodles (ambiguous cartoons) was better when a meaningful interpretation was applied to the material. Given the high distinctiveness of the stimuli to be learned, we feel that these depth-of-processing results clearly implicate an explanation in terms of richness, or number, of elaborations in the memory code.

PROCESSING OF PROSE

It might seem odd to claim that subjects are engaging in so much elaboration, since much less would seem necessary for a typical experiment. After all, it is a very simple thing a subject is asked to do in a typical DOP experiment—e.g., remember a word. Moreover, if a subject brings in a powerful mechanism that generates dozens of propositions, an equally powerful reconstructive mechanism is required to interpret them at test. This has the character of using a sledge-hammer to swat a fly. The reason we posit these mechanisms for this task is because we view them as general mechanisms not especially designed for a verbal-learning experiment or for any memory experiment at all. Rather, we think they are processes critical to dealing with many everyday situations such as comprehension of a message, making an image of a description, predicting what will happen in the future, day-dreaming, finding contradictions, etc. These processes get recruited in the typical memory experiment simply because they are there. One reason that we think it is useful to consider these elaborative processes in the context of prose comprehension is that it provides an additional perspective on their significance.

At the outset, we would like to disavow a certain interpretation of the foregoing remarks and subsequent remarks. There is a position that has been espoused informally and to some degree in print (e.g., Schank & Abelson, 1977; Thorndyke, 1975), which asserts that the "correct" domain to work in is prose processing or, even more specifically, "story" processing; that working with more "impoverished" material leads to distortions of the basic phenomena. This point of view and the methodological imperialism it leads to is nonsense. The human engages in a wide variety of behavior. There is no reason to believe that story comprehension of the kind currently in vogue is more representative of normal processes than is free recall. In fact, there are probably more adult behaviors (e.g., remembering a grocery list) that come close to a free-recall experiment than adult behaviors that come close to reading one of the very simple stories typically employed. The fundamental feature of human behavior is its extreme diversity, and the hallmark of human intelligence is its ability to manage that diversity. It seems silly to regard any paradigm as prototypical. A theorist may miss important generalities in human behavior if the tasks studied are restricted to a narrow paradigm.

At any one time, of course, a psychologist must study human cognition within the context of a particular paradigm. However, this should not obscure the fact that the studied mechanisms operate over a much larger range of tasks than could be produced in one experiment. In trying to understand a mechanism like elaboration, one should learn from all available paradigms. We think that there is a lot to learn from DOP and its typical verbal-learning methodology. However, we feel, too, that there is much that can be added to this knowledge by considering prose processing.

Comprehension of Prose

An important component to the processing of a text is detecting the connections among the sentences of the text. In normal text, there is as much left unstated—to be read between the lines—as there is directly stated. Reading or listening are slow perceptual processes relative to the speed of mental elaboration. Connected discourse almost always consists of the main points and leaves the rest to be filled in by the reader. Consider the following subpassages from Reder (1976):

> 1. Tim wanted a new model airplane. He saw the change lying on his father's dresser.

> 2. The heir to a large hamburger chain worried that his wife did not love him anymore. Perhaps he consumed too much beer and french fries. No, he couldn't give up the fries. Not only were they delicious, he got them for free!

Clearly, in comprehending these texts, one almost automatically makes a large number of connecting inferences. For instance, in 1, the reader infers that the money isn't Tim's; it is his father's money; he wants it so that he can buy a model airplane. In 2, the reader infers that the heir is fat, that his wife may dislike fat men, that he gets his fries from his parents' hamburger chain, etc.

We believe that generation of elaborations is the means by which these connections are made. In addition to the obvious, necessary inferences, it seems that other elaborations spew forth too. These other elaborations are often idiosyncratic. The idiosyncratic elaborations made by the second author (LMR) for (1) include: Tim is about 8 to 12, has a crew cut; the father's dresser is just at Tim's eye level; the model airplane is silver with chevron decals; the father is the absent-minded type who would not notice the change missing but who would be furious if he found out his son took it. For (2) LMR's elaborations include: The hamburger chain is like A & W Rootbeer or Jack-in-the-Box; the wife is pretty and independent, yet had convinced herself before marriage that she loved the heir because she really needed the money; the heir is stupid, lazy, and vaguely miserable about life. Many of these elaborations would only be generated by LMR and are of only moderate plausibility. Some may be useful to connect subsequent lines of the passage with earlier lines. Other elaborations such as Tim's crew cut might seem irrelevant to any comprehension function. However, it is actually difficult to judge in advance what will prove relevant and what will not. Consider the following "trick" story from Reder (1976):

> 3. Alice went to Jimmy's house for lunch. Jimmy's mom served them tunafish sandwiches. Alice liked her sandwich very much and had almost finished it when, all of a sudden, her dentures fell out of her mouth.

Readers quickly detect the humor in this passage, and the comprehender knows why it is funny; however, it is much harder to pinpoint exactly how the anomaly was detected. It is worth considering the introspections LMR reported as to how she detected the anomaly. Part of her elaboration of this passage involved Alice having the smooth skin of a young girl. When LMR heard about the dentures falling out, she elaborated a wrinkled face with an old mouth and exposed gums. The anomaly was detected by noting the contradiction of these two facial features. Thus, elaborations about personal appearance proved critical to detecting the contradiction.

The idea that elaboration may be an important component in human cognition is old. In perception, a similar notion was advanced a century ago by Helmholtz. He proposed that a person combines information from impoverished stimuli with general world knowledge to make inferences about these stimuli. We believe that the predictive and inferential function of the elaborative process is at least as essential as its function in promoting good memory. This function of elaboration is clear when one considers the need to find connections among sentences in prose material, whereas it is not so clear when one considers the free-recall task.

With respect to prose comprehension, it is also clear that it is not functional for people to be good at elaborating orthographic information, whereas it is functional for them to be good at elaborating the semantic content of a passage. That is, there is seldom any payoff for remembering orthographic information, whereas there is frequent payoff for remembering the semantic content of messages. As a consequence, people have learned how to elaborate on semantic content but not on the orthographic. If the nature of our world changed and orthographic information became critical, we would expect to see a gradual change in one's ability to remember orthographic information.

Experimental Evidence

From the point of view of providing strong empirical support for the elaboration theory, a serious problem arises in that the theory implies that an experimenter has poor ability to manipulate the amount and direction of elaboration. For instance, in the typical verbal-learning DOP study, we propose that the amount of elaboration is a function of past experience. This means one must rely on intuition as to what sorts of information subjects are more adept or practiced at elaborating. Unfortunately, in this respect, we have not avoided the unsatisfactory intuitive explanations that have characterized other approaches to DOP.

We believe, on the other hand, that it is possible to obtain more compelling evidence when studying prose material. This is because the richer stimulus material offers more potential to control a subject's processing. We review some of the experimental literature relevant to elaborative processing of prose and then present a summary of some of Reder's work designed to get at these issues.

There are a number of results concerning selectivity in memory that are consistent with an elaboration—plus—reconstruction viewpoint. If subjects have more ability to make certain types of elaborations than others or if subjects are directed to make certain elaborations rather than others, one should see better memory for material consistent with the preferred elaboration and more distortion of material in the direction of the preferred elaboration. The classic example, of course, is the research of Bartlett (1932). He had pre-World War I English subjects study a northwest Indian story, "The War of the Ghosts." He obtained what he interpreted as systematic distortion of the material in the direction of the knowledge of his subjects. This distortion took the form of additions to the material that made the story more consistent with the world view of his subjects, deletion of inconsistent information, and transformations of inconsistent information to make it more consistent with prevailing beliefs.

There has been a long history of debates (e.g., Anderson & Bower, 1973; Gould & Stephenson, 1967; Spiro, 1977) over the extent to which Bartlett's subjects were really misremembering and the degree to which they were knowingly confabulating in respone to perceived task demands. It seems that at least to some degree, subjects are aware of their distortions and are able to assign lower confidence to these than to veridical recalls. However, we feel that this debate misses an important point: The behavior of subjects in Bartlett's task is typical of prose processing. Normally, the reader does not make distinctions between what was actually read in a passage and what is a plausible inference. With most stories, the inferences made are plausible extensions of the story and are not distortions. It was Bartlett's clever story selection that served to highlight the elaborative behavior of subjects.

A number of recent experiments have shown that subjects can be influenced by information they are given about a passage. For instance, Sulin and Dooling (1974) had subjects study identical passages except that the main character was either named Gerald Martin or Adolf Hitler. Subjects showed much greater confusion to foils true of Hitler when they had studied the passage that used Hitler's name. Subjects showed a somewhat similar pattern of confusion when they only learned that the individual was Hitler after reading the passage (Dooling & Christiaansen, 1977). This suggests that distortion can occur at time of test as a reconstructive process and need not operate as an encoding process.

Bower (1976) reports an interesting experiment looking at the effect of prior information on subjects' memory for a passage. Subjects were given a story that consisted of subpassages. Half of the subjects were given prior information that would suggest an interesting, unusual interpretation; half were given no prior information. The story follows the principal character through five episodes: making a cup of coffee in the morning, visiting a doctor, attending a lecture, going shopping in a grocery store, and attending a cocktail party. The meaning of these episodes can be very different depending on whether or not we view the heroine as pregnant. Subjects given the interesting interpretation recalled many more inferences appropriate to the pregnancy theme. They also recalled more of those episodes related to the theme. This is just what we would expect if they were using their information about pregnancy to elaborate. These elaborations should make the text information more redundant and introduce additional inferences.

Hayes (1976) has found a similar correlation between number of intruded inferences and overall memory for text. Hayes and his colleagues tried to find out what mechanisms allow some people to remember more than others. They pretested subjects on their memory for various historical facts and then classified them as those who remember a lot of history and those who do not. The subjects were then given a fictitious history passage to read. The same subjects who knew more veridical history performed better on a test of the fantasy history passage. Subjects were also asked to free recall the passage that they had read. Not only did the subjects with better history memory recall more, they also "recalled" many elaborations that were not asserted. These elaborations were not simple paraphrases of the passage, nor were they simple inferences. The subjects classified as having poor memory for history offered almost no elaborations. From this finding, Hayes conjectured that embellishing the input with elaborations promotes better retention.

A recent experiment by Schallert (1976) makes similar points. She looked at ambiguous passages, either biasing a passage's reading by giving prior information or not biasing it. She found that subjects in the biased group remembered more information consistent with the bias. She introduced an important DOP manipulation in which subjects either processed the sentence at a "shallow" level (counting four-letter words) or a "deep" level (rating for ambiguity). She found that the biased subjects were more likely to remember consistent information when they were processing the material at the semantic level. The elaboration hypothesis predicts that subjects should be generating more elaborations under semantic-orienting instructions. It also claims that elaborations are responsible for this biasing in recall. Therefore, it predicts the interaction found by Schallert between DOP and disambiguating information.

Manipulation of Prose Elaborations

Reder (1976; in press) performed experiments that manipulated quite directly the amount of elaboration given to prose material.[3] She had subjects study short stories of about 20 sentences. An earlier study had shown that subjects have very good memory for these stories even after a week's delay. So the dependent measure chosen was not how well subjects could answer questions, but rather the

---

[3]The most direct manipulation would have been simply to instruct subjects to "elaborate more." This direct manipulation was avoided because of the obvious problems of demand characteristics. It is also uncertain whether subjects could directly relate such a verbal command to the desired underlying operations. Finally, it is a rather bizarre request.

speed with which they could answer questions. The use of reaction-time measures was also important to the additive factors logic that she used. The intent of the study was to encourage subjects to process these stories in the same manner they use outside the experimental setting—which we claim would be a rich elaborative manner. Therefore, subjects were not required to make verbatim memory judgments about the story; rather, they were required to judge the plausibility of the probe with respect to the story. One of the variables of the study was the ease with which subjects could make such plausibility judgments. Three kinds of targets were used. Although these targets were all clearly plausible, they varied in the ease with which they could be judged as plausible. There were verb-based statements that followed directly from the verb of one of the sentences. These are statements that are highly plausible but are seldom spontaneously generated by subjects. (One independent group of subjects generated elaborations to the story, and another rated the plausibility of those generated elaborations.) For instance, if the original text contained: "The heir told his father he wanted no part of his greasy food fortune," the subject might be asked to judge the plausibility of: "The heir communicated with his father."

A second class of statements, called high-plausible statements, were both high in judged plausibility and in frequency of generation. For instance, suppose the original text contained: "The heir decided to join Weight Watchers. Twenty-five pounds later, he realized his wife did love him after all." A high-plausible statement to judge might be: "The heir lost weight."

The third type of statement, the so-called medium-plausible statements, were lower in plausibility than either the high or verb-based statements. They were more frequently generated than the verb-based but less frequently than the high-plausible. For instance, if the subject had studied: "Now he worried that she [his wife] had been after his money all along," the to-be-judged statement was: "The heir had not worried about her motives before marriage."

The average lengths of the three types of probes were equal. For reasons unnecessary to unpack here (but see Reder, 1976), it was expected that both the medium-plausible and verb-based statements would take longer to judge than the high-plausible. Of principal interest was how this variable would interact with the other two variables of the study.

A second variable, called treatment, was a manipulation designed to vary the amount of elaboration relevant to making the judgment. At one extreme, the statement was actually *presented*. This should give the maximal opportunity for elaboration. At the other extreme, the *not-presented* condition, no effort was taken to induce relevant elaborations beyond presenting the story. In the treatment between these two extremes, a question was asked during the story that focused the subject on that part of the story that was relevant to answering the question. This was called the *primed* condition. For instance, the subject might read: "Anyway, real marital strife lay elsewhere. His wife had never revealed before marriage that she was an intellectual, that she read books." Then the subject would be asked to judge the plausibility of: "The heir was delighted that she joined the Book-of-the-Month Club," which is, in fact, not plausible. This question was a prime for judging the plausibility of: "The heir did not like the fact that she read books."

The final variable was the delay at which the subject was asked to make plausibility judgments. The subject would either be asked immediately after the relevant portion of the story or after the story had been completed. In the immediate-presented condition, the statement as a test query followed immediately after its presentation as a statement in the story. The test also followed immediately after asking the prime in the immediate-primed condition. In the delay conditions, the test was approximately 2 minutes after the reading of the relevant portion of the story.

These three variables—plausibility, treatment, and delay—were combined factorially to create 18 conditions. The delay manipulation should affect the availability of information with which to make the plausibility judgment. Treatment (presented versus primed versus not presented) should also manipulate availability of information by affecting amount of elaboration. Therefore, since treatment and delay affect the same process, one would expect them to interact. The plausibility of the statement should affect the ease of making the reconstructive computations that decide plausibility from the elaborations. If one assumes that the subject first retrieves relevant information and then computes plausibility, there is no reason to expect plausibility to interact with the other two variables. It affects a later stage in the information processing.

Figure 18.2 plots reaction time to judge plausible statements as a function of the three variables. "Foil" implausible statements were also used to keep subjects honest, but they did not vary systematically. The pattern of data corresponds quite closely to the predictions of Reder's (1976) model, which is a formal version of the elaboration model. All the main effects are highly significant. Of critical importance, there is a two-way interaction between treatment and delay: $F(2,86) = 35.8; p < 0.001$. The presented condition initially was much faster then the other two, but at a delay, the presented statements took about as long as the primed. The difference between primed and not-presented, on the other hand, grew with delay. The difference between primed and not-presented was significantly bigger in the delay condition than in the immediate, $t(132) = 2.3, p < 0.05$. Therefore, the interaction of treatment with delay is not solely attributable to a big slowdown in the presented statements. That possibility would have made the interaction less interesting: In the immediate-presented conditions, subjects may have been faster due to the repetition of an identical phrase, which may have enabled them to bypass normal comprehension mechanisms.

Plausibility was not affected by treatment or delay; i.e., there was no significant interactions with this factor. The lines, connecting levels of inference type over treatment and delay conditions, are essentially parallel. There is one

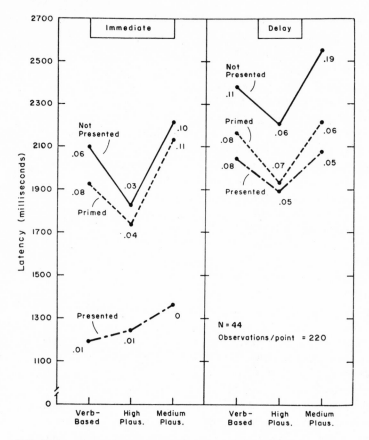

FIG. 18.2.   Mean latencies of correct plausibility judgments (and error rates) as a function of plausibility type, treatment, and delay. From Reder (1976).

exception to the rule of parallel lines, the immediately presented condition. Although there was no overall significant interaction with plausibility, a special contrast was constructed that compared the plausibility effects for the immediate-presented condition with the average effects across treatment and delay. The immediate-presented condition had a different effect due to plausibility than did any other condition, $F(2,172) = 3.54$, $p < 0.05$.

The immediate-presented condition may involve somewhat different processing than the other conditions. For instance, it is possible that subjects were sometimes making their plausibility judgments on the basis of a template match with a verbatim trace of the sentence still active in short-term memory. In none of the other conditions is this likely. It is remarkable how similar the plausibility effect is in these other conditions. The parallel character of these plausibility functions would not have been predicted on one prevalent view of sentence processing (e.g., Anderson & Bower, 1973; Kintsch, 1974; Schank, 1975). This view claims that one tries to verify sentences by simply retrieving them from memory, only resorting to more elaborate inferential reasoning if the statement cannot be found. That view is not consistent with the obtained plausibility effect in the delayed presented condition, since other memory data of Reder mentioned earlier indicates that the presented statements are stored. The reconstructive view of plausibility judgments, on the other hand, is consistent with the results, even the effect in the delayed presented condition.

Upon introspection, it seems clear from everyday examples that plausibility judgments are typically made by means of reconstructive computations and not by means of direct retrieval. For example, to decide if the three characters in *No Exit* were happy or if the young boys in *Lord of the Flies* were savages, one does not search memory for a specific proposition that asserts that the *No Exit* characters were unhappy, nor for a proposition that asserts that the boys in *Lord of the Flies* were savages.

Directions for Future Research

What most impresses us about elaborative processes is that they seem to provide a mechanism for producing powerful effects in overall level of recall. Although measurements using reaction time—as in Reder's experiment— are often theoretically more sensitive, the striking effects should be seen in percent recall. Our respective research endeavors in this area are aimed at discovering what manipulations can increase the amount of relevant elaborative processing that a student can do for prose material and whether these manipulations have their anticipated effects on percent retention. Many mnemonic devices advocated for learning material (see Bower, 1970, for a review) are not directly related to the content of the material. For example, a Roman orator using the method of loci to remember a speech might imagine a puddle of water in front of a temple to prompt discussion about water projects. On the other hand, elaborative processing that also facilitates retention is naturally associated with the studied material. The act of elaborating text is basically "exercising" the reader in thinking about the content. We are excited about the theoretical notions of elaborative processing, because we feel this theoretical analysis may be setting a firm conceptual base for practical applications to human memory.

ACKNOWLEDGMENTS

The preparation of this manuscript was a collaborative effort. The preparation and the research reported were supported by NSF grant BNS76-00959 and ONR grant N00014-72-C-0242 to the first author and by an NSF Graduate Fellowship, a Rackham Dissertation Grant, and an NIMH postdoctoral fellowship to the second author. We would like to thank Miriam Schustack for her comments on the manuscript.

REFERENCES

Anderson, J. R. FRAN: A simulation model of free recall. In G. H. Bower (Ed.), *The psychology of learning and motivation* (Vol. 5). New York: Academic Press, 1972.

Anderson, J. R. *Language, memory, and thought*. Hillsdale, N.J.: Lawrence Erlbaum Associates, 1976.

Anderson, J. R., & Bower, G. H. *Human associative memory*. Washington, D.C.: V. H. Winston, 1973.

Bartlett, F. C. *Remebering: A study in experimental and social psychology*. Cambridge: Cambridge University Press, 1932.

Bobrow, S., & Bower, G. H. Comprehension and recall of sentences. *Journal of Experimental Psychology*, 1969, *80*, 455–461.

Bower, G. H. Analysis of a mnemonic device. *American Scientist*, 1970, *58*, 496–510.

Bower, G. H. *Comprehending and recalling stories*. American Psychological Association, Division 3, Presidential Address, Washington, D.C., Sept. 6, 1976.

Bower, G. H., & Karlin, M. B. Depth of processing pictures of faces and recognition memory. *Journal of Experimental Psychology*, 1974, *103*, 751–757.

Bower, G. H., Karlin, M. B., & Dueck, A. Comprehension and memory for pictures. *Memory & Cognition*, 1975, *3*, 216–220.

Bransford, J. D., & Johnson, M. K. Considerations of some problems of comprehension. In W. Chase (Ed.), *Visual information processing*. New York: Academic Press, 1973.

Craik, F. I. M., & Lockhart, R. S. Levels of processing: A framework for memory research. *Journal of Verbal Learning and Verbal Behavior*, 1972, *11*, 671–684.

Craik, F. I. M., & Tulving, E. Depth of processing and the retention of words in episodic memory. *Journal of Experimental Psychology: General*, 1975, *104*, 268–294.

Dooling, D. J., & Christiaansen, R. E. Episodic and semantic aspects of memory for prose. *Journal of Experimental Psychology: Human Learning and Memory*, 1977, *3*, 428–436.

Fisher, R. P., & Craik, F. I. M. The interaction between encoding and retrieval operations in cued recall. *Journal of Experimental Psychology: Human Learning and Memory*, 1977, *3*, 701–711.

Goldstein, A. G., & Chance, J. E. Visual recognition memory for complex configurations. *Perception & Psychophysics*, 1971, *9*, 237–241.

Gould, A., & Stephenson, G. M. Some experiments relating to Bartlett's theory of remembering. *British Journal of Psychology*, 1967, *58*, 39–49.

Hayes, I. R. Personal communication, 1976.

Hyde, T. S., & Jenkins, J. J. Recall for words as a function of semantic, graphic, and syntactic orienting tasks. *Journal of Verbal Learning and Verbal Behavior*, 1973, *12*, 471–480.

Kintsch, W. *The representation of meaning in memory*. Hillsdale, N.J.: Lawrence Erlbaum Associates, 1974.

Kintsch, W. Memory representations of text. In R. L. Solso (Ed.), *Information processing and cognition*, Hillsdale, N.J.: Lawrence Erlbaum Associates, 1975.

Neisser, U. *Cognitive psychology*. Englewood Cliffs, N.J.: Prentice–Hall, 1967.

Nelson, T. O. Repetition and depth of processing. *Journal of Verbal Learning and Verbal Behavior*, 1977, *16*, 151–171.

Reder, L. M. The role of elaborations in memory for prose. *Cognitive Psychology*, in press.

Reder, L. M. *The role of elaborations in the processing of prose*. Unpublished doctoral dissertation, University of Michigan, 1976.

Schallert, D. L. Improving memory for prose: The relationship between depth of processing and context. *Journal of Verbal Learning and Verbal Behavior*, 1976, *15*, 621–632.

Schank, R. C. *Conceptual information processing*. Amsterdam: North–Holland, 1975.

Schank, R. C., & Abelson, R. P. *Scripts, plans, goals and understanding: An inquiry into human knowledge structures*, Hillsdale, N.J.: Lawrence Erlbaum Associates, 1977.

Spiro, R. J. Inferential reconstruction in memory for connected discourse. In R. C. Anderson, R. J. Spiro, & W. E. Montague (Eds.), *Schooling and the acquisition of knowledge*. Hillsdale, N.J.: Lawrence Erlbaum Associates, 1977.

Sulin, R. A., & Dooling, D. J. Intrusion of a thematic idea in retention of prose. *Journal of Experimental Psychology*, 1974, *103*, 255–262.

Thorndyke, P. W. *Cognitive structures in human story comprehension and memory*. Unpublished PhD dissertation, Stanford University, 1975.

Wickelgren, W. A. The long and the short of memory. *Psychological Bulletin*, 1973, *80*, 425–438.

19 Relation Between Encoding Specificity and Levels of Processing

Endel Tulving
University of Toronto

In this chapter I review the concepts of encoding specificity and levels of processing and discuss the relation between them. The main point of the chapter is that these two sets of ideas are converging on a common fundamental orientation toward phenomena of episodic memory. In this orientation, recollection of an event is a joint function of information stored in memory about the event (the trace) and the information available to the rememberer at the time of attempted retrieval (the cue). Whether or not recollection succeeds depends on the compatibility of the two kinds of information. The major challenge to memory theory lies in the description and understanding of the relation between trace information and retrieval information that underlies remembering of events. Factors such as depth of encoding and distinctiveness or elaboration of memory traces are a part of such description and play a partial role in the attempts to gain such understanding; they need not be considered separately from, or in addition to, the compatibility relation between the trace and the cue.

ENCODING SPECIFICITY

The set of ideas we now know under the label of "encoding specificity" originated in experimental work designed to illuminate the problem of effectiveness of retrieval cues. The original experiment produced results that were interpreted as suggesting that "specific retrieval cues facilitate recall if and only if the information about them and about their relation to the to-be-remembered words is stored at the same time as the information about the membership of the to-be-remembered words in a given list" (Tulving & Osler, 1968, p. 599). The "if and only if" clause in this suggestion was meant to imply a rejection of the then-popular and strongly held belief that one word could serve as an aid for the retrieval of another solely by virtue of the preexperimental relation between them. Under the impact of the results of other experiments and the general acceptance of the idea that words and word-events could be usefully conceptualized as bundles of features or collections of attributes (Bower, 1967; Underwood, 1969), the encoding specificity hypothesis was formulated in more general terms. Thus, for instance, two years later we found it more convenient to suggest that "a specific encoding format of the to-be-remembered item seems to constitute a prerequisite for the effectiveness of any particular retrieval cue" (Thomson & Tulving, 1970, p. 255); we defined the encoding specificity hypothesis as a proposition that "retrieval of event information can only be effected by retrieval cues corresponding to a part of the total encoding pattern representing the perceptual cognitive registration of the occurrence of the event [p. 261]." We wanted to emphasize the fact that the subjects' task was one of remembering the *event* of a word's occurrence in a particular list and that it was stored information about the word-event, rather than about the target word as such, that was critical for cue effectiveness. The phrase, "the total encoding pattern representing the perceptual cognitive registration" of the event, was meant to convey the impression that more was involved in studying a to-be-remembered word than just strengthening, or activating, or adding an occurrence tag to the word's preexperimental representation in memory, although the wording of the idea might have left something to be desired.

In 1973 Donald Thomson and I proposed the encoding specificity principle, asserting that "only that can be retrieved that has been stored, and that how it can be retrieved depends on how it was stored" (Tulving & Thomson, 1973, p. 359); or, in somewhat more elaborate terms, that "specific encoding operations performed on what is perceived determine what is stored, and what is stored determines what retrieval cues are effective in providing access to what is stored [p. 369]." The formulation of the encoding specificity principle is not greatly different from the wording of the encoding specificity hypothesis, although it makes a bit more explicit the dependence of the memory trace on the encoding operations and hence the relation between encoding and retrieval conditions; the difference between the two has to do with their status in the ongoing enterprise of attempting to make sense of the empirical facts. The encoding specificity hypothesis is testable, and it gains or loses credibility depending on experimental outcomes. In order to test the hypothesis, however, the experimenter must know or assume, on whatever basis, exactly what has been encoded in any particular study instance. Such knowledge is not always available; indeed, it is frequently the object of inquiry. This is where the encoding specificity principle enters the picture. We can assume that the encoding specificity hypothesis is in fact true and that a retrieval cue is effective only to the extent that its informational contents match those of the trace; we can then make inferences about what has been encoded, or about the memory trace, on the basis of observed effectiveness of different retrieval cues. In either case—treating encoding specificity as a hypothesis or as a principle—the only facts are provided by observations about the effectiveness of different retrieval cues, whereas two things are unknown— the properties of the trace and the validity of the encoding specificity hypothesis. In order to relate all three principal components of the logical structure of the retrieval situation, we must make some sort of an assumption about one of the two unknown factors. When we use encoding specificity as a hypothesis, we make an assumption about the trace; when we use it as a principle, we make an assumption about the validity of the hypothesis.

Experimental evidence relevant to the evaluation of the encoding specificity hypothesis is derived from a particular type of experiment. The general characteristics of the class of experiments include the requirements that the subject variables and learning materials be held constant in all conditions of the experiment and that both the study (encoding) and test (retrieval) conditions be manipulated in an orthogonal design. The Tulving and Osler (1968) experiment can serve both as an example of a typical encoding specificity experiment and as a source of critical data. Only a part of the complete design is described here, the part relevant to our present purpose.

In the experiment, subjects studied, on a single trial, a list of 24 cue–target pairs and were then tested for their ability to recall the target items in the presence of cues. The cues were either the same that they had seen at the time of study or they were "new," not encountered before in the experiment. There were two encoding conditions: (a) target word accompanied by Cue A, or (b) target word accompanied by Cue B. These two encoding conditions were crossed with two retrieval conditions: (a) Cue A presented, or (b) Cue B presented. Cues A and B were single words that in free associations elicited the target words as a primary response with a probability of 0.01. Two cue words corresponding to any given target word were selected according to normative data and were assigned to the two sets, A and B, on a random basis. Thus, the target words were identical in all four experimental conditions, the cues were equivalent in the two sets, and the relation between the cues and targets in both sets was also equivalent. These features of the design are important in determining the inferences to be drawn from the experimental results.

The results of the experiment, in the form of mean proportions of words recalled, are shown in Table 19.1. The data show a strong "crossover" type interaction between encoding and retrieval conditions: When the retrieval cue matched the encoding cue, subjects recalled 62% of the target words, whereas the mismatch between retrieval cues and encoding cues produced a recall rate of approximately 30%. (This latter figure was lower than free recall of target words in the two encoding conditions considered here, as shown by other experimental conditions not described here.)

There are four general conclusions that can be drawn from these data. First,

TABLE 19.1
Probability of Recall as a Function
of Encoding and Retrieval Conditions
(Tulving & Osler, 1968).

| | Retrieval Cue | |
Encoding Cue	A	B
A	0.62	0.29
B	0.33	0.62

the results clearly show that no absolute answer can be given to the question of which of the two encoding conditions was "better," or produced a stronger memory trace, or led to more efficient remembering. Any answer to such a question must necessarily be qualified by the observed interaction between encoding and retrieval conditions and can only be given in relation to a particular retrieval condition. *The "goodness" of a particular encoding operation depends on the nature of the cues present at the time of retrieval.*

Second, no absolute answer can be given to the question of which of the two retrieval cues, A or B, was more effective. This question, too, can be answered only relative to a particular encoding condition. *Effectiveness of a cue, with respect to a particular target item, depends on the conditions under which the target item was encoded.*

Third, on the unassailable assumption that cue A has more information in common with the trace of the A−T (T for target) pair of studied items than with the trace of the B−T pair, we can say that the probability of successful retrieval of the target item is a monotonically increasing function of informational overlap between the information present at retrieval and the information stored in memory. *Successful recollection of an event depends on the compatibility between the trace and the cue.*

Fourth, since the cues, targets, and the preexperimental (semantic) relations were either identical or equivalent in all four experimental conditions, the observed systematic variability in the effectiveness of retrieval cues cannot be attributed to preexperimentally established relations between cue and target words; it must be determined by processes occurring in the study episode. *The compatibility relation between the trace and the cue, as a necessary condition of recollection of an event, is determined by specific encoding operations at the time of study and not by the properties of cues and target items, and their relations, in semantic memory.*

I would like to propose these four conclusions as defining the essence of the notion of encoding specificity. The central ideas are: (a) the necessity of stipulating *both* encoding and retrieval conditions when describing data or making theoretical inferences from them; (b) the futility of trying to understand processes of remembering, either in general or in any specific situation, in terms of only the encoding or storage processes or only in terms of retrieval processes; and (c) the pivotal role played by phenomena demonstrating *interactions* between encoding and retrieval conditions in shaping theoretical ideas about memory.

LEVELS OF PROCESSING

An interesting feature of psychological thought about memory throughout history has been its preoccupation with the first stage of remembering—that is, acquisition and retention of memorial knowledge, or encoding and storage of mnemonic information. Explaining memory usually has meant explaining how knowledge is acquired and retained, or how information is encoded and stored. There has generally been little concern with the problem of how memorial knowledge affects conscious awareness or behavior, or how the stored information is used. Thus, the second stage of remembering—that is, utilization of stored information, or ecphory, activation of latent memory traces—had received scant attention until only about a decade ago.

The essence of the set of ideas known as "levels of processing" initially also was that memory is a by-product of perception and that goodness of retention of a learned item depends on the conditions under which it was studied. Craik and Lockhart (1972), for instance, proposed that the durability of the memory trace is determined by the depth or level at which stimulus items are processed: "Trace persistence is a function of depth of analysis, with deeper levels of analysis associated with more elaborate, longer lasting, and stronger traces [p. 675]." True to tradition, there was little concern with how the acquired information was utilized, that is, how it was retrieved. It is true that Craik and Lockhart also mentioned the importance of retrieval factors; however, it seems fair to say that at least in the early days of the levels-of-processing era, these factors were not of central interest.

In a typical levels-of-processing experiment, subject variables and preexperimental characteristics of to-be-remembered items are held constant, and the manner in which the learners study to-be-remembered items is varied by manipulating orienting tasks, learning instructions, the context of target items, the learners' expectations about the nature of the retention test, and in other similar ways. It is assumed that these manipulations induce the learner to engage in different mental activities at the time of study, or that they induce the memory system to perform different encoding operations upon the input, resulting in qualitatively different memory traces of to-be-remembered events. It is the characteristics of these traces—depth, spread, elaboration, etc.—that determine how well the item or event is remembered.

The idea that retention depends on how the to-be-remembered material is studied is a familiar one in psychology. For instance, Woodworth (1938), discussing problems in connection with the topic of "memory for form," mentions G. E. Müller's theory, according to which "the memory trace weakens or disintegrates and loses the distinctive characteristics of the original figure, except that a characteristic which was emphasized in perception will persist longer than other characteristics and so be accentuated in the reproduction [p. 81]." Woodworth's (1938) own restatement of Müller's theory includes the following proposition:

> The same objective figure can be seen in a variety of ways according to the features that stand out or are emphasized in perception. What stands out may be either a detail or a character of the whole figure. Both stand out in the common learning process of schema-with-correction. Besides the features specially emphasized, [the observer] may be more or less aware of other details and peculiarities of the figure. . . . The theory . . . assumes a true process of forgetting; the trace weakens or dies out; features which were barely noticed die out more rapidly than those that were emphasized [p. 81].

What is novel and surprising about the elaboration of these old ideas in contemporary research are two facts. First, the same kinds of processes that underlie "emphasizing" of various features of the to-be-remembered complex form also seem to be operating in the "perception" of extremely familiar words when they serve as target items in a memory experiment. The well-known experiments from the Minnesota laboratories (e.g., Hyde & Jenkins, 1969, 1973; Jenkins, 1974; Till & Jenkins, 1973; Walsh & Jenkins, 1973) have shown that free recall of a word can depend greatly on the orienting task in which a subject engages at the time of study. These results suggest that different orienting tasks result in "emphasizing" different features even when the features are not *perceptually* identifiable and distinguishable as they are in the case of complex figures. The classical conception of words was that they were mental or behavioral atoms, basic units not further divisible into components; even today there exist theories in which different words are represented as different nodes in an associative network and in which individual nodes are activated in an all−or−none manner. Second, the effects of encoding operations can be very large. For instance, in some of the experiments described by Craik and Tulving (1975), free recall as well as recognition varied over a range from less than 20% to 70 or 80%, even though all "classical" learning variables were held constant. Variations in performance of this magnitude are difficult to achieve through the manipulation of classical variables such as study time or meaningfulness or ability of subjects; in levels-of-processing experiments, they are brought about by differences in encoding conditions within a few seconds per item. In terms of the sheer magnitude of the effects, encoding operations must be regarded as among the most important determinants of memory performance.

The common theme of levels-of-processing experiments that I am emphasizing here, manifested in large differences in recall or recognition of unitary linguistic units as a function of encoding operations, has emerged over the last few years. Initially the theoretical concerns of the leading proponents of levels-of-processing ideas were somewhat different. For instance, Hyde and Jenkins (1969) presented their experimental findings in the context of the theoretical problem of the locus of organizational effects in free recall. The question was whether organization is determined by certain processes at the time of storage or whether it manifests itself because of what happens at the time of recall. Similarly, Craik and Lockhart (1972) developed their ideas about levels of processing as a theoretical alternative to models of memory postulating separate short-term and long-term memory stores. Neither of these issues, locus of organization or usefulness of the distinction between short-term and long-term stores, is of any great interest to anyone now, whereas experimental work and theoretical speculation about the basic theme of levels of processing still seem to be gathering momentum.

As mentioned earlier, early levels-of-processing experiments involved the manipulation of encoding conditions and the measurement of memory performance in one and the same retention test. Thus, for instance, all of the experiments of Jenkins and his associates (e.g., Hyde & Jenkins, 1969, 1973; Till & Jenkins, 1973; Walsh & Jenkins, 1973) have employed the free-recall test. Similarly, Craik and his associates (e.g., Craik, 1973, 1977; Craik & Tulving, 1975; Moscovitch & Craik, 1976) have usually assessed the effects of encoding operations by free recall or recognition. The logical structure of these experiments is the same as that of one-half of a typical encoding specificity experiment: Encoding conditions are manipulated while retrieval conditions are held constant. For instance, the data in the first data column of Table 19.1, showing the results of the Tulving and Osler (1968) experiment, can be thought of as demonstrating the effects of an encoding operation defined in terms of the particular cue present at the study of the to-be-remembered word. In this somewhat limited view, the encoding conditions exerted a large effect on retention performance.

The problem with the interpretation of the data from typical levels-of-processing experiments is twofold. First, as long as the experiment demonstrates only different retention performances in a single test, resulting from different kinds of orienting tasks, instructions, or contexts, it would be perfectly logical to argue that encoding operations constitute just another way of influencing the strength of the memory trace. Such an experiment cannot provide any evidence in support of the contention that different encoding operations create *qualitatively different* memory traces, an idea central to the current levels-of-processing view. The many terms and ideas now used to interpret levels-of-processing experiments—depth, spread, degree of elaboration, uniqueness, distinctiveness, congruity, meaning, and the like—could be replaced with a single concept such as the strength of the memory trace without any dramatic loss of explanatory power. The second problem is that describing the results of levels-of-processing experiments in terms of the relation between properties of memory traces and probability of retention neglects the critical role played by the retrieval information. When the consequences of some orienting task are said to be the establishment of "deep" or "elaborate" memory traces, and it is argued that such traces endure over a longer period of time than those less deep or elaborate, the implicit assumption is that the nature of conditions at the time of the test does not matter.

The emphasis on the importance of retrieval conditions in the encoding specificity approach and the initial neglect of these factors in the levels-of-processing approach created an obvious discrepancy, if not a conflict, between these two broad frameworks for the study of memory. Now, however, they seem to be converging on the same set of basic ideas shaped by the data from the same kind of experiment. Moscovitch and Craik (1976), for instance, have conducted three experiments to study the relations between retrieval and encoding in a levels-of-processing framework. They pointed out that inasmuch as measured memory performance is "influenced by retrieval factors as well as by encoding operations [p. 447]," the explanation of memory processes suggested by the levels-of-processing framework is incomplete. Another series of experiments by Fisher and Craik (1977) was designed to test the hypothesis that the correlation between encoding operations and retention performance reflects differential compatibility of trace and cue information rather than differential durability of traces. In these experiments, encoding conditions were crossed with retrieval conditions, exactly as in encoding specificity experiments. The results showed that "the retention levels associated with a particular type of encoding were not fixed, but depended heavily on the type of retrieval cue used" (Fisher & Craik, 1977, p. 709). Such an interaction between encoding and retrieval conditions can be appropriately interpreted in terms of qualitative differences in memory traces resulting from different types of encoding; it is not readily reconciled with the notion of unidimensional strength of memory traces.

The initial concern of encoding specificity was with the conditions determining the effectiveness of retrieval cues, whereas the initial thrust of the levels-of-processing approach was directed at the importance of encoding conditions. The more recent levels-of-processing experiments, as we have just seen, are indistinguishable from encoding specificity experiments, and so are the basic beliefs held by theorists representing these two points of view. In the process of convergence, however, some new issues have emerged that have opened the door to a fresh debate. We consider two such issues, but first we must take a closer look at the experimental evidence that has pointed to the critical importance of the interaction between encoding conditions and retrieval processes.

ENCODING/RETRIEVAL INTERACTIONS

There are, as we saw earlier in this chapter, four general conclusions that could be drawn from a simple demonstration experiment such as the one described by Tulving and Osler (1968). The most important of these for what follows later in the paper is the third one: Successful recollection of an event depends on the compatibility between the trace and the cue. But the first two conclusions are also relevant: One cannot make any general statements about "goodness" of encoding operations or about effectiveness of retrieval cues; only relative statements are permissible. The fourth conclusion, concerning the role of specific encoding operations as compared with semantic properties of cues and to-be-remembered items, is of less immediate concern in the present context, since all theorists now accept and make active use of the distinction between preexperimental and experimentally created (or semantic and episodic) components of memory, although they may differ in the details of the manner in which the two kinds of information are conceptualized (see, for instance, Anderson, 1976; Anderson & Ortony, 1975; Crowder, 1976; Kintsch, 1974; Tulving, 1976).

The results of the Tulving and Osler (1968) experiment in some sense were perfectly obvious and hence perhaps trivial; all they showed was that one word can serve as a retrieval cue for another one if an association is formed between them and not otherwise. The generality of the conclusions drawn from the results of such an experiment, therefore, may be questionable. The results of some experiments that I next briefly describe serve to demonstrate that the same general pattern of results can also be obtained with materials and under conditions where the reasons for the outcomes are somewhat less obvious and hence also less trivial. Among other things, they show that encoding conditions determine the effectiveness of retrieval cues even when the cues are strongly related to the to-be-remembered items already before the experiment. The results also show that the compatibility relation between traces and cues that is all-important for successful recollection of the event is created at the time of study of the to-be-remembered material, and that whatever compatibility exists between the cue and the to-be-remembered item otherwise is of no direct relevance.

The first experiment we consider is Experiment 2 reported by Thomson and Tulving (1970). The to-be-remembered items (response words from free-association norms) were presented for study either: (a) singly, one item at a time, with the subjects expecting a free-recall test; or (b) as members of cue—target pairs of the same kind as those used in the Tulving and Osler (1968) experiment, with the subjects expecting to be tested with the cues seen at the time of input. The three retrieval conditions, crossed with the two study conditions, were: (a) no specific cues, that is, free recall; (b) the intralist "weak" cues presented in one of the encoding conditions; and (c) "strong extralist cues," words not encountered by the subjects in the experiment, but strongly associated with target words in semantic memory. The study list was presented once, at the rate of 3 sec/target word, and the retention test was given immediately following the presentation of appropriate recall instructions.

The results, in terms of mean proportions of words recalled, are presented in Table 19.2. Comparing no-cue and weak-cue retrieval conditions, or weak-cue and strong-cue conditions, we observe strong interactions. The most important result is that the strong extralist cues considerably facilitate recall following encoding of single to-be-remembered items in anticipation of free recall (0.68 vs. 0.49), but they do not at all help recall following study of target items in the company of weak cues, under conditions where subjects expected to be tested with weak cues (0.23 vs. 0.30). Thus, effectiveness of cue words strongly associated with target words in *semantic* memory depends greatly on the conditions of *episodic encoding* of target words. Conversely, "goodness" of encoding depends on cue conditions at retrieval.

The second set of data come from Experiment 1 described by Tulving and Thomson (1973). Actually, only one-half of the data come from that experiment—the other half being imaginary, based on data from other experiments in which the same kinds of materials were used. What is again important here is the overall pattern of the data rather than any particular single data point. In the experiment, subjects saw and studied the same kind of list that had been used in the Thomson and Tulving experiments, pairs of weak cues and corresponding target words. The subjects were induced to encode the pairs in the expectation that the recall of the target words would be tested with their weak cues. After the presentation of the list, subjects were asked to produce *free associations* to strong *extralist* associates of target words; many of the words thus produced indeed were copies of the to-be-remembered target words. Subjects then were asked to perform a recognition test on these free associations, under instructions to try to identify the to-be-remembered words from the studied list. After they had finished with this "subject-produced" recognition test, they proceeded to take a cued-recall test in which the weak cues they had seen in the study list were

Table 19.2
Probability of Recall as a Function
of Encoding and Retrieval Conditions
(Thomson & Tulving, 1970, Exp. 2).

	Retrieval Cue		
Encoding Cue	*None*	*Weak*	*Strong*
None	0.49	0.43	0.68
Weak	0.30	0.82	0.23

presented as aids to retrieval of target words. Thus, there were two test situations—recognition and cued recall—or two kinds of cues—copy cues and list cues—given after the encoding of the to-be-remembered item in the presence of weak semantic associates. The imaginery condition, the results of which are indicated in parentheses in Table 19.3, is one in which the subjects see the same to-be-remembered items, but in the absence of any list cues, and in anticipation of, say, a free-recall test. Following this presentation, the subjects are again tested with copy cues, in a recognition test, or with the (now extralist) weak associates. The latter of these two test conditions was a part of the design of the Thomson and Tulving (1970) experiments, and we have a pretty good basis for estimating the results in this condition; the results for the recognition test following the "free-recall" encoding are based on an unpublished experiment done in the Toronto laboratories by Judith Sutcliffe.

The results of this experiment are shown in Table 19.3. Again, there is a strong interaction between encoding and retrieval conditions. The weak retrieval cue, not at all surprisingly, is more effective following the encoding of the target item in the presence of these cues, whereas the copy cue, rather surprisingly, is not only more effective following "free-recall" encoding than "weak-cue" encoding, but is also considerably less effective than the weak cue following "weak-cue" encoding. The overall pattern is very similar to that shown in Table 19.1, despite the fact that one of the cues was the copy of the target item. For reasons of parsimony, I would like to suggest that the interpretation and meaning of this pattern of results are identical with those of the Tulving and Osler (1968) results discussed earlier, including the conclusion about the critical importance of the compatibility of (episodically encoded) traces and retrieval cues.

The third set of data come from an experiment by Bobrow and Light, as described by Bower (1970). Subjects saw a list of 44 ambiguous nouns, each accompanied by an adjective specifying a particular meaning of the noun. Under one condition of study, the adjectives specified the meaning of the nouns in such a fashion that the nouns fell into eight large taxonomic categories (e.g., *chirping*—CARDINAL, *homing*—PIGEON; *lamb*—CHOP, *roast*—HAM),

TABLE 19.3
Probability of Recall as a Function
of Encoding and Retrieval Conditions
(Tulving & Thomson, 1973, Exp. 1).

Encoding Cue	Retrieval Cue	
	Weak	*Copy*
(None)	(0.45)	(0.80)
Weak	0.63	0.24

whereas in the other list, the adjective defined the meanings of the nouns in such a fashion that the nouns were unrelated to one another (e.g., *church*—CARDI-NAL, *stool*—PIGEON; *karate*—CHOP, *theatrical*—HAM). There were two conditions of recall: free recall, or cued recall with the category names appropriate to the categories of the first encoding condition as cues.

The results are summarized in Table 19.4. The interaction between encoding conditions and retrieval cues is again apparent: Category names of to-be-remembered words were effective cues after the corresponding category encoding, but ineffective after "unrelated" encoding.

The next experiment we consider is Experiment 1 by Fisher and Craik (1977). Subjects saw 72 concrete nouns and answered questions about them. One-third of the questions were about rhymes, another third about category membership, and the remaining third about the word fitting into a sentence. Answers to the questions were either "yes" or "no." The six encoding conditions (three kinds of questions and two kinds of answers) were crossed with three retrieval conditions, defined by the presentation of the same three classes of retrieval cues used as questions at the time of study.

Table 19.5 shows the recall of words whose encoding questions were answered affirmatively at the time of study. Proportions of words recalled in the cells along the negative diagonal represent conditions where the retrieval cues were the same cues that the subjects encountered at input, whereas the off-diagonal cells represent data from conditions in which extralist cues were presented. The important point here again is the strong interaction between encoding and retrieval conditions: The "goodness" of encoding depends on the type of cue used at retrieval, and the effectiveness of cues varies with the encoding conditions.

There are other experiments in which interactions between encoding and retrieval conditions have been described (e.g., Anderson, Pichert, Goetz, Schallert, Stevens, & Trollip, 1976; Barclay, Bransford, Franks, McCarrell, & Nitsch, 1974; Morris, Bransford, & Franks, 1977; Moscovitch & Craik, 1976; Nelson, Chapter 3, this volume; Nelson, Wheeler, Borden, & Brooks, 1974; Tulving & Watkins, 1975), but those briefly described here illustrate the main

Table 19.4
Probability of Recall as a Function
of Encoding and Retrieval Conditions
(Bobrow & Light, as reported by Bower, 1970).

		Retrieval Cue
Encoding Condition	*None*	*Category Name*
Category	0.39	0.55
Unrelated	0.27	0.20

Table 19.5
Probability of Recall as a Function of Encoding and
Retrieval Conditions (Fisher & Craik, 1977, Exp. 1).

Encoding Condition	Retrieval Cue		
	Rhyme	Category	Sentence
Rhyme	0.40	0.15	0.10
Category	0.43	0.81	0.50
Sentence	0.29	0.46	0.78

features of such experiments. Many different kinds of cues—rhyming words, category names, strong associates, and even literal copies of targets—can vary widely in their effectiveness, depending on how the target words were stored in memory; conversely, different kinds of encoding operations performed on the input—relating the target to a cue word, interpreting its meaning depending on a biasing adjective, considering the target word as a member of a particular category, interpreting it within a sentence frame—lead to differential recovery of the to-be-remembered items, depending on exactly what retrieval information is available. In short, over a considerable range of experimental conditions, empirical facts show that remembering of events is determined by the interaction between encoding and retrieval; the concordant theoretical conclusion holds that success of recollection of an event depends on the congruence or compatibility between trace information and retrieval information.

In the experiments we have just considered, this interaction manifests itself in an unmistakable form. But we must assume that the processes responsible for the interaction are the same in all situations, including those in which its consequences are not apparent. It makes no sense to assume that the basic principles of memory are different depending on the design of the experiment. It is obviously possible to do experiments in which some of the basic principles are not permitted to manifest themselves, but it does not mean that they are not operative in those situations. For these reasons it makes good sense to assume that the recollection of an event is always determined by the compatibility relation between encoding and retrieval conditions, or the trace information and the cue information. This is the basic premise, accepted by both the encoding specificity and levels-of-processing views of memory, with which all analyses of processes of memory must begin.

DEPTH OF ENCODING AND TRACE/CUE COMPATIBILITY

An appropriate relation between the trace and the cue—we have referred to it as compatibility—is obviously a critical determinant of recollection. But is anything else critical, too? More specifically, is it necessary to be concerned with properties of memory traces or retrieval cues separately from, or in addition to, the compatibility relation between them? In this section we consider two possible answers to this question.

One answer has been given by Fisher and Craik (1977), who hold that a complete account of remembering must include a reference to the depth of processing or the resulting trace in addition to the reference to the relation between encoding operations and retrieval cues. In their words, "both the qualitative nature of the encoding and the degree of compatibility between encoding and cue are apparently necessary to give an adequate account of memory processes [p. 710]," and "no one factor in isolation—the type of encoding, the type of cue, or the compatibility between encoding and cue—is by itself sufficient to describe performance [p. 710]."

Another answer to the earlier question, which I find preferable, is that once we accept the proposition that retrieval of a memory is determined by the compatibility between trace and cue information, there is no need to postulate anything in addition about the relevance of encoding, trace, or retrieval factors. Thus, I would like to argue that the compatibility of trace and retrieval information "in isolation," to use Fisher and Craik's expression, would be sufficient to provide an understanding of memory performance. This position is more parsimonious than Fisher and Craik's, which postulates two factors; it should be explored first and rejected only if it is contrary to empirical facts. For the time being, the insistence on the importance of either the trace or the cue properties separately, in addition to considering their compatibility relation, appears to be logically superfluous; it may also mislead theorists into the traditional preoccupation with trace properties as such, a preoccupation that may have prevented us from making faster progress with understanding of memory.

Fisher and Craik (1977) found support for their conclusion that both compatibility between trace and cue and the depth of the trace were important in three kinds of findings yielded by their experiments. First, as illustrated by the data in Table 19.5, subjects' performance was higher following semantic encoding than rhyme encoding, even when the retrieval conditions were said to be "optimal"—that is, when rhyme-encoded target words were tested with rhymes as cues and associatively encoded target words were tested with their intralist associates as cues. These are the experimental conditions represented by the cells along the negative diagonal in Table 19.5. I return to the concept of "optimal retrieval conditions" later in this chapter; here I would only like to point out that it is incorrect to assume that nominal identity between encoding and retrieval conditions is equivalent to "optimal" retrieval conditions.

The other two important findings come from Fisher and Craik's (1977) Experiment 3. In this experiment, subjects studied target words either in the presence of rhyming context words (e.g., CAT studied in the context of *hat*) or in the presence of associatively related words (CAT studied in the context of *dog*).

Crossed with these two encoding conditions (rhyming encoding and associative encoding) were three kinds of retrieval cues: (a) "identical" cues, the same context words that accompanied the target words in the study list (*hat* as cue after *hat*−CAT encoding and *dog* as cue after *dog*−CAT encoding); (b) "similar" cues, consisting of extralist cues related to the target words along the same dimension that was biased by the encoding situation (e.g., extralist cue *mat* after *hat*−CAT encoding and extralist cue *lion* after *dog*−CAT encoding); and (c) "different" cues, consisting of extralist words related to the target word along the dimension that was not biased at the time of encoding (e.g., cue word *lion* given for the target word CAT encoded in the rhyming condition, and the cue word *mat* given for the target word CAT encoded in the context of *dog* in the associative condition).

The results of this experiment are reproduced in Table 19.6. These results contain two important findings. First, the level of performance in the experimental conditions defined by rhyme encoding and "identical" encoding/retrieval similarity (0.24) was essentially the same as the level of performance in the condition in which associative encoding was combined with "different" encoding/retrieval similarity (0.22). Since the "similarity" between the cue and the encoding condition must have been higher in the former condition than in the latter, identical recall probability suggests the presence of a factor other than encoding/retrieval (or target/cue) similarity. This other factor, according to Fisher and Craik, is the depth of initial encoding.

The second important finding contained in the data in Table 19.6, according to Fisher and Craik, is the fact that the *superiority* of associative over rhyme encoding was positively correlated with the degree of *similarity* between the encoding context and the retrieval cue: As encoding/retrieval similarity is reduced from "identical" through "similar" to "different," the difference between associative and rhyming encoding conditions becomes progressively smaller—from 0.30 to 0.18 to 0.06. Fisher and Craik conclude that "the beneficial effects of similarity between encoding context and cue are greatest with deep, semantic encodings [p. 709]"; it is this interaction between the level of processing (or the nature of the trace) and the degree of similarity between

Table 19.6
Probability of Recall as a Function of Encoding
Condition and Encoding/Retrieval Similarity
(Fisher & Craik, 1977, Exp. 3).

	Encoding/Retrieval Similarity		
Encoding Condition	Identical	Similar	Different
Rhyme	0.24	0.18	0.16
Associate	0.54	0.36	0.22

encoding and retrieval conditions that is taken as evidence that the type of encoding (the type of trace) is important in addition to the trace/cue similarity.

The conclusions that Fisher and Craik have drawn from their findings are logically perfectly consistent with their data. The problem is that the findings are also perfectly logically consistent with two other sets of conclusions that are different from Fisher and Craik's. One is that the other important factor besides the trace/cue compatibility is defined by the retrieval conditions; the other is that it is not necessary to specify any additional factors and that the probability of retrieval always depends only on the nature of the relation between the trace information and the retrieval information.

To illustrate how the first of these two alternative conclusions follows from the data, we take the results of Fisher and Craik's (1977) Experiment 3 from Table 19.6 and rearrange them as shown in Table 19.7. Here one variable is still the similarity between encoding and retrieval conditions, whereas the other variable now is the type of retrieval cue, either rhyme or associate. This arrangement is also perfectly consistent with the design of Fisher and Craik's experiment, but the conclusions we would draw from the data are now quite different. First, we notice that the levels of performance are quite similar in two experimental conditions: one in which the "similar" encoding/retrieval is combined with the rhyme cue (0.18), and the other in which the "different" encoding/retrieval is combined with the associate (0.16). On this basis we could argue that since the trace/cue similarity was greater in the former than in the latter condition, the virtual identity of outcomes suggests that there is another important factor that contributes to performance, namely the type of retrieval cue.

The second important conclusion that follows from the results tabulated in Table 19.7 is that there is apparently an interaction between type of retrieval cue and similarity of cue to encoding context, since the superiority of associative over rhyme cue is greater at higher degrees of similarity.

Thus, on the basis of the data from Fisher and Craik's (1977) Experiment 3,

Table 19.7
Probability of Recall as a Function of Type of
Retrieval Cue and Encoding/Retrieval Similarity
(Fisher & Craik, 1977, Exp. 3).

	Retrieval Cue	
Encoding/Retrieval Similarity	*Rhyme*	*Associate*
Identical	0.24	0.54
Similar	0.18	0.36
Different	0.22	0.16

summarized in Table 19.7, we can conclude that both type of retrieval cue and similarity of cue to encoding context play major roles in determining the level of recall. This last statement is very similar to the one made by Fisher and Craik to the effect that the results of their Experiment 3 confirm that "both type of encoding and similarity of cue to encoding context play a major role in determining the level of recall [p. 708]."

The point of the exercise we have just concluded is very simple: There is no way of deciding on empirical or logical grounds whether one has to specify encoding conditions or the nature of retrieval cues *in addition to* describing the relation between the two as a determinant of remembering. If one finds that recall is higher with Cue X presented after X-encoding than with Cue Y after Y-encoding, one can only say that remembering is more likely in the former situation than in the latter, and try to understand the difference in terms of whatever ideas seem useful. But one cannot say that X-encoding is in any sense superior to Y-encoding, since such an assertion about the effect of one component violates the logic of the observed interaction; it would be equally correct, or equally incorrect, to say that X retrieval cues are more powerful than Y cues.

Granted that experimental results of the kind described by Fisher and Craik cannot be used to distinguish between encoding and retrieval conditions as a factor to be specified in addition to the trace/cue compatibility, would it at least be possible to argue that one of these two factors—either the type of encoding or the type of retrieval cue—must be specified in addition to the trace/cue relation in a complete account of remembering? I would like to suggest that the answer to this question is "no." Fisher and Craik's (1977) findings are logically consistent with our second alternative conclusion, namely that probability of recall is always determined only by the compatibility between the trace information and the retrieval information. If one accepts this conclusion, any insistence on the importance of encoding or retrieval conditions outside the relation between the two makes little sense. The results of Fisher and Craik's (1977) experiments, such as those shown in Tables 19.5, 19.6, and 19.7, can parsimoniously be regarded as showing that in some experimental conditions the compatibility between the trace information and the retrieval information was greater than in others. Thus, for instance, the appropriate interpretation of the data in Table 19.5 is that the compatibility was about the same in category/category and sentence/sentence conditions and higher in these two conditions than in the rhyme/rhyme condition. Similarly, if we are willing to make an assumption about the linearity of the relation between trace/cue compatibility and proportions of target items recalled, we could say, on the basis of the data in Table 19.6, that the difference in the compatibility between associate/identical condition and rhyme/identical condition was greater than the difference between associate/different and rhyme/different conditions. But neither in these two instances, nor in any other imaginable one, are there any logical grounds for making inferences about the superiority or inferiority of different kinds of encoding conditions, their resultant memory traces, or the nature of retrieval information.

It may be useful to consider some simple analogies to the situation in which the successful recollection of an event depends on the compatibility between the trace information and the retrieval information. One such analogy is provided by lock and key: Whether or not a lock can be operated or activated by a certain key depends on the compatibility between the two. The compatibility can be specified by describing both the lock and the key, and in a certain sense, of course, it is the properties of these two objects that determine their compatibility relation. Yet, once we know that a particular lock is or is not compatible with a particular key, any further statements that we might make about either of them are irrelevant to the question of whether the activation of the lock is possible under the conditions specified.

In the lock-and-key analogy, it is difficult to see how the specification of anything other than the appropriate relation between two entities adds anything to the description of the relation and its consequences. In a similar vein, there is no need to try to speculate about the properties of memory traces or retrieval cues separately from, or in addition to, the relation between them. If we want to understand why recollection of event E_1 is easier than that of E_2, we must know why the compatibility between the trace and retrieval information is greater for E_1 than E_2. Knowing something about the properties of the memory traces in these two cases is useful only insofar as it helps to specify the trace/cue compatibility. It does not matter how we describe memory traces—whether in terms of depth, spread, elaboration, uniqueness, distinctiveness, or what not. In the relativity view here proposed, these terms are meaningful and useful only to the extent that they help us specify the extent to which retrieval information in any particular situation is compatible with the information stored about an event.

I should mention parenthetically that a few years ago I wrote a paper (Tulving, 1974) in which I argued that ideas about cue-dependent forgetting were as useful, if not more so, than ideas about trace-dependent forgetting. The general conclusion I offered in that paper—that forgetting is best thought of in terms of inadequate or insufficient cues—no longer appears acceptable. It seems to make more sense now to think about forgetting, too, in terms of the relation between the properties of the memory trace and the characteristics of the (functional) retrieval cue.

TRANSFER-APPROPRIATE PROCESSING?

The arguments I have been advancing here against the idea that retention depends on the depth of processing or properties of the memory trace in addition to the trace/cue relation are very similar to the thoughts expressed by Morris, Bransford, and Franks (1977). These authors, too, question the usefulness of making general statements about the "goodness" of different types of processing and suggest that the value of any processing task must be assessed relative to the demands of the test situation. They base their criticisms of the conventional levels-of-processing ideas on the results of three experiments that show that a "shallow" orienting task (making rhyming judgments about words) leads to higher performance than a "deep" task (making semantic judgments) *if* performance is measured in a recognition test requiring subjects to make use of information about phonetic properties of seen words. Morris et al. propose an alternative to the levels-of-processing framework for interpreting these results, referring to it as "transfer-appropriate processing." The basic idea is that the value of particular acquisition activities depends on particular goals and purposes.

In light of what I have said in this chapter, I am obviously very sympathetic to the ideas of Morris et al., but I do have some reservations about what these authors have to say about "appropriate" and "inappropriate" tests or "optimal" and "nonoptimal" situations for assessing what the learner has learned. Once we are agreed that no absolute statements about efficacy of learning conditions are possible and that performance always depends on, and can only be understood in terms of, the relation between encoding and retrieval conditions (or the trace/cue relation), it is not obvious exactly what is gained by talking about "right" and "wrong" test situations. I think that the traditional research into memory erred by not paying enough attention to retrieval processes and their relation to the products of acquisition, with subjects almost always tested with "training stimuli"; now we should not slip back into the error of insisting that subjects be tested in the "appropriate" or most "optimal" situation. Such a practice would not fit with the emerging relativity theory of remembering.

It may be useful to distinguish between two possible questions that can be asked about a learner in a learning situation:

1. How well or to what extent has the learner acquired some particular information that he or she did not possess before?
2. Exactly what information has the learner acquired in the situation?

Both questions are perfectly legitimate, meaningful, and worth pursuing; the second question logically includes, and goes beyond, the first. The initial levels-of-processing experiments addressed the first question; to address the second, they now have been extended to include different test situations. Morris et al. (1977) also recommend using designs of experiments in which two or more encoding conditions are crossed with (two or more) retrieval conditions. Depending on the choice of the latter, such an extended experiment can provide information relevant to both questions. Thus, if we do wish to find out exactly what the learner has learned in a given learning episode, it will hardly do to test the subject only in what the experimenter *thinks* is the "appropriate" or "optimal" situation; it is necessary to test the subject in many ways, with many queries and many probes.

An added difficulty characterizes concepts such as "test-appropriate strategies" (Lockhart, Craik, & Jacoby, 1976, p. 91), "optimization of retrieval conditions" (Fisher & Craik, 1977; Moscovitch & Craik, 1976), and "optimal test situations" (Morris et al., 1977). Optimal retrieval conditions must exist in an abstract sense, perhaps like absolute zero in physics, but they will never be realized in either the real world or the laboratory. To claim that a particular retrieval situation with respect to a to-be-remembered item encoded in a particular manner is optimal implies that there are no other retrieval cues that could be more effective. Surely we know enough about these things now not to want to make such claims. Not so long ago, it was generally believed that recognition was the most sensitive test of retention and that if a copy cue failed, no other cue could provide access to the trace of a to-be-remembered item. Now recognition failure of recallable words is a well-known fact (e.g., Rabinowitz, Mandler, & Barsalou, 1977; Tulving & Wiseman, 1975). We also know of conditions where a cue that a subject has not seen in the list (an extralist cue) is more effective than a cue that has been paired with a to-be-remembered item (an intralist retrieval cue), a fact demonstrated by Anderson, Pichert, Goetz, Schallert, Stevens, and Trollip (1976). Fisher and Craik (1977, p. 705) referred to the situation where a word was encoded in a rhyme context and tested with a rhyme cue as the "optimal retrieval context," pointing out that performance in this situation was much lower than that provided by appropriately cued "deeper" encodings. As we saw earlier, this was one of the critical findings that led Fisher and Craik to postulate depth of encoding as a second important factor determining the level of retention. But we know, without having to do a special experiment, that a rhyme-encoded word could be more readily retrieved with the aid of a copy cue than a rhyme cue; this fact means that the condition labeled *optimal* is not so in fact. Finally, in the Morris et al. (1977) experiment, subjects did better in the rhyming recognition test after the rhyming encoding task than after the semantic task. This does not mean, however, that the retrieval information was more appropriate or optimal in the former condition than in the latter. Subjects in the semantic encoding condition in the Morris et al. experiment would have been capable of picking out the correct words on the rhyming recognition test as well or better than the subjects in the rhyming encoding group if they had been given more appropriate retrieval information, for instance, semantic or copy cues. It is not true that subjects in the Morris et al. rhyming encoding groups learned something that subjects in the semantic encoding groups did not; the results of the experiments show only that retention performance depends on the compatibility between encoding and retrieval conditions.

Despite these reservations about the set of ideas under the label of transfer-appropriate processing, I find Morris et al. quite correct in their major criticism of the early levels-of-processing point of view: Semantic orienting tasks do not provide inherently stronger memory traces than do nonsemantic orienting tasks. The same objection to the levels-of-processing ideas has been voiced by Douglas Nelson in Chapter 3 of the present volume, backed by a good deal of convincing evidence.

If remembering depends on the relation between encoding and retrieval conditions, or the compatibility of trace and cue, then the problem for theory is to explain the variability in the efficacy of these relations. Why does one relation between encoding and retrieval produce a higher level of performance than another relation? To say that the trace/cue compatibility is greater in one case than another may well describe the situation, but it does not explain it.

Since this particular form of the problem is of relatively recent origin, there are few directly relevant ideas in the literature. Most theoretical ideas about encoding processes and levels-of-processing phenomena have been directed at the question of the interpretation of differences in the ''goodness' of different encoding operations. Just about the only idea that theorists have about the relation between encoding and retrieval conditions is that the nominal identity of these conditions somehow constitutes optimal conditions of remembering. This idea, as I have suggested, is demonstrably wrong. Its replacement with better insights remains a problem for future research.

UNIQUENESS OF TRACES AND RETRIEVAL CUES

One final matter should be mentioned. Many attempts at explanation of encoding effects have been based on the idea that a memory trace can be more readily retrieved, or ''found'' in the store, if it is different from other traces. Terms such as *discrimination*, *differentiation*, and *uniqueness* express this idea; and others, such as *elaboration* and *richness*, are motivated by the same set of considerations. For instance, the thought that there is something ''inherently'' superior in semantic as compared with, say, phonetic encoding can be rationalized by assuming that if not always, then at least frequently, semantic encodings result in richer, more unique, more elaborate, or more readily discriminable memory traces than does phonetic encoding. So, what about uniqueness?

Moscovitch and Craik (1976) have suggested that the concept of uniqueness might be regarded as an alternative to the idea of depth; deep encodings are unique, whereas shallow encodings are less readily discriminable from one another. This suggestion merits careful thought. There is at least one sense in which a concept such as uniqueness, however labeled, may be important even if we believe in the primacy of the relation between encoding and retrieval as a determinant of remembering. It requires, however, that we think of uniqueness not as an alternative to depth of processing, but rather as an orthogonal dimension.

Given the possibility or existence of different encoding operations, the assertion about the critical role played by the relation between encoding and retrieval conditions, like all scientific hypotheses, is based on the (implicit) assumption of the *ceteris paribus* clause: The assertion does not imply that other variables or conditions could not affect the probability of recollection of an event. One such variable is similarity of items in a to-be-remembered collection. If an item I_1 is encoded in situation E_X, then its retrievability in situation R_X may well vary with the number of other similar items I_2, I_3, . . . I_n in the list. This is the classical phenomenon of associative interference, or its modern equivalent of "cue overload." In this case, we can describe the situation by saying that the "uniqueness" of encoded I_1 varies as a function of a variable that is independent of the encoding situation E_X, retrieval condition R_X, and the relation between the two; and in this sense the uniqueness of the trace of an event can be said to be determined by at least two orthogonal factors—the encoding operation performed on I_1 at input and the presence of other related items I_2, I_3, . . . I_n in the same collection. These ideas are discussed and illuminated in some detail by Michael Eysenck in Chapter 5 in the present volume.

What I am saying is rather mundane: It is possible to entertain the hypothesis that characteristics of the memory trace depend both on what the to-be-remembered item is and what encoding operations have been performed on it at the time of its appearance. Hence uniqueness of the trace also is determined by two factors—the similarity of the target item to others and the similarity between the encoding operations performed on all the items in a set. Whether the two factors can be usefully conceptualized as converging into one and the same underlying dimension of uniqueness, however labeled, or whether it is necessary to keep the two factors apart in thinking about problems of encoding and retrieval is something we cannot say at the present time. The problem is important and undoubtedly will come under experimental and theoretical scrutiny. For the time being, we will do well to keep an open mind about it.

ACKNOWLEDGMENT

The author's research is supported by the National Research Council of Canada Grant No. A8632.

REFERENCES

Anderson, J. R. *Language, memory and thought.* Hillsdale, N.J.: Lawrence Erlbaum Associates, 1976.
Anderson, R. C., & Ortony, A. On putting apples into bottles—A problem of polysemy. *Cognitive Psychology,* 1975, *7,* 167–180.
Anderson, R. C., Pichert, J. W., Goetz, E. T., Schallert, D. L., Stevens, K. V., & Trollip, S. R.

Instantiation of general terms. *Journal of Verbal Learning and Verbal Behavior*, 1976, *15*, 667–679.

Barclay, J. R., Bransford, J. D., Franks, J. J., McCarrell, N. S., & Nitsch, K. Comprehension and semantic flexibility. *Journal of Verbal Learning and Verbal Behavior*, 1974, *13*, 471–481.

Bower, G. H. A multicomponent theory of the memory trace. In K. W. Spence & J. T. Spence (Eds.), *The psychology of learning and motivation* (Vol. 1). New York: Academic Press, 1967.

Bower, G. H. Organizational factors in memory. *Cognitive Psychology*, 1970, *1*, 18–46.

Craik, F. I. M. A "levels of analysis" view of memory. In P. Pliner, L. Krames, & T. M. Alloway (Eds.), *Communication and affect: Language and thought*. New York: Academic Press, 1973.

Craik, F. I. M. Depth of processing in recall and recognition. In S. Dornic (Ed.), *Attention and performance VI*. Hillsdale, N.J.: Lawrence Erlbaum Associates, 1977.

Craik, F. I. M., & Lockhart, R. S. Levels of processing: A framework for memory research. *Journal of Verbal Learning and Verbal Behavior*, 1972, *11*, 671–684.

Craik, F. I. M., & Tulving, E. Depth of processing and the retention of words in episodic memory. *Journal of Experimental Psychology: General*, 1975, *104*, 268–294.

Crowder, R. G. *Principles of learning and memory*. Hillsdale, N.J.: Lawrence Erlbaum Associates, 1976.

Fisher, R. P., & Craik, F. I. M. The interaction between encoding and retrieval operations in cued recall. *Journal of Experimental Psychology: Human Learning and Memory*, 1977, *3*, 701–711.

Hyde, T. S., & Jenkins, J. J. Differential effects of incidental tasks on the organization of recall of a list of highly associated words. *Journal of Experimental Psychology*, 1969, *82*, 472–481.

Hyde, T. S., & Jenkins, J. J. Recall for words as a function of semantic, graphic, and syntactic orienting tasks. *Journal of Verbal Learning and Verbal Behavior*, 1973, *12*, 471–480.

Jenkins, J. J. Can we have a theory of meaningful memory? In R. L. Solso (Ed.), *Theories in cognitive psychology: The Loyola Symposium*. Hillsdale, N.J.: Lawrence Erlbaum Associates, 1974.

Kintsch, W. *The representation of meaning in memory*. Hillsdale, N.J.: Lawrence Erlbaum Associates, 1974.

Lockhart, R. S., Craik, F. I. M., & Jacoby, L. Depth of processing, recognition and recall. In J. Brown (Ed.), *Recall and recognition*. London: Wiley, 1976.

Morris, C. D., Bransford, J. D., & Franks, J. J. Levels of processing versus transfer appropriate processing. *Journal of Verbal Learning and Verbal Behavior*, 1977, *16*, 519–533.

Moscovitch, M., & Craik, F. I. M. Depth of processing, retrieval cues, and uniqueness of encoding as factors in recall. *Journal of Verbal Learning and Verbal Behavior*, 1976, *15*, 447–458.

Nelson, D. L., Wheeler, J. W. J., Borden, R. C., & Brooks, D. H. Levels of processing and cuing: Sensory versus meaning features. *Journal of Experimental Psychology*, 1974, *103*, 971–977.

Rabinowitz, J. C., Mandler, G., & Barsalou, L. W. Recognition failure: Another case of retrieval failure. *Journal of Verbal Learning and Verbal Behavior*, 1977, *16*, 639–663.

Thomson, D. M., & Tulving, E. Associative encoding and retrieval: Weak and strong cues. *Journal of Experimental Psychology*, 1970, *86*, 255–262.

Till, R. E., & Jenkins, J. J. The effects of cued orienting tasks on the free recall of words. *Journal of Verbal Learning and Verbal Behavior*, 1973, *12*, 489–498.

Tulving, E. Cue-dependent forgetting. *American Scientist*, 1974, *62*, 74–82.

Tulving, E. Ecphoric processes in recall and recognition. In J. Brown (Ed.), *Recall and recognition*. London: Wiley, 1976.

Tulving, E., & Osler, S. Effectiveness of retrieval cues in memory for words. *Journal of Experimental Psychology*, 1968, *77*, 593–601.

Tulving, E., & Thomson, D. M. Encoding specificity and retrieval processes in episodic memory. *Psychological Review*, 1973, *80*, 352–373.

Tulving, E., & Watkins, M. J. Structure of memory traces. *Psychological Review*, 1975, *82*, 261–275.

Tulving, E., & Wiseman, S. Relation between recognition and recognition failure of recallable words. *Bulletin of the Psychonomic Society*, 1975, *6*, 79–82.

Underwood, B. J. Attributes of memory. *Psychological Review*, 1969, *76*, 559–573.

Walsh, D. A., & Jenkins, J. J. Effects of orienting tasks on free recall in incidental learning: "Difficulty," "effort," and "process" explanations. *Journal of Verbal Learning and Verbal Behavior*, 1973, *12*, 481–488.

Woodworth, R. S. *Experimental psychology*. New York: Holt, 1938.

20 Four Points to Remember: A Tetrahedral Model of Memory Experiments

James J. Jenkins
University of Minnesota

A discussant always hopes to pick up a latent theme in a conference and justify his presence by bringing this theme to the attention of everyone who has been saying it all along. It is to be hoped that this practice is worthwhile, that is, that it is of some use to investigators to have someone say again to them in somewhat different words what they themselves have said. Or perhaps it is the case that the reader of the volume is waiting for the discussant to simplify the issues and make a bald statement that the authors of the original papers were too sophisticated to affirm. In any case, from my point of view a happy situation seems to exist; there does seem to be a latent theme to the conference, and no one seems yet to have boldly asserted what it is. Thus, as a discussant, I am relieved to find that I have a role.

The theme has been manifested partly in what has been said but, just as importantly, in what has not been said. An interesting feature of this conference is that everyone is being extraordinarily reasonable. No one has insisted on his or her particular view of truth or made unqualified strong assertions about laws or rules of memory. Instead of strong, simple claims of relationships, all speakers have presented their ideas surrounded by a host of qualifications. As an old conference attender, I am prompted to ask: Where are the intemperate generalizations of yesteryear? They have been swallowed up in paragraphs that are hedged about with provisos about particular experimental paradigms, with limitations concerning the kinds of materials employed, with cautions concerning the strategies used by subject populations, and with disclaimers relating to particular dependent measures. The strongest sentences that I have heard here have taken the form, "You must not overlook the influence of . . . [fill in your favorite variable]."

The central theme, then, is that no one around this table thinks that memory is simple anymore. No one is looking for "the one rule" or "the primary law" that will capture the important variations in memory experiments. Everyone now knows that memory phenomena are much more complicated and contextually determined than we used to think they were.

Surely, awareness of this theme is good news to researchers in the field and those who apply the findings of research. It means, first, that the field is open to new paradigms and new research ideas in a way that it never was before. It means that one can explore new populations, new tasks, new materials, and new measures without carrying the weight of tradition and the need to show that the new techniques are like the old ones; because we now suspect that new circumstances are not like the old ones. Secondly, it means that applied researchers can legitimately ask for more varied kinds of help from the basic researchers, pointing out that circumstances of application differ from the classical laboratory paradigms and, thus, need special attention. Third, because we are seeing more and more variety, it means that we have more and more to say to the outside world in the way of practical and valid suggestions for people who have specific problems in memory.

On the other side of the ledger, however, we must face the bad news. Memory is extraordinarily complicated. Our hopes that we could "wrap this field up" in a few years of research are gone. All of the variables that we work with appear to bear complex relations to memory phenomena, and even worse, all of the variables interact strongly with each other. It may well tax all our skills to unravel the patterns of interactions that are already before us, much less understand those we see looming in the distance.

The awareness of interaction is by no means confined to the investigators gathered here. I checked the last copy of *Memory & Cognition* to arrive before this conference and found that 11 of the 16 memory studies appearing in that issue had interaction effects as their primary findings. Just to get the flavor, consider half a dozen of these studies: The first paper (Erdelyi, Buschke, & Finkelstein, 1977) deals with hypermnesia (the increase of recall over repeated recall trials). The investigators report that pictured materials show marked hypermnesia and that words show little, *but* words guessed as the result of riddles show the most hypermnesia of all. Baker and Santa (1977), report a series of experiments that lead them to conclude that the effects of retrieval cues vary with the degree to which the initial list is well integrated and with whether the subjects were given instructions to image the words. Connor (1977) finds that type of test (recall and recognition) interacts with the factors of list and test-list organization as well as the subjects' expectations of the type of test they will receive. Stein (1977) reports that encoding instructions significantly affect the subjects' cued recall of members of word pairs and the subjects' performance on a pair-recognition test; however, the same instructions do not influence performance on simple word recall or recognition. Madden and Bastian (1977) show that recognition probes for digits heard dichotically are differentially judged depending on whether they are in the same voice as the originals. Dhawan and Pellegrino,

(1977) find differences in interference effects in memory for words and pictures. Both location and type of interference are different for the different materials.

Even the most cursory survey of the field is sufficient to reveal that research on human learning and memory is far beyond the stage of announcing simple laws. (See McKeachie, 1974, for an earlier elaboration). We are now trying to accept the fact that our field is *context sensitive*. The memory phenomena that we see depend on what kinds of subjects we study, what kinds of acquisition conditions we provide, what kinds of materials we choose to work with, and what kinds of criterial measures we obtain. Furthermore, the dependencies themselves are complex; the variables interact vigorously with one another.

A GENERAL MODEL

In an attempt to keep the variables in some order and to remind myself that even the variables I am currently neglecting have their effects, I have designed a simple "model." It is a useful heuristic, and I offer it to the conference as a framework into which much of the work can be placed. It could be called the "Problem Pyramid" or the "Theorist's Tetrahedron." It appears in Fig. 20.1.

The point of the figure is very simple. In any real problem we must be concerned with the entire tetrahedron, whether we know it or not. Usually we scale down the complexity of the situation by ignoring the (to us) irrelevant aspects of the tetrahedron in the interest of learning something about a restricted area. This procedure is fine, of course, as long as we remember that we performed the simplification. Sometimes, because we cannot change variables at will, we assume that they are "givens" and accept particular values. This, too, is an acceptable practice as long as we remind ourselves that our self-imposed limits are not naturally limited parameters.

The tetrahedron offers us a kind of classification scheme if we want to use it in that way. Each of us has a favorite vertex, and most of us have a favorite edge for research. Consider the vertices, for example. The vertex marked *orienting tasks* is the favored home of students of incidental learning and the levels-of-processing theorists. They are generally content to alter tasks and ask what the effects are on some fixed criterial task. They rarely change subjects, and they are likely to stick with one kind of material.

Investigators who are intrigued with *materials* are likely these days to study words and pictures, running parallel experiments and reporting on the differences observed as they change from one kind of material to another. Alternatively, they may be educational researchers who are concerned with what kind of material to present as well as its structure and organization over time.

Other investigators may be concerned with *subjects*. They may be interested in children versus adults, or educationally disadvantaged children versus normal children, or subjects with a high degree of skill (for instance, in chess) versus novices. Or, alternatively, they may be personnel psychologists interested in

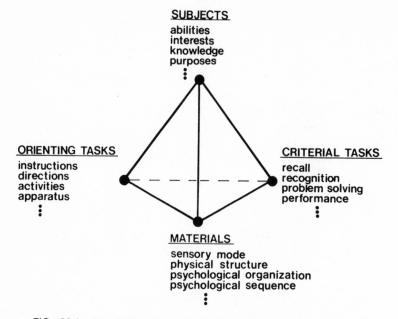

FIG. 20.1. The Problem Pyramid or Theorist's Tetrahedron. Each vertex represents a cluster of variables of a given type. Each edge represents a two-way interaction important to learning and memory. Each plane calls attention to a three-way interaction, and the whole figure represents the four-way interaction of all the variables.

some measured characteristic of a subject population. In most cases, diverse as they seem to be, the investigator is likely to deal with a single paradigm of acquisition, a fixed body of material, and a single dependent measure.

Finally, a few workers are interested in the *criterial tasks*. Such investigators may be concerned with the traditional relationship between recall and recognition, or between memory and problem solving, or the relation between cued versus free recall, or between immediate and delayed measurement of what is learned.

Preferences for interesting problems as shown by a choice of vertices are only the beginning. The problems that grip us most at the present time are the ones that are represented by the interactions along the edges of the tetrahedron. Here we may indeed begin to see the issues of this conference in far more detail than is suggested by the vertices alone. Let us consider these interactions briefly.[1]

---

[1]The writer asks the reader's indulgence for the choice of examples that follow. In the main I have taken examples that are well known to me or conveniently at hand. A complete catalogue would be an entire course in human learning organized along these dimensions, obviously an undertaking for another time and place. The reader may find it instructive to look at a current issue of a journal reporting memory studies and sort the studies into the various categories suggested in the following section.

Orienting Task–Criterial Task Interaction

Clearly the interaction between these two tasks represents the heart of this conference. Theorizing concerned with levels of processing began with the findings that orienting tasks "at different levels" produced differences in free recall. The "deeper," more "semantic" tasks produced superior free recall of words presented in list form, usually in an incidental learning paradigm. The words were medium-frequency-of-usage English words, presented either auditorily or visually. The subjects were college students. But at the same time that these ideas and experiments were being presented, by Craik and Lockhart (1972), Hyde and Jenkins (1973), and Craik and Tulving (1975)—to cite a few canonical studies—the field was aware (and in some cases the same investigator was aware) that the situation was more complex than the framework suggested. The focal argument, of course, was developed by Tulving and his colleagues (e.g., Tulving, Chapter 19, this volume; Tulving & Osler, 1968; Tulving & Thomson, 1973) under the label of *encoding specificity*. This line of research demonstrated that the "same word" (physically) is not always the "same word" (psychologically). Using the cued-recall paradigm and presenting cues in the acquisition list, they showed that the availability of a word for cued recall depends on the "sense" of the word realized by the subject at the time it was presented for learning. If the word *cold* is given in the context of the word *ground* on the original list, for example, it is not readily retrieved in the presence of the cue *hot*, which under other circumstances would be an excellent cue for its recall. Indeed in one study, Tulving and Thomson (1973) found that even the original word itself was sometimes not a good cue for recognition when it was found in a context different from the one in which it was originally presented. Tulving's work hardly needs to be reviewed here. It is enough to recall the intensity with which he has argued at this conference " . . . one canot make any general statements about 'goodness' of encoding operations or about effectiveness of retrieval cues; only relative statements are permissible [Tulving, p. 413]."

   Almost everyone else who presented experimental data at this conference has touched on this crucial interaction. Bransford's arguments concerning "transfer-appropriate processing" direct one to examine the relation between what goes on during the acquisition period and what kinds of processes are required in the later criterial situation (see Morris, Bransford, & Franks, 1977). Moscovitch and Craik (1976) and Fisher and Craik (1977) found powerful interactions between orienting tasks and different kinds of cues that affected recall. The paper by Jacoby and Craik (Chapter 1, this volume) stresses the interactions between distinctive encoding and adequate retrieval information. Battig (Chapter 2, this volume) calls our attention to the fact that items that are difficult to learn may be learned eventually in many different contexts or via several strategies and, thus—all other things being equal—will have a greater likelihood of being recalled in an unspecified context. Eysenck (Chapter 5, this volume) reminds us that word frequency interacts with criterial task (high frequency tends to be good for recall but bad for recognition) and then goes on to show that even that relationship can be wiped out by specified "atypical" processing tasks. To complicate matters even more, however, semantic and phonetic tasks interact with the "typicality of processing" variables.

Outside the domain of word-list recall, there is also considerable interest in the interaction between orienting processes and test processes. Barclay, Bransford, Franks, McCarrell, and Nitsch (1974); Anderson and Ortony (1975); Till (1977); and Verbrugge and McCarrell (1977) have shown in a variety of studies that cued recall may be manipulated in subtle ways depending on the assumed content of the processing involved in understanding sentences. Put most generally, if one knows from logic or intuition the content that listeners must process to understand a sentence they are trying to comprehend, one can use that content as an effective cue in sentence recall, even though the content was originally implicit and does not objectively overlap with the manifest content of the sentence.

One could supply many more examples of work on this particular interaction, but the foregoing are surely sufficient to justify the claim that this interaction is receiving excited attention from many psychologists interested in memory. The ease with which one can obtain very impressive differences through manipulation of the interaction (strongly affirmed by Tulving, Chapter 19, this volume) has made this the second most important notion of the last decade of research, probably exceeded only by the notion of levels of processing itself.

It must be added that the notions of uniqueness, distinctiveness, encoding specificity, elaboration, and so on all make use, explicitly or implicitly, of the interaction of the processes involved in orienting tasks and the processes involved in criterial tasks. Everyone is to some extent struggling with the same sets of problems and working in the same vineyard. Perhaps simple recognition of our concern with exploring these interactions (without too great a preference for "my label" versus "your label") will help us to pursue these interesting problems together.

Orienting-Task–Materials Interaction

It may seem trite to say that whether a given task will be effective in producing recall or not depends on what it is that is to be recalled, but this fact has only recently been appreciated in the laboratory. The current literature seems to be brimming over with studies of the differences between words and pictures as materials in a particular learning–memory situation. A picture may indeed be worth a thousand words, and a diagram may be better understood and retained than a verbal description. Over and over again it has been found that words and pictures are not processed in the same way or with the same effectiveness. Paivio (1975) offered the "dual-encoding hypothesis" to account for some of the observed differences, but the situation seems to be somewhat more complex than that hypothesis would suggest, and many investigators deny that dual coding captures the real differences in materials. Nelson (Chapter 3, this volume) has given us a thorough consideration of some of the differences that are found in particular paradigms in which words and pictures may be used. With the ingenious use of interference evidence, he has shown that words and pictures are often processed differently at acquisition (even under the same instructions). He has gone on to show that under at least one paradigm (ordered-list learning), subjects do verbalize the names of pictures even though they do not do so in another paradigm (when pictures serve as stimuli in paired associates).

There are even more surprising and subtle effects, however, depending on the interrelationships among the items when the materials are "of the same kind." Hyde and Jenkins (1973) used two different word lists in the investigation of orienting tasks, a list of unassociated words and a list containing (nonadjacent) associated pairs such as *table* and *chair*. They found that nonsemantic orienting tasks led to poor recall and semantic tasks led to good recall for both kinds of lists. The list that was associatively related, however, showed a much more marked task effect; the differences between the types of orienting tasks increased. The investigators believed that the added degree of organization or structure exercised a multiplying effect on the usual outcome of the different orienting tasks. Yet, when Strange, Jenkins, and Wilson (1978) asked subjects to perform similar orienting tasks on words that were heard in a paragraph context, the effect of the orienting tasks completely disappeared. One must presume that the orienting tasks failed to exercise a differential effect because all of the subjects processed the words semantically as a result of their being in a story context. It appears that the material demanded and received a kind of processing that overpowered the rating tasks that the subjects were asked to perform. Looking over both of these studies together, we might conclude that as the structure of the material increased, the effect of different orienting tasks was enhanced but then, with further increase in structure, disappeared. As Nelson pointed out forcefully in Chapter 3 (this volume), we cannot assume that the only processing performed by the subject is determined by our instructions as to how to perform the task. In the present case, the material itself demanded and received processing independent of the orienting instructions that was more influential in recall than the processing associated with the instructions.

Materials—Criterial-Task Interaction

The investigation of the interaction between materials and criterial tasks is beset with many difficulties. To begin with, we do not know what criterial tasks are "the same" for different materials. For words, for example, a recall task usually means that the subjects are asked to write or say the orthographic or linguistic characterization of the words they have heard or seen. We do not often ask that the subject keep the same inflection, the same style of type, or any other "irrelevant" aspects of the words that were originally presented. (Yet we know that these variables may make a difference in recognition.) For pictures, on the other hand, we typically ask the subjects to write or say the *name* of the picture they were shown; we do not ask them to reproduce the picture (which on the face of it, would seem to be the closest operation to what we ask with words.) In part, our decision is based on a practical realization that all of our subjects are skilled in saying, in reading, and in writing words and that these skills interpose no obstacle to their displaying what they can recall. We do not suppose that artistic skills are so generously distributed. Indeed, most of us would immediately object to any test of picture recall that demanded accurate reproduction on the grounds that we are simply not skilled enough to reproduce what we actually do remember. (This involves the subject interactions that we consider later, so we may defer this line of argument for the present.)

For most materials, we suppose that recall is more difficult than recognition. If this were just a parametric difference, we could bypass the problem, but it is more than that. With words as materials, recall is usually inferior to recognition (although this relationship has occasionally been reversed; see Tulving & Thomson, 1973). With nonsense figures, however, I am told that the difference is enormous. Recognition is ordinarily excellent, whereas recall is typically abysmal. (One would suppose that the same relationship would hold for recognizing photographs of friends as opposed to drawing their pictures. Most of us would fail to create a faithful representation of any of our friends but would rarely fail to recognize one.)

On the other side of the problem, consider changing the structure of the material while holding the type of material and the criterial task constant. Strange, Jenkins, and Wilson (1978) studied the recognition of target words in the context of synonyms as lures. Across experiments, they varied the structure of the material in which the target words were originally presented. When the target words were presented as specially marked items in a long list of unrelated words, the recognition test showed little false-positive recognition of synonyms (less than one-third of the synonyms were falsely recognized). When the target words were presented as specially marked items in a story context, false recognition of synonyms occurred more than half the time. Further, when the same target words were used in different senses in different stories, the false recognition of synonyms was appropriate to just the meaning used in the story. Subjects who heard Story 1 falsely responded to about half of the appropriate synonyms but responded to only one-fifth of the alternate set of synonyms, whereas subjects who heard Story 2 falsely recognized about half of the second set of synonyms but only about one-fifth of the first set of synonyms.

Another dramatic demonstration of the effect of material structure pertains to picture memory. As is well known, recognition memory for unrelated pictures is excellent. A number of studies have shown that subjects perform with very high accuracy in recognition trials even after viewing thousands of slides (see Shepard, 1967; Standing, 1973; Standing, Conezio, & Haber, 1970). Goldstein and Chance (1970) showed, however, that if all of the slides were taken from the same content category (all faces, or all inkblots, or all snowflakes), recognition accuracy declined precipitously, even with a very small number of slides (14) to be remembered. Jenkins, Wald, and Pittenger (in press) report a series of experiments showing that when the pictures presented for memory were all taken from a single event (like making a cup of tea, answering a phone, or taking a walk), other pictures that belonged to that event were quite likely to be falsely recognized, even though they had not been seen.

We should not rush to conclude that structured material is harder to remember than unstructured material. We know, of course, that exactly the opposite conclusion is justified by the studies of recall. Surely, it would be the case in the last experiment cited that the subject who has seen a set of slides that specify an event will be able to give a more complete account of those slides than a subject who has seen several thousand unrelated slides. The recognition errors that we can elicit from our subjects are "good errors" in the sense that they complete and fill out the structure of the material that they have acquired. (If our students in class did the same kind of thing, we should be happy to call ourselves outstanding teachers!)

Kraft and Jenkins (1977) showed that the positive aspect of structured material can also be observed in a recognition experiment. They were concerned with memory for the left−right orientation of slides. They found that when the slides made a coherent story with movement to the left and right, subjects had no difficulty recognizing the original orientation of the slides. When the slides varied randomly in their original left—right orientation with respect to the story, subjects were reduced to near-chance performance when attempting to recognize the original left−right orientation.

Subject−Orienting-Task Interaction

Examples of this kind of interaction are so plentiful that we often fail to study them in the laboratory, although personnel psychologists capitalize on this interaction as a fundamental "stock in trade." In a sense, all of us know that the subjects' skills, ability, knowledge, intentions, and motivations influence the manner in which they carry out the orienting tasks. It is hardly remarkable, but that, of course, does not make it less important; if anything, it enhances its importance. It is only recently, however, that experimental psychologists have turned attention to such variables in spite of many expressions of the general importance of such investigations (see, for example, Cronbach, 1957, 1975).

Chapters 11 and 12 by Brown and Naus and Halasz (this volume) reflect the importance of this kind of interaction for the developmental psychologist. It is apparent that subjects change with age and experience as they assimilate and accommodate to new cognitive experiences. Brown directs us to consider the interaction between the subject's level of development and his/her ability to employ effective strategies for learning and remembering. Naus and Halasz ask us to distinguish between automatic and deliberate processing as independent components of the cognitive system that are susceptible to different degrees of control. They urge us to think of the memory system as evolving and developing continuously as a result of the child's history of interactions with the meaningful environment.

One of my colleagues, John Flavell, has fascinated me with his studies of "metamemory" in children. Among other things, he has shown that young children do not necessarily behave the same way as older children when they are given identical instructions. Young children, for example, do not do anything different when they are given instructions to "learn" than when they are given instructions to "look at." They attend to what is displayed, but that is all. Older children behave very differently under the two instructions. Similarly, the instruction to "rehearse" leads young children to repeat the last word presented over and over, but it does not lead them to review the preceding words they may still remember. (The young child behaves very much like Cermak's patients with Korsakoff syndrome.) Older children follow the more effective global rehearsal strategy. Thus, the assignment of "the same" orienting task to subjects of different ages results in their doing very diferent things as orienting activities (see Flavell, Friedrichs, & Hoyt, 1970).

A second example is the effect of special skill and knowledge in determining what happens in the orienting task. When chess experts and chess novices look at a chessboard, they literally do not see the same things. The expert sees relations between pieces, positions of strength and weakness, advantages and disadvantages, possible plays, likely outcome of the game, and the like. The novice sees only a scattering of strangely shaped pieces on the checkered board. The instruction to "study the board" or "tell me what you see" is not the same for the two sets of subjects (Chase & Simon, 1973; DeGroot, 1965).

Subject–Material Interaction

The subject–material interaction may be illustrated by a continuation of the last instance just dealt with. The advantage of the chess expert disappears when the material that he/she is asked to study no longer has the appropriate structure of a game. When the pieces are placed at random on the board, the perceptual and memorial advantage of the expert over the novice diminishes. Thus, when the relational structure of the material is appropriate to the skills of the subject, certain effects appear; when the structure of the material is inappropriate, the effects disappear.

Another source of examples concerning special subject skills is, of course, the language we speak. Everyone is, in some sense, an expert in his/her native language, and this expertness confers certain advantages and disadvantages in relation to certain kinds of materials. For example, it is common knowledge that the Japanese language does not make use of the distinction that mature speakers of American English know as the difference between /r/ and /l/. Adult native speakers of Japanese cannot discriminate synthetic speech materials that Americans clearly hear as a series running from /r/ at one end to /l/ at the other with a sudden break from one phoneme to the other in the middle of the series. On the other hand, when one takes the acoustic cue that varies along that series (a high-frequency resonance transition) and plays this sound outside of the speech syllable context, both Japanese and English subjects can discriminate members of the series at a high level of accuracy (see Miyawaki, Strange, Verbrugge, Liberman, Jenkins, & Fujimura, 1975). Although this example may seem too exotic to be included here, I have elected to include it as a dramatic example of language differences that can serve as a reminder of all of the other instances where language interacts with ability to follow directions, understanding materials, having the necessary skills to perform on a criterial test, and so on.

Kolers (Chapter 17, this volume) has tried to sensitize us to the fact that we must deal with the acquisition of skill itself as a form of memory, a form that does not fit into our usual metaphors having to do with the storage of objects or features. As the subject interacts with the special kinds of material that Kolers provides, the subject changes in his/her skills, and those changes themselves result in memorial phenomena.

Subject–Criterial-Task Interaction

We have already touched on this area when we were considering the materials–criterial-task interaction. It is obvious that the results of a memory experiment can be greatly influenced by the skills that the criterial task requires of the subject. What the subject knows or remembers may not be available to the investigator if the criterial task demands supportive skills that the subject does not possess. Reproduction of pictures requires certain levels of motor control and artistic skill. Physics tests commonly presuppose mathematical skills. Fluent writing or typing skills may enable one subject to report more than another subject in the same time interval. Speeded tests of all sorts are known to put the old and the young at a disadvantage relative to the young adult. Even in the laboratory, we know that it makes a difference whether one measures reaction time with the skilled or the unskilled subject.

It is easy for the experimenter to forget or ignore the effects of this interaction when he/she is working with exotic subjects such as small children or members of another culture. Under such circumstances the findings of a criterial task can be misleading with respect to memory. For example, the child's notion of what a story is and what it means to "tell a story" may be the major factor in determining what the child produces under recall instructions. Much of what he/she knows or remembers may not be made available to the experimenter, because the child's notion of telling a story is not in agreement with the experimenter's normative expectations. An instruction that is adequate with a secondary-school subject may be unsuccessful with younger children in terms of revealing what they "really know" about a story just heard.

Probably the most common examples of subject−criterial-task interaction are found in student evaluations. Oral reports are sometimes freely interchanged with written papers, but students have very strong ideas about which they do best. As criterial tasks, it is obvious that in addition to the basic knowledge being displayed, the two kinds of tasks call for very different skills to support the presentation. We are not at all surprised if a student is much better at one kind of performance than the other. In general, all of us associated with educational institutions know that some students have superior test-taking skills and strategies whereas other have lower levels of these skills, less efficient strategies, and perhaps "test anxieties" that prevent them from displaying what they remember. These may be extreme examples, but they may help us recognize that all criterial tasks involve skills and knowledge beyond that of the content that is supposedly being appraised.

It is also known from motor skills research that what is measured by a criterial task, which objectively stays the same, changes with the stage of practice of the learner. Thus, Fleishman (1957) and Fleishman and Hempel (1954) showed that performance on the Complex Coordinator was differentially related to the measured abilities of their subjects at different stages of training. Speed of arm movement, for example, bore little relation to performance on early trials but was fairly strongly related to performance in the later stages of practice. None of us in verbal learning and memory should be surprised to encounter changes in the relation of subject−criterial variables as a function of degree of learning, subject experience, or subject abilities. The most dramatic example in the verbal-learning and memory area is proactive interference, of course, where we find massive effects of earlier experience in retention measures of recently learned material. (See the classic paper by Underwood, 1957.)

Higher Order Interactions

The foregoing illustrations, which could be multiplied many times over, are in themselves simplifications. One could well argue that most of them are not simple interactions but more complex ones, and it is further arguable that the classifications made are arbitrary or incorrect in part. All of that is beside the point. The overwhelming finding is that interactions abound and that straight-forward generalizations about learning and memory are going to be rare. Alternatively, we can say that generalization will be possible only at a very abstract level. Such generalizations must then be projected down to particular situations with a great deal of sophisticated interpretation.

The illustrations above merely say that our four major sources of variation interact vigorously with one another. In addition to the two-way interactions already illustrated, there are of course, 3 three-way interactions (OT × M × CT; OT × M × S; M × S × CT) and 1 overall four-way interaction. I think that all of these interaction patterns are real and may be illustrated readily. But we hardly need to labor the point here.

It is sufficient to say at this time that our statements about learning and memory must be couched in the general form of a four-variable relation: "*If* the Subject . . . and *if* the Orienting Task . . . and *if* the Material . . . and *if* the Criterial Task . . . , then. . . ." For example, I believe that the following statement is generally true: *If* a subject has a standard knowledge of English and standard experience in our culture, and *if* the orienting task requires semantic (rather than formal) processing of the meanings of words, and *if* the materials consist of auditorily presented associated words, and *if* the dependent measure is recall of words, *then* relatively high levels of recall will be observed and the recall will show clustering into associative pairs.

For many purposes, of course, one would not specify all of these parameters, but their specification here is instructive. For example, it reminds us that if the subject does not speak English, nothing else in the expression can save the conclusion. It points out the abstract nature of the classification of the orienting task. What, indeed, is a "semantic" orienting task? Can we make that intuitive notion more precise, or must we leave it as a judgmental matter at present? The reference to associated words in the material phrase assures a strong effect for the orienting tasks and hints at the underlying knowledge that as the strength of the associations employed increases, so also will the amount of recall and the amount of clustering. The reference to auditory presentation obviates a special clause concerning the reading abilities of the subject but also implies that the subject has no hearing deficit, which was presumed in the proviso of "standard knowledge of English." Finally, recall is specified as the dependent measure. Immediate tests of recognition (as opposed to recall) are likely to show no effect of orienting task with this kind of material and, of course, cannot show associative clustering. It could still be argued that this specification is far from complete. Subject age (which is sure to be a variable) has not been specified. The assumption of normality is not explicit, etc. Although the example is labored and faulty, it still may serve to stimulate the reader to explore the limitations of his/her own favorite generalizations.

Consider now an example of another sort. Suppose that we find ourselves in the teacher's position—which I have characterized as having a given assignment, a given population of subjects, and a given criterial task. Can we devise an appropriate orienting task? Linda McCabe and I (McCabe & Jenkins, 1978) took a trivial task to explore, but I think it is instructive. We took as subjects the "standard college sophomore." Our materials consisted of a list of words typed in two different type fonts, Gothic and Script. The criterial task was a recognition task that asked the subject to identify the type font of the words. The subject was shown the complete set of words one at a time. Half of the words were in the typeface in which they had originally been presented, and half were changed to the other face. The subject's task was to identify the ones that had remained the same and the ones that had been changed. (This is admittedly an unusual task and may not be appropriate to any other activity one can think of.) Our task, of course, was to find an orienting task that permitted the subjects to complete the recognition task successfully.

Subjects who were asked to process the words semantically were at the chance level in the recognition task (52% correct, where 50% is chance). Most of them had not even noticed that the words were in different typefaces. Subjects who were asked to count straight and curved lines in the words (and who had no other orienting task to do) performed better (67%) but were still not impressive. McCabe, however, invented an orienting task that produced effortless incidental learning that led to still better recognition (76%). She asked subjects to judge whether the typeface of each word was appropriate to its meaning. (For example, if the word *sheep* were typed in script, that might be appropriate, because sheep have curly wool.) This is a particularly interesting task in that it arranges a fusion of the semantic and nonsemantic aspects of the word and thus provides a basis for the recognition of form that is to come.

The notion that one must consider the whole configuration is not unique to me, of course. When Bransford and his colleagues talk about *transfer-appropriate processing*, they mean to include the other necessary variables. For the processing to be "appropriate" implies that one is already considering the criterial task involved, that one has already thought about the unique properties of the materials, and that one knows what the subject brings to the situation. In short, the notion of *transfer-appropriate processing* can be said to include all of the variables that bear on *appropriateness* and all of the prerequisites that are needed to assure that the processes are or will be as needed to accomplish the task. The only virtue of a "model" such as the one advanced here is that it provides a prompt for one's thinking in a more explicit way than the "transfer of appropriate processing" formulation. It specifically reminds the experimenter that he or she consider each source of variation that contributes to the actual processing involved and the relation of that processing to what will ultimately be required.

Where Do We Go From Here?

If the situation is as interactive as I have suggested that it is, where does the study of memory go? Will there be any solid findings that we can pass along to our students, or will everything have to be held in abeyance until each particular situation of interest has been studied? Is "It depends" the only thing we can say about learning and memory?

On my optimistic days, I believe that we will find sizable areas of consistency. That is, we will find orienting tasks that are effective for several criterial tasks for given classes of materials for large groups of subjects that we care about. This is not an unreasonable expectation given the consistencies that we have already observed with some of our standard laboratory tasks and traditional materials. I do *not* think it is reasonable to expect general laws of memory that will be context free—that is, laws that will be applicable to any subjects whatsoever, to all orienting tasks, to all classes of materials, and to all types of criterial tasks.

How, then, shall we work? Two major possibilities suggest themselves to me. First, we may select problems because of their recognized importance in the world in which we live. It is not that we cannot work with other situations; it is, rather, that there is no assurance that our contrived and artificial situations will ever come to relate to anything that we care about in "the real world." If we can only look for local islands of consistency in the vast ocean of context-dependent situations, one might argue that we ought to be looking for the ones that "count for something" rather than those that simply are convenient for the laboratory.

The second thing we might do as experimenters is attempt to extend our sensitivities and intuitions concerning all aspects of memory and learning by trying to find the extreme cases that test our traditional findings. I have thought from time to time of a "science by challenge" procedure. For example, I believe that most of the people at this conference could arrange an experiment that would overthrow any single-variable generalization about memory if one gave them freedom to select the other three variables as they wished. I think, as a matter of faith, that I could probably defeat any simple two-variable generalization if I could have the other two variables free—and if I could have permission to do a series of pilot experiments to sharpen up my intuitions.

I think such a challenge series could be very exciting and very informative. Surely, at the extreme there will be claims and generalizations involving two or three variables that cannot be overthrown by manipulation of the remaining two variables or single variable. Until further notice, such claims would be regarded as secure. Also, I think it likely that as we explore ways of exploiting interactions, we will come to understand the range, the variation, and the nature of the relationships that abound in the areas of memory phenomena. As Bahrick (Chapter 7, this volume) suggests, clever investigators will find abstract ways of expressing generalizations. These generalizations should capture complex relationships in such a way that, with experience, we can see how they hold across the interactions of specific values of variables.

CONCLUSION

As I see it, the underlying theme of this conference may be characterized as *the context sensitivity of memory*. The generalizations that we have all been trying to establish have proved to be highly vulnerable when they are tested trans-situationally. Investigators in all portions of the field are encountering powerful interactions between variables. The phenomena of learning and memory that we observe are increasingly seen to be dependent on the nature of our subjects, our orienting tasks, the kinds of materials we work with, and the criterial tasks we employ.

We may find either encouragement or discouragement in the state of affairs in our field of research, but however we feel, we cannot long ignore the realities facing us. Simple laws will not capture the phenomena that we have recorded in so many diverse ways. Solid results with orienting tasks for the memory of lists of words cannot lead to *general* conclusions when they may be readily contradicted by changing acquisition paradigms, material, subjects, or criterial tasks. Even a cursory review of the literature shows that our "independent variables" interact in ways that cannot be specified by mere parametric changes. Interaction, contextual sensitivity with respect to all our variables, is the pattern—not the exception.

I believe that we must recognize this state of affairs as one of the major findings of basic research in learning and memory of the last decade or so. We must come to grips with our own findings. Two paths of advance are seen. The first is to concentrate on the range of variables involved in particular problems of importance to us for ecological, practical reasons. The second is to explore the range of applicability of our generalizations through a "science by challenge" procedure. In both of these ways, we can increase our knowledge of the phenomena of learning and memory and our usefulness to workers in related disciplines.

ACKNOWLEDGMENTS

The preparation of this paper was supported in part by the Center for Research in Human Learning, University of Minnesota. The center is supported by grants from the National Science Foundation, the National Institute of Child Health and Human Development, and the Graduate School of the University of Minnesota. The writer is grateful to his colleagues, R. W. Burris, P. W. Fox, P. E. Johnson, W. Strange, J. Blount, and J. Kreps, for comments on an earlier version of these ideas.

REFERENCES

Anderson, R. C., & Ortony, A. On putting apples into bottles—A problem of polysemy. *Cognitive Psychology,* 1975, *7,* 167–180.

Baker, L., & Santa, J. L. Context, integration, and retrieval. *Memory & Cognition,* 1977, *5,* 308–314.

Barclay, J. R., Bransford, J. D., Franks, J. J., McCarrell, N. S., & Nitsch, K. Comprehension and semantic flexibility. *Journal of Verbal Learning and Verbal Behavior,* 1974, *13,* 471–481.

Chase, W. G., & Simon, H. A. Perception in chess. *Cognitive Psychology*, 1973, *4*, 55–81.

Connor, J. M. Effects of organization and expectancy on recall and recognition. *Memory & Cognition*, 1977, *5*, 315–318.

Craik, F. I. M., & Lockhart, R. S. Levels of processing: A framework for memory research. *Journal of Verbal Learning and Verbal Behavior*, 1972, *11*, 671–684.

Craik, F. I. M., & Tulving, E. Depth of processing and the retention of words in episodic memory. *Journal of Experimental Psychology: General*, 1975, *104*, 268–294.

Cronbach, L. J. The two disciplines of scientific psychology. *American Psychologist*, 1957, *12*, 671–684.

Cronbach, L. J. Beyond the two disciplines of scientific psychology. *American Psychologist*, 1975, *30*, 116–127.

DeGroot, A. D. *Thought and choice in chess*. The Hague: Mouton, 1965.

Dhawan, M., & Pellegrino, J. W. Acoustic and semantic interference effects in words and pictures. *Memory & Cognition*, 1977, *5*, 340–346.

Erdelyi, M., Buschke, H., & Finkelstein, S. Hypermnesia for Socratic stimuli: The growth of recall for an internally generated memory list abstracted from a series of riddles. *Memory & Cognition*, 1977, *5*, 283–286.

Fisher, R. P., & Craik, F. I. M. The interaction between encoding and retrieval operations in cued recall. *Journal of Experimental Psychology: Human Learning and Memory*, 1977, *3*, 701–711.

Flavell, J. H., Friedrichs, A. G., & Hoyt, J. D. Developmental changes in memorization processes. *Cognitive Psychology*, 1970, *1*, 324–340.

Fleishman, E. A. A comparative study of aptitude patterns in unskilled and skilled psychomotor performances. *Journal of Applied Psychology*, 1957, *41*, 263–272.

Fleishman, E. A., & Hempel, W. E. Changes in factor structure of a complex psychomotor test as a function of practice. *Psychometrika*, 1954, *19*, 239–252.

Goldstein, A. G., & Chance, J. E. Visual recognition memory for complex configurations. *Perception & Psychophysics*, 1970, *9*, 237–240.

Hyde, T. S., & Jenkins, J. J. Recall for words as a function of semantic, graphic, and syntactic orienting tasks. *Journal of Verbal Learning and Verbal Behavior*, 1973, *12*, 471–480.

Jenkins, J. J., Wald, J., & Pittenger, J. B. Apprehending pictorial events: An instance of psychological cohesion. In C. W. Savage (Ed.), *Minnesota studies in the philosophy of science* (Vol. 9). Minneapolis, Minn.: University of Minnesota Press, in press.

Kraft, R. N., & Jenkins, J. J. Memory for lateral orientation of slides in picture stories. *Memory & Cognition*, 1977, *5*, 397–403.

Madden, D. J., & Bastian, J. Probing echoic memory with different voices. *Memory & Cognition*, 1977, *5*, 331–334.

McCabe, L., & Jenkins, J. J. *Memory for pictures and words: Interactions between orienting tasks, materials and criterial tasks*. Draft paper, Center for Research in Human Learning. Minneapolis, Minn. 55455: University of Minnesota, 1978.

McKeachie, W. J. The decline and fall of the laws of learning. *Educational Researcher*, 1974, *3*, 7–11.

Miyawaki, K., Strange, W., Verbrugge, R., Liberman, A. M., Jenkins, J. J., & Fujimura, O. An effect of linguistic experiences: The discrimination of [r] and [l] by native speakers of Japanese and English. *Perception & Psychophysics*, 1975, *18*, 331–340.

Morris, C. D., Bransford, J. D., & Franks, J. J. Levels of processing versus transfer appropriate processing. *Journal of Verbal Learning and Verbal Behavior*, 1977, *16*, 519–534.

Moscovitch, M., & Craik, F. I. M. Depth of processing, retrieval cues, and uniqueness of encoding as factors in recall. *Journal of Verbal Learning and Verbal Behavior*, 1976, *15*, 447–458.

Paivio, A. Coding distinctions and repetition effects in memory. In G. Bower (Ed.), *The psychology of learning and motivation* (Vol. 9). New York: Academic Press, 1975.

Shepard, R. N. Recognition memory for words, sentences and pictures. *Journal of Verbal Learning and Verbal Behavior*, 1967, *6*, 156–163.

Standing, L. Learning 10,000 pictures. *Quarterly Journal of Experimental Psychology*, 1973, *25*, 207–222.

Standing, L., Conezio, J., & Haber, R. N. Perception and memory for pictures: Single-trial learning of 2500 visual stimuli. *Psychonomic Science*, 1970, *19*, 73–74.

Stein, B. The effects of cue–target uniqueness on cued recall performance. *Memory & Cognition*, 1977, *5*, 319–322.

Strange, W., Jenkins, J. J., & Wilson, B. E. *Context determines word meaning*. Draft paper, Center for Research in Human Learning. Minneapolis, Minn. 55455: University of Minnesota, 1978.

Till, R. E. Sentence memory prompted with inferential recall cues. *Journal of Experimental Psychology: Human Learning and Memory*, 1977, *3*, 129–141.

Tulving, E., & Osler, S. Effectiveness of retrieval cues in memory for words. *Journal of Experimental Psychology*, 1968, *77*, 593–601.

Tulving, E., & Thomson, D. M. Encoding specificity and retrieval processes in episodic memory. *Psychological Review*, 1973, *80*, 352–373.

Underwood, B. J. Interference and forgetting. *Psychological Review*, 1957, *64*, 49–60.

Verbrugge, R. R., & McCarrell, N. S. Metaphoric comprehension: Studies in reminding and resembling. *Cognitive Psychology*, 9, 494–533, 1977.

21 Levels of Processing: Overview and Closing Comments

Fergus I. M. Craik
University of Toronto

When Laird Cermak and I originally planned the Rockport meeting in late 1975, we were hopeful that a representative group of memory theorists could find common ground for agreement and debate within the general framework of a levels-of-processing approach to memory. Despite sundry witty observations made during the course of the Rockport meetings—such as (after a particularly devastating series of "antilevels" comments) "We come to bury levels, not to praise them . . ."; and as a suggested title for the present volume, "Remember that *new* theory of memory? Well, forget it!"—after reading the papers I am even more optimistic that a broad degree of agreement does exist among many memory theorists. Of course, in achieving this degree of consensus, the notions proposed by Craik and Lockhart (1972) have been modified in the direction of other positions at least as much as others' views have changed, so that the agreement I refer to concerns a general "process" view of memory rather than a view that explicitly endorses the notions of levels of analysis as such. It is the purpose of this last chapter to assess the extent of this agreement, to suggest possible ways of bridging gaps between theoretical positions, and to point up differences where such bridging is clearly impossible.

First, there are striking similarities in the chapters by Jacoby and Craik (1), Battig (2), Nelson (3), and Eysenck (5). In this group, all writers stress the basic notions that input processing of an event can be elaborated to a greater or lesser degree; that the degree of elaboration depends on such factors as amount of practice, task-induced processing, and processing produced spontaneously by the subject; and that elaborate processing typically results in a distinctive encoding. Further, provided that the appropriate information is given as a cue at retrieval, such distinctive encodings are associated with high levels of subsequent retention. This change of emphasis—from Craik and Lockhart's suggestion that deeper processing is associated with longer lasting traces to the present group's concern with elaboration, distinctiveness, and compatibility with retrieval conditions—brings the five afore-mentioned authors relatively close to the positions advocated by several other theorists in the present volume. For example, Anderson and Reder (Chapter 18) see elaboration as central to their current position, and Kolers's notion of extensiveness of processing (Chapter 17) has some similarities to elaboration also; although Kolers and Ostry's (1974) stress on "complexity" and "variety" of encoding operations gives their ideas a different emphasis. Again, by acknowledging the necessity for a correspondence between encoding and retrieval conditions, the five authors endorse (in part at least) Tulving's encoding specificity principle (Chapter 19) and the notion of transfer-appropriate processing put forward by Bransford, Franks, Morris, and Stein (Chapter 15) and emphasized by Jenkins (Chapter 20).

There are other clusters of similarity, also, among the views presented here. Several writers spring to the defense of the much-maligned "shallow" or sensory encoding, showing that such information may be far from transient in its effects. The evidence here is presented by Eysenck, Nelson, and Bransford et al. and is especially dramatic in Kolers's demonstrations in which repeated operations facilitate reading up to 1 year later. It now seems clear that my previous generalization that a minimal semantic analysis is more beneficial for memory than is an elaborate structural analysis was too sweeping (although, as detailed later, it still seems that semantic encodings do typically show an advantage in memory). Several authors (e.g., Kolers, Nelson, Treisman [Chap. 14]) rightly point out that Craik and Lockhart's suggestion of a fixed, linear series of analytic levels, with processing that could be "stopped" at various stages, is just not tenable in view of recent work showing recursive operations operating both in a top-down and bottom-up fashion. A further shared view is particularly interesting since it cuts across marked ideological boundaries. On one hand, Bransford et al. (whose views stem from those of J. J. Gibson) question the necessity for memory, as distinct from a progressive refinement of knowledge structures to interpret the incoming pattern of stimulation. On the other hand, Kolers also argues against the necessity for a system of memory traces, but from a different perspective; he takes a "proceduralist" view, claiming that repetition of the pattern-analyzing operations themselves is a sufficient basis for remembering. Finally, although disagreeing on some aspects, Tulving and Bransford et al. share the view that memory can never be described in absolute terms; a particular encoding is "strong" or "weak" only with reference to a particular retrieval condition. The relativity theory of remembering is in the making!

In the foregoing paragraphs, I have pointed out the fairly large areas of agreement I see among many participants at the Rockport meeting. Clearly, many of these shared views are held by other workers also. Two especially relevant views are first—the ideas of Klein and Saltz (1976), who explicitly argue for a "distinctiveness" interpretation of levels-of-processing phenomena—and second—the notions of memory as a "description" put forward by Norman and Bobrow (1977).

Before I turn to a consideration of some specific issues, we should look at some of the terms used by the various authors in this volume. An embarrassing profusion of descriptive terms has been used; it would be useful to determine approximate equivalences between them and to suggest a smaller number of underlying processes to capture the basic notions. The concept of *depth* is dealt with later in this chapter, but it may be briefly noted here that the term refers to qualitatively different codes; the word *depth* was used originally to make the point that the codes were not only different, but were differentially accessible, with deeper levels typically requiring more time and effort to reach, both at encoding and at retrieval. In addition, deeper codes were postulated to be less tied to stimulus qualities and more tied to abstract, derived, semantic characteristics of the incoming information. The value of this concept is examined later. For the moment, it may be noted that Bransford et al. suggest a different sense of "depth," involving degrees of skill and expertise with various types of information. The terms *elaboration*, *breadth* and *spread* of processing, and *richness* and *extensiveness* all seem to refer to greater amounts of processing of the same general type. As such, the concept differs from "depth," which refers to qualitative changes in encoding.

In my own view, the depth to which a stimulus is processed, in conjunction with its degree of elaboration, gives rise to an encoding that is more or less "distinctive" and thus discriminable from other memory traces in the system. The term *uniqueness* has also been used in this sense, but *distinctiveness* is preferable on lexical grounds, since an event can not really be "more or less unique." However, *distinctiveness* is a descriptive term at a somewhat different explanatory level from *depth* and *elaboration*; whereas the latter terms describe the operations carried out during encoding, *distinctiveness* describes the similarity of the product of these operations to other memory traces.

A fourth term that has been used in this general area is the *congruity* of a processed event with either its local context or with the processing system (Schulman, 1974). Craik and Lockhart used *compatibility* in much the same sense, and Nelson's use of *interactiveness* has also something in common with *congruity* (as has the Piagetian concept of *assimilation*). However, whereas *congruity* stresses the extent to which an event fits into current structures and schemas, *interactiveness* stresses the extent to which the system interacts with and modifies the incoming stimulus. For example, a word processed on successive occasions in terms of its phonemic characteristics would result in very similar encodings, whereas if the word is processed semantically, the greater interactiveness of semantic encoding would lead to somewhat different encodings; the exact sense of the encoded word is modified by its context to a much greater degree. Finally, most workers now seem agreed that some concept is required to specify the compatibility, similarity, overlap, or correlation between trace and retrieval information (or between encoding and retrieval operations). This point is stressed most strongly in the present volume by Bransford et al., by Kolers, and by Tulving.

In my view these five descriptive dimensions—depth, elaboration, distinctiveness, congruity, and compatibility between encoding and retrieval—reflect the basic concepts used by most contributors to the present volume. Of course, not all contributors use all of the concepts, and some authors explicitly deny the need for some descriptions. Thus, Kolers as well as Anderson and Reder see the quantitative amount, or number, of elaborations as being sufficient to describe encoding—they see no need for the notion of depth. Tulving goes even further and claims that the nature of the relation between trace information and retrieval-cue information is sufficient to give an adequate account of remembering. Those workers who do use two or more of the five descriptors often posit some relation between the dimensions. Thus Anderson and Reder suggest that "deep" processing simply allows for a greater number of elaborations. The notions of elaboration and distinctiveness are obviously related—greater degrees of elaboration typically yield more distinctive encodings—but the terms are not synonymous, since elaborating the stimulus in some ways (e.g., deeper, semantic ways) leads to an encoding that is more distinctive from other encoded events than elaborating the stimulus in other less semantic ways (see also Anderson and Reder's Fig. 18.1). Finally, Eysenck in his Fig. 5.1 ties together distinctiveness and encoding/retrieval compatibility in a simple and useful formulation.

My conclusion from surveying the ideas and concepts used by the present contributors is that although there are substantial differences in approach and emphasis among the views put forward, the contributions are more remarkable for their underlying similarity than for their differences.

SOME SPECIFIC ISSUES

Development of Memory

The chapters by Brown (11), Naus and Halasz (12), and Hagen (13) also show a great deal of agreement among themselves as to the important issues and on a theme common to all contributors—the stress on the particular mental activities carried out during input and retrieval processing. In addition to this latter point, Brown emphasizes the importance of the *goal* of that activity and illustrates this point by examples from the Soviet literature, and Hagen shows how the levels-of-processing notions can be utilized to study developmental changes. But in general, the three chapters put as much stress on the value of developmental work in understanding adult cognitive processes as on the usefulness of general models of memory to illuminate developmental problems.

The two major areas discussed by Brown and by Naus and Halasz are first—the distinction between voluntary and involuntary processing in memory—and second—the distinction between semantic and episodic memory. The first distinction is of great interest to the present group, since extensive use has been made of incidental orienting tasks to control the type of processing carried out during encoding (e.g., Craik & Tulving, 1975; Hyde & Jenkins, 1969). In the work with adults, it seems generally true that intentional learning yields retention levels approximately equivalent to those found after giving a "semantic" orienting task. Thus adults have typically learned how to learn; they make reasonably good use of their processing capabilities. The growth of this knowledge is an extremely important issue for developmental psychologists; Naus and Halasz raise a further important issue—namely, how is this knowledge represented in the system, where does it "fit" in a levels framework? My colleagues and I have implicitly treated such effects of strategy and metamemory as being somehow superordinate to the processing system. This view may well turn out to be unsatisfactory, however; the acquisition and use of skilled procedures must be inherent in the knowledge system itself. The chapters by Kolers and by Bransford et al. contain some thoughts on how this state of affairs may come about.

The writers of the three chapters on development all agree that the distinction between semantic and episodic memory is too abrupt in its present form. As I understand it, Tulving (1972) proposed the distinction to emphasize that the encoding of a specific event was in most cases very different from a simple activation or tagging of that event's preexisting mental components. Further, the specific context in which an event occurs determines both its encoding and retrieval in important ways; the word *black* is encoded very differently in the pair *train—black* than in the pair *white—black* (Thomson & Tulving, 1970). In this sense the distinction between context-specific and prototypical representations has been illuminating and useful. However, when the structure of the memory system is considered, the implied break between two memory systems is unsatisfactory. Whereas the occurrence of a specific event is tied to a particular time and place, there may well be clusters of events that share many features of the context; there are scripts of "things to do" in particular settings, and this type of knowledge seems intermediate between the representation of individual episodes and the representation of context-free general knowledge about the world (Brown, Chapter 11, this volume; Schonfield & Stones, in press). One solution is suggested in the chapters by Naus and Halasz and by Jacoby and Craik; these authors suggest a continuum of representation, running from highly context-specific episodes at one extreme to abstract generalized knowledge at the other. As a further speculation, Jacoby and Craik suggest that the portion of the continuum utilized in any transaction with the outside world will determine whether the system is being used in an interpretive mode (that is, when generalized stored information is used to understand the incoming stimulus pattern) or in a memory mode (that is, when the incoming stimulation is used to reactivate the representation of a specific context-dependent episode). Finally, both Brown and Naus and Halasz point out the congruity between information-processing views of semantic memory interpreting incoming stimuli and being changed by them, and Piaget's notions of accommodation and assimilation.

Levels of Processing in Language Comprehension

Both Perfetti (Chapter 8) and the Lachmans (Chapter 9) point out that notions on levels of processing have had little relevance to theoretical work on comprehension. The Lachmans go on to provide a very useful account of recent developments in that area; perhaps one bridge between their approach and work on memory will be the idea of the synthesized code—from a "levels" point of view, the memory trace is the record of the operations performed on the input, and this view of the trace is quite similar to the synthesized code discussed by the Lachmans. Perfetti describes a sequence of analytic stages for language processing but makes it clear that there is no simple relation between the *logical* order he describes and either the order of processing or the order in which information at various levels becomes accessible to conscious awareness (these important points are also stressed by Kolers, Kintsch, [Chap. 10] and Treisman). The relative ease of processing at different levels of analysis in Perfetti's scheme and the type of information rendered "opaque" (that is, consciously accessed) depends largely on the task and on the extent to which the particular material can be processed automatically. Where no automatized processes are available, focal attention must be brought to bear; this in turn involves present awareness of the analytic operations and subsequent memory for those operations (Shiffrin & Schneider, 1977). Perfetti makes the additional interesting suggestion that in comprehension, conscious awareness does not typically operate at the highest logical level; both lower levels (e.g., phonological, syntactic) and higher levels (e.g., associations and inferences) may proceed automatically and unconsciously—although presumably the effects of these automatic operations are reflected in the nature of the conscious percept and its memory record.

Kintsch is more hopeful about the applicability of levels-of-processing notions to language and urges that more memory studies should be carried out using sentences and text as materials. In a discussion of his own model, Kintsch is sympathetic to a description in terms of levels of analysis but, like Kolers, he emphasizes that the levels can be accessed in parallel, rather than serially. If this is so, in what sense are they "levels"? Kintsch again makes it clear that a distinction must be drawn between the logical description and the processing sequence.

Are Memory Traces Necessary?

In the chapters by Kolers and by Bransford et al., the notion of memory traces is seriously questioned. Bransford et al. take the Gibsonian position that learning reflects increases in the cognitive system's ability to differentiate aspects of the stimulus array, but there need be no system of records associated with remembered events (see also Bransford, McCarrell, Franks, & Nitsch, 1977). Kolers further develops his position that remembering consists of repeating the same pattern-analyzing operations; he stresses the importance of the apparently peripheral (surface) aspects of perceived events. Kolers's elegant experiments have shown beyond doubt that the surface shell, as well as the semantic pearl, plays an important role in remembering.

As I understand these authors' views, it appears possible to account for recognition of familiar events in their terms. Well-known events or situations are analyzed skillfully and easily by well-practiced analytic operations; it follows that feelings of familiarity could be correlates of the ease with which the analyzing routines are executed. However, I do not see how such accounts can handle remembering a specific episode. What corresponds to the knowledge that something similar to a present experience has occurred previously, perhaps in a somewhat different context? In pattern-analyzing terms, how can a fragmentary retrieval cue in recall lead to the successful reconstitution of the original experience? Of course, no extant theory gives an adequate account of how remembering takes place, but it seems necessary to postulate some specific change in the system corresponding to perception of an episodic event, and to further postulate that the change (call it a "trace" without any commitment as to its nature) retains its specificity and is not assimilated generally into the system. When the event recurs, the processing operations involved in its perception must somehow contact and reactivate the trace of the previous occurrence. In short, the present experience must incorporate some knowledge of a specific *past* episode; if remembering consisted only of skilled processing of events, there would be no way to distinguish past from present, except that some stimuli would feel familiar and others would not. Kolers appears to acknowledge the need for some form of record of the initial occurrence when he suggests that "recognition is achieved by virtue of the correlation between the operations carried out on two encounters with a stimulus event. The more similar the operations, the readier the recognition [p. 383]." By this account, activity has been preserved in some form from the first occurrence to correlate with activity induced by the second occurrence. It is possible, of course, that the "trace" is represented by a pattern of activity in the system; in this way, the attractive features of Kolers's account of remembering in terms of correlated sets of operations could be retained.

On another issue, Kolers argues convincingly for the importance of "surface" or sensory information in remembering. On the basis of his evidence as well as the evidence of other workers (e.g., Morris, Bransford, & Franks, 1977), it must be conceded that sensory codes can be associated with high levels of retention. But is it the enhanced extensiveness of *graphemic* analysis that supports the excellent retention of inverted sentences, or is it the subject's greater involvement of semantic operations to aid him or her in decoding the difficult script? It seems clear from Kolers's results that graphemic analysis plays an important part in the recognition process, but the results of Masson and Sala (1978), described by Kintsch, show that semantic processing also plays a crucial role. It seems reasonable, as Nelson suggests, that "sensory" aspects of the stimulus (e.g., graphemic, phonological, pictorial, spatial) and semantic aspects (i.e., abstract, context-free qualities) should *both* contribute to remembering. It also seems reasonable that the various operations or codes contribute differentially to memory performance depending on how adequately they support discrimination of the wanted trace from others in the system. Thus when the task necessitates extensive, distinctive processing of "surface" features but allows cursory analysis of semantic aspects, remembering will depend more on the former (Kolers, Eysenck), although it seems likely that the more usual state of affairs is that semantic processing supports more distinctive differentiation (see the next section).

At the end of Chapter 17, Kolers agrees that memory for semantic context is usually superior to memory for the graphemics. His point is that by inducing more extensive processing of graphemic information, he has led his subjects to produce deeper and richer representations of the sentences, which are then correspondingly memorable.

> The conclusion thus seems to be that the semantic is not necessarily a deeper or richer or more elaborate level of processing by virtue of its kind or nature. The semantic is usually remembered better, not because it is semantic, but because its acquisition requires particular analysis. . . . What is remembered better is what was analyzed more; the analytical operations themselves, their extent, and complexity account for performance [p. 384].

One major difficulty in this debate is the lack of an adequate definition of "semantic." Is pictorial information sensory or semantic? Although initial processing of a scene could reasonably be described as sensory, it seems clear that subjects make deep, abstract, inferential judgments in processing pictures just as they do with words (see also Paivio, 1971, Chap. 3). Similarly when well-learned "sensory" distinctions become associated with other rich sources of information (recognizing a friend's voice, face, or handwriting, for example), it seems that the processes brought to bear on the analysis are semantic and "deep" as much as they are shallow and sensory.

It is apparent that Kolers intends his usage of the term *pattern-analyzing operations* to apply to abstract, modality-free forms of representation as well as to the surface form of the perceived event. After all, there is no doubt that a word presented visually will be recognized later, even though the test modality is auditory. On the other hand, the word *jam* in the context "traffic jam" is poorly recognized if it was first presented in the context "strawberry jam" (Light & Carter−Sobell, 1970). Clearly, repetition of the operations mediating perception of surface form cannot by itself constitute a sufficient basis for an account of remembering. Given that Kolers includes "semantic" forms of representation in his use of the term *pattern-analyzing operations*, there appear to be two major differences between his theoretical position and a position that describes memory performance in terms of the match between trace information and retrieval information: First, Kolers describes remembering in terms of the mental operations themselves, rather than in terms of their products; second, he stresses the importance of surface form for memory performance under conditions that encourage a complex and extensive analysis of the surface form. The first difference constitutes a radical shift in viewpoint when compared with the majority of information-processing models of memory; it has already been successful in suggesting rather different kinds of experiments, but a final judgment on "traces versus operations" must await further data and arguments. The second difference can be assimilated into other current models, although Kolers's results do disconfirm Craik and Lockhart's original postulate that surface form is rapidly forgotten. The relative contribution to remembering of various types of information is considered further in the next section.

Equality of Traces?[1]

One question raised by several authors is whether any one type of information is inherently better suited to support good retention than any other type; as Lockhart puts it, are all traces "born equal?" This question strikes at the roots of the viewpoint advocated by Craik and Lockhart (1972), since their major suggestion was that deeper levels of processing are associated with higher levels of retention. Although there is certainly evidence to support this position (Craik & Tulving, 1975; Hyde & Jenkins, 1969), both Bransford et al. and Tulving in the present volume point out that the conditions at retrieval very often favored the deeper encoding conditions; both authors demonstrate situations where the apparently "poorer" encoding condition nevertheless yielded higher retention levels when the test was appropriate.

However, the data of Morris, Bransford, and Franks (1977) and Fisher and Craik (1977) show that whereas a word encoded phonemically is better retrieved via a phonemic cue than via a semantic cue, and that under such phonemic retrieval conditions, phonemic encodings are superior to semantic encodings, nevertheless semantic encodings with semantic cues yield higher levels of

---

[1]This section was written in collaboration with Ronald P. Fisher.

retention than do phonemic encodings with phonemic cues. Thus we would agree that the notions of transfer-appropriate processing and encoding specificity are important. But does Tulving go too far in suggesting that successful recollection depends only on the compatibility of trace information and cue information and that factors such as depth, elaboration, and distinctiveness need not be considered separately from, or in addition to, this compatibility relation? Let us consider Tulving's arguments.

The debate centers on the issue of whether one principle—that of compatibility between trace and retrieval information—is sufficient for an understanding of the process of remembering; or whether two basic notions are necessary—encoding/retrieval compatibility plus a qualitative description of the trace itself. Fisher and Craik (1977) postulated that both factors were necessary to describe the pattern of data shown in Table 19.6 of Tulving's chapter, whereas Tulving argues that the compatibility relation between the trace and the cue is sufficient by itself. Tulving makes the point that if one is to supplement the encoding/retrieval compatibility factor with a second factor to explain the Fisher and Craik data, one can equally well select type of retrieval cue as type of encoding operation; both descriptions are perfectly consistent with the data (Tulving, this volume, Tables 19.6 and 19.7). We agree with this point; in two out of the three conditions shown in Tulving's Table 19.6, encoding type is confounded with cue type; thus the pattern of data shown in Table 19.7 is quite similar to that shown in Table 19.6. Whether the position is stated in terms of encoding or in terms of cues is not central to our argument, however. Our point is that two factors are required for an adequate description of the data shown in Tulving's Table 19.6—one to capture the principle of compatibility between trace and cue and the other to describe the qualitative nature of the trace. Since we accept the encoding specificity principle, it follows that the nature of the trace is determined by the type of encoding operation performed and that it determines, in turn, the type of cue that will be effective.

Why do we insist that two factors are necessary to describe the data? Our argument is that when degree of similarity between encoding conditions and retrieval conditions is held constant, substantial differences in performance level remain. For example, the combination of semantic encoding with a semantic test yields higher levels of retention than the combination of phonemic encoding conditions with an appropriate phonemic test (Fisher & Craik, 1977, Exps. 1, 2, & 3; Morris, Bransford, & Franks, 1977; Nelson, Wheeler, Borden, & Brooks, 1974). What underlies this difference in performance level? A conjecture that fits in with at least some of the views put forward by others in this volume and elsewhere (e.g., Battig, Eysenck, Nelson; Klein & Saltz, 1976) is that semantic traces are *typically* more discriminable from other traces in the system than are such "shallower" traces as phonemic information. If shallow codes are characterized as sharing many features with past encodings (possibly because of a relatively restricted repertory or "alphabet" of encoding operations), then in terms of Eysenck's Fig. 5.1, the information contained in the present encoding (B) would overlap substantially with information from past encodings (A). In this case, even when there is a high degree of compatibility between the trace B and the retrieval information C, performance will not be high, since the retrieval information also "overlaps" with many past encodings. Put in a slightly different way, there is more built-in cue overload for shallow encodings. Even with perfect overlap of C and B (Eysenck, Fig. 5.1), there is a functional ceiling on performance owing to the lack of distinctiveness of the present trace from past encodings. This is not to assert that "sensory" codes can *never* be made more distinctive—they clearly can, as the work of Eysenck, Kolers, and Nelson has shown. The point of the present argument, rather, is to give some theoretical account of the typical finding—in the outside world as well as in the laboratory—that events are well remembered to the extent that they are processed in a way that stresses their meaning and significance.

To return to the initial quetion: Do some types of trace information inherently support higher retention levels than some other types? Our answer to this question is "yes." Whereas Tulving suggests that the patterns of data shown in his Tables 19.5, 19.6, and 19.7 "can parsimoniously be regarded as showing that in some experimental conditions, the compatibility between the trace information and the retrieval information was greater than in others" (Tulving, this volume, p. 421), we wish to speculate on *why* there is greater compatibility in some cases than in others. For example, why do "deeper" encodings, when tested appropriately, yield higher performance levels than do combinations of shallow encodings and cues? Our argument (and also that of Klein & Saltz, 1976; and Eysenck, Chapter 5, this volume) is that semantic traces are more distinctive in the memory system than are sensory and phonemic traces; it is this enhanced distinctiveness that lies behind their higher levels of retention.

Depth and Distinctiveness

Given the emphasis in this book on the notions of elaboration and distinctiveness, is the concept of "depth of processing" outmoded and redundant? I would argue that the metaphor of depth is still a useful one to express the idea that analysis of an event takes place gradually, and that the qualitatively different internal forms of representation of the stimulus can be ordered from those concerned with sensory, "surface" qualities to those concerned with the abstract, symbolic properties of the event. Similar positions are propounded in the present volume by Treisman (whose 1964 "levels-of-analysis" theory of attention was a major influence on the view of memory suggested by Craik & Lockhart, 1972) and also by Rumelhart (1977). However, my own views have changed somewhat since 1972. First, it no longer seems reasonable to suggest one inflexible processing sequence that proceeds in a bottom-up fashion and is "stopped" at the level induced by the task. Treisman and others in this volume have pointed out that whereas levels of analysis can be ordered logically from shallow to deep, the processing sequence is likely to reflect interactions and recursive operations among the various levels and types of representation. Such interactive processing will proceed until appropriate action can be taken, but the particular analyses performed will depend very much on the task, leaving a record reflecting differential activity at various depths, rather than a linear sequence that proceeds to a certain level and then stops. The differential activity of particular types of operation is captured by notions such as extensiveness and elaboration. It seems particularly important to note that "semantic processing" is not an all-or-none phenomenon; there are degrees of involvement of meaning just as any other qualitative type of analysis can be carried out more or less fully. Treisman also points out that the various possible senses in which depth has been used—to reflect greater semanticity and expertise, more effort or processing capacity expended, order of processing, lateness in time, or order of conscious access—are only loosely related. It is a challenging empirical and conceptual task for the future to work out their interrelations and dependencies.

The second main way in which my thinking about levels of processing has changed over the last few years is to accommodate a more complex relationship between depth of processing and subsequent memory performance. After reading several of the chapters in this book, it is clear that memory reflects elaboration as well as depth and that extensive "sensory" analysis *can* lead to higher levels of retention than minimal semantic analysis. Ordinarily, however, it seems that deeper processing will be associated with higher performance levels, either because deeper levels afford greater potential for distinctiveness (Eysenck, Chapter 5; Jacoby & Craik, Chapter 1), or because at deeper levels, encoding operations are more richly interconnected and articulated, thereby facilitating both elaboration at input and redintegrative reconstruction at retrieval (Anderson & Reder, Chapter 18).

What about distinctiveness—the heir apparent in the "levels" order of succession? Are we in for 5 years of research showing "distinctive encodings are remembered better"? Whereas many contributors to the present volume see the notion of distinctiveness as useful and integrative, others (e.g., Baddeley, Chapter 16; Lockhart, Chapter 4) warn of the continuing dangers of circularity and difficulty of definition. Personally, despite these valid criticisms, I see several positive reasons for exploring the concept further; first, its use stresses the close relations between perception and memory; second, recent work in the measurement of similarity and discriminability in perceptual and conceptual contexts (e.g., Garner, 1974; Tversky, 1977) provides some hope that memory theory can also benefit from these workers' efforts; third, the description of traces in terms of distinctiveness allows a way of integrating present lines of research with previous work on similarity in memory—especially with classic interference theory concepts and results (Battig, Chapter 2, this volume; Postman, 1976).

Finally, what of the future of the levels-of-processing approach to memory? On this score I feel optimistic, since ideas derived from a levels point of view are being applied quite widely in many different contexts: for instance, in studies of child development (Hagen, Chapter 13, this volume), in the study of amnesia (Cermak, Chapter 6, this volume), aging (Perlmutter, 1978), schizophrenia (Koh & Peterson, 1978), the effects of alcohol (Hartley, Birnbaum, & Parker, 1978), individual differences (Battig, Chapter 2, this volume), and research on personality (Rogers, Kuiper, & Kirker, 1977). In addition, the notions are being extended in various ways—principally, perhaps, to make contact with theory and data on retrieval (Bartlett, 1977; Fisher & Craik, 1977; Whitten, 1974). The major objection to the levels-of-processing approach has been that the theorizing it engenders is very loose and global; that the approach deals with general principles rather than with tight, predictive, falsifiable models (T. O. Nelson, 1977) or with specifiable mechanisms that can be elucidated through experiment (Baddeley, 1978). These criticisms are valid and undeniable. However, in Chapter 7, Bahrick points to a way in which global principles can usefully advance our understanding of memory processes. His main point is that the attempt to "prove" or "disprove" general principles is misguided and wasteful; rather, the global ideas should be used to provide a theoretical perspective that is used in turn to discover and elucidate patterns of empirical relations over a broad range of tasks and situations. Within this broad framework, it is possible to postulate more detailed and specific theoretical ideas that *are* testable and falsifiable in a more traditionally scientific fashion. One example of this development within the levels-of-processing framework is the work on maintenance processing and its effects on retention (Craik & Watkins, 1973; Glenberg, Smith, & Green, 1977; T. O. Nelson, 1977; Rundus, 1977).

In conclusion, although it is evident that the particular version of the levels-of-processing view of memory advanced by Craik and Lockhart (1972) has evolved and changed in many respects over the last 6 years, that is as it should be. It is noteworthy that many of the changes described in this final chapter and elsewhere have come about as a consequence of experimental work suggested by the "levels" framework (e.g., Craik & Tulving, 1975; Fisher & Craik, 1977; Moscovitch & Craik, 1976). Thus the ideas have shown themselves to be amenable to refinement and modification through empirical work, much as we had originally hoped. In addition to stimulating research questions in our own laboratories, the levels framework has helped to generate experimental work carried out by others. In some cases the results have been taken to support a levels-of-processing view; in other cases the experimenters have been strongly critical of our position. Overall, however, there can be no doubt that the framework has fulfilled a heuristic purpose—again, much as we had hoped. The liveliness and richness of the debate reported in the present volume is an excellent illustration of the view that the levels-of-processing framework has helped to provide and develop a milieu of thought that has led to substantial advances in memory research.

ACKNOWLEDGMENTS

Preparation of this chapter was facilitated by Grant A8261 from the National Research Council of Canada. The report was written while the author was on research leave at Stanford University.

REFERENCES

Baddeley, A. D. The trouble with "levels": A re-examination of Craik and Lockhart's framework for memory research. *Psychological Review*, 1978, *85*, 139–152.

Bartlett, J. C. Effects of immediate testing on delayed retrieval: Search and recovery operations with four types of cue. *Journal of Experimental Psychology: Human Learning and Memory*, 1977, *3*, 719–732.

Bransford, J. D., McCarrell, N. S., Franks, J. J., & Nitsch, K. E. Toward unexplaining memory. In R. Shaw & J. Bransford (Eds.), *Perceiving, acting, and knowing*. Hillsdale, N.J.: Lawrence Erlbaum Associates, 1977.

Craik, F. I. M., & Lockhart, R. S. Levels of processing: A framework for memory research. *Journal of Verbal Learning and Verbal Behavior*, 1972, *11*, 671–684.

Craik, F. I. M., & Tulving, E. Depth of processing and the retention of words in episodic memory. *Journal of Experimental Psychology: General*, 1975, *104*, 268–294.

Craik, F. I. M., & Watkins, M. J. The role of rehearsal in short-term memory. *Journal of Verbal Learning and Verbal Behavior*, 1973, *12*, 599–607.

Fisher, R. P., & Craik, F. I. M. Interaction between encoding and retrieval operations in cued recall. *Journal of Experimental Psychology*, 1977: Human Learning and Memory *3*, 701–711.

Garner, W. R. *The processing of information and structure*. Hillsdale, N.J.: Lawrence Erlbaum Associates, 1974.

Glenberg, A., Smith, S. M., & Green, C. Type I rehearsal: Maintenance and more. *Journal of Verbal Learning and Verbal Behavior*, 1977, *16*, 339–352.

Hartley, J. T., Birnbaum, I. M., & Parker, E. S. *Alcohol and storage deficits: Kind of processing?* Journal of Verbal Learning and Verbal Behavior, 1978 (in press).

Hyde, T. S., & Jenkins, J. J. Differential effects of incidental tasks on the organization of recall of a list of highly associated words. *Journal of Experimental Psychology*, 1969, *82*, 472–481.

Klein, K., & Saltz, E. Specifying the mechanisms in a levels-of-processing approach to memory. *Journal of Experimental Psychology: Human Learning and Memory*, 1976, *2*, 671–679.

Koh, S. D., & Peterson, R. A. Encoding orientation and the remembering of schizophrenic young adults. *Journal of Abnormal Psychology*, 1978, *87*, 303–313.

Kolers, P. A., & Ostry, D. J. Time course of loss of information regarding pattern analyzing operations. *Journal of Verbal Learning and Verbal Behavior*, 1974, *13*, 599–612.

Light, L. L., & Carter–Sobell, L. Effects of changed semantic context on recognition memory. *Journal of Verbal Learning and Verbal Behavior*, 1970, *9*, 1–11.

Masson, M. E. J., & Sala, L. S. Interactive processes in sentence comprehension and recognition. *Cognitive Psychology*, 1978, *10*, 244–270.

Morris, C. D., Bransford, J. D., & Franks, J. J. Levels of processing versus transfer appropriate processing. *Journal of Verbal Learning and Verbal Behavior*, 1977, *16*, 519–533.

Moscovitch, M., & Craik, F. I. M. Depth of processing, retrieval cues, and uniqueness of encoding as factors in recall. *Journal of Verbal Learning and Verbal Behavior*, 1976, *15*, 447–458.

Nelson, D. L., Wheeler, J. W., Fr., Borden, R. C., & Brooks, D. M. Levels of processing and cuing: Sensory versus meaning features. *Journal of Experimental Psychology*, 1974, *103*, 971−977.

Nelson, T. O. Repetition and depth of processing. *Journal of Verbal Learning and Verbal Behavior*, 1977, *16*, 151−171.

Norman, D. A., & Bobrow, D. G. *Descriptions: A basis for memory acquisition and retrieval.* Technical Report 74, Center for Human Information Processing, 1977.

Paivio, A. U. *Imagery and verbal processes*. New York: Holt, Rinehart and Winston, 1971.

Perlmutter, M. What is memory aging the aging of? *Developmental Psychology*. 1978, *14*, 330−345.

Postman, L. Methodology of human learning. In W. K. Estes (Ed.), *Handbook of learning and cognitive processes* (Vol. 3). Hillsdale, N.J.: Lawrence Erlbaum Associates, 1976.

Rogers, T. B., Kuiper, N. A., & Kirker, W. S. Self-reference and the encoding of personal information. *Journal of Personality and Social Psychology*, 1977, *35*, 677−688.

Rumelhart, D. E. Toward an interactive model of reading. In S. Dornic (Ed.), *Attention and performance VI*. Hillsdale, N.J.: Lawrence Erlbaum Associates, 1977.

Rundus, D. Maintenance rehearsal and single-level processing. *Journal of Verbal Learning and Verbal Behavior*, 1977, *16*, 665−681.

Schonfield, A. E. D., & Stones, M. J. Remembering and aging. In J. F. Kihlstrom & F. J. Evans (Eds.), *Functional disorders of memory*. Hillsdale, N.J.: Lawrence Erlbaum Associates, in press.

Schulman, A. I. Memory for words recently classified. *Memory & Cognition*, 1974, *2*, 47−52.

Shiffrin, R. M., & Schneider, W. Controlled and automatic processing: II. Perceptual learning, automatic attending, and a general theory. *Psychological Review*, 1977, *84*, 127−190.

Thomson, D. M., & Tulving, E. Associative encoding and retrieval: Weak and strong cues. *Journal of Experimental Psychology*, 1970, *86*, 255−262.

Tulving, E. Episodic and semantic memory. In E. Tulving & W. Donaldson (Eds.), *Organization of memory*. New York: Academic Press, 1972.

Tversky, A. Features of similarity. *Psychological Review*, 1977, *84*, 327−352.

Whitten, W. B. *Retrieval "depth" and retrieval component processes: A levels-of-processing interpretation of learning during retrieval*. (Tech. Rep. 54). Ann Arbor, Mich.: University of Michigan, Human Performance Center, 1974.

Author Index

463

D

E

F

Subject Index